Price Guide to Country Antiques & American Primitives

Dorothy Hammond

To my husband Robert,
who provided the original incentives.

Price Guide to Country Antiques & American Primitives

Dorothy Hammond

FUNK & WAGNALLS *New York*

Books by Dorothy Hammond

Confusing Collectibles

More Confusing Collectibles

Collectible Advertising

Mustache Cups, Their History & Marks

Library of Congress Catalog Card Number: 75-13602
ISBN: 0-308-10183-9 (hardcover)
0-308-10184-7 (softcover)

Prepared and Produced by Everybodys Press, Inc.
Printed in the United States of America

This Edition Prepared for Distribution by
Funk & Wagnalls Publishing Company, Inc.

Contents

Introduction

Price Guide To Country Antiques & American Primitives has been written because of the outgrowth of interest in this field during recent years. As more and more Americans become aware of their heritage, young and old alike diligently search for objects that carry with them fascinating clues to America's past. Moreover, collectors have quickly discovered that because of the demand for these objects, prices are steadily increasing, making their purchases very worthwhile investments. Because no general price guide available can possibly cover every category in this entire spectrum, keeping up with values of country pieces has become a very frustrating activity for the antiques dealer as well as the collector nowadays. Therefore, the writer felt that a comprehensive, well-illustrated guide should be written now, since the field has never been covered in a publication of its very own.

The bulk of the listings include American-made pieces of furniture and related objects — most of which are still commonplace. Every listing was recorded from an antiques shop, auction, flea market or antiques show, from all parts of the country, between April 1974 and March 1975 and every entry is in fine saleable condition unless otherwise noted.

Although many collectors of antiques use prices paid at auctions as an indication of current market trends, it is quite important that these prices be evaluated carefully. As a general rule, wholesale prices are paid for the ordinary object, while retail prices are generally paid for rarities. And because it is here that the rarest of Americana is offered, the extraordinary piece often fetches an impressive figure. It is this element of surprise that makes auctions worthwhile.

Since prices vary greatly due to geographic differences, the writer has created a new concept in pricing which should be very helpful to readers. Letters in parentheses are shown after each entry, which indicates either a dealer's asking price, or an auction price, in addition to the region or the state that the object was located. For example: **Rolling pin,** cherry, 1-pc., 18" L. (D-MW) $22.00. In this instance, a "Dealer's" price has been quoted, and the location is in the Midwest.

A glossary of terms has been included at the back of the book to aid the reader, since the names of different objects sprang into existence with the making of different pieces; therefore, only those living in certain localities could explain their meaning.

Every effort has been made to record prices as accurately as possible in this publication. However, the writer cannot be responsible for any clerical or typographical errors that may occur. And, finally, this book should be considered as merely a guide to prices of objects in this broad field, and in no way constitutes an appraisal.

Dorothy Hammond

Key to Abbreviations

Every item listed is keyed to either a dealer price, or an auction value. The letter "D" denotes "Dealer", whereas the letter "A" denotes "Auction" price. And the different letters that follow will indicate the locality each item was found to be priced by an antiques dealer, or sold at an auction. The various area letters are:

E, East   S, South
MW, Midwest   SE, Southeast
N, North   SW, Southwest
NE, Northeast   W, West
NW, Northwest

EDITOR'S NOTE: For greater ease in study and appraisal, the prices listed in this guide have been rounded off to the nearest dollar.

Acknowledgments

The author expresses deepest appreciation to all of those who have so generously provided information and photograph illustrations to make this project a reality. Thanks are especially due to: Catherine M. Pennypacker for the many photos from the late James G. Pennypacker estate auction; Charles Pennypacker of the Pennypacker Auction Centre, Kenhorst, Reading, Pennsylvania; George R. Morrill, Morrill Auctions, Harrison, Maine; Tom Porter, Garth's Auction Barn, Inc., Delaware, Ohio; Richard A. Bourne Company, Inc., Hyannis, Massachusetts; The Western Reserve Historical Society, Cleveland, Ohio; Joan Cawley (American Indian objects), White Buffalo Gallery, Wichita, Kansas; Ruth Troiani (chalkware), Pound Ridge, New York; Elizabeth Stokes (hooked rugs), Weare, New Hampshire; David Y. Ellinger (theorem paintings), Pottstown, Pennsylvania; Donald Hobart, Savogran (tools), Norwood, Massachusetts; the Cunninghams, David and Sue (quilts and coverlets), Denver, Pennsylvania; Samuel Pennington, Editor, Maine Antique Digest, Inc., Waldoboro, Maine; Rufus Foshee (spongeware), Camden, Maine; and Mr. and Mrs. Jerome Blum (furniture and accessories), Lisbon, Connecticut. And to the many others who helped along the way. I am grateful to Helen McClure, May Moore, Grace Colvin, Carolyn Lerke, Louise Pendergrass, Betty L. Mylchreest, Mr. and Mrs. John Glahn, Stan and Clara Jean Davis, Hopkinton, New Hampshire, and to my secretary Barbara Hart, who gave unselfishly of her time and for assuming additional responsibilities in order that deadlines could be met.

Banks

The adage "a penny saved is a penny earned" has represented an important part of Americana from the time of Benjamin Franklin. Parents taught their children the art of saving at a very early age, by giving them "penny" banks—first of pottery and stoneware, followed by tin, glass and iron, the "still" type and the "mechanical." The "still" banks are those with no moving parts, while the "mechanicals" have parts that move when a coin is inserted in the slot.

Although all types of penny banks are extremely collectible today, the surviving examples made of pottery and stoneware during the eighteenth and nineteenth centuries are of particular interest to the collectors of American primitives. Once commonplace, these banks have become increasingly scarce—commanding high prices today when found at shops, shows, or at auctions. They were made in a variety of interesting forms. Some were shaped like birds or animals, while others resemble a small boat, a cabin or a house.

* * *

Apple shape, redware, 3½" diam. (D-E)	$ 65
Barrel, redware, painted decor., 3½" (D-NE)	10
Barrel, tin, "Happy Days" (D-S)	5
Bear, iron, standing (A-E)	45
Buffalo, iron, 5½" h. (A-E)	38
Cow, iron, 4½"h. (A-E)	40
Deer, iron (A-MW)	25
Dog, chalkware (A-E)	27

Penny banks, pottery, Bennington, flint enamel, dogs w/coleslaw hair on head & tail ends & decor. w/bright green, brown & tan glaze (A-E) $1150

Penny bank, pottery, Jonah & the Whale, expertly crafted piece of folk art (A-E) $2600

Dog, pottery (A-E) ....$ 190
Dogs, pottery, pair, green, brown & tan decor., coleslaw hair on head & tail ends, rare, ex. cond. (A-E) 1150
Egg, redware, 4"h. (D-E) 80
Elephant, iron (D-E) 65
Elephant, iron, 7½"h. (A-MW) 32
Elephant, iron, w/howdah (A-E) 22
Football player, iron (D-NE) 47
Head of black man, redware, painted (D-E) 65
Head, woman's, chalkware, 3½" (A-MW) 50
Horse, iron (A-MW) 42
Jug, pottery, blk. splash decor., 5½" (A-E) 75
Jug, redware, w/stopper (A-E) 40
Mule, iron (A-E) 70
Penny, redware, form of handled jug w/stopper, red glaze (A-E) 40
Penny, redware, jug, black splash decor., 5½" (A-E) 75
Penny, dogs, redware, green, brown & tan decor., Cole Slaw hair on head & tail ends, rare, ex. cond., pr. (A-E) 1150
Pig, chalkware, 18"h. (A-E) 30
Pig, iron (D-E) 25
Redware, 8"h. (A-E) 80
Redware, gray to brown ground w/black specks, 3¼" (A-NE) 200
Safe, iron, 4½"h. (A-NE) 22
Safe, tin, with lock (A-MW) 17
Santa Claus, pottery, painted red & white (A-NE) 17
Shoe, woman's, brass w/nickel plating, C.1880, 5½"l. (D-E) 48
Trunk, iron (A-E) 25
U.S. Mailbox, iron, painted (A-E) 25
World, tin, painted (A-E) 15

Baskets

The art of basketry was one of our earliest crafts which is recognized today as yet another interesting form of folk art. Since basketry was common on the Continent — many of the first settlers were experienced basketmakers, — and they quickly adopted new techniques from the Indians who were also excellent basketmakers. ·

During the decades following the first colonization, the need for containers and storage facilities was immense. Since materials were abundant, the art of basketmaking flourished until around the turn of the present century when basket factories became established and mass-produced containers became available.

A variety of materials were used to produce baskets of various shapes and sizes down through the years, including reeds, grass, straw, pine needles, roots, vines, cornshucks, split and unsplit willow and porcupine quills. However, the

Penna. Dutch rye straw baskets (D-MW), *left:* **basket,** 5½" deep, 8½" diam. $39; *right:* **basket,** 3" deep, 9" diam. $32

sturdy splint baskets are among the earliest types made by the colonists. The hand-cut splints, usually of oak, ash or hickory, were flexible strips of wood, but thick and irregular. This characteristic is helpful to identify the earlier baskets, in addition to the handles. The first were carved by hand, and will show tool marks left by the maker. Moreover, the earliest baskets were held together with natural materials, mostly thin strips of wood or animal sinew, followed by handwrought nails and copper tacks. String and thread became popular binding materials, along with rattan during the early part of the nineteenth century. Eventually metal bails and bands were added for bracing.

Early baskets were made to be used. Constant wear left splintered edges, broken or missing pieces, and oftentimes stains which reveal the purpose for which they were originally made.

Among the most desirable baskets of interest to collectors are the so-called Nantucket, Shaker, American Indian and the coiled rye straw. The latter type is characteristically Pennsylvania Dutch, formed by coiled ropes of rye straw, laced with fine oak strips. Rye straw baskets were made in many shapes and sizes for multiple purposes ranging from small berry, nut, fruit and egg baskets, to a variety of bread baskets and large beehive-shaped hampers with covers. These were used for holding dried fruit, feathers, grain, etc.

Lightship men — retired or active — and retired whalemen are to be credited for the so-called "Nantucket Lightship" baskets. Their lack of decoration, simplicity of design and construction are characteristic of the Quaker tradition. Sizes run from as small as a pint up to as large as twelve quarts. Some were fitted with wooden lids, and some were made in nests, totaling eight baskets. Other than varnish, no finish or paint was used on these baskets. Their construction was started from the bottom with staves inserted into the grooved edges of the bottom board. Woods used for the board were pine, mahogany, sycamore and black walnut. Staves were of white oak, ash and hickory, with weaving strands and lavings of rattan. The handles were known as "ears," and some baskets had metal attachments of brass or copper.

Shaker baskets are especially noted for their fine workmanship. They made and sold a wide variety of round, square and rectangular baskets, with or without

Left: **berry basket,** splint, small, ½-pt. (D-E) $8; *right:* **willow basket,** covered, w/handle (D-E) $18.

Apple basket, Shaker, ½-bushel (D-MW) $45.

handles and covers. The larger utility baskets were made of splint hickory, ash, curly maple or poplar, while rush and reed palm were used for making some of the smaller baskets.

The American Indians had achieved artistic excellence as basket weavers long before the white man came. (See *Indian* category.) Born of Mother Earth, their makings included the rough foliage of sparse terrain, the yucca plant, bear grass, reeds of river beds, the willow, rabbit brush or sumac, vines and splint, oftentimes decorated with dyes made from wild berries, roots or bark. From these makings came beautiful distinctive shapes and designs, sought after by today's collectors of basketry.

Baskets are presently enjoying much popularity among collectors, especially the younger generation. An interesting collection can be assembled over a relatively short period of time, inexpensively, unless one's taste preference includes one of the four types mentioned above or examples of fisherman's basketry.

* * *

Apple, walnut, bushel (A-E) ....$ 15
Berry, splint, handled, 3"×3½" (D-W) 15
Cheese, drying, ex. cond. (D-NE) 65
Cradle, woven splint of natural & blue, splint 1"w., early 19th C., hooded, man-made headed nails, 19"×8" (D-NE) 85

Baskets, (A-E), *top row, left to right:* **oyster basket,** 12 3/4″ diam., 12½″ h., $60; **oyster basket,** 13″ diam., 14″ h., $70; **oyster basket,** painted blue & red, 16½″ h., $40; *center row:* **basket,** large, overall height, 16½″, 18″ diam., $60; **basket,** circular, 21″ diam., 14½″ h., $75; *bottom row:* **oyster basket,** circular, marked, E M G, 12½″ diam., 13″ h., $90; **oyster basket,** circular, early, 14″ diam., 13″ h., $90; **oyster basket,** flat-top, 1-pc. handle, 11″ h., 14½″ diam., $60

Double-butted, handled, old green-gray paint 10″ diam. (D-NE)	$ 24
Double-butted, handled, small, 7″ h. old green paint (A-NE)	90
Double-butted, splint, med. size, stained brown w/flat handle (D-MW)	8
Drying, splint, openwork, splint bottom, 16½″×4″ (D-NE)	30
Drying, square, 7″ (D-NE)	8
Drying, square, 6½″ (D-NE)	8
Fruit, 1½ bushel, flat attached handles, early (D-MW)	85
Fruit, or vegetable, w/hinged bottom, 19th C., 20″ (A-NE)	150
Goose feather, covered, large, 22″t., 18″ diam. (D-NE)	50
Goose feather, covered, 22″ (D-E)	55
Handled, split willow, old green paint, 12″ h. (A-NE)	40
Handled, splint, old white paint, 13″ (D-NE)	28
Handled, old white paint, 12½″ h. (D-E)	28
Handled, sweetgrass, porcupine twist in blue at bottom, 4″ diam., 2″ t. (D-NE)	12
Handled, thin bark 7″, sq. bottom (D-NE)	19
Hanging, splint comb case, blue decor., 8½″×8½″ (D-E)	35
Hickory, splint, urn shape w/cover, small, 6″h. (D-E)	22
Kettle shape, splint, w/handle (D-E)	32
Lettuce, splint, w/handles, 10″ h. (A-NE)	160
Maine, covered, woven of ¼″ splint, greenish-blue paint, 9½″×13″ (D-NE)	30

Melon shape, splint, flat, 11″ (D-NE) ....$ 15
Miniature, handled, splint weave 4″×2¼″ (D-NE)   12
Miniature, splint, swing handle, kele shape like early iron, 3 legs, 4″×3″ (D-E)   24
Miniature, split willow, 2-handled w/lid, decor. on side (A-E)   35
Nantucket, early type handle joint, nut brown patina, round, 10″×4¾″ (D-NE)........   225
Nantucket, handled, early, 6″ diam., 4¼″ t. (D-NE)   210
Nantucket, handled, early type extensions for handles, perfect cond., 9½″ diam. (D-NE)   235
Nantucket, handled, round (D-NE)   150
Nantucket, M. Ray label (D-NE)   185
Nantucket, oval, 13″ diam. (D-E)   185
Nantucket, oval, 12″ (D-E)   175
Nantucket, oval, wood bottom, handle, good cond., 10″×7½″, 5″ across center (D-E)   135
Open, small, combination of narrow splint & braided grass, weather gray color, shaped like
    redware bean pot, 5″×5″ (D-E)   14
Peach, splint, shallow, old green paint, ½ bu. (D-NE)   16
Root, twisted, 6″ diam. 4″ deep (D-MW)   22
Rope, twisted, resembles Nantuckets (D-NE)   75
Rye straw, assembled w/colored string, 16″×10″×4½″ (D-W)   28
Rye straw, beehive shape, 26″ high (D-E)   95
Rye straw, breadbasket, 6″ w., 6″ d., 20″ l., handles (D-MW)   85
Rye straw, bushel w/wood handles & base rim (D-E)   55
Rye straw, 5″ deep, 12″ diam. top (D-MW)   32
Rye straw, flared, 8″ h., 12″ top diam., handles (D-E)   28
Rye straw, flared, 6″ h., 10″ top diam., handles (D-MW)   45
Rye straw, 4″ deep, 12″ diam. top (D-E)   18
Rye straw, grain sowers, kidney shape w/handles, 7″ deep, 26″ long, 8-12″ widths (D-W)   100
Rye straw, hamper covered, 20″ diam., 24″ high (D-E)   125
Rye straw, oval, 6″×12½″ (D-MW)   55
Rye straw, pair, matched, 3″ d., 11″ diam. (D-MW)   55
Rye straw, round, w/lid, 18″ d. (A-E)...   55
Rye straw, winnowing, round, ex. cond., 22″×4″ (D-E)   60
Sewing, split willow, small open compartments around top (inside), 11¾″ (D-NE)   18
Sewing, tin & oak, lined w/ticking (D-SW)...   60
Shaker, 2-handled, splint, approx. 30″ diam. (D-NE)   225
Shaker, splint, 2-handled, 26″×13″ (D-S)   110
Shaker, laundry, splint, 28″×15″×14″ (D-E)   125
Shaker, splint, rectangular, handle over top, green paint, 11″×16″ (D-E)   22
Shaker, sewing, splint, marked "Sabbathday Lake" (A-E)   50
Shaker, splint, signed "S. Fisk", top handle, tight weave, 11″ diam. × 8″ (D-NE)................   45
Shaker, stationary handle, darkened splint, 11″ diam. (D-E)   35
Shaker, swing handle, darkened splint, 13″×8½″ (D-E)   45
Shaker, splint, top handle, open work, reinforced bottom, 11″ diam. × 8″ (D-NE)   34
Shaker, top handle, tight weave, 9½″ diam. × 7″ (D-NE)   32
Splint, berry, approx. 1½ cup size (D-E)   8
Splint, covered, woven, pumpkin shape, old red veg. dye, unusual (D-NE)   20
Splint, egg, 12″ h. including handle (D-E)   20
Splint, fruit/berry w/handle, approx. 1 qt. size (D-E)   12
Splint, goose, w/cover, ovoid shape, 24″ h. (D-MW)   45
Splint, half-melon shape, tightly woven, handle holes, 22″×21″×8″ (D-NE)   12
Splint, narrow, wood handle, 10″ d., 8″ diam. (D-SW)   35
Splint, rect., handled, small w/brass nails (D-W)..   9
Splint, rect., stenciled, 9″×13″×6″ (D-E)   18
Splint, swing handle, rare old yellow paint, 14½″×7″ (D-NE)   65
Splint, vegetable dyes in orange & blue, 8″ diam., 3″ t. (D-NE).............................   16
Wall, splint, boat shaped, 13¼″, old pale gray paint (D-NE)....................................   12
Wall, sweetgrass, 7½″ (D-NE)   9
Winnowing, splint, square 18″ (D-NE)   55
Woven, split willow, primitive, handled, old lt. blue, 12″ (D-NE)   24
Woven, split willow, side handles, 19″ diam., 13½″ t. (D-NE)..................................   50

Bennington

The first pottery works in Bennington, Vermont was established by Captain John Norton in 1793 and for 101 years it was owned and operated by succeeding generations of Nortons. Today, the term "Bennington" is synonymous with the finest in American ceramics, because the center was the home of several pottery operations during the last century, each producing under different labels, and their collectible artistry is now conveniently, if inaccurately, dubbed "Bennington."

The most popular of all ware produced at Bennington was the handsome utilitarian objects first made by Christopher Webber Fenton—related by marriage to the son of the founder of the Norton pottery. Fenton broke away from the

Bennington (A-NE), *top row, left to right:* **frames,** oval, pr. $325; **frame,** square, $150; **tiebacks,** $110. *Middle row, left to right:* **nameplate,** $80; **frame,** small, flint enamel, $400; **nameplate,** $40; **frame,** Rockingham, $275; **tile,** flint enamel, $330. *Bottom row, left to right:* **tiebacks,** $175; **frame,** flint enamel, large, $575.

Left to right: **bowls,** Rockingham glaze, nest of 5, $200; **mug,** Rockingham glaze, $39; **quart jar,** Peoria pottery, $12 (all items D-ME)

Bowl, Bennington, Rockingham glazed, w/pouring lip, large (D-NE) $165

older stoneware tradition, producing many fine decorative items. During the 1840s, he began the production of plain yellow clay crockery for household use—known as "yellowware," and his rich, dark brown glazed wares called "Rockingham," followed. It is believed that the latter term originated in England at an earthenworks named after the Duke of Rockingham, on whose property the factory was located.

The first pieces of Rockingham produced here were hand-dipped, and later the objects were spattered as they revolved in a rotating vat. It is easy to understand why no two pieces of this very desirable ware are exactly alike in glazing.

Fenton patented his famous "flint" enamel glaze in 1849—decorating the ordinary Rockingham finish with yellow, blue, orange, and green overtones

Left: **lion,** Bennington, flint enamel (A-NE) $1350; *right:* **poodle,** Bennington, flint enamel (A-NE) $1650

through the use of metallic oxides. Examples of this ware are rarely found on the open market.

Because the pottery produced at Bennington was of outstanding quality, a host of United States potteries turned out similar wares up until the late 1800s, making it difficult for anyone to attribute an object to a Bennington firm unless it was marked at the time of production. It has been estimated that only about one-fifth of the Fenton pottery was marked in any way, but examples of flint enameled wares were frequently marked. Other wares produced at Bennington include redware, stoneware, scroddled ware, graniteware, common white, parian porcelain, mortar ware, white and colored porcelain.

One of the most helpful books available to the collector of this type ware is Richard Carter Barrett's *Bennington Pottery and Porcelain* (Bonanza Books, New York). Over 2,000 items are illustrated, and there is a chronological listing of the various markings.

Pottery being produced in Bennington today by David Gil is actually the only pottery in Vermont to carry the precise name of "Bennington." These contemporary objects should never cause any problems in this field, as they are well-marked and shapes are very modern; but on several occasions, I have discovered one of Gil's plates in an antiques shop. His trademark resembles a long handled fork, and directly beside the mark "Bennington Potters, Inc., Bennington, Vermont."

* * *

Basin, flint enamel, 12-sided, marked Lyman Fenton & Co., Fenton's enamel, Pat. 1849, Bennington, Vt., 12¾" diam. (A-MW) ....$ 250
Basin, wash, flint enamel, overflow pipe & drain fitting in bottom (A-E)   550
Bottle, coachman's, Fenton's 1849 mark (A-E)...   230
Bottle, coachman's, mkd. Lyman Fenton & Co., Pat. 1849, Bennington, Vt., 10⅝" h. (A-MW).   400
Bottle, coachman's, flint enamel, 10½" h. (A-NE)...   425
Bowl, mixing, Rockingham mottled glaze, footed, 5¼" diam. (D-MW)...................................   28
Bowl, mixing, Rockingham mottled glaze, rounded sides, 8½" diam. (D-S)   38
Bowl, mixing, Rockingham mottled glaze, rounded sides, footed, 8½" diam. (D-N)   32
Bowl, mixing, Rockingham mottled glaze, rounded sides, footed, 9½" diam. (D-W)..............   32
Bowl, mixing, Rockingham mottled glaze, rounded sides, 10" diam. (D-NE)..........................   35
Bowl, mixing, Rockingham mottled glaze, rounded sides, 12" diam. (D-MW)   95
Bowl, mixing, Rockingham mottled glaze, sloping sides, 8½" diam. (A-MW)   27
Bowl, mixing, Rockingham mottled glaze, sloping sides, 5¼" diam. (D-MW)   38
Bowl, mixing, Rockingham mottled glaze, sloping sides, 9" diam. (D-MW)   45

Bowl, mixing, Rockingham mottled glaze, sloping sides, 9" diam. (D-W) ....$ 40
Bowl, mixing, Rockingham mottled glaze, sloping sides, 10⅜" diam. (D-MW)......................   85
Bowl, mixing, Rockingham mottled glaze, sloping sides, 13" diam. (D-E)............................   85
Churn, stoneware, 3-gal. floral, E. Norton (A-E)   125
Coffeepot, flint enamel, 14" (A-E)   375
Cookie jar, Rockingham mottled glaze (D-E)   45
Creamer, cow, flint enamel (A-NE)   375
Creamer, cow, light brown glaze (A-E)   170
Creamer, cow, Rockingham glaze (A-MW)   80
Crock, stoneware, bird decor. (A-E)   130
Crock, stoneware, blue decor., 4-gal. (A-E)...   130
Crock, stoneware, blue floral decor., E. Norton (D-NE)..   160
Crock, stoneware, deer & house decor. (D-NE)..   550
Crock, stoneware, handpainted blue decor., 1½ gal. (D-E)..   40
Croup kettle, flint enamel (D-E)   175
Cup, custard, Rockingham mottled glaze, 2" h., 3¼" diam. (D-MW)   18
Cup, custard, Rockingham mottled glaze, 2" h., 3¼" diam. (D-NE)..................................   28
Curtain tiebacks, flint enamel, pr., 4½" l., 4" diam. (A-NE)..   110
Curtain tiebacks, Rockingham mottled glaze, pr. (A-E)..   115
Cuspidor, Rockingham mottled glaze, raised eagles, minor chips, 9¾" h. (A-E)   35
Cuspidor, Rockingham mottled glaze, 9" diam., 4" h. (D-MW)   35
Cuspidor, Rockingham mottled glaze, shells, 7½" d. (A-E)...   40

Bennington, flint enamel (A-NE, *top row, left to right:* **creamer,** $325; **milk pitcher,** ribbed, $450; **water pitcher,** repaired spout, $200; **milk pitcher,** ribbed, $275; **milk pitcher,** ribbed damaged, $80. *Second row, left to right:* **miniature pitcher,** $400; **teapot,** ribbed, signed, $1000; **teapot,** ribbed, signed, $875; **teapot,** ribbed, $350

Bennington, (A-NE), *top row, left to right:* **book flasks:** flint enamel, pint, $400; **pint,** $275; **2-quart,** $150; **Ladies' Companion,** 4-qt., $275; **Departed Spirits,** flint enamel, 2-qt., $825; **pint,** $275; **pint,** flint enamel, $425; *bottom row, left to right:* **pint,** $275; **pint,** $225; **pint,** flint enamel, $425

Dish, baking, oblong, 11"×12", Rockingham mottled glaze (D-MW)   45
Dish, relish, flint enamel, traces of orange coloring (D-MW)   200
Dish, serving, Rockingham mottled glaze, octagon, 3" d., 14" l., dk. brown glaze, 1849 mark on
    bottom (A-E)..   490
Dish, soap, Rockingham mottled glaze, 1 pc. 8½×6" (D-E)..   35
Dish, soap, Rockingham mottled glaze, insert (A-E)   35

Dishes, celery, Rockingham mottled glaze, shell design, pr. (A-E).......................\$ 680
Dog, seated, Rockingham mottled glaze, 11" h. (A-E) 70
Dog, seated, Rockingham mottled glaze, shaped octagonal base, shows restoration, 10½" h.
(A-MW) 80
Doorknob, Rockingham mottled glaze (D-MW)... 18
Doorknobs, Rockingham mottled glaze, pr. (A-NE) 70
Flask, book, Rockingham mottled glaze (A-E) 250
Flask, book, "Coming Through The Rye", blue glaze (A-E)... 140
Flask, book, "Departed Spirits", Rockingham mottled glaze (D-MW) 200
Flask, book, "Departed Spirits", Rockingham mottled glaze, 2 qt., 8" h. (A-NE) 825
Flask, book, flint enamel (D-MW).. 225
Flask, book, flint enamel, 1 qt., 5½" h. (A-NE) 275
Flask, book, flint enamel, 2 qt., 8" h. (A-NE) 150
Flask, book, "Ladies Companion", flint enamel, 4 qt. (A-NE) 275
Flask book, "Ladies Companion", flint enamel, 1 qt. (D-E) 350
Flask, tavern, flint enamel (A-NE) 375
Inkwell, brown glaze, figures in relief, 3¼" d. (A-E)... 20
Jug, stoneware, E. Norton, floral, 3-gal. (A-E) 90
Jug, stoneware, J.P. Norton (D-MW) 90
Jug, J.P. Norton, blue decor. of house & trees (D-E)... 420
Lion, flint enamel, coleslaw mane (A-NE) 1350
Mold, Turkshead, Rockingham mottled glaze, 9" diam. (D-MW)............................... 45
Muffin pan, flint enamel, 12-hole, green, yellow/brown glazes, 10"×14½" (D-E).................... 950
Mug, flint enamel, 3¼" h. (A-MW) 40
Mugs, concave sides w/strap handles, pr. 2¾" h. (A-MW)... 110
Name plate, flint enamel, shield shape, 8" l., 3¾" h. (A-NE) 40
Name plate, Rockingham, 7¼" l., 3¼" h. (A-NE).. 80
Pans, milk, Rockingham mottled glaze, flared sides, 11" diam., pr. (A-MW) 90
Paperweight, flint enamel, 1849 mark, dog motif (A-E).. 375
Picture frame, flint enamel, ivy vine pattern, scalloped edge, 11¾" h., 9" w., rare (A-NE) 150
Picture frame, flint enamel, rococo, 11" h., 9½" w. (A-NE)... 575
Picture frame, flint enamel, scalloped edge, 12" h., 9½" w. (A-NE)............................. 400
Picture frame, Rockingham mottled glaze, oval, 9½" h. (A-MW) 160
Picture frame, rectangular, 5"×8" (A-E) 380
Picture frame, Rockingham, 11¾" h., 10½" w. (A-NE)... 275
Picture frame, Rockingham glaze, oval (D-MW) 220
Picture frames, Rockingham mottled glaze, oval, pr. 11½" h. (A-E) 325
Picture frames, Rockingham, pr. 7⅞" h., 6⅝" w. (A-NE) 325
Pitcher, flint enamel, 5⅝" h. (A-NE) 325
Pitcher, flint enamel, scalloped rib pattern, 9" h. (A-NE)... 275
Pitcher, flint enamel, swirled alternate rib pattern, 10" h. (A-NE) 400
Pitcher, flint enamel, tulip & heart pattern (A-NE).. 400
Pitcher, hound handle, hunt scene decor. in relief, 7" h. (A-MW)............................... 110
Pitcher, mixing, footed w/handle, Rockingham glaze (D-E)... 75
Pitcher, water, hound handle, dk. brown glaze (A-E) 400
Pitcher, water, hound handle, embossed deer & dog, Rockingham mottling (D-MW)............. 50
Pitcher, water, Rockingham mottled glaze, hunter w/his dogs in relief decor., 9¼" h. (A-MW) 80
Pitcher, water, tankard shape w/6 matching mugs, Rockingham mottled glaze (D-MW).......... 75
Pitcher, water, Rockingham mottled glaze, tulips in relief decor., 10" h. (A-MW) 90
Plate, pie, flint enamel, 9⅜" (D-E) 175
Plate, pie, flint enamel, signed, 9⅜" (A-E) 420
Plate, pie, Rockingham glaze, 9½" (A-MW).. 65
Plate, pie, Rockingham glaze 9½" (D-S)... 38
Plate, pie, Rockingham glaze 10" (D-N)... 90
Plate, pie, Rockingham mottled glaze, 8" (D-MW) 48
Plate, pie, Rockingham mottled glaze, 9⅜" (D-W).. 45
Plate, pie, Rockingham mottled glaze, 9½" (D-MW) 45
Plate, pie, Rockingham mottled glaze, 10¾" (D-MW).. 85
Plates, pie, Rockingham mottled glaze, pr., 10" diam. (A-MW) 135

Bennington (A-NE), *top row, left to right:* **Toby, Wellington,** $175; **coachman's bottle,** $425; **Ben Franklin Toby,** $175; *bottom row, left to right:* **Toby snuff bottle,** flint enamel, $525; **doorknobs,** $70; **Toby, Ben Franklin,** flint enamel, $500; **creamer,** cow, flint enamel, $375; **Toby, pitcher,** Rockingham, $45; **tavern flask,** Rockingham, $375

Poodle, Rockingham mottled glaze, 8" h. (A-NE) ....$ 1650
Snuff jar, flint enamel, signed (A-E) 425
Snuff jar, Toby, flint enamel, 4¼" h. (A-NE) 525
Teapot, flint enamel, alternate rib pattern, 7⅝" h. (A-NE) 350
Teapot, flint enamel, alternate rib pattern, 6½" h. (A-NE) 875
Teapot, flint enamel, alternate rib pattern, 6¾" h. (A-NE) 1000
Tea set, teapot, cake plate, sugar, creamer, 6 cups & saucers, Rockingham glaze (D-E).......... 475
Tile, flint enamel, olive-green, 7" square (A-NE).. 330
Tobacco jar, flint enamel, covered, canister shape, ribbed & reeded, side handled, marked Lyman
    Fenton & Co., Fenton's enamel, pat. 1849, Bennington, Vt., 7" h. (A-MW) 225
Toby, flint enamel, Ben Franklin pattern, boot handle, 5¾" h. (A-NE)................................. 175
Toby, flint enamel, Ben Franklin pattern, grapevine handle, 5¾" h. (A-NE) 500
Toby, Rockingham mottled glaze, 5⅞" h. (A-NE)... 45
Toby, flint enamel, signed, small repair (A-E) 440
Toby, "The Snuff Takers", 9½" h. (A-MW) 55
Toby, Wellington, Rockingham mottled glaze, 6" h. (A-NE).. 175
Urn, flint enamel, panel design, yellow & green glaze (A-E).. 450
Washboard, Rockingham mottling (D-W)... 65
Washbowl & Pitcher, Rockingham mottled glaze, panel design, 1849 mark (A-E) 500

Blue-White Stoneware

Both the prices and the popularity of American shaded blue-white stoneware are rapidly moving upward. It was produced in quantity for utilitarian purposes from the late 1800s, well into the present century. Similar objects having a brown or shaded green glaze were produced, but it is the blue-and-white pieces that enjoy the greatest popularity among collectors. Marked examples of this type of stoneware are scarce, and it really has no specific name. Through the years it has been called German blue stoneware, blue crockery, salt glaze pottery and blue Flemish. The latter term was noted in a 1914 Lee catalog. And in 1924, the American Wholesalers Corporation catalog listed it as merely tinted blue and white stoneware.

Decoration varies from a shaded smooth surface to attractive embossed patterns. Some collectors have found as many as 80 different patterns including figures, buildings, trees, flowers, animals and birds. Examples of the latter are presently commanding the highest prices.

* * *

Bedpan (A-E) ....$	8
Bedpan (D-MW)	10
Bean pot w/cover, handle on side (D-MW)	50
Bowl, large, bail handle (D-MW)	15
Bowl, large mixing, embossed love bird decor. (D-S)	50
Bowl, large mixing, flying bird decor. embossed (D-SE)	25
Bowl & pitcher set, basket-weave decor. (D-S)	75
Bowls, set of 4, embossed apricot design (D-SE)	45
Bowls, set of 6, mixing, embossed wedding band decor. (D-MW)	60
Butter tub, w/cover & bail, embossed Greek column decor. (D-MW)	38
Butter tub, w/cover, embossed love birds (D-MW)	65
Butter tub, without cover, embossed love birds (D-E)	28
Canister set, w/lids, 6-pc., basket-weave decor. (D-MW)	50
Chamber pot, w/cover, adult's, embossed basket-weave design (D-S)	40
Chamber pot, w/cover, child's, embossed basket-weave design (D-MW)	18
Cookie jar, w/cover, flying bird embossed on side (D-MW)	55

Blue-white pottery (D-MW), *left:* **milk pitcher,** $35; *right:* **bowl,** $12

Blue-white pottery (D-MW), *left:* **covered butter,** damaged, $18; *right:* **water pitcher,** $28

Crock, embossed polar bear decor. (D-S) ....$	90
Foot warmer (D-S)	40
Foot warmer (D-W)..	32
Foot warmer, salesman's sample or child's, 6" (D-W)	45
Jardiniere & base, embossed tulip decor. (D-MW)	75
Mug, barrel shape (D-S)	18
Pie plate (D-S)	28
Pitcher, milk, embossed Dutch boy & girl (D-E)	35
Pitcher, milk, embossed head of Lincoln (D-MW)................................	55
Pitcher, milk, embossed rose w/bead decor. (D-S)................................	35
Pitcher, 6 matching mugs, embossed flying bird design (D-S)	185
Pitcher, water, barrel shape, banded (D-MW)....................................	30
Pitcher, water, bulbous shape, daisy decor. (D-MW)	50
Pitcher, water, embossed apricots (D-S)...	35
Pitcher, water, embossed basket weave decor. (D-E)	20
Pitcher, water, embossed butterfly decor. (D-MW)	28
Pitcher, water, embossed head of Indian chief (D-S)...........................	50
Pitcher, water, embossed love birds (D-MW).....................................	45
Pitcher, water, embossed swan (D-S)	45
Pitcher, water, embossed tulip decoration (D-W)	25
Rolling pin, banded & floral decor. (D-MW)	35
Salt, hanging w/cover (D-MW)	20
Salt, hanging w/cover, embossed apricot design (D-SE)	30
Salt, hanging w/cover, embossed Indian good luck sign (D-SE)................	40
Salt, hanging, w/lid, embossed basket weave & grape decor. (D-SE).........	32
Salt, w/lid, oak leaf decor. (D-S)	32
Soap dish, lid, basket-weave embossed decor. (D-S)	22
Soap dish, lion's head embossed in center (D-S)................................	20
Spittoon, basket-weave design (D-MW)..	12
Teapot, w/cover (D-E)	22
Teapot, w/cover (D-SW)..	15
Toothbrush holder, basket-weave decor. (D-MW)	12
Water cooler, w/cover, embossed cupid & scroll decor. (D-S)	175
Water cooler, w/cover, embossed deer—"Sanitary Water Keg." (D-E).......	130
Water cooler, w/cover, embossed words "Ice Water" (D-S)	100

Boxes

Boxes are fascinating collectibles. They come in a variety of shapes, sizes and materials, and have been used for various purposes throughout our recorded history. Finding two early examples exactly alike is almost an impossibility, except for those that were made on molds or in wood factories during the last century.

Wooden boxes are favorites of the country collector. Wood used for making these containers was generally pine, birch, maple, ash or beech, since these were the more common trees in the New England areas. For assembling the earliest boxes, short wooden pegs were used to fasten the bottom to the side and the top

Saltbox, hanging, cherry, orig. finish (D-MW) $175

Saltbox, pine & cherry striped wood (D-W) $45

Knife box, walnut, dovetailed, hinged covers, orig. porcelain pulls, refinished (D-MW) $55

to the rim. Later examples were fastened with copper or iron nails. Round boxes were the most common shape. These were used in pantries and in kitchens for storage, and were rarely decorated. Most were made in nesting sizes, ranging from 2 inches for pills and other numerous small items, to medium size examples for storing herbs, sugar and meal, to the large 18 and 24 inch sizes for storing cheese.

Then we have the very desirable oval Shaker boxes, first made about 1798. Their construction was errorless. These were sold in graduated sizes or "nests" and, if equipped with handles, they were known as "carriers." Shaker boxes can be identified by their projecting "fingers" or laps, which were always evenly cut and matched, and secured by wrought-iron or copper rivets. Some were var-

Spice box, pine, orig. old red
stained finish (D-W) $70

Spice box, hanging, pine & maple,
8-drawer, refinished (D-MW) $69

nished, while others were painted. The reds and yellows were the most common, while blues or greens of the mellowest hue are considered rarer. Fine Shaker boxes are still being made, but they can be easily identified as each box is branded to protect the integrity of the original. (See *Shaker* category.)

Spice boxes — metal or wooden — are especially favored by collectors. Occasionally, the odor of a box that hasn't been used for many years will be a clue to its original use. Boxes assembled in groups, whether made for hanging, to be placed on a cabinet top, or large enough to be set on the floor, are of much interest. Of this type, there is a wide variance in sizes and arrangements of the small interior drawers. Some are called spice cabinets or chests, and those dating from the late 1700s well into the last century often reflect in miniature the furniture styles of the period.

Many boxes were made specifically for different purposes, such as the candleboxes with their sliding covers, knife boxes for wall or tables, salt and pipe boxes for hanging, writing, sewing, snuff and trinket boxes, and interesting Bible boxes, oftentimes decorated with carving, inlay or painting.

Bright and delightfully colored boxes were popular during the last century. Fancy bride's boxes decorated with gay flowers, birds and figures were common in the Pennsylvania German areas. And, from the same region, we have the fine decorated boxes in various sizes made by Jacob Weber, around the 1850s. And finally we have the extremely popular bandbox, oftentimes covered with color printed papers depicting topical and historical events and well-known sights. These were used for storage as well as transporting clothing, hats, and other personal effects.

Amazingly, it is still possible to assemble an interesting collection of boxes that spans at least one hundred and fifty years or more. But, the novice collector should avoid making quick and expensive purchases, especially if spice boxes are preferred. Both the round wood-bound style holding round, small spice containers, as well as a variety of new hanging boxes (assembled in groups of six or eight boxes) are on the market. Like furniture, early spice boxes, as well as other types, carries, plainly written over its various parts and surfaces, an accurate record of age and treatment. The eye and fingertips working together can distinguish stains, tiny scratches, and bruises which give wooden surfaces a mellow quality of color and texture that cannot be imitated or hurried. And finally, your nose in an asset too, as old wood has a distinct odor that cannot be duplicated.

Apple, footed, smoke decor., splayed outward from base (A-NE) ....$ 225
Apple, pine, old green paint, 11"×8½" (A-NE) 40
Ballot, black balls (D-N) 25
Ballot, mahogany, mortised joints, handled, early, 9"×6"×4½" (D-NW) 25
Ballot, maple, sliding dovetailed top, slat in sliding lid, oblong (D-E) 85
Ballot, pine, orig. red paint, 12" sq., 24" h. (D-W)... 22
Bandbox, "Bucher" type, 9"×6", decor. w/school house & tree on lid (A-E)............ 1350
Bandbox, faded blue, red & green floral pattern, oval, stenciled (D-NE) 55
Bandbox, floral decor. very faded, cond. good. 6" round (A-E)........................... 200
Bandbox, large, decor. w/flowers on branches (A-E) 2000

Spice box, hanging,
oak (D-MW) $79

Bride's box, painted tulip decor. on dk. green
ground, dated 1817 (D-MW) $200

Bandbox, large, decor. w/man & woman w/flowers on lid, sides decor. w/tulips, (A-E)........... 1050
Bandbox, large, marked Hannah Davis (A-E) 125
Bandbox, New York State House decor. (D-E) 145
Bandbox, rare design on lid; hunter shooting deer, large (A-E)............................ 525
Bandbox, wood, old dk. green, oval, rare, 19½"×12" t. (D-NE) 38
Banded, decor., 12½" (A-E) 90
Banded, decor. w/bright colors, 9½"×7" (A-E) 150
Banded, tulips & flowers, man & woman, 19" diam. (A-D)................................ 300
Banded, wallpaper, ex. large (A-E).. 30
Bee, elaborate (D-E) 45
Bee, hickory wood, 2 slides, ca. 1830, 4"×6" (D-E) 25
Bee, tin (D-W) 22
Bee-finder's, sliding lid, refinished, 10"×4", rare (D-MW) 70
Bible, dated 1732 (D-E) 195
Bible, oak, hand carved, bird & heart motif (D-NE) 275
Bible, round top, dov. const. brown/black sponge decor. (A-E)........................... 50
Brass, leather covered, coffin shape (A-E) 30
Brass, leather covered, studded, coffin shape (A-E) 30
Brass, octagonal, handle (D-W).. 27
Bride's, New England, domed top, cotter pinned, covered w/orig. colorful wallpaper, well pre-
    served, 12" l., 6" d., 5¾" h., late 18th C. (D-E) 145
Bride's, oval, wooden, 19th C. (D-E) 230
Bride's, painted bride & groom amid floral & emblematical decor., 18" oval (D-E) 350
Bride's, painted, Dutch legend (D-E).. 230
Bride's, sponge decor., initialed, C.1840–, 27" long (D-E) 250

Bride's, tulip & floral decor. on sides, bride's decor. on top, 18½" l., 11" w., 7" h. (D-E) ....$ 300
Butter, w/6 individual containers, 1 pound (D-MW) 95
Button, wood w/floral decor. (A-E)... 35
Candle, cherry, chip carved, scalloped arch, sunburst, dovt. (D-E) 385
Candle, chip carved, sliding lid, orig. dark finish, dovt. const. (D-E) 175
Candle, chip carved, no lid (A-E) 50
Candle, geometric tree & heart, carved & inlaid decor., 8" (A-NE)...................................... 90
Candle, hanging, high back, dovt., orig. dark finish, lid (D-E) 95
Candle, hanging, oak, sliding front (D-MW) 75
Candle, hanging, orig. dk. green finish, sliding lid (A-MW) 65
Candle, hanging, painted red, (old) 15½" h. (D-MW).. 80
Candle, hanging, pine, 1 large & 1 small box attached to backboard, dovetailed & refinished
  (D-MW) 85
Candle, hanging, pine, slant lid & simple arched back w/hole for hanging, orig. finish worn, fine
  patina, 14½" l., 6½" d., 12¼"h., early 18th C. (A-E) 135
Candle, hanging, pine, sliding front, refinished, 12" h. (A-NE).. 62
Candle, hanging, tin, line decor., round (A-E) 190
Candle, hanging, tole, cylindrical, orig. fine decor. w/lid (A-E).. 350
Candle, hanging, 2-tier, old mustard paint, triangular back shield, 6"×11"×16" (D-NE) 95
Candle, hanging, wood, dov. const., orig. old med. blue paint, 15¼"×7½"×5" (D-NE).......... 75
Candle, pine, 13⅛" l., 9⅝" w., 4¾" d. (D-E) 20
Candle, pine, dovetailed (D-W)... 45

Domed box, decor. w/floral bird & drape, 25½" l.,
12½" d., 14" h. (A-E) $275

Candle box, hanging, sliding
front, 16½ h., 5¾ w. (D-MW) $85

Candle, pine, sliding lid, cream ground w/dk. green sponged decor., red border, knob on lid,
  14¼" l. (A-E).. 350
Candle, pine, sliding lid, large dovt. const., refinished (D-MW) 60
Candle, pine, sliding lid, orig. red paint, dov. const. (A-E)... 62
Candle, pine, sliding lid, refinished, 13⅛" l., 9⅝" w., 4¾" d. (D-W).................................... 38
Candle, walnut, sliding lid, refinished, 13½" l., 10¼" w. (D-W) 38
Candle, slide cover, floral decor., dk. green, white & red, 10¼"×7" (D-NE).......................... 36

Candle, sliding lid, decor. w/tulip buds & flowers, dov. const. (A-E)............................$ 400
Candle, sliding lid, floral decor., dk. green, white & red, 10¼"×7" (D-NE).......................... 136
Candle, sliding lid, flower decor. on lid & sides; front panel decor. w/school house & trees (A-E). 900
Candle, sliding lid, molded base, orig. dk. green paint, 11"×6½"×7¼" (D-NE)..................... 55
Candle, sliding lid, red paint old, 13" l. (A-E).. 80
Candle, table model, slide lid, painted red, 6½"×7"×13" (D-E) 65
Candle, tin, oblong, brass studded (A-E)... 20
Candle, tin, orig. asphaltum paint, 11" l., 4½" w. (D-E)... 195
Candle, tin, pierced w/stars, hanging, round (D-E) 165
Candle, tin, wall (D-NE)... 95
Candle, tin, wall, w/line decor., round (A-E).. 190
Candle, wood, wall, painted red, 15½" l. (D-E) 81
Candle, wood, sliding lid, dovt. const. (A-E) 45
Cardboard, Centennial w/presidents up to 1876 & picture of Capitol bldg. (A-E) 30
Change-cash, cherry, long, narrow w/2 sliding lids & finger holes (D-SE).............................. 135
Cash, tole, flat top, orig. stenciled decor. w/owner's initials, 9"×6"×5½" (D-NE) 15
Cheese, large, old red stain (D-N).. 45
Cheese, round, w/scratched carved tree & leaf design on top, blk. & green incl. orange band w/mahogany diamond inlays, label, "G.E.P. Hinkley", 7" diam. (A-E) 350
Cheese, small, old blue paint (D-N)... 28
Coal, brass, w/ball feet (A-NE) 75
Cobbler's w/tools (A-E) 27
Coffee bin, pine w/slant top (D-MW) 38
Coin, money changer, oak, dated 1823 (D-MW) 225
Comb, wall, decor. w/blue & yellow (A-E) 260
Comb, wall, inlaid w/birds in relief (A-E) 220
Cookie, Pa. Dutch, circular w/wooden lid, decor. w/floral motif & doves, handle (D-W) 265
Covered, birds'-eye & tiger maple, oval, white w/blue sponge (D-NE)................................... 20
Deed, flat top, all orig., stenciled w/"Fidelity" on top, 6½"×4"×2½" (D-NE) 28
Deed, pine, wallpaper covered, rounded top & tin hinges & latch (A-E) 150
Deed, toleware, decor. (A-E)... 60
Deed, toleware, mini-rose stencil, blue japanned, 3½"×2"×2¼" (D-E) 35
Deed, toleware, orig. flowers & bird decor. 8½" (D-NE) 75
Deed, toleware, round top, colorful decor. (A-E)... 135
Deed, wood, carved sides, front & top (A-E).. 50
Deed, wood, coffin type; tulip & floral decor. (A-E)... 375
Deed, wood, decor. w/flowers & birds on top w/bldg. & men on horseback on front; tulip & daisy decor. on sides (A-E) 320
Deed, wood, rounded top (A-E) 15
Deed, wood, rounded top, covered w/wallpaper (A-E).. 30
Desk, mahogany, w/compartments for pens, pencil & inkwell, 5"×4½"×14¼", orig. brass escutcheon (D-MW).. 265
Desk, old dk. green, handplaned slant cover, molded back shelf inside, tin hasp & hinges (D-W) 50
Desk, pine, dk. green paint shows handplaning, tin hinges & hasp, slant cover w/molded back & front cover, shelf inside, 13¼" w., 10½"d. (D-NE)... 55
Desk, pine, red, w/dk. brown brush decor., w/eye shapes centered on lid & sides, 2 decor. interior drawers, 17"×18" (A-NE) 300
Desk, slant lid, old red paint, 17½" w. (A-E)... 80
Document, toleware, decor. w/red, white, black & gold on asphaltum base, 6½"l.×4"t.×3"w. (D-S).. 75
Document, toleware, floral decor. (A-E) 110
Document, toleware, good decor., hasp catch missing (A-E)... 100
Document, toleware, orig. decor., good cond. (D-NE) 95
Document, toleware, decor., red, white, black & gold on asphaltum base, 6½"l.×4"t.×3"w. (D-S) 75
Document, toleware, red & yellow decor., (A-E).. 220
Document, toleware, signed Hannah Barber, bright decor. w/lg. bird, rare (A-E) 675
Document, toleware, small (A-E) 57
Document, walnut, dated 1761, H.I.P. (A-E)... 130
Dome-top, black paint, decor. w/red streaked line (A-NE).. 300

Trinket box, decor., slide lid 9¾ × 5¼″ (A-E) $4150; **date board,** wooden, (A-E) $50; **comb box,** wall, decor., in blue & yellow (A-E) $260; **dome-lid box,** decor. birds on front & back, 10″ l. (A-E) $425

Dome-top, cream colored ground w/bold red swirled & sponged decor., 29″×29″ (A-NE)..........$ 550

Dome-top, decor. birds on front & back, 10″ l. (A-E) 425

Dome-top, decor. in lt. blue-green & white, 29½″ (A-NE)... 275

Dome-top, decor orig. paint, good cond. (A-E)... 30

Dome-top, decor., orig. paint, large (A-E).. 50

Dome-top, elaborate sponged earth colored decor., dov. const. 18″ (A-NE) 175

Dome-top, green w/smoke decor., 16″ (A-NE).. 175

Dome-top, large, profuse decor., blue-green background (A-E).. 3,200

Dome-top, lock & hasp decor., w/form of reeding over top, 4 reeded panels & heart on front in old gr. paint, lg., dov. con. (A-E).. 425

Dome-top, ochre ground & bold green wavy line decor., 18″ (A-NE) 300

Dome-top, original black/red swirl grained finish, brass hdw. orig., 13″×13″×28″ (D-E) 200

Dome-top, overhanging top & scalloped & moulded bracket base, amber painted veneer, orig. lock & key, 9½″ (A-NE).. 425

Dome-top, painted in red, green, ochre & white, dov. const. 28″ (A-NE) 1850

Dome-top, potato decor., 18″ l. (A-E) 800

Dome-top, reeding on lid & front, panels & hearts, dov. const., rare (A-E)............................ 500

Dome-top, toleware, painted, (D-MW) 225

Dome-top, yellow ochre ground w/black fan sponged decor., w/overlying blue-green borders, 20″, dov. const. (A-NE)... 875

Dome-top, yellow w/red, blue & blk. brushed decor., 24″, orig. hardware (A-NE) 425

Dough, pine, orig. dark paint (D-S) 65

Dough, pine, orig. roseheaded nails (A-MW) 250

Dovetailed, old blue paint, early nails, lined w/old wallpaper, 12″×23½″×9½″ (D-NE)........... 48

Dovetailed, orig. blue paint, 14½″×8″×6½″ (D-NE)... 20

Dovetailed, walnut, 1-drawer, 13″×9″×7″ (A-E).. 75

Flat, small, decor. w/simulated veneer graining, inscr. "Grace Knapp, West Dummerston, Vt." (A-NE).. 150

Flat-top, green ground, ochre seaweed decor. & red spots, dovt. const., 24″ (A-NE) 575

Flat-top, ochre w/dk. green brushed spots, red dry-brush decor. overall w/orig. hdwe., 30″ (A-NE) 285

Glove, small, wallpaper covered (D-E)... 70

Grained, over orig. green, Pa. origin, ca. 1850, 18″ l., 6½″ h. (D-E) 325

Grain, pine, w/handmade nails (D-E) 130

Hanging, pine & poplar, slant lid & 1 drawer, dovetailed, orig. paint, 12¼″ w., 15″ l., 10½″ w. (A-E) 175

Hat, cardboard, covered w/floral wallpaper, print of cow on inside cover, handstitched, 6½″ oval × 4″ h. (D-NE) 30

Hat, covered w/blue paper w/birds (D-E) 110

Hat, cardboard, old bonnet inside, wallpapered w/floral paper in pink & blue on beige, oval, (bonnet, gray satin) 9½″ h. × 12″ (D-NE).. 25

Hat, decor. w/bird, dog, flower basket on black gr., 13½″×9″×7″ (D-E)................................ 210

Hat, Hannah Davis, 10″ (D-NE) 125

Hat, historical, wood, 18″×14″, merchant's ex., N.Y., amber-white on yellow (D-E) ....$ 275
Hat, joys of rural life (papered), rose, white, umber on blue ground (D-E) 200
Hat, pine, ladies, sq. domed top w/strap handle, 19th C., 16½″ l. (A-MW)..................... 150
Hat, tall wallpaper style (D-E) 90
Hat, tin, original paint, oval, blue interior, dark russet mustard outside (D-NE) 25
Hat, tin, raw sienna paint outside, blue inside, all orig., oval (D-NE)................................. 25
Hat, wood, stage coach, orig. finish, lock & key, Ca. 1874-90 (A-E) 80
Herb, Shaker, copper tacks, oval & open, straight lap, handplaned bottom, 12½×7¼×2¾″
  (D-NE).. 35
Herb, oval/shallow w/shaped laps, orig. lid, traces of orig. red paint (D-E) 250
Knife, burl, decor. w/black trim (D-SE).. 75
Knife, black w/striping in old yellow, olive green & red, 15″×7½″×4″ (D-NE)....................... 45
Knife cleaning, hanging, old red, black & yellow line decor. (D-E)..................................... 45
Knife cleaning, 2 slide lid boxes, 9½″×14″ (D-E) 45
Knife, curly maple, dovt. const. (A-E) 40
Knife, hinged, opening in center w/orig. paint, dovt. ends, rare (A-E).............................. 140
Knife, old red paint, strawberry decor. on sides, 12″×9″ (D-NE) 18
Knife, old red, slanted sides, 12″×11″×4″ (D-NE) 33
Knife, pine, cut-out handle & shaped ends, yellow & red sponge decor. (A-NE) 250
Knife, pine, scalloped double wooden, dovt. const. (D-E)... 135
Knife, scalloped edges, 18th C. (A-E) 70
Knife/pumice, hanging (D-MW) 42
Knife/pumice, w/lip (D-E) 35
Knife sharpening & storage, 10½″ l., 5¼″ w., 3¾″ d. (D-E).. 24
Knife, walnut, carved handle-like wings (D-SE)... 75
Lift-top, handcarved, decor. w/birds & animals (D-NE) 75
Lunch, toleware, blue japanned, red striping, 6½″×3″×3″ (D-E)...................................... 45
Lunch, oval, covered, 19th C. (A-MW) 35
Match, wood, handcarved, 5″ h. (D-MW)... 20
Open, hanging, hand carved, hewn from solid piece wood, 10″ l., 7¼″ h., (D-S)................. 95
Open, 2-compartment, decor. w/cherries, apple, pear, peach & plum; dov. con., chamfered top
  inside edges, 10″ l. (A-E) 300
Painted, w/primitive lion on lid, painted flower decor. front & sides, framed in green, 9″ w.
  (A-NE).. 650
Pantry, birch bark, 1848 Maine newspaper on cover & inside lining, oval, 12″×6″ (D-E) 36
Pantry, black, 7¼″×3″ (D-NE) 20
Pantry, blue, 13½″×6½″ (D-E) 28
Pantry, blue, old orig. paint, 8″×4″ (D-MW) 20
Pantry, bright green, 10″×5″ (D-NE) 22
Pantry, colonial, stitched (D-W).. 22
Pantry, dk. green, 8½″×4″ (D-E)... 16
Pantry, dk. green, 6″×2¾″ (D-E) 14
Pantry, dk. green, v-lap, 7″×2¾″ (D-NE) 24
Pantry, dk. leaf green, 9″×5″ (D-NE) 18
Pantry, darkened to nut brown, v-lap top, stitched bottom, 5″ (D-NE) 30
Pantry, gray blue, v-lap top, 8″×3½″ (D-NE) 20
Pantry, lt. olive green, 6½″×2½″ (D-NE) 14
Pantry, lt. pearl gray, oval, 14″×11″×5½″ (D-NE) 35
Pantry, marked J. Brown, early nails, 5″ (D-NE) 15
Pantry, med. green, 8½″ (D-NE) 18
Pantry, med. green, 14½″×7½″ (D-NE) 45
Pantry, med. green, inset bottom 9″×4½″ (D-NE) 30
Pantry, med. green, 6″ (D-NE) 14
Pantry, med. gray, 6¾″×2¾″ (D-E) 14
Pantry, med. mustard brown, 8¾″×4″ (D-NE) 16
Paper, theorem on velvet on top, 5″×2½″ (D-NE).. 18
Pencil, child's, w/pen, pencil & eraser (A-E).. 12
Pencil, slide lid, hand-hewn, pine, small (D-E) 15
Pencil, sliding top, dov. const. (D-E).. 15

Pantry, old dk. blue, 11" (D-NE) .... $ 18
Pantry, old lt. gray, 5¾" (D-NE) 14
Pantry, old red, 12½"×6¾" (D-NE) 40
Pantry, old red color, worn on top, 6" (D-NE) 14
Pantry, oval, lt. blue-gray, 14"×11"×5½" (D-E) 35
Pantry, oval, stitched, 10" (D-NE) 40
Pantry, red, 8¾"×3½" (D-E) 16
Pantry, steel gray, 9¾"×4½" (D-NE) 18
Pantry, unusual shade of orangy ochre, 8½" (D-NE) 25
Pantry, v-lap, old dk. green, 7½" (D-NE) 25

Saltbox, wall, decor., 2-drawer, scrolled top (A-E) $800

Wall box, decor. w/scalloped cut-outs (A-E) $725

Pantry, white, 6¾"×3" (D-E) 18
Pine, rectangular w/1 long upper drawer over slant compartmented section, 28" w., 18" d., 29½" h. (A-MW) 350
Pipe, cherry, orig. finish, dated 1767 (D-NE) 800
Pipe, pine w/drawer, dovt. const., orig. dk. finish, fish-tail back (D-MW) 300
Pipe, traveling, orig. grained paint (A-E) 70
Poplar, blue-green paint w/yellow & red dec. of primitive bird & flowers & "Cordelia S. Gilliland", no lid, 8½"×6½"×5¼" (A-E) 325
Poplar, dovt. const., red & black graining, hdwe. incomplete, 31"×14½"×31" (A-E) 95
Receipt, wagonmaster's, orig. blue finish, Lancaster Co., Penna., ca. 1850 (D-E) 90
Round, early, decor. (A-E) 50
Salt, burnt wood, "poker work" (D-S) 8
Salt, flat back, curved front, old red painted finish (D-E) 45
Salt, hanging, maple & cherry, striped wood, pin hinged cherry top (D-MW) 35
Salt, hanging, maple & cherry, striped wood, pin hinged cover (D-E) 90
Salt, hanging, orig. red paint, curved front sawed almost through wood to make shape, dovt. const., dated 1725, sgn. F.M., pin hinged top (D-MW) 200
Salt, hanging, pine, dovt. const., open, refinished (D-E) 75
Salt, hanging, pine, dov. const., 2 compartments, (A-E) 45
Salt, hanging, staved, wooden bands, orig. old red finish good (D-NE) 85
Salt, hanging, walnut, slant top, dovetail drawer below (D-MW) 125
Salt, open, 2 compartments, Pa. Dutch hex sign & initialed (D-MW) 150
Salt, pine, hinged cover, cut out back, in the rough (A-E) 27
Salt, pine, hinged lid (A-N) 32
Salt, treen, early & crude, open, 2½" h. (D-E) 42

Salt, wall, 2 drawers, scrolled top (A-E) ....$ 800
Salt, walnut, 1 drawer, hinged (A-E) 37
Seed, compartments, sliding lid (D-E) 110
Sewing, maple, sliding lid (A-NE) 55
Sewing, maple, sliding lid (D-NE) 50
Sewing, pine, handmade, w/incised & colored hex sign decor. (A-E) 115
Shaving, w/brush, early treen (A-NE) 35
Slide-cover, w/child's game inside, handmade (D-NE) 10
Slide-lid, "Bucher", decor. w/red & white tulips, black background (A-E) 850
Slide-lid, burl maple, dov. const. (A-E) 62
Slide-lid, cherry, dovt. const. (A-E) 45
Slide-lid, pine, decor. w/green leaves & roses (A-E) 120
Slide-lid, decor. w/tulips, dov. const. (A-E) 130
Small, dk. green, w/olive & gold striping, free hand brush decor. on box top & sides, 9"×7"×4"
    (A-NE) 225
Snuff, burl, ovoid (D-E) 45
Snuff, handcarved wood, hinged (A-MW) 32
Snuff, pewter, oval, engraved repoussé (D-E) 18
Snuff, tin, handpainted red, double head of Washington (D-NE) 35
Snuff, tin, oval, hinged, dated 1860, 2¼"×3¼" (D-W) 15
Snuff, toleware, handpainted red, double head of Washington (D-NE) 30
Spice, cherry, 9-drawer w/1 long drawer at base, orig. finish good, 13" h., 12" w. (D-E) 135
Spice, curly maple, 12-drawer, orig. sm. brass pulls, molded top & base, ref. (D-MW)........... 290
Spice, hanging, 8-drawers, orig. black paint (D-W) 75
Spice, hanging, oak, 8-drawer, orig. wooden pulls, refinished (D-MW) 75
Spice, hanging, oak, 8-drawer, w/wooden pulls (D-MW).. 65
Spice, hanging, pine, 8-drawer, porcelain knobs (D-NE) 80
Spice, hanging, pine, 8-drawer, porcelain knobs new, refinished (D-W) 78
Spice, hanging, tin, 8-drawer, orig. black painted finish (D-S) 85
Spice, hanging, tin, 8-drawer, orig. black paint, knobs (D-W) 75
Spice, hanging, walnut, 2-drawer, hinged lid, scalloped eagle heads on back & dove tail (A-E). 275
Spice, hinged cover w/containers for spices & grater in center, complete, japanned (D-MW)... 38
Spice, oak, 8-drawer, orig. wood pulls, ex. cond., refinished (D-MW) 68
Spice, pine, 8-drawer, dovetailed, orig. white porcelain pulls badly worn, refinished (D-E).... 95
Spice, hanging, pine, 8-drawer, horizontal, orig. wooden pulls, ref. (D-W) 55
Spice, pine, new porcelain pulls, orig. dark red finish (D-N).. 75
Spice, pine, 9-drawer, orig. red paint & wooden pulls, 13¾" h., 13" w., 6½" d., refinished (D-N) 75
Spice, pine, painted white, 8-drawer, 16½" h. (A-MW) 16
Spice, pine, refinished, 8-drawer, white porcelain pulls orig., dovetailed drawers (D-E) 95
Spice, pine, unpainted, 5-drawer, dovetailed boxes, 16¼" h., 8" w. (A-NE) 72
Spice, tin, covered w/containers for spices & grater in center, japanned (D-E)...................... 40
Spice, tin, round, hinged cover, complete w/grater, orig. japanning good (D-E) 37
Spice, tin, round, hinged lid, 7 containers, complete w/grater (D-W) 22
Spice, tin, round w/spice containers, complete, cond. fair (D-S) 18
Spice, tin, 7 small, round spice containers, stenciled w/contents, grater in center, 10" diam. (D-S) 22
Spice, tin, wire handle, oblong, 6 round spice boxes (D-E) 28
Spice, toleware, 6 interior containers (D-E) 20
Spice & salt, hanging, cherry, wall, dov. const. (A-E)... 110
Spice & salt, hanging, lift lid, 2 small compartmented drawers; back designed like cocked hat
    (A-E) 170
Stamp, brass, w/hinged cover, footed (A-NE) 35
Stamp, copper, hinged w/1 compartment (A-MW)... 17
Stamp, pewter, w/center hinged top (A-E) 50
Sugar, toleware, orig. yellow & red basket flowers stencil, 12" diam., twist off cover (D-E)..... 125
Sugar, wood, screw type lid, fixed handle, red, 10" diam. (D-NE) 100
Tin, for plumed cocked hat of Army officer, 19th C. (D-MW) 85
Tin, old red, small, some black striping, 3¼"×2"×2½" (D-NE) 20
Tobacco, w/orig. Pa. paint work, 11" w., 19" h., 8" d. (D-MW) 40
Tramp art, geometric, footed, drawer & hinged top, 14"×15" (A-NE) 160

Bandbox, fine Bucher type,
painted flowers, trees, &
schoolhouse, 9"×6" (A-E) $1350

Spice box, walnut, scalloped eagle heads on
backboard, dovetailed (A-E) $275

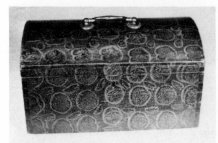

Domed box, pine, brown & buff sponge decor.,
dovetailed, 12" l. (D-MW) $275

Trinket, grained & painted, 1-drawer (D-E) ....$ 275
Trinket, green wood, carved all sides, slide lid (A-E) 260
Trinket, miniature, domed lid, blue-green background, 5½" l. (A-E) 525
Trinket, slide lid, decor., 9¾"×5¼" (A-E)..150
Trinket, slide lid, decor. w/tulips, tree of life, blk. birds w/red & green wings, initials "M"H.",
   8½" long (A-E)..2500
Trinket, slide lid, orange background, blue & white decor., 8¾" l. (A-E) 325
Trinket, slide-lid, wood, carved w/tulips, 6" l. (A-E)..275
Voting, oak, shape of lg. pot w/handle & tray w/hole in middle (D-E)................................33
Wall, attached spoon rail, blue-gray, 16" (A-NE)..275
Wall, back w/scrolled cut-outs, lid, front & sides decor. w/flowers (A-E) 725
Wall, hanging, 3-tiered, old green paint, 25" h. × 19" w. (A-NE) 450
Wall, miniature, old oxblood red, 5¼"×7½" (A-NE)..275
Wall, pine, gray-brown w/black squiggles, 12" h. (A-NE) 400
Wall, pine, red stain, 19" h. (A-NE) 175
Wall, wood, 5 compartments, 16" w., decor. similar to toleware, rare (A-E) 275
Weber, decor. w/birds, tulips & grapes, 19¼" l., 13" d., 12" h. (D-E) 225
Weber, decor. w/tulips on yellow background, miniature (A-E)...270
Weber, floral bird & drape decor., 25½" w., 12½" h., 14" d. (A-E)....................................275
Weber, miniature, decor. w/house, trees & tulips, yellow background, orig. hasp (A-E) 825
Weber, tulip & bird decor. along sides & pot of flowers on top, 11¼" h., 19" l., 9¾" d. (A-E) .250
Wood, birds'-eye maple w/painted flowers (A-E) 80
Wooden, coffin shape, w/wallpaper decor. (A-E)..60
Wooden, cotter pin hinges, orig. dark finish, 14½" l., 6" d., 5¼" h. (D-W) 42
Workbox, burl mulberry, bat-wing shape (A-E)..90
Writing, Shaker, side drawer & ink drawer (D-MW)...100

Brass

Early pieces of golden yellow American brass ware have been used for a wide range of cooking utensils since the 1700s. Collectors of country antiques have discovered that the primarily utilitarian objects—long-handled skimmers, forks, ladles, teakettles, kettles, pans, etc.—are extremely decorative. And, like other fine old collectibles in this vast field, they are becoming scarcer and more expensive with each passing year.

Brass is an alloy of copper and zinc with other elements added for special uses. It is a sturdy metal and generally, regardless of the age, an early piece is in good condition when found.

It is not a difficult task to determine early examples of brass from later pieces, as color is a true indication of age. Contemporary brass pieces have a tendency to turn reddish in color when they become tarnished, whereas an early piece will not discolor in this manner.

A tremendous amount of new brassware has been made in recent years, including attractive long-handled warming pans and coal scuttles with Delft handles.

* * *

Andirons, ball, turned spire, 18th C., 16″ (D-NE)	$ 165
Andirons, Chippendale, ball turning, small (A-E)	300
Andirons, Chippendale, early (A-E)	95
Andirons, claw feet (A-E)	60
Andirons, deer feet (A-E)	100
Andirons, double top (A-E)	450
Andirons, marked Hunneman Boston, ca. 1810, 16″ t. (D-NE)	675
Andirons, Queen Anne, ex. cond. (A-E)	47
Andirons, Queen Anne, w/leg stop finial, 12″ (A-E)	85
Andirons, small (A-E)	120
Andirons, small, early (A-E)	80
Andirons, steeple-top (A-E)	200
Barometer, ship's (D-MW)	75
Bedwarmer, circular form w/turned wood handle, 19th C., 41½″ l. (A-MW)	110
Bedwarmer, engraved & pierced (A-E)	55
Bedwarmer, iron handle (D-NE)	35
Bedwarmer, large, good design on lid incl. large tulip (A-E)	175
Bedwarmer, maple handle (A-E)	80
Bell, church, 26″ h. (A-E)	130
Bell, elephant, engraved (D-NE)	10
Bell, hand, 3″ (A-E)	27
Bell, hand, 3¼″ (A-E)	27
Bell, school, 12″ h., 6½″ diam. (D-MW)	65
Bell, school, large (A-E)	32
Bells, sleigh, double string, 46 bells (A-E)	150
Bells, sleigh, 1 large string (A-E)	37
Bells, sleigh, string of 15 w/leather strap (A-E)	35
Bells, sleigh, string of 54, nickel plated, on unused leather harness (D-N)	75
Bells, sleigh, string of 30 (A-E)	72
Bell, teacher's, 8″ (A-E)	12
Bell, tap, teacher's (D-E)	15
Bowl, 8″ diam. (A-MW)	30
Bowl, candy, round w/2 handles (A-E)	20

Chestnut roaster, brass (D-MW) $80

Skimmer, brass, shaped iron handle (D-MW) $45

Sleigh bells, brass, orig. strap (D-N) $90

Bowl, large, w/handles (A-E)	$ 25
Bowl, round, w/wrought iron handles, 12½" (A-E)	27
Bowl, taster, good cond. (A-E)	40
Bucket, dated 1851 (D-NW)	55
Bucket, hand forged iron bail & supporting top ring, 6" diam. (A-E)	28
Bucket, handmade, iron band at top, bail handle, 18th C., 7½" diam. × 5" (D-NE)	45
Bucket, iron bail, marked H.W. Hayden, 1851 (D-E)	48
Bucket, rat-tail handle (A-E)	45
Bugle, fireman's, engraved Adams Fire Dept. N.Y.S., 20" (D-E)	140
Button, uniform, Indian service (A-E)	5
Cake turner, Penna., wrought iron handle (D-MW)	22
Clothes tree, tall (A-E)	50
Cowbell, 4" h. (A-E)	17
Cowbell, w/leather neck strap (A-E)	18
Dipper, iron handle, scrolled hook, 5¾" diam., 19" l. (D-E)	65
Dipper, iron hook handle (A-N)	15
Dipper, large (A-E)	25
Doorbell (A-E)	15
Eagle, for flagpole (D-E)	30
Fender, large (A-E)	25
Fender, pierced, lion feet, 48" (D-NE)	115
Fender, pierced, lion head feet, 42" (D-NE)	120
Fender, pierced (D-NE)	70
Fender, reeded feet, rounded, 44", 8" h. (D-NE)	105
Fixtures, fireplace, andirons, railing, screen, tools (A-E)	300
Flatiron holder, bird & leaf pattern (A-E)	35
Foot warmer (A-E)	22
Funnel, round w/long spout, 9½" (D-E)	36
Goffering iron, complete (D-E)	130
Grater, on iron frame, 18th C., 12½" l. (D-E)	65
Grater, kitchen, pierced, 18th C., 13" (D-E)	50
Hall tree, ex. cond. (D-MW)	135
Hinges, H-L, pr. 11"×15" (A-E)	95
Jardiniere (A-E)	40
Kettle, brass handle, marked & dated (A-E)	47
Kettle, cast wrought iron bail riveted on, 10" diam. (A-E)	78
Kettle, 8½"×5" (D-E)	45
Kettle, iron bail (D-W)	125
Kettle, iron handle, marked & dated (A-E)	32
Kettle, jelly, cast iron handles, 11" diam. (A-E)	25
Kettle, large wrought iron loop handles at each side, 7½" diam., 2½" deep (D-W)	35
Kettle, singed, Hiram W. Hayden, Waterbury, Conn., pat. Dec. 16, 1851, 5¾" h., 8½" across (D-E)	45
Kettle, small, 7" across, 5" h. (A-E)	80
Kettle, spun exterior, 10" d. (D-W)	45
Kettle, 10"×6½" (D-E)	65

Kettle, wrought iron bail handle, 24½" d. (A-E) ....$ 140
Key, ship's, 4" (A-E) 5
Ladle, handwrought iron handle, decor. (A-E)... 150
Ladle, iron handle, 1846 (A-E)... 85
Ladle, iron handle 18" long (D-MW)... 38
Ladle, strainer lip & iron handle, 18½" l. (D-E) 65
Ladle, wrought iron handle, signed J Schmidt 1842 (A-E)................................ 230
Ladle, wrought iron handle, small (A-E).. 42
Ladle, wrought iron handle, small (A-MW) 40
Letter opener, on tray (D-MW)... 45
Letter scale, hanging (A-E) 27
Lock, Eagle Lock Co. (A-E) 15
Lock, 5"×8" (A-E) 65
Lock, 5¼"×8¼" (A-E) 140
Lock, rare, 6"×9½" (A-E).. 150
Mantel ornament, figure, pr. of lions (A-E) 1200
Match holder, w/2 compartments (A-E).. 30
Match safe, mouse figure (D-NE)... 80
Match safe, owl face figure (D-NE) 100
Match safe, punch w/hunch back figure (D-NE)... 95
Match safe, workshoe (A-E) 78
Mortar & Pestle, w/wooden frame, 1 drawer (D-MW) 35
Nutcracker (D-MW) 17
Pan, iron handle, round (A-E) 15
Picture frame, oval, small (D-E) 15
Plant stand, tray decor. w/embossed flower des. (D-W)..................................... 30
Rose basket of flowers, cast (A-E) 130
Scales, hanging store type, 2 pans 1" diam. (D-MW) 50
Scales, drugstore, complete (A-E) 42
Scales, wooden platform (A-E) 75
Screen, fireplace (A-E) 175
Scuttle, coal, boat-shaped, handled, 19th C. (A-MW) 115
Scuttle, fireplace (A-E) 52
Skimmer, hand forged, 21" (D-E) 39
Skimmer, perforated bowl, iron hook handle, 6" diam. (A-MW) 18
Skimmer, pierced, iron handle, 8" l. (D-E) 50
Skimmer, pierced, iron handle, 5¼" diam., 21½" l. (D-E) 65
Spatula, iron hook handle (D-E) 30
Spatula, wrought iron handle, signed "F.B.S. Canton, Ohio, pat. Jan. 28, '88", 14½" l. (A-E) . 55
Spit, fireplace, wind-up, marked "John Linwood" (A-E) 60
Spit jack, "salters", 13" (D-E) 80
String holder, sand weighted, ball shape (D-W) 28
Taxi horn (A-E)... 10
Teakettle, four bun feet, w/"C" scroll, 19th C. (A-MW)..................................... 90
Teakettle, gooseneck spout, footed (A-E) 65
Tool holder, for fireplace, brass ship model top stand (A-E) 30
Tools, fireplace, 5 pc. (D-E) 125
Tray, round, 10¼" diam. (D-W) 35
Trivet, early, ca. 1820, 6½" w., 9¼" l.,5" h. (D-E) 55
Trivet, heart handle, S/"H. Barton" (A-E)... 22
Trivet, heart shape w/bird & harp center (A-E) 40
Trivet, tiger pattern, ca. 1850, 3¾" w., 10" l., 5" h. (D-E) 65
Umbrella stand (A-E) 37
Umbrella stand, ornate handles (D-NE) 18
Utensil holders, for fireplace, rect., 3-column, twist fluted, 19th C. (A-MW) 110
Warming pan, floral pierced top, 9½" d., 30" handle, orig. (D-MW)...................... 125
Warming pan, large, good design on lid incl. large tulip (A-E) 175
Warming pan, wrought iron handle, pierced cover, 18th C. (D-E) 90
Watering can, w/half lift lid, 2 handled, old (A-E) 45

Chalkware

"Chalk" ornaments—actually plaster of Paris—are decorative figures attributed to the Pennsylvania Dutch, even though the first known examples were imported from England. Figures, and other ornaments of pottery and parian, were so popular there that they were inevitably copied in the much less expensive chalkware. Molds were even made of some original porcelain figures and the plaster objects were made in quantity. By the late 1700s, these English ornaments were being advertised in eastern newspapers as "images."

The majority of the American chalkware examples available to collectors dates from the 1850-1890 period, when peddlers traveled through the country selling their decorative wares. Most of their figures were cast in two-part molds having a

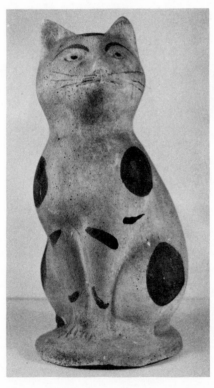

Cat, chalkware, 10¼" h. (D-E) $2500

hollow center. Because the objects were lightweight, often top-heavy, and extremely fragile, occasionally bases were partially or completely filled with clay for added stability. When the pieces were joined, they were brightly decorated in a sometimes garish, haphazard manner, without sizing, in bright red, green, yellow, brown and black paint.

Among the different forms most frequently found are birds and animals, which seem to be the most popular subjects. Other subjects included fruit arrangements, houses, or angels, which are considered rarities. Often the small animals have slots that indicate they were once "penny" banks.

Although chalkware, like almost everything else collectible, has been reproduced, a curious fact is that only age brings about a change in the texture of the surface to which color has been applied, that no artificial aging process can duplicate.

* * *

Bird on nest, mint cond. (D-E)	$ 245
Cat, colorful, 10½" (A-E)	150
Centerpiece, urn & fruit topped w/2 kissing doves, red, green, black & yellow, 11" h. (A-E)	500
Deer, colorful, 9"×9½" (A-E)	425
Deer, resting position (D-E)	200
Dog, early, 8½" (A-E)	57
Dog, seated, red & black paint, 6" h. (A-E)	75
Dog, sitting, paint fine, base slightly worn, detail good, 5"×5¼" (D-NE)	80
Dogs, standing poodles (2), 7¾" h. (A-MW)	150
Dove, w/yellow & green wings, 6" (A-E)	225
Lambs, reclining sheep w/lamb, on rectangular plinth, 6½" h. (A-MW)	110
Owl, standing, 12½" h. (A-MW)	175
Owl, traces of polychrome, 18¾" h. (A-E)	250
Parrot, rare, fine cond., 10½" h. (A-E)	1050
Pug dog (D-E)	35
Rooster, colorful, 6" h. (A-E)	325
Spaniel (D-E)	40
Spaniel, w/pipe, seated, 9" h. (A-MW)	70
Spaniels, pr., seated, 8½" h. (A-MW)	70
Squirrel, colorful (A-E)	140
Stags, pr., seated, on rectangular plinths, 10" h. (A-MW)	100
Stags, pr., seated on rectangular plinths, 10¾" h. (A-MW)	200

Clocks

The earliest clocks came to America with the first settlers. At that point in our history, a clock had more prestige than practical value because time meant very little to the colonist who spent his daylight hours building a homestead or tilling the soil.

Over the years, America has added its fair share of illustrious names to the world's great clockmakers. Some craftsmen were working here as early as the seventeenth century and, during the eighteenth century, every colony had a clockmaker. It took months to produce a single clock because each of its innumerable parts was carefully made by hand.

The two main district communities producing clocks during the eighteenth century were Philadelphia and Boston. The early craftsmen—Dutch, English, and German descendants, followed the traditional styles they had learned while

Pillar & scroll clock, Eli Terry (A-E) $2000

Mantel clock, "The Boston," 8-day, half-hour strike (D-MW) $90

apprentices; therefore, at first sight it is difficult to distinguish the colonial long-case clock from its progenitor in Europe. But, with the passage of time, these two great clockmaking centers developed their own recognizable styles.

The four major types of clocks are *tower, tall, wall* and *shelf*. Records indicate that large tower or turret clocks were in use as early as 1650. These were mounted on the steeple of a church or on some portion of a public building not only to show the time of day to everyone who passed by, but also to strike the hours.

Early American-made clocks for the home were called "tall," "long case," or "wall" clocks. The finest hardwoods were chosen for the cases which hid the pendulum and weights. Walnut, mahogany and chery were preferred, with satinwood and other exotic hardwoods being used for inlay decoration. The very early tall clocks had square tops, but during the 1700s the arched top became popular. The making of tall clocks continued well into the nineteenth century. Their height varied from around five feet to eight feet or more, with the latter being the most common. The term "grandfather's clock" didn't become popular until 1875, after Henry Clay Work wrote the song titled "Grandfather's Clock." The smaller tall-case clocks are oftentimes called "grandmother" clocks, and most of these date from the early years of the nineteenth century. Their height never exceeded four feet, and sometimes less.

Clocks that were made to hang on the wall are known as "wall" clocks. They were made in a variety of styles and shapes, the earliest of which is the "Wag-on-Wall," which exposes the clock movements. They resemble the tall clocks, without the case. Around 1783, Simon Willard made the thirty-hour

Left to right: **blinking eye clock,** Sambo, (A-E) $500; **blinking eye clock,** Terry, 30-hour (A-E) $650; **blinking eye clock,** Continental soldier (A-E) $650

Banjo clock, Aaron Willard, reversed painting (A-E) $2300

brass-movement wall clock. Its evolution is an interesting piece of American history. In its second state of development, it was cased in Massachusetts shelf or half clock cases. And, in 1802, Willard patented his famous banjo clock. Most of these were merely "timepieces" recording time only, whereas, in addition, the true clock strikes the hours. Striking banjo clocks were made later. These have a wider throat to accommodate the necessary two weights. Many were housed in fine ornate cases.

Finally, we have the shelf clock which was made to stand on a shelf, mantel or table. These were produced in an extraordinary variety of styles, from the early bracket clock to the round, tin alarm of the present century. The earliest American shelf clock was the type known as the Massachusetts Shelf Clock, made by the Willards and others after the Revolutionary War. The largest number of these clocks was made by Connecticut clockmakers.

Clocks did not become common in American homes until after the 1800s. Their manufacture in quantity began in 1840, fathered by Chauncey Jerome, a Waterbury clockmaker. His new methods of manufacture quickly replaced wooden movements with rugged interchangeable brass-geared works which eventually

Banjo clock, Howard, mahogany, reversed ship painting on door & panel (A-E) $2100

8-day clock, cherry, time & striker, moon phase & calendar (A-E) $1500

Clock in box case, Eli Terry (A-E) $2100

led to mass production. Today, older styles of wall and tall clocks occasionally become available, but nineteenth century shelf clocks are still in plentiful supply. The four things that add to the value and authenticity of an old clock are: the paper label—usually pasted inside the case—which identifies the maker and approximate date of manufacture; second, the tablet or glass front panel, oftentimes decorated with a reverse painting, should be the original; third, the case should be the original, as well as the movement; and finally, the clock should be in good running order, still ticking off the minutes and striking the hour. Be cautious of purchasing a clock that is not running, as repairs are often expensive.

* * *

Anniversary, brass, pendulum signed "D.R.G.M.", 11" h. (A-E)	$ 75
Astronomical, month dial w/sunrise & set chart, gale (A-E)	2400
Balance wheel, Marine Clock Co., time & strike on one mainspring, 2 escape wheels, ripple case (A-E)	350
Balance wheel, Terry, Davies & Burwell, in iron case w/mother-of-pearl inlay (A-E)	60
Balloon, Seth Thomas, inlaid fleur-de-lis & shell pat., brass feet, 13" h. (A-E)	100
Banjo, American Clock & Clock Makers, "diamond head", time & alarm, reverse painting on glass (A-E)	2750
Banjo, Curtis & Dunning (A-E)	900
Banjo, Curtis & Dunning (A-E)	2100
Banjo, J.L. Dunning, weight-driven, wood panel door & throat (A-E)	2500
Banjo, J. Dyar (A-E)	1900
Banjo, E. Howard & Co. (A-E)	750
Banjo, E. Howard & Co., mahogany, reverse ship painting on glass, door & panel (A-E)	2100
Banjo, Hull; mahogany case w/eagle finial, brass mountings, center panel w/shield & eagle reverse painting on glass (A-E)	900
Banjo, Daniel Munroe (A-E)	1300
Banjo, Aaron Willard, reverse painting on glass (A-E)	1900
Banjo, Aaron Willard, t-bridge w/reverse painting on glass (A-E)	2300
Banjo, Simon Willard, t-bridge, reverse painting on glass (A-E)	1700

Banjo, Simon Willard, t-bridge (D-E) ....$ 2000
Banjo, David Wood, primitive painting (A-E) 1200
Box case, Eli Terry (A-E).. 2100
Beehive, J.C. Brown, time & striker (A-E) 130
Beehive, Gilbert, 8-day, time & striker (A-E).. 140
Beehive, New Haven Clock Co., 8-day, time & striker (A-E) 100
Beehive case, Brewster & Ingraham, fusee rack & snail in Ives pat. (A-E)........... 900
Black wood case, Ingraham, flat top (A-E) 25
Blinking eye timepiece, Terry, 30-hour, rare (A-E) 650
Bobbing doll clock, Ansonia, 30-hour timepiece, pat. Dec. 4, 1886, up & down motion of doll acts
as pendulum (A-E) 450
Box case, Waterbury, w/iron front (A-E) 55
Brass, Silas Hoadley (A-E) 130
Bronze, Tucker, w/Conn. movement, balance wheel (A-E)........................ 85
Calendar, Ansonia (A-E) 625
Calendar, E. Ingraham Co., B.B. Lewis patent (A-E).............................. 675
Calendar, E. Ingraham & Co., perpetual 8-day, time & striker (A-E)............ 775
Calendar, Ithaca, parlor (A-E).. 1900
Calendar, Ithaca, wall or shelf (A-E) 525
Calendar clock, Ithaca, Norton patent (A-E) 450
Calendar, B.B. Lewis, spring driven, 8-day time & strike (A-E) 600
Calendar, Jerome & Darrow, experimental (A-E) 250
Calendar, B.B. Lewis (A-E) 575
Calendar, perpetual, Ingraham Co., parlor (A-E) 825
Calendar, perpetual, Welch Spring & Co., time of day, day of week, etc. (A-E)..................... 2400
Calendar, Seth Thomas, peanut, small fig. 8, double dial (A-E)................. 1400
Calendar, Waterbury Clock Co., day of week, day of month, pat. 1880 (A-E) 575
Calendar, Welch Spring Co., time only (A-E) 400
Carved columns & splat, Rodney Brace, glass painting, good label, Torrington movement (A-E) . 625
Case, tall, mahogany, scrolled pediment, dentil molding, reeded columns, fluted quarter col-
umns, painted dial, signed "Benjamin Clark", Phila. (D-E) 2200
Case, tall, Aaron Willard, mahogany, orig. brass finials, pierced fretwork top, corner columns,
brass capitals (D-NE) 5500
Clock, Henry C. Smith, w/carved case (A-E).. 275
Columns, Henry Hart, stenciled splat (A-E) 180
Column & splat, Boardman & Wells (A-E) 120
Columns & splat, Boardman & Wells, good paper (A-E) 100
Columns & splat, Eli Terry & Son, stencil, carfed feet (A-E) 275
Cottage, Ansonia, 8-day, time & striker (A-E) 90
Cottage, N.W. Atkins & Co., cigar box (A-E) 75
Cottage, Chauncey Jones, 8-day, time & striker (A-E) 80
Cottage, Gilbert (A-E) 55
Cottage, Gilbert Mfg. Co., time & striker, 30-hour (A-E) 60
Cottage, grain painted steeple shaped case w/glass panel door, lower half w/floral eglomise
painting, 19th C., 10¼" h. × 7" w. (A-MW) 120
Cottage, Smith & Goodrich, large, 8-day, time & strike (A-E) 140
Cottage, Smith & Goldrich on dial, 30-hour, glass sides (A-E) 160
Cottage, C. S. Spring Clock Co. (A-E) 100
Cottage, S.B. Terry, painted w/red barn paint (A-E) 110
Cottage, Seth Thomas, 8-day, large (A-E) 140
Cottage, Seth Thomas, 8-day, lyre movement (A-E) 200
Cottage, Seth Thomas, 8-day, time & striker (A-E) 90
Cottage, Waterbury, balance wheel, 8-day (A-E) 65
Cut-out of old locomotive, Seth Thomas (A-E) 50
Daguerreotype, Jerome, 1-day, round top (A-E) 100
Daguerreotype, Jerome, square top (A-E).. 140
Deck, Seth Thomas, U.S. Navy (A-E) 95
Dew drop, walnut, E. Ingraham & Co. (D-NE) 140
Double case, Henry Terry, 2 doors, gilt columns, stenciled splat, good paper & painting (A-E) . 180

Wall clock, acorn,
w/reverse painting
(A-E) $3000

Double decker, J.J. & W. Beals, unusual O.G. case (A-E) ....$ 180
Double decker, Spencer Hotchkiss, Salem bridge movement (A-E).. 500
Double-decker, Asa Munger, labeled, open escapement, signed on dial (A-E) 800
Drop octagon timepiece, Jerome, hand setter on bottom of case (A-E)................................. 170
8-day, Ansonia, lyre type movement (A-E)... 100
8-day, Atkins Clock Co. (A-E) 250
8-day, Jerome, box w/papier-mâché front, mother-of-pearl (A-E) 90
8-day, Jerome, w/double door (A-E) 100
8-day, Eli Terry, Jr. (A-E)... 450
Farmer's calendar, Ithaca (A-E)... 475
Figure 8 style, Gilbert, rare, all orig. brass trim & rosewood, ex. cond. (D-MW).................... 280
Gallery, Botsford (A-E).. 150
Gallery, Chauncey Jerome, gilt case (A-E)... 180
Gallery, S. B. Terry (A-E) 50
Gallery, Simon Willard, weight driven, stencilled, made for public buildings (A-E) 400
Grandfather, J. Barnett, mahogany case, chamfered fluted corners, arch hooded fret work top,
brass finials, brass moon dial, 8-day works (A-E).. 1600
Grandfather, Samuel Breneisen, Lancaster, Pa., sweep second hand, name on dial, curly maple
case (A-E)... 2300
Grandfather, Chippendale, fluted corners, O.G. feet, scroll top, flame finial & carved rosettes,
moon dial, 4 corners having painted woman profile, mahogany, John Owen, 73 Arch St., Phila.
(A-E)... 3500
Grandfather, curly maple, inlaid, 8-day w/moon dial (A-E) 1800
Grandfather, Gottleib Eberman, Lancaster; case attrib. to Bachman (A-E)............................. 4100
Grandfather, Jacob Ely, moon dial, cherry case w/inlay, name on dial-Manheim (A-E).......... 6500
Grandfather, Christian Hall, Lititz, Pa., curly maple case (A-E) 2400
Grandfather, Wm. Cooper Hamilton, mahogany case, 8-day, scroll top, inlay on door & base,
painted dial w/ships & flowers (A-E)... 725
Grandfather, S. Hoadley, Plymouth, pine, case dec. in red & black w/door sponge dec. in green &
yellow, 7' overall height (A-NE) 1800

Grandfather, S. Hoadley, Plymouth, pine, face w/painted eagle motif above & town view below, case of reeded columns on bonnet, dec. in tan, brown & dk. brown, 6'10" h. (A-NE)..........$ 1250

Grandfather, Ithaca, oak case (A-E)... 230

Grandfather, Richard Koch, York, Pa. (A-E) 2200

Grandfather, Isiah Luke, bell cast by John Willbank, walnut hepplewhite case (A-E) 2000

Grandfather, Benjamin Morris, walnut case, scroll top, fluted corners, turtle panel on base, ogee feet (A-E) 2000

Grandfather, David Rittenhouse, Phila., Pa., mahogany & cherry case, scroll top, 83" t. (A-E). 5500

Grandfather, Martin Schreiner, in corners, walnut cased, inlay in base on bottom panel & below face, w/carved apron & bracket feet, arched door & square top, 2 turned columns & oval windows on sides, face w/8-day works moon dial & gold dec. (A-E).. 2500

Grandfather, Daniel Shade, curly maple, turtle shell on base, French feet, scroll top door & top, hood w/finials, carved rosettes, moon dial, 8-day works (A-E) 3300

Grandfather, Shaker (A-E) 550

Grandfather, Waterbury, oak, weight-driven, time & striker (A-E) 425

Grandfather, Riley Whiting, Winchester, Conn.; pine case w/red & black decor., 6'11" h. (A-NE) 1700

Grandmother, Joshua Wilder, new case (A-E)... 450

Half column, Jerome, 1-day (A-E).. 140

Half pillar & scroll, Seth Thomas (A-E) 150

Hollow column, Brewster & Ingraham (A-E) 200

Hollow column, Jonathan Frost (A-E)... 350

Hollow column, Chauncey Jerome, small (A-E) 210

Ink stand, by J. J. Davies (A-E) 32

Iron base, Terry Clock Co. (A-E).. 470

Iron pot-belly stove case, A. L. Swift Co. (A-E) 55

Kitchen, Gilbert, time & striker (A-E) 80

Kitchen, Ingraham, 8-day, time & striker (A-E) 65

Kitchen, E. Ingraham & Co., "Gila" calendar (A-E) 130

Kitchen, E. Ingraham Co., "Vesta" (A-E) 85

Kitchen, New Haven, 8-day, ca. 1880, carved oak (D-NE) 195

Kitchen, New Haven, time & striker (A-E) 65

Kitchen, Seth Thomas on dial, 8-day (A-E) 65

Kitchen, Seth Thomas, painted green (A-E).. 90

Lever escapement in wood case, Seth Thomas, 10" dial, time only (A-E) 70

Lock & key, Jerome (A-E).. 105

Lyre, Connecticut, rare wall acorn, fusee time & strike (A-E).. 2500

Lyre, Curtis, Concord, Mass., 1811-1818 (A-E)... 3100

Lyre, John Swain (A-E) 3000

Lyre striker, Tifft, mahogany (A-E) 3300

Mahogany, J. C. Brown, dec. w/children & rabbits (D-NE) 75

Mantel, Eli Terry, Jr. & Co., mahogany, w/orig. dial, half pillars at sides & cut-out top (D-NE) . 65

Mantel, Seth Thomas, 8-day, time & striker (A-E).. 35

Mantel, Seth Thomas, mahogany case, gold leaf on wood, reverse painting on door (A-E) 65

Mantel, Waterbury, 8-day, time & striker (A-E) 25

Marine, E. N. Welch, lever escapement, 1855 (A-E) 90

Metal case, Eli Terry, w/mother-of-pearl inlay, torsion movement (A-E) 375

Metal case, Seth Thomas, shape of house (A-E) 50

Mirror, Burr & Chittenden, eagle hands, stenciled pillars & splat, time & striker (A-E) 175

Mirror, Stephen Collins, time & striker (A-E) 1700

Mirror, Ephraim Downes, wooden works (A-E) 125

Mirror, George Hill, marine, 30-hour, balance wheel w/double escape wheel, cast iron back plate (A-E) 900

Mirror, Silas Hoadley, triple decker, painting on lower glass, stenciled splat & columns, brass bushings (A-E) 600

Mirror, Erastus Hodges, weight-driven, time & striker, columns, stenciled splat, good paper (A-E) 120

Mirror, Joseph Ives, frame movements (A-E) 150

Mirror, Ives, short pendulum (A-E)... 1250

Mirror, Ives, 30-hour, roller pinion (A-E).. 875

Grandfather's clock, by S. Hoadley, Plymouth, case decor. in red & black, door sponge decor. in green & yellow, 7' overall height (A-NE) $1800

Grandfather's clock, rare curly maple case, painted moon dial, 8-day works by Daniel Shade, Somneytown, 8' h. (A-E) $5300

Grandfather's clock, by David Rittenhouse, Phila., cherry & mahogany, 83" h. (A-E) $6500

Mirror, Northup & Smith, 30-hour, wooden works (A-E)	$ 195
Mirror, Daniel Pratt, bell on top, groner, wooden movement (A-E)	150
Mirror, Daniel Pratt, weight-driven, time & striker (A-E)	150
Mirror, Seymour, Williams & Porter (A-E)	140
Mirror, Samuel Terry (A-E)	200
Mirror, Riley Whiting, time & striker, small, stenciled columns & splat (A-E)	260
Mirror, Samuel Abbott (A-E)	2300
Mirror, Ives, C & L, triple decker, gilt columns, carved eagle painting on door (A-E)	325
Mirror, Benjamin Morrell, New Hampshire (A-E)	2600
Molded metal, American Clock Co., decor. w/green paint (A-E)	160
Music box, drum, castanets; 7 bells, plays 12 tunes, fine inlaid case (A-E)	1250
Octagonal, E. N. Welch, balance wheel, time only (A-E)	60
O.G., J. C. Brown, weight-driven, time & striker (A-E)	110
O.G., W. N. Johnson, weight-driven, miniature (A-E)	270

O.G. case, D. S. Crosby, time & striker (A-E)...$ 50
O.G. case, Forestville Mfg. Co. (A-E)   85
O.G. case, Forestville Mfg. Co. (A-E)   100
O.G. case, Hills & Goodrich, w/J. Ives movement (A-E)   400
O.G. case, Jerome, time & strike, orig. Geo. Washington painting, weight-driven (A-E)   85
O.G. case, Sperry & Shaw (A-E)   75
O.G. case, Silas B. Terry, time & strike, 8-day, reverse (A-E)..........................   260
O.G. case, Waterbury, time & strike (A-E)   65
O.G. case, Waterbury, weight-driven, time & striker (A-E)   50
Papier-mâché, 8-day, inlay, picture of J. C. Brown on door (A-E)   500
Pendulum, Ives, mirror, time & strike (A-E) 2500
Pendulum, Jerome, small (A-E)   32
Pillar & scroll, Bishop & Bradley (A-E)   900
Pillar & scroll, Heman Clark (A-E).. 1000
Pillar & scroll, Heman Clark (A-E).. 1050
Pillar & scroll, Clark & Morse, Plymouth, Conn. (A-E)   950
Pillar & scroll, Ephraim Downes (A-E)   950
Pillar & scroll, Silas Hoadley (A-E) 1350
Pillar & scroll, Erastus Hodges, Torrington, Conn. (A-E) 1100
Pillar & scroll, Chauncey Ives (A-E)   950
Pillar & scroll, Hugh Kearney (A-E) 1000
Pillar & scroll, Mark Levenworth (A-E) 1050
Pillar & scroll, George Mitchell (A-E)   950
Pillar & scroll, Ethel North, small (A-E) 1700
Pillar & scroll, Norris North (A-E) 1000
Pillar & scroll, Eli Terry, early (A-E) 2000
Pillar & scroll, Eli Terry & Son (A-E) 1200
Pillar & scroll, Samuel Terry, good label (A-E) 1450
Pillar & scroll, Seth Thomas (A-E) 1250
Pillar & scroll, Seth Thomas, off-center (A-E) 1500
Pillar & scroll, Riley Whiting (A-E) 1200
Pillars & splat, Marsh Gilbert & Co., stenciled (A-E)   125
Presentation, Aaron Willard, orig. gold finish w/painted glass in door, time only (A-E) 1400
Regulator, H. Ash, hanging timepiece (A-E)   200
Regulator, E. Howard & Co. (A-E) 1350
Regulator, E. Howard-on dial, astronomical, large (A-E) 2000
Regulator, pendulum, Atkins-Bristol, 8-day, brass works, paper on floor, large (A-E)   400
Regulator, Daniel Pratt & Son, Boston (A-E)   500
Regulator, Seth Thomas (A-E)   350
Regulator, wall, E. Howard & Co. (A-E)... 1000
Regulator, wall, S. B. Terry, winds at 2 (A-E)   700
Regulator, wall, Aaron Willard, 8-day (A-E)... 1350
School, Seth Thomas, oak (A-NE)   155
Schoolhouse, Seth Thomas (A-E)   145
Shelf, American Clock Co., small w/metal front on wooden box, decor. & inlay (A-E)...........   50
Shelf, Atkins Clock Co., Bristol, Conn., fusee (A-E)   380
Shelf, J. J. Beals, Boston, Mass.; rippled front, twin steepled, round (A-E) 1200
Shelf, Bridgewater, mirrored door (D-NE)   150
Shelf, J. C. Brown, rippled front, standard type steeple, fusee movement (A-E)   575
Shelf, J. C. Brown, rippled front, standard type steeple, fusee movement (D-E)   725
Shelf, J. C. Brown, rippled front, standard type steeple, painting of residence on front glass (A-E) .   725
Shelf, Burr & Chittenden, large, gilt & black pillars (A-E)   140
Shelf, empire type, mahogany, made at Forestville, Bristol, Conn., 3' (A-E)   85
Shelf, Forestville, 8-day, O.G. case, weight-driven, time & striker (A-E)................   80
Shelf, Forestville Mfg. Co. on dial (A-E)   60
Shelf, E. O. Goodwin (A-E)   110
Shelf, Silas Hoadley, Plymouth, Conn., ca. 1830 (A-E)................................   160
Shelf, Erastus Hodges, 30-hour, time & striker, columns, splat & carved feet (A-E)   550
Shelf, Jerome & Darrow, 30-hour, wooden works, bird's-eye maple & walnut case (A-E)   375

Shelf, Jerome, weight-driven, time only (A-E)..$ 260
Shelf, Ingraham, time & striker, Doric trademark (A-E) 190
Shelf, Ingraham, walnut (A-E) 70
Shelf, Chauncey Jones, fusee movement, pearl inlay (A-E)..................................... 230
Shelf, Noah Pomeroy, Bristol, Conn. (A-E) 140
Shelf, Pratt & Frost, weight-driven, stencil glass, splat & columns, time & striker (A-E)........ 160
Shelf, William Sherman, wooden works, scroll top, side columns, in two sections (A-E)........ 300
Shelf, William Sherman, wooden works, scroll type top, turned pillars & feet, 30-hour (A-E) . 325
Shelf, Sperry & Shaw, weight-driven, small, O.G., time & striker (A-E) 140
Shelf, Eli Terry, Jr., 1-day, time & striker, pewter pinions (A-E)...................................... 375
Shelf, Eli Terry & Sons, 30-hour, weight-driven, wooden works, columns, splat (A-E)........... 250
Shelf, Samuel Terry, carved eagle & columns, primitive painting (A-E) 275
Shelf, S. B. Terry, time piece, metal case w/mother-of-pearl inlay & stenciling (A-E) 175
Shelf, Terry, time & striker (A-E) 140
Shelf, Terry, wagon spring, pineapple finials, stencil columns (A-E) 1400
Shelf, Seth Thomas, mahogany, hand-painted center panel, 32" h., 16" w., 5" d. (A-E).......... 175
Shelf, Seth Thomas, pillow (A-E).. 70
Shelf, Seth Thomas, timepiece, iron case w/mother-of-pearl inlay (A-E) 100
Shelf, Teutonia Clock Mfg. Co., yellow & ochre decor., 7¾" w. × 11¾" h. (A-NE)................. 150
Shelf, Waterbury, small, early balance wheel (A-E).. 90
Shelf, E. N. Welch, rippled front, twin steepled, round Gothic (A-E) 750
Shelf, Riley Whiting, carved eagle, good tablet & label (A-E)....................................... 525
Shelf, Simon Willard, mahogany, weight-driven, 30-hour, 18" h., early (D-E) 9200
Shelf, David Wood, mahogany (A-E).. 4500
Shelf, beehive, J. C. Brown, rippled front (A-E)... 550
Shelf, beehive, E. N. Welch, rippled front (A-E)... 500
Shelf, looking glass, double decker, free standing pilasters flank mirror which is divided from
   wooden dec. face by reverse painted panel, empire splat top w/small longitudinal mirror, paper
   label "David Dutton, Mont Vernon, N.H., March 1836", 34" h. (A-E)................................. 225
Shelf, looking glass, Samuel Terry, carved pineapple finials (A-E) 225
Shelf, mirror, Eli Terry (A-E)... 145
Shelf, pillar, Joseph L. Smith (A-E)... 200
Shelf-on-shelf, Ezekiel Jones, burl walnut (A-E)... 4900
Ship's, Seth Thomas, brass (D-MW)... 150
Ship's, Seth Thomas, 8-day, brass case (D-E) 110
Ship's, Seth Thomas, 8-day, lever escapement, brass case (A-E)..................................... 150
Ship's, Seth Thomas, 8-day, lever escapement, time only, nickel-plated base (A-E) 95
Ship's bell, Seth Thomas, 30-hour, metal case, bell below strikes ship's bells, not the hour (A-E). 190
Solar timepiece, by T. R. Timby (A-E)... 1700
Spring calendar, Welch (A-E)... 600
Steeple, Chauncey Boardman, 1-day w/fusee movement (A-E) 225
Steeple, Chauncey Boardman, 8-day, fusee works (A-E) 220
Steeple, Boardman & Wells, 30-hour, fusee movement (A-E).. 240
Steeple, Brewster & Ingraham, sharp Gothic (A-E) 130
Steeple, J. C. Brown (A-E) 90
Steeple, Gilbert Clock Co., small (A-E)... 80
Steeple, E. & A. Ingraham, Gothic, 1-day, time & striker (A-E) 120
Steeple, Jerome & Co., New Haven, Conn., small (A-E) 100
Steeple, Jerome & Co., small (A-E) 140
Steeple, Chauncey Jones, 8-day, time & striker, over-pasted label, good tablet, veneer (A-E).. 145
Steeple, William Markham, double candlestick, wagon spring, cord instead of chain (A-E) 2100
Steeple, New Haven Clock Co., hand painted glass bottom panel, orig. label, 20" h., 11" w., 5" d.
   (A-NE).. 115
Steeple, E. N. Welch (A-E) 75
Steeple, E. N. Welch, 8-day, time & striker (A-E) 175
Steeple, E. N. Welch, sharp Gothic, miniature (A-E).. 200
Steeple, twin, Brewster & Ingraham, 8-day, patent spring, round Gothic (A-E)................... 625
Steeple, twin, Brewster & Ingraham, 8-day, sharp Gothic (A-E) 625
Tall, R. Brackett, Maine; maple w/moon phase (A-E)... 2900

30-day, Atkins Clock Co., w/fusee movement, time & striker (A-E) 950
30-hour, Blakeslee, weight-driven, columns, splat, carved feet (A-E)..$ 275
30-hour, J. C. Brown, spring brass movement, miniature, in half ripple case (A-E)............... 220
30-hour, Friesland, painted pewter & cast dial, animated figures (A-E) 2400
30-hour, Ives, w/wood works, stenciled columns, & splat, good label (A-E) 230
30-hour, Smith & Goodrich, small, O.B., w/fusee movement (A-E) 240
30-hour, E. N. Welch, all orig., ca. 1865 (A-E).. 70
Time, by International Time Recording Co., N.Y. (A-E).. 85
Timepiece, E. Howard Co., figure of 8 (A-E) 1800
Timepiece, round, gilt, Jerome, escape wheel in back of back plate (A-E)............................ 100
Time & strike, Jerome, walnut case, small (A-E) 80
Time & strike, Noah Pomeroy, w/painted glass door (A-E).. 110
Time & strike, Silas B. Terry, 1-day (A-E)... 475
Time & striker, Terry, iron case (A-E) 340
Time & striker, Seth Thomas, 8-day (A-E) 90
Torsion pendulum, J. R. Mills & Co., designed by Aaron D. Carne (A-E) 575
Triple decker, Barnes-Bartholomew, w/carved eagle (A-E) 525
Triple decker, Birge & Gilbert, carved black & gold dial (A-E) 325
Triple decker, Birge & Fuller, 8-day, strap movement, carved top (A-E)............................... 250
Triple decker, J. C. Brown (A-E).. 300
Triple decker, Ives, early, 8-day, strap movement, w/carved eagle (A-E) 450
Triple decker, Jerome (A-E) 325
Triple decker, Northrup & Smith, wooden works (A-E)... 160
Triple decker, Eli Terry, 1-day time & strike, wooden works (A-E)....................................... 185
Triple decker, Samuel Terry, weight-driven, 2 mirrors, time & striker (A-E)......................... 325
Triple decker, S. B. Terry (A-E) 300
Triple decker, Seth Thomas, 8-day, curly maple columns (A-E)... 175
Violin, Seth Thomas (A-E)... 650
Wagon spring, J. J. & W. Beals (A-E)... 1900
Wagon spring, Birge & Fuller, 8-day (A-E)... 2300
Wagon spring, Birge & Fuller, 30-hour (A-E) 1500
Wagon spring, by John Hunt, Gothic (A-E) 1750
Wagon spring, Ives, hour glass, 1-day (A-E)... 3600
Wagon spring under dome, Ives (A-E).. 1050
Wall, Wm. L. Gilbert Clock Co., tall (A-E) 375
Wall, Chauncey Jerome, key-hole, small (A-E)... 575
Wall, Chauncey Jerome, octagon shape, dated 1845 (D-MW) 80
Wall, Kroeber (A-E).. 450
Wall, Sessions, iron front (A-E).. 175
Wall, calendar, Ansonia, octagon drop timepiece (A-E) 360
Wall, calendar, days of month & week, Galusha Maranville, Mar. 5, 1861, Winsted, Conn. (A-E). 600
Wall, calendar, H. B. Horton patent, Itahca, 30-day (A-E) 725
Wall, calendar, H. B. Horton patent, Ithaca, 30-day, time & striker (A-E)............................ 750
Wall, calendar, Ithaca, iron case, rare (A-E) 2200
Wall, calendar, Seth Thomas (A-E) 525
Weight-driven, Atkins Clock Co., time & striker (A-E) 140
Weight-driven, Erastus Hodges, stenciled pillars & splat, time & striker (A-E)...................... 190
Weight-driven, Jerome, time & striker (A-E) 250
Weight-driven, Mark Levenworth, time & strike, good label, stenciled splat & columns (A-E). 140
Weight-driven, Seth Thomas, time & strike, columns, gilt & stencil (A-E) 80
Weight-driven, Seth Thomas, time & strike, columns & splat (A-E) 300
Weight-driven, Seth Thomas, 30-hour (A-E) 100
Weight-driven, Riley Whiting, time & strike, stenciled columns & splat, tall (A-E) 140
Weight-driven, Riley Whiting, rime & strike, turned columns, good label (A-E)...................... 220
Wood hands, G. W. Bartholomew, early (A-E).. 130
Wooden works, Seth Thomas (A-NE) 800
Wooden works, Seth Thomas, ca. 1816, figure of Revolutionary soldier painted on the glass, (D-MW) 375
Year, Year Clock Co., N.Y., needs winding once each year (A-E) 125

Copper

Copper has been used essentially for utilitarian articles since the early eighteenth century, according to advertisements of early makers. The different objects mentioned in their newspaper ads included coffeepots, teakettles, skillets, baking pans, kettles, ladles, skimmers, stew pans, cake molds and warming pans. These objects were both hammered and cast.

A variety of new ware is available today; however, its appearance is so different from the earlier examples that identification is usually very easy for collectors. The contemporary examples lack the inimitable patina that a genuinely old piece acquires from usage . . . the bruises, dents, and frequently the telltale "verdigris," a greenish surface discoloration usually found in seams.

Other clues that identify earlier wares are the irregularities of shape, hammer marks, hand-riveting, dovetailed joints, and handwrought handles.

* * *

Bedwarmer, peafowl & floral decor. (A-E)	$ 390
Bedwarmer, punched heart top w/turned handle, 42" (D-E)	175
Boiler, large (A-E)	37
Boiler, wash, complete (D-N)	48
Boiler, wash, lid (A-MW)	25
Boiler, wash, lid (D-W)	42
Boiler, wash, lid (D-MW)	35
Boiler, wash, lid (D-SW)	40
Boiler, wash, no lid (D-MW)	18
Bottle, hot water, 11" l. (A-MW)	32
Bowl, ring for hanging, 11½" diam. (A-E)	70
Bucket, brass lid, spout, & bands, 14" h. (D-E)	90
Bucket, iron bail, 14" diam. (D-N)	85
Bucket, iron bail, 9" diam. (D-S)	45
Bucket, iron bail, tin lined, copper lid (D-W)	35
Chafing dish w/matching tray, wooden handles, complete, mkd. Manning-Bowman (D-MW)	45
Coal hod w/shovel (A-E)	150
Coffeepot, orig. nickel-plated, stripped (A-MW)	22
Coffeepot, orig. nickel-plated, stripped (D-MW)	21
Coffeepot, orig. nickel-plated, stripped (D-N)	32

Left: **Teakettle,** copper, gooseneck (D-MW) $75; *right:* **coffeepot,** copper, hinged brass covered spout (D-MW) $38

Kettle, copper, brass tulip rings & wrought iron handle, 3 different types of metal, 16" diam. (A-E) $500

Coffeepot, orig. nickel-plated, stripped (D-S) ....$ 25

Coffeepot, wooden finial & handle, brass hinged spout cover, mkd. "Rochester" (D-MW) 38

Cup, hot toddy, w/flared sides, 3½"×5" (D-NE) 20

Dipper, milk (A-E) 17

Dipper, wrought iron handle, 20" l. (A-E) 50

Dipper, wrought iron long handle (A-E)... 30

Eagle, mounted on wooden base (A-MW) 60

Glue pot (D-E) 55

Jug, milk, dovetailed seam & broad strap handle, 9" h. (D-W) 85

Jug, water, w/hinged cover, strap handle (D-MW) 65

Kettle, apple butter, dovetailed, iron bail (D-S) 245

Kettle, apple butter, dovetailed, iron bail (A-N) 105

Kettle, apple butter, dovetailed, iron bail (D-MW) 265

Kettle, apple butter, dovetailed, iron bail, 28"×18" (D-MW) 285

Kettle, apple butter, dovetailed, iron bails, 24"×16" (D-MW) 235

Kettle, apple butter, large (A-E) 70

Kettle, apple butter, large (A-W) 150

Kettle, dovetailed, wrought iron bail, well preserved, 12" diam., 7" deep (D-W).............. 175

Kettle, handle, cleaned, 19" (A-E) 70

Kettle, iron tripod stand, med. size (D-E) 425

Kettle, large (A-E) 110

Kettle, rare tulip brass rings, wrought iron handle, 16" diam. (A-E) 500

Kettle, used for carrying liquids, rare & unique, signed "I. Witman", 19th C. (A-E).......... 850

Measure, handled, tin lined, wide lip, 1 qt. size, marked N.Y. City (D-W)..................... 40

Measure, 1 gal., ca. 1840 (A-E) 95

Measure, 2 gallon (A-MW)... 75

Measures, set of 4, brass lip & handle, 2 qt., 1 qt., pint, ½ pt. (D-MW)..................... 155

Mold, cake, large (A-E) 40

Mold, cheese, 12" diam. (A-MW) 25

Mold, fish (D-NE) 25

Mold, pudding, coffeepot in relief, 8" diam. (D-E) 65

Mug, handled, pink lustre band inside, 3" (D-E).. 30

Oil can, unusual shape w/wood handle (A-E) 30

Pan, stew, handle (A-E)... 40

Pan, stew, wrought iron handle, 5½" (A-E) 37

Pan, stew, wrought iron handles, 9", marked "I. Olac & Sons, Phila." (D-E)................. 175

Pitcher, dovetailed, heavy (A-E) 30

Pot, large, w/lid (A-E) 35

Pot, large, oval w/wrought iron bail (D-W).. 115

Pot, loop handles, tinned, dovetailed seams, 9" diam., 4" deep (A-NE) 45

Pot, stew, large w/wrought iron handles, 12" (D-E)... 135

Pot, straight sided w/copper loop handle, tinned interior, 12" diam., 6" deep (A-E).............. 65

Samovar, canister shape w/flared urn top, porcelain handles, some brass, 19th C., 22¼" h.
(A-MW) 150

Saucepan, dovetailed bottom, copper handle, 4 qt. size (D-W) 62

Saucepan, dovetailed bottom, 2 qt. size (D-E) 48

Skillet, iron handle, 10" diam. (D-MW) 65

Skimmer, cream, hammered, oval, 1-pc., 4"×4½" (D-E) 35

Spatula, wrought iron handle, signed "D. Rohrer" (A-E) 260

Still, complete & in working order (D-S) 80

Strainer, broad flat handle, 22" l., 8" diam. (A-E) 95

Strainer, ladle, handwrought iron decor. handle (A-E) 120

Strainer, wood handle, tinned, 18th C., 42" l., strainer diam. 8½" (D-E)..................... 85

Tankard, strap handle, early, 8½" h. (D-E).. 38

Teakettle, J. Babb, Reading, Pa., ca. 1816 (A-E) 230

Teakettle, dovetailed, small, unsigned, 5" diam. (A-E) 250

Teakettle, dovetailed, small, unsigned, 5¼" diam. (D-E) 200

Teakettle, A. Gillespie, 1807 (D-E) 395

Teakettle, gooseneck, brass & copper handle (D-MW) 55

Tray, copper, hammered, brass handles, 12″ × 17½″ (D-MW) $39

Copper & brass utensils (A-E), *top row, left to right;* bell metal **skillet,** 3 cast legs, marked Taylor & Richmond, 18th C., 8½″ diam., handle 11″, $425; bell metal **skillet,** 3 cast legs, 8″ diam., 10″ l., $50; *second row, left to right:* **double boiler,** copper, dovetailed, 8″ diam., 6″ h., $25; **double boiler,** copper, dovetailed, bottom, 8″ diam., 6″ h. $80; *third row, left to right:* **skillet,** copper, mounted on 4″ legs, dovetailed, handle 7″ l., $50; **pot,** copper, tinned, loop handles, dovetailed seams, 9″ diam., 4″ h., $35; *fourth row, left to right:* **pitcher,** copper, tinned inside, 9″ h., $70; **jam kettle,** brass, iron bail riveted on, 10″ diam., $45; *fifth row:* **pot,** copper, large, 1 loop handle, tinned, 12″ diam., 6″ d., $25. (Objects are displayed on rare **Shaker step,** pine, painted red, 42″ h., 36″ w., $125)

Teakettle, gooseneck, signed D. Bentley, Phila. (D-N)	$ 290
Teakettle, gooseneck, dovetailed, signed John Getz, 8½″ diam. (A-E)	250
Teakettle, gooseneck, dovetailed, signed "I.S." (D-E)	350
Teakettle, gooseneck, dovetailed, signed Kiefer, 9″ diam. (A-E)	275
Teakettle, gooseneck, dovetailed, signed Shenfelder, Reading, Pa. (A-E)	310
Teakettle, gooseneck, dovetailed, signed G. Tryon, Phila. (A-E)	250
Teakettle, gooseneck, unmarked (A-E)	155
Teakettle, gooseneck, unmarked, dents on sides & spout (A-MW)	75
Teakettle, A. Keeney-Carlisle, med. 7″ diam., ex. cond. (A-E)	375
Teakettle, orig. nickel-plated, stripped, bail handle w/wood grip (D-MW)	35
Teakettle, orig. nickel-plated, stripped, chuckwagon-type, 2 gal. (D-W)	55
Teakettle, small, fixed bail (A-MW)	65
Teakettle, J. P. Thompson, dovetailed, handle (A-E)	275
Teakettle, unsigned, small, 5″ diam. (A-E)	250
Teakettle, wooden base (A-E)	22
Teapot, brass stand (A-NE)	140
Teapot, brass tray (A-MW)	115
Tray, brass handles, mkd. hand hammered, 11½″ w., 17½″ l. (D-W)	28
Tray, oval, raised handles (A-MW)	32
Tub, oval (D-NE)	150
Warming pan, turned handle, pierced edge (A-MW)	80
Warming pan, wooden handle (A-E)	50
Wash kit, 17th C. (D-MW)	65

Decoys

Decoys are choice items of collectors and decorators who diligently search for these pieces of floating and sitting sculpture, realizing that many are still roosting quietly in old abandoned sheds, waterfront shacks, attics, basements and barns.

Many producers of decoys claimed that the most effective decoy was a realistic one, carved and painted to resemble a particular type of bird, while others believed that details didn't really matter; so the difference of opinions resulted in a great variety of decoy styles made from wood, metal, papier-mâché, canvas and rubber, all of which are very collectible.

Decoy-making can be called a truly American craft, because it actually began with the Indian tribes and was further developed by the pioneers who quickly learned that the decoys lured waterfowl within gunshot. By 1800, the white settlers were making their own decoys—whittling them from whatever was available—a piece of driftwood, an old fence post, or a cedar root. The floating decoys were intended to deceive waterfowl and were originally called "blocks," "trollers," and "stools." The latter type was a stick-up, intended to attract shorebirds such as sandpipers, snipe, etc.

Today, serious collectors prefer to collect the early, hand-carved varieties which have become scarce and expensive. However, there are still many of those examples which were produced on lathes to be found, since they were turned out in greater numbers. Happily for the collector, these can still be acquired at fairly modest prices.

* * *

Beach bird, papier-mâché, very rare, type-written label w/name "Mackey" on bottom (A-E)... $ 125
Beach bird, small, ex. cond., orig. paint, unusued cond. (A-E) 375
Beach bird, small, Thomas H. Gelston, cork body w/head tilted down, weathered cond., paint worn off (A-E)... 50
Beach bird, small, reddish breast & gray back, orig. wire mount, orig. paint worn (A-E) 150
Black duck, Animal Trap Co., Pascagoula, Miss., orig. paint worn (A-E) 20
Black duck, Barnegat Bay area, New Jersey, branded "price" on bottom, repainted, ex. cond. (A-E) 60
Black duck, carved & painted head & body w/eel grass, held on by net, old, good cond., minor repair (A-E) 60
Black duck, carved wings, oversized, orig. paint worn off (A-E) 40
Black duck, carved wings, wide body, large, good cond. (A-E)... 125
Black duck, Cobb Island, early, w/tucked-in sleepy head, carved wing tips, weathered, orig. paint good (A-E)... 125
Black duck, Cobb Island, primitive, all orig. (A-E)... 70
Black duck, A. Elmer Crowell, oval brand signature, repainted, ex. cond. (A-E) 75
Black duck, early, cork body, carved wooden head & keel, c.1880, carved w/initials "C.E.R.", good orig. paint (A-E).. 40
Black duck, early, oversized, fair cond., paint worn to natural wood (A-E) 50
Black duck, early, turned head & carved wings, much used w/orig. paint worn (A-E)............ 70
Black duck, early, 2-pc. cork body, ex. cond., w/good orig. paint (A-E) 75
Black duck, good cond., minor wear, repainted (A-E) 130
Black duck, good cond., orig. paint worn off (A-E)... 60
Black duck, hollow carved, aluminum head, worn cond. (A-E)... 40
Black duck, hollow carved, Ken Anger, Dunnville, Ontario, carved wing details, good used cond. (A-E) 275
Black duck, hollow carved, Jake Barrett, good cond., paint weathered (A-E)......................... 40

Decoys (A-NE), *top row, left to right:* **black-breasted plover,** 11″ h., $325; **Canadian goose,** 25″ h. × 12″ h., $200; **old squaw,** primitive, 12″, $150; *bottom row, left to right:* **hollow brant,** $275; **shore bird,** unusual head, 11¼″, $275; **canvasback sleeper,** orig. paint, $250; **blue bill,** attributed to Frank Sterey, ca. 1920, $150.

Black duck, hollow carved, Jake Barrett, New Jersey, ex. cond. (A-E) ....$ 70
Black duck, hollow carved, carved wing tips, ex. cond. w/worn orig. paint (A-E)................. 110
Black duck, hollow carved, carved wing tips & tail feathers, good cond. (A-E) 75
Black-duck, hollow carved, Connecticut, brand signature of K. Peck, 1933, orig. paint good (A-E). 200
Black duck, hollow carved, Connecticut, w/head tucked down, ex. orig. cond., orig. paint good (A-E) 75
Black duck, hollow carved, Connecticut, w/head turned slightly to right, looking down, carved eyes, ex. cond., orig. paint weathered (A-E)... 150
Black duck, hollow carved, early, orig. paint good, ex. cond. (A-E)..................................... 225
Black duck, hollow carved, ex. cond., orig. paint worn (A-E) 40
Black duck, hollow carved, good cond. w/minor wear, ex. orig. paint (A-E) 110
Black duck, hollow carved, good used cond. w/paint weathered (A-E)................................. 40
Black duck, hollow carved, graceful neck & full breast, ex. cond., good orig. paint (A-E) 75
Black duck, hollow carved, Stanley Grant, New Jersey, barmegat (D.1960), orig. paint, ex. cond. (A-E) 90
Black duck, hollow carved, Ellis Harper, ex. cond., traces orig. paint (A-E) 40
Black duck, hollow carved, John Heisler, tucked-down head, carved wing & tail feathers, ex. orig. cond. (A-E)... 300
Black duck, hollow carved, John Heisler, tucked-down head, carved wing & tail feathers, ex. orig. paint (A-E) 275
Black duck, hollow carved, inletted bill const., glass eyes, good cond. (A-E) 50
Black duck, hollow carved, Albert Laing, Connecticut, ca. 1870-1880, rare, minor wear, ex. cond. w/fine orig. paint (A-E) 2500
Black duck, hollow carved, New Jersey, ex. cond., w/good orig. paint (A-E).......................... 80
Black duck, hollow carved, New Jersey, minor wear, orig. paint fair (A-E)............................ 85
Black duck, hollow carved, orig. paint fair, restored (A-E) 110
Black duck, hollow carved, primitive, good used cond., orig. paint weathered (A-E)............. 80
Black duck, hollow carved, restored & repainted, good cond. (A-E) 60
Black duck, hollow carved, Harry V. Shourds, ex. cond., in-use, repainted (A-E)................. 125
Black duck, hollow carved, Harry V. Shourds, New Jersey, rare, repainted, ex. cond. (A-E) ... 75
Black duck, hollow carved, Harry V. Shourds, Tuckerton, N.J. (1861-1920), glass eyes, orig. paint fair (A-E)... 100
Black duck, hollow carved, Rhoades Truax, Absecon, N.J., orig. paint worn, good cond. (A-E). 100
Black duck, hollow carved, Rhoades Truax, early, slight wear, paint weathered w/age (A-E)... 50
Black duck, hollow carved, John Van Dyke, orig. paint fair, ex. cond. (A-E)......................... 80
Black duck, Ira Hudson, rare, bird standing on cast metal feet w/wings spread, turned head, extended neck, ex. cond., w/fine orig. paint (A-E)... 1250
Black duck, in-use, repainted, ex. cond. (A-E) 90
Black duck, Joseph W. Lincoln, rare, Accord, Mass. (1859-1938), orig. paint worn, ex. cond. (A-E). 200
Black duck, late factory, orig. paint, good cond. (A-E)... 20

Black duck, Mason's, made in 2 halves, good used cond., orig. paint worn (A-E) ....$ 40

Black duck, Mason's, repainted, slight wear (A-E) 50

Black duck, sleeper, Delaware River, ex. carving, painted (A-NE).. 250

Black duck, sleeper, string of 5, incl. bobbing head, turned head, etc., carved, painted &
sculptured w/orig. paint & weights (A-NE) 750

Black duck, sleeping, branded w/names "Brice", "H. B. Endicott", "W. S. Bigelow", good cond.,
no finish (A-E) 50

Black duck, sleeping, shadow decoy, metal mounting marked "Chase", ex. cond., little use (A-E). 30

Black duck, sleepy w/head tucked down, paperweight glass eyes, marked w/name "Thomas
Chambers" & "Gordon Sears Rig", orig. paint worn off (A-E) 40

Black duck, solid body w/initials "H.D." carved under tail, carved wing tips, good used cond.,
orig. paint weathered (A-E) 90

Black duck, swimming, Down East Decoy Co., carved wings, orig. paint weathered (A-E)..... 100

Black duck, Taylor-Johnson, Bay Head, N.J., hollow-carved, orig. paint weathered, good cond.
(A-E) 80

Black duck, turned head, ex. cond., orig. paint weathered (A-E) 70

Black duck, turned head, orig. paint (A-NE) 250

Blue bill, attrib. to Frank Sterey, orig. paint, ca. 1920 (A-NE).. 150

Blue jay, A. Elmer Crowell, life-sized, very rare, minnow in bill, signed in pen on bottom, ex.
cond. (A-E).. 1100

Brant, "Gus Bishop" branded at bottom, glass eyes, wide body, fair cond. (A-E) 40

Brant, canvas-covered, head in looking down position, stenciled w/"Ronald Stowe", orig. paint
(A-E) 30

Brant, carved wings, Cobb Island, minor repair, orig. paint worn off (A-E).......................... 100

Brant, carved wings, New Jersey, ex. cond., orig. paint (A-E).. 275

Brant, carved wing tips, Cobb Island, w/head downward, good cond., orig. paint worn (A-E) 150

Brant, carved wings & head, Virginia, ex. cond., orig. paint weathering (A-E) 290

Brant, carved wing tips, head tilted in feeding position, signed J. B., solid body, ex. cond. (A-E) 110

Brant, carved wing tips, rare, Mares Island, orig. paint worn (A-E)................................... 100

Brant, good carving, painted (A-NE).. 125

Brant, hollow carved, New Jersey, Capt. Jess Birdsall, Barnegat, good cond., traces orig. paint
(A-E) 75

Brant, hollow carved, New Jersey, branded E. B. Cobb, good cond., orig. paint worn (A-E) ... 80

Brant, hollow carved, New Jersey, branded E. B. Cobb, good cond., orig. paint worn (A-E) ... 75

Brant, hollow carved, New Jersey, branded B. T. Morris, ex. cond., good orig. paint (A-E) 175

Brant, hollow carved, flat back, wide body, orig. paint worn (A-E) 50

Brant, hollow carved, head drawn back, looking down, weathered, traces orig. paint (A-E).... 75

Brant, hollow carved, New Jersey, carved wing tips, graceful head, orig. paint (A-E)............. 250

Brant, hollow carved, New Jersey, good cond., orig. paint back & sides (A-E) 60

Brant, hollow carved, New Jersey, good used cond., traces orig. paint (A-E) 100

Brant, hollow carved, New Jersey, high neck, ex. cond., orig. paint good (A-E) 70

Brant, hollow carved, New Jersey, stick-up, ex. cond., orig. paint (A-E) 475

Brant, hollow carved, New Jersey, swimming position, extended neck, minor repair, orig. paint
good (A-E).. 325

Brant, hollow carved, painted, orig. cond. (A-E).. 275

Brant, hollow carved, Harry Shrouds, head in downward position, minor wear (A-E)............ 130

Brant, inletted head, good cond., orig. paint worn off (A-E).. 50

Brant, Long Island, cork body, good cond. (A-E).. 125

Brant, Mason's, rare, paint worn, weathered (A-E).. 60

Brant, New Jersey, branded on back w/"Sinbad", ex. cond., traces orig. paint (A-E).............. 150

Brant, New Jersey, good cond., orig. paint weathered (A-E).. 60

Brant, New Jersey, minor repair, old paint, ex. cond. (A-E).. 90

Brant, New Jersey, solid body, minor repair, traces orig. paint (A-E)................................... 40

Brant, New Jersey, solid body, root-head const., fair cond., traces orig. paint (A-E) 30

Brant, New Jersey, 2-part solid const., branded w/"Accomac Gunning Club", minor wear, orig.
paint (A-E) 70

Brant, primitive, from natural formed piece wood, good cond., orig. paint worn (A-E).......... 100

Brant, primitive, solid body, minor wear, orig. paint worn off (A-E).................................... 150

Brant, solid body const., carved head, glass eyes, minor repair, good orig. paint (A-E).......... 80

Decoys (A-E) top row, *left to right:* pair of pintails, by Ward Bros., ca. 1920s, $6500; *second row, left to right:* pintail drake, by Robert White, "W" brand on bottom, $275; pintail drake, by Amiel Garibaldi, ca. 1930, $325; *third row:* pintail drake, swimmer, large, by David Simaldi, signed, $150; *fourth row, left to right:* mallard drake, by Lem & Lee Dudley, neck repaired, rare, $550; gadwall drake, cork, by Harold Haertel, signed, $500

Above: bird, decoy (A-E) $25; *Below:* Shore bird decoys, pr. (A-E) $550

Brant, swimming, carved wing details, extended neck, good cond., orig. paint good (A-E) ....$ 150
Brant, swimming, early, w/wide body, cylindrical weight set into bottom, good cond., some orig. paint (A-E)   100
Brant, wide body, hollow carved, filled w/cork, minor wear, orig. paint worn (A-E)   120
Broadbill, New Jersey, early, hollow carved, orig. paint weathered (A-E)..............................   40
Broadbill, Chauncey Wheeler, good used cond., orig. paint (A-E)......................................   200
Bufflehead, drake, carved wings, small, orig. circular weight, orig. paint good (A-E)   45
Bufflehead, drake, early, balsa wood, plump body, minor wear, in-use repainting (A-E).......   60
Bufflehead, drake, early, exaggerated head & flat body, ex. cond., minor wear, good old paint (A-E)   40
Bufflehead, drake, early, 5-pc. laminated body, head made in 2 halves, good used cond., traces orig. paint (A-E)..   50
Bufflehead, drake, early, good used cond., orig. paint worn (A-E)......................................   110
Bufflehead, drake, early, hollow, forward tilted flat head, 100 yrs. old, traces orig. paint, ex. cond. (A-E)   130
Bufflehead, drake, early, hollow const., ex. cond. w/good orig. paint (A-E)..........................   70
Bufflehead, drake, early & rough-hewn, head tucked down, good used cond., orig. paint weathered (A-E)...   50
Bufflehead, drake, early, traces orig. paint, ex. cond. (A-E)   130
Bufflehead, drake, hollow carved, early, fine orig. cond., orig. paint weathered (A-E)...........   40
Bufflehead, drake, hollow carved, New Jersey, Charles Parker, ex. cond., repainted (A-E)   225
Bufflehead, drake, Doug Jester, ex. cond., paint good cond. (A-E)....................................   60
Bufflehead, drake, Doug Jester, much used cond., orig. paint weathered (A-E)   70
Bufflehead, drake, Mason's, rare, professionally repainted (A-E)   50
Bufflehead, drake, primitive, Oscar Ayers, New Jersey, head held high, ex. cond., orig. paint worn (A-E)   60
Bufflehead, drake, primitive, slightly turned head & squat plump body, orig. cond., good orig. paint (A-E)   80

Bufflehead, drake, primitive, small, approx. 100 yrs. old, good used cond., orig. paint worn off (A-E) ....$ 100

Bufflehead, drake, primitive, 2-pc. body & 1-pc. head, traces orig. paint (A-E) 60

Bufflehead, drake, rare, ex. used cond., orig. paint good (A-E) 450

Canvasback, bob-tail, hen, Ill. River, ex. used cond., little wear to paint (A-E) 50

Canvasback, drake, balsa body, carved, sleepy head version, ex. cond., little use (A-E) 50

Canvasback, drake, balsa, head looking down, glass eyes, carved, ex. cond., unused (A-E).... 50

Canvasback, drake, balsa wood, Harry Megargy, w/"to Bill Mackey/from Harry Megargy/Jan. 4, 1968" on bottom, also branded "H.P.M.", cond. like new (A-E).. 50

Canvasback, drake, Samuel Barnes, fair cond., orig. paint weathered, 19th C. (A-E).............. 30

Canvasback, drake, bob-tail, Ill. River, balsa body, orig. paint good (A-E)............................ 40

Canvasback, drake, Samuel Denny, N.Y., minor wear w/ex. orig. paint (A-E)........................ 170

Canvasback, drake, fat body, much used, orig. paint (A-E)... 25

Canvasback, drake, feather carving, Ill. River, cast metal head, orig. paint, ex. cond. (A-E).... 100

Canvasback, drake, feeding, miniature, by A. Elmer Crowell, early rubber stamp signature, perfect cond. (A-E) 350

Canvasback, drake, full-bodied w/solid block, large, branded w/"P.A. Club", shows wear, traces orig. paint (A-E).. 60

Canvasback, drake, glass eyes, good cond., orig. paint weathered (A-E) 30

Canvasback, drake, Joe Heaps, minor repair, repainted, early (A-E) 50

Canvasback, drake, hole drilled in tail, lg. carved head, fair cond., paint worn off (A-E)........ 50

Canvasback, drake, hollow carved, early prim., orig. paint fair, good cond. (A-E).................. 650

Canvasback, drake, hollow carved, glass eyes, worn cond. (A-E) 50

Canvasback, drake, hollow carved, wing details, turned head, oversized, 29½" l., ex. cond. w/good orig. paint (A-E).. 1700

Canvasback, drake, Mason's Dec. Fact., Detroit, Mich., minor wear, fine orig. paint (A-E) 200

Canvasback, drake, Mason's, rig of D. B. Day, minor wear, good orig. paint (A-E) 100

Canvasback, drake, Bob McGaw, Maryland, 1885-1952, ex. cond., traces orig. paint (A-E)..... 60

Canvasback, drake, Michigan bobtail, rare, ex. cond., minor repair, orig. paint weathered (A-E) 60

Canvasback, drake, Michigan bob-tail, w/wide body, flat bottom, heavy keel, good cond. w/orig. paint (A-E) 110

Canvasback, drake, Madison Mitchell, Maryland; good cond. w/orig. paint (A-E) 100

Canvasback, drake, North Carolina, good cond., orig. paint weathered, ca. 1880 (A-E) 50

Canvasback, drake, North Carolina, A. Grandy, carved w/name "Henley", ex. cond. w/good orig. paint, ca. 1915 (A-E) 450

Canvasback, drake, old factory, used as a wing duck, considerable wear (A-E) 80

Canvasback, drake, old, much used, repainted (A-E) 35

Canvasback, drake, sleepy turned head, ex. cond. w/good orig. paint (A-E) 150

Canvasback, drake, solid body w/head resting on back, ex. orig. cond. (A-E) 90

Canvasback, drake, "wing duck", rare, well preserved, orig. paint (A-E) 125

Canvasback, drakes, folding cardboard, marked w/"Johnson's Folding Fiberboard Decoys, mfg. by William R. Johnson Co., Seattle", good cond., minor wear, pr. (A-E) 50

Canvasback, hen, canvas-covered, C. V. Wells Decoy Co., Wis., good cond., fine orig. paint (A-E) 40

Canvasback, hen, early, fair cond., orig. paint worn off (A-E) 30

Canvasback, hen, Mason factory (A-E) 55

Canvasback, hen, Michigan, movable head, ex. cond., orig. paint good (A-E) 25

Canvasback, hollow carved, Illinois River, orig. paint good, ex. cond. (A-E).......................... 75

Canvasback, primitive, oversized, ex. cond., orig. paint worn away (A-E) 40

Canvasback, sleeper, primitive, orig. paint (A-NE) 250

Canvasback, Stevens Dec. Fac., Stevens brand visible on bottom, repainted, good cond. (A-E). 50

Coot, American, factory, repainted, rough finish, fair cond. (A-E).. 35

Coot, American, Mason's, good orig. paint, minor wear (A-E).. 250

Coot, Maine, inletted head, horseshoe weight, carved w/initials "HT" on bottom, very old, repainted (A-E) 70

Coot, Maine, unusual head constr., orig. paint good, minor wear (A-E)................................ 50

Coot, mud, Evans, good cond. (D-MW) 45

Coot, primitive, w/turned head, ex. cond., orig. paint bold (A-E)... 70

Coot, sea, hollow carved, New England, orig. paint fair, slight wear (A-E)............................ 75

Cradle, hooded, molded edges, robins' egg blue interior (A-NE) 175

Shore bird decoys (A-E), *top row, left to right:* **black-bellied plover,** by William Matthews, $225; **yellowlegs,** by William Matthews, carved wing detail, $225; *second row, left to right:* **yellowlegs,** early, probably New Jersey, $110; **ruddy turnstone,** very early, New Jersey, $175; *third row, left to right:* **yellowlegs,** long rough-hewn body, primitive, $270; **black-bellied plover,** Virginia, $100; *fourth row:* **black-bellied plover,** Virginia, by Capt. B. Burton, early, $175; **golden plover,** New England, $290; *fifth row:* **curlew,** Cobb Island, orig. paint faded & worn away, rare, $600; **robin snipe,** humorous, primitive, $170

Crow, carved wing tips, body made in 3 parts, minor wear, ex. cond. (A-E) ....$	75
Crow, carved wing tips & cocked head, large, unused cond. (A-E)	60
Crow, carved wood w/glass eyes, 15", ca. 1900 (D-E)...	375
Crow, hollow carved, common, orig. wire legs, unused cond., by Charles H. Perdew Company (A-E)	250
Crow, hollow carved, New Jersey, large, ex. unused cond., ca. 1920 (A-E)...........................	275
Crow, large, almost unused (A-E)	75
Crow, large, solid const., never used (A-E)	40
Crow, shadow, flat, simple const., good cond., orig. paint worn (A-E)	25
Curlew, Barnegat, early, orig. paint unrestored but weathered, minor wear (A-E).................	500
Curlew, Cobb Island, early, carved wings, orig. paint worn, ex. cond. (A-E)........................	200
Curlew, Cobb Island, early, running position w/carved wing detail, orig., paint fair (A-E)	700
Curlew, Cobb Island, rough-hewn const., w/carved wing tips, fair orig. paint (A-E)..............	150
Curlew, early, brand "JSL" under tail, minor wear, orig. paint good (A-E)...........................	120
Curlew, early, large, bill missing, orig. paint good cond. (A-E)	110
Curlew, early, rough-hewn, used cond., orig. paint worn off (A-E)	85
Curlew, early, w/spike for bill, good orig. paint, ex. cond. (A-E)......................................	175
Curlew, eastern shore, early, old nail for bill, minor wear, orig. paint fair (A-E)	125

Curlew, Eskimo, flat w/nail for bill, early w/feather painting, all orig., good cond. (A-E)........$ 120

Curlew, Eskimo, rare, w/carved wings & hole in center for mounting of wings, initials "H.D." on
bottom, traces orig. paint, ex. cond. (A-E) 625

Curlew, flat, early, w/spike for bill, ex. cond., orig. paint weathered (A-E) 100

Curlew, Hudsonian, Cape May Co., New Jersey, orig. paint, good cond. (A-E) 600

Curlew, Hudsonian, early, aged & weathered, orig. paint fair (A-E).................................... 275

Curlew, Hudsonian, early, orig. paint, no damage, ex. cond. (A-E)...................................... 500

Curlew, Hudsonian, rare, w/carved wing outlines & wing tips, ex. orig. cond., black glass eyes,
orig. paint good (A-E) 375

Curlew, Mason, rare, ex. cond., good orig. paint, orig. glass eyes (A-E) 2300

Curlew, New Jersey, early, rare, w/iron spike for bill, orig. paint good, ex. cond. (A-E)......... 550

Curlew, primitive w/flat body, good orig. cond., orig. paint weathered (A-E)....................... 200

Curlew, primitive, rough-hewn, w/burlap covering, bill missing, unused (A-E).................... 35

Curlew, shadow, rare, early, minor wear, orig. bill, ex. cond. w/fine orig. paint (A-E)........... 175

Curlew, Virginia, branded w/"OW", fair cond., orig. paint worn off (A-E)............................ 100

Decoy, handmade, head turns, wings & tail detailed, good old paint, black, gray, white (D-NE) . 30

Dowitcher, Cobb Island, early, carved wings, initial "W" under tail, ex. cond., orig. paint worn
(A-E) 100

Dowitcher, flat, dated 1910, ex. cond. w/bold orig. paint (A-E) 25

Dowitcher, Long Island, early, outstanding orig. cond., little use (A-E) 175

Dowitcher, primitive, shows age, orig. paint worn (A-E)... 10

Dowitcher, running, rare, Cobb Island, paint worn (A-E) 200

Duck, black & silver body, red head, silver bill, glass eyes, repainted (D-S) 12

Duck, hollow carved, Jake Barret w/branded signature on bottom, repainted (A-E)............. 40

Duck, Labrador, primitive, hollow w/carved wings, ex. cond., w/good orig. paint (A-E) 700

Duck, marked "FCC" (A-E) 17

Duck, marked J. H. Whitney, large (A-E) 50

Duck, papier-mâché, large, gray/brown/white, glass eyes (D-MW).................................... 12

Duck, ruddy, rare, good cond., w/much orig. paint remaining (A-E) 500

Duck, triple shadow, folds into one (D-MW).. 45

Duck, wing, canvasback drake, iron, fair cond., no paint (A-E) 75

Duck, wing, iron, weight 25 lb., ex. cond., no paint (A-E).. 350

Duck, wing, rare (canvasback drake), used on floating rig, ex. cond. w/good orig. paint (A-E) 150

Duck, wing, (scaup drake), chestnut body, good used cond., traces orig. paint (A-E) 35

Duck, wood, decor. (A-E).. 20

Duck, wood, 11½" (A-E) 30

Duck, wood, 15½" (A-E) 27

Duck, wood, 14" (A-E) 25

Eider duck, primitive, w/inletted head constr., all orig., minor wear, good orig. paint (A-E)... 100

Eider, hen, good carving, orig. paint, 18" (A-NE)... 100

Eider, Maine, drake, 17" l., w/orig. paint (A-NE) 725

Eider, primitive, inletted head, repainted, minor wear (A-E) 75

Gadwall, hen, Ken Anger, w/slightly turned head, carved wing details, branded on bottom
w/initials, "P.M.P.", good used cond., paint weathered (A-E) 200

Geese, Canadian, w/orig. paint, pr., 18" h., 23" l. (A-NE).. 475

Godwit, Eastern Shore, rare, carved wings, orig. paint worn, minor wear, ex. cond. (A-E)..... 160

Godwit, Hudsonian, rare, 1" thick body w/applied wings, made in 3 parts, all orig. w/minor wear,
good paint (A-E) 1000

Goldeneye, drake, early, branded w/name "A.F. Bishop", much used, orig. paint fair (A-E) .. 80

Goldeneye, drake, early, much used, orig. paint worn (A-E).. 50

Goldeneye, drake, ex. cond., good orig. paint (A-E) 80

Goldeneye, drake, ex. cond., orig. paint fair (A-E)... 60

Goldeneye, drake, hollow carved, early, chipped, orig. paint flaking (A-E) 70

Goldeneye, drake, hollow carved, early, flat body & head, orig. paint fair (A-E).................. 60

Goldeneye, drake, hollow carved, early, good cond., orig. paint fair (A-E).......................... 75

Goldeneye, drake, hollow carved, orig. paint good, minor wear, ex. cond. (A-E) 300

Goldeneye, drake, hollow carved, orig. paint worn (A-E) 60

Goldeneye, drake, Mason's, ex. orig. paint, minor wear (A-E).. 230

Goldeneye, drake, primitive, Maine, inletted head, repainted, ex. cond. (A-E) 40

Goldeneye, drake, Stevens Dec. Fac., orig. paint, ex. cond. (A-E) ....$ 350

Goldeneye, hen, early, w/carved eyes, branded w/name, "A. F. Bishop", good used cond., orig. paint weathered (A-E).. 125

Goldeneye, hen, early, w/carved wings, minor wear, good cond., orig. paint good (A-E) 75

Goldeneye, hen, excellent cond., well preserved (A-E).. 160

Goldeneye, hen, hollow carved, glass eyes, carved wings, light & fitted w/metal bottom, good cond., orig. paint worn (A-E)... 60

Goldeneye, hen, hollow carved, Harry Shourds, good used cond., traces orig. paint (A-E) 50

Goldeneye, hen, Harry Shourds, good orig. used cond., orig. paint weathered (A-E) 100

Goldeneye, hen, Bob White, Tullytown, Pa., turned head, new cond., signed in lead weight (A-E) 250

Goose, Canadian, carved from 1 pc. wood, except head, orig. paint, 21" l. (D-NE) 78

Goose, Canadian, carved head & tail, orig. paint, 25" l., 12" h. (A-NE) 200

Goose, Canadian, carved, hollow, traces of orig. paint, early, 12"×25" (D-E) 575

Goose, Canadian, Cobb Island, rare, by Nathan Cobb, w/carved "N" sgn., minor repair, orig. paint good (A-E) 350

Goose, Canadian, early w/head tucked down, hollow carved, much used, paint worn (A-E) ... 120

Goose, Canadian, fair cond., orig. paint weathered (A-E) 75

Mallard drake decoy, by Charles E. Wheeler, superb, bird features a pair of copper curled tail feathers, never used (A-E) $2200

Goose, Canadian, hollow carved, minor repair, orig. paint (A-E) 225

Goose, Canadian, hollow carved, New Jersey, ex. cond., good orig. paint (A-E) 120

Goose, Canadian, hollow carved, New Jersey, ex. cond., orig. paint fair (A-E)...................... 100

Goose, Canadian, hollow carved, New Jersey, John Furlow, ex. cond., good orig. paint (A-E) 175

Goose, Canadian, hollow carved, New Jersey, good cond., orig. paint worn off (A-E)............ 125

Goose, Canadian, hollow carved, New Jersey, old, good cond., minor repair, orig. paint worn (A-E) 250

Goose, Canadian, hollow carved, New Jersey, orig. paint worn off (A-E) 190

Goose, Canadian, hollow carved, New Jersey, Harry V. Shourds, good cond., minor repair, traces orig. paint (A-E)... 250

Goose, Canadian, hollow carved, New Jersey, stick-up, w/plump body, curved neck & small bill, repainted (A-E) 125

Goose, Canadian, hollow carved, painted as Brant, good cond., traces orig. paint (A-E)......... 100

Goose, Canadian, hollow carved, rare, ex. cond., minor repair, ex. orig. paint (A-E) 825

Goose, Canadian, hollow carved, wide body, branded w/initials "SRD", good used cond., orig. paint fair (A-E)... 75

Goose, Canadian, hollow carved, Charles E. "Shang" Wheeler, Stratford, Conn., 1872-1949, 27" l., rare, pine, turned head, unused, ex. cond. (A-E) 8000

Goose, Canadian, Mason factory, solid wood, 18½" l. (D-MW)... 135

Goose, Canadian, New Jersey, solid body, orig. paint worn (A-E) 175

Goose, Canadian, primitive, wide, flat body, orig. paint worn off (A-E) 75

Goose, Canadian, solid body cons., weathered paint, minor wear (A-E) 70

Goose, Canadian, swimming, rare, signed w/carved "N" on bottom, ex. cond., minor repair, orig. paint good, ca. 1880 (A-E) 1600

Goose, Canadian, tin, orig. paint fine (D-MW) ....$ 32
Goose, Canadian, watch gander, fair cond., paint worn (A-E) 175
Goose, pine, refinished (D-W) 45
Goose, slat, canvas-covered, good used cond., repainted (A-E) 150
Goose, snow, rare, stick-up w/head extended in horizontal position, ex. cond., little use (A-E). 650
Goose, swimming, hollow carved, New Jersey, ex. cond., old, orig. paint good (A-E)............ 275
Heron, primitive, w/naturally formed head, orig. paint worn, orig. w/minor repair to neck (A-E) 550
Herring gull, w/glass eyes & turned head, ex. cond., orig. paint weathered (A-E) 175
Mallard, drake, collapsible, canvas, w/wooden bottom, ex. cond., w/bright orig. paint (A-E).. 20
Mallard, drake, covered w/skin & feathers of real mallard, well preserved (A-E).................. 10
Mallard, drake, J. N. Dodge Decoy Factory, Detroit, Mich., orig. paint, minor wear, ex. cond.(A-E)
Mallard, drake, J. N. Dodge Decoy Factory, Detroit Mich., orig. paint, minor wear (A-E) 40
Mallard, drake, early, w/small head, orig. paint good though weathered (A-E) 50
Mallard, drake, early, wooden, paint good (D-MW) 30
Mallard, drake, hollow carved, Ill. River, orig. paint fair (A-E) 150
Mallard, drake, hollow carved, Old Illinois River, orig. paint excellent, minor wear (A-E)...... 300
Mallard, drake, hollow carved, solid const., fair cond. (A-E) 60
Mallard, drake, Illinois River, Charles H. Perdew, Henry, Ill. (1874-1963), "O.J.C." on bottom,
   ex. cond. (A-E) 450
Mallard, drake, Mason's, ex. cond., orig. paint, minor wear (A-E) 270
Mallard, drake, Mason's, orig. paint, worn cond. (A-E) 60
Mallard, drake, tin, orig. paint good (D-MW) 22
Mallard, hen, hollow carved body w/tin head, oversized, branded w/names "Keith" & "L.C.
   Fenno", used cond., orig. paint worn (A-E) 10
Mallard, hen, hollow carved, Mason's, good cond., w/ex. orig. paint (A-E) 40
Mallard, hen, tin, orig. paint good (D-MW) 18
Mallard, painted, head raised, bill open in calling position, 17" (A-NE) 250
Merganser, American, early New Jersey, turned head, fine cond., orig. paint (A-E)............. 220
Merganser, drake, American, early, primitive, turned head, wide flat body, carved initials "RW"
   in bottom, orig. paint (A-E) 150
Merganser, drake, American, hollow carved, early, New Jersey, paint worn, good cond. (A-E). 60
Merganser, American, hollow carved, early, orig. paint, ex. cond. (A-E) 300
Merganser, drake, factory, balsa, ex. cond., unused (A-E).. 70
Merganser, drake, red-breasted, carved w/initials "R.P.", good used cond., traces orig. paint
   (A-E) 150
Merganser, drake, red-breasted, early, eastern shore, orig. paint, minor wear, good cond. (A-E) 60
Merganser, drake, red-breasted, early, good cond. w/orig. paint (A-E)........................... 150
Merganser, drake, red-breasted, early, good cond. w/orig. paint worn (A-E) 150
Merganser, drake, red-breasted, hollow carved, branded w/"H. Conklin, N. J.", turned head,
   unused cond. (A-E) 125
Merganser, drake, red-breasted, hollow carved, early, orig. paint good, minor wear (A-E) 525
Merganser, drake, red-breasted, Long Island, early, cork body, repainted, minor wear (A-E).. 60
Merganser, drake, w/3-pc. cork body, carved head, all orig., good cond., paint worn (A-E).... 100
Merganser, hen, hollow carved, branded w/initials "MAS", early, w/minor repair & good orig.
   paint (A-E) 120
Merganser, hooded, early, primitive, orig. paint good cond., minor wear (A-E).................... 75
Merganser, hooded, hen, rare, Doug Jester, Chincoteague, Virg., orig. paint good (A-E)........ 400
Merganser, Long Island, early, branded w/name "A. F. Ristiop", carved eyes & bill, orig. paint
   good (A-E)... 125
Merganser, Long Island, early, rare, natural form root head, orig. paint good (A-E) 290
Merganser, Long Island, early, root head, orig. paint worn away, minor wear (A-E) 125
Merganser, red breasted, hollow carved, New Jersey, early, orig. paint fair, ex. cond. (A-E)... 150
Merganser, red-breasted, hollow carved, New Jersey, early, rare, orig. paint, ex. cond. (A-E). 175
Merganser, red-breasted, hollow carved, New Jersey, rare, repainted, good cond. (A-E) 230
Merganser, Virginia, early, oversized, orig. paint worn, minor wear (A-E).......................... 100
Merganser, Virginia, branded "R Chute" on bottom, orig. paint worn (A-E) 75
Mergansers, hooded, by Harold Haertel, Dundee, Ill., both w/carved wing tips, incised feather
   design, matched pr., hen preening breast, drake w/head turned left, both in mint cond. w/no
   wear, pr. (A-E)... 2000

Decoys (A-NE), *top row:* **Canadian geese,** primitive, orig. paint, matched pr., 18" h., 23" l., $475; *bottom row, left to right:* **black duck,** sleeper, Delaware River, $250; **robin,** on gold ball, Maine, carved wood, metal legs, bill broken, 9" h., $155; **black duck,** turned head, orig. paint good, $250

Nodding goose, tin (D-MW) ....$	35
Old squaw, drake, Frank Dobbins of Maine, w/carved "F" signature, marked on bottom "Old Squaw/Merrymeeting/Bay/Maine/, like new cond. (A-E)..	60
Old squaw, drake, hollow carved, early, New Jersey, good used cond., minor repair, traces orig. paint, (A-E)...	140
Old squaw, drake, hollow carved, Mark English, signed "M.E." under tail, orig. paint, minor wear (A-E)..	700
Old squaw, drake, Maine, inletted head, repainted, minor wear (A-E)	50
Old squaw, hen, hollow carved, w/initials "M.E." on tail, orig. paint, ex. cond. (A-E)..........	850
Old squaw, hen, Maine, repainted, slight wear, ex. cond. (A-E)	40
Old squaw, New England, primitive, orig. paint fair (A-E)...	40
Old squaw, primitive w/orig. paint, 12" l. (A-NE)...	150
Owl, balsa w/paperweight glass eyes, minor wear, orig. paint fair (A-E)............................	375
Pigeon, passenger, Lou Schifferell, w/glass eye (D-E)...	200
Pintail decoy body, A. Elmer Crowell, oval brand signature, orig. paint fair, good cond. (A-E) .	80
Pintail drake, body & neck, Joseph W. Lincoln, repainted, slight wear, ex. cond. (A-E).........	30
Pintail, drake, canvas covered & filled, good cond. (A-E)...	20
Pintail, drake, carved wing & tail feathers, tucked-down sleepy head, good cond., ex. orig. paint (A-E)	200
Pintail, drake, A. Elmer Crowell, East Harwich, Mass. (1862-1952), early brand signature, repainted, ex. cond. (A-E)	150
Pintail, drake, by A. Elmer Crowell, w/oval brand signature, head turned to left, ex. cond., repainted (A-E)	125
Pintail, drake, early, branded w/name "Harrington", carved wing & tail feathers, orig. paint worn (A-E)...	200
Pintail, drake, early, good cond., orig. paint (A-E)..	50
Pintail, drake, Ira Hudson, good orig. paint, ex. cond. (A-E)..	750
Pintail, drake, Mason's, orig. paint, slight wear (A-E)	100
Pintail, drake, Lem & Steve Ward, rare, w/broad tail & hump back, Crisfield, Maryland, 1930, minor wear, well preserved, good orig. paint (A-E)	2300
Pintail, drake, Wildfowler Decoys, Inc., Conn., paperweight glass eyes, ex. cond., never painted (A-E)	20
Pintail, drake, wooden w/glass eyes, factory made (D-MW)..	15
Pintail, hen, Mason's, rare, orig. paint, slight wear, good cond. (A-E)................................	100

Pintail, hen, rare, good used cond., orig. paint (A-E) ....$ 325

Pintail, hen, Lem & Steve Ward, w/hump back & broad tail, rare, turned head, "Ward Decoy, Crisfield, Md." written under tail, minor repair, orig. paint good, slight weathering (A-E)..   1200

Pintail, Virginia, ex. cond., orig. paint worn off (A-E)..   100

Pintails, shadow, set of 3, fold-up, 2 drakes & 1 hen, mounted on 3-way stretcher, J. W. Reynolds Patent, ca. 1900, orig. 3-way spring mount, good used cond. (A-E)   80

Plover, attrib. to George Boyd, good cond., w/fine orig. paint (A-E)   350

Plover, black-bellied, Bellport, Long Island, H. F. Osborn, carved wing details, branded w/initials "C.V.", minor wear, ex. cond. w/ex. orig. paint (A-E).....................................   750

Plover, black-bellied, Cobb Island, carved wings, initials "JJ" under tail, minor wear, orig. paint worn off (A-E)...   150

Plover, black-bellied, Cobb Island, Luther Nottingham, Cape Charles, Va., carved sgn. "LLN" under tail, carved wing details, ex. cond., orig. paint worn (A-E)   375

Plover, black-bellied, Cobb Island, prof. repainted, ex. cond. (A-E)....................................   225

Plover, black-bellied, early w/carved wings, good cond. w/ex. orig. paint (A-E)....................   150

Plover, black-bellied, early, carved wing tips, prof. repainted, minor wear (A-E)..................   150

Plover, black-bellied, early, ex. cond. (A-E)   125

Plover, black-bellied, early, lg. carved "D" on bottom, good used cond., paint good (A-E)   75

Plover, black-bellied, New Jersey, early, good orig. paint (A-E)   100

Plover, black-bellied, early, movable wing arrangement, prof. repainted, ex. cond. (A-E)   60

Plover, black-bellied, New Jersey, early, w/hole in tail, good used cond., orig. paint worn (A-E).   100

Plover, black-bellied, early Virginia, plump, carved wing outline, repainted (A-E)   75

Plover, black-bellied, ex. cond., good orig. paint (A-E)   300

Plover, black-bellied, ex. cond., repainted (A-E)   60

Plover, black-bellied, fine cond. w/ex. orig. paint (A-E)   175

Plover, black-bellied, Wm. Matthews, carved wings, ex. cond., orig. paint good (A-E)..........   250

Plover, black-bellied, New Jersey, carved wings & eyes, minor wear, traces orig. paint (A-E)   150

Plover, black-bellied, New Jersey, early, w/letter "H" under tail, minor wear, ex. orig. paint (A-E)   125

Plover, black-bellied, primitive, sq. head, plump, all orig., no damage, orig. paint ex. (A-E).   80

Plover, black-bellied, rare, attributed to Leeds, carved wing & tail outlines, orig. paint, ex. cond. (A-E)   450

Plover, black-bellied, shore bird, white ground, yellow & blk. spotting, ex. cond. (A-NE).....   250

Plover, black-bellied, Charles E. "Shang" Wheeler, rare w/balsa wood, sleepy attitude w/head turned back, glass eyes (A-E)   1200

Plover, black-breasted (D-W)   25

Plover, black-breasted, orig. paint, ex. cond., wood base, 11" (A-NE)................................   325

Plover, George Boyd, early, minor wear, ex. cond. w/fine orig. paint (A-E)   350

Plover, Geo. Boyd, early, New Hampshire, good cond., orig. paint (A-E)   350

Plover, Cobb Island, carved eyes & wing tips, worn to natural wood finish (A-E)   150

Plover, Dodge Decoy Factory, ex. cond., orig. paint, glass eyes (A-E)   525

Plover, Dodge Decoy Factory, ex. cond., good orig. paint (A-E)..   250

Plover, early, carved wings, ex. cond. w/bold orig. paint (A-E)...   150

Plover, early, full bodied w/split tail (D-MW)   135

Plover, early, good cond., orig. paint worn (A-E)..   75

Plover, early, incised wing outlines, orig. paint worn off, ex. cond. (A-E)............................   175

Plover, early, primitive, plump bird, orig. paint worn, fine cond. (A-E)   400

Plover, early, replaced bill, good orig. paint (A-E)   150

Plover, factory, ex. cond. w/orig. paint, little wear (A-E)...   275

Plover, factory, w/incised feather & wing details, made w/2 halves joined together, ex. cond., good orig. paint (A-E)   50

Plover, feeding, Cobb Island, w/turned head bent forward, carved wings, orig. paint worn away (A-E)   175

Plover, golden, early, Nantucket, w/hole for stringing rig, made in 2 halves, w/orig. iron stick up, orig. paint worn (A-E)...   225

Plover, golden, early, Nantucket Island, Mass., drilled hole w/orig. iron mount, good used cond., orig. paint worn (A-E)   175

Plover, golden, early, New England, slight wear, orig. paint weathered (A-E)   175

Plover, golden, early, rare, papier-mâché, orig. paint, minor wear, good cond. (A-E)   75

Plover, golden, Nantucket Island, Mass., ex. cond. almost unused (A-E)..............................   225

Plover, golden, orig. paint good (D-MW)..$ 30

Plover, killdeer, A. Elmer Crowell, life-sized, unusual hewn base, ex. cond. (A-E)............... 700

Plover, Wm. Matthews, rare, w/turned head & carved wings, minor wear, ex. cond., paint worn
one side (A-E).. 750

Plover, Nantucket, rare, early, Mackey's typewritten label, drilled w/2 holes, good cond. w/ex.
orig. paint (A-E) 1000

Plover, New Jersey, branded w/name "J. Nickerson", glass eyes, minor wear, orig. paint worn off
(A-E) 130

Plover, New Jersey, made in 3 parts, body w/each wing applied separately, good orig. used cond.,
orig. paint weathered (A-E) 75

Decoy, eider drake, orig. paint, from Monhegan Island, Maine (A-NE) $725

Plover, New Jersey, w/orig. wire mount, thick & flat, good used cond., paint worn (A-E) 90

Plover, pressed fiber, rare, molded feather details, worn with age, good cond. (A-E)............. 30

Plover, primitive, drilled hole in center for stringing rig, repainted (A-E) 100

Plover, primitive, early, orig. paint, minor wear, ex. cond. (A-E).. 125

Plover, primitive, lg., in-use repainting (A-E) 75

Plover, primitive, very early, attributed to Leeds, orig. paint, ex. cond. (A-E) 125

Plover, Harry V. Shourdes, rare, minor wear, good cond., ex. orig. paint (A-E) 550

Plover, thick & flat w/carved wings, fair cond. (A-E) 150

Plover, tin, 2-pc., orig. paint (D-E) 28

Plover, Virginia, early, plump, ex. cond., paint worn off (A-E) 150

Redhead, drake, carved wing tips, dated 1948, good cond., paint worn (A-E)...................... 80

Redhead, drake, cork body w/wooden head, by Thomas Gelston (D-E) 90

Redhead, drake, hollow carved, bill repaired, prof. repainted, ex. cond. (A-E)..................... 70

Redhead, drake, hollow carved, Lloyd Parker, New Jersey, orig. paint weathered (A-E)......... 60

Redhead, drake, hollow carved, rare, w/carved wing tips, "N" signature on bottom, orig. paint
worn, ex. cond. (A-E).. 950

Redhead, drake, Mason's, good cond., orig. paint, minor wear (A-E) 260

Redhead, drake, Mason's, orig. paint, well preserved, slight wear (A-E) 100

Redhead, drake, sleeper, balsa body, incised wing details, ex. cond., little use (A-E) 70

Redhead, drake, sleeper, Jim Keleen, balsa body w/head tucked down, good used cond. (A-E) . 60

Redhead, drake, sleeper, Jim Keleen, balsa body, unused cond. (A-E)................................ 50

Redhead, drake, sleepy head type, Mason's, minor wear, good cond., orig. paint worn (A-E) 275

Redhead, drake, very rare, w/"L D" signature, body repaired, good orig. paint (A-E)........... 625

Redhead duck, tin silhouette (D-N) 18

Redhead, half-pattern, used by Armstrong Stove & Foundry Co. when casting redhead wing duck,
aged natural wood finish (A-E)...
60

Redhead, hen, Ill. River, hollow constr., orig. paint fair (A-E) 100

Redhead, hen, New York state, minor wear, ex. cond., orig. paint weathered, ca. 1880 (A-E) .$ 100
Redhead, hen, Nate Quillen, Rockwood, Mich., for J. C. Morse in 1894, hollow w/brand, "Point Mouillee Shooting Club," good orig. cond., minor wear, good paint (A-E)....................... 400
Redhead, hen, Wm. M. Rumble, early, Bloomfield, Ontario, ca. 1880-90, hollow carved, ex. cond., orig. paint good (A-E) 50
Redhead, rare, orig. paint worn off, ca. 1865 (A-E).. 300
Ringbill, hen, sleeper, hollow carved, branded w/name, "H. Conklin", unused cond. (A-E)... 100
Sanderling, A. Elmer Crowell, life-sized, penned signature & impressed rectangular stamp on bottom, ex. cond. (A-E) 700
Sanderling, early, Taylor Johnson, ex. cond., fine orig. paint, minor wear (A-E) 200
Sanderling, Long Island, branded w/initials "JWC", carved eyes, all orig., good cond. (A-E).. 125
Sanderling, New Jersey, fair cond., in-use repainting (A-E) 100
Sanderling, New Jersey, old, minor wear, good cond., traces orig. paint (A-E) 150
Sanderling, primitive, good cond., orig. paint worn (A-E) 50
Sandpiper, Cobb Island, w/carved wing details, good cond., traces orig. paint (A-E) 150
Sandpiper, least, feeding, rare, ex. cond. (A-E) 325
Sandpiper, least, feeding, S. Jersey, good used cond., orig. paint (A-E) 275
Sandpiper, pectoral, minor wear, ex. orig. paint (A-E) 150
Sandpiper, pectoral, New Jersey, early, w/carved wing details, initials "NJS" under tail, ex. cond., orig. paint worn off (A-E) 50
Sandpiper, pectoral, New Jersey, ex. cond., old, little use (A-E).. 150
Sandpiper, pectoral, Virginia, carved "W" on bottom, minor wear, orig. paint weathered (A-E) . 175
Sandpiper, pectoral, Virginia, early, ex. original paint, worn, well preserved (A-E) 150
Sandpiper, pectora, Virginia, orig. cond. good, orig. paint weathered (A-E)......................... 125
Sandpiper, pectoral, Virginia, orig. paint worn, good cond. (A-E) 150
Sandpiper, Virginia, early, orig. paint weathered (A-E) 170
Sandpiper, pectoral, Virginia, replaced bill, orig. paint good (A-E) 225
Sandpiper, pectoral, Virginia, early, signed w/carved initial "W", paint worn, minor wear, good cond. (A-E)... 125
Sandpiper, primitive, orig. paint, much used (A-E) 40
Scoup, blue bill, good cond. (A-E) 50
Scaup, drake, Ken Anger, w/carved wing details, branded "D.S." in bottom, new cond. (A-E) . 150
Scaup, drake, carved wing & tailfeathers, fair cond. (A-E) 60
Scaup, drake, carved wing & tail feathers, tucked head, ex. cond. (A-E) 100
Scaup, drake, carved wings & turned head, branded w/name "C. T. Sprague", good cond., orig. paint fair (A-E)... 125
Scaup, drake, ex. used cond., good orig. paint (A-E).. 125
Scaup, drake, good orig. paint, minor wear (A-E)... 200
Scaup, drake, good used cond., orig. paint (A-E)... 50
Scaup, drake, hollow carved, all orig., paint weathered & worn (A-E) 40
Scaup, drake, hollow carved, carved wing tips, good used cond., orig. paint fair (A-E) 50
Scaup, drake, hollow carved, Bart Clayton, New Jersey, minor repair, orig. paint worn (A-E). 100
Scaup, drake, hollow carved, Connecticut, good used cond., traces orig. paint (A-E)............. 35
Scaup, drake, hollow carved, deep-bodied, orig. cond., like new (A-E) 400
Scaup, drake, hollow carved, early, ex. cond., w/fine orig. paint (A-E) 175
Scaup, drake, hollow carved, Dan English, carved tail feathers, good used cond., orig. paint good (A-E) 275
Scaup, drake, hollow carved, John Furlow, Atantic City, New Jersey, orig. paint, good cond. (A-E) 75
Scaup, drake, hollow carved, ex. cond. w/good orig. paint (A-E)... 60
Scaup, drake, hollow carved, Henry Grant, orig. cond., little use (A-E) 500
Scaup, drake, hollow carved, Henry Kilpatrick, Barnegat, New Jersey, orig. paint weathered, slight wear (A-E) 70
Scaup, drake, hollow carved, Joe King, much used, orig. paint fair (A-E)............................. 50
Scaup, drake, hollow carved, minor repair, good orig. paint (A-E)... 30
Scaup, drake, hollow carved, New Jersey, repainted, ex. cond. (A-E) 125
Scaup, drake, hollow carved, old attached label, "made by Francis Burritt, Stratford, Conn., 1876", good orig. cond., paint weathered (A-E) 300
Scaup, drake, hollow carved, orig. paint good, minor wear (A-E) 350

Scaup, drake, hollow carved, Lloyd Parker, good cond., w/ex. orig. paint (A-E) 225

Scaup, drake, hollow carved, rare, carved tail feathers, orig. paint, ex. cond. (A-E) ....$ 1500

Scaup, drake, hollow carved, restored & repainted (A-E) 40

Scaup, drake, hollow carved, Harry Shourds, ex. cond., repainted (A-E)............................. 80

Scaup, drake, hollow carved, Harry V. Shourds, minor repair, orig. paint good (A-E) 300

Scaup, drake, Roland Horner, ex. used cond., good orig. paint (A-E) 325

Scaup, drake, Ira Hudson, minor repair, good cond., paint weathered (A-E) 250

Scaup, drake, Joe King, Parkertown, New Jersey, hollow carved, orig. paint weathered (A-E). 40

Scaup, drake, Ogdensburg, hump-back style, orig. paint, slight wear (A-E) 40

Scaup, drake, rare, Ill. River, branded "GJC" on bottom, minor wear, fine orig. paint (A-E) .. 250

Scaup, drake, Harry V. Shourds, New Jersey, carved "WMJC" on bottom, orig. paint weathered, ex. cond. (A-E)... 175

Scaup, drake, solid, marked by Mr. Mackey on bottom "Burch, Willis Wharf", orig. paint, worn areas (A-E) 65

Scaup, early, Connecticut, repainted, minor wear (A-E)... 70

Scaup, greater, drake, Rhoades Truax, New Jersey, hollow carved, some orig. paint, minor wear (A-E) 50

Scaup, greater, Mason's, ex. cond. w/fine orig. paint (A-E) 300

Scaup, hen, R. I. Culver, branded twice with name, fine orig. cond., orig. paint weathered (A-E) 150

Scaup, hen, hollow carved, John Furlow, brand sign. on bottom, ex. cond. w/good paint (A-E). 60

Scaup, hen, hollow carved, Mark Kerr, Linwood, New Jersey, good used cond., orig. paint weathered (A-E) 70

Scaup, hen, hollow carved, New Jersey, ex. cond., minor wear (A-E) 50

Scaup, hen, hollow carved, Harry Shourds, shows use, orig. paint fair (A-E)........................ 80

Scaup, hen, Roland Horner, Manahawkin, New Jersey, hollow carved, ex. cond. (A-E).......... 350

Scaup, hen, Mason's, challenge quality head, orig. paint, minor wear, good cond. (A-E) 100

Scaup, hen, Mason's, orig. paint, well preserved, minor wear, ex. cond. (A-E) 450

Scaup, hen, Lloyd Parker, Parkertown, New Jersey, hollow carved, orig. paint fair, good cond. (A-E) 150

Scaup, hen, well formed & carved, orig. paint good, ex. cond. (A-E)................................... 325

Scaup, hen, Chauncey Wheeler, New York, ex. cond., fine orig. paint (A-E) 175

Scaup, lesser, drake, Mason's, rare sleepy head type, orig. paint, minor wear, ex. cond. (A-E) . 350

Scaup, Long Island, rare. w/head back, carved from 1 piece wood, good cond., repainted (A-E) 950

Scaup, Mason's, good cond. w/ex. orig. paint (A-E) 70

Scaup, Mason's, orig. paint, slight wear, excellent condition (A-E)..................................... 370

Scaup, Mason's, orig. paint, slight wear, well preserved (A-E)... 50

Scoter, Maine, w/inletted constr., old, orig. paint weathered (A-E) 50

Scoter, white-winged, rare, w/carved wings, graceful head, minor wear, good cond., w/ex. orig. paint (A-E) 1200

Shadow decoys, set of 3, mounted on 3-way stretcher, J. W. Reynolds patent, ca. 1900, mallards — 2 drakes, 1 hen; good used cond. (A-E) 70

Shadow, flat (Va. Yellowlegs), minor wear, ex. cond., orig. paint weathered (A-E)................ 30

Shadow, stick-up, flat, w/orig. stick-up wire, ex. cond., orig. paint dull w/weathering (A-E) .. 25

Shadow, tin, lot of 3, dowitcher & 2 plovers; good cond., plovers w/orig. twisted stands, dowitcher never used (A-E) 100

Shadow, tin, w/removable wings & fold down stick, fair orig. paint (A-E) 20

Shore bird, carved, minor wear, repainted (A-E) 50

Shore bird, cork, nail for bill, repainted (A-E) 50

Shore bird, cork body, rare, feeding, 3 parts, worn cond., traces orig. paint (A-E) 125

Shore bird, Dodge Factory, repainted, good cond. (A-E) 60

Shore bird, early, primitive, orig. paint fair (A-E) 70

Shore bird, hand carved, gray & black, 13", mounted (D-NE) 100

Shore bird, made in 2 halves, flat sided, orig. paint weathered (A-E) 30

Shore bird, painted, carved head, crest w/glass eyes, 11¼" l. (A-NE)................................... 275

Shore birds, heavy black bills, orig. paint, 1 much worn, 1 good cond., pr. (A-E) 15

Shore birds, w/orig. decor., pr. (A-E) 25

Snipe, early, w/brass tack eyes, ex. cond. (A-E) 125

Snipe, early, ex. orig. paint, minor wear, ex. cond. (A-E) 60

Snipe, early, primitive, nail for bill, traces orig. paint, worn (A-E)....................................... 30

Snipe, Virginia, early, w/tilted head, good cond., traces orig. gray paint (A-E) ....$ 125
Snipe, flat, primitive, orig. stick, worn cond. (A-E)   60
Snipe, robin, early Cobb Island, w/carved tail, much used cond., orig. paint fair (A-E)..........   300
Snipe, robin, Cobb Island, carved wings, old & worn (A-E)...   100
Snipe, robin, Cobb Island, carved wings, orig. paint good (A-E)   175
Snipe, robin, Dodge Decoy Factory, ex. cond., repainted (A-E)..   100
Snipe, robin, Dodge Decoy Factory, minor repair, good orig. paint (A-E)   100
Snipe, robin, Dodge Decoy Factory, minor repair, good orig. paint (A-E)   200
Snipe, robin, Cobb Island, early, orig. paint, minor wear, ex. cond. (A-E)   140
Snipe, robin, early, ex. cond. w/good orig. paint (A-E)..   200
Snipe, robin, early, head fastened by peg, repainted (A-E)   125
Snipe, robin, early, nail for bill, most paint orig., ex. cond. (A-E)..................................   90
Snipe, robin, Joe King, ex. cond., orig. paint worn (A-E)..   175
Snipe, robin, primitive, 3 parts, all orig., worn cond. (A-E)   70
Snipe, robin, primitive, w/turned head, rough hewn, orig. paint good (A-E)......................   100
Snipe, robin, rare, branded w/"E.C." under tail, ex. cond. w/orig. glass eyes & bill, finish worn to
   natural wood (A-E)   150
Snipe, robin, rough hewn, ex. cond. w/orig. paint (A-E)..   100
Snipe, robin, Virginia, carved initial "R" under tail, repainted, ex. cond. (A-E)....................   100
Snipe, robin, Virginia, early, good cond. w/orig. paint (A-E)..   125
Snipe, robin, Virginia, early, initial "W" carved under tail, orig. paint fair, good cond. (A-E)   75
Snipe, robin, Virginia, early, orig. wire mount, orig. paint, worn (A-E)   20
Snipe, robin, Virginia, plump, rough-hewn, minor wear, repainted (A-E)   125
Snipe, robin, Virginia, plump, well formed, minor wear, orig. paint, ex. cond. (A-E)............   130
Snipe, robin, well made, thin, orig. paint ex., minor wear (A-E)   90
Snipe, tin (D-W)   28
Swan, hollow carved w/tin bottom, large, good used cond., orig. paint weathered (A-E)........   750
Swan, solid body construction, primitive, turned head, orig. paint fair (A-E)   250
Swan, Virginia, orig. paint (D-MW)   1000
Teal, blue-winged, composition, Victor Decoy Co., marked w/"Victor Veri-Lite", 1946, ex. orig.
   paint, minor wear (A-E)   25
Teal, blue-winged, drake, Mason's, rare, orig. paint, ex. cond. (A-E)................................   600
Teal, blue-winged, drake, orig. paint, slight wear, ex. cond. (A-E)   175
Teal, blue-winged, hen, Mason's, good cond., orig. paint worn slightly (A-E)......................   600
Teal, green-winged, drake, hollow carved, early, carved wing tips, good orig. paint (A-E).....   375
Teal, green-winged, drake, Mason's, orig. paint worn off, fair cond. (A-E)   110
Teal, green-winged, drake, Mason's, worn, well-preserved, repainted (A-E)   90
Teal, green-winged, hen, Mason's, orig. paint worn away, fair cond. (A-E)   60
Teal, green-winged, hollow carved, New Jersey, w/head back in sleeping position, ex. cond.
   (A-E)   90
Teal, green-winged, rare, small, ex. cond., orig. paint (A-E)   180
Tern, A. Elmer Crowell, life-sized, penned signature of Mr. Crowell on base, ex. cond. (A-E)   900
Turnstone, hollow, early, made in 2 halves, orig. paint, minor wear, ex. cond. (A-E)   125
Turnstone, ruddy, early & branded w/name "Accomac Club, Va.", minor wear, ex. orig. paint
   (A-E)   210
Turnstone, ruddy, early, carved wing tips, orig. paint ex., slight wear (A-E)   40
Turnstone, ruddy, good cond. w/fine orig. paint (A-E)   225
Turnstone, ruddy, Long Island, early, ex. cond. & orig. paint (A-E)   800
Turnstone, ruddy, New Jersey, carved wings & initials "DH", minor wear, orig. paint good (A-E)   300
Turnstone, ruddy, New Jersey, early, good used cond., orig. paint worn (A-E)......................   150
Turnstone, ruddy, New Jersey, ex. orig. cond., little use (A-E)   225
Turnstone, ruddy, New Jersey, nail for bill, orig. paint good, ex. cond. (A-E)......................   150
Turnstone, ruddy, New Jersey, orig. paint good (A-E)..   100
Widgeon, drake, A. Elmer Crowell, very early, repainted, ex. cond. (A-E)...........................   75
Widgeon, drake, Mason's, very rare, repainted and restored, slight wear (A-E)   50
Widgeon, hen, A. Elmer Crowell, oval brand signature, repainted, slight wear, ex. cond. (A-E)   75
Willet, early, w/carved wings, bill replaced, minor wear, orig. paint w/little wear (A-E)   275
Woodpecker, downy, A. Elmer Crowell, life-sized, mounted on heavy piece of pine bark, signed
   on back in pen, ex. cond. (A-E)..   500

Yellowlegs, Lou Barkelow, New Jersey, early, carved wings, good cond., w/ex. orig. paint (A-E) .$ 450
Yellowlegs, carved wings, ex. cond., minor wear, paint orig. & ex. (A-E) 125
Yellowlegs, A. Elmer Crowell, rare, sleeping, bill fully carved, w/glass eyes, ex. cond. almost unused, paint worn on sides (A-E) 1750
Yellowlegs, early, carved wing tips, good used cond., orig. paint worn off (A-E) 110
Yellowlegs, early, deeply carved wings, orig. paint, minor wear, ex. cond. (A-E) 100
Yellowlegs, early, Mass., w/peg in wishbone tail, worn cond. orig. paint (A-E) 200
Yellowlegs, feeding, New Jersey, w/carved wings, ex. cond. (A-E) 120
Yellowlegs, feeding, curlew like bill, glass eyes & incised wing outline, good cond. (A-E) 190
Yellowlegs, feeding, S. Jersey, rare, good orig. paint (A-E) 110
Yellowlegs, "fish-in-throat" appearance, minor wear (A-E) 250
Yellowlegs, flat, early, minor wear, orig. paint good (A-E) 50
Yellowlegs, flat, hole drilled in center, ex. cond., orig. paint (A-E) 40
Yellowlegs, flat, Long Island, signed "BC" under tail, ex. orig. cond., ex paint (A-E) 175
Yellowlegs, flat, orig. paint excellent, very good cond. (A-E) 90
Yellowlegs, flat, primitive, bill damaged, orig. paint worn (A-E) 60
Yellowlegs, Thomas H. Gelston, cork, minor wear, good cond. w/ex. orig. paint (A-E) 200
Yellowlegs, Thomas H. Gelston, rare, cork, good cond., ex. orig. paint (A-E) 150
Yellowlegs, greater, early, primitive, orig. paint good, ex. cond. (A-E) 120
Yellowlegs, greater, orig. paint excellent, slight wear (A-E) 10
Yellowlegs, Ira Hudson, rare, good cond., w/ex. orig. paint (A-E) 525
Yellowlegs, Joe King, rare, ex. cond., orig. paint worn (A-E) 150
Yellowlegs, lesser, carved wings, all orig. & good cond., paint good (A-E) 475
Yellowlegs, lesser, early, Bay Head, New Jersey, good cond., w/orig. paint, minor wear (A-E).. 175
Yellowlegs, lesser, early, ex. cond., orig. paint weathered (A-E) 300
Yellowlegs, lesser, early, orig. feather painting, ex. cond. (A-E) 45
Yellowlegs, lesser, Mason, ex. cond., good orig. paint, little wear (A-E) 550
Yellowlegs, lesser, Wm. Matthews, w/carved wings, minor wear, ex. orig. paint (A-E) 250
Yellowlegs, lesser, nail for bill, orig. paint one side only, slight wear (A-E) 30
Yellowlegs, lesser, primitive, shows age, orig. paint good (A-E) 40
Yellowlegs, lesser, 2, both missing bills, both retain orig. paint (A-E) 60
Yellowlegs, lesser, wire for bill, tiny head, slight wear, repainted (A-E) 50
Yellowlegs, Wm. Matthews, Virginia, early w/carved wings, minor wear, ex. cond. w/good orig. paint (A-E) 270
Yellowlegs, Wm. Matthews, Virginia, early w/carved wings, minor wear, good cond., orig. paint fair (A-E) 200
Yellowlegs, Wm. Matthews, early, w/carved wing tips, ex. cond., orig. paint w/minor wear (A-E) . 275
Yellowlegs, New Jersey, branded w/"Accomac Club, Va.", minor wear, repainted (A-E) 125
Yellowlegs, New Jersey, early, carved eyes, minor wear w/ex. orig. paint (A-E) 275
Yellowlegs, New Jersey, early, worn, repainted (A-E) 70
Yellowlegs, New Jersey, like new, orig. paint, no damage (A-E) 90
Yellowlegs, New Jersey, little wear & use, paint orig. & excellent (A-E) 60
Yellowlegs, New Jersey, made in 2 halves w/slender neck, orig. paint fair (A-E) 150
Yellowlegs, papier-mâché, early w/glass eyes, good cond., orig. paint (A-E) 150
Yellowlegs, New Jersey, Lloyd Parker, carved wing details, good used cond. w/orig. paint (A-E) 410
Yellowlegs, New Jersey, B. Seninio, made in 2 halves, w/nail for bill, orig. paint worn (A-E) . 225
Yellowlegs, New Jersey, very early and primitive eyes formed by drilled hole, ex. cond. (A-E) . 150
Yellowlegs, primitive, angled hole in tail, ex. cond., orig. paint worn off (A-E) 200
Yellowlegs, primitive, early, orig. paint good, slight wear (A-E) 65
Yellowlegs, primitive, ex. cond. w/orig. paint (A-E) 60
Yellowlegs, primitive, half-moon shape, nail for bill, ex. cond. w/good orig. paint (A-E) 110
Yellowlegs, primitive, humorous, excellent condition (A-E) 100
Yellowlegs, primitive, orig. heavy wire mount, orig. paint fair (A-E) 40
Yellowlegs, rare, minor wear, orig. paint good, ex. cond., ca. 1897 (A-E) 100
Yellowlegs, Virginia, carved wings, ex. cond., much orig. paint, weathered (A-E) 275
Yellowlegs, Virginia, early, glass eyes, orig. paint good, ex. cond. (A-E) 50
Yellowlegs, Virginia, early, plump, carved wing detail, orig. paint fair (A-E) 150
Yellowlegs, Virginia, orig. bill, minor wear, 2 drilled holes, ex. orig. paint (A-E)................... 650
Yellowlegs, Virginia, orig. paint good, well preserved (A-E) 30

Fraktur

Illuminated manuscript writings are commonly known as "Fraktur," a distinctive style of penmanship, combined with bright pictorial embellishments, so naively drawn and decorated that existing examples are considered to be one of our most delightfully beautiful forms of folk art.

This type of highly stylized lettering and decoration was introduced in America by German immigrants during the early eighteenth century. The art flourished in parts of Pennsylvania and the Shenandoah Valley for approximately one hundred years. The work of the Pennsylvania German calligraphers is particularly prized today, with good examples of Fraktur costing thousands of dollars.

The earlier examples appear to have been made by ministers, schoolmasters and untrained layman (written mostly in German script) and range in size up to about twelve by fifteen inches. The pen-and-ink outlines of the figures were

Fraktur, bookmark, tulip & heart, framed, dated 1834 (A-E) $280

Fraktur, double bookmark, quails & flowers, bird's-eye frame (A-E) $130

done first, then filled in with colors, hence the term *illuminated.* Most of the remaining examples have retained their original intensity to a remarkable degree over the years.

Fraktur falls into several categories. The interesting handwriting specimens were used for teaching the younger set the alphabet; this is known as *vorschrift.* The birth or baptismal certificate, a *taufschein,* and the house blessing, a *haus sagen.* And, of course, there is a large group of the more common types of Fraktur—which includes bookplates, rewards of merit, valentines, bookmarks, or a family record.

Another form of Fraktur that is gaining in popularity—and prices are rising rapidly—is the printed birth or baptismal certificate. This type has printed verses, is flanked by angels on two sides, in addition to flowers or baskets of flowers, harps, wreaths, birds and hearts, all of which are colored by hand. The spaces are filled with handwritten names and the place of birth. These certificates were printed from the late 1700s up until around the middle of the nineteenth century. Some of the better known printers of these forms were: G. S. Peters;

Lutz & Scheffer of Harrisburg, Pennsylvania; Blumer & Leisenring of Allentown, Pennsylvania; Johann Ritter, (from about 1808-1825); Gottlieb Jungmann and his partners, Benjamin Johnson & Thomas Barton; as well as George D. Gerrish and Jacob Schneider, all of Reading, Pennsylvania.

* * *

Baptismal certificate, Chambersburg, Pa., German writing, colorful, 1814 (A-E)....................$ 100
Bird on branch, curly maple frame, w/flowers (A-E) 200
Birth certificate, Johannes Bolfinger, 1803, Berks Co., circle center w/tulips, flowers (A-E) 290
Birth certificate, Anna Maria, 1807, signed "Martin Brechall" (A-E)....................................... 275
Birth certificate, Susanna Baucher, 1806, Ephrata imprint, hand drawn, birds & flowers (A-E) 150
Birth certificate, Bedminster Twp., Bucks Co., decor. w/red & yellow birds & tulips w/dots & lines, 1821 (A-E).. 1500
Birth certificate, Margretha Berger, 1825, decor. w/tulips & green grapes (A-E) 3800
Birth certificate, blank form, decor. w/rampant red lions (A-E) 1400
Birth certificate, block print, 1836, decor. w/blue & red-winged angels (A-E) 250
Birth certificate, Samuel Boffemeyer, 1829, dec. w/face & clock (A-E) 1900
Birth certificate, Levi Bobp, 1824, block print, by Philip Hantsch, Reading, Pa. (A-E)............ 160
Birth certificate, Catherina, 1815, Berks Co., Pa., signed "Martin Brechall", stylized flowers, red & blue (A-E) 1400
Birth certificate, Calvin Catherman, 1855, Centre County, roses w/wreath of small flowers (A-E). 200
Birth certificate, colorful, 1789, signed "Martin Brechall" (A-E) 1100
Birth certificate, curly maple frame, flower & diamond colored border w/flowers & writing in center, dated 1834 (A-E) 325
Birth certificate, dated 1818, large central urn w/flowers, ex. old frame (A-E) 675
Birth certificate, dated 1860, printed, decor. w/birds & hearts (A-E)................................... 575
Birth certificate, decor. w/birds on flower pots & heart w/weeping tulips, 1774 (A-E)............. 750
Birth certificate, decor. w/candle chandelier, shield of floral designs, flowerpots & plants, 1797, rare (A-E) 1300
Birth certificate, decor. w/houses, fences, flowers & birds, exc. frame, 1829 (A-E)................. 4000
Birth certificate, decor., w/parrots & two stars w/faces, by Krebs, 1803 (A-E) 1100
Birth certificate, decor., birds, parrot & tulip, dated 1762, colorful, printed (A-E) 200
Birth certificate, decor. w/star flowers, 4 distelfinks, hearts; nice frame, signed "A.W. (Adam Wuertz)", 1835 (A-E).. 1100
Birth certificate, decor. w/tulips & birds, old frame, 1811 (A-E)... 1300
Birth certificate, Henrich Delang, 1807, by Krebs, decor. w/decals (A-E).............................. 475
Birth certificate, Anna Maria Drager, 1790, borders w/clusters of flowers, hearts & birds (A-E) 3000
Birth certificate, Sarah Eschleman, Oct. 5, 1828, handmade, central heart, floral border (A-E) . 475

Fraktur, Taufschein, printed by Johann Ritter & Co., dated 1838 (D-MW) $90

Fraktur, New Year's wish to parents, dated 1846 (D-MW) $1800

Birth certificate, Catherine Frank, 1816, Centre County, red, yellow & green tulips, good frame
(A-E) ....$ 625
Birth certificate, George Friederich, 1812, Hanover Twp., decor. w/parrots, faces & flowers, frame
(A-E) 550
Birth certificate, Thomas Gehmeyer, 1803, decor. w/"Ehre Fater Und Mutter", colorful (A-E) .. 1400
Birth certificate, Johannes Gehringer, 1814, by Martin Brechall, tulips, pomegranites (A-E) 350
Birth certificate, Jacob Gerhard, 1787, decor. w/pelicans & flowers (A-E) 2100
Birth certificate, German, 1821, decor. w/stars, tulips, angels, Lancaster Co. (A-E)................. 650
Birth certificate, Johannes Givler, 1807, three human bust portraits (A-E)............................. 1600
Birth register, Gottschall family, 1786 to 1816, frame (A-E) 475
Birth certificate, Adam Graple, Heidelberg Twp., decor. w/pots of tulips & flowers, 1804 (A-E). 200
Birth certificate, by Sara Grillin, 1787, heart shape center w/2 figures of men holding flowers, bird
& flower in center, parrots, sunflowers on base (A-E).. 900
Birth certificate, Isabell Grim, 1834, block print, by Johann Ritter, Reading, Pa. (A-E) 45
Birth certificate, Palli Griszinger, 1837, block print w/hand drawn birds on sides (A-E).......... 100
Birth certificate, Sara Hautz, 1794, block print, large angels on black clouds (A-E)................. 100
Birth certificate, George Heiger, 1776, decor. w/parrots, moon & stars, frame (A-E) 800
Birth certificate, heart, angel, birds, ladies, dated 1812 (A-E) 800
Birth certificate, Elizabeth Heilman, 1810, Lebanon Co., decor. w/tulips, acorns & child, frame
(A-E) 850
Birth certificate, Paulus Heller, 1784, decor. w/checkered pots, tulips & floral border (A-E)..... 2200
Birth certificate, Rubin Herbst, 1818, decor. w/tulips, top border w/sun, moon & stars (A-E) .. 1500
Birth certificate, Samuel Hoch, 1799, decor. w/flying angels, flowers & birds, words of hymn in
German, rare (A-E).. 5000
Birth certificate, Sara Hochin, Berks Co., decor. w/blue flowers, thistles & 2 distelfinks (A-E). 750
Birth certificate, Maria Huber, born 1787, printed w/wood block birds & flowers, hand decor.,
dated 1805, pine frame, 16½"×19¼" (A-E) 375
Birth certificate, Esther Immel, 1810, decor. w/angels, birds & flowers & tulips in pots (A-E).. 140
Birth certificate, in German w/eagles in each corner, bird & flowers on base, oval center,
13½"×16½", 1825 (A-E) 210
Birth certificate, Sara Ann Kaufman, 1845, decor. w/tulips & other flowers (A-E).................. 475
Birth certificate, Maria Catherina Lang, 1826, Northampton Co., decor. w/birds & tulips (A-E). 900
Birth certificate, Ann Lippincott, 1797, daughter of Arney & Lydia, a Phila. Quaker family,
funeral invitation of father, Arney, attached, figures of man & woman, brown cow under green
tree, vase & flowers, in English (A-E).. 2700
Birth certificate, Feyanna Lenher, 1820, decor. w/urn & flowers, good frame (A-E) 1300
Birth certificate, Elizabeth Lescherin, 1822, decor. w/angel cherub w/trumpet, birds (A-E)...... 900
Birth certificate, Esther Linthemuth, 1822, angels, baptismal scene, birds on sprigs & statue in
garden pavilion (D-E).. 80
Birth certificate, Anna Loscherin, 1768, decor. w/wreath of tulips & flowers, 2 angels w/trumpets
(A-E) 7000
Birth certificate, Magadalenn, 1811, Adam & Eve, hand drawn, two birds & flowers, two angels
w/trumpets (A-E) 160
Birth certificate, Elizabeth Mann, 1796, decor. w/heart, birds & flowers, multi-colored lettering
(A-E) 550
Birth certificate, Maria Anna Martin, 1833, clock design, rare (A-E).................................... 800
Birth certificate, Hannah Meirel, 1802, two red-breasted robins at top & multi-colored tulips at
bottom, Lancaster Co., Pa., green & yellow border (A-E) 525
Birth certificate, Maria Hanna Meissel, decor. w/tulips & birds, eagle & shield w/motto, "America
alone" (A-E) 1600
Birth certificate, Peter Metz, 1829, block print, 2 red-robed angels, Noah's ark w/dove & olive
branch, baptismal scene (A-E) 100
Birth certificate, Anna Meyer, 1809, 2 male angels, 1 with trumpet in hand, 1 with tulip, red, blue,
green & yellow (A-E) 4500
Birth certificate, Georg Miller, 1804, early Krebs type (A-E).. 275
Birth certificate, Henrich Miller, 1817, Columbia Co., two distelfinks holding flowers in bills,
rooster & hen (A-E) 3600
Birth certificate, Jacob Miller, 1808, handmade, decor. w/hearts, tulips, floral border, unusual
writing (A-E) 1200

Fraktur, songbook plate of Veronica Rohrerin, written April 15, 1822 (A-E) $325

Fraktur, small drawing in red, green, yellow (A-E) $1100

Birth certificate, Jacob Miller, 1805, handmade, portion missing (A-E) ....$ 200

Birth certificate, Valentin Miller, 1761, Lancaster Co., Pa., by Henrich Otto, profuse decor. (A-E) 2000

Birth certificate, Margaretha Mohn, 1813, decor. w/star & tulip surrounding heart ceotie & dove & tulip edge (A-E) 625

Birth certificate, Joseph Nunkesser, April 10, 1815, handmade, two crouching birds on bases of flowers (A-E) 525

Birth certificate, Catherine Paul, July 1835, Lancaster Co., colorful (A-E) 80

Birth certificate, Magdalene Raberin, 1775, decor. w/tulips & lg. Pa. Dutch heart, figures of 5 women (A-E) 2300

Birth certificate, Johannes Reichert, 1820, green leaf circle, birds on wreath, pots of flowers (A-E).. 300

Birth certificate, Maria Reichert, 1793, Barton & Jungman, Reading, Pa. (A-E) 600

Birth certificate, Leonard Reitz, 1822, decor. w/2 lg. angels, eagle & shield, printed by Johann S. Wiestling, Harrisburg, Pa. (A-E)... 105

Birth certificate, Carolus Renninger, 1836, Mahantango Twp., Schuykill Co., old red frame, decor. w/angels (A-E) 950

Birth certificate, Maria Renninger, 1833, handmade, from Mahantongo Twp., ex. old frame (A-E) . 400

Birth certificate, Jonal Ritter, 1805, by Martin Brechall, hand made, old black frame, side pillars w/capitals, molded at top & bottom (A-E) 525

Birth certificate, Eleonor Rothermel, 1809, by Samuel Baumann, Ephrata, Pa., blue color w/designs of birds, deer & flowers (A-E)... 250

Birth certificate, Sara Ruhmen, 1831, red roses w/tulips, two angels w/trumpets (A-E)........... 200

Birth certificate, Johannes Schaeffer, 1807, Schaeffers Taun, Libanon Co., handmade w/good color & caligraphy (A-E) 2200

Birth certificate, Catherina Schweigert, 1834, colorful (A-E) 1300

Birth certificate, Susanna, 1806, Northumberland Co., decor. w/tulips, flowers & shields, signed "Martin Brechall" (A-E) 1000

Birth certificate, Union Co., Abner Middlesworth, pillars w/girls each side, covered vase top of pillars, colorful, 1839 (A-E)... 250

Birth certificate, Daniel Wannemacher, 1815, decor. w/birds & floral sprigs, block print, small vignettes (A-E)... 200

Birth certificate, Henrich Werner, 1805, decor. w/tulips & large Pa. Dutch heart (A-E) 2100

Birth certificate, Daniel Widman, 1826, decor. w/women figures, birds & flowers (A-E) 3500

Birth certificate, Sybilla Wittmeyer, 1834, block prints, children, butterflies, fruit & flowers; by Joseph Schnee, Lebanon, Pa. (A-E) 160

Birth record, John Landis, 1832 (A-E) 100

Bookmark, bird's-eye maple frame, quail & flower (A-E) 130

Bookmark, bird's-eye maple frame, tulip & onion pattern flower, small (A-E)...................... 300

Bookmark, curly maple frame, pot of tulips, small (A-E).. 450

Bookmark, drawing of grandfather clock w/moon face at top, floral clock panel (A-E) 750

Bookmark, frame, belted kingfisher (A-E)... 95

Bookmark, frame, decor. w/parrot on branch (A-E) 60

Bookmark, frame, by Johannes Hauffer, 1853 (A-E)... 175

Bookmark, frame, tulip & heart, dated 1834 (A-E).. 280

Fraktur, birth certificate of Henrich Delang, by Krebs, dated 1807 (A-E) $600

Fraktur, birth certificate, interesting
angelic forms, framed, dated 1817 (D-E)
$1800

Bookmark, hearts & flowers, 1841 (A-E) ....$	275
Bookmark, mahogany frame, flowers, small (A-E)...	35
Bookmark, parrot & font, small (A-E)..	175
Bookmark, pot of tulips, flowers & birds (A-E)..	160
Bookmark, religious precept, heart & tulip (A-E)	650
Bookmark, tiger maple frame, bird perched on tulip, small (A-E)...........................	400
Bookmark, tulip decor., small (A-E)..	95
Bookplate, double, of Jacob Ritzman, 1818; farm scene, thatched roofed barn, tile roofed house w/rows of trees (A-E)	1950
Bookplate, Maria Hofflerin, 1832 (A-E)	200
Bookplate, George Hough, crowned cartouche at top w/initials "G.S.", 1708, two red columns holding blue balls & floral border w/birds, early (A-E)...	675
Bookplate, of Anna Hunsicker, 1835, decor. w/fine lettering & floral border (A-E)	750
Bookplate, little portion (A-E)...	375
Bookplate, song, Veronia Rohrerin, written April 15, 1822 (A-E)...........................	325
Christmas card, dated Dec. 25, 1787, rare (A-E)	250
Christmas card, rare, 18th C. (A-E)	90
Drawing, decor. w/birds, tulips in pot & flowers, good frame (A-E)	375
Drawing, for Elizabeth Fisher, Nov. 1829, by A. Hall; decor. w/birds, flowers & trees (A-E) ...	350
Drawing, man & woman in two cartouches; two floral channels, two unicorns & three hearts (A-E)	1100
Drawing, red, green, & yellow birds, rare (A-E)	1100
Drawing, two red & yellow roosters on perches w/green sprigs, framed (A-E)......................	3600
House blessing, Peter Bank, 1802, old red frame (A-E)..	925
House blessing, by Henrich Otto, 1785; twelve hearts for the hours of day; lg. heart w/traditional prayer (A-E)...	1600
Imprint, by Johannes Armbrust; 2 wood blocks depict Christ falling w/weight of cross & Simon of Cyrene carrying the cross for Christ (A-E)...	550
Legal bond, dated 1785, between Jacob Greedy, Lancaster, Co., Pa., & Joyner & Thomas Fisher, decorated (A-E)	325
New year's wish, 1769, 2 pillars arch, 3 urns holding flowers, sprigs of flowers on side, ex. pen work, rare (A-E)	850
Song, perhaps Ephrata, rare (A-E)	120
Valentine, by John H. Wagner, Hummelstown, Pa.; flint lock rifle & many designs (A-E)	95
Valentine, to Miss Rebecca Bowman, Hummelstown, Dauphin Co., from John Wagner; decor. w/red heart & hand (A-E)	105
Vorschrift, decorated w/birds & tulips (A-E)...	1100
Vorschrift, fine capital letters, dated 1818 (A-E)	140
Vorschrift, interlaced letters w/elaborate capital letter, dated 1814 (A-E)	725
Vorschrift, Johannes Gluck, decor. w/flowers, eagle & symbol of lamp & pennant (A-E).........	2400
Vorschrift, calligraphy, 1831, yellow & red, side panel w/tulip & heart; floral border (A-E)	1050
Vorschrift, calligraphy, pen work, decor. w/green, red & yellow animals, hearts & tulips (A-E) .	2700
Writer's paint box, barrel shape, 3½" diam., 6½" h., conical at top; circular line inlay, compartments w/bottles of dried up ink, rare (A-E)	150

Furniture

The furnishings of America's past had a particular flair — functionalism that was the natural design expression of a country where practicality meant survival. Pieces produced here were a combination of Yankee ingenuity in adapting revered Old World styling to New World materials, resulting in furniture having a timeless appeal in uniqueness that is purely American, with simplicity of line being its most characteristic feature. What remains is a part of our heritage, almost always so beautifully put together that it has never gone out of style — nor ever will.

The term "country furniture" means many things to many people. Opinions on the subject are as varied as the interesting examples they attempt to define. Pieces may be either sophisticated or naive, exhibiting many graduations of

Blanket chest, pine, orig. red paint, New England, ca. 1730-50 (D-NE) $1200

Gateleg table, pine top, oak base, ca. 1740 (D-NE) $6000

quality and style. Although many obviously lack the perfect proportions and technical skills of a master craftsman, the term "country" should never be regarded as "crude." This term should be applied only to those first primitive furnishings which were created in haste to serve the basic needs of the earliest settlers — from New England to the Far West. From all accounts, their furnishings were simple makeshifts that were discarded as more substantial furniture became available.

The earliest rural cabinetmakers were usually itinerant craftsmen who borrowed their ideas from several periods, oftentimes adding a bit of individuality all their own. Undoubtedly, the first articles made here were six-board chests, which not only provided necessary storage, but often served as a seat, table and bed. Then came the handmade cupboards, tables, benches, stools and settles. The bulk of the early furniture was utilitarian and commonplace, made to serve a useful purpose. Woods used were native, depending upon what was available to the area.

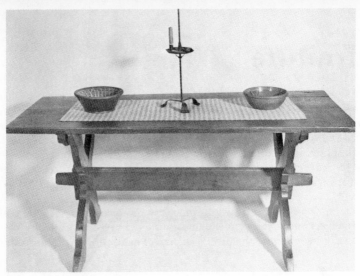

Sawbuck table, pine, excellently shaped legs, which can be taken apart, top 30″ × 60″ (A-E) $8900

By the mid-1600s, six of the thirteen colonies had been established and the standard of living had improved greatly. Many well-trained cabinetmakers had arrived — mostly English — so for the next two hundred years, when furniture-making was a major craft in America, English styles dominated.

However, American-made furniture was always simpler and less ornate than its European counterparts. Beginning with the earliest style period designated as Jacobean, with oak being the principal wood used, the other periods that followed included the William and Mary, Queen Anne, Chippendale, Hepplewhite, Sheraton, Federal, Empire and Victorian.

The principal cabinetmaking centers were Boston, Salem and Newburyport, Massachusetts; Philadelphia, Pennsylvania; Newport, Rhode Island; New York City and Charleston, South Carolina.

As cities grew, some of the rural craftsmen were near enough to the main centers of cabinetmaking to keep in touch with changing styles, so that some of the country pieces became rather formal in style. Their methods of construction varied according to the background and capability of the individual artisan.

Each region had its own version of country pieces which is helpful to the collector, but dating this furniture is rather difficult because designs and methods of construction remained the same for many years. Moreover, it is impossible to set a terminal date, since individual craftsmen lingered on in regions far from cities.

There are many interesting old pieces available that originated in New England, Pennsylvania and New York. But, frontier country furniture is scarce. For many years this vast area was inhabited only by Indians and, later, Spaniards. It wasn't until the last century that it became a magnetic force for attracting explorers, soldiers, traders, trappers, sodbusters, ranchers and homesteaders simply looking for a new home. Since little furniture could be brought along, it was made upon arrival. Most of the frontier craftsmen made an earnest effort to reproduce forms they remembered, but many were merely images. Furniture, as other objects made and used by those who wrestled with the perils of frontier life, is as varied as the Western landscape itself.

Country painted furniture ran the gamut. Most collectors feel that painted decoration is the most distinguishing attribution of country furniture. In recent years, the "original paint" has become as desirable as "original patina" has always been.

During the 1700s, and well into the mid-1800s, an enormous amount of almost every type of furniture was grained, stenciled, japanned, gaily painted or gilded. Today, these surviving examples are sought by the advanced collector, with most fetching lofty prices when sold. Values are determined by condition and the amount of the original decoration remaining.

Among the earliest painted, sophisticated pieces were japanned highboys, clocks, chairs, etc., decorated with gold leaf or bronze powders, varnished and highly polished in the Oriental fashion. This type decoration was practiced on the elegant furniture of the Queen Anne or Chippendale periods.

The term "graining" denotes the painted imitation of different woods. Much of this type decoration was a coarse imitation of the finer woods, actually never intended to deceive, while other pieces were painted with an exact painstaking duplication of expensive woods. Some of the methods used to create the different effects included turkey feathers, dried corncobs and smoking candles. Over the wet pigment — usually a light background — the candle-painter manipulated a smoking candle to imprint swirls.

The Pennsylvania Germans loved color. Their gay, imaginatively decorated furnishings, dating approximately from 1750-1850 — and including the fine old dower chests that were the pride of every maiden — are especially desirable. Favorite designs included the tulip, heart, star, unicorn, peacock, turtledove and eagle.

During the early years of the ninteenth century — brilliant free-hand decoration, in oils and bronze powders, ornamented New England country furniture, as well as "fancy" Sheraton chairs, washstands, settees, etc. Stenciled furniture had its hey-day during the early years of the nineteenth century, reaching its height of popularity in the attractive painted furniture made by Lambert Hitchcock.

During this period, native woods were used with respectful understanding. Therefore, it isn't uncommon to find a painted piece made of a variety of woods, especially chairs.

Cupboard, pine, large
(A-NE) $1250

Blanket chest, poplar, inside compartment, small, refinished, 22" h., 11" h., (D-MW) $55

Until recent years, children's furniture has been a neglected field, mostly for lack of interest. Today there is a scarcity of the earlier pieces, with mostly interesting small chairs and charming old cradles remaining. But, during the last decade, there has developed a growing interest in the available nineteenth century pieces and, suddenly they have become respectable collectibles. During the second half of the nineteenth century, a number of furniture manufacturers produced children's furnishings. Like the earlier examples, most were essentially scaled-down versions of the imposing Victorian pieces.

Oak furniture began staging a comeback during the '50s when the younger collectors discovered its merits. Oak was a favorite of the middle class from the latter part of the nineteenth century, until the 1930s. There was a tremendous

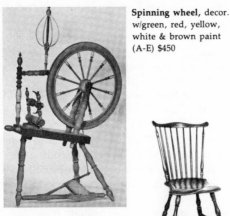

Spinning wheel, decor. w/green, red, yellow, white & brown paint (A-E) $450

Side chair, Windsor, comb back, 7-spindle, refinished (D-MW) $390

Armchair, Windsor, bow back, orig. finish (D-MW) $650

amount made and, because of its durability, most of the pieces made are still with us, and are structurally sound as when first made. There are still many pieces available to the collector at realistic prices, but values for fancy patterned back chairs and round tables with claw feet are constantly on the increase.

In summary, quality country furnishings, from the 1700s up until about 1850, are at the top of the market in popularity and price. It is these objects that will continue to appreciate in value most on a percentage basis.

Becoming an expert in this field requires much time and the development of all five senses used intelligently. The crucial differences between the fake and the genuine antique is obvious when one knows what to look for. There is nothing wrong with buying a reproduction, a piece that has some restoration — or an old form made from old woods — when you know what you are buying. But, it is getting duped that hurts.

When considering a purchase, here are a few helpful clues to age: 1) From a visual point of view, the patina of old wood is a good indicator of age. Through usage, it acquires a thin layer of tiny scratches, dents and bruises which give it a

Settee, Windsor, orig. fine finish (A-E) $650

Side chairs, decor., cane seats, 2 of a set of 6 (A-E) $300

mellow quality of color and texture that cannot be hurried or imitated. 2) Observe closely the edges on furniture. Once sharp, they will be rounded by usage, as these areas erode and soften with age. 3) Do not be afraid to pull out drawers and examine carefully. The underside will be worn smooth from decades of friction. Moreover, these protected areas should be the same color, having a natural all-over shading. And too, because wood shrinks with age, many of the drawers in early pieces fit loosely. 4) The backs of chairs, as well as the front rungs and legs, are good indicators of age. These are areas that show wear first. 5) Turn large pieces upside down and study the under structure which, because of more exposure to air and sometimes moisture, will be darker. 6) Screws are also helpful to determine age. The earliest, of course, were wooden. The first metal screws had uneven threads and the narrow slot in the head was oftentimes off center. Blunt end machine made screws date from the first quarter of the last century, whereas the pointed screw became available around 1850. 7) Wooden pegs on early pieces were oblong or square, none perfectly rounded. Pegs on reproductions appear perfectly round, and are cut off exactly flush with the surface. On the early pieces, the pegs usually projected from the surface, or were recessed slightly below the surface from shrinkage. 8) Sawmarks are another tell-tale sign of age. The earliest were straight, with coarse teeth, leaving a clear pattern of straight parallel scratches. During the mid-19th century, the circular power-driven saw came into usage. This type left circular scratches in the wood. Sawmarks are usually quite obvious on the backside of large case pieces, or on the underside of drawers.

Dovetail joints used for joining drawers was a good indication of age up until recent years. The earliest was one large dovetail which fit into a corresponding open mortise. With the passage of time, three to five dovetails appeared on drawers, each cut by hand, but the spacing and sizes were different. Today, a variety of new pieces with dovetail construction are being marketed. These include hanging salt boxes, pipe and candle boxes. The dovetails on these pieces compare to those found on objects made in factories during the late nineteenth century — machine-cut and evenly spaced.

Making furniture from old wood to resemble the early forms — dry sinks, dough troughs and small hanging cupboards — has been practiced for sometime. But, the biggest "rip-off" currently taking place across the country is the practice of converting wall and corner cupboards into dry sinks. These are the pieces, deliberately made to deceive, that create the biggest problem for the collector.

As noted earlier, becoming an expert in this field requires much time and the development of all five senses. This, combined with actual experience, will help the serious collector to develop a sixth sense which will serve as a guide in distinguishing the spurious from the respectable antique.

Armchair, banister back, 5 vertical slats, rolled arms, fine turnings, black paint worn, new rush seat, early 18th C. (A-SW)..$ 350

Armchair, banister back, Spanish foot, w/rams horn arms & bulbous turnings, Prince of Wales crest in orig. brown paint, gold decor., ex. cond. (A-NE) 11,000

Armchair, Carver, early (A-E).. 75

Armchair, Chippendale, walnut, early Penna., vase type open splat, carved earls & knuckle arms, sq. legs, H stretcher (A-E).. 400

Armchair, Chippendale, walnut, Penna., open splat back, scalloped apron, sq. legs, H-stretcher (A-E) 400

Armchair, ladder back, ball finials, turned legs (D-E) 435

Armchair, ladder back, 4-slat, ash seat, sausage turns, orig. black paint, back 50″ h. (A-NE)... 400

Armchair, ladder back, 4-slat, large ball turnings on front stretcher, blk. paint, splint seat (A-E).. 425

Armchair, ladderback, 5-slat, ball turning, rush seat, pad feet, rare (A-E).......................... 350

Armchair, ladder back, 5-slat, ball turnings on base, rush seat (A-E) 425

Armchair, ladder back, 5-slat, scalloped apron & base, ball turned feet & center, rush seat, all orig. (A-E) 275

Armchair, ladder back, maple, orig. rockers, sausage & ring turned supports, shaped finials, 4 arched slats, shaped arms, new rush seat & turned front stretcher (A-E) 200

Armchair, ladder back, maple, refinished (A-N) 150

Armchair, ladder back, rocker, child's, orig. finish worn smooth (A-E) 200

Armchair, ladder back, rocker, curly maple, fine turnings, splint seat (A-E).......................... 80

Armchair, ladder back, rocker, fine turnings & arms (A-E).. 250

Armchair, ladder back, rocker, 4-slat, sausage turnings, old blk. paint, 18th C. (A-NE).......... 175

Armchair, ladder back, rocker, 5-slat, turned finials, curved & scrolled arm rests, rush seat, bold stretcher turnings (A-E) 575

Armchair, ladder back, rocker, intricate turnings, refinished (D-MW) 125

Armchair, ladder back, rocker, orig. old red paint good, sausage turned (A-NE) 700

Armchair, ladder back, rocker, orig. red, sausage turned, good paint (A-NE).......................... 700

Armchair, ladder back, sausage turned, black paint (A-NE).. 225

Armchair, ladder back, sausage turned, orig. old red painted finish (A-E) 700

Armchair, ladder back, Shaker, 4-slat, rush seat, New England style (D-E) 300

Armchair, ladder back, turned stretcher in front, old black paint (A-NE)................................ 525

Armchair, rush seat, black, sausage turned, 4-splat, 49″ (A-NE) 375

Armchair, slat-back, orig. cond., ca. 1720 (D-NE).. 640

Armchair, Wainscot, raised panel back, ca. 1665 (A-E).. 500

Armchair, Wainscot, wooden seat, sausage turning, H-stretchers, 3 scalloped slats, top slat carved w/names & date (A-E) 155

Armchair, Windsor, arrowback, converted into potty chair (A-E) 75

Armchair, Windsor, arrowback, half-spindle (A-MW).. 75

Armchair, Windsor, arrowback, writing arm, rocker, tall, grain decor. w/yellow striping & fruit decor. on slat (A-NE) 550

Armchair, Windsor, bar, hickory & pine, turned spindles, shaped legs & box stretcher, 19th C. (A-MW) 50

Armchair, Windsor, birdcage, ladies', refinished (D-MW).. 160

Armchair, Windsor, bow back, bamboo turnings, 9 spindles, saddle seat repaired (A-E)........ 290

Armchair, Windsor, bow back, bold turnings, modified knuckle arms, black paint over old green (A-NE).. 800

Armchair, Windsor, bow back, saddle seat, all orig. traces of black paint (A-MW)................ 278

Armchair, Windsor, bow back, saddle seat w/camfer, turned legs & end posts, sgn. O. M. Bowen, old red paint (A-E) ....$ 1200

Armchair, Windsor, bow back, 7-spindle, legs & stretchers restored (A-E) 250

Armchair, Windsor, bow back, 7-spindle, vase turnings (A-E) 650

Armchair, Windsor, bow back, 7-spindle, vase turnings, old black paint & line dec., saddle seat, orig. (A-E) 500

Armchair, Windsor, bow back, writing arm, orig. old paint (D-E)................................ 750

Armchair, Windsor, brace back, bold turnings in orig. green paint (A-NE) 650

Armchair, Windsor, butterfly, 7-spindle, duck bill type arms, lg. butterfly & acorn knobs on posts, converted from rocker (A-E) 180

Armchair, Windsor, comb back, rocker, rabbit ears, old red paint (A-NE).......................... 325

Armchair, Windsor, continuous, bold turnings, back legs only extended 1", refinished (D-W).$ 450
Armchair, Windsor, double comb back, decor. (A-E) 200
Armchair, Windsor, double comb back, carved ears, saddle seat, marked "R.D." on base of seat (A-E) 80
Armchair, Windsor, double comb back, N.E., knuckle arms, flared comb w/scrolled ears, signed, 18th C. (D-E) 1850
Armchair, Windsor, double comb back, knuckle arms, saddle seat, carved ears, H-stretcher (A-E) 450
Armchair, Windsor, double comb back, rocker, conv. to commode chair, refinished (D-W) 90
Armchair, Windsor, double fanback, knuckle arms, fine turnings, H-stretchers (A-E) 575
Armchair, Windsor, fanback, 9-spindle, H-stretcher, late 19th C. (D-E) 60
Armchair, Windsor, fanback, 9-spindle, saddle seat, H-stretcher, late 19th C. unfinished state (D-E) 78
Armchair, Windsor, fanback, 9-spindle, split seat (A-E) 190
Armchair, Windsor, fanback, 7-spindle, conv. to commode chair, refinished (D-E) 70

Spool cabinet, cherry, 6-drawer, pressed wood drawer fronts, orig. brass pulls, refinished (D-MW) $300

Bolt cabinet, pine, new pulls, 2 sections, refinished, late 19th C., 38" h., 37" w. (D-MW) $300

Armchair, Windsor, fanback, 7-spindle, early, primitive (D-MW) 275
Armchair, Windsor, fanback, 7-spindle, refinished (D-MW) 140
Armchair, Windsor, 5-spindle back, bamboo turned legs & stretchers, 19th C. (A-MW) 225
Armchair, Windsor, hoop back, old black paint (A-E) 975
Armchair, Windsor, 6-spindle, molded seat, hickory, pine & maple, ex. design, Rhode Island orig., 18th C. (A-E) 4800
Armchair, Windsor, step-down, converted into potty chair (A-E) 75
Armchair, wing, Hepplewhite, old frame, new covering (A-E) 625
Armchair, writing arm, Windsor, pine, half-spindle bamboo turnings, refinished, 19th C. (A-MW) 225
Armchair, writing, Windsor, bow back, orig. black paint (D-E) 750
Armchair, writing, Windsor, drawer under seat, ca. 1840 (D-MW) 700
Armchair, writing, Windsor, drawer under seat, refinished, ca. 1840 (D-E) 600
Armchair, writing, Hitchcock type, arrow back spindles, small drawer under writing arm, rare, decorated (A-E) 725
Baby bed, rope, Hepplewhite style, orig. oxblood red, 22" h.×44" l. (A-NE) 200
Baby bed, roped, orig. oxblood red, 22" h., 44" l. (A-NE) 200
Baby buggy, 4-poster model, 1824 (A-NE) 200
Baby buggy, 4-wheel, dog-drawn (A-E) 1000
Baby buggy, 4-wheel push model (A-NE) 175
Baby buggy, 4-wheel push model, "big babies" (A-NE) 275
Baby buggy, 4-wheel push model, canopy (A-NE) 425
Baby buggy, 4-wheel push model, canopy, 1880 (A-NE) 325
Baby buggy, 4-wheel push model, canopy, 1876 (A-NE) 475
Baby buggy, 4-wheel push model, 1877 (A-NE) 1000

Side chair, rabbit ear, yellow, stenciled & freehand decor., striping, signed "F. Brooks, Warranted," 1 of a set of 6 (A-MW) $1500

Pie safe, walnut, refinished (D-MW) $190

Baby buggy, 4-wheel push model, 1897 (A-NE)	$ 450
Baby buggy, 4-wheel push model, narrow front, 1870 (A-NE)	350
Baby buggy, 4-wheel push model, reed body (A-NE)	650
Baby buggy, 4-wheel push model, small, 1872 (A-NE)	300
Baby buggy, 4-wheel push model, tilting, 1870 (A-NE)	450
Baby buggy, stroller-highchair combination, 1901 (A-NE)	350
Baby buggy, 3-wheel pull type, 1860 (A-NE)	375
Baby buggy, 2-wheel model, 1811-1828 (A-NE)	150
Baby buggy, 2-wheel model, 1826 (A-NE)	80
Baby buggy, 2-wheel pull model, 1860 (A-NE)	200
Baby buggy, 2-wheel pull model, 1865 (A-NE)	225
Baby chair, ladder back, 18th C. (D-E)	125
Baby tender, pine, worn blue-gray paint w/seat, early 19th C. (A-NE)	110
Baby walker, Windsor, orig. cond. (A-E)	75
Bed, bench, pine, pegged, combination bench and bed, traces of orig. red paint (A-W)	350
Bed, brass, double, ornate, burnished (D-MW)	425
Bed, brass, double, ornate, unburnished (D-S)	200
Bed, brass, full-size, burnished (D-W)	390
Bed, brass, full-size, ornate, burnished (D-MW)	525
Bed, brass, heavy & large designs, spun brass mounts & knobs, swell-foot end (D-W)	355
Bed, brass, twin-size, very ornate, unburnished (D-S)	190
Bed, cannon ball, maple, twin, wood rails, refinished (D-MW)	180
Bed, cannon ball, maple, full-size, wood rails, orig. finish (D-E)	350
Bed, cannon ball, maple, rope, ¾ size, orig. round rails w/screw ends, orig. finish ex. (D-W)	275
Bed, cannon ball, painted red finish orig. untouched, scrolled headboard, 37" posts (D-NW)	225
Bed, cannon ball, painted red finish orig. w/trundle, wooden wheels (D-NE)	375
Bed, cannon ball, pine, full-size, old red stained finish, urn carving on headboard (D-E)	650
Bed, canopy, brass, center crown (D-NE)	975
Bed, canopy, maple, bird's-eye maple paneled headboard w/turned post, ca. 1830, 74" h., 81" l., 59" w. (A-E)	325
Bed, canopy, tiger maple, headboard of curly maple (D-NE)	1450
Bed, canopy, tiger maple, refinished, Pa. full-size, ca. 1835 (D-E)	750

Bed, **country,** maple, full-size, green paint (A-NE) ....$ 500
Bed, **country,** pine & maple, scalloped headboard, old red paint (A-NE)   450
Bed, **country,** turned, old green paint, single-size (A-NE)   325
Bed, **day,** pine, scroll back rest w/turned finials, turned shaped legs, from Amana Colonies, 19th
  C., 17" l. (A-MW)   625
Bed, **day,** Windsor, ball turnings, rush seat, tilted back rest (A-E)...............................   725
Bed, **field,** curly maple, tester top, octagonal head posts, double-size (D-NE)   750
Bed, **field,** pine, four posts, refinished (D-E)...   180
Bed, **field,** Sheraton, maple w/vase-turned & baluster posts, traces old red paint, ca. 1800, 60" h.
  (A-E)   375
Bed, **folding,** pine & maple, 6-legged, unpainted (A-NE)...   250
Bed, **4-poster,** maple, ¾-size, turned headboard & footboard, metal side rails, 19th C. (A-MW)   268
Bed, **4-poster,** poplar, Sheraton style, 6' to top of tester (D-E)...............................   600
Bed, **4-poster,** tiger maple & walnut (D-E)   450
Bed, **4-poster,** walnut, handmade, hewn panel in headboard, ca. 1850 (D-S).......................   600
Bed, **high post,** curly maple, all orig., full-size, complete (D-E)..............................   450
Bed, **high post,** high head board, orig. black finish, Penna., ca. 1860 (D-E)   500
Bed, **high post,** mahogany, pencil post, w/box spring & mattress (A-E)...........................   425
Bed, **high post,** maple, twin-size, orig. finish good (D-W)   350
Bed, **iron,** full-size, ornate, painted white (D-MW)   300
Bed, **iron,** ornate, finished in white painted enamel, head 55" h., foot 41", brass knobs & rods
  (D-MW)   165
Bed, **iron,** twin, ornate (A-MW)   36
Bed, **low post,** curly maple, full-size, new rails, orig. rope converted (D-MW)   450
Bed, **low post,** maple, ¾-size, orig. red painted finish (D-S)   150
Bed, **low post,** maple, ¾-size, tiger striping in headboard, headboard 43" h., 51" w. (D-MW).   200
Bed, **low post,** painted w/stencil decor., ca. 1830 (D-N)..   900
Bed, **low post,** walnut, ¾-size, rope, orig. finish (D-W)   125
Bed, **maple,** mushroom turned, extended rails (D-NE)   225
Bed, **maple,** single, shaped headboard, 61" h. (D-NE)...   395
Bed, **maple,** twin-size, fine turnings, shaped headboard, med. dk. brown finish (D-NE)   375
Bed, **maple,** twin-size, refinished, steel rails (A-E)   60
Bed, **oak,** Eastlake style, matching dresser, bevel mirror, brass pulls, orig. untouched cond. good
  (D-MW)   255
Bed, **oak,** fancy carved head & footboard, 6½' h., finish fair (D-W)   170
Bed, **pencil post,** New England type (A-E)...   675
Bed, **pencil post,** pine & maple w/orig. coloring, 51" w. (A-E).................................   525

Pewter cupboard, orig. red
paint, New England (A-E) $625
(Brass andirons, doubletops (A-E) $450)

Blanket chest, pine, decor. (A-E) $3500
Box, colorfully decor., tulip & bird along
sides, pot of flowers on top, 11¼ h., 19" l.,
9¾" deep (A-E) $250

Bed, rope, early, old red stain (D-E) ....$ 260
Bed, rope, maple, 4-poster, urn finials, turned & shaped headboard & supports, orig. finish good
    (D-W) 325
Bed, rope, 4-poster, pine, full-size (D-E).. 290
Bed, rope, fruitwood, all orig., ca. 1830 (D-S) 350
Bed, rope, high poster, maple, w/mattress, vase turnings (A-E) 275
Bed, rope, old yellow grained paint (D-NE) 485
Bed, Sheraton, mahogany, 47″ posts acorn carved & reeded, headposts acorns w/spool turnings,
    orig. ¾-size, ca. 1800 (D-NE) 475
Bed, Sheraton, maple, tester, turned posts w/urn tops, pine headboard, footposts w/turned roll,
    small, ref., 41″ h. (D-E) 225
Bed, sleigh, mahogany, ¾-size (D-NE) 115
Bed, spool, canopy, walnut, high poster (A-E) 525
Bed, spool, maple, low post, full-size, in rough (A-MW) 45
Bed, spool, maple & pine, low post, ¾-size, refinished, complete (D-MW) 225
Bed, spool, maple, ¾-size, refinished, 19th C. (A-MW)... 400
Bed, spool, maple, low post, twin, fine turnings, refinished, complete (D-MW).................... 200
Bed, spool, walnut, full-size, turned corners (D-MW) 90
Bed, urn & ball, maple & pine, full-size, decor. in red & black w/stenciled basket of fruit outlined
    in yellow on headboard & footboard, Maine (A-NE)... 700
Bed, queen size, rare, ex. cond. (D-MW) 1000
Bed & wardrobe, oak, combination, folds up in back, lg. wardrobe space w/hooks, 18″×40″
    German bevel mirror door, open, 4′ w., 6′3″, woven wire mattress, orig. finish (A-NE) 325
Bench, bucket, pine, long (A-E) 75
Bench, bucket, pine, rectangular w/slant front, 19th C., 33″ l. × 14″ d. × 33″ h. (A-MW) 175
Bench, bucket, pine, refinished, 36″ h., 32″ w. (A-E) 100
Bench, bucket, pine, w/3 shelves (D-NE) 275
Bench, bucket, pine w/3 shelves & 3 drawers below, orig. painted finish (D-E)..................... 575
Bench, bucket, poplar (D-W).. 65
Bench, bucket, scalloped, 38″ h., 18″ d., 29″ h. (A-E) 575
Bench, bucket, shelves w/rounded scallops at end, 2 doors on cupboard sect. (A-E).............. 1300
Bench, cobbler's, all orig., leather seat, 1 drawer, Penna., ca. 1825 (D-MW)......................... 350
Bench, cobbler's, large, orig. leather seat, & finish, 6 drawers, complete w/tools (D-N) 525
Bench, cobbler's, large, orig. finish, leather seat & tools, 6 drawers, good cond. (D-NE) 500
Bench, cobbler's, pine, 37″ l., 19½″ w. (A-E) 90
Bench, cobbler's, pine, stand-up & sit-down work surface, four drawers, solid ends, crude &
    early, refinished (D-MW) 550
Bench, cobbler's, pine, 3-drawer (D-E) 650
Bench, cobbler's, refinished (A-E) 170
Bench, cobbler's, pine, 10 drawers, various sizes, orig. pulls, refinished (D-E) 380
Bench, cobbler's, pine, 3-drawer, splayed legs, all original w/leather seat (D-E) 650
Bench, cobbler's, pine, stand-up & sit-down work surface, 4 drawers, solid ends, crude, re-
    finished (D-MW) 550
Bench, cut-out, oval top decor. w/hearts & bird, sulphur inlay (A-E) 270
Bench, deacon's, Vermont, orig. dark finish, 90″ l. (D-NE) 110
Bench, deacon's, Vermont, refinished, 10′ l., orig. (D-MW)... 200
Bench, fireside, pine, w/18″ deep seat & 59″ back, scalloped on ends (top & base) (A-E)......... 375
Bench, fireside, walnut, scalloped arms & 13½″ back, all orig. (A-E) 230
Bench, foot, from N. E. Church, 48″×6½″ (D-NE) 25
Bench, Jacobean oak, turned legs, flat stretchers, 17″w.×51″l.×19″ h. (D-NE) 300
Bench, Mammy, rocker, orig. black finish & stencil decor. 6 ft. l. (A-E) 525
Bench, Mammy's, rocker, orig. paint, removable fence guard, dated 1830 (D-MW) 350
Bench, milk, w/orig. buttermilk paint (D-NE).. 225
Bench, Pa. Dutch, gray, rectangular hinged cover, crib & secret drawer, bracket feet, 19th C., 29½″
    l., 15″ d., 18″ h. (A-MW) 225
Bench, pine, cut-out ends, refinished, 3′ (A-E) 50
Bench, pine, orig. gray paint w/boot-jack cut out ends, 6′9″×13″ (A-NE) 120
Bench, pine, pegged, orig. old red paint, scalloped ends, straight skirt, 62″ l. (D-MW)........... 110
Bench, pine, rectangular, shaped frieze, 19th C., 71″ l. (A-MW) 175

Bench, pine, rectangular top, trestle base, 19th C., 41¾" l., 17" h. (A-MW) ....$ 85
Bench, pine, large, scalloped base (A-E)   45
Bench, pine, slipper feet, early (A-E)   55
Bench, pine, solid back, primitive, refinished, 5½ ft. l. (D-E)   135
Bench, pine, tapered shape, for pottery (A-E)   60
Bench, porch, pine, heeled through seat, scalloped undersides, refinished, 54" l. (A-E)   100
Bench, porch, pine, heeled through seat, refinished, 86" l. (A-E)   115
Bench, porch, pine, heeled through seat, 63" l., refinished (A-E)   30
Bench, porch, pine, long (A-E)   37
Bench, porch, pine, scalloped undersides, refinished, 58" l. (A-E)   135
Bench, porch, small, dov. const. (D-E)   75
Bench, porch, wood, 17"×61" (A-E)   40

Icebox, oak, handsomely carved,
orig. brass hdwe., large (D-E) $300

Rolltop cabinet, oak, 12" h., 16" l., 11" d. (D-W)
$65

Bench, prayer, cut out ends & apron, 27"×7"×15" (D-NE)   44
Bench, saddler's (D-E)   65
Bench, settle, armed, w/bracket base, 4-paneled back, old brown paint, 18th C. (A-NE)   450
Bench, stepdown, Windsor, w/knuckle arms & orig. stenciling (D-NE)   950
Bench, table, cut out legs (A-E)   350
Bench, table, scalloped legs, old green paint (D-E)   490
Bench, table, trestle, poplar, orig. finish, ca. 1820 (D-NE)   395
Bench, vestibule, oak (D-MW)   85
Bench, water, 4-shelf, cut-out, rare, traces orig. red paint, 33" w., 59½" h. (A-E)   375
Bench, water, orig. buttermilk red paint (D-N)   225
Bench, water, pine & poplar, 3 side by side drawers, 2 cupboards, shelf in each, large base for milk
pans (D-E)   1200
Bench, water, pine, 3 upper drawers, shaped back, 2 doors below & shelf, refinished (A-MW) .   155
Bench, water, pine, 2 shelves, heeled through top & sides & tapered front, 5'1" w., 3'10" h. (A-E)   210
Bench, water, primitive, 4 shelves, curved end (A-E)   210
Bench, water, rare, w/cupboard, shaped end, other end includes cupboard, two drawers w/brass
knobs, dovt. const., raised panel door (A-E)   825
Bench, Windsor, Conn., orig. decor., ca. 1870, 7' (A-S)   275
Bench, Windsor, orig. finish, 33 spindles (A-E)   1850
Bench, Windsor, poplar, 8 legs w/bamboo turnings & 31 spindles in back, seat board, old finish,
18½"×94"×37" h., ca. 1800 (D-E)   1250
Bookcase, oak, hand carved, adjustable shelves, heavy molding around top, glass doors, 5'h., 6"
w. (D-W)   315

Bookcase, oak, hand carved, heavy base, rope molding at top, adjustable shelves, glass doors, 60"
h., 36" w., orig. finish (D-MW)...$ 265
Bookcase, oak, hand carved w/3 lg. glass doors, small drawer, open lattice work in top center door,
adjustable drawers, 6'3" h., 5'3" w., orig. finish (D-S)... 310
Bookcase, oak, 2 French bevel mirrors, 6"×12", glass door; glass cabinet w/door in top & large
shelf; 6' h., 2'7" w., orig. finish (A-E)... 190
Bookcase-writing desk, oak, 3 lg. drawers w/swell front, 16"×24" French bevel mirror, adj.
shelves, shaped glass in door; desk w/pigeon holes & drawers, 6'2" h., 3'10" w. (D-MW) 166

Blanket or coverlet rack, maple, refinished (D-MW) $55

Side table, maple, refinished (D-MW) $80

Cabinet, w/towel bar, oak (D-W) $85

Bookcase-writing desk, oak, 3 swell front drawers, cast brass handles under desk, 16"×22" French
bevel mirror, adj. shelves, 6' h., 4'1" w. (A-E) 195
Breakfront, pine, New England, refinished, pegged door; top 51½" w., 58" h. w/glass doors,
adjustable shelves, base w/solid doors, 1 shelf, 32" h., 60" w. (D-MW) 1200
Bureau, cherry bow front, all orig. red paint, brasses, bracket feet, thumb molded top w/hair line
reeding, 4 beaded drawers (A-E) 1700
Bureau, Chippendale, mahogany, 4-drawer, bracket feet, old brasses (A-E) 500
Bureau, Chippendale, pine, bow front rectangular top, 3 long drawers, ogee bracket feet, 18th C.,
35½" w., 19" d., 36¼" h., restored (A-MW) 925
Bureau, cottage, 4-drawer, refinished (A-E)... 65
Bureau, cottage, pine, dovt. const. w/6 drawers (A-E).. 45
Bureau, cottage, pine, small, 3-drawer (A-E) 55
Bureau, decorated, 3 large graded drawers, 2 small drawers, one of which has orig. wooden spring
clip lock, orig. brasses & feet, ex. cond. (A-E) 1550
Bureau, 4 tiger striped drawers, orig. bracket feet w/minor repair, molded top 38½" l., 18" d, 35" h.
(A-E) 1400
Bureau, Hepplewhite, pine, 4-drawer, rectangular, shaped apron, bracket feet, 19th C., 40" l., 19"
d., 38¼" h. (A-MW)... 425
Bureau, mahogany, 4-drawer, bamboo turned legs, wood pulls, 52" w. (D-NE)...................... 255
Bureau, walnut, 4 graded overlapping drawers w/curly walnut front, molded top, fluted quarter
columns, ogee feet, 38" w×36½" h×21" d. (A-E) 900
Cabinet, barber's, oak, wall, drop front, 1 drawer, brass pulls (D-E)....................................... 45
Cabinet, barber's, wall, pine, drop front, 1 drawer, brass pull refinished (D-MW).................. 45
Cabinet, bolt, 40-drawer, chest type, pine w/wooden pulls (D-MW) 375
Cabinet, bolt, oak, octagon shape, iron base, 64 pie-shaped drawers, orig. labels & porcelain pulls
(D-MW) 475
Cabinet, bolt, oak, octagon shape, revolving, 64 pie-shaped drawers, refinished, new pulls (D-W) 575
Cabinet, bolt, oak, revolving, pyramid shape, 102 drawers, orig. wooden pulls, refinished
(D-MW) 625
Cabinet, hanging, pine, good cond. (A-E).. 50
Cabinet, hanging, pine, Penna. perfectly proportioned, crown molding, 1 shelf, rat-tail hinges,
wrought iron escutcheon, 1 door w/2 panels (A-E)... 6900

Desk, slant top, cherry, on frame, cabriole legs, ball & claw feet, New England (A-E) $8900

Chair with writing arm, arrowback, decor. $1500

Cabinet, corner, hanging, pine, Pa. Dutch, molded frieze above 1 door w/heart cut-outs, 2 shelves, 19th C., 32½" h. × 18½" d. (A-MW) ....$ 250

Cabinet, hanging, walnut, receipt holder, pigeon holes, dovetailed ends (A-E) 85

Cabinet, hutch, pine, upper section w/4 open shelves above 2 door base section, 19th C., 43¼" w. × 20½" d., × 76" h. (A-MW)... 525

Cabinet, medicine, pine w/mirror (A-W)... 45

Cabinet, medicine, pine, 3 shelves, open, primitive (A-E).. 35

Cabinet, needle, oak, orig. finish, porcelain pulls & stencil — CROWLEY NEEDLES, 14"×16"×6" (D-MW) 68

Cabinet, needle, oak, 2-drawer, 12" sq., 6½" h. (D-W)... 55

Cabinet, parlor, oak, hand carved, French bevel mirror, 8×8 & one 10×18; 57" h., 32" w. (D-W) 135

Cabinet, smoke decor., 17 drawers, dovt. const., 18" w., 6½" d., 17" h. (A-E) 750

Cabinet, spice, hanging, pine w/14 drawers (D-E) 300

Cabinet, spice, orig. red finish, w/15 drawers, ca. 1810 (D-E).. 350

Cabinet, spice, pine, grained, w/1 long drawer & 3 columns of 4 smaller drawers, dov. top & bottom, 21" h., 21" w. (A-E) 325

Cabinet, spice, pine, turnip feet, orig. red paint good, 9 small drawers inside cabinet, butterfly hinges on panel door front (A-E) 425

Cabinet, spice, raised panel door, interior has 4 small, 2 lg. drawers, butterfly hinges, ball feet (A-E) 230

Cabinet, spice, 6-drawer, green & white knobs, some drawers show name of spices (A-E) 125

Cabinet, wall, oak, 4 shelves, 2 French bevel mirrors 8" diam., 24"×24", ref. (D-MW) 55

Cabinet, wall, oak, turned spindles, brass brackets at end of front railing, 3 shelves, 17"×21", refinished (D-S)... 55

Cabinet, spice, wall, pine w/orig. red paint, molded frieze over 3 rows of 3 short drawers, 2 long drawers, orig. pulls, 24½" h. (A-MW) 170

Cabinet, spool, cherry, pressed wood fronts on 7 drawers, ex. cond. J. & P. Coats (D-W)....... 375

Cabinet, spool, oak, Clark's O N T, swivel base, roll-up sides, glass front, 19th C. (D-E) 300

Cabinet, spool, oak, 4-drawer (D-E) 140

Cabinet, spool, oak, 4-drawer, refinished (D-MW).. 140

Cabinet, spool, oak, 6-drawer, refinished (D-MW).. 350

Cabinet, spool, oak, 6-drawer, Clark & White, refinished (D-E)... 245

Cabinet, spool, pine, early, solid plank ends, scalloped apron front, 7 drawers, refinished, 40" h., 15" d., 21" w. (D-W)... 200

Cabinet, spool, pine, 8-drawer, refinished, from old N. E. country store (D-E) 250

Cabinet, spool, pine, 7-drawer, refinished, used in store, ex. cond. (D-W)............................ 200

Cradle, hooded, pine, Penna. Dutch, dovetailed (D-E) $250

Child's dresser, 31" h., (D-E) $180

Corner cupboard, pine, orig. finish (D-W) $135

Cabinet, spool, pine, 10-drawer, early, Pa. Dutch, orig. porcelain pulls, nice scalloped front apron, orig. finish (D-E) ....$ 285

Candlestand, brown paint over old red, primitive make-do legged base, 18th C. (A-NE)........ 175

Candlestand, cherry, chamfered corners, turned pedestal over spider legs, ca. 1750, 18½"×15½"×27" h. (D-NE) 250

Candlestand, cherry, circular top on turned maple standard, tripod base, snake feet, 18¾" diam., 25¾" h. (A-MW).. 275

Candlestand, cherry, circular top, turned standard, tripod base, snake feet, 19th C., 15½" diam., 26½" h. (A-MW) 250

Candlestand, cherry, spider leg, fine turnings (A-E)... 200

Candlestand, cherry, square w/snake feet (D-MW) 275

Candlestand, cherry, tilt top, star inlaid, spider leg, fine turnings, round top (D-E)............... 450

Candlestand, cherry, tripod snake feet, base turnings (A-E) 160

Candlestand, circular pine top, maple post turned, pine cross & raised base, ref., 18th C., 28" h. (A-MW) 295

Candlestand, curly maple, dish top, spider leg, 16¼" top (A-E) 375

Candlestand, Hepplewhite, grained finish, red & brownish paint (A-NE) 350

Candlestand, Hepplewhite, round smoke decor. top, 1 small drawer, early white paint over old red (A-NE) 1000

Candlestand, Hepplewhite, tilt-top, w/shaped corner top of tiger maple, orig. finish (A-NE) .. 1050

Candlestand, mahogany, dish top, spider leg (A-E).. 95

Candlestand, mahogany, tilt-top (D-W) 90

Candlestand, maple base, pine top (A-E) 62

Candlestand, maple, circular top on urn-shaped standard, quadruped base, 19th C., 24½" diam., 28¼" h. (A-MW).. 100

Candlestand, maple, stretcher base, sq. legs w/outside stretchers, oval top, 25" h., 20"×20" top (A-E) 210

Candlestand, maple, swivel type, tall, 3-leg (A-E) 130

Candlestand, maple top, tiger maple base, New England, ca. 1760 (D-MW)........................... 295

Candlestand, maple, turned legs, stretcher base, oval top, all orig., rare (A-E) 575

Candlestand, oak, ratchet, for 2 candles (A-E) 190

Candlestand, old brownish-red paint, block turnings below shaft & dish top, 3-legged (A-NE). 500

Candlestand, pine, early, crossed base w/squared taper, stop chamfered post, circular top, refinished, 28" h. (A-NE) 275

Candlestand, pine, low X table base, oval top (A-E)..$ 65

Candlestand, pine, Penna., urn pedestal w/blunt arrow feet, 18th C. (D-NW)....................... 850

Candlestand, pine, painted white over old red, early (A-E).. 1000

Candlestand, pine, spider leg, round top (A-E) 120

Candlestand, pine, tall X table base, oval top (A-E).. 55

Candlestand, pine, tilt-top, round, center pedestal on sq. base (A-E)................................ 100

Candlestand, pine, tilt-top, turned standard, tripod base, 19th C., 21″ sq. top, 28″ h. (A-MW) 150

Candlestand, pine top, maple turned post, pine cross raised base, bracket feet, refinished, 18th C., 28″ h. (A-MW) 295

Candlestand, pine & walnut, oval top w/dowel & octagonal standard, X footed base, 14″ oval top, 18th C., 27½″ h. (A-MW) 150

Candlestand, primitive, turned pedestal & shaped top formed from 1 pc. wood, blue-green paint, 30″ h., 20½″ d. (D-E) 175

Candlestand, screw top, tripod base (A-E) 290

Candlestand, Sheraton, pine, orig. varnish finish, Penna., ca. 1835 (D-E)........................... 395

Candlestand, walnut, dish top (A-E) 240

Candlestand, walnut, dish top w/birdcage, snake feet, 22″ top (A-E).................................. 400

Candlestand, walnut, spider legs, inlaid top & legs (A-E) 75

Candlestand, walnut, tilt-top, oval, tripod base, ca. 1800 (D-E) 625

Case-of-drawers, Chippendale, high, all orig. except hdwe. (A-E)..................................... 1300

Chair, arrowback, rabbit ear w/multi-colored decor. on black ground (A-E) 250

Chair, baluster back, w/ball turnings & stretcher base, maple (A-E) 130

Chair, banister back, old paint (A-E).. 220

Chair, banister back w/shaped crest (A-E).. 190

Chair, bench, fireside, slipper feet, pine (D-E) 950

Chair, captain's, pine, full-size, shaped rolled back (D-NE)... 135

Chair, captain's, swivels (D-E) 100

Chair, chamber, Windsor, orig. decor., painted black, ca. 1840 (D-MW)............................. 200

Chair, corner, cherry w/rush seat, country, 18th C. (D-NE).. 250

Chair, corner, Chippendale, mahogany w/molded legs & stretchers, open work, splat (D-NE). 325

Chair, corner, Chippendale, rush seat, sq. leg, stretcher base, open splat back w/rail back, curled arms (A-E) 250

Chair, corner, maple, New England, orig. rush seat, ca. 1730 (D-E) 350

Chair, corner, pine & elm w/splint seat, fine orig. cond. (D-MW)..................................... 249

Chair, corner, Sheraton, maple, yolk shaped crest-rail, turned legs & stretchers w/reed seat, 19th C. (A-MW) 525

Chair, Hitchcock, orig. dark finish & stenciling, ca. 1840 (D-E)... 275

Chair, kitchen, Windsor type, refinished (A-E)... 25

Corner cupboard, pine, Penna. Dutch, 2-pc., refinished (D-MW) $850

Sewing cabinet, oak, lift top, 2 drawers front, 11″ w., 12″ h., 11½″ deep (D-W) $45

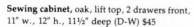

Chair, ladies', w/gold stencil incl. basket of fruit & ochre decor. seat (A-NE) ....$ 175
Chair, low back w/rush seat (A-E)... 52
Chair, oak, bentwood, orig. finish (A-MW).. 27
Chair, oak, hoop back, refinished (D-MW).. 18
Chair, oak, pressed back, fine detail, refinished (D-MW) 45
Chair, rocker, arrowback w/engraved decor., tall, primitive (D-E) 290
Chair, rocker, balloon back, orig. black finish (D-E)... 75
Chair, rocker, Boston, decor. w/stencils & basket of fruit on crest; red & black, general decor.,
   yellow & red decor. rolled on seat (A-NE) 325
Chair, rocker, Boston, refinished (A-E) 100
Chair, rocker, Boston, rolled seat, w/arms, orig. black finish & stenciling good (D-E)............. 225
Chair, rocker, Boston, scalloped back & half spindles (A-E)... 100
Chair, rocker, Boston, spindleback (D-E) 125
Chair, rocker, comb back, shaped comb back over 7-spindle turned back w/molded seat, outward
   flared turned legs w/stretcher and rockers, orig. paint, 18th C. (A-MW) 375
Chair, rocker, curly maple, upholstered (new) Hitchcock-type (D-E) 185
Chair, rocker, decor., cane seat, rolled arms (D-E) 150
Chair, rocker, early, cane seat, 5-spindle back, roll seat (D-NE) 22
Chair, rocker, ladder back, ash, refinished, rush seat good (D-MW) 49
Chair, rocker, ladder back, ash, rush seat, in the rough (D-MW).. 35
Chair, rocker, ladder back, maple, rush seat, refinished (D-MW) 80
Chair, rocker, ladder back, pine, rush seat, 19th C. (A-MW) 200
Chair, rocker, ladder back, pine, rush seat, orig. dark finish, 19th C. (A-MW)...................... 200
Chair, rocker, ladder back, pine, rush seat, unfinished cond. (D-MW) 32
Chair, rocker, ladder back, rush seat, orig. finish, thin, knife blade rockers, ex. cond. (D-MW). 95
Chair, rocker, oak, high arms, leather seat & back, carved, refinished (D-MW) 110
Chair, rocker, oak, high back, rope spindles & posts, spring seat (D-MW) 100
Chair, rocker, oak, rope spindles, carved, orig. finish (D-MW)... 97
Chair, rocker, oak, saddle wood seat, refinished (D-W) 95
Chair, rocker, Penna., tall, lyre back (A-E).. 60
Chair, rocker, Salem, red, black & gold grained & decor. (A-NE) 375
Chair, rocker, Salem, shaped crest, stenciled fruit & free hand florishes on yellow ground, w/arms
   (A-E) 375
Chair, rocker, sewing, balloon back, all orig. (A-E)... 50
Chair, rocker, sewing, good cond. (A-E) 27
Chair, rocker, sewing, plank seat (A-E) 27
Chair, rocker, sewing, red flower decor. (A-E).. 40
Chair, rocker, sewing, Windsor, spindle runner (A-E) 37
Chair, rocker, shoe-foot, Hudson Valley, old green paint (D-E).. 300
Chair, rocker, Windsor, arrowback, red & black paint (A-E)... 300
Chair, rocker, Windsor, continuous arm, all orig., Mass., ca. 1760-1780 (D-E) 375
Chair, rocker, Windsor, orig. decor., high back (A-E)... 85
Chair, rocker, Windsor, pine & ash, w/arms, rod back (A-E) 285
Chair, rocker, Windsor, step down, high back (D-E) 200
Chair, side, arrowback, middle front stretcher splat, rare yellow background (A-E) 350
Chair, side, arrowback, orig. cond. good, yellow/green painted finish w/morning glory center
   back, plank seat, high shaped ears (D-MW) 155
Chair, side, arrowback, plank seat, orig. decor. poor (A-E) 40
Chair, side, balloon back, plank seat, orig. dark finish & stenciling (D-MW) 75
Chair, side, balloon back, plank seat, orig. finish good (A-MW) 75
Chair, side, Chippendale, country version, rush seat, unfinished, 18th C. (D-MW) 100
Chair, side, Chippendale, walnut, sq. legs, H-stretchers, open splat back (A-E) 350
Chair, side, dining room, bird's-eye maple back, cane seat (A-E)... 45
Chair, side, highback, seat replaced, old invalid chair (D-E)... 50
Chair, side, Hitchcock, maple, plank seat (D-E) 135
Chair, side, Hitchcock, maple, rush seat (D-E)... 175
Chair, side, Hitchcock, orig. black paint w/painted red/green/yellow decor. on crest (A-E) 175
Chair, side, Hitchcock, rush seat, fruit decor. all orig. (D-W)... 150
Chair, side, ladder back, cherry, rush seat, orig. finish, light, late 18th C. (D-NE)................. 250

12-drawer chest, walnut & pine, dovetailed frame, orig. porcelain pulls, 24″ × 24″ × 9¼″ (D-MW) $300

Chest of drawers, oak, wishbone mirror, refinished (D-MW) $90

Chair, side, ladder back, curly maple, Pa., 4 splat back w/rush seat, refinished (A-NE) ....$ 200
Chair, side, ladder back, curly maple, turned finials, bulbous front stretcher, orig. Patina ex. (A-E) 1200
Chair, side, ladder back, curved slats, Penna., ca. 1820 (D-E) 150
Chair, side, ladder back, maple, balloon cane seat, 19th C. (A-MW) 87
Chair, side, ladder back, maple, rush seat, ball turnings (A-MW).. 100
Chair, side, ladder back, Penna., early, 5 graduated arched slats, orig. black paint, well-preserved finish (A-E) 290
Chair, side, ladder back, rush seat, ball turnings (A-E) 130
Chair, side, ladder back, rush seat, ball turnings (D-E) 100
Chair, side, ladder back, rush seat, ball turnings in front (A-E) 80
Chair, side, ladder back, rush seat, orig. finish (A-E) 65
Chair, side, ladder back, sausage turned, ca. 1740 (D-E) 225
Chair, side, ladder back, splint seat, turned legs & front base (D-MW) 175
Chair, side, ladder back, turned finials, bold ball & point feet, stretcher w/bold turnings, old Patina ex. (A-E)... 750
Chair, side, Queen Anne, biscuit foot, rush seat, splat back & ball turning in center (A-E)..... 425
Chair, side, Queen Anne, cherry, rush seat, in the rough, 18th C. (D-E) 400
Chair, side, tiger maple, cane seat, button feet on front legs (A-E) 50
Chair, side, tiger maple, curved crest rail, wide front stretcher, cane seat (D-MW) 95
Chair, side, walnut, William & Mary, carved, ca. 1690, good cond. (D-SW) 1600
Chair, side, Windsor, arrowback, maple, refinished (A-E)... 50
Chair, side, Windsor, arrowback, painted yellow ochre, w/black-brown striping, brushed on arrows & fruit on slat (A-NE) 150
Chair, side, Windsor, birdcage, 5-spindle, orig. finish ex. (D-E) 95
Chair, side, Windsor, birdcage, New England, orig. finish, ca. 1780 (D-MW) 150
Chair, side, Windsor, birdcage, 7-spindle, old red paint (A-E).. 300
Chair, side, Windsor, birdcage, shaped seat, bamboo turnings, traces orig. cream paint & vining decor. (A-E) 200
Chair, side, Windsor, bow back, bamboo turnings, plank seat, orig. finish good (D-MW)...... 375
Chair, side, Windsor, bow back, bamboo turnings, plank seat, 5-spindle back, refinished (D-W) 132
Chair, side, Windsor, bow back, 8-spindle, orig. black finish, ca. 1800 (D-E)....................... 450
Chair, side, Windsor, bow back, 8-spindle, orig. black finish good, bulbous turnings, N. Eng. orig. (D-NE) 475
Chair, side, Windsor, bow back, H-stretcher, saddle seat, refinished (A-E) 70

Chair, side, Windsor, bow back, 9-spindle, shaped seat, painted black w/traces of orig. green paint bleeding through (A-MW) ....$ 175

Chair, side, Windsor, bow back, 7-spindle, H-stretcher, all orig. (A-E) 110

Chair, side, Windsor, bow back, 7-spindle, orig. black paint (D-S) 250

Chair, side, Windsor, bow back, 7-spindle, outside stretchers (D-MW)................................ 100

Chair, side, Windsor, bow back, shaped saddle seat, worn red painted finish (A-E)............... 275

Chair, side, Windsor, brace back, cont. arm, bulbous turnings (D-NE) 875

Chair, side, Windsor, brace back, New England orig., orig. black finish good (A-E)............... 1500

Chair, side, Windsor, brace back, saddle seat, refinished (A-E) 400

Chair, side, Windsor, butterfly, 5-spindle (A-E)... 100

Chair, side, Windsor, butterfly, 7-spindle (D-MW).. 150

Chair, side, Windsor, comb back, saddle seat, turnings, H-stretchers (A-E)......................... 225

Chair, side, Windsor, comb back, 7-spindle, saddle seat (A-E) 275

Chair, side, Windsor, comb back, 7-spindle, saddle seat, vase turnings on spindle end posts (A-E) 475

Chair, side, Windsor, comb back, shaped spindles, orig. finish (D-MW).............................. 395

Chair, side, Windsor, comb back, turned legs, saddle seat, flaring curves (A-E).................... 500

Chair, side, Windsor, double comb back, carved ears, saddle seat, H-stretchers (A-E) 525

Chair, side, Windsor, fanback, 9-spindle, bamboo turnings, signed "I. Lackey" (A-E)........... 325

Chair, side, Windsor, fanback, 9-spindle, comb rail w/carved ears, saddle seat, chamfered edge (A-E) 800

Chair, side, Windsor, fanback, 9-spindle, H-stretcher, orig. finish (D-MW).......................... 225

Chair, side, Windsor, fanback, 9-spindle, saddle seat, H-stretcher, refinished (A-MW) 80

Chair, side, Windsor, fanback, outside stretchers (D-MW) 240

Chair, side, Windsor, fanback, primitive, rough, old finish (A-E) 195

Chair, side, Windsor, fanback, round seat, rare, orig. paint (D-E) 600

Chair, side, Windsor, fanback, 7-spindle (A-E).. 65

Chair, side, Windsor, fanback, 7-spindle, bulbous vase turnings, saddle seat, signed "Fahy" (A-E) 725

Chair, side, Windsor, fanback, 7-spindle, delicate turnings, New Eng., ca. 1820 (D-E) 1800

Chair, side, Windsor, fanback, 7-spindle, H-stretcher (D-MW) 200

Chair, side, Windsor, fanback, 7-spindle, saddle seat, H-stretchers (D-E)............................ 125

Chair, side, Windsor, fanback, shaped seat, worn orig. black paint (D-E) 300

Chair, side, Windsor, rabbit ear, raked, decorated w/triple red leaf & gold stencil on yellow ground (A-NE).. 275

Chair, side, Windsor, step down, 5-spindle, orig. finish good (D-W) 125

Chair, weaver's, fine turnings, woven split seat (A-E) 175

Chair, weaver's, Windsor, rare, 5-spindle, rake to legs (A-E) 375

Chair, Windsor, arrowback, half-spindle, green paint orig. (A-MW).................................... 60

Chair, Windsor, bow back, bar-room, saddle seats, H-stretchers, Windsor turnings (A-E) 85

Chair, Windsor, bow back, 7-spindle, saddle seat (A-E).. 140

Chair, Windsor, comb back, saddle seat, stretchers (A-E).. 185

Chair, Windsor, comb back, 7-spindle, saddle seat, vase turnings, old black paint (A-E)........ 400

Chair, Windsor, low back, continuous arm w/applied crest, supported by 16 spindles, bulbous turnings, orig. finish (D-E) 400

Chair, wing, Sheraton, fireside w/sweeping wings (A-NE) 475

Chairs, arrowback, set of 6, slant back, redecorated (A-E) 540

Chairs, arrowback, slant back, orig. yellow decor., pr. (D-E) 675

Chairs, Baltimore style, set of 6, cane seats (A-E) 300

Chairs, Chippendale, set of 4, oak, early (A-E) 200

Chairs, decorated, set of 6, half rod, plank seat, orig. yellow paint & stencil decor. (D-E)....... 375

Chairs, Hitchcock, set of 6, gold & brown grained leaf decor. (A-E)................................... 420

Chairs, Hitchcock, set of 6, orig. black painted & stenciled decor. 5 side & 1 arm (D-E) 1200

Chairs, Hitchcock type, arm chair & 5 matching side, black w/orig. stenciled decor., fine (D-W) 650

Chairs, oak, bentwood, ex. cond., set of 6, refinished (D-MW) 200

Chairs, oak, fancy pressed backs, set of 6, orig. finish fair (A-MW).................................... 105

Chairs, oak, high pressed backs, caned seats, set of 6, refinished (D-MW) 350

Chairs, side, balloon back, set of 6, orig. decor. (D-E) 1200

Chairs, side, balloon back, set of 6, orig. fruit decor., plank seats (A-E)............................... 330

Chairs, side, curly maple, pair, ladderback w/rush seats, 2-slat (A-E)................................... 170

Chairs, side, half spindle, set of 4, yellow paint & stenciled decor. orig. (D-MW)..................$ 350
Chairs, side, half-spindle, set of 6, decor. in pale yellow w/orig. handpainted decor. (A-E)..... 345
Chairs, side, half-spindle, set of 6, orig. decor. finish ex., ca. 1860 (D-E) 1900
Chairs, side, set of 6, yellow decor., stenciled & free hand decor. w/stripping, all marked
"warranted", one signed "F. Brooks" (A-E).. 1500
Chairs, side, Sheraton, set of 4, painted w/orig. decor. (A-E) 120
Chairs, side, Windsor, arrowback, set of 6, plank seat, bamboo spindles (D-E) 245
Chairs, side, Windsor, birdcage, set of 4, bamboo turned, refinished (D-E)......................... 125
Chairs, side, Windsor, brace back, pair (D-W).. 300

Desk, slant top,
William & Mary, on
frame, tulip feet, all
orig. (A-E) $950

Jelly cupboard,
poplar, pegged,
dovetailed drawers,
refinished (D-MW)
$225

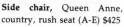

Side chair, Queen Anne,
country, rush seat (A-E) $425

Chairs, side, Windsor, brace back, set of 8, 6 side & 2 cont. arm w/knuckles, orig. green paint,
labeled Wallace Nutting (A-E) 2200
Chairs, side, Windsor, fanback, heavy turnings, pair (A-E).. 600
Chairs, side, Windsor, hoop back, set of 6, saddle seat, ca. 1800 (D-MW).......................... 850
Chairs, side, Windsor, set of 6, 7-spindle, yellow pencil lines on seat, ring turnings on legs,
stretchers & spindles (A-E) 950
Chairs, side, Windsor, stepdown, set of 6, 2 arm & 4 side chairs (D-NE) 950
Chairs, Windsor, arrowback, set of 4, brown base w/yellow, green decor., yellow & green
pineapple on crest rail (A-NE).. 950
Chairs, Windsor, brace back, oak & yew, set of 6 (D-MW) 450
Chairs, Windsor, brace back, pair, 1 arm, 1 side, all orig. refinished (A-E)......................... 1000
Chairs, Windsor, stepdown, pair, maple w/bamboo turnings, pine seat, 32½" h. (D-NE) 230
Chest, apothecary, door above & doors on either side of 6-center drawers (D-E) 495
Chest, apothecary, oak, pewter handles, 24 drawers, orig. dark finish good, bun feet, ca. 1835
(D-NE) 875
Chest, apothecary, oak, 64-drawer, orig. porcelain pulls, refinished (D-W).......................... 600
Chest, apothecary, pine, 80-drawer w/orig. labels & porcelain pulls (D-MW) 575
Chest, apothecary, pine, orig. dark finish good, orig. wood pulls, 25 drawers, 40" h., 36" w., 10" d.
(D-E) 650
Chest, apothecary, pine, orig. paint & bun feet, 12 drawers, wooden pulls, 30" w., 42" h. (D-W) .. 500
Chest, apothecary, pine, wooden knobs, orig., 28-drawer, refinished, 48" h., 35" w., 12" d.
(D-MW) 475
Chest, apothecary, poplar, 60-drawer, ex. cond. (A-MW) 550
Chest, apothecary, step-back, yellow & green paint, double paneled doors, 14 drawers below,
signed "Henry M. Kimball, Esq. Solon, Maine, Nov. 17, 1827" (A-NE)............................. 1700

Desk, pine, country, 58" h., 31" w. (D-MW) $195

Drop leaf table, Chippendale, walnut, w/19" leaves, cabriole legs, ball & claw feet, scalloped ends, all orig. (A-NE) $1800

Chest, ash, 3 drawers, small mirror, oak leaf pulls (D-NE) ....$	95
Chest, bachelor, cherry, w/1 lg. & 4 sm. drawers in base, bracket feet, chamfered corners, orig. brasses, 32" h., 17½" d., 30" w. (A-E)	625
Chest, birch, 4-drawer w/bowed top, wide overhang, bracket base, holly string inlay on drawers, Chippendale brasses, ca. 1750, 36" w., 35" h., 17½" d. (D-NE)	925
Chest, bird's-eye maple, 4-drawer, orig. feet (A-NE)	550
Chest, bird's-eye maple, 6 drawers, 5½' h. (A-NE)	315
Chest, bird's-eye maple & walnut, old red stain, ca. 1825 (D-E)	300
Chest, blanket, bracket feet, grained finish, bread board ends on top, Penna., ca. 1840 (D-E).	450
Chest, blanket, cherry, rectangular top w/hinged cover over 2 false drawers & 2 graduating long drawers, bracket feet, wooden drawer pulls, 19th C., 42¾" l., 18½" d., 44" h. (A-MW)........	175
Chest, blanket, country Hepplewhite w/3 drawers, curved French bracket feet, short strap hinges, interior w/2 drawers under till box, orig. red finish, good cond., Penna., ca. 1810 (D-E)......	650
Chest, blanket, decor., bracket feet, dated 1825 on lid (A-E)	300
Chest, blanket, decor., bracket feet w/spurs & two drawers w/two brass handles each, 49½" l., 30" h. (A-E)...	325
Chest, blanket, decor., 2 drawers w/brasses, ogee feet (A-E)...	375
Chest, blanket, dome top w/green spotted & sponged decor. on light ground, dov. const., 25" (A-NE)	150
Chest, blanket, dovetailed, iron carrying handles at each end, orig. dark green paint, 26"×14"×9" (D-NE)..	32
Chest, blanket, grained oak, buff & brown, handwrought hinges & heart shaped handles, 24½" l., 17½" d., 15¾" h. (D-W)...	55
Chest, blanket, grained, orange & yellow sponge decor., painted arch panel w/"Kriebel, 1823"; 2 drawers, ogee feet, old hdwe. (A-E)	2500
Chest, blanket, Hepplewhite, 2-drawer w/white & gray smoked decor. (A-NE).....................	1500
Chest, blanket, long strap hinges, dovetailed bracket feet, orig. wavy red decor. finish, heavy moldings, rosehead nails, Penna., ca. 1780 (D-E)	350
Chest, blanket, med. size, stippled in yellow (A-E)...	575
Chest, blanket, orig. brown painted finish, 2 drawers, bracket base, cotter pin hinges, hardware replaced, early 18th C. (A-NE)	575
Chest, blanket, orig. grained finish, small, dovetailed, Penna., ca. 1850 (D-E)	450
Chest, blanket, orig. graining, black on mustard, footed (D-MW)	195
Chest, blanket, orig. red paint good, six board, inside comp. (D-MW)	75
Chest, blanket, painted, orig. red, good cond., 6-board, 48" l., dov. const. (D-MW)	350
Chest, blanket, painted, orig. red/yellow good, 9 raised panels in front, 4 on each side (A-E).	550
Chest, blanket, pine, bracket feet, jaw lock, strap hinges (A-E)......................................	70
Chest, blanket, pine, bracket feet, jaw lock, strap hinges, refinished (D-MW).......................	87
Chest, blanket, pine, bracket feet, strap hinges, floral decor. (A-E)	200
Chest, blanket, pine, bracket feet, strap hinges, marked "Susi Scheile, 1804", 4' w., 22" d. (A-E).	160

Chest, blanket, pine, decor., ochre & yellow, orig., dovetailed, bracket feet, jaw lock, strap hinges (A-N) ....$ 260

Chest, blanket, pine, decor., umber on ochre gr., w/red spotting, one drawer, ex. cond., 36" l. (A-E) 2800

Chest, blanket, pine, domed top w/nail decor. w/initial "D. Donn", iron handles & lock, 29¼" l., 15½" d., 13½" h., 19th C. (A-MW).. 70

Chest, blanket, pine, domed, wrought iron side mounted handles, 18th C., refinished, 27" l., 19½" d., 23¼" h. (A-MW)... 225

Chest, blanket, pine, dovetailed, turned feet, dark graining w/geometric striping at ends, front has 3 arched sections painted white & dec. w/tulips & foliage, wrought iron bear trap lock & strap hinges, till is incomplete, 52" l., 23½" w., 24½" d. (A-E) 550

Chest, blanket, pine, early, 3 arcaded panels, tulip & flower decor., 1777, molding, bracket feet, strap hinges (A-E) 450

Chest, blanket, pine, 5-lipped drawers, bracket base w/solid single board sides & top, Chippendale brass pulls & escutcheons on all drawers, 36" w. × 46" h. × 18" d. (D-NE)................. 575

Chest, blanket, pine, grained (A-E) 90

Chest, blanket, pine, grained finish orig., gray w/green spots, signed E.J.M. 1809; 32" l. (A-NE) . 450

Chest, blanket, pine, jaw lock & strap hinges (A-E) 200

Chest, blanket, pine, lift top w/cotter pin hinges, 4 drawers in base, beading around each, bracket feet, 18th C. (D-NE) 575

Chest, blanket, pine, old hdwe., in rough (A-MW) 55

Chest, blanket, pine, small, green & black, hinged lid w/metal side handles, 19th C., 22" l. (A-MW) 125

Tavern table, barrel, walnut, lift top, dual purpose; when not used to hold liquor barrels, top folds down to serve as table (A-E) $350

Flour & sugar bin, pine, divider & tray in top section, storage space below for utensils, refinished (D-MW) $250

Tavern table, 1-board scrub top (A-E) $1350

Chest, blanket, old hdwe., round top, soft wood, dov. const. (D-E) 125

Chest, blanket, pine & maple, rectangular, turned legs, 36½" l., 24" h. (A-MW)................... 125

Chest, blanket, pine, 1-drawer, ca. 1780, 29" h., 19" d., 37" l. (D-NE).................................... 285

Chest, blanket, pine, painted, lt. ochre w/burnt sienna squiggles, one drawer, 36" l. (A-NE) .. 900

Chest, blanket, pine, Queen Anne, American, 2 full-width drawers at bottom, 2 simulated drawer fronts in upper section, lift top w/pin hinges, early 18th C., 38″ l., 18″ d., 45″ h. (A-E) .$ 550

Chest, blanket, pine, round feet, 2 drawers, old lock & strap hinges (A-E) 130

Chest, blanket, pine, 6-board, 39″ l., 14″ w. (D-NE) 95

Chest, blanket, pine, 6-board, dov. const., round feet, inner compartment, 1820-1840 (D-NE) 195

Chest, blanket, pine, strap hinges, 2 drawers (A-E) 175

Chest, blanket, pine, strap rat-tail hinges, small (D-MW) 75

Chest, blanket, pine, tall, top half w/false drawers, 1 drawer below, ball feet, refinished (A-E).. 275

Chest, blanket, pine, 3-drawer, bracket feet, willow brasses, jaw lock & curled strap hinges (A-E) . 395

Chest, blanket, pine, 3 drawer, jaw lock & strap hinges (A-E) 190

Chest, blanket, pine, 3-drawer, jaw lock, strap hinges, ogee feet, old brasses (A-E) 260

Chest, blanket, pine, 3-drawer, ogee feet, old brasses & hdwe., strap hinges, jaw lock (A-E).. 280

Chest, blanket, pine, 2-drawer, grained in red & black, w/gold stencils on face, inscr. ″New Portland, Maine″ in center top & bordered by stencils in gold of dogs chasing deer, 37″ (A-NE) 1450

Chest, blanket, pine, 2-drawer, ogee feet, jaw lock & strap hinges, initialed ″E.B.″ in white on front (A-E) 170

Chest, blanket, pine, 2 raised panels on front, 1 on each side, bun feet, orig. old red paint striped w/black (D-E) 450

Chest, blanket, pine, white, black & gray smoked decor., 2-drawer (A-E) 1500

Chest, blanket, pine, yellow smoked painted decor., 6 board, dov. const., Sheraton leg, 33″ w., 21½″ h., 15½″ d. (A-NE) 2300

Chest, blanket, poplar, grained decor., ex. cond. (D-N) 525

Chest, blanket, red, incised, 1820 (A-MW) 225

Chest, blanket, round top, decor. w/tulips, birds & flowers (A-E) 400

Chest, blanket, scalloped apron, dovetails, strap hinges & lock, refinished (D-E) 375

Chest, blanket, secret drawers, 2 panels on front & one on each side, w/columns holding checkered arches, checkered flower pots w/plants, flowers & fans, center front has decor. flower pot, buds, flowers & star (A-E) 1000

Chest, blanket, 6-board w/orig. blue paint (D-E) 295

Chest, blanket, small, orig. dec. in yellow on brown & tree on top (D-NE) 175

Chest, blanket, small panel type, orig. red finish, Penna., ca. 1860 (D-E) 200

Chest, blanket, small, two stippled panels & two half moons on front, one panel on top, 30″ l., 14″ h. (A-E) 450

Secretary, cherry (D-NE) $2300

Desk, cherry (A-NE) $1600

Chest, blanket, softwood, decor. w/house, pine tree & tulips, 8½"×11" (A-E) ....$ 155
Chest, blanket, softwood, turned feet, molding at base & on lid, orig. painted panel w/"G.S. 1835" (D-E).. 140
Chest, blanket, sponge decor., red/black, ball feet, ex. cond. (A-E)...................................... 370
Chest, blanket, sponge grain decor., old red & black, lined w/old print, 31" l. (D-W) 300
Chest, blanket, stippled, yellow, red & black (A-E).. 160
Chest, blanket, strap hinges, jaw lock, French feet (A-E) 80
Chest, blanket, 3-drawer, ogee feet, strap hinges, all orig., green & red trim w/narrow panel, dated 1804, "Daniel Rohr" (A-E).. 330
Chest, blanket, 2-drawer, bracket feet, red paint, 39½" l., 24" h. (A-E) 375
Chest, blanket, 2 panels on front decor. w/running deer, lined w/green, orig. finish, dov. const. inside comp. (A-E) 725
Chest, blanket, tiger maple grained finish, 2 overlapping drawers, turned feet, good cond., Penna., ca. 1850 (D-E) 400

Blanket chest, pine, dovetailed, strap hinges & interior compartment (D-MW) $125

Tool chest, pine, compartments & sliding tray, dovetailed, small, refinished, 22" × 10" × 12" (D-MW) $75

Pie cupboard, 7 vented shelves, small, refinished (D-MW) $75

Chest, blanket, turned legs, decor. in red & yellow, Penna., ca. 1840 (D-E) 550
Chest, blanket, walnut, dov. const. ends, bracket base, 2 drawers, refinished, Penna., ca. 1780 (D-S).. 250
Chest, blanket, walnut, 5 raised panels front, 2 raised panels either side, sulphur inlay, 1779, molding, tall round legs (A-E) 200
Chest, blanket, walnut, front panel inlaid w/design of pitcher, flowers & stems, Penna., ca. 1790 (A-E) 600
Chest, blanket, walnut, (mule type), orig. finish, 1 drawer, wooden pulls, early (D-NE) 200
Chest, blanket, walnut, 3 drawers in base, strap tulip hinges, jaw lock, turnip feet (A-E)....... 240
Chest, blanket, walnut, 3 drawers, round feet, jaw lock & strap hinges, 49"l., 27"h., 22" d. (A-E).. 275
Chest, blanket, walnut, 3 sunken arched panels, heavy molding, inlay on lid "PF" w/tulip (A-E). 625
Chest, cherry, bracket feet, fine molding, four lg. drawers, two med., three sm., w/bale brasses, 40" w., 5'4½" h., 23" d., all orig. (D-NE) 950
Chest, Chippendale, butternut, 3-drawer (D-NE) 130
Chest, Chippendale, cherry, dainty ball & claw feet, orig. brasses, 36" h., 39½" l., 20" D. (A-E) . 3300
Chest, Chippendale, cherry, dovetailed frame, bracket feet, orig. finish, 4 grad. drawers, 3½ ft. h. (D-E) 1000

Chairs, armchair & side chair, yoke back, matching pr. (A-NE) $2900

Table, Queen Anne, pine (A-NE) $2900

Chest, Chippendale, cherry, fluted quarter columns (A-E) ....$ 600

Chest, Chippendale, cherry, 4-drawer w/fluted corners, ball & ball brasses, 38″ w., 41″ h. (A-E)   375

Chest, Chippendale, cherry, ogee feet, ball brasses, 40″×21″×34″ h. (A-E)   525

Chest, Chippendale, cherry, 6-drawer, bracket feet, orig. hdw. & finish, 55½″ h., 38″ w., 21½″ d. (A-E)   1350

Chest, Chippendale, 4 graduated drawers, fluted corners, ogee feet, fine molding, all orig. except brasses, 35½″ h., 36″ w., 20″ d. (A-E)   2800

Chest, Chippendale, mahogany, fine molding on top piece w/2 small & 3 large drawers; base w/3 drawers, top drawers w/butler's desk w/fine interior, bracket feet, in-the-rough (D-E)   1400

Chest, Chippendale, mahogany, 4 drawers, fluted corners, ogee feet, brasses (A-E)   1050

Chest, Chippendale, mahogany, molded top w/split tongue corners, reeded quarter columns, orig. ogee feet, 4 drawers (A-E)   3200

Chest, Chippendale, mahogany, 2 small & 4 large drawers, ogee feet, fluted corners, 47½″ h., 20½″ d., 41″ w. (A-E)   325

Chest, Chippendale, maple & cherry, fluted corners, new brasses, 6 drawers, 4½′ h. (A-E)   600

Chest, Chippendale, maple, grad. drawers, bracket base, orig. finish good (D-E)   1400

Chest, Chippendale, maple, grad. 6-drawer, w/bracket base, moulded top, old brown paint (A-NE)   1300

Chest, Chippendale, pine, 5-drawer, bracket base, moulded top, decor. in varying colors of brown; drawers outlined w/yellow stripe, ea. drawer w/different application of decor. (A-NE).   900

Chest, Chippendale, solid ends dovetailed, 4 drawers, orig. dark finish (D-W)   150

Chest, Chippendale, tiger curly maple, Phila. molded top, fluted quarter columns, overlapping drawers, O.G. feet, orig. brasses, 41″ w., 20″ d., 39″ h., restored, rare (A-E)   1650

Chest, Chippendale, walnut, chamfered corners, ogee feet, willow brasses, fine molding, 3 sm., 2 med., & 4 lg. drawers, orig. finish (A-E)   875

Chest, Chippendale, walnut, fluted corners, reeded & scalloped, ogee feet, brass handles, 3 sm., 2 med., 3 lg. dov. drawers, 66″ h., orig. finish (A-E)   950

Chest, Chippendale, walnut, orig. cond., rare racing greyhound brasses, 3 drawers, molded till, strap hinges, Penna., ca. 1840 (D-E)   1100

Chest, curly maple, bracket feet, molding, 6 drawers, large (A-E).....................................   750

Chest, curly maple, 4-drawer, inch molded overhang top, solid sides to floor, bracket base, diamond escutcheons bird's-eye maple, ca. 1725, 42″ w. × 42″ h., 20½″ d. (D-NE)   1600

Chest, curly maple, 4 grad. drawers, orig. pulls, 42″ w., 42″ h., 20½″ d., Plymouth, Mass., ca. 1725 (D-E)   1600

Chest, curly maple, 6-drawer, Penna., ca. 1770 (D-NE)   2500

Chest, dower, black eagle w/red eyes holding federal shield & clutching tulip & conventional star design in talons, stippled background w/circular & quarter circles on sides, front & lid, 50″ w., 26½″ h., feet not orig., 1807 (A-E)...   975

Chest, dower, decor. w/hearts & tulips, dated 1805 (D-MW) ....$ 1800
Chest, dower, decor., Penna., shoe feet, dated 1776 (A-E) 550
Chest, dower, Elizabeth Lutz, 1787, secret drawer (A-E) 3500
Chest, dower, Montgomery Co., Penna., 1788, 3 panels front, 1 each end; two drawers, 3 secret
    drawers, orig. bracket feet, decor. w/flower pots, tulips, fans & birds (A-E)........................ 880
Chest, dower, pine & decor., 3 blue painted on panels on front showing tulip & floral decor. sides
    w/6 pointed star & floral decor., ends w/painted pinwheel in circle, dated 1811, bracket feet,
    dovetailed, jaw lock & strap hinges (A-E) 3500

Dower chest, Penna. Dutch, 3 sunken panels, initialed A B H R 1787, incised carving on pilasters, ogee feet, in the rough (A-E) $4000

Dower chest, decor., ca. 1800 (D-NE) $2500

Chest, dower, pine, Penna. origin, painted blue, 3 floral white panels decor. w/flowers on front,
    dovetailed, shoe feet (D-E)... 3800
Chest, dower, pine, Penna., orig. sponge painting in tulip design, 3 drawers at base, hinged
    upper lid, short legs, 32" h., 51" w., 22" d. (D-MW) 450
Chest, dower, red background w/3 decor. Gothic arch panels outlined in yellow; orig. hand-
    wrought iron lock & key w/tulip strap hinges, Penna., ca. 1780 (D-E) 1900
Chest, dower, 3 sunken architectural panels initialed A.B.H.R., 1787, decor. w/tulips & flowers in
    vases, incised carving on pilasters, ogee feet, 18th C. (A-E)... 4000
Chest, dower, tulip decor., lt. blue, white & gray, Penna., ca. 1800 (D-E)............................... 2200
Chest, dower, Johannes Trump, 1779, decor. w/snowflakes & flowers, 4 galloping horsemen, ex.
    cond. (A-E)... 4300
Chest, dower, Maria Zukil, painted red, 2 drawers, round feet, white oblong panel style w/tulips
    on each side, dated 1784 (A-E) 300
Chest, Empire, cherry, orig. varnish finish, Penna., ca. 1840 (D-E)...................................... 350
Chest, Empire, stipple decor., Penna., ca. 1860 (D-E) 650
Chest, Empire, tiger maple & cherry, very small, in-the-rough, Penna., ca. 1840 (D-E)........... 600
Chest, Empire, walnut, 3 drawers across top, ca. 1840 (D-E)... 265
Chest, federal period, black walnut & pine, 4 drawers, acorn brasses, Shenandoah Valley origin,
    ca. 1800 (D-SW).. 1150
Chest, flour, dough box & bread board, orig. decor. finish, Penna., ca. 1880 (D-E) 650
Chest, flour, pine, lift top, three bins for flours & meal, two compartments below for pans, orig.
    finish (D-MW) 250
Chest, flour, pine, slant top, dovetailed, bun feet, orig. dark finish good (D-N)................... 285
Chest, flour, slant top, dovetailed w/2 panel doors at bottom, in-the-rough, Penna., ca. 1840 (D-E) 325
Chest, grain, pine, mortise & tenon joints, panel const. ref. (D-W)..................................... 125
Chest, grained, 4 small & 3 large drawers, miniature (D-E) 625
Chest, Hepplewhite, cherry, inlay good, Ky. origin, ca. 1790 (D-S)...................................... 800
Chest, Hepplewhite, cherry & pine, orig. red finish, New England, ca. 1820 (D-E) 800
Chest, Hepplewhite, cherry, 7 drawers, chamfered corners, bracket feet, oval brasses, all orig.,
    76" h. (A-E)... 1300
Chest, Hepplewhite, 4-drawer, inlaid key escutcheons, orig. oval brasses, French feet, scalloped
    apron w/inlaid butterfly, 40" w., 20" d., 37½" h. (A-E) 550

Chest, Hepplewhite, pine, 4-drawer, red/brown & black striped decor. w/yellow & green outlines on drawers & chest, 39" h. (A-NE) ....$ 5250

Chest, Hepplewhite, pine, rectangular top, 2 short drawers, 3 graduating long drawers, shaped apron, splayed bracket feet, 18th C., 35¾" l., 17¾" d., 39¾" h. (A-MW) 350

Chest, Hepplewhite, 3 small & 4 large drawers, chamfer corners, scalloped apron, French feet, 40" w., 54" h., 21" d. (A-E) 450

Chest, Hepplewhite, tiger maple, bow front, signed orig. brasses, rare (D-NE)..................... 1650

Chest, Hepplewhite, walnut, French feet, scalloped apron, overlapping drawers, molding, 42" w., 43" h., 21½" d. (A-E) 475

Chest, immigrant's, initialed, orig. painted decor., ca. 1800 (D-W) 250

Chest, jewelry, ladies, 4 drawers (2 false), yellow ground, red trim, gold stenciled w/scalloped edges (A-NE) 475

Chest, maple, graduated drawer, old red paint, turned feet & splashboard, ca. 1825, 36" (A-NE) 600

Chest, mule, poplar, reddish brown flame graining on yellow background, 2 drawers, 38"×38"×18" (A-E) 325

Chest, oak, 5-drawer, graduating, orig. finish (A-MW)... 30

Chest, oak, 4 large drawers, 3 small, 54" h., refinished (D-MW) 75

Chest, oak, strap hinges, carving of birds, animals, houses, trees & people, ca. 1680, 28" l., 13½" w., 12" h. (A-E) 155

Chest, oak, swelled top drawers, brass hdw., bevel mirror, 6' 8" h. (D-W) 180

Chest, on frame, walnut, 6 lg. drawers, all orig. brasses, molding, scalloped base w/Queen Anne web foot legs, 71" h. overall, 38" w., 21½" d. (A-E)... 1700

Chest, pine, all orig. except hardware, plank end (A-E) 200

Chest, pine, 4 drawers, decorated w/Penna. Dutch floral motif, ca. 1880 (D-E) 450

Chest, pine, New England, 4-drawer, all orig. except brasses (D-NE) 650

Chest, pine, small, 4-drawer, dov. const. (D-MW).. 325

Chest, pine, small 4-drawer, old red paint, brass pulls, bracket base, 35" h. (D-E) 425

Chest, pine, 6 grad. drawers, dovetailed, bracket base, orig. finish good (D-E) 1275

Chest, pine, 3-drawer, bracket base, tan ground w/black & brown striping, 27" (A-NE).......... 475

Chest, pine, 3-drawer, orig. wood pulls, ogee feet, in rough (A-E) 220

Chest, poplar, New England, 8-drawer, bootjack ends, ca. 1750 (D-E)................................. 250

Chest, Sheraton, cherry, bow front, panel ends, 4 graded drawers, 42" w., 20" d., 41½" h. (A-E) 435

Chest, Sheraton, mahogany, orig. varnish finish, Penna., ca. 1830 (D-E) 750

Chest, Sheraton, mahogany, swell front, 4-drawer, opposed rope turnings, lipped drawers, shaped backboard, oval brasses, ca. 1800 (D-NE) 425

Chest, Sheraton, orig. red finish, ¾ size high chest w/2 drawers over 3, Penna., ca. 1830 (D-E). 700

Chest, Sheraton, tiger maple & cherry, ¾ size high chest, in the rough, Penna., ca. 1840 (D-E). 390

Chest, Sheraton, tiger maple & cherry & walnut, orig. red painted finish, Penna., ca. 1850 (D-E). 1400

Chest, sugar, cherry, dovetailed drawer, working lock, refinished, ca. 1800 (D-S).................. 590

Chest, sugar, pine, dovetailed drawer, lock, refinished (D-MW) 325

Chest, tiger maple, 6 drawers, brass handles, bracket feet, 57" h., 35¾" w., 19" d. (A-E) 1250

Chest, tool, pine, complete, in the rough (D-E) 28

Chest, tool, pine, early, 2 compartments, refinished (D-MW) 65

Chest, walnut, bracket feet, molding, 9 drawers, chain inlay, orig. brasses, signed "A.T. 1779" (A-E) 1550

Chest, walnut, 3-drawer, cut-out base, in the rough (A-E) 125

Chest-on-chest, captain's, pine, lift-top w/compartment, 2 sm. drawers, 1 secret; base has 1 lg., 2 med., & 3 sm. drawers w/locks, scalloped skirt on front, layered bun feet, refinished, 35" h., base 38" w. (D-MW).. 800

Chest-on-chest, Chippendale, curly maple, upper part w/fine molded top w/2 small, 3 med. & 3 lg. drawers, chamfered corners; lower part w/2 lg. drawers, chamfered corners & O.G. feet (A-E).. 2500

Chest-on-chest, Chippendale, walnut, double fluted corners, inlay on drawers, diamond inlay top & base, ogee feet, 5 drawers, 64" h., 21" d., 42" w. (A-E) 900

Chest-on-chest, walnut, overlapping drawers, 7 drawers top sec., 2 drawers base, line inlay on chamfered corners (A-E) 2900

Chiffonier, oak, hand carved, 5 large drawers, 14"×22" French bevel mirror, shaped top drawer & brass handles, top 21"×30" (D-MW)... 134

Child's armchair, ladder back, orig. finish worn smooth (A-E) 65

Child's armchair, ladder back, splint seat, 3 slats (A-E)... 32

Dutch cupboard, walnut, 2 parts, 6′ × 10″ × 35″ (A-E) $1900

Dutch cupboard, colorful orange-red painted decor., 2 parts, hinges replaced (A-E) $3700

Child's armchair, ladder back, turned finials, new seat, painted dark green (A-E) ....$ 85
Child's armchair, rush seat, early (A-E) 62
Child's armchair, Windsor, H-stretcher, duck bill (A-E)... 65
Child's armchair, Windsor, turned spindles, shaped legs, painted, 19th C. (A-MW) 50
Child's bed, brass, fancy w/large posts, 48″ l. (D-S) 250
Child's bed, old blue paint, w/patriotic child's coverlet, 29″ l. × 24″ h. (A-NE)...................... 1000
Child's bed, spool, maple, low post, refinished, complete (D-MW) 300
Child's blanket chest, pine, inside comp., refinished, 28″ l. (D-MW) 45
Child's blanket chest, stippled in red & yellow (A-E) 280
Child's blanket chest, walnut, 2 drawers, orig. bracket feet, 22″ l., 13″ d., 15″ h., dov. const. (A-E) .. 2000
Child's bureau, bird's-eye maple, 4-drawers w/brass pulls (D-E) 225
Child's bureau, walnut, 4 beaded drawers, flaring feet, apron & brasses restored, 24″ l., 13½″ d.,
  27″ h. (A-E)... 2500
Child's chair, Hitchcock, orig. black finish & stencil decor. good (D-NE) 95
Child's chair, Hitchcock, stencil decor. (D-NE) 85
Child's chair, ladder back, 18th C. (D-E).. 125
Child's chair, ladder back, rush seat (D-E) 250
Child's chair, ladder back, rush seat, cut out slat, arms, ca. 1760 (D-N)............................... 165
Child's chair, plank seat, green paint (D-E) 50
Child's chair, plank seat, 3 arrowback spindles (A-E) 40
Child's chair, primitive, rush seat & orig. decor. (A-E)... 52
Child's chair, primitive, shaped arms, heart cut out, lid & door restored (A-E) 95
Child's chair, rail back, Windsor, bamboo turnings, signed "Frazer", 12½″ seat height, red strip
  decor. (A-E)... 350
Child's chair, rocker, arrowback, orig. stenciling (D-MW)... 95
Child's chair, rocker, bentwood & wicker, fan shaped wicker back, wicker seat, spool turned legs,
  front stretcher (D-MW)... 175
Child's chair, rocker, Boston, cane seat, orig. finish, Vermont (D-E).................................... 75
Child's chair, rocker, Boston, cane seat, orig. finish, Vermont (D-MW)................................ 50
Child's chair, rocker, ladder back, arms, old finish worn smooth (A-E)................................ 200
Child's chair, rocker, maple, cane seat & back, 18th C. (A-E).. 75
Child's chair, rocker, plank seat (A-E) 55
Child's chair, rocker, plank seat (D-E) 55
Child's chair, rocker, plank seat, decorated (A-E).. 80

Child's chair, rocker, Boston, red w/white striping (D-E) ....$ 65
Child's chair, rocker, slat back, tiger maple & hickory, turned arms & finials (D-NE)............ 30
Child's chair, rocker, Vermont, cane seat, orig. red finish (D-MW)..................................... 50
Child's chair, rocker, Windsor, cheese-cutter type, good turnings, tiger stripe decor., back splat
    decor. w/3 apples & tray, 9½" seat height (A-E) 575
Child's chair, rush seat, orig. decor., primitive, miniature (A-E).. 52
Child's chair, rush seat, small (A-E)... 35
Child's chair, side, balloon back, plank seat, refinished (D-E) 200
Child's chair, side, Windsor, bow back, 7-spindle, bamboo turnings, saddle seat, 12½" h., good
    chamfer (A-E) 475
Child's chair, side, Windsor, comb back, maroon legs w/bulbous vase turnings, end posts w/bold
    vase turnings, 13" to top of saddle seat (A-E).. 1400
Child's chair, side, Windsor, 6-spindle, bow back, bamboo turned legs & stretcher, good seat,
    11½" h. (A-E).. 750
Child's chair, spindle, splat back, black, small (A-E) 35
Child's chair, Windsor, bamboo turnings, signed "Frazer", 12½" seat height, red stripe decor.
    (A-E) 350
Child's chair, Windsor, bow back, 7-spindle, bamboo turnings, saddle seat, 12½" h., all orig.
    (D-E) 400
Child's chair, Windsor, bow back, 7-spindle, bamboo turnings, 11½" h. (A-E)...................... 750
Child's chair, Windsor, 5-spindle, flared back, bamboo turnings, decor. on legs (A-E)........... 60
Child's chair, Windsor, orig. colors of blue, ochre & salmon, early (D-NE)........................... 350
Child's chest, pine, 3 drawers (A-E)... 25
Child's cupboard, Dutch, pine, one pc., orig. finish, step back, closed front, pegged (D-W)... 125
Child's cupboard, 4-shelf w/door below, decor. in burnt yellow & brown, 2 keys & nail painted on
    side, pine, 31½" w. × 53" h. (A-NE).. 800
Child's deacon bench, old green paint (D-E) 200
Child's dresser, 3-drawer, yellow pine, oval swivel mirror (D-E)... 95

Settle, pine,
ca. 1750 (D-NE) $2000

Child's highchair, arrow back (A-E).. 45
Child's highchair, arrow back, plank seat (D-E) 50
Child's highchair, black paint over old brown, sausage turned, dated 1789, 38" h. (A-NE)...... 1600
Child's highchair, Chippendale, ball & claw feet (A-E) 210
Child's highchair, fanback, 5-spindle, carved arms, H-stretchers, saddle seat (A-E) 240
Child's highchair, folding w/metal wheels, oak, refinished (D-MW) 150
Child's highchair, ladder back, early turnings, red paint, new split seat (A-E) 200

Chair, Windsor, decor., yellow ground, step-down back splat, bamboo turnings, 1 of a set of 6 (A-E) $1800

Windsor chairs, (A-E), *left to right:* **side chair,** comb back, 7-spindle, saddle seat, $275; **side chair,** bow back, 9-spindle, braced back, signed "E. Tracy," $575; **side chair,** comb back, 7-spindle, saddle seat, vase turnings, orig. old black paint, $400.

Child's highchair, maple, w/orig. finish, ca. 1810 (D-MW)	$ 225
Child's highchair, oak, w/cane seat (D-E)	45
Child's highchair, plank seat, scroll arms, modified arrow back, orig. decor. good (A-NE)	58
Child's highchair, rush seat & old red stain (D-E)	160
Child's highchair, split-seat, 35" h., unpainted (D-E)	115
Child's highchair, Windsor, bow back, yellow w/red & white striping, signed "I. C. Tuttle of Salem, Mass.", 33½" h. (A-E)	2000
Child's highchair, Windsor, New England, ca. 1770 (D-E)	180
Child's highchair, Windsor, New England, ca. 1770 (D-E)	195
Child's highchair, Windsor, old paint, bamboo turned legs, bulbous stretcher turnings (A-E).	775
Child's highchair, Windsor, pine, orig. finish, 19th C. (A-MW)	137
Child's potty-chair, old blue paint, high back, early (D-E)	385
Child's potty-chair, orig. grained paint (A-E)	45
Child's potty-chair, orig. grained mustard painted finish (A-E)	45
Child's potty-chair, pine (D-MW)	28
Child's potty-chair, pine, primitive, fireside style (D-E)	65
Child's potty-chair, traces of old yellow paint (A-NE)	185
Child's sideboard, walnut, ca. 1890 (D-NE)	110
Child's table, ice cream, w/4 chairs (D-E)	148
Child's table, ice cream, w/4 chairs, ex. cond. early (D-MW)	148
Child's wing chair, pine, shaped frieze over two slanting wings, 18th C., 24½" h. (A-MW)....	90
China cabinet, oak, corner, spiral fluted & twisted pillars, 35" wide front, 65" h., orig. finish (D-MW)	360
China cabinet, oak, hand carved w/lg. claw feet, swell-shaped glass in ends, 6' h., 4'6" w., orig. finish (D-MW)	455
China cabinet, oak, spiral fluted & twisted pillars, shaped glass in ends, 5'6" h., 3'6" w., orig. finish (A-E)	415
Church pew, oak, unfinished, 6' l. (D-S)	45
Church pew, pine, made from 18" boards, refinished, 39" l. (D-W)	169
Church pew, pine, refinished, 4' l. (D-W)	100
Coffee table, made from large pine bellows (D-W)	200
Commode, lift top, pine, door & drawer (A-E)	75
Commode, lift top, pine, 2-pc., small drawers in top sect., door in base (D-W)	90
Commode, oak, cast brass handles, drawer locks, hand carved (D-W)	137
Commode, oak, cast brass handles, drawer locks, serpentine fronts, orig. finish (D-S)	137
Commode, pine, refinished, all orig. (A-E)	155
Commode, pine, small, refinished, 2 spool towel rods (D-NE)	50

Commode, pine, w/red & black graining, gold stenciled decor., incls. splash board, drawer, ball feet, double tiered, 36" w. (A-NE) ....$ 375

Commode, pine w/tiger maple graining, 25" h. (A-E) 135

Commode, walnut, bow front, flower decor., 1 drawer & 1 door (A-E) 55

Cradle, cherry, hand windup rocker system, 18th C. (D-MW) 100

Cradle, cherry, heart & scalloping, dove tailed (D-E) 300

Cradle, hickory, ca. 1870 (D-S) 125

Cradle, hooded, dov. const., orig. paint & stenciling (D-MW) 135

Cradle, hooded, molded edges & robins' egg blue interior (A-NE) 175

Cradle, pine, birch posters, ca. 1780 (A-NE).. 2100

Cradle, pine, hand holes, shaped top, dov. const. (D-NE).. 45

Cradle, pine, hooded, painted side decor., 32" l., 18" w. at top (D-W)................................ 125

Cradle, pine, orig. finish, scalloped w/hearts & acorns (A-E) 180

Cradle, small, spindle (A-E)... 110

Cradle, walnut, canted sides, turned finials, heart cut outs in ends, 1 rocker repaired & reattached, 39" l. (A-E) 125

Cradle, walnut, hooded (A-E) 200

Crib, spool turnings, orig. dark finish, ca. 1850 (D-MW).. 135

Cupboard, bucket bench, all orig., old red paint (D-E) 575

Cupboard, cherry, primitive, orig. finish fine, 1 drawer, 2 doors, orig. lock & key (S-W) 310

Cupboard, cherry, 2 glass doors at top, 6 lights each, pie shelf, 3 drawers & 2 paneled doors below (D-E) 975

Cupboard, cherry, 2-pc., paneled doors, 2 drawers, pie shelf, 9 small paned doors, scrolled apron (D-E) 675

Cupboard, clothes, 2 doors over 2 drawers, dovetailed case, applied bracket foot, orig. decor. finish, Penna., ca. 1840 (D-E) 1450

Cupboard, corner, cherry, broken arch, all orig. (A-E) 1200

Cupboard, corner, cherry, broken arch, bracket foot, 12 panes, 2 drawers, 2 doors, 102" h., 42" wide (D-E)... 1200

Cupboard, corner, cherry, Kentucky-made, ca. 1820, 7'8" t. (D-S)..................................... 800

Cupboard, corner, cherry, scroll top w/3 finials arch door, molding-top piece; lower part w/2 doors, round feet, 45" w., 7'5" t., 26" d. (A-E) 2100

Cupboard, corner, cherry, top door w/12 panes, ogee molding; lower part w/2 doors, scalloped base w/bracket feet, 7'6" h., 46" w. (A-E).. 975

Cupboard, corner, cherry, 12 glass panes, orig. unfinished cond. (A-E) 975

Cupboard, corner, cherry, 2-pc. small panes in upper section (D-NW)................................ 750

Cupboard, corner, cherry, 2-pc., glass doors, Va., ca. 1800, 6' h., 3'4" w. (D-E)..................... 750

Cupboard, corner, cherry, 2-pc., top part w/2 oval doors & butterfly shelves; lower part w/2 drawers, 2 doors, bracket feet, all orig., 99" h., 56" w., 34" d. (A-E) 1750

Cupboard, corner, cherry, 2-pc., top w/2 arcaded doors, ea. door w/8 panes, "H" hinges; base w/3 drawers, 2 doors w/4 mirror panel ea. door, "H" hinges, bracket feet, scalloped apron, 72" h., 4'5" w. (A-E).. 3800

Cupboard, corner, cherry, unrestored, 6½' h. (D-N) 750

Blanket chest, pine, grain decor., New England, ca. 1800 (D-NE) $900

Stretcher table, walnut, removable top, feet restored, 60" × 32½" (A-E) $1300

Cupboard, open, pine, primitive, large (A-E) $950

Schoolmaster's desk, slant top, pine, w/drawer (A-E) $425

Cupboard, corner, crown molding, 12-pane glass door, fluted stiles & sunburst carving, 2 raised panel doors, bracket feet (A-E) ....$ 900

Cupboard, corner, grain painted, 2-pc., solid doors (D-NE)... 650

Cupboard, corner, grain painted, 2-pc., 12 panes of glass, 3 drawers in center, 2 doors at bottom w/cut-outs on feet, beveled doors w/simulated fan in ea. corner, ca. 1840-60 (D-NE) 1250

Cupboard, corner, hanging, cherry, fishtail, Maine (A-E)... 170

Cupboard, corner, hanging, pine, early, New England, 1 door w/2 raised panels, fitted molding across top, refinished, 36"×30" (D-MW) 490

Cupboard, corner, hanging, pine, H-hinges, in rough (D-MW)... 190

Cupboard, corner, hanging, pine, H-hinges, orig. finish, early 19th C., 14" w., 30" h. (D-W) .. 350

Cupboard, corner, hanging, pine, H-hinges, worn paint, 2-pc., orig. untouched finish good, Va. orig., 35½" h., 29½" w., 19" d. (A-E)... 375

Cupboard, corner, hanging, pine, paneled doors, 4 shelves, 32"×55", refinished (D-W).......... 300

Cupboard, corner, hanging, pine, raised panel, chamfered, fine molding w/drawers inside, 18"×21", orig. finish (D-E) 900

Cupboard, corner, hanging, pine, rat-tail hinges, orig. dark finish fair (A-E)...................... 475

Cupboard, corner, hanging, pine, stripped, unfinished 30"×30" (D-N) 225

Cupboard, corner, hanging, rare, butterfly shelves, 4 standard — 2 half size glass in door, molded base, 2 pilasters extending to crown molding (A-E) 4100

Cupboard, corner, hanging, walnut, blue-gray paint (A-E)... 300

Cupboard, corner, maple, 2-pc., solid paneled doors on top & base (A-E) 260

Cupboard, corner, old red paint, crown molding, 2-pc. 4 reeded quarter columns, beaded drawer, 2 raised panel doors, 12-pane glass door, patina, 7'8½" h. (A-E).. 2200

Cupboard, corner, orig. blue & mustard yellow, 2-pc., top w/two 8-pane glass doors; bottom w/2 panel doors, curved shelves, backboards, dovetailed & wedged (A-E)............................... 750

Cupboard, corner, orig. cond., arch door, glass & reeding, shaped shelves (A-E) 1100

Cupboard, corner, orig. red, feather swirled, painted finish, 2-pc., top w/9 pane glass door & 3 drawers; bottom w/2 paneled doors (A-E) 650

Cupboard, corner, pine, barrel back, butterfly shelves (D-MW)... 1400

Cupboard, corner, pine, 4 shelves over raised panel door, H & L hinges, Mass., ca. 1720, 7'7" h., 42" w., 13" d. (D-E) 575

Cupboard, corner, pine, glazed doors, carved button molding, large ogee bracket, chamfer, clover leaf shelves, 30" front, 6½' tall (A-E) 850

Cupboard, corner, pine, 1-pc. (D-E)..$ 595

Cupboard, corner, pine, orig. red paint, shaped shelves, top doors w/small glass panes; bottom door-wood, 84" h. × 46" w. × 26" d. (D-MW) 900

Cupboard, corner, pine, overhang molding, keystone & fretwork, 2 half moon doors, butterfly shelves, 2 doors lower sec., paneled sides & front, 59" w., 7'6" h. (A-E) 500

Cupboard, corner, pine (pumpkin), Penna. Dutch, 2-pc. (A-N).. 168

Cupboard, corner, pine, scroll top, base 1-door, fluted panels; top-arch door, fluted pillow flower type above door, 85" h., 41" w. (A-E).. 1150

Cupboard, corner, pine, 2-pc., base w/2 fine raised panel doors, top w/9 panes, old red finish, in the rough, Penna., ca. 1800 (D-E).. 800

Cupboard, corner, pine, 2-pc., H-hinges, 3 arcaded panes at top, 7'2" t. (D-E) 3500

Cupboard, corner, pine, 2-pc., paneled w/good orig. untouched finish, 49" w., 22" d., 82" h. (D-S) . 450

Cupboard, corner, pine, 2-pc., top part, 12-pane glass door, H-hinges; lower part, raised panel door, rat-tail hinges, dovetailed drawer, 7' h., 46" w. (A-E)... 1025

Cupboard, corner, pine, unfinished, 2-part, 12 panes glass (A-E)... 400

Cupboard, corner, pine & chestnut, 1-pc., blind front w/new paint inside (D-MW) 425

Cupboard, corner, small, 2-part, paneled door below, 6-pane door above, simple cornice, old dark worn finish, green interior, 77" h., 18½" d., 32" w. (A-E) 1025

Cupboard, corner, softwood, 2-pc., arcaded windows, 2 doors, lower sec., 82" h. (A-E) 525

Cupboard, corner, softwood, 2-pc., molding on top, 12 panes, raised panel door in base, bracket feet, 82" h., 43" w. (A-E) 525

Yarn winder, pine & maple, upright, adjustable, New England (D-MW) $55

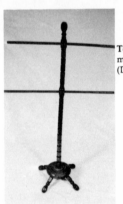

Towel rack, maple, refinished (D-MW) $39

Cupboard, corner, softwood, 2-pc., top part w/1 door w/12 glass panes; base w/2 doors, cut out apron, bracket feet, 7'×5' (A-E).. 700

Cupboard, corner, walnut, 1-pc., 4 single panel doors, H-hinges, in the rough, Penna., ca. 1800 (D-E) 900

Cupboard, corner, walnut, 1-pc., 1 door w/4 raised panels, rat-tail hinges, cut-out shelves, bracket feet, 29"×22"×67" (A-E) 875

Cupboard, corner, walnut, top w/raised panel doors, butterfly shelves, scalloped apron, cabriole legs & web feet, 6' h., orig. finish good (A-E) 750

Cupboard, crown molding, bracket feet, brass knobs, old blue paint, 26¾" h. (A-E).............. 700

Cupboard, Dutch, cherry, rat-tail hinges at top & base; upper part w/ogee molding, 2 doors w/nine panes each; lower part w/4 drawers w/2 mirror panel doors, champhered corners, solid ends, ca. 1750 to 1760, 59" w., 75" h. (A-E)... 4000

Cupboard, Dutch, cherry, 2 8-pane doors on top; 3 drawers over 2 doors on bottom, wooden "knob" pulls, all orig., Penna., ca. 1800, 90" h., 62" w., 22" d. (A-E) 1350

Cupboard, Dutch, cherry, 2-pc., top part w/2 paneled doors; base w/3 drawers & 2 doors, bracket feet (A-E) 600

Cupboard, Dutch, child's, early, top w/2 glass doors w/overhang molding, base w/3 drawers & 2 doors, bracket feet (D-E).. 350

Table, Sheraton-style, New
England ca. 1815 (D-NE)
$550

Windsor chairs, (A-E), *left to right:* side chair,
birdcage back, early red paint, $300; armchair,
bow back, vase turnings $650; side chair,
butterfly, $150

Footstool, walnut, in the
rough, w/few minor repairs,
Penna., ca. 1750 (A-E) $5300

Cupboard, Dutch, decor., w/orange, red & yellow, 2 parts, sunburst panels on doors, 3 beaded
drawers, 5 spice drawers, 2 glass doors w/6 panes each, crown molding (A-E) ....$ 8000
Cupboard, Dutch, keystone molding, 1770, w/A.D.B. & tulip decor. in sulphur inlay, 2 doors w/9
panes ea.; 2 doors w/raised panels, 3 drawers, H-hinges, bracket feet (A-E).......................10,000
Cupboard, Dutch, lower part, 2 paneled doors & 3 drawers; top part, crown molding & Sheraton
reeding, 2 6-pane each doors, 65″ w., 87″ h. (A-E) 900
Cupboard, Dutch, orange-red decor., top part, 2 6-pane doors, 3-pane arched center piece; lower
part, 2 drawers, 2 panel doors, bracket feet, 6′6½″ h., 58″ w. (A-E) 3700
Cupboard, Dutch, orig. red painted finish, 12-pane top w/pie shelf, lower part has solid ends w/2
doors & 2 drawers, Penna., ca. 1860 (D-E)... 950
Cupboard, Dutch, pine, early, top w/2 doors w/6-pane glass openings, spoon racks, cup & saucer
shelf, reeded base w/3 overlapping dovetailed drawers & 2 doors w/raised panels, partially
restored (D-NE)... 200
Cupboard, Dutch, pine, orig., center panel, 6′ l. (A-E) 1500
Cupboard, Dutch, pine, 2-parts, top part w/2 glass doors; lower part w/4 drawers, 2 doors, 68″ w.,
painted white on top, brown on base (A-E) 700
Cupboard, Dutch, poplar, single 9-pane glass door, 2 drawers, orig. bracket feet, spoon rack on
two shelves, dovetailed case, Penna., ca. 1800, 7′3″ t., 42″ w. (D-MW) 750
Cupboard, Dutch, primitive, old red paint, 1 pc., 4 paneled doors, molding around top (A-E) 1400
Cupboard, Dutch, softwood, orig. leaf & flower design on moldings & all doors, Penna., dated
1873 (A-E) 1600
Cupboard, Dutch, softwood, 2-pc., top part w/2 doors w/6 panes ea. door, lower part w/3 drawers,
2 doors, round feet, 4′2″ w., 20″ d., 7′4″ h. (A-E).. 750
Cupboard, Dutch, top, one 6-pane door; bottom w/1 panel door, 1 drawer, 47″ w., 77″ h. (A-E). 1500
Cupboard, Dutch, top part, 1 door w/9 pane glass, crown molding, lower part, 2 beveled drawers,
1 double sunken panel door, turned feet, 6′ h., 35″ w. (A-E).. 1900
Cupboard, Dutch, 2-pc., vertical ¾ columns, bracket feet, 2 paneled doors, 2 drawers, one 9-pane
glass door (A-E) 2700
Cupboard, Dutch, walnut, top part, two 9-pane glass doors & 5 drawers; base, 3 drawers, 2
paneled doors, chamfered corners, bracket feet, 59″ w., 76½″ h., slight restoration (A-E)..... 3100

Cupboard, Dutch, walnut, 2-pc., top fine molding, 2 doors, 12 panes, fluted stiles ea. side; base w/2 mirror paneled doors, bracket feet, 5 small drawers, 5'3" w., 69" h., 18" deep (A-E).......$ 445

Cupboard, Dutch, walnut, 2-pc., top part w/1 door w/9 panes; lower part w/2 drawers, 1 door, chamfered corners, 8'4" h., 3'8" w., 23" deep (A-E) 775

Cupboard, early, 1-pc., top sect., 2 doors w/iron bars, strap hinges, dovetailed drawers; base, 2 drawers & 2 doors w/strap hinges, ea. door has 8 raised panels, 14 raised panels on each end, 53½" w., 6'6" h. (A-E) 400

Cupboard, grained, 2 doors, 61" h., 4' w. (D-MW) 190

Cupboard, hanging, cherry, 34" w., 31" h. (A-E) 260

Cupboard, hanging, pine, cut-out shelf below, 1 door (A-E).. 190

Cupboard, hanging, pine, keystone molding, paneled, 1 door, 9 panes, solid panel & pie board (A-E) 170

Cupboard, hanging, pine, molded top, scalloped apron & shelf & double raised panel door, 48" l., 12" d., 11" w. (A-E) 275

Cupboard, hanging, pine, 1 door & 1 drawer, scalloped base & shelf (A-E) 275

Cupboard, hanging, pine, 1 double panel door, Penna., ca. 1850 (D-E)................................. 400

Cupboard, hanging, pine, orig. old red paint, leather hinges, 2 shelves, open back, flat top, early, 16½" h., 10" d., 24½" w. (D-NE)... 288

Cupboard, hanging, pine, raised panel door, dovetailed drawer, scalloped sides & base w/shelf, all orig., 23"×35½" (A-E) 550

Cupboard, hanging, pine, small w/glass door (A-E).. 55

Cupboard, hanging, rare, cut-out shelf, 1 drawer (A-E) 1850

Cupboard, hanging, raised paneled arch, panel decor. w/blue, red & flowers on door, date inside door, 1781, A. H. Blodd, old hdwe. (A-E) 850

Corner cupboard, hanging, maple, orig. mirror, small, 16½" l., 12¼" w. (D-MW) $100

Shelf, hanging, w/cherry tree & 2 cardinals observed by a cat standing near ladder at base, painted green, red & gold (A-NE) $300

Cupboard, hanging, raised panel door, large molding, old hardware, softwood, 36" h., 31" w. (A-E) 350

Cupboard, hanging, rat-tail hinges, raised panel door, 31"×29", walnut (A-E)...................... 300

Cupboard, hanging, shelf & cut out base, pine, 1-door (A-E) 150

Cupboard, hanging, walnut, 1 raised panel door, wrought H L hinges, 33" w., 39" l. (A-E)..... 240

Cupboard, jelly, Amish, pine, refinished (D-W)... 90

Cupboard, jelly, cherry, 2 dovetailed drawers top, 2 doors, ball feet, scalloped top, orig. finish fair (A-MW) 195

Cupboard, jelly, pine, 4 round screened air vents on sides, 2 drawers & 2 doors, refinished (A-MW) 185

Cupboard, jelly, pine, 2 dovetailed drawers, 2 doors, orig. red paint (D-MW) ....$ 200

Cupboard, jelly, pine, 2 drawers top, 2 doors below, 2" backboard, 4" holes on sides for vent., screened, refinished (D-MW) 225

Cupboard, jelly, pine, 2 drawers, 2 doors, paneled ends (A-E) 70

Cupboard, jelly, pine, 2 paneled doors, paneled ends, round turned feet, 54" h., 42½" w., 19½" d., orig. red paint (A-E) 500

Cupboard, jelly, solid ends w/back, 2 doors & 2 drawers, pine, Penna., ca. 1860 (D-E) 290

Cupboard, jelly, tiger maple, ca. 1830 (D-E) 585

Cupboard, kitchen, oak, 2 frosted glass doors above, 4 spice drawers, 2 long drawers below work surface, & 2 doors, refinished (D-MW) 275

Cupboard, linen, 1 double panel door, dovetailed case w/graduated shelves, orig. red finish, ex. cond., Penna., ca. 1820 (D-E) 950

Cupboard, linen, rat-tail hinges, old blue paint, bracket feet, all orig. (D-S) 975

Cupboard, linen, 2 double panel doors, chamfered corners, old iron hdwe., orig. red finish, Penna., ca. 1800 (D-E) 800

Dressing stand, tiger maple, 28" h. (A-E) $625

Dough trough, pine, on legs, dovetailed & pegged, refinished (D-MW) $265

Spice cabinet, maple, 12-drawer, orig. brass pulls, refinished, 17" × 14½" (D-MW) $150

Cupboard, maple, 1 pc., 2-door (A-E)... 180

Cupboard, milk, dovetailed pine case, 1 double panel door, Penna., ca. 1820 (D-E).............. 590

Cupboard, molded top & base, 2 mirror panels on 2 doors, old hdwe., 43" w., 13" d., 53" h. (A-E). 75

Cupboard, open, cherry, solid covered lower doors, 7' h. (D-S) 650

Cupboard, open cutout, rare, bottom drawer w/H-hinges, crown molding, ogee cutouts on sides shelves beaded, old red paint, 32½" w., 77" h., dated 1793 (A-E) 1500

Cupboard, open, pine, molding, 2 drawers, 6'1" h., 25" d., 39" w., ca. 1790 (D-NE) 475

Cupboard, painted & grained, Vermont, 2-part, ca. 1850 (D-E) 795

Cupboard, painted blue, orig., 2 doors, above & below, H-hinges (A-E)............................ 350

Cupboard, painted red & black, orig. finish, 2 pc., top w/3 double panel doors, pie shelf & spoon slots, base w/2 doors & 2 drawers, Penna. ca. 1840, ex. cond. (D-E).................................. 1200

Cupboard, painted red finish orig., 2 pc., top has single panel door, pie shelf, spoon slots; base w/2 doors & 3 drawers, Penna., ca. 1830 (D-E).. 875

Cupboard, pantry, large, old red paint (A-E) 150

Cupboard, Pa. Dutch, raised panel, 3-pc., decor. w/tulips & floral sprigs in orig. cond., 2 doors & 2 drawers above, 2 doors below, ca. 1750 (A-E).. 2300

Cupboard, pewter, dk. aged pine, 1-pc. 1 wide door at bottom, dovetailed top, flat molding surrounds open top, 38" w., 71" h. (D-W)...$ 575

Cupboard, pewter, early pine, open top w/3 shelves, alcove on extended base w/2 paneled doors (A-E) ....

Cupboard, pewter, pine, hutch top w/2 shelves, 2-door base, paneled door fronts, plank feet, 51¾" w., 50¾" d., 67½" h., 18th C. (A-MW) 400

Cupboard, pewter, hanging, scalloped on each side, tapered base, 3 shelves, 53"×34" (A-E) ... 150

Cupboard, pewter, N. Y., ca. 1800 (A-N) 975

Cupboard, pewter, open top, cherry, 2-pc., fine molding w/2 shelves; lower part w/2 doors & 2 drawers, scalloped base, bracket feet, 7'1" t., 6'3" w., base 23", desk top post 15" deep (D-E) 2850

Cupboard, pewter, pine, orig. old red paint fair, New Eng. orig. (A-E) 625

Cupboard, pewter, pine, orig., open top, 3 drawers & open shelf at bottom, 60" w., 7' h., ca. 1820 (D-N)... 825

Cupboard, pewter, pine, rosehead nails, orig. iron "HL" hinges, orig. finish, ca. 1765, 6' h., 48" w. (D-NE) 1200

Cupboard, pewter, pine, wide shelf at top, 7'×5½', orig. red paint (D-NE) 2200

Cupboard, pewter, softwood, 2-pc., scalloped side, base w/2 doors & 2 drawers (D-E)........... 850

Cupboard, pine, Dutch, base 56" w., 20" d. w/3 drawers & 2 doors (D-E) 650

Cupboard, pine, 4 grooved shelves over raised panel door, molded top, edge boards at front taper to top, 31" w., 13" d., 6'9" h. (D-NE).. 425

Cupboard, pine, graining in brown & ochre, shaped apron, 37" w., 15½" d., 44½" h. (A-NE). 500

Cupboard, pine, lower part has solid ends w/2 doors & 2 drawers; top w/2 single panel doors & pie shelf, stripped, unfinished, small, Penna., ca. 1850 (D-E) 750

Cupboard, pine, old green exterior & old red interior, 2 panel doors below & 2 double panel doors above, 51" w. × 19" d., 62" h. (A-NE) 1700

Cupboard, pine, old mustard yellow, primitive (A-NE) 295

Cupboard, pine, 1 door, fine molding, scrolled rat-tail hinges, 50" h., 26" w. (A-E)............... 260

Cupboard, pine, 1 door, raised panel door (A-E) 110

Cupboard, pine, 1-pc., double arched glass door, sq. fluted pillars, butterfly shelves, H hinges, 57" w., 8½' t. (A-E) 240

Cupboard, pine, 1-pc., top part scalloped out w/1 shelf, lower part, raised panel doors, h hinges, 3 raised panels on ea. side, 17½" d., 45½" w., 6'5" h. (A-E) 425

Cupboard, pine, orig. hdwe. & glass panes, stripped, 19th C., 42" w., 78" h., 16" d. (D-MW).. 290

Cupboard, pine, Penna. Dutch, shaped cornice, 2 arched panel doors, 1 long drawer, 2 bottom doors decor. w/carved cut-out heart, bracket feet, 86" h., 39½" w., 17" d. (A-MW) 925

Cupboard, pine, 2 doors over shaped aproned base, stepback top w/shelf & apron, orig. brown paint, Plymouth, Mass., ca. 1800, 31½" w., 50" h. (D-NE) 350

Cupboard, pine, Penna. Dutch, 2 doors w/12 orig. glass panes; 2 drawers & 2 doors in bottom part, ca. 1830 (D-MW) 995

Cupboard, pine, raised panel doors & sides, on frame (A-E) 280

Cupboard, pine, rat-tail hinges, bracket feet, 4 paneled doors, 1 pc., 74" h., 36" w., orig. finish ex. (D-MW) 1400

Cupboard, pine, shaped top over four shelves, H & L hinges, solid doors below, ca. 1780, 7'7" h., 42" w. (D-NE) 575

Cupboard, pine, small, early built, raised panel door, beaded frame & good molding, one interior shelf, 28½" h., 17¼" w., 22" l. (A-E)... 100

Cupboard, pine, step-back, keeping room, orig. cond., ca. 1820, 6'3", 5'6" (D-NE)................. 550

Cupboard, pine, tall & narrow, 1-door (A-E) 130

Cupboard, pine, 2 doors over aproned base, stepback top w/shelf, 31½" w. × 50" h. × 15" d. (D-NE) 325

Cupboard, pine, 2 dovetailed drawers, 2 raised panel doors, handwrought H hinges & paneled sides in the rough, 46½" × 56" (A-E)... 200

Cupboard, pine, 2 paneled drawers, 2 raised panel doors w/rat-tail hinges & old brasses, raised panel sides, molding top & base, 4' w., 54" h. (A-E).. 240

Cupboard, poplar, old varnish finish, early Va., paneled doors w/orig. H-hinges, fluting, dentil molding & good cornice, molding at bottom orig. part of bracket feet, 73½" t., 41" w., 17" d. (A-E) 525

Cupboard, poplar, pierced tin doors, 2 drawers dove., solid doors below, refinished (D-MW) 200

Cupboard, raised panel door, bracket feet, old hardware & red paint, 35"×53", 19" d. (A-E).... 140

Cupboard, raised panel door, rat-tail hinges, 1 drawer, walnut (A-E) ....$ 165
Cupboard, raised panel w/molded outline, 6 shelves in lt. green paint, 18th C. (A-NE) 200
Cupboard, secretary, set-back, pine, w/2 full & 1 split drawer below & 4 open shelves above, old
red paint w/black decor., 37½" w. × 77" t. (A-NE) 1100
Cupboard, small, Penna., decorated w/tulips, heart, urn & flowers; facial profile in green on
yellow ground (D-E) 1200

Welsh dresser, raised panel
doors, refinished, 71" h.,
47½" w. (A-E) $2800

Table, Country Queen Anne, pine oval
top, maple bass, pad feet (A-E) $725

Cupboard, spice, hanging, pine, Penna., 15 small drawers, brass knobs, scrolled brackets,
beaded crown molding, butterfly shelf, old blue paint, 23" h. × 13¼" w. (A-E) 2100
Cupboard, spice, pine, cornice, applied bracket foot, dovetailed case, 18th C., Penna., ca. 1830
(D-E) 850
Cupboard, step-back, closed front, pine, 1-pc., raised panel doors, orig. finish good, 18th C., 78"
h., 37½" w. (A-E) 450
Cupboard, step-back, open top, orig. blue paint w/3 shelves, 67" h., 34" w. (A-NE) 900
Cupboard, step-back, pine, w/tapered upper sect., interior in old green paint, 18th C., 6'8" h.
(A-NE) 2500
Cupboard, 3 shelves, old green, double raised paneled doors & sides, beaded shelves, end post
construction, shaped molding top & bottom (A-E) 475
Cupboard, wall, hanging, smoke grained pine, 2 double paneled doors, 2 small drawers below,
24½"×35" (A-E) 475
Cupboard, wall, 1-pc., fold out shelf, 3 drawers, cockbeaded frame, paneled sides match bottom
doors, graining removed to show orig. old yellow finish, 67½" h., 46½" l., 17¾" d. (A-E)... 750
Cupboard, wall, pine, dk, stained finish, 2 panel doors top, 2 drawers & 2 doors in base, 2-pc.,
Penna., ca. 1880 (D-E) 800
Cupboard, wall, pine, old red painted finish, paneled doors, pie shelf, 4 spice drawers, ogee feet,
84½" h., 44" w. (A-E) 1000
Cupboard, walnut, 8 pine panels in door, crown molding, 38" w., 56" h., good cond. (A-E).... 475
Cupboard, walnut, 1 door & 1 drawer, rat-tail hinges (door missing) (A-E) 35
Cupboard, water bench, pine & poplar, 18th C., 6' h. (D-E) 185
Cupboard, yellow pine, 2 doors on scalloped base, 18th C. (A-E) 795
Desk, butler's, cherry, ex. cond. (D-S).. 500
Desk, butler's, Mass., inlaid w/orig. eagle brasses (A-E) 2200
Desk, cherry, 4-drawers & 4 individual compartments, dated 1841 (A-E).............................. 400

Open cupboard, H-hinges, beaded shelves, dated 1793 on back, 77" h., 32½ w. (A-E) $1500

Chair table, shoe foot, orig. old red paint, 18th C., 44" diam., 28" h. (A-NE) $2750

Desk, Chippendale, cherry, 4 grad. drawers on bracket base, interior of 7 drawers over Queen Anne shaped apron & 3 cubbyholes, 38" w. × 43½" h. × 20" d., writing lid 31½" h., ca. 1730 (D-NE) ....$ 1850

Desk, clerk's, cash drawer, nat. pine (D-E) 340

Desk, country, pumpkin pine, 19th C., 50" h., 42" w. (D-NE) 855

Desk, empire secretary, curly maple, 2 pc., solid doors top (2), one drawer only below writing surface, turned legs, refinished (A-MW) 390

Desk, field, chestnut, 2-pc., ca. 1860 (A-E) 185

Desk, handmade, sits on table, religious motif, stenciling (D-NE) 70

Desk, lap, slant lid, early, wrought strap hinges w/shaped ends, ball feet, 18" l., 10½" d., 10" h. orig. finish (D-NE) 165

Desk, oak, flat top, drawer below writing bed, 4 side drawers, 42" l., refinished (A-MW) 65

Desk, oak, flat top, 4 drawers on each end, sliding arm rests, wooden pulls, 48" l., orig. finish (D-MW) 250

Desk, oak, hand carved drop leaf, pigeon holes & drawer inside, 1 lg. drawer w/cast brass handles & railing on top, 27" w. (D-W) 136

Desk, oak, 1 drawer, partitioned pigeon holes & 1 drawer inside, orig. finish (D-MW) 132

Desk, roll top, oak, arm rests, lock, 8-drawer, 50" h., 54" l., refinished (D-MW) 500

Desk, roll top, oak, 22 pigeon holes, solid oak writing bed, auto. lock, 8 drawers, 5' l., 50" h., refinished (D-MW) 700

Desk, on frame, stretcher base, slant top, old hardware, 6 sm. drawers (A-E) 60

Desk, paymaster, walnut, inlaid key holes, ca. 1840 (D-S) 500

Desk, school, w/solid top, pull out tray on one side, 4-drawers w/wooden handles (D-NE)..... 110

Desk, schoolmaster's, black paint, early 19th C. (D-E) 340

Desk, schoolmaster's, bookcase top, turned legs, mahogany, ca. 1840 (D-E) 390

Desk, schoolmaster's, drawer, round legs, cherry (A-E) 200

Desk, schoolmaster's, orig. black paint, early 19th C., New England (D-N) 340

Desk, schoolmaster's, pine, refinished (D-MW).. 185

Armchair, Windsor, butterfly, duckbill-type arms, acorn knobs on posts, converted from rocker matching side chair on right, pr. (A-E) $180

Library stool, walnut, primitive, legs heeled through top (A-E) $165

Desk, schoolmaster's, pine & cherry, secret drawer, swing-out shelf for ink bottle, ca. 1830 (D-E)$ 320

Desk, schoolmaster's, slant top, curly maple, square legs (A-E) 160

Desk, schoolmaster's, 2-pc., maple (A-E) 120

Desk, secretary, pine, rectangular upper sect. w/stepped frieze over 2 paneled doors (shelves, pigeonholes & slides), base sect. w/folding slanted writing surface, 3 long drawers, scroll bracket feet, wooden drawer pulls, 19th C., 37½" w., 19½" d., 77" h. (A-MW) 800

Desk, Sheraton, mahogany w/4 grad. drawers over bracket base, holly line inlay on drawers; 2 long drawers ea. side center door, 4 cubbyholes, dov. con., ca. 1790, 40" w. × 43" h. × 19½" d, writing lid 33" h. (D-NE) 1650

Desk, slant top, cherry, 4-graduated drawers, all orig. (D-NE) 2100

Desk, slant top, cherry, inside section finished w/bird's eye maple (D-S) 550

Desk, slant top, cherry, rare New Engl. style, on frame w/bookcase top w/scalloped apron on frame w/cabriole legs & ball & claw feet; desk w/4 graded drawers w/willow brasses & 2 slides, scalloped pigeon holes, sm. drawers; bookcase w/2 arched raised panel doors, 2 sliding candle stick holders w/broken arch top, carved rosette in center, flame finial, inside arch door has rising sun carving (A-E) 8900

Desk, slant top, Chippendale, cherry, ogee bracket feet, fluted quarter columns & overlapping drawers w/orig. bail brasses; interior w/stepped gallery w/2 rows of drawers, center drawer has carved sunburst w/conforming fluting flanked by 2 fluted half columns, writing height 32½"; 41¾" h. × 40" l. × 20½" w. (A-E) 3500

Desk, slant top, Chippendale, maple, w/orig. ogee bracket feet (A-E) 1700

Desk, slant top, Chippendale, Va. walnut, shaped ogee feet, cockbeaded dovetailed drawers & chamferred corners, interior w/serpentine arrangement of drawers & secret compartment, slant top missing, stand up writing height 42½"; 43" l., 23" w., 54½" h. (A-E)............................. 1700

Desk, slant top, Chippendale, walnut, w/fluted quarter columns, ogee feet, 32" writing height (A-E) 3000

Desk, slant top, mahogany, ca. 1800 (A-E).. 675

Desk, slant top, maple, orig. bracket feet & brasses, 4 graded overlapping drawers; 8 drawers inside, 8 pigeon holes, 2 half column upright drawers 36" w, writing height, 30½" (A-E) 1650

Desk, slant top, New England, primitive William & Mary style, maple, 3 lg. drawers w/willow brasses, 29" h., 15" d., interior w/4 step down drawers & pigeon holes (A-E) 275

Desk, slant top, William & Mary, on frame w/fine pigeon hole & drawer interior, base w/2 large drawers, turnip feet, all orig., rare (A-E).. 950

Desk, slant top, wood bookcase on top, cherry, top part w/molding, 2 mirror panel doors & 2 drawers; base w/4 drawers, French feet, scalloped, orig. brasses; 31" h. to writing board, 70" h. w/top of bookcase (A-E).. 1600

Desk, slant top, writing, maple, 4 drawers, bracket feet, shell carving, all orig., 41" w., 22" d. (A-E) 975

Desk, slant top, writing board, 4-graded drawers, fr. bracket feet, inlaid diamond pattern around base of molding, brass knobs, curly maple interior, arch panel door (A-E) 1500

Desk, surveyor's field, dov. const., carved top, eagle & shield decor. (A-E)........................... 40

Desk, travel, initials "M. D.", slant top, oak, carved, butterfly hinges, 15"×24" (A-E) 75

Desk, walnut, orig. finish, mint cond. (D-SW) ....$ 900
Dough bin, pine, covered, breadboard, in the rough (D-W) 45
Dough bin, pine, covered, breadboard, refinished (D-MW)... 90
Dough cupboard, oak, spice drawers above roll back top, breadboard work top, two storage bins
below, ref. (D-S)... 300
Dough cupboard, oak, storage bins, roll top w/slide out board (A-NE)............................... 350
Dough trough, cherry, w/legs, dovetailed, turned legs, orig. finish ex. (D-E) 425
Dough trough, maple, w/legs, dovetailed, legs pegged to frame, refinished (D-MW)............. 300
Dough trough, maple, w/legs, 1-pc., set in legs & ends, sliding top, 33" h., 38" l., refinished
(D-MW) 390
Dough trough, pine, w/legs, dovetailed box, orig. dark finish good, ca. 1840 (D-N)............... 325
Dough trough, pine, w/legs, dovetailed box, turned legs, 1-pc., orig. dark finish, Penna. Dutch,
ca. 1840 (A-NE) 355
Dough trough, pine, w/legs, dovetailed, 1-pc., tapered & splayed legs pegged to frame, refinished
(D-MW) 400
Dough trough, pine, w/legs, dovetailed, turned legs, refinished, ex. cond. (D-E)................... 295
Dough trough, pine, w/legs, dovetailed, turned splayed legs, orig. grained finish good, but top
worn down (D-NE) 390
Dough trough, pine, w/legs, grained finish, buff & brown, good, one piece, pegged legs,
dovetailed box (A-E) 457
Dough trough, pine, w/legs, orig. old dk. red finish fair, sq. tapered legs (D-N) 200
Dough trough, pine, w/legs, orig. red finish good, scrubbed top, dovetailed box, sq. tapered legs
worn (D-NE)... 195
Dough trough, pine, w/legs, tapered sq. legs, warped top, small, refinished (D-MW) 160

Rocking armchair, rabbit ear, comb
back & cutouts in old red paint
(A-NE) $325

Chairs, arrow back, redecor., 2 from set of 6 (A-E) $540

Dough trough, pine, w/legs, turned cherry legs, pegged to frame, refinished (D-S)................ 175
Dough trough, pine, w/legs, sliding top supported by butterfly swinging leg, rare shape, re-
finished (D-W).. 335
Dough trough, turned & splayed legs, orig. red painted finish worn smooth, large (D-S) 145
Dough trough, lift top, dovetailed, orig. black painted finish worn, small (D-MW)................ 65
Dough trough, lift top, pine, dovetailed, traces of orig. red paint (D-E) 165
Dough trough, orig. red painted finish good, 36" l., handle grips (D-MW) 75
Dough trough, pine, hand hwen, 30" l., handle grips on each end (D-SW) 35

High chest of drawers,
walnut, 63″ h., 21½″ d., 41″
w. (A-E) $2400

Low chest of drawers, Chippendale, walnut, all orig., 35″ h., 36″
w., 19″ d. (A-E) $3300

Dough trough, pine, dovetailed box, small, refinished, 20″ l. (D-NW) ....$ 90

Dresser, oak, bevel mirror, cast brass handles, drawer locks, serpentine front, dresser top, 24″×50″ (D-S) 134

Dresser, oak, bevel mirror, top, 20″×46″ (A-E) 122

Dresser, oak, hand carved, bevel mirror, brass handles, drawer locks, serpentine front, top 21″×44″, orig. finish (D-W) 170

Dresser, oak, hand carved, 24″×30″ French bevel mirror, drawer locks, cast brass handles, top drawers w/swell front, top 21″×44″ (D-W) 127

Dresser, pewter, pine, 2-pc., open top, step back, w/molding flush to floor; cornice moulded top w/3 drawer & 2 compartments below, old brown paint, 66″ w. × 83″ h. (A-NE) 1100

Dresser, pine, 4 drawers, 3 doors, fine orig. cond., New England, ca. 1780, 7′ h., 5½″ w., top 11″ d., base 22″ d. (D-E) 2500

Dresser, pine, 2 raised panel doors & 2 drawers in base, top w/½ moon overhang scalloping & spoon rack, refinished, 47½″ w., 71″ h. (A-E) 2800

Dresser, Welsh, pine, 1-pc., open, deep scalloping, cut-out curved spoon rack, base w/2 raised panel doors, rat-tail hinges, bracket feet, 38″ w., 16″ d., 68½″ h. (A-E) 2600

Dressing table, oak, ladies′, hand carved, shaped drawer w/cast brass handles, 14″×22″ French bevel mirror, ornamental, top 16″×32″ (D-MW) 125

Dry sink, cherry, splash board, 1 door, refinished, ca. 1860 (D-E) 350

Dry sink, cherry, splash board back, 1 drawer, dovetailed, two doors, refinished (D-NE) 280

Dry sink, chestnut, tall, w/3 drawers & 2 doors on top; 2 drawers in bottom (D-E) 675

Dry sink, corner, orig. mustard paint, 28″ h., 27½″ w., 18″ d. (center) (D-W) 750

Dry sink, Hepplewhite, pine, orig. green paint & hdwe. w/plank door & inset molded top, 44″ w. × 19″ d. (A-NE) 450

Dry sink, high back, dovetailed base w/2 doors & 2 drawers; top w/2 shelves, orig. red finish, Penna., ca. 1825 (D-E) 500

Dry sink, oak, high back, 3 drawers across top, shelf at center, well w/drawer at side & 2 drawers below (A-E) 200

Dry sink, high back, Pa., orig. red stain, candle drawer & 2 doors below (D-NW) 375

Dry sink, high back, 3 spice drawers, stripped, ready for refinishing, Penna., ca. 1825 (D-E) . 400

Dry sink, lift top, dov. const., high bracket foot & skirt, orig. red/blue/green finish, Penna., ca. 1840 (D-E) 650

Dry sink, lift top, pine, 1 drawer, 2 doors, refinished, 38″ w. (D-W) 150

Dry sink, lift top, pine, 2-pc. (A-E) 325

Dry sink, low, w/scalloped back rail, 2 paneled doors & drawers (A-E) ....$ 135
Dry sink, pine, 5″ deep well w/3 deep grooves & drain hole, flared sides, top not joined to base, w/1
shelf, closed front, refinished (D-W).. 390
Dry sink, pine, in the rough, four center drawers, door on each side, 48″ l. (D-MW) 285
Dry sink, pine, 1 drawer to right of well, grooved w/drain center, refinished (D-W).............. 290
Dry sink, pine, orig. finish good, 7 storage drawers at top of back board, 2 doors below sink (D-S) . 390
Dry sink, pine, orig. old blue paint, H-stretcher incomplete, 45″ l. × 22½″ 2. × 29″ h. (A-E) .. 275
Dry sink, pine-poplar, 34″ l., two doors, ref. (D-MW)... 200
Dry sink, pine, rectangular galleried top over 2 doors, bracket feet, 19th C., 42½″l., 16¼″ d., 31″ h.
(A-MW) 200
Dry sink, pine, small, 1 door, pegged, refinished (D-MW) 225
Dry sink, pine, splashboard & 5 small drawers across top, two doors below well, refinished
(D-NW)... 850
Dry sink, pine, unfinished, 2 doors, 42″ l., 19½″ d. (A-W) 35
Dry sink, pumpkin pine, bootjack shaped feet, solid plank doors, ca. 1800 (D-E) 260
Dry sink, poplar, orig. finish, two doors, ca. 1880 (D-MW) 75
Dry sink, poplar, 2 drawers w/wood pulls, 2 doors below sink (D-W)................................ 150
Dry sink, 2 doors below, backboards repaired, orig. deep brown finish, Penna. origin, 37″ w., 41″
h., 15″ d. (D-E).. 280
Dry sink, waterbench, Pa. pine, 2 cupboard doors bottom sec., deep brown color, 37″ w., 41″ h.,
15″ d. (D-NE) 375
Flour bin, pine, Penna. Dutch, orig. finish, slant top, ca. 1830 (D-E) 260
Flour bin, slant top, 2 doors at base for utensils, refinished (D-W) 100
Footstool, curly maple (A-E)... 65
Footstool, decor. w/white & red daisy design, 3-legged (A-E) 150
Footstool, early, oblong, finished (D-W) 45
Footstool, early, round, in the rough (D-W) 30
Footstool, figure eight, 4-legged (D-E) 55
Footstool, inlaid design (A-E).. 15
Footstool, maple, heeled through top w/drawer (A-E) 32
Footstool, miniature, old green paint, 4¼″ h. (A-NE) 100
Footstool, oblong, orig. blue paint (D-W) 30
Footstool, small, decorated (A-E)... 42
Footstool, tiger maple, 1 drawer, curved legs, heeled through top (A-E)............................ 160
Footstool, walnut (A-E)... 25
Frame, mirror, walnut, Chippendale (A-E) 85
Frame, picture, curly maple, flat, orig. finish, 16″×17½″×2½″ (D-E)................................. 50
Frame, picture, curly maple, inside measurement 10″×8¼″ (A-E) 30
Frame, picture, curly maple, inside measurement 12″×14″ (A-E) 35
Frame, picture, grain painted 18″×23″×2″ (D-NE) 45
Frame, picture, pine, hand carved, 8½″×12″×2″ (D-E) 28
Frame, picture, pine, oval, stripped of plaster-of-paris decor. & refinished, 15½″×22″×3″ (D-MW) 38
Frame, picture, pine, shadow box type, refinished, 12″×14″×3″ (D-MW) 24
Frame, picture, walnut, brass liner, 27″×37″ (A-MW)... 36
Frame, picture, walnut, oval, approx. 8″×12″×2″ (D-E)... 15
Frame, picture, walnut, 10″×14″ (D-E).. 25
Frames, picture, bird's-eye maple, 16½″×21″×5″, pair (D-W)... 125
Hall tree, oak, hand carved, 16″ circle French bevel mirror, 4 double hat hooks, umbrella holder,
seat w/lid for rubbers, 78″ h., 38″ w. (D-MW) 230
Hall tree, oak, hand carved, 16″×26″ German bevel mirror, 4 double hooks & umbrella holder, seat
w/lid for rubbers, 6′8″ h., 37″ w. (D-W)... 180
Hall tree, oak, hand carved, 18″×26″ French bevel mirror, 4 lg. double hat hooks, umbrella holder,
lid to seat, 6′ h., 3′2″ w. (D-W) 280
Hall tree, oak, hand carved, 18″×40″ French bevel mirror, umbrella holder, 4 double hooks & lid to
seat, 6′10″ h., 3′ w. (D-W) 167
Hall tree, oak, hand carved, 24″×30″ French bevel mirror, 4 lg. double hat hooks, umbrella holder,
seat w/lid for rubbers, 7′2″ h., 3′9″ w., orig finish (A-E)... 295
Hall tree, oak, hand carved, 34″×38″ French bevel mirror, 4 double hat hooks, seat w/lid for
rubbers, 7′ h., 4′6″ w. (D-MW).. 300

Highboy, Chippendale, base w/cabriole legs, 4 drawers & old brasses (A-E) ....$ 220
Highboy, mahogany, Queen Anne bonnet type (A-E)... 775
Highboy, maple w/fan, 5'10" (D-S) 4500
Highboy, maple, orig. finish & hdwe., ca. 1770 (A-NE) 1250
Highboy, Queen Anne, low boy base w/2 long drawers, swastika carved center; top part w/2 sm. drawers each side w/swastika carved sq. drawer in center & 3 lg. drawers, 74"h., 19" d., 37" w. (A-E) 1450
Highboy, maple, Queen Anne, small, refinished (D-NE).. 3200
Highboy, tiger maple, Queen Anne, New England, orig. brasses, cabriole legs w/lg. pad ft., ca. 1740, 5'8" h., 40" w., 21" d. (D-E) 10,500
Highboy, walnut, Queen Anne, fan carved drawer, tear drop, 35" h., 31½" d., 38" w. (A-E) ... 275
Hour glass, oak, 2-hour, mounted (A-E) 300

Dry sink, pine, pegged, small, refinished 27½" h., 30" w. (D-MW) $300

Apothecary chest, oak, orig. pulls, dated 1904, refinished (D-MW) $200

Cupboard, jelly, pine, 4" diam. screen holes on side for ventilation, small, refinished (D-MW) $225

Icebox, oak, handsomely carved exterior, 48" h., brass hdwe., refinished (D-MW)................. 125
Icebox, oak, in the rough, metal hdwe., 40" h. (A-MW) 20
Icebox, oak, large, brass hdwe., refinished (D-W)... 150
Icebox, oak, orig. finish good, 45" h. (D-N).. 48
Icebox, oak, porcelain castors, polished brass hdwe., refinished (D-MW) 75
Ice chest, oak, lift top, refinished (D-W) 68
Kas, molding on top & base, 2 raised panel doors, rat-tail hinges, 2 drawers, old brasses, old red & green paint (A-E) 600
Kas, pine, large, 2 doors w/butterfly hinges, mirror panel sides & doors, 2 drawers, bracket feet (A-E) 475
Kas, poplar w/orig. red paint, Penna. Dutch (D-SE)... 650
Kas, softwood, 1-6 panel door & lg. drawer, ogee feet, 39" w., 20" d., 6'2" h. (A-E)............... 180
Kas, softwood, 2 parts, quarter columns on corners, 2 raised panel doors w/rat-tail hinges; lower part w/2 drawers on molded base (A-E) 575
Kas, walnut, overhang molding, fluted corners, 2 raised panel doors, 3 sm. & 1 large drawer, O.G. feet, 10" h. overall dim. 8'1" h., 20" deep, 4'3" w. (D-A) 2000

Kas, walnut, 2 raised panel doors, H-hinges, 7 drawers, ogee feet, panel sides, 7'1" w., 2' d., 8" h. (A-E) ....$ 825

Kas, William & Mary style, curly maple, 3-sect., overhang ogee molding, 2 raised panel doors, set-on panels on doors & corners, 2 small & 1 lg. drawer w/willow brasses & large turnip feet, rare (A-E) 3400

Kitchen safe, pine, pegged panel doors on front round, screened side vents, refinished, 75½" h., 68½" w., ca. 1865 (D-MW) 290

Kitchen safe, poplar, 6 pierced tin panels in top, 2 drawers, 2 doors base (1-pc.), orig. finish good (D-MW) 300

Kitchen safe, walnut, glass doors above, solid panel doors below, round 4" holes on sides for ventilation, refinished (D-MW)... 375

Kitchen safe, yellow pine, screen 4" round holes on sides for ventilation, 2 drawers, 2 doors below, unfinished (A-MW) 65

Linen press, early, primitive, refinished, 14½" d., 70" t., 42" w. (D-E) 2800

Linen press, pine, painted (D-NE) 265

Linen press, pine, 2-pc., 2-doors in top sect., 5 drawers in bottom sect., orig. brass hdwe., ca. 1790, 6'7" h., 42" w. (D-S) 575

Linen press, pine, 2 raised panel doors, rat-tail hinges, sq. fluted legs, orig. paint (A-E)........ 410

Linen press & wardrobe combination, walnut, top part, 2 panel doors, 2 small drawers; lower part, 4 lg. drawers, French feet, 66" w., 92" h., ex. cond. (A-E).. 925

Mantel, carved, fluting & dentil molding, 51" w., 62" h., fireplace opening 3×3 (A-E)............ 82

Mantel, New Jersey, large, (in the rough), 18th C. (A-E) 180

Mirror, carved, pine, motifs include primitive lion, fish, leopard, figure w/mandolin, etc., 19th C., 12"×14" overall, 30" h. (A-NE) 95

Mirror, Constitution, 2-panel, upper panel w/églomisé landscape painting, orig. Hitchcock stencil decor., signed (William Goodwin, maker, Auburn), 19th C., 22½" h., 11" w. (A-MW). 155

Mirror, courting, painted w/gold & red spotted decor., w/19th C. watercolor silhouette, 18th C. (A-NE) 525

Mirror, empire, pine, 2-panel, upper section w/seascape, painted, 30" h., 13½" w. (A-MW).... 70

Mirror, federal, round w/eagle, ca. 1830 (A-NE) 170

Mirror, federal, small w/reverse painting of ship, frame decor. in red & yellow marbleized graining (A-NE) 450

Mirror, grained frame, reverse painting above w/lake & trees (A-E)...................................... 110

Mirror, hand, primitive (D-NE) 48

Mirror, painted black frame, 18th C., 11"×13¼" (A-NE) 180

Mirror, pine frame, mortised & pinned, 10"×13" (D-E) 55

Mirror, pewter case w/embossed eagle, small, round, 2¾" d. (A-E) 120

Mirror, Queen Anne, mahogany, gold leaf, scroll base, carved flowers & leaves, scroll top w/Phoenix bird (A-E) 1300

Mirror, shaving, pine, Chippendale, drawer, dov. const. (D-E)... 95

Mirror, shaving, hand type, magnifying, turned handle, tin backed, 19th C. (D-NE) 40

Mirror, shaving, on stand, primitive (A-E)... 50

Mirror, shaving, tiger maple & cherry frame, swinging type w/single drawer in base, 21" h., 16" w. (D-MW) 125

Mirror, shaving, 2 drawers (A-E) 65

Mirror, thick pine frame, rectangular, wood pegs, 10½"×13½" (D-NE) 60

Mirror, tiger maple grained frame, 17½"×24½", good cond. (A-E) 240

Mirror, tiger stripe frame (A-E) 225

Mirror, wall, Chippendale (A-E)... 375

Mirror, wall, Chippendale, walnut frame, all orig., label on back, 21"×13" (A-E) 285

Mirror, wall, curly maple frame (A-E) 175

Mirror, wall, Empire, mahogany frame (A-W) 27

Mirror, wall, Federal w/reverse painting of ship, frame decorated in red & yellow marbleized graining (A-NE) 450

Mirror, wall, mahogany frame w/reverse painting on glass of lake & farm scene (A-E)........... 110

Mirror, wall, pewter frame, circular w/ring for hanging, 4⅛" diam. (D-NE)............................ 675

Mirror, wall, pine, 19th C., 18"×25" (A-MW)... 50

Mirror, wall, pine, 19th C., 19"×14" (A-MW)... 60

Mirror, wall, pine, 19th C., 21"×30" (A-MW)... 80

Mirror, wall, Queen Anne, curly maple frame, scalloped top, 19″×53″ (A-E) ....$ 475
Mirror, wall, Queen Anne, small (A-E) 150
Mirror, wall, reverse painting on glass, girl & swan at lake (A-NE) 40
Mirror, wall, reverse painting on glass, grained frame (A-E) 140
Mirror, wall, reverse painting on glass, houses & birds in trees scene, green & yellow background (A-E) 75
Mirror, wall, reverse painting on glass, houses, birds, trees w/green & yellow background, mahogany frame (A-NE).. 75
Mirror, wall, reverse painting on glass of schoolhouse & trees (A-E) 70
Mirror, wall, Sheraton, reverse painting on glass, fluted frame (A-E)............................... 110
Mirror, wall, Sheraton, reverse painting on glass, girl holding wreath of flowers & standing by tree, mahogany frame (A-E) 160
Mirror, wall, Sheraton, small w/painting on glass (A-E) 105
Mirror, wall, Sheraton, 2-part, carved mahogany frame (A-E).. 60
Mirror, wall, 38 carved stars on frame, black paint (A-NE) 60
Mirror, wall, tiger stripe frame (A-E) 25
Nightstand, Hepplewhite, cherry, dovetailed drawers, square legs, 16½″×16½″×27″ (A-E)..... 275
Panel, from blanket chest, framed wood, decor. w/motifs: tulips, lions, distelfinks, hearts (A-E) . 200
Pie safe, butternut, pierced tin panels, w/lacy bellflower & vine, refinished, ca. 1840 (D-E) 275
Pie safe, cherry, pierced tin front panels & side, 1 drawer below, refinished (D-MW)........... 200
Pie safe, cherry, pierced tin side panels & front, good, refinished (D-MW).......................... 265
Pie safe, curly maple, pierced tin doors & side panels, ex. cond., 2 drawers above, in the rough (D-E) 400
Pie safe, heart & blazing sun pattern, ca. 1800-20 (A-E) 300
Pie safe, pine, lift top, two doors w/pierced tin panels w/sugar & creamer (rare), refinished, 6′2″ h., 40″ w. (D-W).. 400
Pie safe, pine, 1 drawer top, solid ends, pierced tin front panels good (D-E) 195
Pie safe, pine, pierced tin front & sides, drawer below dovetailed, painted white finish (A-MW) 25
Pie safe, pine, pierced tin front & side panels, sunburst, two drawers, dovetailed at top (D-E).. 225
Pie safe, pine, pierced tin front & side panels, tulips & hearts, 1 drawer below, dovetailed, refinished (D-MW) 185
Pie safe, pine, pierced tin front w/sugar & creamer (rare), solid ends, lift top, drawer below, refinished (D-SW)... 400
Pie safe, pine, wooden grill front (rare), refinished, 60″ h., 38″ w. (D-S)............................ 375
Pie safe, pine, solid ends, 2 drawers above two pierced tin panel doors, good & orig., refinished (D-MW) 295
Pie safe, pine, 2 drawers, pierced tin panels new, refinished (D-S) 80
Pie safe, poplar, 8 pierced tin panels, dark, refinished (D-SW) 100
Pie safe, poplar, pierced tin panels w/star, refinished (D-MW)... 90
Pie safe, walnut, Penna., 2 doors, pierced tin below 1 full-width drawer, 37″ w., 46″ h.; 13″ deep (D-E) 250
Pie safe, walnut, 2 doors, pierced tin, single full-width drawer below, 37″ w., 46″ h., 13″ d. (D-NE). 235
Plate rack, hanging, w/scalloped ends, orig. paint (A-E) 75
Screen, fire, mahogany, cabriole legs w/carved knees, pad feet, oblong screen covered w/red felt w/crewel work of peacock feathers & flowers, 18th C. (D-NE) 295
Secretary/bookcase, pine, 2 glass doors & drop front desk in upper section, two doors below, pegged, early, refinished (D-E)... 1200
Secretary/bookcase, pine, 2 paned doors above orig., drop front w/2 drawers & pigeonholes, two doors in base section, pegged, orig. dark finish ext., cream painted int. (A-MW)......... 200
Secretary, grained yellow paint good, Vermont origin, 2-pc. glass panes top, orig. (D-E) 950
Secretary, maple & pine, upper part w/shaped corners, 2 panel doors, 2 shelves; lower part w/fold-top writing surface, 1 drawer, sq. tapering legs, 19th C., 26¼″ w., 16¾″ d., 61½″ h. (A-MW) 425
Secretary, pine, pegged, cathedral panel doors w/orig. panes, refinished, early (D-MW)......... 650
Secretary, slant top, pegged, walnut & pine, brass pulls, refinished (D-N) 550
Secretary, sleigh front, pine, w/cathedral panel doors above, fine graining (A-NE) 525
Secretary, tiger maple & cherry, Mass., all orig. ex. cond. (A-E)... 3500
Server, country, Hepplewhite, curly maple top w/breadboard ends over 1 long & 2 short drawers, tapered legs w/shelf between, ca. 1780 (D-NE) 435

Server, pine, paneled, 3-drawer & 2 door (A-E) ....$ 150

Server, Queen Anne, oak, single drawer, shaped aprons over flat sided cabriole legs, drake feet,
    Chippendale brass, top 30½″ w., 32½″ h., 17½″ d. (D-NE) 595

Settee, arrowback, large, orig. decor., 8-legged, 6′7″ l., 20½″ d. (D-E).................................... 1400

Settee bed, maple, combination settee & double bed, primitive, pegged, rare (D-MW) 500

Settee, bent arrowback, w/orig. graining, floral decor., rush seat, arm spindles (A-E) 375

Settee, black paint w/orig. stenciling on back, des. on seat, 8′ 1. (A-E) 195

Settee, half-spindle back, green flowers decor. (A-E) 180

Settee, half-spindle, decor., needs repair (A-E) 57

Settee, half-spindle, heart cut-outs, deep plank seat (A-E).. 260

Settee, Hitchcock, orig. cond., incl. rush seat & decor. (A-E) 575

Settee, lyre back, orig. decor., 72″ l. (A-E) 425

Settee, lyre back, Penna. floral decor., orig. (A-E) 300

Settee, Mammy's, pine, hickory, oak & maple, spindle back w/shaped spindle arms, H-stretchers,
    oak rockers, 42″ l. (A-MW) 360

Settee, spindleback, painted green (D-E) 850

Settee, Windsor, arrowback, 25 spindle, painted light green (A-E) 375

Settee, Windsor, low back w/deep plank seat, orig. (A-E).. 650

Settee, Windsor, minor repair, 60″ l., 37″ h. (A-E) 1450

Settee, Windsor, plank seat, stick back, butterfly top rail, 8 leg (D-E) 650

Settee, Windsor, 30-spindle, 8-legged (A-E) 410

Settle, New England, orig. blue paint (D-E) 1200

Settle, pine, New England, orig. blue paint (D-E) 1250

Settle, pine, orig. finish good, 44″ h., seat 46½″ l. (D-MW) 300

Settle, pine, paneled back w/orig. finish (D-MW).. 650

Sewing box, oak, lift top, 2 drawers below, sm. brass pulls, orig. finish good, 11½″ sq., 10″ h.
    (D-MW) 48

Shelf, jigsaw cut, cherry tree, 2 cardinals, cat near ladder at base of tree; orig. painted finish,
    signed & dated 1875 (A-NE)... 300

Shelf, wall, large scallop cut out (A-E) 525

Shelf, wall, 2 cut-out stars & scalloped front, ex. cond. (A-E) 1600

Shelf, wall, 2-tier, old blue decor. (A-E) 650

Shelf, whatnot, corner, 5-shelf, walnut (A-E) 130

Shoemaker's table, pine, from Amana Colonies, rect. top, three quarter gallery over frieze, 2
    drawers, trestle shelf base, 34″ w., 16″ d., 21½″ h., 19th C. (A-MW) 250

Shuttle, weaving, signed & dated 1795, 11″ (D-N) 32

Sideboard, butler's, tiger maple, New Hampshire, ca. 1790, 48″ w., 19″ d. (D-NE).................. 2500

Sideboard, Hepplewhite, fan inlay w/brasses all over inlaid (A-E) 800

Sideboard, oak, hand carved, 18″×40″ oval French bevel mirror, cast brass handles, lower doors &
    top drawers w/swell front, velvet-lined drawer, top, 25″×48″ (D-W) 255

Sideboard, oak, 18″×40″ French bevel mirror, 2 sm. drawers, 1 partioned & lined for silverware, 1
    long drawer, 2 doors in base (A-E)... 227

Sideboard, oak, 16″ × 44″ French bevel mirror, 1 long drawer, 3 sm. drawers, double closet in base,
    4′6″ w., 5′1″ h. (D-W) 220

Sideboard, Sheraton, mahogany, fluted base, 4 doors & 3 drawers, rail top (A-E).................. 150

Sideboard-china cabinet, oak, bevel mirror, cabinet w/lg. glass door & glass ends, adj. shelves;
    sideboard w/swell front, 2 drawers & 2 doors, brass handles, orig. finish (D-MW).............. 225

Sideboard-china cabinet, oak, French bevel mirrors, shaped base w/swell front, 6′6″ h., orig.
    finish (D-W) 285

Sideboard-china cabinet, oak, glass in top, 12″×44″ French bevel mirror; 4 drawers w/swell front,
    cast brass handles, drawer locks, 5′10″ h. (D-MW).. 200

Spinning wheel, all orig. (D-N) 185

Spinning wheel, fine turnings, unpainted, signed, "PW", ex. cond. (A-E) 310

Spinning wheel, high, good turnings, connecting rod restored (A-E).................................... 425

Spinning wheel, large wheel, complete, refinished (D-N) 280

Spinning wheel, maple, ex. cond., early 19th C. (D-NE) 250

Spinning wheel, rare, good cond., green, yellow, white & brown paint (A-E) 450

Spinning wheel, restored (D-N) 170

Spinning wheel, small bobbin, orig. finish, complete (D-MW) 225

Cabinet, hanging, oak, 1-drawer, dovetailed frame, small, refinished, 16¼" h., 9¾" w. (D-MW) $90

Chest-on-chest, Chippendale, curly maple, chamfered corners, ogee feet, rare (A-E) $2500

Spoon rack, pine, chip carved, Penna. Dutch, w/8 unmarked pewter spoons, early (D-MW) ...$ 250
Spoon rack, pine, 8 carved slots for spoons, hanging, orig. dark finish, 18th C. (D-NE) 185
Spoon rack, walnut, chip carving, Penna. Dutch, hex signs (D-MW) 125
Stand, shaving, curly maple, 1 drawer & mirror, small (A-E) 200
Stand, shaving, mahogany, rectangular swing mirror w/reeded slanted brace, rectangular base w/2 drawers, bracket feet, ivory drawer pulls, string inlay, inlaid key guards, 19th C., 24¾" l. (A-MW) 110
Stand, wig, mahogany (A-E) 10
Stool, farm, small, primitive (A-E).. 90
Stool, joint (D-E).. 195
Stool, library, walnut, heeled through top, primitive (A-E) 165
Stool, milking (A-E) 25
Stool, milking, carved from single block of wood (D-W).. 35
Stool, milking, early, 4-legged (A-E).. 27
Stool, milking, 4 straight legs, hole in protruding handle for hanging (D-MW)..................... 35
Stool, milking, swivel seat w/3 legs (D-MW)... 12
Stool, pine, top 7"×13", 1¾" thick, 4 carved legs pegged to top, 6½" high, side skirts, traces of blue paint (D-MW) 38
Stool, rush seat, rungs rounded by plane, 1½" square maple legs w/⅜" chamfer at each corner, 24" h., 13" square (A-E) 85
Stool, pine & maple, refinished, 4 legs (D-E)... 35
Stool, top joint, octagonal, maple, good turnings, outside stretchers (A-E) 185
Stool, tall, 4-leg (A-E) 25
Stool, Windsor, painted, ca. 1820, 33" h. (D-NE) 135
Stool, Windsor, refinished, 3-leg (D-MW)... 75
Stool, Windsor, 3-leg 2" thick top, Windsor turnings, H-stretcher, dished board in base, v-shape (A-E) 375
Table, bedside, decor. w/turned legs & drawer (A-E)... 325
Table, butcher block, w/2 benches to match, refinished, rare, 34" w., 77" l., 28" h., w/3" top (A-E). 410
Table, butterfly, drop leaf, dated 1680-1720, w/leaves down, 30" w. 11" d. (D-E)................... 4500
Table, butterfly, pine & maple, refinished w/fine patina, 35" top (D-E) 675
Table, butterfly, maple & butternut, rare, ca. 1700 (D-E)... 975
Table, butterfly, pine, orig. finish good, top 38" diam. (D-MW) 200
Table, chair, oblong top, breadboard ends, 44" l., chair w/plank seat & splayed legs, pine w/black painted finish worn (D-E)... 440
Table, Chippendale, maple, old green paint, chamfered legs, 2-board top (A-NE) 425
Table, Chippendale, orig. red finish, molded leg, 1 drawer, Penna., ca. 1800 (D-E) 390
Table, console, curly maple, square legs, lift top, 1 drawer, old hdwe., orig. cond. (A-E)....... 575
Table, dining, cherry, drop leaf, 6-legged w/simple turned legs, folded: 24" w., 29" h., 48" l., width of leaves 23½" (D-MW) 225
Table, dining, cherry, Hepplewhite tapered legs, 40"×19"×49" w/leaves extended, ca. 1775 (D-NE)... 375
Table, dining, Sheraton, mahogany, w/concealed drawer, molded edges, pedestal, splayed legs, brass finished feet, 53"×45", ca. 1820 (D-NE) 415
Table, dressing, country, old yellow paint w/orig. grain, stencil decor., 1 drawer (D-W) 175
Table, dressing, country Sheraton, w/lg. step-up drawer in center of splashboard, lt. red, brown & black decor. (A-NE) 750

Table, dressing, Hepplewhite, pine, w/1 split drawer, 3-sided splash board, olive-green paint outlined in blue, bisected w/black line (A-NE) ....$ 375

Table, dressing, maple, slender legs, 1 divided drawer, 28" w., 17½" d., 28½" h. (A-E)   625

Table, dressing, pine (A-E)   50

Table, dressing, pine, w/turned legs, scalloped back, 3-dovetailed drawers, refinished (D-E) ..   150

Table, dressing, Sheraton, pine & maple, 2-drawer in step-up splashboard, old yellow paint, free hand & stencil decor., form of swans & morning glory, 35" w. × 39" h. (A-NE).................   525

Table, drop leaf, butternut, traces old red paint (A-E)   195

Table, drop leaf, butternut, turned legs, refinished (D-W)   75

Table, drop leaf, cherry, rectangular, turned legs, 2 14⅛" "D" shaped drop leaves, 20" w., 36¼" h. (A-MW)...   175

Table, drop leaf, cherry, 4-leg (A-E)..   100

Table, drop leaf, cherry, mahogany front, single leaf (A-E)   75

Table, drop leaf, cherry, round, 4-leg, fine turnings (D-E)   250

Table, drop leaf, cherry, 6-leg, 63" leaf open, 21½" leaf, 20" top, refinished (A-E)...................   280

Table, drop leaf, cherry, 6-leg, fine turnings, 18" top, 22" leaves (D-E)..................................   600

Table, drop leaf, cherry, 6-leg, fine turnings, 29" h., 41" w., 20" leaves, 18½" top, 58½" open (A-E) .   250

Table, drop leaf, cherry, 6-leg, in the rough (D-E)   200

Table, drop leaf, cherry, 6-leg, w/drawer, 21½" top, 21½" leaves, 46" l., 62" open (A-E)   350

Table, drop leaf, cherry top, 4-leg, curly maple base, w/drawer (D-MW)   340

Table, drop leaf, cherry, turned legs, ca. 1825 (D-MW)   500

Table, drop leaf, cherry, w/turned legs (A-E)   135

Table, drop leaf, Chippendale, scalloped ends, ball & claw foot, walnut, 4' l., 53" top, open (A-E) ..   1975

Table, drop leaf, Chippendale, walnut, Marlboro leg, 4-leg, w/drawers (A-E)   1100

Table, drop leaf, Chippendale, walnut, molded legs inside chamfer, cutout ogee apron 15" w. at ends; w/leaves down, 41" l. (A-E)   350

Table, drop leaf, Chippendale, web foot (A-E)   425

Table, drop leaf, curly maple (D-MW)   525

Table, drop leaf, curly maple, 4-leg (A-E)   425

Table, drop leaf, curly maple & bird's-eye maple (D-MW)   325

Table, drop leaf, curly maple, cut corner top (A-W)   82

Table, drop leaf, extension, w/red & yellow decor. finish, opens to 84", signed & dated 1881 (D-E) .   850

Table, drop leaf, gate leg, cherry, 6-leg in orig. red finish, Penna., ca. 1825 (D-E)...............   350

Table, drop leaf, gate leg, maple, slipper foot, swing leg (A-E)   1800

Table, drop leaf, gate leg, oak, w/outside stretchers, turnings, oval (A-E)..............................   80

Table, drop leaf, gate leg, oval top, 32"×29" h. (A-E)..   175

Table, drop leaf, gate leg, pine, 3-cornered, w/oval fine turnings, T-stretcher, split leg opening into full size table, scalloped apron, 27" h., 34"×35" table top open 3' wide (A-E).....................   225

Table, drop leaf, gate leg, walnut, 6-leg, drawer, refinished, Penna., ca. 1850 (D-E)   225

Table, drop leaf, gate leg, walnut, swing leg, scalloped ends w/drawer, 54" l., 54" diam. when top open (A-E)...   375

Table, drop leaf, mahogany, cross-stretchers, 1-drawer, Hepplewhite, ca. 1770, ex. cond. (D-E)   650

Table, drop leaf, mahogany w/rope legs, brass casters, molded edges w/single drawer, 36"×18" closed, 12" leaves, ca. 1810 (D-NE)   325

Table, drop leaf, maple, biscuit foot (A-E)   150

Table, drop leaf, oval, mahogany satin wood, bell inlay on legs & star, inlaid on tops & leaves, 28" l., 37" w/leaves open, 18" closed, w/bow ends (A-E)   1500

Table, drop leaf, Pembroke, maple, tapered legs, refinished, 35" l. opened, 31⅝" w., 27¼" l., ca. 1800 (D-E)   450

Table, drop-leaf, Pembroke, walnut, cross stretcher, square tapered legs, 1 drawer, all orig., 30" l., 27½" h., 32" open top (A-E)   475

Table, drop leaf, Pembroke, walnut inlaid, 36" l., 19" w; 36" open (A-E)   240

Table, drop leaf, pine, all orig. (A-E)   110

Table, drop leaf, pine, cut-out corners, turned legs (A-E)   95

Table, drop leaf, pine, 5 inches across top when leaves dropped, open, 42" d., refinished (D-MW).   85

Table, drop leaf, pine, 1 drawer, swing-legs, ca. 1840, refinished (D-W)...............................   200

Table, drop leaf, pine, tapered legs, refinished (D-MW)   175

Table, drop leaf, pine, turned legs, refinished (D-E)   295

Table, drop leaf, pine, turned legs, w/2 dovetailed drawers, in the rough (D-W)...................   80

Table, drop leaf, Queen Anne, maple, biscuit foot, 46" l., 51" oval top when open, 27½" h. (A-E) ....$ 875

Table, drop leaf, Sheraton style, curly maple, refinished (D-MW) 375

Table, drop leaf, walnut, 4-leg, 1 drawer, refinished (A-E).. 160

Table, drop leaf, walnut, 1 drawer, flat stretcher base, orig. dk. finish (A-E) 325

Table, drop leaf, walnut, pedestal base, porcelain casters, all orig., ca. 1800 (D-E)............... 285

Table, extension, oak, pedestal base w/claw feet, refinished, 48" sq. (D-MW)....................... 390

Table, game, inlaid console card table, green felt missing on top (A-E)................................. 180

Table, game, Queen Anne, mahogany, rounded legs, duck feet, two rear legs swing; oblong top, closed, 28" w., 13½" d. (D-E)... 550

Table, game, Queen Anne, oak, handkerchief style, one leg draws out from back to support felted top (D-NE) 395

Table, gate leg, walnut, 2 drawers, cut-out ends, 40" l., 29" h. (A-E).................................. 675

Table, handkerchief, walnut, sq. top, notched corners, cabriole legs, slipper feet, 26" sq., 27½" h., 18th C. (A-MW)... 325

Table, handkerchief, oak, gate leg, 3-leg corner, ca. 1690-1740 (A-E) 360

Table, harvest, pine, five sq. legs, H-stretchers on base, 1 drop leaf (A-E) 220

Table, harvest, cherry (D-E) 250

Table, Hepplewhite, country, pine, tapered leg, chamfered top decor. in form of checkerboard, apron decor. w/trees, initialed A.D., in red & black (A-NE).. 650

Table, Hepplewhite, country, 2-drawer, refinished (A-E)... 225

Table, hutch, orig. green paint, scrubbed top (D-NE).. 875

Table, hutch, orig. painted red surface worn, hinged seat 28" l., scrubbed top (D-NE) 725

Table, hutch, orig. red paint, ca. 1790 (A-E) 755

Table, hutch, orig. red paint w/scrubbed top 36"×54" (D-W).. 400

Table, hutch, Penna., orig. green paint (D-MW) 200

Table, hutch, pine, all orig. including pins, refinished (D-W)... 350

Table, hutch, pine, circular top opening to reveal cupboard, trestle base, 36" diam. × 28" h., 19th C. (A-MW) 400

Table, hutch, pine, orig. red painted finish fair, enclosed box base, molded cleats under top, 30½" h., 48" top (A-NE).. 1900

Table, hutch, pine, oval top, compartmented base, shoe feet, 46½" l., 38¾" w., 26¾" h., 18th C. (A-MW) 2300

Table, hutch, round, 47½" diam., old green paint, ca. 1730 (D-E) 950

Table, hutch, pine, round top 44", shoe foot, orig. old red paint, 28" h. (A-NE) 2750

Table, hutch, pine, seat framed w/1⅝" sq. maple, mortised & tenoned, 3-plank pine top w/breadboard ends, pinned to arms w/wooden pegs, shoe feet, 29¾" h., top is 48"×58½" (A-NE)... 1200

Table, hutch, pine, storage box below, rail feet, crude, orig. untouched cond. (D-E) 200

Table, hutch, pine, 3-board round top, in the rough, box base (A-E)................................... 230

Table, hutch, round pine top, poplar & pine base, shoe feet, refinished (D-MW)................... 350

Table, hutch, scrub-top, traces old blue paint (D-E) 850

Table, hutch, shoe foot, orig. old red paint good, scrub top w/fine patina (D-E)................... 1200

Table, hutch, 2-board top, old red paint, bench base hinged (D-MW) 425

Table, hutch, pine, 2-board top, orig. pins & cleats, bench base w/hinged cover, rail feet, refinished, Penna. (D-E) 1000

Table, kitchen, orig. old red finish, scrubbed top, 2 drawers, Penna. origin (D-E) 250

Table, kitchen, pine, drop leaf, tapered legs, ca. 1890, refinished, skinned down (A-E) 90

Table, kitchen, pine, drop leaf, 2 drawers, round turned legs (A-MW) 90

Table, kitchen, pine, H-stretcher, 2-drawer, dovetailed, refinished (D-E)............................ 550

Table, kitchen, pine, pegged, H-stretcher base (A-E) 325

Table, kitchen, pine & tiger maple, rectangular top over frieze w/1 drawer, sq. tapering legs, 46" l., 31" w., 28" h., 19th C. (A-MW) 325

Table, kitchen wall, folding, unpainted pine, 1 leg & single board shaped top, 62" l. × 22" w. × 32½" h. (A-NE) 225

Table, kitchen, walnut, drop leaf, 2 drawers, turned legs, in the rough (D-E) 190

Table, library, bird's-eye maple, large (D-MW) 475

Table, library, drop leaf, mahogany, 1 drawer, rope leg w/brass cap casters, 17" center, leaf 12", 42"×41" open, ca. 1815 (D-NE).. 260

Table, library, oak, lg. lower shelf, 1 drawer, cast brass handles, top, 24"×36" (D-W) ....$ 55

Table, library, oak, shaped top w/fancy supports, good stock w/swell ends & sides, top, 32"×32" (D-MW)   82

Table, middle stretcher, old red paint, top 21"×32" w/molded edge, legs reeded on outside corners, chamfered inside edge, ca. 1760 (A-E)   750

Table, middle stretcher, turned, soft wood, red, two lg. drawers, dust proof bottom, 36" w., 72" l., restored above drawer fronts (A-E)   1050

Table, maple, square leg, refinished, primitive, small (A-E)   65

Table, oak, heavy rope design legs, brass feet, 26"×26" oval top (D-MW)   75

Table, oak, round, 3 boards, refinished, 48" (D-MW)   175

Table, oak, round, 28" top w/inlaid lines (D-MW)   67

Table, pedestal, cherry, 36" tilt top, round, ca. 1830 (D-SW)   895

Table, pedestal oak, round, fine carved claw feet, refinished, 42" (D-SW)...........................   390

Table, pedestal, oak, round, claw feet, orig. finish, 54" (A-E)   48

Table, pedestal, oak, round, 54", claw feet, refinished (D-W)...   350

Table, pedestal, oak, round, curved legs, refinished, 42" (D-S)   190

Table, pedestal, oak, round, 48", refinished (D-W)..   175

Table, pedestal, oak, round, 3 ex. boards, refinished, 48" (D-MW)   195

Table, Pembroke, mahogany, cookie corner leaves, Chippendale tapered legs, lt. brown, orig. (D-NE)..   250

Table, Pembroke, walnut, delicate turned legs & cut-out leaves, refinished, Penna., ca. 1825 (D-E)   275

Table, Pembroke, walnut, w/string inlay, turned legs, in the rough (D-E)   125

Table, pine, half-round, scrubbed top, 3 tapered legs, base w/old brown paint, 27½" h., 43" l. (A-NE)   375

Table, pine, 1-drawer, old blue paint, splayed legs, beaded trim on drawer (A-E).................   625

Table, pine, Queen Anne country, oval top, maple base, splayed legs w/pad feet (A-E)   725

Table, pine, round, 65" diam., w/lazy susan, pegged splayed legs, refinished (D-E)...............   550

Table, pine, sq. checkerboard top, painted, 26½" sq. (D-MW)..   65

Table, Queen Anne, maple base, pine scrubbed top 30"×39", red painted base, splayed legs, button foot (A-NE)   1000

Table, sawbuck, breadboard ends & scrubbed top (D-E)..   235

Table, sawbuck, pine, 1 drawer, ca. 1800 (D-NE)..   670

Table, sawbuck, pine, X-shaped legs, molded stretcher, top 30 × 60" (A-E)..........................   8900

Table, settle, pine & maple, w/35½"×6' single board scrubbed top & base in old gray-green paint (A-NE)...   2400

Table, sewing, cherry, drop leaf, 2-drawer, fine turnings (A-E)   170

Table, sewing, maple, w/orig. red paint, sandwich pulls (D-MW)   325

Table, sewing, raised edge molding, splayed legs, beaded drawer (A-E)   1200

Table, sewing, tripod foot, 2 drawers, drops at corners (D-E)   95

Table, Sheraton, country, maple & birch, decor. w/narrow red, black & yellow stripes (A-NE)   375

Table, Sheraton, country, pine, 1 drawer, black w/yellow sponged shell decor. on top surface (A-NE)   500

Table, Sheraton-style, serving, decor. w/hand painted flowers on black, ca. 1815, Maryland (D-E) .   550

Table, shoemaker's, pine, from Amana Colonies, rectangular top w/three-quarter gallery, over frieze w/2 drawers, trestle shelf base, 19th C., 34" w., 16" d., 21½" h. (A-MW)   250

Table, side, birch, drop leaf, w/2 curly maple drawer fronts, fine turned legs (A-E)   115

Table, side, birch, 1 drawer, sq. legs, stripped (A-MW)..   35

Table, side, cherry, drop leaf, 2-drawer, fine turned legs (D-SE)   190

Table, side, cherry, drop leaves, 2 drawers, spool turned legs, 27" h. (D-MW)   150

Table, side, cherry, 1 drawer (D-W)   175

Table, side, cherry, 1 drawer, tapered legs, early (A-E)...   285

Table, side, cherry & tiger maple, 3 drawers, turned legs, small, Penna., ca. 1825 (D-E).........   450

Table, side, curly maple, 16" sq. top, 2 drawers (D-NE)   350

Table, side, grained orange & red, 1 drawer, tapered leg (A-E)..   230

Table, side, Hepplewhite, country pine, w/cut out sides & back; red & black graining w/red & yellow rolled decor. on single drawer (A-NE)   600

Table, side, Hepplewhite, maple w/overhang, curly drawer, tapered legs, 18th C., case 16"×16"; top 19½"×27" h. (D-NE)   275

Table, side, Hepplewhite, pine, 1 drawer, orig. red & black grained finish good (A-E)   550

Table, side, maple, drop leaf, single drawer, refinished (D-MW) ....$ 85
Table, side, maple, grained, splayed legs (A-S)   60
Table, side, maple, 1 drawer, tapered sq. legs, painted pink (A-MW)..............................   21
Table, side, maple, 1 drawer, turned legs, refinished (D-W)...   90
Table, side, orig. red finish, turned legs, small, Penna., ca. 1840 (D-E) 290
Table, side, orig. red painted finish good, sq. tapered legs, small, Penna., ca. 1830 (D-NE).... 275
Table, side, pine, 1 drawer, turned legs, painted white over green (D-W)   28
Table, side, pine, sq. leg, outside stretchers, 1 drawer dovetailed (A-SE)   85
Table, side, scalloped backboard, 26" l., pine, pegged, one drawer, tapered legs, refinished
(D-MW) 125
Table, side, Sheraton, pine & maple w/smoke decor., 2 drawers (A-NE) 575
Table, side, tiger maple, 1 drawer, tapered legs, ca. 1790 (D-N).................................... 390
Table, side, tray top, splayed leg, traces of old yellow paint, ca. 1810 (D-NE) 285
Table, side, 2-drawer, feather grained, Penna. origin (A-E).. 195
Table, side, walnut, 1 drawer (D-E)   75
Table, side, walnut, 1 drawer, turned legs, in the rough (D-W)   32
Table, side, walnut, 1 drawer, turned legs, refinished (D-MW).......................................   48
Table, stand, cherry, 1 drawer, tapered legs, early (A-E).. 280
Table, stretcher, scalloping on apron all 4 sides, orig. ball feet, ex. cond., top 30" × 47" (A-E). 4400
Table, stretcher, walnut, upright stretchers all 4 sides, removable top, 60" × 32½", turned legs, 2
drawers w/orig. brasses (A-E)... 1300
Table, tavern, barrel, walnut, used to hold liquor barrels & top folds down to serve as table, lift top
(A-E) 350
Table, tavern, bread board ends, stretcher base, 1 drawer (D-MW) 650
Table, tavern, cherry, round top w/drawer, no stretchers, early (D-E) 4800
Table, tavern, cherry, single drawer, boxed stretcher base, square legs, 31" l., 20" d., 29" h. (D-E) 490
Table, tavern, curly maple, round top, drawer, turned legs, no stretchers, rare (D-E)............. 4800
Table, tavern, lift top, arched corners on top, base w/fine turnings & ball feet, scalloped apron &
flat stretcher, 86" l., 29½" w., 30" t. (A-E) 2000
Table, tavern, lift top, tapered legs (A-E).. 130
Table, tavern, maple base w/orig. red paint, breadboard ends, scrubbed top, Mass., ca. 1700,
21½"×33½"×25¾" h. (D-E)... 1800
Table, tavern, maple, button feet, large drawer, ex. orig. top w/breadboard ends (A-E).......... 500
Table, tavern, maple, stretcher base, orig. black paint (D-MW)...................................... 1200
Table, tavern, oak, early, molded top, 18th C., 35½" w., 17½" d., 29" h. (D-MW) 700
Table, tavern, oak, 4 turned stretcher legs (A-E)   60
Table, tavern, oak, round, 1 drawer, stretchers, refinished, 35" (D-W) 225
Table, tavern, oak, round pine top w/3 oak tapered legs, shelf & stretchers, refinished (D-W). 225
Table, tavern, oak, turned stretcher legs (A-E)..   85
Table, tavern, 1-board scrub top, turned legs, stretcher base, refinished (A-E)...................... 1350
Table, tavern, outside stretchers, chamfered legs (D-NE) 1250
Table, tavern, outside stretchers, 2 drawers, scalloped apron, early, 28"×28" (A-E) 200
Table, tavern, pegged breadboard ends, stretchers, w/drawer, orig. finish (D-E) 650
Table, tavern, pine, breadboard ends, 1 drawer & 1 board top, old red on base, scrub top (A-E) .. 850
Table, tavern, pine, drop leaf, w/drawer, stretchers, refinished (D-MW) 400
Table, tavern, pine, early Dutch, lift top, sq. chamfered legs, 3 dovetailed drawers, sunken panels
on either side & ends, 6'6" long, 36" w. (A-E).. 210
Table, tavern, pine, hexagonal top (A-E) 250
Table, tavern, pine, pegged top, Penna., ca. 1820 (D-E)... 525
Table, tavern, pine, rectangular top, grooved box frieze, sq. grooved legs w/H-stretcher, 35" l., 24"
w., 27½" h., 18th C. (A-MW) 250
Table, tavern, pine, rectangular top, molded edge, apron w/1 long drawer, sq. legs, box stretcher,
orig. finish (A-MW).. 250
Table, tavern, pine round top, three oak sq. legs, pine triangle stretchers (D-MW)................ 250
Table, tavern, pine top w/maple frame, New England, breadboard ends, ca. 1780 (D-MW) 550
Table, tavern, Queen Anne, button foot, 1 board top w/shaped corners, shaped apron, orig. finish,
34¼"×23½"×27" (D-NE) 1700
Table, tavern, Queen Anne, maple, American, turned legs w/full width drawer in base, scrubbed
maple top w/breadboard ends, orig. cond. good., 18th C., 45"l., 25" w., 28" h. (A-MW)....... 850

Table, tavern, Queen Anne style, walnut, pad feet, lift top, 1 drawer, 39"×27½" top, 22"×29" base
(A-E) ....$ 700
Table, tavern, Pa., splay stretcher base, top 24"×26" h.; 24" scrubbed top (D-E) 1200
Table, tavern, tapered legs, red paint (A-E)... 70
Table, tavern, walnut base w/cherry top, lift top, 1 drawer, turned legs, flat stretcher & flat ball
feet, 60½"×36" (A-E) 300
Table, tavern, walnut, cross-stretchers & drawer, 29½"×57", cut out top, base, 23"×33" (A-E). 700
Table, tavern, walnut, Penna. orig., unfinished (D-MW) 135
Table, tavern, walnut, 3-leg, stretcher base, butterfly supports (A-E) 575
Table, tavern, walnut, turned legs, 2 drawers w/orig. pulls, top w/2 wide boards, Penna., ca. 1800,
30" h., 59" top, 35" w. (A-NE) 400
Table, tavern, walnut, turned stretchers, dovetailed drawer, 38" round top (D-MW) 190
Table, tilt-top, birdcage, walnut, w/old patina, circular top w/molded edge, padded feet, Penna.,
ca. 1840, 20½" diam., 24" h. (A-E).. 5800
Table, tilt-top, cherry, cut-out top w/pad feet (A-E)... 120
Table, tilt-top, cut out corners, snake foot (D-NE).. 100
Table, trestle, pine, backed, w/matching benches, orig. non-painted cond. good., ca. 1800, table
7' l., 24" w. (D-MW)... 800
Table, trestle, pine, ex. cond., refinished (D-MW) 350
Table, trestle, pine, orig. green paint worn, top 49" l., 32" w., 30" h. (A-NE) 550
Table, trestle, pine, rectangular, 18th C., 58" l., 16½" w., 29½" h. (A-MW) 325
Table, turned splay legs, orig. red finish, small, Penna., ca. 1840 (D-E) 225
Table, walnut, Dutch, lift top, 2 drawers, round tapered legs, top 54"×35" (A-E) 170
Table, walnut, lift & pegged top & 1 drawer, fine turnings w/outside stretchers & ball feet,
refinished orig. cond. (A-E) 1050
Table, walnut, New England, turned splayed legs, small (A-E) 100
Table, walnut, oval top, 3 legs (A-E) 60
Table, walnut, round slender legs, 1 small & 1 large drawer, 30" w. base, 27½" h., 27" d; 40" w. top,
31" d. (A-E)... 200
Table, walnut, small, splayed legs, top replaced w/boards from old Queen Anne table (A-E) .. 1400
Table, walnut, turned legs, 1 center drawer, 46" diam., refinished (D-MW) 135
Table, work, Hepplewhite, pine & maple, serpentine hinged top, 1 false long drawer, & 1 long
drawer, turned legs w/three-quarter stretcher, restored, 19th C., 21" w., 14½" d., 30½" h.
(A-MW) 150
Table, work, pine, 1-board top 28" w., turned legs, 2 long dovetailed drawers, stripped, un-
finished (D-W).. 90
Table, work, pine, rectangular, 2 short drawers, sq. tapered legs, 21¾" w., 19" d., 28½" h.
(A-MW) 160
Table, work, pine, sq. top w/straight apron, 4 sq. legs, 19th C., 18¾" w., 16¾" d., 29¾" h. (A-MW) 150
Table, work, walnut, H-stretcher, 2-drawer (A-MW) 58
Table, work, walnut, turned legs, 2 dovetailed drawers & removable 3-board top, old patina,
66"×37", 27" h. (A-E).. 525
Table, Windsor, pine & maple, 3 legs, green paint, 31" h. (A-NE) 350
Tea caddy, walnut, casket shape, bun feet, 2 covered compartments, 19th C., 7¾" l. (A-MW). 50
Towel rack, walnut, refinished (A-E) 37
Tray, butler's, walnut, 18th C., 25" l. (A-MW) 70
Trunk, antique horsehair covered, hump back, iron fittings, 36" l., 17" h. (D-MW)................. 55
Trunk box, smoke-grain painted, 23" l., 10¼" h. (A-E) 80
Trunk, decor. w/red, blue & green flowers & angels, dated 1793, wrought iron handles, heart
shape strap hinges & decor. inside lid (A-E) 575
Trunk, decor. w/yellow & brown graining (D-NW) 165
Trunk, domed lid, large, completely restored, exterior red w/white trim, interior lined w/red
calico (D-W).. 200
Trunk, domed lid, large, orig. untouched cond., lined w/1882 New York paper, good (A-MW) . 33
Trunk, domed lid, metal w/brass trim, large, orig. untouched cond. fair (A-MW).................. 12
Trunk, domed lid, pine, covered w/leather, brass nails & hdwe., orig. cond. good (D-NE) 325
Trunk, domed lid, pine, dovetailed & old blue paint, lock missing, 36½" l., 19" w., 17" h. (A-E) 40
Trunk, domed lid, pine, stripped of orig. tin covering, refinished & lined in red calico, 22" l., 18"
h. (D-MW)... 75

Bed, 4-poster, walnut (D-S) $690

Rope bed, walnut, interesting hand-carved eagle headboard, orig. finish, excellent condition, ¾-size (A-E) $1200

Trunk, domed lid, small, M.O.P. green tin cover, good, brass trim, lock, inside comp. untouched cond. (D-W)..$ 78

Trunk, domed lid, wallpaper covered, 19th C. (D-E) 95

Trunk, immigrant, orig. brown painted finish, handwrought hinges & handles, unfinished (D-W).. 75

Trunk, immigrant, pine w/orig. old blue painted finish worn, handwrought hinges & handles, large (D-W).. 68

Trunk, ladies', all orig., sponged orange & brown painted finish fair, complete w/tray (D-NE) . 95

Trunk, ladies', pine, brass bound, new interior lining, complete w/tray, refinished (D-S) 90

Trunk, leather, brass bound (A-E) 285

Trunk, leather, brass bound, 28″ l., 15½″ h. (D-MW).. 62

Trunk, leather covered, brass trim, small, orig. cond. fair (A-MW)................................. 48

Trunk, leather, decor. w/black iron strips & studded w/brass nails, 26″ l., 15″ h. (D-MW) 45

Trunk, pine, metal straps, binding & handles, on metal rollers, 19th C., 28″ l., 15″ w., 15¼″ h. (A-MW) 80

Wagon seat, hickory, double chair, spindle back, knob finials, turned spindle arms, rawhide basketweave seat, 6 stretchered circular legs w/rockers, 18th C., 34″ w. (A-MW)................. 325

Wagon seat, maple, orig. rush seat, slat back, signed, early 19th C. (D-E) 450

Wardrobe, oak, door & drawer, fitted w/hooks, ornamental, 7′4″ h., 3′1″ w. (A-E) 180

Wardrobe, oak, hand carved, 2 doors & 2 drawers, fitted w/hooks, 8′ h., 4′3″ w. (D-W) 280

Wardrobe, oak, 2 doors & 2 drawers, French bevel mirrors in doors, ornamental, 7′9″ h., 4′ w. (D-MW).. 284

Washstand, corner, Hepplewhite, mahogany, 18th C., refinished (D-E) 1250

Washstand, corner, pine, sloping top above 1 door, bracket feet, 19th C., 26″ d. × 37″ h. (A-MW) 250

Washstand, corner, Sheraton, bow front, 1-drawer, cut-out back (A-E) 225

Washstand, corner, Sheraton, maple, refinished (D-MW) 550

Washstand, Hepplewhite, maple, orig. finish (D-E)... 180

Washstand, lift-top, orig. false graining, flower decor. (A-E)... 95

Washstand, maple, 1 drawer (A-E) 150

Washstand, opening for basin, shelf & drawer below, orig. black finish & stencil good (D-MW).. 235

Washstand, opening for basin, shelf & drawer below, orig. decoration restored, ex. cond. (D-W) 90

Washstand, pine, bow front, ca. 1830 (D-E).. 295

Washstand, pine, bow front, w/yellow ground, free hand & rolled earth colored decor. (A-NE) . 400

Washstand, pine, 1 drawer, 2 doors, refinished (A-E)... 75

Washstand, pine, opening for basin, gallery shelf top, shelf below & drawer, painted white, 38″ h. (D-E)... 185

Washstand, pine, opening for basin, 1 shelf below, shaped back, refinished, 38″ w. (D-W) 175

Washstand, pine, tapered legs, towel bars, 1 drawer, refinished (D-MW)............................. 65

Washstand, pine & tiger maple, galleried rectangular top, 1 long drawer, 1 shelf, turned legs, 24¾″ l., 13¾″ d., 30″ h. (A-MW)... 200

Washstand, pine, towel bars, 1 drawer, stripped (D-W)... 70

Washstand, pine, towel bars, tapered legs, 1 drawer, orig. red paint (D-E)......................... 90

Washstand, Sheraton, yellow & green w/gold stenciled bowl of fruit on splash board (A-NE).. 425

Washstand, spool leg, 1 drawer w/towel rack arms (A-E).. 90

Washstand, walnut, opening for basin, shelf & drawer, refinished (D-N)............................. 90

Woodbox, spindle back, turned feet, in the rough (A-E)... 180

Gaudy Dutch

Gaudy Dutch is the most spectacular of all Staffordshire products made especially for the Pennsylvania Dutch market from about 1785 to around 1820. It was originally intended to imitate the fine Imari-type porcelain produced at Derby and Worcester during the same period.

Gaudy Dutch can be characterized by its colorful, bold designs having an Oriental influence. It is a soft paste tableware, very lightweight and frail in appearance. Its rich cobalt blue decoration was applied to the biscuit, then glazed and fired. To complete the pattern, other colors such as bright red, orange, pink, yellow, and green were applied over the glaze, then the object was fired again. No lustre is included with the decoration.

Among the well-known patterns are Butterfly, Carnation, Dahlia, Double Rose, Dove, Grape, Leaf, Oyster, Primrose, Single Rose, Strawflower, Sunflower, Urn, War Bonnet and Zinnia.

* * *

Bowl, carnation pattern, 6½″ diam. (D-E)	\$ 450
Bowl, carnation pattern, 6¼″ diam. (A-E)	400
Bowl, double rose pattern, 6¼″ (A-E)	375
Bowl, Dutch urn pattern, 6½″ (D-E)	385
Bowl, oyster pattern, 5½″ (A-E)	290
Bowl, single rose pattern, 5½″ diam. (D-E)	175
Bowl, single rose pattern, 6″ diam. (D-E)	225
Bowl, sunflower pattern, rare, 6½″ (D-E)	425
Bowl, sugar, double rose pattern (A-E)	115
Bowl, sugar, double rose pattern, covered (A-E)	140
Bowl, sugar, grape pattern, covered, rare (A-E)	450
Bowl, sugar, oak leaf pattern, covered (A-E)	150
Bowl, sugar, war bonnet pattern, covered, rare (A-E)	190
Coffeepot, oyster pattern, 12″ t. (A-E)	525
Creamer, butterfly pattern, rare (A-E)	2000
Creamer, carnation pattern, rectangular, 5½″ l., 5″ h. (D-E)	450
Creamer, double rose pattern (A-E)	230
Creamer, double rose pattern (A-E)	240
Creamer, grape pattern (A-E)	270
Creamer, oyster pattern (A-E)	360
Cup plate, double rose pattern, 3½″ (A-E)	825
Cup & saucer, butterfly pattern (A-E)	325
Cup & saucer, carnation pattern (A-E)	250
Cup & saucer, carnation pattern (N-E)	275
Cup & saucer, carnation pattern (A-E)	325
Cup & saucer, dahlia pattern (A-E)	215
Cup & saucer, dahlia pattern (A-E)	300
Cup & saucer, double rose pattern (A-E)	180
Cup & saucer, double rose pattern (A-E)	225
Cup & saucer, double rose pattern (A-E)	250
Cup & saucer, dove pattern (A-E)	160
Cup & saucer, grape patten (A-E)	275
Cup & saucer, grape pattern (A-E)	180
Cup & saucer, grape pattern, large (A-E)	130
Cup & saucer, oak leaf pattern (A-E)	370
Cup & saucer, oyster pattern (A-E)	220

Gaudy Dutch, King's rose pattern (A-E), *left:* **pair of matching cups & saucers,** $250; *center,* **large plate,** 9¾" diam., $150; *below center:* **small plate,** 5¾" diam., $120; *right,* **pair of matching cups & saucers,** $300

Gaudy Dutch (A-E), *top row:* **sugar bowl,** Carnation pattern, damaged, $125; *plate,* Single Rose pattern, 9¾" diam., $450; **creamer,** Butterfly pattern, rare, $2000; *bottom row:* **plate,** Urn pattern, 8" diam., $280; *plate,* Single Rose pattern, 6¾" diam., $175

Gaudy Dutch (A-E), *top row, left to right:* **plate,** Carnation pattern, blue & white border, 8½" diam., $325; **plate,** Urn pattern, 8" diam., $280; *bottom row, left to right:* **cup & saucer,** War Bonnet pattern, $425; **bowl,** Single Rose pattern, 5½" diam., $400; **cup & saucer,** Double Rose pattern, $250

Cup & saucer, single rose pattern (A-E)..$	200
Cup & saucer, single rose pattern (A-E)..	165
Cup & saucer, single rose pattern (A-E)..	200
Cup & saucer, single rose pattern (A-E)..	250
Cup & saucer, urn pattern (A-E)...	280
Cup & saucer, war bonnet pattern (A-E)...	280
Cup & saucer, war bonnet pattern (A-E)...	275
Cup & saucer, war bonnet pattern (A-E)...	425
Cups & saucers, single rose pattern, set of 6 (A-E)	850
Plate, bread & butter, grape pattern, 6" (D-E)...	390
Plate, bread & butter, single rose pattern (A-E)	160
Plate, butterfly pattern, rare, 6½" (A-E)	950
Plate, butterfly pattern, 6½" (A-E)	450
Plate, butterfly pattern, 8½" (A-E)	400
Plate, carnation pattern , 6½" (A-E)	210
Plate, carnation pattern, 9¾" (A-E)	400
Plate, carnation pattern, 9¾" (D-E)	350
Plate, carnation pattern, blue & white border, 8¼" (A-E)	325
Plate, cup or toddy, rare oyster pattern, 5½" (D-E)...	425
Plate, cup or toddy, single rose pattern, 5¼" (D-E)...	240
Plate, dahlia pattern, 6¼" diam. (D-E)	200
Plate, double rose pattern, 8" (A-E)	120
Plate, double rose pattern, 8¼" (A-E)	220
Plate, double rose pattern, 10" (A-E)..	200
Plate, double rose pattern, 10" diam. (D-E)..	325

Plate, dove pattern, 6½" (A-E)..$ 270
Plate, dove pattern, 10" (D-E) 550
Plate, dove pattern, rare, 6¼" (D-E) 275
Plate, Dutch urn pattern, 8¼" (D-E) 295
Plate, grape pattern, 6¼" (A-E).. 200
Plate, grape pattern, 6¼" (D-E).. 195
Plate, grape pattern, 7" (A-E)... 200
Plate, grape pattern, 9¾" (A-E) 200
Plate, grape pattern, 10" (A-E) 220
Plate, oak leaf pattern, 6¾" (A-E)... 260
Plate, oyster pattern, 10" (D-E) 475
Plate, oyster pattern, 10" (D-E) 300
Plate, single rose pattern, 6½" (A-E) 200
Plate, single rose pattern, 7" diam. (D-E) 290
Plate, single rose pattern, 7¾" (D-E) 195
Plate, single rose pattern, blue & white border, 9¾" (A-E) 300
Plate, single rose pattern, lt. blue & white border, 6¾" (A-E) 175
Plate, single rose pattern, marked Riley, 10" (D-E)............................ 435
Plate, single rose pattern, marked Riley , 10" (D-E) 450
Plate, single rose pattern, mint cond., 6⅜" diam. (D-NE).................... 120
Plate, strawflower pattern, marked "Riley", 10" (D-E) 650
Plate, strawflower pattern, marked "Riley", 10" (A-E) 550
Plate, strawflower pattern, marked "Riley", blue & white border, 9¾" (A-E) 450
Plate, soup, carnation pattern, 10" (D-E) 425
Plate, soup, double rose pattern, 9½" (A-E) 250
Plate soup, grape pattern, 7" deep (A-E) 190
Plate, soup, grape pattern, 10" (A-E) 270
Plate, soup, grape pattern, 10" (D-E) 350
Plate, soup, war bonnet pattern, 8" (A-E) 260
Plate, soup, war bonnet pattern, 8¼" (A-E) 200
Plate, soup, war bonnet pattern, 10" (A-E) 285
Plate, soup, war bonnet pattern, mint. cond., 7" (A-E)........................ 500
Plate, soup, zinnia pattern, marked "Riley", 10" (D-E)........................ 650
Plate, toddy, primrose pattern, 4½", mint cond. (A-E) 700
Plate, urn pattern, 6½" (A-E) 200
Plate, urn pattern, 6½" (A-E) 225
Plate, urn pattern, 7½" (A-E) 180
Plate, urn pattern, 8" (A-E) 280
Plate, urn pattern, 8" (D-E) 295
Plate, urn pattern, blocked border, 10" (A-E) 425
Plate, war bonnet pattern, 5¼" (A-E) 225
Plate, war bonnet pattern, 7¼" (A-E) 210
Plate, war bonnet pattern, 9½" diam. (D-MW) 350
Plate, war bonnet pattern, 9½" diam. (D-SE)..................................... 450
Plate, war bonnet pattern, 10" (D-E) 395
Plate, zinnia pattern, marked "Riley", 8½" (A-E) 475
Quill holder, single rose pattern, covered, rare (A-E) 2500
Sugar bowl, carnation pattern, covered (D-S) 125
Sugar bowl, dove pattern, covered (D-E) 425
Teapot, double rose pattern (A-E) 210
Teapot, double rose pattern, age mark on lid (A-E) 290
Teapot, oak leaf pattern, covered, large (A-E) 750
Teapot, single rose pattern (A-E) 550
Toddy plate, double rose pattern, 4½" (A-E) 500
Toddy plate, double rose pattern, 4½" (A-E) 250
Toddy plate, grape pattern, 6¼" (A-E)... 170
Toddy plate, "Indian bonnet," 4½" (D-E) 350
Toddy plate, war bonnet pattern, 5¼" (A-E) 390
Toddy plate, war bonnet pattern, 4½" (A-E) 400

Gaudy Welsh

Among other tablewares considered to be typical of the so-called Pennsylvania Dutch wares is Gaudy Welsh, produced in England from about 1830 well into the third quarter of the last century. It resembles Gaudy Dutch in decoration, having large flowers and leaves freely painted in the same colors. However, the ware is weighty, designs are cruder, its texture more comparable to that of spatterware, and "lustre" is usually included in the decoration. Hence, it has not been as popular with collectors as other gaudy wares; but it certainly deserves more attention while prices are reasonable.

Patterns include Flower Basket, Morning Glory, Grape, Oyster, Shanghai, Strawberry, Tulip, Urn and Wagon Wheel. Plates are irregular in shape, cups are straight-sided with handles, and the hollow pieces frequently have short feet.

* * *

Pitcher,
Gaudy Welsh, 7" h.
(D-MW) $45

Bowl, grape pattern, early, 5¼" (A-E)	$ 32
Bowl, oyster pattern (A-E)	25
Bowl, sugar, pin wheel pattern, w/lid (A-E)	55
Bowl, tulip pattern, 6¼" (A-E)	28
Bowl, waste, dahlia pattern, 3½" h., 6" diam. (D-NE)	49
Bowl, waste, pin wheel pattern (A-E)	32
Coffeepot, pin wheel pattern, 9" t. (A-E)	190
Creamer, oyster pattern, 3½" (A-E)	20
Creamer, oyster pattern, 4" (A-E)	45

Creamer, pin wheel pattern (A-E) ....$ 110
Creamer, tulip pattern, 3″ (A-E) 15
Creamer, tulip pattern, 4½″ (A-E) 17
Cup & saucer, dahlia pattern, wishbone handle (D-NE).. 40
Cup & saucer, pin wheel pattern (A-E)... 35
Cup & saucer, seeing eye pattern (A-E) 55
Cup & saucer, tulip pattern, handled (A-E) 20
Pitcher, cream, dahlia pattern (A-E) 30
Pitcher, milk, dahlia pattern, 8″ (A-E) 65
Pitcher, pin wheel pattern, 7½″ (A-E)... 145
Pitcher, milk, oyster pattern, early, 7½″ (A-E) 55
Plate, cake, dahlia pattern, 9″ diam. (D-E).. 40
Plate, flower basket pattern, 8½″ (A-E) 70
Plate, grape pattern, 5¼″ (A-E)... 45
Plate, oyster pattern, 10¼″ (A-E) 25
Plate, soup, oyster pattern, 10¼″ (A-E)... 50
Plate, pin wheel pattern, 6½″ (A-E) 27
Plate, pin wheel pattern, 7½″ (D-MW) 35
Plate, pin wheel pattern, 7½″ (D-S).. 30
Plate, pin wheel pattern, 8″ (A-E) 25
Plate, pin wheel pattern, 9½″ (A-E) 30
Plate, soup, pin wheel pattern, 10½″ (A-E) 38
Plate, seeing eye pattern, 6¼″ (A-W)... 15
Plate, seeing eye pattern, 6½″ (A-E).. 75
Plate, seeing eye pattern, 8¼″ (A-E).. 30
Plate, strawberry pattern, mint cond., 8½″ (A-E) 75
Plate, strawberry pattern, mint cond., 8¾″ (D-MW) 45
Plate, strawberry pattern, mint, 8¾″ (D-NW) 70
Plate, strawberry pattern, 9″ (A-E) 37
Plate, strawberry pattern, 8″ (A-E) 40
Plate, soup, strawberry pattern, 9″ (A-E).. 75
Platter, morning glory pattern, 11″ (A-E).. 75

Graniteware

Graniteware—often referred to as enamel or agate cooking ware—was manufactured in quantity by numerous firms from the late 1800s well into the present century. It remained popular until the 1930s, when it was replaced by gleaming aluminumware. Unfortunately, graniteware chipped quite easily, and the chances of finding a perfect old piece today are very remote.

The United States produced more of this ware for utilitarian purposes than any other country in the world. One of the first major firms to make graniteware was Lalance & Grosjean Manufacturing Company, New York, Chicago and Boston. In 1878 the firm won the Grand Gold Medal at the Paris Exposition for their fine blue-and-white mottled enamelware kitchen utensils.

Because of its popularity, colors became quite important to customers and manufacturers began giving their products fanciful names such as "Onyx Ware," a rich brown color with white mottling, "Shamrock Ware," shaded from sea-green to moss green, "Blue Diamond," a mottled blue on white, "Thistle Ware," having violet shades, "White Diamond," white with black trim, etc.

There has been a revival of interest in graniteware in recent years, when many discovered the bounty of country living. Suddenly, its appeal spread from the country village to metropolitan highrise, and a vast amount of new graniteware found its way to the production lines. Many of the new pieces are deliberate copies of earlier wares, but it is quite easy for collectors to distinguish the new from the old, because new graniteware *looks* new.

* * *

Bedpan, green & white (D-E)	$ 3
Boiler, lift-out rack, bail handle, gray (D-W)	6
Bottle, flask w/screw top, turquoise (D-E)	30
Bowl, blue & white, 2 qt. (D-MW)	5
Bowl, brown, 2 qt. (D-S)	3
Bowl, ladle, blue & white speckles (D-E)	12
Bowl, mixing, purple shaded, 2 qt. (D-MW)	8
Bowl, mixing, yellow & white, 2 qt. (D-W)	15
Bowl, sugar, pewter cover & trim, gray (D-E)	25
Bowl & pitcher, blue & white (D-MW)	22
Bowl & pitcher, brown & white (D-MW)	30
Bowl & pitcher, green & white, shaded (D-W)	28
Bucket, blue (D-E)	8
Bucket, blue, bail handle (D-W)	9
Bucket, brown, bail handle, lid, 4" h. (D-S)	5
Bucket, blue, bail handle, lid, 6" h. (D-MW)	6
Bucket, water, blue & white, w/bail, wooden handle (D-MW)	8
Bucket, water, brown & white, w/bail, wooden handle (D-W)	10
Can, cream, blue, dome lid, bail handle, qt. (D-MW)	18
Caster set, 4 enameled gray bottles w/pewter tops, set in pewter frame (D-W)	145
Coffee boiler, blue & white, w/cover & wire bail, wood handle (D-MW)	20
Coffee boiler, brown & white, w/cover & wire bail, wood handle (D-W)	22
Coffeepot, blue & white (D-MW)	18
Coffeepot, blue & white, (biggin) (D-W)	18
Coffeepot, blue & white speckles, 10½" h. (A-E)	42
Coffeepot, brown, hinged dome lid, 4-cup (D-E)	22

Coffeepot, brown & white (D-W) ....$ 22
Coffeepot, brown & white (D-W)   25
Coffeepot, gray (D-S)...   12
Coffeepot, gray (D-SW)   10
Coffeepot, gray & white, 10" h. (D-E)   20
Coffeepot, red & white (D-MW)   12
Coffeepot, turquoise, hinged lid, 8-cup (D-MW)   28
Colander, blue & white, large, handled (D-W)......................................   12
Colander, brown & white, handled (D-W)   18
Colander, brown, side handles (D-E)   12
Creamer, gray, pewter trim (D-E)   18
Cup & saucer, brown & white (D-MW)   8
Cup & saucer, gray (D-W)   5
Cup, baby's, blue & white (D-MW)   5
Cup, black & white, qt. (A-W)   33
Cup, blue & white, can-shaped (D-MW)..   3
Cup, dark green, shaded (D-W)   1
Cup, gray, sloping side (D-MW)..   1
Dipper, blue & white, wooden handle, small bowl (D-MW)   12
Dipper, brown & white, enameled, hook (D-MW)   4
Dipper, gray, wooden handle (D-MW)   5
Dish, baking, blue & white, oblong (D-S)..   6
Dish, soap, brown, hanging type w/holes (D-MW)   6
Dustpan, blue & white (D-MW)   6
Foot tub, gray, bail handle (D-MW)   3
Funnel, blue & white, small (D-W)   6
Funnel, gray, large (D-MW)   2
Hangrack w/tool set, green & white, complete w/ladles, etc. (D-MW)........   25
Kettle, blue & white, w/bail & orig. cover (D-MW)   6
Kettle, blue, preserving type w/bail handle & lid, large (D-S)   12
Kettle, milk, blue, w/wooden handle & bail, dome lid, 2 qt. (D-MW)   18
Kettle, white, w/bail & orig. cover (D-MW)   4
Ladle, gray, ½-cup size (D-MW)   4
Lunch box, blue, w/bail handle, wooden knob (D-E)   22
Measure, blue, 1 qt. (D-MW)   9
Measure, blue & white, qt. size (D-MW)   18
Measure, brown, qt. (D-E)   10
Measure, brown & white, qt. size (D-W)   22
Measure, gray, qt. size (D-MW)   15
Measure, turquoise, cup (D-SW)...   5
Measure, turquoise, pint (D-MW)..   8
Measure, white, qt. size (D-S)...   3
Measure, turquoise, ½-cup (D-SW)   4
Milk pail, blue & white (D-MW)   18
Milk pail, brown & white (D-W)   20
Milk pail, shaded blue (D-MW)   22
Milk pail, white (D-S)..   4
Mold, cake, gray, tube, fluted (D-MW)..   8
Mold, Turks head, gray (D-MW)   12
Mold, Turks head, gray (D-S)   10
Muffin pan, blue & white, 8-muffin size (D-MW)................................   8
Muffin pan, brown & white, 8-muffin size (D-W)................................   10
Muffin tin, gray, 6-hole (D-S)...   7
Muffin tin, brown, w/fluted cups, 12-hole (D-MW)............................   8
Mug, gray, handled (D-NE)   2
Pail, gray, dinner (D-E)   10
Pail, gray, lunch, w/cover (D-E)   9
Pan, cake, blue & white (D-MW)   6
Pan, cake, brown & white (D-MW)...   10

Graniteware, with pewter trim
(D-MW), *left to right:* **teapot,**
gray, $65; **mug,** lavender, $25;
coffeepot, gray, $75

Graniteware (D-MW), *left to right:*
milk pail, shaded blue, qt., $23; **pie
pan,** brown/white, 9", $8.00;
coffeepot, brown/white, $18

Pan, cake, brown & white (D-W) ....$	14
Pan, cake, gray, 8-sided w/tube (D-S)..	18
Pan, milk, blue & white (D-MW)...	5
Pitcher, blue & white, small (D-W)	3
Pitcher, brown & white, small (D-W)	8
Pitcher, gray, small (D-S)...	3
Pitcher, green shaded, small (D-S)	6
Plate, pie, brown, 10" diam. (D-MW)	8
Plate, pie, turquoise, 9" diam. (D-SW)..	8
Pot, blue & white, large (D-E)	12
Saucepan, turquoise, w/pouring lip, 1 qt. size (D-S)......................................	4
Scoop, grocer's, blue & white (D-MW)	6
Skimmer, brown, long handle, perforated bowl (D-W)	10
Spatula, turquoise, long handle, perforated blade (D-W)	5
Teakettle, blue & white (D-MW)	25
Teakettle, brown & white (D-S)...	28
Teakettle, brown, wooden handle, swan spout, 6½ qt. (D-MW)	22
Teakettle, gray (D-S)	12
Teakettle, gray & white, 9" t. (D-E)	7
Teakettle, gray, wooden handle, swan spout, 9 qt. (D-S)	10
Teakettle, turquoise, wooden handle, swan spout, 5½ qt. (D-E)	22
Teapot, blue & white (D-MW)...	12
Teapot, brown & white (D-MW)...	16
Teapot, granite & pewter (D-W)	45
Teapot, gray (D-W)...	10
Teapot, gray, pewter cover & trim (D-E)	25
Teapot, red (D-MW)	8
Teapot, white (D-W)	6
Teapot, yellow (D-S)	12
Tea steeper, blue & white, covered (D-W)..	12
Tea steeper, white covered (D-MW)	8
Toilet set, gray, 7-pcs., bowl, pitcher, covered chamber, small pitcher, cov. soap dish, tooth brush holder & cup (D-MW)	68
Turk's head, gray, cake mold, 3 qt. (D-MW)	15
Water pitcher, turquoise, w/lip guard (D-W)	18

Indian Collectibles

With interest in the American Indian aroused by recent publicity—including that surrounding the controversial stand at Wounded Knee—there has been a growing acceptance of Indian work as a major American art form. Moreover, collectors have discovered that genuine American Indian workmanship is equivalent, if not superior to other ethnic art forms. As a result, there has been an increased demand for early examples of beadwork, baskets, jewelry, rugs, etc., and prices have soared.

Since the demand for Indian objects exceeds the supply, many new articles have been imported from Hong Kong, Taiwan, Japan and Mexico, falsely labeled as American Indian. Beware of anything that has one of the following phrases attached to it: *Indian-design, Indian-inspired,* or *Indian-type.*

New Navajo rugs and jewelry have caused the greatest problem in this field. Good quality turquoise is in short supply, hence there is an increasing amount of fake, synthetic, and poor quality jewelry available. When considering a piece of turquoise jewelry, it is suggested that the following points be considered: 1) if a turquoise stone is opaque, it is generally of high quality and will have a mirror-like shine; 2) when a stone is translucent this usually indicates that it has been treated, and could possibly be synthetic, examples of the latter are usually soft and will scratch easily; 3) a good piece of turquoise will scratch, but not very easily. Many collectors prefer the "knifeblade" test, and if this is done, the test should be made on the edge of the stone; 4) a turquoise stone should rise well above the bezel (the silver strip that holds the stone in place), and should fit well; 5) note edges of the silver mounting—there should be no rough edges, and the mounting should be weighty, have clean, simple lines; and 6) earlier turquoise stones often show cracks, because the stones are brittle and can be damaged by rough handling.

It should also be mentioned that a good turquoise stone can be damaged easily when subjected to a flame. Heat can permanently whiten or alter the color of turquoise, or even crack it.

The contrast between Navajo and Mexican woven rugs becomes very apparent when the loom techniques, raw materials, and the finishing processes are compared.

Navajo weaving traditionally involves the usage of hand-cleaned and hand-spun yarns, retaining much of the lanolin that exists in the original fleece. The commercially prepared Mexican yarn is devoid of natural lanolin because it has been exposed to cleaning chemicals. It is the presence of the lanolin that adds weight to the genuine Navajo rug, and gives it a certain look, feel and odor (from the sheep), that does not exist in Mexican-made rugs of the same size.

A second area of comparison is the uniformity of color that is found in the Mexican rugs as a result of commercial dyes. For instance, gray is used regularly in their imitations: one light and one dark shade. In both instances, colors are uniform, no streaking, and the lighter shade of gray will have an occasional color-fleck—sometimes yellow or pink—which aids in identification.

Another important area of comparison is the weaving method, since the Navajo loom employs a warp that is mounted vertically, whereas the Mexican loom is set up with a horizontal warp which does not permit intensive packing, thus producing a more loosely woven rug. Moreover, several warp groups at the sides of weaving are used to compensate for reduced loom tension in maintaining straight edges.

Finally, the presence of multiple warpings and weaving on the Mexican loom results in fringed ends which are rethreaded. The 3-1-3-1 warp clusters give a ridged external texture to the top and bottom inch of the weaving, clearly indicating Mexican origin.

The federal government has twice tried programs of labeling Navajo rugs with attached tags with lead seals, but both experiments failed after a short period. Known misleading labels are: *Genuine Indian Made, Genuine Navajo Made,* or *Genuine Indian Maid* which pictures a Navajo weaver at her loom (stapled to Mexican rug).

Unfortunately, the only way a beginning collector of Indian crafts can protect himself is to make certain that he is dealing with a reputable and authentic store. The Arts & Crafts Division, U. S. Interior Department, Washington, D.C., maintains a list of reliable dealers, free for the writing.

* * *

Apron, Chippewa, hide w/front surface beaded in floral & leaf des. on black velvet background, back surface painted w/geometric design in red, hide fringe & ties, 16" w. (A-SW) ....\$ 250

Baby bonnet, Sioux, hide & cloth, fully beaded w/multicolored glass beads in geometric design, ca. 1890-1900, 12" circumference (A-SW) 350

Bag, Plateau, rectangular form, front surface fully beaded w/multicolored floral design on white background, cloth lined, 14"×16" (A-SW) 200

Bag, Plateau, rectangular form, front surface fully beaded w/multicolored floral design on white background, cloth lined, 13"×14" (A-SW) 150

Bag, strike-a-light, Apache, hide, blue & white beads in terraced pattern w/tin cone tinklers, ca. 1900, 5" l., 3½" w. (A-SW) 200

Basket, Pima
(D-W) \$210

Basket, Hopi, large coil, 6½" h. (D-W) \$225

Basket, Apache, oblong (D-W) \$225

Bag, strike-a-light, Plains, hide w/multicolored beads in floral design & w/pine cone tinklers, ca. 1890-1900, 4½"×4" (A-SW) 100

Bag, Umatilla, cloth, front fully beaded w/multicolored geometric designs on white background, ca. 1900, 12½"×13" (A-SW) 175

Bandolier bag, Chippewa, cloth, front stitched w/multicolored beads in floral pattern on white background, bugle bead tassels, ca. 1890, 41" l. (A-SW) 600

Bandolier bag, Chippewa, wide cloth bag & shoulder strap fully beaded w/floral design on white background, fringe of beads & yarn tassels, 47" l. (A-SW) 600

Bandolier bag, Chippewa, wide cloth bag & shoulder strap stitched overall w/multicolored glass beads, floral & leaf design, trim & fringe of loomed beadwork & yarn tassels, ca. 1890, 48" l. (A-SW) 850

Bandolier bag, Chippewa, wide cloth bag & shoulder strap, full beaded panel w/floral design on black velvet, beaded yarn tassels, ca. 1890, 48" l. (A-SW) 400

Basket, Apache, coiled grain barrel, diamond design, 19" h. (A-SW) 1050

Basket, Apache, coiled grain barrel, 4-color polychrome geometric design, 23" h. (A-SW) 3250

Basket, Apache, coiled bowl, various geometric designs radiating from central floral motif, 25½" diam. (A-SW) 1500

Basket, Apache, coiled shallow bowl, concentric flower petal motif, 25" diam. (A-SW) 1750

Basket, Apache, coiled shallow bowl, motif of dogs & crosses w/geometric designs, 17" diam. (A-SW) 650

Basket, Apache, coiled shallow bowl, motif of dogs interspersed w/geometric designs, 13" diam. (A-SW) 500

Basket, Apache, coiled grain barrel, motif of dogs & stars interspersed w/geometric designs, 16½" h. (A-SW) 2200

Basket, Apache, coiled shallow bowl, motif of horses & crosses, geometric designs, 23" diam. (A-SW) 1500

Basket, Apache, coiled shallow bowl, motif of men & concentric bands of geometric design, 22" diam. (A-SW) 900

Basket, Apache, coiled shallow bowl, motif of men, deer, dogs & crosses interspersed w/geometric designs, 18" diam. (A-SW) 400

Basket, Apache, coiled shallow bowl, motif of men, deer & dogs interspersed w/geometric designs, 19" diam. (A-SW) 900

Basket, Apache, coiled shallow bowl, negative & positive motif of men & dogs, geometric designs, 17" diam. (A-SW) 750

Basket, Apache, coiled shallow bowl, whirlwind design of comb-like motifs, 19½" diam. (A-SW) . 600

Basket, Apache, twined burden basket, hide reinforced bottom & suspensions of hide fringe & hawk bells, beaded tump-line, 11" h. (A-SW) 300

Basket, Apache, twined burden basket, hide reinforced bottom & suspensions of hide fringe, woven bands of design, 12" h. (A-SW) 450

Basket, Apache, twined burden basket, hide reinforced bottom & suspensions of hide fringe, woven & painted bands of design, 10" h. (A-SW) 200

Basket, Chemehuevi, coiled shallow bowl w/geometric designs, 12¾" diam. (A-SW) 800

Basket, coiled deep bowl w/ovoid form & embricated w/birds & geometric designs 14" h. (A-SW) 500

Basket, feather, round, 31" t. (A-NE) 35

Basket, form of doll's rocking cradle, w/blue decor. (A-NE) 275

Basket, hanging, red & brown stain w/stepped back, 13" h. × 6" w. (A-NE) 120

Basket, Hopi, coiled bowl, polychrome floral design, 9½" diam. (A-SW) 125

Basket, Hopi, coiled bowl, polychrome floral motif, 10" diam. (A-SW) 200

Basket, Hopi, coiled deep bowl, motif of polychrome kachina masks & deer, 6½" h. (A-SW) .. 250

Basket, Hopi, coiled deep bowl, polychrome geometric design, 7" diam. (A-SW) 150

Basket, Hopi, coiled deep bowl, polychrome geometric design, 6" diam. (A-SW) 125

Basket, Hopi, coiled deep bowl, 2 rows polychrome kachina masks, 15½" diam. (A-SW) 700

Basket, Hopi, coiled plaque, Navajo wedding basket design, 10" diam. (A-SW) 100

Basket, Hopi, coiled plaque, polychrome feather motif, 11" diam. (A-SW) 150

Basket, Hopi, coiled plaque, polychrome geometric design, 14½" diam. (A-SW) 200

Basket, Hopi, coiled plaque, polychrome geometric design, 7½" diam. (A-SW)......................... 50

Basket, Hopi, wicker bowl, polychrome geometric design, 7" diam. (A-SW) 75

Basket, Maidew tribe, water (D-E) 250

Basket, Maine, birch bark, interwoven w/white & brown, 9¼"×4¾" (D-NE) 18

Basket, Maine, covered, large, yellow & brown decor. (A-NE) 60
Basket, Maine, covered, round, painted; yellow & green stain w/decor., 12" h. × 15" diam. (A-NE) 80
Basket, Maine, early, shaped like stubby milkcan, splint turned gray, 18th C., 10"×8½" (D-E) 58
Basket, Maine, large, green, blue & yellow decor. (A-NE) 125
Basket, Maine, loom, double container, "porcupine" twist, pyramid shape, 21" overall, remnants red veg. dye (D-NE) 65
Basket, Maine, med. size, green & blue decor. (A-NE) 90
Basket, Maine, natural w/dk. blue bands, square, 10½"×11" (D-NE) 18
Basket, Maine, painted & decor., 12" × 18" (A-NE) 60
Basket, Maine, round, covered, blue-green, pink banding, 15½"×8½" (D-NE) 35
Basket, Maine, round, natural, pink, aqua banding, 10½"×12" (D-NE) 28
Basket, Maine, splint, square, covered, yellow, dk. gray & red, potato stencil in blue & red on alternate plain squares, 7"×8" (D-E) 25
Basket, Mono, coiled bowl w/2 bands of geometric design, 16" diam. (A-SW) 400
Basket, wedding, Navajo (D-W) 160
Basket, Northeast, red & blue stain, stamped decor. (A-NE) 55

Bean pot,
Picuris (D-W) $40

Basket, Northeast, red & green decor., 16"×7½" (A-NE) 80
Basket, open splint, wide bands of dk. blue, 16" diam., 13" h. (D-NE) 28
Basket, painted, cover in red & green w/stamped leaf decor. (A-NE) 190
Basket, painted, green & blue stain decor., 6" h. × 7" w. (A-NE) 120
Basket, painted, red & green stain w/stamped designs (A-E) 25
Basket, painted, red & yellow decor. (A-NE) 90
Basket, Papago, ca. 1840 (D-E) 50
Basket, Papago, ca. 1900, 12" diam., 4" d. (D-E) 50
Basket, Papago, coiled cylinder w/lid, geometric design, 15" h. (A-SW) 300
Basket, Penobscot, w/potato decor. (D-W) 35
Basket, "Pidgeon", loosely woven of bark, handled, 6" h., 7" diam. (D-NE) 25
Basket, Pima, animals & geometric design, rectangular, 15" l. (A-SW) 115
Basket, Pima, coiled bowl, fret design, decor. w/turquoise chunks & silver beads, 5" h. (A-SW) 350
Basket, Pima, coiled deep bowl, ovoid form, decor. w/embricated dog & bird motifs, 13½" h. (A-SW) 350
Basket, Pima, coiled jar, fret designs, 12" h. (A-SW) 350
Basket, Pima, coiled plaque, man-in-the-maze design, 10" diam. (A-SW) 275
Basket, Pima, coiled shallow bowl, complex geometric design, radiating from center, 21½" diam. (A-SW) 650
Basket, Pima, coiled shallow bowl, 5-armed fret design, 17½" diam. (A-SW) 350
Basket, Pima, coiled shallow bowl, 5-pointed star design, 18" diam. (A-SW) 400
Basket, Pima, coiled shallow bowl, 4-armed fret design, 18" diam. (A-SW) 350
Basket, Pima, coiled shallow bowl, 4-armed fret design, 10½" diam. (A-SW) 250
Basket, Pima, coiled shallow bowl, 4-petal squash blossom design, 18" diam. (A-SW) 600
Basket, Pima, coiled shallow bowl, fret design, 17¾" diam. (A-SW) 400
Basket, Pima, coiled shallow bowl, maze-like geometric design, 20" diam. (A-SW) 150
Basket, Pima, coiled shallow bowl, modified 5-petal squash blossom design, 13¼" diam. (A-SW) . 350
Basket, Pima, coiled shallow bowl, motif of butterfly wings, 10½" diam. (A-SW) 200
Basket, Pima, coiled shallow bowl, swastika design, 19" diam. (A-SW) 450
Basket, Pima, coiled shallow bowl, swastika design, 17" diam. (A-SW) 450

Basket, Pima, coiled shallow bowl, swastiska design, 20" diam. (A-SW) ....$ 500

Basket, Pima, coiled shallow bowl, whirlwind design, 15½" diam. (A-SW) 450

Basket, Pima, coiled shallow bowl, whirlwind design, 14¾" diam. (A-SW) 300

Basket, Pima, coiled tray, man-in-the-maze design, 10¼" diam. (A-SW) 350

Basket, Pima, flared, cylindrical shape w/swallow tail design (A-SW) 40

Basket, Pima, geometric design, 11½" diam. (A-SW) 35

Basket, Pima, geometric design, 5½" diam. (D-MW) 15

Basket, Paiute, coiled bowl, exterior covered w/beads in polychrome design, 5" diam. (A-SW) 300

Basket, porcupine twist, weathered gray color, handled, 5½"×4" (D-E) 18

Basket, red berry stain bands & natural, 2 handles, 22" × 14" × 9½" (D-NE) 28

Basket, small, old green paint, 9½" w. × 4" h. (A-NE) 30

Basket, small, orange & green paint, 2½" h. (A-NE) 60

Basket, Southwest Indian, seed, eagle pattern on bottom shelf (A-E) 185

Basket, splint, deep, 3-handled, will hang on wall, 11"×19" (D-NE) 19

Basket, square, covered, lined w/1829 Maine newspaper, wide splint in grape red w/grape red brush stroke decor., 15" sq. (D-E) 45

Basket, Yavapai, coiled grain barrel w/motifs of deer, birds & cacti, interspersed w/geometric designs, 22½" h. (A-SW) 6500

Basketry wallet, Nez Perce, twined of corn husks w/polychrome designs, 15½" l. (A-SW) 150

Basketry wallet, Nez Perce, twined of corn husks w/polychrome designs of dyed wool embroidery, 21½" l. (A-SW) 225

Beaded yoke, Blackfoot, hide, fully beaded w/multicolored beads in geometric design on white background, tassels of "Padre" beads, fringe on edges, post-1900, 35" w., 15" l. (A-SW)...... 500

Blanket, Navajo, chief's blanket pattern of stripes & terraced elements in red, black, blue, purple, brown & white, aniline dyed & natural wool colors, 6'8"×4'11" (A-SW) 2600

Blanket, Navajo, green background w/red designs in late serape style, aniline dyed handspun yarn, ca. 1875-1880, 6'4" × 4'1" (A-SW) 3000

Blanket, Navajo, late serape style design of terraces & stripes in red, orange, green, yellow & white, aniline dyed handspun yarn, ca. 1875, 6'10"×4'7" (A-SW)..................................... 4250

Blanket, Navajo, red background w/banded design, indigo blue, yellow & white, handspun yarn, 5'6"×4'2", ca. 1880 (A-SW) 1100

Blanket, Navajo, red & brown stripes on cream ground, 2'9"×5'2" (A-SW) 85

Blanket, Navajo, red background w/black and white wavy stripes, handspun, ca. 1900, 5'8" × 4'6" (D-MW).. 525

Blanket, Navajo, reds & browns against cream background, 4'11"×2'11" (A-SW) 190

Blanket, Navajo, Saxony yarn & raveled Bayeta, red background w/yellow, and black stripes on orange-red ground (D-NW).. 650

Blanket, Navajo, undamaged cond., mid-19th C. (D-W) 95

Blanket, Rio Grande, banded design in pink, yellow, white & green, vegetal dyed, handspun yarn, pre-1900, 8'×4'2" (A-SW).. 250

Blanket, saddle, Navajo, double, diamond twill in brown, black & white natural wool colors (A-SW).. 100

Blanket, saddle, Navajo, double, diamond twill in red, purple, blue, green & white w/green yarn tassels as corners, aniline dyed & natural wool colors (A-SW) 150

Blanket, saddle, Navajo, double, narrow strips of black & white, white yarn fringe at corners (A-SW).. 100

Blanket, saddle, Navajo, double, red background w/banded design in orange, green, yellow, black, gray & white, diamond twill weave, aniline dyed & natural colors, ca. 1910 (A-SW).. 450

Blanket, saddle, Sioux, hide, wide beaded strips of multicolored beads in geometric design, black satin center, 70" l. (A-SW) 1700

Bow & arrows, Hopi, painted wood, sinew wrapped, used in dances, post-1900, 25" l. (A-SW).. 50

Bowl, Navajo, stamped design, signed, "B. T.", ca. 1960, 13" diam. (A-SW) 100

Bowl, Navajo, copper w/stamped design, signed, "B. T.", ca. 1960, 13" diam. (A-SW) 100

Bridal set, horsehair (D-MW) 165

Box, Indian, oval, birch, lined w/Maine paper, ca. 1830s-40s (D-NE) 45

Cane, Great Basin, wood, fully beaded w/multicolored beads & beaded tassels, shell casing tip, ca. 1900, 37" l. (A-SW).. 350

Coat, Crow, painted yellow hide, front, back & sleeves sewn w/multicolored glass beads in floral des., trimmed w/otter fur & red & green ribbon, fringed, ca. 1870, 39" l. (A-SW)................ 2000

Coat, man's, Woodlands, hide, multicolored beads in floral design on cuffs, shoulder & strip up front, fringe on pockets, shoulders & cuffs, ca. 1900, 56"×30" (A-SW) ....$ 650

Cradle cover, Sioux, hide, flannel lined, w/outer area beaded w/multicolored design on white background, trimmed w/hide fringe & hawk bells, sinew sewn, post-1900, 22" l. (A-SW)..... 800

Dance wand, Plains, 2 inverted buffalo horns partially wrapped in hide & cloth, attached to wooden handle w/multicolored beadwork, ca. 1890, 22" l. (A-SW) 200

Doll, carved, Hopi, God of the sky, white case mask w/peaked headdress, holding lighting frame & bull-roarer, 14½" h. (A-SW)... 125

Doll, carved, Hopi, mudhead clown, seated & holding drum, 7½" h. (A-SW)........................ 125

Doll, carved, Hopi, snake dance figure, antelope priest, holding feathers & bag, 10" h. (A-SW). 125

Doll, kachina, Hopi, black ogre (Nata-aska) w/blue case mask, wearing hide & holding axe & staff, 17½" t. (A-SW)... 200

Doll, kachina, Hopi, butterfly, elaborate tableta w/figure in traditional garb, in dance movement, 15" h. (A-SW)... 300

Doll, kachina, Hopi, cow, gray & black case mask w/horns & bead necklace, rigid posture, 12" h. (A-SW).. 350

Doll, kachina, Hopi, cow holding staff, green case mask & painted kilt, 18" h. (A-SW).......... 200

Doll, kachina, Hopi, cross-legged, brown case mask w/lambskin wig, extended arms, 14½" h. (A-SW).. 300

Doll, kachina, Hopi, early morning, figure holding bow & yucca leaves, mask w/badger tracks, 18" h. (A-SW)... 225

Doll, kachina, Hopi, Heheya, green case mask w/white body in movement, 13" h. (A-SW) 125

Doll, kachina, Hopi, Hemis, surrounded by elaborate tableta, in dance movement, 16" h. (A-SW). 150

Doll, kachina, Hopi, Hototo, second mesa, horns & snout on mask, rigid posture, 12½" h. (A-SW) 250

Doll, kachina, Hopi, hummingbird, green case mask w/beak, bird on top of head, holding blossom & rattle, 14" h. (A-SW) 125

Doll, kachina, Hopi, hummingbird (Tocha), striped case mask w/feathered tableta, holding staff & ring, mounted on base, 15" h. (A-SW) 200

Doll, kachina, Hopi, long hair, traditional garb, holding rattle & sprig of Douglas fir, 17½" h. (A-SW).. 200

Doll, kachina, Hopi, mad or stone eater, from third mesa, black face mask w/snout, rigid posture, 10" h. (A-SW) 125

Doll, kachina, Hopi, mountain sheep holding cane, white case mask, 15½" h. (A-SW).......... 150

Doll, kachina, Hopi, ogre (Chaveyo) holding axe & bow from first mesa, w/black case mask, mounted on base, 13½" h. (A-SW)... 125

Doll, kachina, Hopi, red-tailed hawk, red tufts of horsehair protruding from mask, holding rattle, 17" h. (A-SW)... 250

Doll, kachina, Hopi, three horns on top of head w/snout, in dance movement, 11" h. (A-SW) 100

Rug, Navajo, red, black & white, ca. 1910, 38" × 55" (D-W) $250

Rug, 2 Gray Hills design, 24" w., 35" l., (D-W) $850

Doll, Navajo, stuffed figure of woman in traditional dress, 14″ h. (A-SW) ....$ 50

Dress, Apache, 2-piece, hide, top beaded & painted w/fringe, multicolored ½″ strip of beads, sinew sewn; skirt has tassels w/fringe & tin can tinklers, yoke 21″, skirt 20″ w., 24″ l., ca. 1890, (A-SW)..   900

Dress, Cheyenne, hide, yoke w/3 beaded strips in geometric design, w/white background, body of dress w/row of animal teeth & beadwork strips, fringe, ca. 1900, 45″ l., yoke 31″ w. (A-SW)   450

Dress, Navajo, 1-piece, black center w/terraced designs in red & blue at both ends, ca. 1885, 4′9″×4′3″ (A-SW)   2000

Dress, Navajo, 2-piece, black center w/terraced & striped design in blue & red at both ends, ca. 1885, 4′×2′5″ (A-SW)..   750

Dress, Navajo, 2-piece, black center w/terraced design in blue & red at both ends, aniline dyed & natural wool colors, 3′11″×2′9″ (A-SW)   450

Dress, Navajo, 2-piece, black center w/terraced design in blue & red at both ends, 4′3″×2′2″ (A-SW)...   350

Dress, Plains, hide, narrow strips of beadwork in geometric design, large trade beads & fringe, 39″ l. (A-SW)...   250

Drill, Pueblo, wooden hand tool used for drilling beads, 15½″ l.)A-SW)   250

Drum, hide & wood, drum head painted w/motif of bird, 4½″×19″ (A-SW).........................   150

Drum, Pueblo, hide on cottonwood w/painted geometric design, 7″×8″ (A-SW).....................   75

Drum & beater, Pueblo, painted wood w/drum heads & carrying loops of hide, wood & hide beater, 25″ l. (A-SW)   300

Drum & beater, Pueblo, painted wood w/drum heads & carrying loops of hide, beater of wood & hide, ca. 1930, 12½″ h. (A-SW)...   125

Drum rattle, Plains (D-W)   175

Kilt, Hopi, white cotton background w/red, green & black design, embroidered on ends w/woolen yarn, 3′8″×1′11″ (A-SW)   250

Knife sheath, Plains, hide, multicolored beads in geometric designs, sinew sewn, ca. 1900, 7½″ l. (A-SW)...   200

Leggings, Kiowa, hide, 2½″ strip of multicolored beadwork in terraced design on white background on one end, fringe on side, ca. 1890, 19″ l., 6″ w. (A-SW)   175

Loom, beadwork, Apache, w/wooden rollers & posts, complete, 11¾″ l., 4¼″ w. (D-W).......   65

Martingale, Sioux, hide w/cloth lining, long beaded strip forming loop w/geometric design, in multicolored glass beadwork, suspensions of tin cones w/dyed horsehair tassels & "scalp", 36″ l., ca. 1885 (A-SW)..   2000

Moccasins, Apache, woman's, painted yellow hide w/strips of beadwork, "cactus kicker" toes w/silver buttons, attached leggings, ca. 1890, 16½″ h. (A-SW)   300

Moccasins, Navajo, hide, high-topped, ankle flaps secured by 3 metal buttons each, 10¼″ l. (A-SW)..   50

Moccasins, Plains, hide, beaded w/multicolored beads in open work des., painted parfleche soles, 10″ l., ca. 1890 (A-SW)   400

Moccasins, Plains, hide, geometric, floral & life-form design, multicolored glass beadwork, sinew sewn (A-SW)..   60

Moccasins, Sioux, burial, child's, hide, ankle flaps & attached leggings, fully beaded w/geometric design in red, green, blue, yellow & white, sinew sewn, ca. 1890, 8″ l. (A-SW)..   500

Moccasins, Sioux, burial, hide, fully beaded w/geometric design in multicolored glass beads, sinew sewn, 6″ l. (A-SW)   300

Moccasins, Sioux, man's, hide, fully beaded w/geometric design in multicolored glass beads on white background, sinew sewn, ca. 1895, 11″ l. (A-SW)   150

Pipe & stem, Plains, round wooden stem, no decor., w/plain catlinite pipe bowl, ca. 1890, 25½″ l. (A-SW)...   100

Pipe bag, Northern Plains, hide, rect. beaded panels both sides w/geometric des. in red, blue, green & yellow on white background, quilled fringe, sinew sewn, 31″ l.)A-SW)......   400

Pipe bag, Sioux, hide, body w/multicolored beads in geometric design on white background, beaded strips on edges, dyed quill fringe, sinew sewn, ca. 1890-1900, 21″ l.)A-SW)..   450

Pipe bag, Sioux, hide, rect. beaded panels on both surfaces w/cross & bar design in multicolored glass beads on white background; quilled fringe w/matching cross design, ca. 1890, 25″ l. (A-SW)   400

Water jug, Apache, piñon pitch glaze, 12" h. (D-W) $250

Urn, Apache (D-W) $1800

Tray, Hopi, 14" diam., (D-W) $175

Pouch, Apache, hide, saguaro & ocotillo design in red & green glass beads, & band of geometric beaded trim, loomed beadwor, carrying strap, 6" l.)A-SW) ....$ 225

Pouch, Arapahoe, hide w/bands of multicolored beads in gometric design, ca. 1890, 9½"×7" (A-SW) 175

Pouch, hide w/floral arrangement in multicolored glass beads, fringed, 12" l.)A-SW) 150

Pouch, Navajo, medicine man, leather w/silver buttons, 55 half-inch & 1 one-&-one-half inch buttons on flap; 70 three-eights inch buttons on strap, pouch, 7½"×5¼", strap, 52" l., ca. 1890 (A-SW) 2500

Rattle, Plains, hide, wooden handle, body painted black, ca. 1890-1900, 7" l. (A-SW)........... 25

Rug, Navajo, banded designs, black, aniline dyed & natural wool colors, white background, 8'2"×5'6" (A-SW) 400

Rug, Navajo, banded designs, brown, black & white, vegetal dyed & natural wool colors, lt. brown background, 4'7" × 2'11" (A-SW) 200

Rug, Navajo, banded designs, brown, gold, gray & white, vegetal dyed & natural wool colors, 5'11"×a3'4" (A-SW)... 400

Rug, Navajo, banded designs, brown, gold, red, pink, gray & white, vegetal dyed & natural wool colors, 11'6"×9' (A-SW) 3000

Rug, Navajo, banded designs, brown, green, gray & white, vegetal dyed & natural wool colors, gold background, 8'4"×5'3" (A-SW) 750

Rug, Navajo, banded designs, gold, lavender & green, vegetal dyed colors, 6'4"×3'10" (A-SW).. 450

Rug, Navajo, banded designs, gold & white, gray background, vegetal dyed & natural wool colors, 4'4"×2'6" (A-SW)... 150

Rug, Navajo, banded designs, gray, green & white, vegetal dyed & natural wool colors, 5'3"×3'7" (A-SW)... 850

Rug, Navajo, banded designs, gray, green, pink, brown & white, vegetal dyed & natural wool colors, 4'6"×3'2" (A-SW) 250

Rug, Navajo, banded designs, green, brown & white, vegetal dyed & natural wool colors, gold background, 5'4"×3'5" (A-SW) 650

Rug, Navajo, banded designs, green, brown, gray & white, vegetal dyed & natural wool colors, gold background, 5'4"×3'6" (A-SW) 600

Rug, Navajo, banded designs, green, brown, gray & white, vegetal dyed & natural wool colors, gold background, 6'9"×4'3" (A-SW) 1000

Rug, Navajo, banded designs, green, gold, gray & white, vegetal dyed & natural wool colors, 5'2½"×3'5" (A-SW)... 450

Rug, Navajo, banded designs, lt. brown, gray & white, vegetal dyed & natural wool colors, by Alice Jones, Pine Springs (A-SW) 450

Rug, Navajo, banded designs, red, black & white, diamond twill weave, 4'8"×2'8" (A-SW).. 150

Rug, banded designs in red, blue, orange, black, gray & white, ca. 1900, 4'3"×3'1" (A-SW) . 300

Rug, Navajo, banded designs, red, pink, green, brown & white, vegetal dyed & natural wool colors; 7' × 3'10" (A-SW) 550

Rug, Navajo, chief's blanket pattern, stripes & terraces, red, blue, black & white, aniline dyed & natural wool handspun yarn, ca. 1900, 6'8"×5'1" (A-SW) 2500

Rug, Navajo, framed, red background w/serrated diamonds & interlocking designs, black, red, blue, brown & purple, ca. 1885, 3'2"×2'3" (A-SW) 600

Rug, Navajo, gray background, 4 yei figures in bright aniline dyed & natural wool colors, 6'9"×4'2" (A-SW)... 950

Rug, Navajo, gray background, outlined geometric designs in red, blue, green, black, brown, gray & white, teec nos pos style, aniline dyed & natural wool, 7'7"×3'8" (A-SW) ....$ 1200

Rug, Navajo, gray background, serrated diamonds, red, brown, black, gray & white, aniline dyed & natural wool colors, 8'8"×4'1" (A-SW) 350

Rug, Navajo, pink background w/diamond, square & chevron design, brown, black & white, aniline & vegetal dyed yarns, 8'7"×4'7" (A-SW) 850

Rug, Navajo, red background, 5 yei figures, pink, black, gray & white, wide black border w/stylized life forms in pink, green & white, aniline dyed & natural wool colors, 6'×3'10" (A-SW).. 1200

Rug, Navajo, red background, terraced & serrated diamonds in red, blue, orange, yellow, black & white, aniline dyed handspun & Germantown yarn, 6'4" × 4'6", ca. 1885 (A-SW) ... 2700

Rug, Navajo, teec nos pos style, geometric designs, red, blue, green, black, brown, gray & white, aniline dyed & natural wool, gray background, 7'7"×3'8" (A-SW) 1200

Rug, Navajo, 2 gray hills design, 5'9" × 7'10" (A-SW)... 800

Rug, Navajo, 2 gray hills design, black, gray, white, red & brown, aniline dyed & natural wool colors, lt. brown background, 7'×5'2" (A-SW).. 1200

Rug, Navajo, 2 gray hills design, black, white, brown & gray, natural wool colors, gray background, 11'6" × 4'5" (A-SW) 1250

Rug, Navajo, 2 gray hills design, brown, black, gray & white, natural wool & vegetal dyed colors, gray background, 8'×5'2½" (A-SW).. 2000

Rug, Navajo, 2 gray hills design, wide border of black & white, natural wool colors, brown background, 4'9"×3'6" (A-SW) 800

Rug, Navajo, white background, 3 yei figures, surrounded by rainbow god, bright aniline dyed & natural wool colors, 2'8"×2'6½" (A-SW)... 300

Rug, Navajo, white background, 3 yei figures surrounded by rainbow god, bright aniline colors, 2'6½" × 2'5" (A-SW) 400

Rug, Navajo, white background, 2 yei figures surrounded by rainbow god in bright aniline colors, 3'2"×2'5½" (A-SW)... 250

Rug, Navajo, zig-zag designs in red, blue, orange, green, black & white, aniline dyed handspun yarn, ca. 1885-1890, 6'8"×4'2" (A-SW) 1300

Rug, Navajo, zig-zag designs, red, orange, brown & white, aniline dyed & natural wool colors in pulled-warp weave, ca. 1885, 7'4"×5'3" (A-SW).. 2000

Saddle throw, Navajo, complex geometric design in red, blue, green, brown, black & white, aniline dyed 4-ply Germantown yarn, fringe & tassels, ca. 1890-1900 (A-SW) 650

Saddle throw, Navajo, feather, terrace & fret design in bright aniline colors, decorative fringe & tassels (A-SW) 400

Saddle throw, Navajo, gray background & red border w/design in orange, blue, black, gray & white, fringe & tassels (A-SW) 400

Saddle throw, Navajo, framed, red background w/serrated & rectangular design in blue, green, yellow & white, Germantown yarn, ca. 1880 (A-SW)... 800

Saddle throw, Navajo, star & floral design in red, orange, brown, blue, black & white, aniline dyed & natural wool colors, fringe & tassesls (A-SW) 144

Saddle throw, Navajo, swastika & fret designs in various bright colors, fringe & tassels (A-SW)... 500

Saddle throw, Navajo, white background w/geometric design in blue, orange, brown & white, aniline dyed & natural wool (A-SW).. 350

Sash, Hopi, woven of red & green woolen & white cotton yarns, 9' l. (A-SW).................... 50

Shawl, Hopi, white cotton center w/wide marginal bands of red & black woolen yarn, 4'×4'2" (A-SW) 300

Shirt, Crow, man's, hide, front & back decor. w/wide beaded strips w/geometric decor. in black, red, & blue beads on blue background, triangular neckflaps red & blue trade cloth w/beaded trim & fringe, sleeves w/beaded strips, tassels of ermine hide & tails, post-1900, 30½" l. (A-SW) 1500

Trencher, Indian, early, hollowed out of log, bark still adheres, flat ends, 31"×9½" (D-NE) 45

Vessel, Acoma, pottery, jar w/black geometric designs on white slip, ca. 1900-1910, 10½" h., diam. at shoulder 13" (A-SW) 400

Vessel, Santa Clara, pottery, polished black jar, no decor., 9½" h., diam. at shoulder 8" (A-SW)... 150

Vessel, Zuni, pottery, canteen w/floral medallion design, brown, white & red, 4" diam. (A-SW)... 175

Iron

From the time the first ironworks opened, about 1650, blacksmiths began producing a variety of interesting objects, both utilitarian and functional. During those early years, the fireplace was the only source of heat and, as a result, many fine iron articles collected today are directly related to the hearth—trammels, grills, trivets, skewers, cranes, toasters, waffle irons, tongs, log hooks, toasting forks, pokers, pie lifters, shovels, a variety of cooking utensils, and hardware, such as hinges, latches, straps, etc.

Blacksmiths rarely finished their handforged creations, leaving the filing, chasing, polishing, or any engravings, to the "whitesmith." Occasionally, however, there were craftsmen who carried out both procedures. These well-designed, decoratively engraved objects have become increasingly scarce and expensive in recent years.

Coffee grinder, iron, Enterprise, all orig. & working (D-W) $90

Scales, iron, brass pan orig. japanning fine (D-MW) $65

Iron hardware for furniture and construction was widely produced. The fittings which the collector seeks today are fine examples of the blacksmith's art.

Nothing enhances a piece of furniture more than the correct hardware, just as nothing detracts from it more than incorrect hardware. Metal fittings were originally intended to strengthen the large, heavily constructed objects such as chests, cupboards, and cabinets. These fittings quickly became decorative features. Most of the early chests have beautifully handwrought iron hinges, locks, straps and corners, as well as hasps and keys. During the early years of the seventeenth century, only two types of hinges were used on chests, the common bent wire or staple hinge, and the hardwood dowel. The first H-hinges were imported from England, but soon blacksmiths here were turning out these hinges. The smithy frequently produced rare and decorative forms of hardware, especially hinges. Here we have the intricately crafted butterfly, cock's head, hoop, dolphin, rat-tail, and the fanciful H- and LHL-hinges. These decorative features were especially popular in rural districts.

During the eighteenth century, brass and bronze embellishments began to replace iron fittings, and wooden pulls were gradually replaced by ivory, glass, and porcelain.

The shortage of good decorative cast and handwrought iron objects has naturally brought reproductions on the scene, and some very authentic-looking examples have been made in recent years. The best guide in determining whether a piece is old or new is its condition. Collectors should be extremely cautious of objects showing rusted, corroded, or rough surfaces, as many pieces have been artificially aged by exposure to moisture and chemicals, which produces a surface that is impossible to clean. The early objects were made to be used, and those pieces that have been associated with everyday living will have a smooth, worn surface appearance that is extremely difficult to duplicate until it has been used for a long period of time.

New iron objects which create the most problems for collectors today are trammels, skewer rests, hooks, Betty lamp spikes, balance scales 13" across, double crusie type lamps (many having pattern backs), handforged iron fireplace shovels, revolving fireplace trivets with pothandle rest, and rotating broilers or toasters. The majority of the new larger types listed are being made in the United States, but many smaller pieces are being imported.

* * *

Andirons, brass finials (A-E)	$ 130
Andirons, eagle, cast, 12" h., 15" l. (A-E)	65
Andirons, eagle, marked & dated (A-E)	70
Andirons, Franklin stove, ring finials, line decor. (A-E)	50
Andirons, good cond. (A-E)	60
Andirons, gooseneck, 23" l. (D-S)	48
Andirons, gooseneck, ball top, small feet, 18th C., 18½" d., 19½" h. (D-NE)	95
Andirons, gooseneck, handwrought, faceted tops & double spit holders, 21" h. (A-NE)	550
Andirons, gooseneck, handwrought, flattened iron blobs finials, 18th C., 16½" h. (D-NE)	95
Andirons, handwrought, dog feet (A-E)	65
Andirons, handwrought, Maine origin, 18th C. (A-NE)	200
Andirons, handwrought, multi-sided knobs on curved neck finials, wide flat frontal piece (A-E)	130
Andirons, handwrought, penny feet, diamond finials on bent neck, line decor., 8" (A-E)	675
Andirons, handwrought, pig tail, 14" (A-NE)	450
Andirons, pig tail, rare (A-E)	425
Andirons, scroll, footed base, early, 11" t., 13" backs (D-NE)	85
Andirons, twist form w/diamond baluster finials, 18th C., 16" h. (A-MW)	90
Andirons, 27" tall (A-E)	325
Apple dicer, cast (D-MW)	8
Apple peeler, clamp-on (D-E)	20
Apple peeler (D-E)	18
Apple peeler, dated May 24, '89 (D-N)	16
Back plate, fireplace, cast, relief decor. of the three witches, w/inscrip. "double, double, toil & trouble, fire burn & caldron bubble", marked A. Cox Stove Co., Chicago, pat pend., 19th C., 28½"×28½" (A-MW)	180
Bar, handwrought, tooled, 31½" l. (A-E)	50
Bell, dinner, on stand (A-W)	125
Bell, dinner, w/yoke (D-SE)	35
Bell, school, large (A-E)	45
Bell, sheep, 4½" h. (A-E)	15
Bell, ship's, cast (A-E)	50
Bill spindle, hanging, scrolled (D-MW)	8
Bird roaster, w/frame supports, 8"×12", 2 sections, for fireplace cooking (D-E)	30
Bird spit, w/heart, adjustable (A-E)	300
Book ends, dog, cast, 5½" h. (A-E)	25
Bootjack, beetle (D-MW)	22

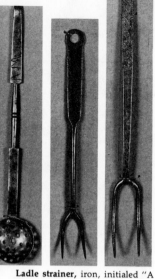

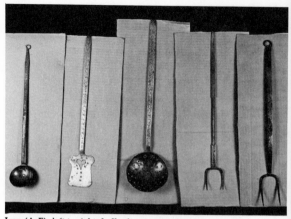

Ladle strainer, iron, initialed "A M", small (A-E) $210; **fork,** wrought iron, small (A-E) $65; **fork,** wrought iron, decor. handle, small (A-E) $50

Iron (A-E), *left to right:* **ladle,** brass, w/wrought iron handle, signed & dated, J. Schmidt 1842, $230; **spatula,** iron, fancy decor. handle, 1-pc., $270; **ladle strainer,** copper, wrought iron decor. handle, large, $120; **fork,** wrought iron, copper inlay, "P S 1831", $140; **fork,** wrought iron, full signature of John Derr, $425

Bootjack, beetle design (D-W)	$ 35
Bootjack, Naughty Nellie (D-MW)	28
Bootjack, Naughty Nellie (D-N)	25
Bootjack, Naughty Nellie (D-W)	38
Bootjack, Naughty Nellie, orig. decor., red/gilt (D-W)	25
Bootjack, pistol shaped, folding (D-MW)	32
Bootjack, steer's head (D-W)	15
Bootjack, triple heart, cast, 9½" (D-E)	65
Bootscraper, Terrier dog (D-W)	18
Bootscrapers, handwrought, pr. (A-E)	30
Bottle opener, shape of fish, 5½" (D-MW)	10
Bowl, 11¼" (D-NE)	38
Bowl, late 18th C., early 19th C., 10½" (D-NE)	36
Bowl, late 18th C., early 19th C., 11" (D-NE)	38
Bowl, table, 18th C., cast, 9½" diam. (D-E)	45
Bowl, table, 18th C., 10¾" (D-NE)	40
Bowl, table, 18th C., 14" (D-NE)	45
Bowl, table, late 18th, early 19th C., 10⅝" (D-NE)	38
Bowl, 10¼" (D-NE)	36
Brace trough, handwrought, ornamental (A-E)	52
Branding iron, handle, handwrought (D-E)	12
Brazier stand, handwrought, 17th C. (D-E)	75
Broiler, fish/meat, w/swivel joint & long iron handle (D-NE)	150
Broiler, handwrought, primitive (A-E)	240
Broiler, swivel type w/heart cut-out on top of handle (A-E)	180
Broiler, whirling, down-hearth, handwrought, round expanded hand grip w/raised center ridge (D-MW)	139
Broiler, whirling, early, round, waving grid pivoting on center pin & spit collar on handle (D-E)	110
Broiler, whirling, handwrought, wavy grid, 13"×20" (D-E)	85
Broiler, whirling, revolving rack, wavy bars, 4" legs, 18" handle, handwrought (A-E)	100

Buggy step, handwrought, w/wrought heart, 18½" l. (D-NE) ....$ 29
Bullet mold (A-E)..   17
Butter mold, glass plunger w/cow design, rare (D-MW)   55
Butter print, basket of flowers, 4¼" diam., round (D-NE)   30
Butter print, round, 3 ferns, rare (D-E)   50
Chain, w/hook, handwrought, to hang early lantern, 13" (D-E)   10
Chair, bow-back Windsor type made of solid iron (D-MW).....................................   18
Charcoal iron, w/one chimney (D-MW)   56
Charcoal roaster, iron/metal w/revolving handle, rarity (D-MW)   88
Cheese tester, 17½" (D-S)   15
Cherry pitter, single (D-N)   9
Cherry stoner, Enterprise, cast (D-E)   15
Chopper, early, 8½" blade, handwrought w/wooden handle (D-NE)........................   15
Chopper, food, w/side "L" shaped handle, handwrought, 6"×7" (D-NE)   20
Coal hod, w/hinged lid, cast (A-E)   50
Coal scoop, w/lid & wood handle (A-E)   22
Coffee grinder, box type, mkd. Crown no. 1, orig. black enamel finish good, brass cover
polished, working (D-NE)..   18
Coffee grinder, box type, Universal no. 110 attached handle, complete & working (D-S)   22
Coffee grinder, box, "Universal Coffee Mill, one pound", 7½" h., 6" sq. base, drawer (D-W) .   35
Coffee grinder, red, mkd. "Grand Union Tea Co.," (D-E)..   75
Coffee grinder, wall, American, Clark pat. (D-E)   45
Coffee mill, Enterprise, no. 1, complete & working (A-E)   135
Coffee mill, Enterprise, no. 1, complete w/drawer, all orig. (D-MW).....................   90
Coffee mill, Enterprise, no. 2, complete & working, two wheels, orig. paint good (D-MW)   185
Coffee mill, Enterprise, no. 3, complete & working, two wheels, orig. japanning ex. (D-E)   250
Coffee mill, Enterprise, no. 3, double wheels, orig. decor., ex., working (D-E)   255
Coffee mill, Enterprise, no. 3, new paint (black), wooden drawer & cover (D-W)..................   55
Coffee mill, Enterprise, no. 3, orig. paint faded but good, complete (D-SE)..........................   150
Coffee mill, Enterprise, no. 9, eagle finial, orig. paint proof, complete (D-MW)   300
Coffee mill, Enterprise, no. 12, store type w/eagle on hopper, two wheels, orig. japanning good,
working (D-MW)   350
Coffee mill, Enterprise no. 350, wall type, complete w/pan & working (A-MW)   67
Coffee mill, "Ever Ready" no. 2, complete w/orig. canister & cup, japanned, good, working
(D-MW)   420
Coffee mill, Universal, clamp on table, complete & working (D-MW)   38
Coffee mill, Universal no. 0012, sheet iron w/black enamel finish, wall type, comp. &
working (D-N)..   32
Coffee roaster, cylinder-shaped, sits on stove lid (D-E)..   55
Coffee roaster, early, round sheet iron container w/sliding door & pivot on base to revolve,
long handle, 60" l. (A-E)   85
Coffee roaster, long handle, spike end, 18th C., 49" l. (D-NE)   145
Coffee roaster, rare ball shape, 4" iron spike on base & short iron handle, 10" l. (D-S).........   85
Coffee roaster, rare ball shaped form w/4" iron spike on base & short handle opposite end,
10" l. (D-E)   85
Cookie board, eagles & flowers, hollow, cast (D-E)   75
Cookie cutter, lyre shape, oval, 5¼" (D-N)..   38
Cookie cutter, Santa Claus (D-MW)   95
Cookie mold, basket of flowers, oval, handwrought (D-E)   45
Cowbell, 5" h. (D-S)...   12
Cowbell, ball clapper, 7" h. (D-W)   17
Crane plate, footed, stationary, wrought handle, w/swivel top, 13½" diam. × 16" t. (D-E)   65
Cup, tin lined, marked (D-S)..   42
Curlers, wig, handwrought, ball ends (D-E)   15
Curling iron, crimper, early (D-W)..   4
Curling iron, handwrought (D-E)   65
Cuspidor, cast (D-NE)...   15
Dipper, brass bowl attached to wrought handle, forged ring for hanging, 19" l., diam. of bowl 4½"
(A-NE)   35

Dipper, ice cream (D-E)	$ 3
Dipper pan, handled, thin iron, 7″ bowl, 8″ handle (D-NE)	22
Dog collar, handwrought, stone rattles, 18th C. (A-NE)	40
Doorknocker, ring 6″ diam., hand forged (D-E)	28
Door latch, large double tulip, rare (A-E)	300
Doorstop, basket of flowers, 8¾″ h. (D-NE)	12
Doorstop, bulldog, 3½″ h. (A-E)	12
Doorstop, elephant (A-E)	22
Doorstop, frog (A-E)	15
Doorstop, Mayflower ship (D-NE)	30
Doorstop, Mayflower ship, orig. paint, 12″ h. (D-W)	18
Doorstop, peacock, w/spread tail (D-NE)	15
Doorstop, scottie (D-MW)	35
Doorstop, shape of lion, cast (A-E)	30
Doorstop, soldier figure (D-MW)	15

Muffin pan, iron, heart-shaped molds (D-MW) $19

Muffin pan, cast iron, fruit & vegetable-shaped designs (D-MW) $80

Dough scraper, brass & iron, dated & signed "P. D., 1848" (A-E)	250
Dough scraper, brass & iron, signed "P. D." (A-E)	90
Dutch oven, cast (D-E)	8
Dutch oven, perfect bottom w/orig. high flange cover, chipped corner, 18th C. (D-NE)	45
Eagle, spread-winged, over-door plaque, 19th C., 21″ w. (D-W)	150
Eagle, 3-dimensional (D-E)	35
Eagles, snow, dated, cast, pr. (D-E)	25
Ember carrier, punched tin floral decor. on cover (D-E)	65
Ember carrier, wooden handle, perforated top (D-W)	35
Escutcheon, handwrought, w/rooster head (A-E)	230
Firedogs, handwrought, 17th C., 33″×11½″ (D-NE)	135
Fire marker, oval, F. A. w/fire plug & hose (D-E)	90
Fire tongs, handwrought, long handled (A-E)	40
Flatiron, box-type, insert for heating (A-NE)	28
Flatiron, charcoal, twisted handle mkd. 5w (D-MW)	20
Flatiron, small, red, dated 1877 (D-E)	30
Flatiron, used by tailors, large (D-E)	20
Flatiron, wood handle (D-S)	4
Flatiron, wood handle (D-W)	7
Fluting iron, double, complete w/holder (D-W)	50
Fluting iron, Geneva hand, base marked "heat time", pat'd. 1866 (D-MW)	22
Fluting iron, Geneva, 2-part, complete (D-E)	20
Fluting iron, rocking, "the best", 2-part, complete (D-E)	20
Fluting iron, 2-part (D-E)	16
Food chopper, early, 12″ l. (D-E)	20
Food grinder, clamp on table, complete & working (D-MW)	12
Footscraper, cast, set in marble, from Baltimore, 22″ l. × 13″ with 14¼″ leaves, 28½″ h. (A-E).	90
Footscraper, handwrought, small, rooster tail, wing nut (A-E)	25

Footscraper, wrought, ramshorn, curled tops (D-MW) ....$ 32
Fork, handwrought, brass inlay "Jo. Seacer" (A-E)... 90
Fork, handwrought, 39" l. (D-E).. 25
Fork, handwrought, copper inlay "P S 1831" (A-E) 140
Fork, handwrought, med. size, rams horns & curved hook (A-E) 200
Fork, handwrought, nice decoration (A-E) 27
Fork, handwrought, rare, signed John Derr (A-E) 425
Fork, handwrought, small (A-E) 65
Fork, handwrought, small, decorated handle (A-E).. 50
Fork, handwrought, 3-tine, 17" (D-E) 22
Fork, handwrought, 2-tine, rat-tail end (D-E) 22
Fork, large (A-E) 52
Fork, large, good decor. on handle completely filled (A-E) 80
Fork, med. size, round to flattened handle (A-E) .... 30.
Fork, med. size, well-crafted, elongated diamond shaped handle (A-E).......................... 55
Fork, resting, hearth, w/tripod base (A-E) 80
Fork, 3-tine, handwrought, 12" l. (A-E)... 18
Fork, "X" decor., heavy, handwrought, 13" deep (D-E) 35
Fork & spatula, combination, rare, w/heart, 1809 (A-E)... 625
Fork & spatula, set, early, wrought, 15" & 18" l. (D-E) 50
Fork, toasting, w/legs, for use on hearth, twisted handle, 30" l. (D-MW) 65
Frog, cast, political — "I croak for the Webster wagon" (A-E)...................................... 345
Fry pan, handwrought, long handled, 19th C., handle 36" l., pan 10" diam. (A-MW)............. 38
Fry pan, handwrought, long handled, 1-pc., 40" l., pan 11¼" (D-NE)............................ 95
Fry pan, marked "Whitfield" (A-E).. 12
Fry pan, on three legs (A-E) 37
Goffering iron (D-MW) 40
Goffering iron, ram's horn curl decor., spear end, double, handwrought, 13" t. (D-E)............ 175
Grating, window, lacy iron, w/hearts, stars, 21"×11" (D-E) 10
Griddle, pancake, 3-legged (D-E)... 125
Griddle, "plate", handled, 9" (D-NE)... 16
Griddle, projections for handles, 18"×9" (D-NE) 6
Grill, decorated handle, closed, cast, 13¾" (A-E) 45
Grill, fireplace, double & reversible, handwrought, 23" l. (A-NE)................................. 150
Grill, footed, fireplace, grease trough & 10 hollow bars for grease, ca. 1850, 12" sq., handle 17" l.
  (A-E) 48
Grill, heart cut out handle, signed "C. B.", 21" l., handwrought (A-NE) 140
Grill, large, cast, solid, 15" diam. (A-E) 35
Grill, open w/four shaped feet, handwrought, 10½" (A-E)... 40
Grisette, handwrought, 22" handle, pan 7" diam. (D-E).. 48
Grisette, wrought, 20" handle (D-E) 90
Grist mill, "black hawk", table, complete & working (D-S) 28
Handle, rare, top cusp w/no hole for thumb piece, tulip cusp at top, well-shaped heart at bottom
  (A-E) 350
Hanger, for roasting birds, handwrought, small w/4 prongs, 2½" ring (A-NE) 18
Hanger, handwrought w/2 hooks (A-E)... 15
Hearth pan, handwrought, 12½" diam., 5" deep, tripod, handle 18" l. (A-E) 125
Hinge, frogs legs, handwrought (A-E).. 65
Hinges, barn, scrolled, pr. (A-E).. 42
Hinges, bird head, good escutcheon & one H-hinge w/designed finials, mounted on board, pr.
  (A-E) 210
Hinges, blanket chest, handwrought, pr. (A-E)... 27
Hinges, butterfly, covered, handwrought, pr. (A-E) 70
Hinges, cross-garnet, handwrought, tulip plant & flower design, pr. (A-E)............... 2900
Hinges, for wagon box, pr. (A-E).. 17
Hinges, handwrought, narrow w/tulip bud motif, pr. 22" (D-W) 55
Hinges, "H", handwrought, rare, scroll-rooster head, pr. (A-E)................................... 170
Hinges, handwrought, small, pr. (A-E)... 55
Hinges, rams horn, cross-garnet, pr. (A-E)... 40

Hinges, shutter, handwrought, eleven (A-E)	$ 22
Hinges, single, three (A-E)	37
Hinges, strap, blanket chest escutcheon, red paint, pr. (A-E)	50
Hinges, strap, frogs legs pintles, small, pr. (A-E)	45
Hinges, strap, handwrought, w/bird head pintles, pr. (A-E)	225
Hinges, strap, long, four (A-E)	27
Hinges, strap, rams horn pintles, pr. (A-E)	40
Hinges, tulip strap, large, pr. (A-E)	25
Hinges, "water buffalo scroll" type, pr. (A-E)	30
Hitching block, horses (D-W)	6
Hitching post, horse, 51" h. (A-E)	275
Hitching post, horse head (D-SE)	70
Hitching post, horsehead & rings, early (D-E)	160
Hook, barn, handwrought, tulip design (A-E)	230
Hook, devil's tail, handwrought (A-NE)	50
Hook, door, handwrought (D-NE)	1
Hook, handwrought, 4-pronged, 9½" (A-NE)	70
Hook, form of snake, early, handwrought, 14" h., (39" in actuality) (A-NE)	200
Hook, hunter's, handwrought, orig. strap to carry over shoulder, held rabbits or fowl, early 19th C. (A-E)	55
Hook, kettle, handwrought, pr. (A-E)	55
Hook, kettle lifting, twisted shaft & wood handle, 5"×4½" (D-E)	50
Hook, "S", for crane, 7" (D-NE)	7
Hook, "S", for crane, 7½" (D-NE)	8
Hook, "S", good cond., 8" (D-NE)	7
Hook, "S", handwrought, 8" (D-NE)	8
Hook, "S", handwrought, 14" (D-NE)	10
Hook, "S", handwrought, 6" (D-NE)	8
Hook, "S", handwrought, 6¾" (D-NE)	8
Horseshoe, large work horse (D-MW)	3
Hot plate, oval, cast, 10" d. (A-E)	22
Humidor, round, standing general figure, signed Crowley (D-E)	30

Iron (A-E), *top row, left to right:* **toaster,** rotating, wrought iron, 14" w., 17" l., $190; **toaster,** wrought iron, revolving, used on down-hearth, early 18th C., **$300;** *bottom row, left to right:* **camp broiler** or charcoal stove, oak handle, Revolutionary War period, $225; **trivet to toaster,** wrought iron, rare, adjustable, 10" h., $350

Bird spit, wrought iron, adjustable (A-E) $175

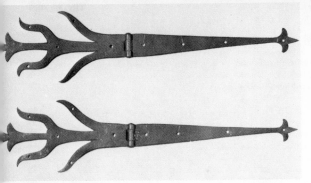

Hinges, wrought iron, cross garnet type, 18th C. (A-NE) $2900

Wrought iron hardware (A-E), *left to right:* **latch lock,** tulip, $70; **door latch, double tulip,** $300; **latch lock,** tulip, $60

Ice chopper (D-E) ....$	3
Ice skates, curved runners, 18th C. (D-E)	65
Kettle, butchering, large, cast (D-E)	35
Kettle, bundt, w/bail, footed, 10″ (D-E)	85
Kettle, cast, 3-legged w/swinging handle (D-MW)	35
Kettle, 4 legs, lid & brail, 14″ diam. (D-NE)	55
Kettle, Gypsy, 3-legs, 12″ diam. (D-SW)	25
Kettle hanger, used on trammel in fireplace, 13½″ l. (D-E)	35
Kettle, swinging handle & side ring (D-MW)	42
Kettle, 3 legs, w/handle, 24″ diam. (D-MW)	35
Kettle tilter, for crane, handwrought, 18th C. (D-E)	140
Kettle tilter (D-NE)	155
Kettle, witch's, w/lid, cast, no bail handle, 9½″ (A-NE)	110
Ladle, for lead, large (D-MW)	12
Ladle, good shape, initialed "E. B.", small (A-E)	120
Ladle, handwrought, ex. design on handle, serrated line border, 1822 (A-E)	275
Ladle, handwrought, initialed "J. W.", heart design, 1840 (A-E)	425
Ladle, handwrought w/2 legs that extend 4″ each side just before hand grip, rare form (A-NE)	68
Ladle, shaped handle, profusely decor. (A-E)	130
Ladle, small, initialed "AM" (A-E)	180
Ladle, straining, decor. in form of 8-pointed star (A-E)	130
Ladle, tasting, signed J Schmidt, 1846, support tongue under ladle cup (A-E)	200
Ladles, skimming, (2) 1 w/well-shaped handle (A-E)	65
Latch, arrowhead, Suffolk, w/flattened handle lined in middle (A-E)..............	100
Latch bars, handwrought, one beehive form, pr. (A-E)	50
Latch, "bean", handwrought (D-NE)..	4
Latch, crescent moon at top (A-E)	125
Latch, door, Suffolk tulip bud, handwrought (A-E)	40
Latch, Suffolk, form of spear head w/full compliment (A-E)	75
Latch, Suffolk, handwrought w/excellent design (A-E)....................................	110
Latch, tulip, handwrought (D-E)...	140
Latch, tulip, Suffolk, w/full compliment (D-E)...	125
Latch, tulip, Suffolk, w/full compliment (A-E)...	500
Lid, stove, 5″ diam. (D-S)	4
Lid, stove, 9″ diam. (D-S)	5
Lock, brass knobs, double wrought iron, 12″ (A-E)	35
Lock, door, handwrought, chased handle (A-E)	45
Lock, door, handwrought, decor. (A-E)	35
Lock, door, w/key, 18th C., 11¼″×5½″ (D-W)	40
Lock, latch, signed "W B", good design (A-E)	35
Lock, house, tulip latch (A-E)..	60
Lock, latch, tulip, handwrought (A-E)	70
Locks, door, pr. (A-E)	45

Match holder, stove shape (D-NE) ....$ 25

Match holder, wall, single compartment (D-NE)   15

Match holder, wall, 2 compartments (D-E)   12

Match safe, cast "Crown Jewel stoves", high button shoe, 6"×6" (D-E)   35

Match safe, cast, half circle, hanging, open, 5½"×2½"×1" (D-W)   25

Match safe, wall, striker in front (D-MW)   22

Mold, lamb (D-S)   22

Mortar & pestle, cast, 7¼" h. (A-E)..   40

Mortar & pestle, cylindrical shaped mortar, wood pestle (D-MW)   22

Mortar & pestle, cylindrical, square side handles (D-MW)   22

Mortar & pestle, large, early, 8" diam., 8¼" h. (D-NE)..   45

Mortar & pestle, urn shaped mortar on pedestal base w/iron pestle (D-MW).......................   18

Muffin pan, corn, 8-mold (D-MW)..   12

Muffin pan, 8 holes, assorted fruit & vegetables (D-E)..   75

Muffin pan, 8 shallow ovals, early (D-W)   22

Muffin pan, for 7 muffins, side handle, 3-legged, round (D-MW)   35

Muffin pan, for fireplace, shallow, flat bottom cups, 3-2-3 rows, hanging handle (D-W)   22

Muffin pan, round w/6 heart shaped holes, center w/star, 6" handle, cast (D-MW).................   20

Muffin pan, 7 cornsticks (D-S)   18

Muffin pan, 7 small, deep, round bottom cups, 2-3-2, hanging handle, round, early (D-NE) ..   25

Muffin pan, shallow, flat bottom cups, 3-2-3 rows, hanging handle, 1 long foot at back, pan slants
  on flat surface, for fireplace (D-NE)..   25

Muffin pan, shallow ovals (8), w/hole for hanging, ca. 1840 (D-E)   22

Mulling iron, brass knob & curved end, 18th C., 15" l. (D-E)..   38

Mustache curling set w/alcohol burner, complete (D-E)   35

Niddy-noddy, handwrought, good cond. (D-E)   28

Nutcracker, dog, cast (D-MW)   18

Nutcracker, dog (D-NE)..   18

Nutcracker, parrot (D-MW)   28

Nutcracker, squirrel, cast (D-MW)   20

Nutcracker, table clamp on type (D-MW)   15

Pan, feet (D-E)   30

Pan, 3-spike-legs, 8" handle (A-E)   65

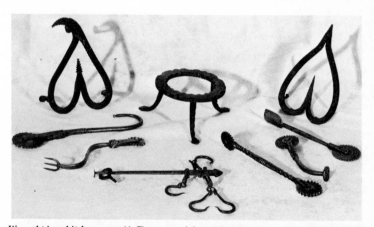

Wrought iron kitchenwares (A-E), *top row, left to right:* **trivet,** heart-shaped, penny feet .
& rattler-tail design at point of heart, rare, $180; **trivet,** round, flaring legs terminating in
arrow feet, $100; **trivet,** heart-shaped, penny feet, $90; *bottom row, left to right:* **pie
crimper,** $75; **pie crimper** w/wheel on 1 end & 3-pronged fork on other end for decor. pie
crust, $250; **miniature hanging scales,** $65; **double wheel pie crimper,** $65; **pie crimper**
w/curved extension having rare cloverleaf print, $200; **pie crimper,** rare wrought iron,
with serrated spoon, crimper at opposite end, $330

Pancake turner, handwrought, hook handle w/curlicue, 18" l. (D-MW) ....$ 35
Peel, bake oven, handwrought, scrolled top, 39½" (A-NE)   100
Peel, bread, 18th c. (D-NE)   75
Peel, handwrought w/twisted handle (A-E)   20
Peel, pie (D-E)   75
Pie crimper, double wheel, handwrought w/decor. handle (A-E)   65
Pie crimper, handwrought, design on handle, rare clover leaf print (A-E)............................   200
Pie crimper, handwrought, good design w/unusual crook (A-E)   75
Pie crimper, handwrought, rare, serrated spoon crimper w/eagle & shield design, line decor. on handle, brass wheel (A-E)   330
Pie crimper, handwrought, wheel one end & curved 3-pronged fork other end (A-E).............   250
Pie crimper, 4" l. (D-W)   22
Pie lifter, cast, 19th C. (D-MW)   18
Plaque, overdoor, spreadwinged eagle, 19th C., 21" w. (D-W) ....   150.
Plate, table, 8" (D-NE)   40
Plate warmer, handwrought, made to hang on crane or fire bar, rare (A-E)   120
Porringer, cast, handled, signed Kenrick, 5½" (D-E)   70
Porringer, oversize, straight sprue on bottom, early casting, handled like a porringer/support pieces under handle, 8" (D-NE)   65
Porringer, signed Kenrick, 5" (D-NE)..   55
Porringer, signed Kenrick, 5½" (D-NE)...   55
Posnet, early, 8" (D-NE)..   28
Posnet, early, 10" (D-NE)..   32
Posnet, long handled (D-E)   75
Posnet, 3 feet, straight handle, 8" (D-NE)   28
Pot, cooking, cast, fireplace, 11" diam., w/lid (A-E)   62
Pot, cooking, cast, w/lid, 11" diam. (A-NE)   62
Pot, cooking, long handle, marked "Seitle" (A-E)   32
Pot, handwrought, 3-legged, 9½" diam. (D-NE)..   28
Pot lifter, 5" circular wooden handle, lifter clinched at end of handle, handwrought (D-W).....   18
Pot lifter, half-round handle, 5" drop at right angle w/decor. twist, hook w/1" opening, 6" l. (D-E)   28
Pot, 9" brass spigot & hook to hang from crane, marked w/"R", 27" h. (A-NE)   200
Pot, on 3 legs w/side handle (D-MW)   40
Pot, side handle, cast (D-MW)...   28
Pot, stew, w/cover (D-E)   50
Pudding mold, handled (D-MW)   25
Pump stay, w/twisted braces, handwrought (A-E)   60
Rabbit roaster, w/frame supports, 12"×16", 2 sections for cooking each half of rabbit in front of fire (D-MW)   35
Rack, 14 assorted metal & iron cooking implements, 19th C. (A-MW)................................   60
Razor, men's, handwrought, rare (A-E)   30
Receipt spindle (D-MW)...   10
Roaster, charcoal, w/revolving handle (D-MW)   88
Rolling pin, cast, 18" l. (D-E)   12
Sausage grinder, Enterprise no. 32 (D-W)   12
Sausage stuffer, paint worn (D-MW)..   15
Scale, brass pans, 19th C., 22" l. (A-MW)..   120
Scale, 2 brass pans, 19th C., 20" l. (A-MW)   115
Scale, counter type, brass pan, iron wts., orig. japanning good (D-MW)   65
Scale, counter type, cast iron, brass weights (D-MW)   30
Scale, counter type, weights up to 15 lbs., orig. brass pan & iron weights, japanning ex. cond. (D-W)   65
Scale, druggist's, milk glass, 4" diam., flat plates, mkd. complete (D-MW)   60
Scale, meat, small, decor. (D-E)   45
Scuttle, coal (A-E)   17
Sewing bird, handwrought, extended tongue, decor. w/punch work, thumbscrew shape of heart w/2 love birds (A-E)   825
Shears, handwrought, 12" l. (A-E)..   20
Shears, handwrought, 18th C., 12" l. (D-E)..   35

Shears, handwrought, 18th C. (D-E)...$ 30
Shoe, button, for mannekin, 6½" h. D(-W)   22
Shoes, high button, cast, pr., 8×10" (D-E)...   50
Shoe scraper, handwrought, ex. large curls (A-E)   65
Shoe scraper, large flowing curls (A-E)   125
Shoe scraper, rat-tail pattern, handwrought (A-E)   45
Shoe scraper, scroll on ends (A-E)..   27
Shovel, fireplace, handwrought, heart shaped handle (A-E)   75
Shovel, fireplace, handwrought, rams horn decor. at top of handle (A-E)...........................   55

Trammel, wrought iron,
Penna. Dutch, incised heart
decor. (A-E) $500

Foot tub, iron,
small (D-MW) $38

Pan, cast iron, unusual design (D-MW) $22

Shovel, fireplace, rams horns on handle (A-E)..   130
Shovel, handwrought, heart shaped, handle (A-E)   75
Sign, hex, for barn (A-E)   40
Skewer holder, complete w/skewers (D-E)...   250
Skewer holder, handwrought, 5 skewers, rare (A-E)..   525
Skewer set, handwrought, holder, 4 skewers 9-5" l. (D-MW)   350
Skewers, set of 5, handwrought, ca. 1700, orig. holder (A-NE)   79
Skillet, cast, early, supported by 3 legs w/straight 8" handle; 6" h., 7" diam. (A-E).................   65
Skillet, cast, 3 legs & straight 4" handle, 4½" diam., 3½" h. (D-E)   38
Skillet, cast, 3 legs & straight 7" handle, 5" diam., 6" h. (D-W)................   30
Skillet, on three legs w/side handle (D-MW)   18
Skillet, on 3 legs, 10" diam. (D-NE)..   22
Skimmer, handwrought, w/deep bowl, holes in bowl, 17" (D-E)..............   22
Snow eagles, cast, pr. (A-NE)   37
Snow eagles, handwrought, pr. (D-E)   50
Snow eagles, small size, pr. (D-MW)...   22
Spatula, elaborate decor. on handle filled even to spatula part (A-E)....................   270
Spatula, handwrought, 18", signed "Cook" (D-W)   20
Spatula, handwrought, iron handle, brass flipper, 12" (D-NE)   66
Spatula, handwrought, signed "S. Wolf" (A-E)..   40

Spatula, handwrought, 16" l. (D-E) ....$ 15
Spatula, handwrought, twisted handle, 18th C., 16¾" l. (D-E)   38
Spatula, handwrought, well-shaped handle (A-E)   30
Spatula, fork and ladle, handwrought, set (A-E) 125
Spoon, early, long handle/rat-tail hook, 20¼" (D-NE)   16
Spoon, handwrought (D-W)   22
Spoon, large, with decor. (A-E)   45
Spread eagles, cast, w/10" wingspan, pr. (A-E)   85
Squeezer, lemon (D-MW)   16
Squeezer, lemon, squeezes ½ lemon, 8½" (D-E)   15
Staples, handwrought, lg., use w/"S" hooks for hanging lanterns, etc. (D-NE)   1
Stew pan, 3-legged (A-E)   45
Stove, charcoal, early, small, complete (D-N)   65
Stove, charcoal, supported by 4 scrolled feet, wooden handle & latch rest supports for pan, 8" sq.,
   9" h. (D-E)   80
Stove, heating, parlor, shape of house, good cond. (D-MW)   85
Stove, kitchen range, Richmond Stove Co., complete & usable (D-MW) 175
Stove, parlor, small, cast, marked "C. W. Warnick, pat. 1848", 16" h., 23" l. (D-E) 300
Stove plate, American eagle 18"×22" (D-NE) 325
Stove plate, children & animals in relief, 20"×22" (D-E) 200
Stove plate, name, date & tulip decor. (A-E)   95
Stove plate, name, date & decor. (D-MW)   80
Stove poker (D-N)   5
Stove poker, spring handle, handwrought (A-E)   20
Stove, Shaker design, w/4 tapering round legs, cast (A-E) 500
Stove, toy iron nickel plated "Royal," complete w/cook pots & stove pipe (D-SE)   65
Stove, wood, large, on base marked "Philadelphia Stove Works" (A-E)   50
Strainer, handwrought, 26" l. (A-E)   20
Strainer, ladle, small, handle initialed "A M" (A-E) 210
Strawberry huller, cast (D-E)   6
String holder, ball shape w/hinge (D-E)   28
String holder, beehive type, 5" h. (D-W)   25
String holder, beehive type, 6½" × 7½" (D-E   40
String holder, beehive type, complete (D-MW)   32
String holder, hanging store type (D-MW)   12
Tallow scoop, concave w/turned wooden handle, 25" l. (A-NE) 150
Target, billy goat (D-E)   15
Teakettle, cast, very early, on 3 legs w/wrought iron bail, 9" diam. (D-W)   38
Teakettle, gooseneck spout (D-W)   25
Teakettle, marked "J. Savery, New York" (A-E)   27
Teakettle, sliding cover, dated 1861 (D-NE)   25
Teakettle, sliding cover, 4-qt. (D-W)   20
Teakettle, 2 handles, marked "J. B." on side of kettle (D-E)   40
Teakettle, tripod, cast, twisted handle, 7½" h. (A-NE) 100
Toaster, fireplace, handwrought, decor. w/6 hearts & 4 drooping branches, 4 curved
   arches, curved rod, blunt feet w/1 in form of arrowhead (D-E) 1500
Toaster, footed, swing handled, twisted tree-like motif, 27" (A-NE) 150
Toaster, handwrought, 42" l. oak handle (A-E) 115
Toaster, handwrought, marked & dated 1818 on both sides, hinged bottom, handle (D-NE) ... 210
Toaster, handwrought, ram's horn design, 20½" l. (D-E) 130
Toaster head, revolves, handle made in 1 piece w/base (D-E)   75
Toaster, rotating, handwrought (A-E)   75
Toaster, rotating, hearth (D-E) 175
Toaster, rotating, hearth (D-MW)   65
Toaster, rotating, hearth, fancy (D-E) 175
Toaster, swivel, footed, twisted iron arches (A-E)   75
Toaster, swivel, handwrought (A-E)   70
Toaster, swivel, handwrought, footed w/handle, rack w/grad. twisted loops (D-E) 150
Toaster, swivel, handwrought, footed w/long handle, rack w/fleur-de-lis & loop design (D-E). 175

Trivet, iron, Penna. Dutch (D-MW) $38   **Trivet,** iron, footed (D-MW) $35

Toaster, swivel, handwrought, footed w/long handle, rack w/heart design (D-MW)..............$ 200
Toaster, swivel, hearth, handwrought, footed, drooping branches (D-E) 110
Toaster, swivel, hearth, handwrought, footed, hearts & branches (D-MW) 155
Toaster, swivel, hearth, handwrought, footed, twisted bars (D-S) 65
Toasting fork, w/legs, twisted handle, 30" l., for fireplace (D-MW) 65
Tobacco cutter, general store type, signed "Star", orig. japanned black & gold (D-E) 20
Toddy, in goffering iron stand (D-E) 55
Tongs, baked potato, flat round ends, 14" l. (D-E).. 12
Tongs, ember (D-MW) 15
Tongs, ember, expansion, 3" when closed, 20½" open (D-MW).. 145
Tongs, ember, or pipe tongs, long, narrow & self closing w/spring action, handwrought, 15" l. (D-MW) 35
Tongs, ember, pocket type, late 18th C., 6" l. (D-NE).. 32
Tongs, ember, scissors type, handwrought, 10" l. (D-NE)... 28
Tongs, ember, tulip shaped, w/spring action, handwrought, rare, 16¾" l. (A-E).................... 65
Tongs, pipe, fireplace, used to hold a pipe in fire to bake out, handwrought, 24" l. (D-E) 135
Tongs, pipe, pocket (A-E).. 35
Tongs, cut out tulip & pinwheel, handwrought, marked "S. B." (A-E).................................. 32
Tongs, hearth, w/small shovel (A-E) 20
Tongs & shovel, fireplace, brass ball tops, 18th C., 20" l. pr. (D-E) 20
Top hat, cast, 7"×11" (D-E) 45
Trammel, chimney, sawtooth adjustments, complete (D-E) 40
Trammel, early, 28½" closed (D-NE) 35
Trammel, fireplace, handwrought, good cond. (A-E) 65
Trammel, fireplace, sawtooth, late 18th C., 26½" l. (A-E)... 28
Trammel, fireplace, 10 holes for adjustment, 37" l. (D-MW) 35
Trammel, good cond. (A-E) 35
Trammel, Penna., incised heart decor. (A-E) 500
Trammel, small, for parlor fireplace or to hang lantern (D-W).. 42
Trivet, cast, "1889" (A-E).. 22
Trivet, cast, "1881" (A-E).. 22
Trivet, circle w/6 point star, footed, cast, good molding, round, 5½" diam. (D-NE) 12
Trivet, cloverleaf, handwrought, 18th C. (A-NE).. 120
Trivet, colt (D-MW) 45
Trivet, cricket, handwrought, round, footed (D-E) 35
Trivet, eagle & roses, paw feet (D-S) 22
Trivet, heart, handmade, w/pad feet (A-E) 95
Trivet, heart, handmade, w/round feet (A-E) 40
Trivet, handwrought, 4 cross bars w/handle (A-E).. 55
Trivet, heart, handwrought (A-E) 90
Trivet, heart, handwrought, 18th C. (A-NE) 190
Trivet, handwrought, heart, footed, 7" (A-NE).. 80
Trivet, heart, handwrought, penny feet, rattlesnake tail design (A-E) 180
Trivet, heart, handwrought, w/snake head (A-E) 80
Trivet, heart, handwrought, w/2 small hearts (A-E) 325
Trivet, heart design, small, footed, handled (D-W) 18
Trivet, heart, turned wood handle, 18th C. (D-N) 85
Trivet, heart/pan, handwrought, footed (D-E) 45

Waffle iron, cast iron,
3-pc., complete
(D-W) $35

Wine press, cast iron,
Enterprise, orig.
japanning, complete
& working (D-W) $65

Trivet, heart, handwrought, 10" sq. w/7 round bars, long handle, footed (D-E) ....$	35
Trivet, hearts (intertwined), early, cast, round, footed, 7½" (D-NE)............................	15
Trivet, hex sign, 6-pointed star, round, 3-footed, 5¼" diam. (D-NE)	10
Trivet, horse & eagle, "good luck", cast (A-E)	30
Trivet, lacy design, cast, 12" l. (A-E)...	20
Trivet, Lantz no. 5, cast (D-S)	6
Trivet, Lantz no. 6, cast (D-W)	5
Trivet, marked "Owens" (A-E)..	45
Trivet, portrait of Washington, rare, 9½" (D-NE)	35
Trivet, rams horn design, square shape (A-NE)	70
Trivet, rectangular cathedral, cast (D-MW)	25
Trivet, revolving, w/wavy broiling surface, handwrought, 18th C., 12" w., 3 penny feet (D-S).	75
Trivet, round, handwrought, edges cut-out, 3 flaring legs, arrow feet, 4½" (A-E)	100
Trivet, spade shape, wrought, back bar & handle mort. & riveted to 1-pc. frame, ca. 1800 (D-E)	45
Trivet, spade shape, handwrought, footed (D-MW)...	15
Trivet, spade shape, footed, handwrought (A-E)	22
Trivet, spoon rest, 18th C. (D-S)	95
Trivet, 3 cross bars, handwrought, penny feet w/handle (A-E)	65
Trivet, triangular, handwrought, leg extensions on sides, 18th C. (D-W)............................	18
Trivet, triangular, handwrought, 2 cross bars, curled feet (A-E)	35
Trivet, triangular, handwrought, footed, 18th C., 9" (D-NE)	20
Trivet, triple arrow head, handwrought (A-E)	22
Trivet, wooden handle, handwrought, lg. (A-E)..	22
Trivet or broiler, 6 round cross bars, handwrought, curved cut outs & lines both top & bottom, handle incised w/two impressed eagle hall marks, signed Elizabeth Bower, July 4th, 1834 (A-E)..	275
Urn, flower, on base (A-E)	50
Utensil holder, 5-hook, handwrought, rare (A-NE)	250
Utensil holder, 3 inverted hearts as hooks (D-E)	45
Wafer, showing religious symbols, 24" handles (D-W)	30
Wafer, showing well-executed eagle on each disc, 20" handles (D-E)..................................	150
Wafer iron, handwrought, incised design of hearts, ball top on handle, handle 31½" l., 18th C. (A-NE)...	120
Waffle iron, "crescent", wood handles, japanned base, for stove top (D-MW)	20
Waffle iron, flower design (A-E)...	62
Waffle iron, 4 different griddle designs, w/24" handle (D-MW)	50
Waffle iron, geometric pattern, hearth type w/long handle (D-E)	50
Waffle iron, geometric pattern, long handle (D-N)	60
Waffle iron, heart pattern, stove top w/handle (D-S)...	22
Waffle iron, heart pattern, stove top, handle (A-MW)...	30
Waffle iron, heart shaped plates, handwrought, 36" handle (fireplace) (D-E)	85
Waffle iron, large bold fat Penna. Dutch type heart, beautiful designs inside (A-E)...............	2100
Waffle iron, marked "BW Chatham", scarce (D-NE)..	65
Waffle iron, stove top, mkd. (D-W)	12
Waffle iron, tulip design, long handle, round (D-MW)	85
Washboard, iron, cut-out top for hanging (D-MW)..	30
Wing nuts, Conestoga wagon type, (3), handwrought (A-E)	27

Lighting

Between the rush light holders of the early settlers, and the fancy kerosene lamps of the late Victorian era, there exists an immense range of interesting lighting collectibles and accessories, most of which are readily adaptable for modern decorative and functional usage.

The commodities for producing light in colonial America were splints of wood — usually pine, and animal and vegetable oils, depending upon their availability. The oils were used as burning fluids in various forms of shallow flat grease lamps. The "Betty" was the first of this type, followed by the Phoebe or crusie. Candles were expensive and in short supply. When the colonies were being supplied with British goods, a prime request was for tallow for candles. The major difficulty in making candles was finding a substitute for beef tallow, since domestic animals were not plentiful in America until the late 1600s. Among the substitutes for tallow was beeswax found in small amounts, the waxy substance known as "spermaceti" which was obtained from the head of the sperm whale, and bayberry wax. The berries — found growing in clusters on stems of the bay shrub — are covered with a greenish-white wax. The berries were boiled slowly and skimmed repeatedly until the wax took on a light greenish color. The bayberry candle was a favorite because of its fragrant aroma when lit. But, regardless of what method of lighting was used by the colonists, the prime necessity was to keep the hearth fire burning; from this, all lights were kindled.

The tinderbox was a necessity in the home. It contained a piece of steel, flint, and a disc to cover pieces of tinder, scraps of shredded cloth or pine splinters which would ignite readily. The flint and steel were struck together until a spark flew into the disc protected tinder in the bottom of the box. From this flame, splinters of wood or twists of paper were carried to the hearth. When sulphur was available, the wood splinters were tipped with it. These were our earliest matches, known as "spunks." Although the spunks could not be lit by striking, the sulphur prolonged the life of the flame.

There is still a variety of early lighting collectibles available to the collector — including examples of the popular Betty lamp. It is said that the first governor of the Plymouth Colony brought with him an iron Betty lamp from Holland. The source of its name is much debated, but perhaps it comes from the word "betying," meaning crude fat or leavings.

Candlemolds are fascinating to collect. The most common contains 4, 6, 8 or 12 tubes. These were usually constructed of tin or pewter. Copper molds were also made, but extremely scarce. The most sought after candlemolds are those with an odd number of tubes, or with unusual arrangements of tubes within the mold.

A seemingly endless variety of candlesticks were made. Tin, wood and pewter were used in the kitchen; while brass, silver, glass and porcelain examples were used in the parlor. Most were made for holding only one candle, but there were the candelabras for two or more, and the quaint tin hanging chandeliers with four, six or more graceful extending arms, each tipped with a socket for holding the candle.

Sconces with backplates of pewter, tin, or bits of looking glass that reflected the candlelight, are extremely desirable collectibles. And so are the early wooden candlestands which permitted height adjustments. See the *Furniture* category.

Lanterns fitted with candles became fashionable during the 1700s. They can be divided into two groups; portable and fixed. The latter group included ship's lanterns, carriage lamps, hall, street lanterns, etc. The portable types are classified by the purpose for which they were made, their material, or shape.

The availability of whale oil transformed lamp designs during the late 1700s, and remained the most important type of fuel for lamps well into the 1800s. The earliest and simplest whale oil lamps had closed reservoirs with either one or two round wicks passing through the neck. The interesting little peg and petticoat lamps had whale oil burners. Peg lamps make interesting collections. They were made by fitting a ball-shaped reservoir with a protruding end which fit into the socket of a regular candlestick. The term is American, but they were used in England long before they were made here, and were called "stand and socket" lamps.

Camphene lamps came into use during the second quarter of the last century. They resemble the whale oil lamps, but their wick tubes are set at opposing angles — "V" shape — to compensate for the extreme combustibility of the fuel, which was a mixture of turpentine and alcohol. From the 1830s, the Argand whale oil burner, an invention of a Swiss scientist, dominated lamp designs until the 1860s when kerosene eventually replaced all other fuels.

* * *

Candelabra, brass, 5-branch, lion paw feet, 22" h. (A-E) ....$ 75

Candelabra, brass, 3-pc. set, marble base, prisms (A-E)... 80

Candleholder, brass, chimney (A-E).. 30

Candleholder, brass, Chippendale w/push rod & snuffer (A-E) 175

Candleholder, brass, saucer-based w/large ring handle & thumb piece, ca. 1890, 9" diam. (D-W). 55

Candleholder, graniteware, saucer type w/handle, brown (D-E) 18

Candleholder, handle, 3½" h. (A-E) 450

Candleholder, iron, bird cage type, adjustable (D-MW) 185

Candleholder, iron, bird cage type, square base, 7½" h. (A-E) 175

Candleholder, iron, handwrought, 9" l., w/trivet, heart shaped, turned legs, 18th C., 13½" l. (A-MW) 160

Candleholder, iron, handwrought, rush light pinchers, spring clip length adjustment, rare (A-E) . 325

Candleholder, iron, handwrought, spring clip on slide, sq. base on four curved legs & ball ft. (A-E) 375

Candleholder, iron, handwrought, 3-legged, primitive (D-E)... 250

Candleholder, iron, jam hook at top (D-E) 125

Candleholder, iron, spiral, adjustable, wood base, 8" h. (D-S) 145

Candleholder, redware, handle, marked I. Stahl, 1941, "the weather, rain & warm" (A-E)...... 230

Candleholder, Rockingham mottled glaze (A-S) 55

Candleholder, tin, birdcage, w/turned wooden base, 10" t. (D-E) 125

Candleholder, tin, cone, sand weighted, step lift (D-E).. 85

Candleholder, tin, crimped edge, 3"×1¾" (D-NE) 14

Candleholder, tin, hanging, punched star decor., 13"×13¼" (A-E) 55

Candleholder, tin, sand cone filled, w/tin snuffer, adjustable tray, rare (A-E)....................... 1150

Candleholder, tin, table model, spring trammel w/sand weighted base, curved transporting rod (D-E) 375

Candleholder, tin, tinderbox, complete w/douser & strike, 3½" h., 4" w. (D-S) 125

Candleholder, tin, tinderbox w/damper, strike, etc., handled (D-E) 150

Candleholder, tin, wall, curved w/fluted top (A-E) 75

Candleholder, tin, tinder box incl., flint piece iron & stones, rags for igniting, sulphur tipped sticks, 3-ring lid finial inside (A-E) 190

Candleholder, tin, turned wooden base, 8" t. (D-E)... 110

Candleholder, miner's or cooper's, iron, w/spring catch, handwrought, decor. w/initials "F.L.J."/ (A-E) ....$ 130

Candleholder & rush, iron, 3-legged, penny feet, twisted on candle arm & upright, 8½" (D-NE) . 135

Candleholder, tavern, toleware, floor type, crossbar for 5 candles on weighted cone base, 4'3" h. (D-E) 350

Candleholders, brass, push rod, pr., early (A-E) 60

Candle mold, pewter, wood frame, 18th C. (A-E) 495

Candle mold, tin, round top, 18" (D-E) 150

Candle mold, tin, 1-tube, patty pan, crimped top & handle (A-E) 20

Candle mold, tin, 1-tube, perf. cond., 11" l. (D-E)... 50

Candle mold, tin, 1-tube, strap handle (D-MW)... 75

Candle mold, tin, 1-tube, strap handle, straight (D-E) 68

Candle mold, tin, 1-tube, strap handle, straight (D-MW) 75

Candle mold, tin, 1-tube, strap handle, straight (D-SW) 21

Candle mold, tin, 12-tube, 2 handles & 4 splayed feet, early (D-MW) 125

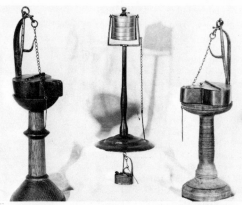

Early lighting examples (A-E), *left to right:* Betty lamp, copper, Peter Derr, dated 1835, $950; **Betty lamp stand,** wooden, Peter Derr type, $150; **gallows lamp,** Peter Derr, signed "P.D. 1843", $1600; **Betty lamp,** miniature, rare, $320; **Betty lamp,** brass, Peter Derr, dated 1845; $750; **Betty lamp stand,** wooden, $180

Lantern, wooden, pegged, 3 orig. glass panes, pin hinges & door pull, early (D-MW) $85

Candle mold, tin, 2-stand, handled (D-E) 30

Candle mold, tin, 2-tube (D-NE) 34

Candle mold, tin, 2-tube, complete & early (D-NE)... 34

Candle mold, tin, 2-tube, scalloped base, 10⅜" h. (A-E)... 45

Candle mold, tin, 2-tube, strap handle, tapered (D-E) 30

Candle mold, tin, 2-tube, strap handle, tapered (D-NE)... 34

Candle mold, tin, 2-tube, strap handle, tapered (D-NW)... 22

Candle mold, tin, 2-tube, strap handle, tapered, some rust (D-NE) 25

Candle mold, tin, 2-tube, tapered (D-NE)... 30

Candle mold, tin, 3-tube, complete & early (D-NE) 28

Candle mold, tin, 3-tube, complete & early, handle missing (D-MW) 35

Candle mold, tin, 3-tube, complete & early, straight (A-E) 45

Candle mold, tin, 4 rows of 3 tubes each, 10⅝" h. (A-E)... 55

Candle mold, tin, 4-tube, complete, early, regular (D-NE)... 28

Candle mold, tin, 4-tube, complete, early, tapered, 2 rows of 2 (D-E) 30

Candle mold, tin, 4-tube, complete, early, tapered, 2 rows of 2 (D-NE)............................. 30

Candlemold, tin, 4-tube, early, strap handle, straight (D-MW) 38

Candle mold, tin, 4-tube, square base, handle, 10⅜" h. (A-NE)............................. 38

Candle mold, tin, 4-tube, square base, handle, 10¾" h. (A-E) 38

Candle mold, tin, 4-tube, straight (D-NE)... 28

Candle mold, tin, 4-tube, straight (D-NE)...$ 38
Candle mold, tin, 4-tube, tapered (D-NE)   30
Candle mold, tin, 4-tube, tapered, strap handle (D-S)   25
Candle mold, tin, 4-tube, tapered, strap handle, some rust (D-SE)   18
Candle mold, tin, 6-tube, curved feet, rare (D-E)   95
Candle mold, tin, 6-tube, curved feet, straight, mint (A-E)   95
Candle mold, tin, 6-tube, complete, early, regular, 2 rows of 3 (D-NE)   30
Candle mold, tin, 6-tube, complete, early, tapered, 2 rows of 3 (D-NE)..................   32
Candle mold, tin, 6-tube, straight (D-NE)..   32
Candle mold, tin, 6-tube, straight, complete (A-MW)   42
Candle mold, tin, 6-tube, straight, strap handle (D-NE)...   38
Candle mold, tin, 6-tube, tapered (D-NE)   32
Candle mold, tin, 6-tube, tapered, strap handle (D-SW)   48
Candle mold, tin, 6-tube, tapered, strap handle, painted black (D-W)   22
Candle mold, tin, 7-tube, tapered, circular form w/crimped top & bottom rims, rare form (D-NE)   200
Candle mold, tin, 8-tube, arched base (D-E)   70
Candle mold, tin, 8-tube, arched base, tapered (D-E)   70
Candle mold, tin, 8-tube, round, 11¼ h., top 6¼″ diam., base 5¾″ w/handle, rare (D-E)   155
Candle mold, tin, 8-tube, straight, strap handle (A-E)   55
Candle mold, tin, 12-tube, complete, early, regular (D-NE)   40
Candle mold, tin, 12-tube, complete, early, tapered, 2 rows of 6 (D-NE)   42
Candle mold, tin, 12-tube, early, 4 splayed feet, 2 handles (D-MW)   134
Candle mold, tin, 12-tube, early, straight, some rust (D-MW)................................   40
Candle mold, tin, 12-tube, on curved base (D-S)   95
Candle mold, tin, 12-tube, on curved base, tapered (D-S)   95
Candle mold, tin, 12-tube, straight (D-NE)   40
Candle mold, tin, 12-tube, striaght, complete (D-N)..   62
Candle mold, tin, 12-tube, tapered (D-NE)   42
Candle mold, tin, 12-tube, tapered, complete (D-NW)   42
Candle mold, tin, 12-tube, tapered, early & complete (D-NE)   40
Candle mold, tin, 12-tube, tapered, 2 strap handles, painted black (D-MW)   30
Candle mold, pewter, wooden frame, 13-tube, restored (D-NE)   185
Candle mold, tin, 24-tube, circular form rare, tapered, cond. ex. (D-E)   375
Candle mold, tin, 24-tube, complete, early, regular (D-NE)   85
Candle mold, tin, 24-tube, straight (D-NE)   78
Candle mold, tin, 24-tube, straight, complete (D-NE)   78
Candle mold, tin, 24-tube, straight, wire handles, early (A-MW)   75
Candle mold, tin, 24-tube, tapered, early & complete (D-MW)   85
Candle mold, tin, 24-tube, wood frame, tapered (D-E)   400
Candle mold, pewter, 36-tube, tapered, set in wooden frame (D-E)........................   350
Candle mold, tin, 48-tube, ex. cond. (D-E)..   200
Candle mold, tin, 48-tube, set in wooden frame, complete (D-E)   160
Candle mold, tin, 48-tube, set in wooden frame, ex. cond. (D-E)   200
Candle mold, tin, 50-tube (D-MW)   225
Candle mold, tin, 50-tube, square frame, tapered holes, complete (D-MW)   225
Candle mold, tin, 72-tube (D-E)   175
Candle mold, tin, 72-tube, tapered, set in wooden frame (D-E)   175
Candle snuffer, brass, gadroon border, 9¼″ l., 4″ w. (D-E)   8
Candle snuffer, iron (D-E)   45
Candle snuffer, iron, early, footed (D-W)   22
Candle snuffer, iron, handwrought, 18th C. (D-E)   25
Candle snuffer, iron, tiny cone, handled (D-NE)   10
Candle snuffer, tin, old black paint, early, 8¾″ (D-NE)   15
Candle snuffer, tin, orig. blue decor. (D-NE)   32
Candle snuffer, red background, gold decor. (D-NE)..   38
Candle snuffer, tin, tin cone, ring handle, 3½″ h. (D-E)   38
Candlestick, iron, birdcage, across turned wooden base, 9″ t. × 3½″, 18th C. (D-S)............   145
Candlestand, iron, handwrought, adj. octagonal tray w/1 candleholder & 1 well for floating rush,
   bold carved feet (A-E)   900

Left to right: **lantern,** tin, removable well, $200; **candle box,** tin, cylindrical, wall, decor. lid, $340; **kettle lamp,** brass, on iron stand, rare, $475 (all items A-E)

Candlestand, iron, handwrought, 3-footed base, 5-sided drip tray, twisted & crook top hand holder, spring clip candleholder (A-E) ....$ 275

Candlestand, tin, birdcage, adjustable (A-E) 100

Candlestand, tin, cone, adjustable, double candle tray (A-E) 375

Candlestand, tin, cone, adjustable, sand filled, crimped drip pan (A-E) 400

Candlestand, tin, cone, arrow point adjusting handle & glass globe (A-E) 275

Candlestick, brass, bell base, 5″ (D-E) 65

Candlestick, brass, bell-bottom, 18th C. (D-E) 125

Candlestick, brass, Chippendale (A-E) 55

Candlestick, brass, circular standard w/large square base, 19th C., 6″ h. (A-MW) 60

Candlestick, brass, circular standard w/spur handle at top, deep saucer base, adjustable slide, 19th C., 9″ h. (A-MW) 120

Candlestick, brass, hogscraper, wedding band (D-E)... 60

Candlestick, brass, shaped standard w/collar, large drip pan, bell base, 19th C., 11″ h. (A-MW) 110

Candlestick, brass, spiral w/wood base, lip & lift (D-E) 120

Candlestick, brass, three claw foot, rare (A-E) 70

Candlestick, hogscraper, iron, brass ring, marked, made w/no hanging hook, 7″ (D-NE) 85

Candlestick, hogscraper, iron (A-E) 28

Candlesticks, fruitwood, early, pr. (A-E) 55

Candlestick, copper, hand-hammered, dovetailed (A-E).. 17

Candlestick, hogscraper, iron, 7″ h. (D-MW) 18

Candlestick, hogscraper, iron, complete, signed "Bili", 8″ h. (D-E)................................... 75

Candlestick, hogscraper, iron, orig. & complete, 5¼″ to 7″ (D-NE) 34

Candlesticks, hogscraper, iron, wedding band, pr. 8½″ t. (D-E) 150

Candlestick, iron, Tommy, handwrought, 7½″ (D-E).. 65

Candlestick, spiral, iron, early, handwrought, 7½″ t. × 4″ across turned wooden base (D-S) .. 120

Candlestick, spiral, iron, 7½″ t. × 5″ across crimped saucer base, complete (D-S).................. 85

Candlestick, spiral, iron, w/wood base, 7″ t. (D-E) 120

Candlestick, tin, cone bottom, sand filled, wax catcher restored, 8½″ (D-NE) 22

Candlestick, tin, handled, fluted edge (D-E).. 38

Candlestick, tin, saucer, handled w/push-up (D-W) 28

Candlestick, tin, whale oil lamp, japanned (D-E) 65

Candlestick, wood w/smoke decor., 31″ (A-NE) 425

Candlesticks, brass, altar, pr., decor. standards w/center collar, tripod bases, paw feet, star shaped bobeche, 19th C., 19″ h. (A-MW) 50

Candlesticks, brass, beehive, octagonal base, pr., 19th C., 10¾″ h. (A-MW)......................... 85

Candlesticks, brass, beehive turned standards, octagonal base, 19th C., pr., 11¾″ h. (A-MW). 120

Candlesticks, brass, pr., ca. 1830, 14″ (D-MW) 245

Candlesticks, brass, Chippendale, marked "Bayley" (A-E) 100

Candlesticks, brass, early (about 1800), pr. (A-E) 80

Candlesticks, brass, old push-up style, pr. (A-E) 45

Candlesticks, brass, push-up rods, pr., ca. 1860, 10¼″ h. (D-E) 85

Early lanterns (A-E), *top row, left to right:* **pierced tin,** 2 doors, 1 rounded, 1 flat w/glass, ca. 1800, 14″ h., $80; **pierced tin,** so-called Paul Revere type, $110; *bottom row, left to right:* **lanthorn,** tin, English, marked, 19th C., 8″ diam., 15″ h., $70; **lanthorn,** tin, English, early 19th C., $90

Early lighting (A-E), *top row, left to right:* **sconce,** tin, rectangular, single socket, ca. 1845, 13⅜″ h., $90; **candle lantern,** tin, ca. 1850, 11½″ h., $130; **sconce,** tin, oval, single socket, crimped edges, ca. 1845, 8½″ h., $140; *bottom row, left to right:* **grease lamp,** 2-part sheet brass canting, French, early, overall H. 8½″, $40; **wall lamp,** kerosene, ca. 1890, 8½″ H., $35; **Betty lamp,** tin, pear-shaped, ca. 1825, 11¼″ h., $150

Candlesticks, brass, turned standards, sq. bases, pr., 19th C., 10¼″ h. (A-MW)..................$	75
Candlesticks, brown glaze, pr. (A-E)...	310
Candlesticks, maple, early, refinished, pr., 7¾″ h. (D-MW)	42
Candlesticks, pr., 8″ (A-E)	350
Candlesticks, pewter, American pushups, minor repair, ca. 1790, 9½″ h. (D-E)	155
Candlesticks, pewter, marked Bush & Perkins, pr., ca. 1775, 9½″ t. (A-E)	375
Candlesticks, pewter, pr. (A-E)	160
Candlesticks, pewter, push-up type w/attached bobeches, pr., 8″ h. (D-MW)...................	120
Candlesticks, pewter, push-up, unmarked, 8″ t. (A-NE)...	140
Candlesticks, pewter, Roswell Gleason, good design, pr., 6¾″ (A-E)	275
Candlesticks, pewter, single, w/rounded bases & plain baluster columns ending in vase shaped sockets, pr., 13″ h. (D-MW)..	125
Candlesticks, pewter, unmarked, pr., 8¾″ (D-E)	100
Chamberstick, brass, American, 6″, sq. base w/pierced gallery 1″ h. (D-W)	95
Chamberstick, brass, snuffer, square, 7″ (A-E)	60
Chamberstick, pewter, circular base w/upturned edge, gadroon border, round handle, ca. 1800, 6″ diam., 4½″ h. (D-MW)	35
Chamberstick, pewter, push-up type, circular domed base w/flaring rim & round handle, ca. 1850, 4″ h., 5½″ diam. (D-MW)...	145
Chamberstick, pewter, saucer base, handle, ca. 1850 (D-MW).......................................	60
Chamberstick, redware, orange-brown w/brown decor., 3¼″ (A-NE)	150
Chamberstick, tin, brass trim (A-E)	135
Chamberstick, tin, rectangular base, push-up style, 6¾″×5″×4″ t., handled (D-NE)...............	35
Candlestick, tin, saucer base, japanned finish worn, sliding ejector, ca. 1870, 4¾″ h., 6½″ diam. (A-NE)..	32
Chamberstick, tin, saucer based, japanned finish worn, sliding ejector, ca. 1870, 4¾″ h., 6½″ diam. (D-MW)...	22
Chambersticks, tin, suacer base, pair, 5¾″ × 4″ t. (D-E)	50
Chandelier, candle, hanging, floral design, branches, wooden center & candle holders (A-E)..	275
Chandelier, candle, iron (A-E)	180
Chandelier, candle, wood, fine turnings, curly maple potty pans for candles (A-E)...............	230
Fat lamp filler, tin, spouted (A-E)..	35
House, tin, for lighting, rare form, ca. 1820 (D-E)	275
Lamp, Betty, brass, Peter Derr, hook & chain w/pick, 1845 (A-E)	750
Lamp, Betty, copper, iron hanger, 11″ (A-E)	65

Lamp, Betty, copper, Peter Derr, 1835 (A-E) ....$ 800
Lamp, Betty, copper, Peter Derr, decor. hook, 1835 (A-E)... 950
Lamp, Betty, iron, double wrought, decor., twisted hook (A-E) 110
Lamp, Betty, iron, handwrought, brass sliding lid, signed "made by M. I. Long-George Ruhill,
    1847" (A-E)... 1000
Lamp, Betty, iron, handwrought, lid missing, hook not orig. (A-E)..................................... 22
Lamp, Betty, iron, handwrought, rare, signed "J D", twisted hook & wick pick, rod & loop type
    chain holding pick (A-E) 950
Lamp, Betty, iron, handwrought, rooster on lid, twisted hook on chain (A-E) 150
Lamp, Betty, iron, handwrought, saw tooth trammel w/curved hook at end (A-E) 150
Lamp, Betty, iron, handwrought, twisted hook, chain & wick pick, bird on lid (A-E)............ 150
Lamp, Betty, iron, handwrought, twisted rod on hook, 14" l. (A-E) 95
Lamp, Betty, iron, hanging, rooster on oil cup (A-E) 45
Lamp, Betty, iron, heavy gauge wire hanging hook & pick (D-E)... 70
Lamp, Betty, iron, open pan w/handwrought handle (A-E)... 90
Lamp, Betty, iron, Peter Derr, signed "P. D. 1843" (A-E)... 800
Lamp, Betty, iron, twisted wrought iron hanger, ca. 1850, 10¼" h. (A-NE).......................... 85
Lamp, Betty, iron, wooden Betty lamp stand (A-E) 160
Lamp, Betty, pewter, traditional form, handled, 10¾" h. (A-MW) 140
Lamp, Betty, tin (D-NE) 110

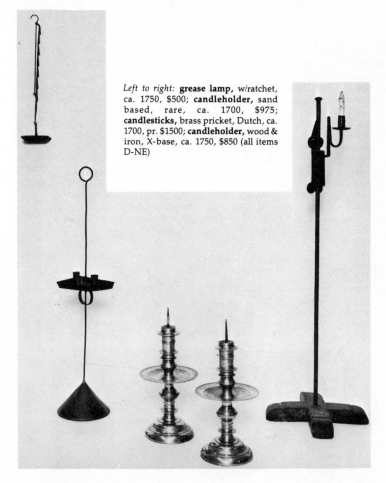

Left to right: **grease lamp,** w/ratchet, ca. 1750, $500; **candleholder,** sand based, rare, ca. 1700, $975; **candlesticks,** brass pricket, Dutch, ca. 1700, pr. $1500; **candleholder,** wood & iron, X-base, ca. 1750, $850 (all items D-NE)

Lamp, Betty, tin, Ipswich, w/tidy top, 12" t. (D-E)...$ 250

Lamp, Betty, tin, on cone stand in dish (A-E) 120

Lamp, Betty, tin, pear-shaped, early, solid cover, hinged flap & handle on cover w/slot for wick
support, half-bail hanger w/hook & wick pick fastened to upper end, mounted on cylindrical
column, saucer base, 11½" h. (A-E)... 220

Lamp, Betty, tin, rare wooden Betty lamp holder (A-E).. 100

Lamp, Betty, tin, stand, scalloped top (A-E) 95

Lamp, Betty, tin, tin stand (D-S) 265

Lamp, Betty & holder, tin, Ipswich, 10" h., 6½" across saucer base, complete w/pickwick (D-S) 145

Lamp, boiler inspector, tin, whale oil, w/wire handle, square (D-NE).................................... 36

Lamp, camphene guest, tin, 3 burners w/pewter snuffers, 3½" h., 4" w. (D-S) 75

Lamp, camphene, pewter (D-E) 230

Lamp, carriage, tin (A-E) 20

Lamp, cast iron, kerosene w/hurricane shade, 19th C., 19½" h. (A-MW) 27

Lamp, coach, brass, decor. w/spread eagle finial (A-E)... 125

Lamp, fat, brass, iron handle, marked & dated P.D. 1842 (A-E) 825

Lamp, fat, brass, signed, Peter Derr, ca. 1860 (D-MW)... 300

Lamp, fat, copper, unmarked (A-E)... 110

Lamp, fat, iron, hanging w/saw tooth trammel, handwrought (A-E) 190

Lamp, fat, iron, tri-form pan, hanging w/handwrought stem & saw tooth trammel (A-E) 300

Lamp, fat, iron, tri-form pan, twisted stem decor., saw tooth trammel, hook w/curl (A-E) 275

Lamp, fat, tin, whale oil, witches, japanned, hinged cylinder, tin & mica shield (D-E) 75

Lamp, fat, witches, toleware (A-E).. 27

Lamp filler, fat, copper (A-E) 80

Lamp filler, whale oil, tin (D-NE) 18

Lamp, floor, iron (A-E) 30

Lamp, grease, iron, open, handwrought, footed w/hanging rod (D-E) 225

Lamp, grease, pottery, mottled brown glaze (D-E)... 165

Lamp, grease, tin, black japanned finish, cylindrical font w/single burner, saucer base w/flat ring
handle, 7¾" h. (D-E)... 65

Lamp, grease, tin, "Davis Patent", 1856 (D-W) 95

Lamp, grease, tin, early, double wick w/ventilator in the support, 8" h. (A-NE) 65

Lamp, grease, tin, 9" h., 5" across saucer base, side handle (D-MW) 55

Lamp, grease, tin, pedestal base, saucer bottom, handled, ca. 1840-50 (D-E) 115

Lamp, grease, tin, rare, inverted cone shape w/saucer base & flat strap handle, 4¾" h. (A-NE).. 55

Lamp, grease, tin, table, complete w/shade, rare form, 10" h. (A-E) 38

Lamp, guest, tin, whale oil, 3 wick (D-NE) 45

Lamp, hall, brass, hanging, candle, w/glass hurricane shade (A-E) 55

Lamp, hanging, brass, milk glass type shade & hurricane shade, adjustable, 19th C. (A-MW). 130

Candle chandelier, tavern, wood
& tin, Penna., ca. 1800 (D-NE)
$2500

Post lamp, tin, Dietz,
eagle finial, large
(A-E) $260

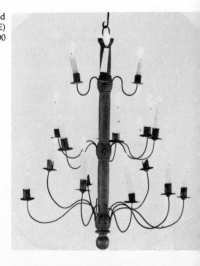

Lamp, hanging, brass, smoke bell, clear font, old yellow bird shade (A-E) ....$ 90
Lamp, hanging, brass, soot bell, glass shade (D-NE)   40
Lamp, hat, tin, whale oil, witches, japanned, hinged cylinder, tin & mica shield (D-E)   75
Lamp, hot, witches, toleware (A-E)   27
Lamp, kettle, brass, iron stand, designed rod, 4 curved legs, blunt arrow feet, rare (A-E) 475
Lamp, lard oil, tin, 7½" t. (D-E)   75
Lamp, lard oil, tin, Kinnear Patent (D-E)   65
Lamp, lard stand, tin, large saucer base, inverted conical font w/strap ring handle, ca. 1850, 8" h.
   (A-SW)   32
Lamp, miner's, tin, marked "Dunlap's-Pittsburgh", ca. 1890, 3½" h. (A-NE)   75

Grease lamp, tin, w/cover, small (D-E) $33

Candlesticks, Bennington, flint enamel (A-NE), *left to right:* **pair of candlesticks,** $657; **single candlestick,** $325; **pair of candlesticks,** $475

Lamp, miner's, tin, w/tall spout & flat strap handle, 4¼" h. (A-NE).......................................   90
Lamp, miner's, tin, whale oil (D-E)...   15
Lamp, nurse's, toleware, all orig. colorful decor. (D-NE)   75
Lamp, oil, brass, hurricane shade of iridescent milk glass, swirl decor., 19th C., 22½" h. (A-MW)..   75
Lamp, oil, brass, milk glass ribbed hurricane shade, electrified, 19th C., 21½" h. (A-MW)   50
Lamp, oil, brass, tall (A-E)..   55
Lamp, oil, brass, turned standard w/urn shape font, milk glass shade, 19th C., 20¼" h. (A-MW) .   90
Lamp, oil, iron, handwrought, clear glass reservoir, milk glass hurricane shade, 19th C., 13" h.,
   w/frame & bracket (A-MW) 100
Lamp, oil, pewter base w/green glass reservoir & hurricane shade, 18½" h., together w/pressed
   glass oil lamp, hurricane shade, 16¼" h. (A-MW)   90
Lamp, oil, pewter, cylindrical oil font, saucer base, ring handle, marked Capen & Molineux, New
   York, 1844, 7" h. (D-MW)..   90
Lamp, oil, pewter, twin wick, 5½", unmarked (D-E) 290
Lamp, old chimney (A-E)   17
Lamp, pan, brass, table model, spring trammel (D-E) 200
Lamp, pan, iron, handwrought, 17" l. (D-E) 125
Lamp, pan, iron, on standard, handwrought, cloverleaf shaped pan adjustable in height, 18th C.,
   20" overall (D-S) 165
Lamp, pedestal, tin, whale oil, 6¼" (D-NE)...   70
Lamp, peg, tin, "People's Lamp", w/hogscraper candlestick (A-E)......................................   50
Lamp, peg, tin base, glass, complete w/wick holder, 8½" h., 4" across funnel base (D-S) 150
Lamp, peg, tin, whale oil, flat, slide section of cover allows burner to life out for filling (D-NE)   36
Lamp, peg, tin, whale oil, used in hogscrapers, etc. (D-NE)   48
Lamp, peg, wood, bronze base, maple pedestal, drop burner, 7" t. (D-E) 160
Lamp, petticoat, tin, complete (D-E)...   38
Lamp, petticoat, tin, complete, proof (D-NE)...   50
Lamp, petticoat, tin, 3-tube whale oil burner, vertical filler tube w/plug attached to side, round
   peg in bottom for mounting in candle socket (A-NE)..   85
Lamp, pewter (A-E) 110

Lamp, pewter, Betty w/wick pick & chain (D-SE) ....$ 165
Lamp, pewter, camphene burner, brass cap on chain, 2¼" h. (D-NE) 210
Lamp, pewter, Capen & Molineux, camphene burner, brass cap on chain, 2¼" h. (D-E) 200
Lamp, pewter, double crusie w/hanging spike & chain (D-MW).. 75
Lamp, pewter, unmarked, lard oil burner, 6½" t. (D-NE) 240
Lamp, pewter, whale oil burner, R. Dunham, 4½" h. (D-NE) 250
Lamp, pewter, whale oil burner, marked Gleason (D-NE) 245
Lamp, pewter, whale oil burner, saucer base, 5½" h. (D-N) 135
Lamp, pin-up, brass, glass font, old green 7" shade (A-E) 20
Lamp, privy, Shaker, double-drop whale oil burner & screw top, 9¼" l. (D-E)...................... 90
Lamp, rush, iron, wooden base (A-E)... 75
Lamp, sewing, brass, candle type, collared circular standard w/candle hood, stepped circular
base, 19th C., 13½" h. (A-MW) 100
Lamp, ship's oil, brass, wall mounted, hurricane shade, 10½" h., together w/wall mounted brass
oil lamp w/milk glass & hurricane shade, 19th C., 19" h. (A-MW)................................ 180
Lamp, skater's, tin, round handle on top w/octagon-shaped globe (A-E) 70
Lamp, sparking, pewter, brass single wick insert complete with snuffer, 3½" h., 3½" across
saucer base (D-MW).. 190
Lamp, sparking, pewter, column shaped lamp w/flaring base, circular handle, screw type cap,
brass fittings, 3" diam., 3½" h. (D-MW).. 165
Lamp, sparking, pewter, round-tiered pedestal base w/round font, circular handle w/thumb rest,
2½" diam. (D-MW) 170
Lamp, sparking, pewter, signed, Reed & Barton, 6" t. × 2¾" across base (D-S)..................... 75
Lamp, sparking, pewter, small sand box, hinged dome lid, 19th C., 4" h. × 2⅜" diam. (A-MW) 80
Lamp, sparking, pewter, unmarked, s/snuffer, 3½" h. × 3½" across saucer base (D-S) 125
Lamp, spout, brass, w/weighted base, Penna., 11" h. (D-MW) 57
Lamp stand, tin, whale oil, crimped top, pedestal base, for petticoat lamp or small whale oil
lamps, blue asphaltum, rare, 2¾" h. × 4" top (D-NE) 65
Lamp, store, brass, hanging, kerosene, tin shade, 19th C. (A-MW) 100
Lamp, store, brass, w/tin, kerosene, 19th C. (A-MW)... 80
Lamp, store, tin, hanging, w/brass bowl (A-E).. 42
Lamp, student, brass, old Bristol glass shade, 19th C., 26" h. (A-MW) 250
Lamp, student, brass, single, green shade (A-E) 140
Lamp, student, brass, old green 10" shade, w/gold dragons (A-E)............................. 210
Lamp, student, brass, single, w/orig. chimney, dated 1879 (A-E)............................. 180
Lamp, swivel, brass, for ship, electrified (A-E) 17
Lamp, swivel, pewter (A-E) 100
Lamp, table, brass, kerosene, ribbed milk type shade w/hurricane shade, 19th C., 19½" h.
(A-MW) 80
Lamp, tin, tin reflector (D-E).. 125
Lamp, traveler's, brass, kerosene, fitted for electricity, 19th C. (A-MW) 85
Lamp, vapor & pump, iron & tin exhaust, complete (D-E) 125
Lamp, wall, tin, kerosene, very good cond., late 19th C., 8½" h. (A-E) 30
Lamp, weavers, iron, flattened circular reservoir w/strap handle & hook, rooster finial, 19th C.,
20½" h. (A-MW)... 50
Lamp, whale oil, brass (A-E) 52
Lamp, whale oil, tin, handled saucer base, Trunnion or Gimbal (D-E)......................... 155
Lamp, whale oil, iron, marble base flint, brass column, 9½" h. (D-MW) 115
Lamp, whale oil, pewter, 6" h. (D-E) 85
Lamp, whale oil, pewter, burner, R. Gleason, 6" t. (D-E) 350
Lamp, whale oil, pewter, cylinder form w/fluted pedestal base, 19th C., 6⅜" h. (D-E) 95
Lamp, whale oil, pewter, footed w/orig. wooden handle (D-W) 185
Lamp, whale oil, pewter, Roswell Gleason, ca. 1845, 6" high (D-E)........................... 135
Lamp, whale oil, pewter, on saucer base, 6¾" h. (A-E) 165
Lamp, whale oil, pewter, pedestal, 8½" t. (D-E) 150
Lamp, whale oil, pewter, signed Morey & Ober (A-E).. 150
Lamp, whale oil, pewter, signed Morey & Ober (D-E).. 385
Lamp, whale oil, pewter, signed, Yale & Curtis, New York (D-E) 750
Lamp, whale oil, pewter, unmarked, 6" (D-E).. 200

Lamp, **whale oil,** pewter, unsigned, ca. 1825, 8" t., 4" base (D-S) ....$ 125

Lamp, **whale oil,** tin, hinged wind cover w/mica window, orig. blue paint (D-E)................. 75

Lamp, **whale oil,** tin, on base, 6½" (D-E)... 70

Lamp, **whale oil,** tin, pear shaped, peg lamp w/threaded opening at top containing whale oil burner, ca. 1825, 4" h. (D-MW) 28

Lamp, **whale oil,** tin, pottery pan base (A-E)... 80

Lamp, **whale oil,** tin, guest, 3 wicks (D-NE)... 45

Lamp, **whale oil,** tin, 3 wicks, handled, work light, 6"×2¼" (D-NE) 55

Lamp, **whale oil,** tin, 2 wicks, guest room (D-E) 65

Lamps, kerosene, tin, decor., w/chimneys, pr. (A-E) 55

Lamps, peg, copper pedestal bases, spun brass fonts, 5½" h., pr. (D-W)............................... 45

Candle snuffer, iron, fancy (D-S) $55

Whale oil lamps, pewter, unmarked, pr. (D-MW) $225

Lamps, **peg,** pewter, clear blown flint collars, crystal, ca. 1845, pr., 5½" (D-W) 80

Lamps, pewter, matched pair, burners marked Newell, Caldwell, Coffin pat., 4⅛" h. (D-E).... 390

Lamps, pewter, unmarked, orig. screening inside bell-shaped font, pr., good cond., 4⅛" h. (D-NE).. 390

Lamps, pewter, unmarked, whale oil burners, pr., 2¾" h. (D-NE)...................................... 225

Lamps, pewter, unmarked, whale oil burners, saucer base & urn font, pr., 6⅝" h. (D-NE) 300

Lamps, **safety oil,** brass, with globes, pr. (A-E) 42

Lamps, **whale oil,** pewter, marked "Rufus Dunham, Westbrook, Me.", pr., ca. 1840, 6" t. × 3¾" across base (D-S) 650

Lamps, **whale oil,** pewter, pr., 8" h. (D-MW) 180

Lamps, **whale oil,** pewter, twin wicks, 8½" h., unmarked (D-MW) 395

Lantern, **candle,** cherry & hickory, 7"×7"×19" (D-E) 395

Lantern, **candle,** copper, embossed w/tulips, w/horn inserts, unusual, small, 12" h. overall (D-S). 200

Lantern, **candle,** pine, rectangular, 4 glass panes (A-E) 425

Lantern, **candle,** pine, square w/4 glass panes, pin hinges, hoop handle, pegged (D-MW)...... 85

Lantern, **candle,** tin, campaign (D-E).. 50

Lantern, **candle,** tin, folding, mica sides, handled, Miners pat., 1865 (D-E) 35

Lantern, **candle,** tin, folding pocket, w/mica windows, signed "Minors patent 1855", 5" t. (D-S) 50

Lantern, **candle,** tin, 4 rows wire window guards, 5"×5"×16" (D-E) 125

Lantern, **candle,** tin, glass lens, orig. asphaltum finish, 4½" t. (D-E) 35

Lantern, **candle,** tin, half-round glass front, 4"×7"×13" (D-E).. 135

Lantern, **candle,** tin, old red paint, wooden feet (A-E)... 45

Lantern, **candle,** tin, Paul Revere, punched 13" (A-E)... 75

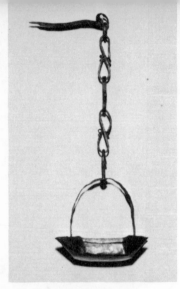

Fat lamp, hanging, made to hold 4 wicks, sq. (D-E) $35

Lantern, candle, tin, Paul Revere, punched, dated "J. B. 1833", rare (A-E) ....$ 95
Lantern, candle, tin, Paul Revere, punched, small (A-E) 95
Lantern, candle, tin, pierced, cylindrical shape w/conical top, rectangular door, thick candle socket, circular flat strapped handle at top, 13½" h. (A-NE)... 80
Lantern, candle, tin, pierced, w/outside candle socket, traces old red paint, 5½" diam., 14½" t. (D-E) 325
Lantern, candle, tin, round w/7 panes (A-E)... 125
Lantern, candle, tin, semicircular, punched tin heart & circle designs around back & flat front w/sliding glass window, flat strapped handle, ca. 1850, 10" h. (A-NE)............................... 75
Lantern, candle, tin, 6 lights of glass, shallow tin base, domed top, w/American circa 1850, 10½" h. (A-SE)... 90
Lantern, candle, tin, square (A-E)... 50
Lantern, candle, tin, 3 glass sides (A-E).. 42
Lantern, candle, tin, 3 glass sides, 4 protecting rings (A-E) 50
Lantern, candle, toleware, campaign (D-E).. 50
Lantern, candle, wood, top & bottom pine w/oak corner posts fastened in place by wooden pegs, glass panels, wire hinges & door latch, wire bail, ca. 1800, 10" h. (A-E) 125
Lantern, candle, wood, tin strap hinges, wire bail, 18th C., 12" h., 7½" w., 7" d. (D-S).......... 95
Lantern, half-moon, tin (A-E) 75
Lantern, half-moon, tin, Paul Revere type, perforated tin (A-E) 240
Lantern, tin, half round one side glass, rear door w/punched design (A-E) 110
Lantern, horn, tin (D-E) 200
Lantern, iron, 4-pane, w/tin (D-MW).. 65
Lantern, tin, old red paint (A-E)... 130
Lantern, onion, tin, 12" h. (D-N) 125
Lantern, onion, tin, glass 5" across, 12" h. (D-NE).. 120
Lantern, pierced, tin, candleholder & round bail (D-MW).. 80
Lantern, pierced, tin, complete, some rust (D-W)... 38
Lantern, pierced, tin, early, 17" (D-NE).. 85
Lantern, pierced, tin, early, 13½" (D-NE).. 85
Lantern, pierced, tin, 14½" (D-MW).. 85
Lantern, pierced, tin, cylindrical shape w/conical top, circular strap handle, simple punched decor., ca. 1875, 11" h. (A-SW) 60
Lantern, pierced, tin, cylindrical shape w/conical top, detailed & excellent punched decor., rectangular door, candle socket in center of base, flat circular strap handle, ca. 1840, 15" h. (A-SW)... 55
Lantern, pierced, tin, early, cylindrical shape w/conical top, detailed punched decor., rectangular door in side, candle socket in center of base, circular strap handle, ca. 1840, 14½" h. (D-MW) 55

Lantern, pierced, tin, early, cylindrical shape w/conical top, simple punched decor., rectangular door in side, socket mounted in center, some rust, handle missing, 10½″ h. (A-E) ....$ 45

Lantern, pierced, tin, hearts & sunbursts in mint condition (D-MW)   155

Lantern, pierced, tin, Revere (D-MW)   85

Lantern, pierced, tin, rosettes pattern, ex. cond., 15″ t. (D-E)...   90

Lantern, pierced, tin, well punched, 14½″ (D-NE)...   85

Lantern, round, tin & glass w/inside betty lamp (A-E)   115

Lantern, round, tin & glass & small w/betty lamp cup inside (A-E)....................................   160

Lantern, ship's, brass, white enameled reflector, 19th C. (A-MW)   65

Lantern, signal, tin, free-blown jar-shaped glove w/projecting tin collars at top & bottom, orig. whale oil burner, circular flat ring handle, ca. 1840, 11″ h. (A-NE)....................................   125

Lantern, signal, tin, free-blown, onion-shaped globe w/removable tin base w/conical oil lamp & burner, conical shaped tin top w/ring handle, ca. 1840, 10″ h. (A-MW)..............................   45

Lantern, skater's, brass, burner & wick intact, polished, 7½″ (D-NE)   20

Lantern, tin, red glass, candleholder 4¼″ (D-NE)   32

Lantern, tin, removable well, early round globe (A-E)   200

Lantern, tin, small, pierced (A-E)..   150

Lantern, tin, tri-corner (D-E)   125

Lantern, tin, 2 sides glass, flat narrow form (A-E)   70

Lantern, wall, tin, w/cupola (D-MW)..   45

Lantern, wood, w/rosehead nails, 4 windows made from broken pieces of glass, unpainted, 18th C. (A-NE)..   850

Light, lumberman's, brass, whale oil, trunnion, w/wrought iron hook & spike, 12″ overall, 2½″ diam. (D-NE)   75

Lighter, Cape Cod, brass, w/tray (A-E)   22

Oven light for candle, tin, w/long wooden handle (D-E)   75

Rush holder, iron, handwrought, candle socket, twisted stem & arm w/penny feet, 9½″ t. (D-E)..   225

Rush holder, iron, handwrought, 8″ t. (D-E)   110

Rush holder, iron, jab & candleholder, rare (A-E)   87

Rush holder, iron, handwrought, on 3 legs, 3-toed feet show wear, 7″ t. (D-S)......................   135

Rush holder, iron, handwrought, spring loaded jaws, rams head thumb press, 8½″ h., 4″ across base (D-S)   185

Rush holder, iron, handwrought, twisted stem & arm, cast iron base, 9″ t. (D-E)   150

Rush & candle holder, iron, handwrought, tripod base, candle socket provides counter-balance, feet rolled outward, 18th C., 8″ h. (A-MW)..   165

Rush & candle holder, iron, handwrought, twisted, wooden base, 14″ h. (A-NE)..................   200

Rushlight holder, iron, dated 1721, 7″ h. (A-E)   225

Rushlight holder, iron, twisted w/wooden base (D-W)   59

Rushlight holder, iron, twisted wrought iron stems, wooden base, 13″ h., 4″ across (D-MW)..   145

Rushlight & candle holder, iron, crown base, handwrought, 12″ h. (D-E)   75

Rushlight & candle holder, iron, slide spring trammel loom light, 18th C., complete, extends to 33″ (D-E)   250

Rushlight & candle holder, iron, wooden base (D-W)   85

Sconce, brass, hanging, 3-branch (A-E)   35

Sconce, brass, 2-candle, w/mirror (D-E)   65

Sconce, candle, tin, 14″ (A-E)   65

Sparking lamp, pewter, w/brass snuffer, unmarked (D-MW) $185

Sconce, candle, tin, 10"×4" (D-NE)...$ 80
Sconce, candle, tin, 13½" (A-E)   70
Sconce, candle, tin, crimped leaf shape crown (A-E)   175
Sconce, candle, tin, crimped shell top (D-E)   90
Sconce, candle, tin, crimped top, 6"×14" (D-MW)   35
Sconce, candle, tin, line decor. (A-E)   130
Sconce, candle, tin, New England, all orig., 13½" (D-N)   125
Sconce, candle, tin, round crimped crown (A-E)   125
Sconce, candle, tin, round, rare, 11½" (A-E)   225
Sconce, candle, tin, semi-circular back, carying handle on front, 9" h., 4½" w. (D-MW)   55
Sconce, tin, candle socket, single, circular fluted reflector, 14" h. (A-NE).......................   40
Sconce, tin, crimped candleholder & rectangular back, 9"×13" (A-NE)   250
Sconce, tin, crimped edges on pan & buttoned reflector back, 11" h., 6½" w. (D-MW)   150
Sconce, tin, crimped edges on pan & reflector back, 11" h., 6½" w. (D-E)......................   115
Sconce, tin, early, 13½"×4" (D-E)   125
Sconce, tin, fluted reflector (D-E)   45
Sconce, tin, lard oil (D-E)   50
Sconce, tin, single socket, rectangular, half-round drip tray, 13½" h. (A-NE)   28
Sconce, tin, single socket, rectangular, half-round drip tray w/raised edge, 13½" h. (D-MW) ..   55
Sconce, tin, small (A-E)..   95
Sconce, tin, whale oil, black paint, w/free blown peg lamp, 14" (A-NE).........................   175
Sconces, candle, tin, pr., 9½" (A-E)   325
Sconces, candle, tin, pr., 13½" h. (A-E)   200
Sconces, candle, tin, shield & star punched tin w/overhang, pr. (A-E)   140
Sconces, candle, toleware, oval, crimped shields, red, pr. (D-NE)   450
Sconces, tin, all orig., pr. (A-E)   115
Sconces, tin, crimped overhang, pr. (A-E)...   140
Sconces, tin, diamond shape, pr., 14" (A-E)   230
Sconces, tin, decor., pr. (A-E)   25
Sconces, tin, mirror back, early, pr. (A-E)..   260
Sconces, tin, mirror back, pr. (D-MW)..   200
Sconces, tin, mirrored, round, pr., 18th C., 9½" diam. (D-E)   525
Sconces, tin, patty pan candleholders & shield backs, pr. (A-E)   250
Sconces, tin, rare, tulip shape, pr. (A-E)   410
Sconces, tin, scalloped overhang, ex. cond., pr., 14" h. (jA-E)......................................   300
Socket, candle, iron, handwrought, single, twisted hanging, 12" l. (D-E)   180
Spill/splint box, tin, w/tab, hanging, oval, 4½"×8½" (D-E)   25
Splint holder, iron, handwrought, w/spike end, 18th C., 13" l. (A-NE)...........................   225
Stand, Betty lamp, tin (D-NE)..   165
Stand, Betty lamp, wood, tin cup betty (A-E)..   65
Stand, fat lamp, 8½" (A-E)   160
Stand, fat lamp, 4½" (A-E)   25
Stand, fat lamp, iron, handwrought, curved feet, adjustable fat wells (A-E)..........................   225
Tinderbox, copper, oval, ca. 1830, 6" l., 3½" w. (D-E)   65
Tinderbox, iron, complete w/1 compartment (D-MW)   45
Tinderbox, iron, flintlock w/2 compartments, cylindrical, 2"×4½" (D-E)   160
Tinderbox, maple, hanging, w/drawer (D-E)   195
Tinderbox, metal, complete (D-E)   185
Tinderbox, tin, candleholder top, striker & flint, crimped edge cover inside, complete (D-NE)   145
Tinderbox, pewter, hinged (D-E)   75
Tinderbox, tin, cover & insert (A-E)..   140
Tinderbox & candleholder, tin, round, complete w/damper, strike, flint, tinder 4" diam. (D-E).   175
Tinder lighter, iron, handwrought (A-E)...   290
Tinder pouch, leather (D-MW)   35
Torch, tin, handled, 9" l. (D-NE)...   10
Torches, iron, railroad, hanging, complete w/handle (D-MW)   36
Torches, tin, railroad, w/handle (D-MW)..   18
Trammel, Betty lamp, sawtooth, rare, patina ex. (A-E)..   300

Miniatures

Miniatures of any object, made prior to the turn of the century, attract and hold a special fascination for collectors nowadays. And, the growing scarcity of the more respectable examples has influenced prices to the extent that it has put a strain on even well-padded purses.

For generations, children have always enjoyed creating their very own toy microcosm of the adult life about them; so the cabinetmaker, as well as the potter, woodcarver and even the tinsmith, turned to miniatures, either as playthings for their own children, or for those of their customers.

A fantastically mixed bag of miniatures was produced that can only be classified as "toys." Then, we have the larger pieces that oftentimes come under the heading of "children's furnishings," made on a scale readily usable by a child. Objects include a variety of small chairs, blankets chests, settees, tables, beds, or chests-of-drawers, to name a few.

Finally, we have the so-called "salesman's" samples which were carried about the countryside to illustrate the style and ability of the cabinetmaker, or the "display" samples that were used in shopwindows, since early shopwindows were much smaller. Scale models were necessary during the eighteenth and early nineteenth centuries in order that the "window-shopper" might see the entire piece. When larger plate-glass windows became common, the miniature display samples were no longer made. These pieces are particularly sought today by collectors.

* * *

Anvil and hammer, signed "J Perry 1902" (A-E) ....$	50
Anvil, 2 hammers (A-E)	100
Bandbox, decor. (A-E)...	50
Basket, berry, splint, handled, 3"×3½" (D-W)	15
Basket, handled, splint weave, 4"×2¼" (D-NE)...	12
Basket, Indian, Pima, coiled shallow bowl, whirlwind design, 4½" diam. (A-SW)..................	200
Basket, 2-handled, lid, decor. on side (A-E)	210
Basket, Indian, orange & green paint, 2½" h. (A-NE)...	60
Basket, kettle, shaped like early iron kettle, 3 legs, swing handle, 4"×3" (D-NE)	24
Bench, decor. w/green, red & white lines, ends w/gouged cut outs, ogee apron (A-E)	125
Bird whistle, pottery (A-E)	950
Bowl, deep, slip decor., green, black & white, repaired, 4½" (A-E)	45
Bowl, pouring, pottery, 2½" (A-E)...	25
Bowl, pouring, redware, w/handle, circular line coggle indentation decor., 4½" (A-E)............	210
Bowl, redware, black sponge decor., 2½" (A-E)	150
Bowl, redware, black sponge decor., incised coggle circle, 3¼" (A-E)	130
Bowl, redware, black stripe decor. on rim, 4½" diam. (A-E)..	350
Bowl, redware, dark glaze, 3½" (A-E)	35
Bowl, redware, red & black, 3" (A-E)..	35
Box, dome-top, pine, dk. green w/yellow & black quilted brushed decor., 6"×3" (A-NE)	225
Box, music, plays 3 tunes (A-E)...	52
Box, trinket, domed lid, blue-green background, profuse decor., 5½" l. (A-E)	525
Box, wall, old oxblood red, 5¼"×7½" (A-NE)	275
Box, "Weber", decor. w/house, trees & tulips, yellow background, orig. hasp (A-E)	825
Box, "Weber", decor. w/tulips on yellow background (A-E)...	270
Bucket, wood, blue w/red stars, flags, horses, 3½" h. (D-E)...	45
Bureau, decor., 3 lg., 2 sm. drawers, dov. const., 11½" w., 15½" h. (A-E)............................	95

Case-of-drawers, rare, "Bachman", Lancaster Co., Pa., carved quarter columns, drawer fronts, burl walnut, orig. ogee feet, ex. cond., ca. 1780 (A-E) 6600

Chest, blanket, cherry, dov. const., footed, 9½" h., 10" w., 15" l. (D-E) 90

Chest, blanket, grained, dov. const., bracket feet (A-E) 230

Chest, blanket, pine, dov. const., 12" h., 12½" w., 18" l. (D-W) 45

Chest, blanket, poplar, dovetailed & turned feet, sanded & refinished, 8¼"×12½"×9½" (A-E) . 65

Chest, coffin shape, decor. w/tulip design, 8"×12" (A-E) 360

Chest, early, brown & buff grained, American, dovetailed & domed top, handmade hinges, ca. 1800, 20" l., 10" d., 8" h. (D-E) 200

Chest, grained fish eye pattern, dk. & lt. brown, initials "HM, 1847" on lid, 9½"×17"×12" (A-E). 260

Chest, grained, 4 small & 3 large drawers (D-E) 625

Chest, Shaker, pine, 3-drawer, 19th C., 11¼" w., 12½" h. (A-MW) 85

Chest, softwood, old green paint, coffin style (D-E).. 290

Clamp, screws 6" l., ⅜" diam., jaw 4" l. (D-E).. 25

Cleaver, meat, iron, w/human form handle (A-E) 475

Clock, O.G., weight-driven, W. N. Johnson & Co. (A-E).. 270

High chest of drawers, Chippendale, walnut, miniature, 20" h., 14" w. (A-E) $1500

Chest, walnut, miniature, attributed to Bachman of Lancaster County, Penna., ca. 1780, rare (A-E) $6600

Clock, steeple, Gothic, E. N. Welch (A-E).. 200

Clock, 30-hour, J. C. Brown, spring brass movement, in half ripple case (A-E) 220

Coffee mill, tin, punched decor. w/drawer, 2¼×2¼×2" (D-E).. 35

Coffeepot, tin, 3 rings on lid, inside strainer & inside support in handle, line decor. on body & spout (A-E)... 115

Coffeepot, tole (D-E).. 22

Cookie cutter, tin, round (D-MW)... 17

Creamer, spatterware, peafowl pattern, green spatter, miniature, 2" h. (D-E) 145

Crock, open (A-E) 15

Crock, pottery, 1½" (A-E)... 22

Crock, redware, 1⅝" (A-E).. 22

Crock, stoneware, brown glaze, 2½" t. (D-E).. 12

Cup & beaker, tole, red, handled (A-E).. 145

Cupboard, Dutch, early, top w/2 glass doors w/overhang molding, base w/3 drawers & 2 doors, bracket feet (D-E) 350

Cupboard, pine, step-back, old green paint w/ipen top, 14" w. × 16" h. × 6" d. (A-NE) 375

Cupboard, red, 15" w., 16" h. (A-E)... 385

Cuspidor, redware, 2¾" (A-E)... 40

Conestoga wagon, miniature, 6 carved horses & driver, cloth on wagon top advertising "George Smith, Schuylkill Mills 1818" (A-E) $1600

Decoy, Baltimore Oriole, by A. Elmer Crowell, early rubber stamp signature, perfect cond. (A-E) .	150
Decoy, Baltimore Oriole, by A. Elmer Crowell, impressed rectangular stamp, perfect cond. (A-E) .	150
Decoy, blackbird, red-winged, by A. Elmer Crowell, impressed rectangular signature, perfect cond. (A-E)	125
Decoy, bluebird, by A. Elmer Crowell, impressed rectangular stamp, ex. cond. (A-E)	325
Decoy, black duck, flying, rare, by A. Elmer Crowell, unsigned, perfect cond. (A-E)	200
Decoy, blue jay, by A. Elmer Crowell, impressed rectangular signature, ex. cond. (A-E)	170
Decoy, blue jay, by A. Elmer Crowell, unsigned, minor wear, early, ex. cond. (A-E)	75
Decoy, bobolink, by A. Elmer Crowell, early rubber stamp signature, perfect cond. (A-E)	150
Decoy, brown thrasher, by A. Elmer Crowell, early rubber stamp signature, perfect cond. (A-E) .	125
Decoy, cedar waxwing, by A. Elmer Crowell, early, unsigned, small base, perfect cond. (A-E)	125
Decoy, chickadee, by A. Elmer Crowell, impressed rectangular stamp, mint cond. (A-E)	150
Decoy, feeding canvasback drake, by A. Elmer Crowell, early rubber stamp signature, perfect cond. (A-E)	350
Decoy, flying black duck, A. Elmer Crowell, unsigned, rare, perfect cond. (A-E)	200
Decoy, flying goldeneye drake, by A. Elmer Crowell, unsigned, ex. cond. (A-E)	200
Decoy, goldfinch, A. Elmer Crowell, impressed rectangular signature, early, perfect cond. (A-E)	200
Decoy, Kentucky warbler, by A. Elmer Crowell, early, unsigned, perfect cond. (A-E)	100
Decoy, Kentucky warbler, by A. Elmer Crowell, impressed rectangular stamp, perfect cond. (A-E)	150
Decoy, Northern flicker, by A. Elmer Crowell, early rubber stamp signature, minor wear, ex. cond. (A-E)	150
Decoy, Northern flicker, by A. Elmer Crowell, impressed rectangular signature, perfect cond. (A-E)	150
Decoy, nuthatch, by A. Elmer Crowell, impressed rectangular signature, ex. cond. (A-E)	275
Decoy, owl, one eye half shut, fitted w/sandwich glass cup plate for use as ash try, ex. cond. (A-E) .	450
Decoy, pheasant, rare, by A. Elmer Crowell, early rubber stamp, minor wear, ex. cond. (A-E)	170
Decoy, red-breasted Merganser drake, by A. Elmer Crowell, early rubber stamp signature, perfect cond. (A-E)	250
Decoy, red-winged blackbird, by A. Elmer Crowell, impressed rectangular signature, perfect cond. (A-E)	125
Decoy, scarlet tanager, early, by A. Elmer Crowell, rubber stamp signature, ex. cond. (A-E) ..	175
Decoy, tern, early, mounted on clam shell, by A. Elmer Crowell, early oval rubber stamp signature, perfect cond. (A-E)	350
Decoy, downy woodpecker, by A. Elmer Crowell, impressed rectangular signature, ex. cond. (A-E)	170
Decoy, wood thrush, by A. Elmer Crowell, impressed rectangular signature, ex. cond. (A-E)..	200
Desk, rare, ogival skirt, 1 drawer, ca. 1790 (A-E)	850
Dishpan, tin, w/2 handles, 6½" (A-E)	15
Dry sink, pine, 1 door 17¾" wide, 23" h. w/3" deep well, refinished (D-MW)	125
Footstool, well-shaped, old green paint, 4¼" h. (A-NE)	100
Fork, wrought iron, decor. (A-E)	45
Goffering iron, brass tube, lacy base, 4" h. (D-E)	60
Goffering stand, iron, brass slub holder, 2¾"×4¼" (D-NE)	60

Iron and crimping iron (A-E) ....$ 40
Iron and trivet, red swan w/white feathers (A-E)...................................... 32
Jar, redware, name in black slip "S. J. McKee," 2" (A-E) 325
Jug, olive to orange glaze w/brown decor. (A-E) 40
Jug, redware, 3" (A-E) 35
Knife, bleeding, in case (A-E) 22
Lamp, Betty, on saw-tooth trammel (A-E).. 275
Lamp, Betty, redware, on tray w/handle, turned stem (A-E)..................... 475
Lamp, Betty, redware, black splash decor. (A-E) 625
Lamp, Betty, redware, w/handle & spout (A-E) 385
Lamp, Betty, tin, w/hook, chain w/pick (A-E) 320
Mold, butter, "circle", round, 1⅛" diam., wood (D-E)............................. 20
Mold, butter, wood, "over-ripened pineapple", round, 1⅓" diam. (D-E) 22
Mold, butter, wood, sheaf of wheat, 2" (A-E) 42
Mold, candle, 6-tube, handled, very rare, 5¾"×5½"×3¼" (D-E)............... 125
Mold, candle, 6-tube & shaped handle, hanging ring (A-E)...................... 300
Mold, food, greenish-brown dripping glaze, impressed "John Bell, Waynesboro", 4¼" d. (A-E). 190
Mortar & pestle, iron, 4" t. (D-NE)... 25
Mortar & pestle, maple (A-E) 55
Mousetrap, wire, squirrel cage design (D-E)... 28
Muffineer, tin, 4½" t. (D-NE) 16
Mug, redware, glazed inside only, white & green lines, unusual, 2¾" (A-E).......... 70
Painting, oil on canvas, brown robed monk opening bottle of wine, ornate gilt frame, ca. 1860,
    overall 4½"×6" (D-E) 60
Painting, oil on ivory, portrait of man (A-E).. 55
Painting, on ivory, "nobleman", "lady", pr., 3¼"×2½", signed "J. Zanava" (A-MW) 150
Penny bank, pottery, black dot decor., 3½" (A-E) 230
Pitcher, dark glaze, 3½" (A-E) 80
Pitcher, pottery, 2¼" (A-E) 35
Pitcher, redware, 2¾" (A-E) 37
Pitcher, pottery, 2⅜" (A-E) 45
Pitcher, pottery, 3" (A-E) 75
Pitcher, pottery, 3" (A-E) 45
Pitcher, pottery, 3¼" (A-E) 120
Pitcher, redware, handled, orange glaze, 2¼" h. (A-NE) 75
Plate, cup, slip decor., pottery, 4" (A-E) 175
Plate, cup, slip decor., pottery, 4" (A-E) 180
Plate, orange, brown & black decor. (A-NE)... 45
Plate, pottery, dot slip decor., 4½" (A-E) 230
Plate, pottery, 6-line slip decor., 4½" (A-E) 130
Plate, pottery, slip decor., 4" (A-E) 350
Plate, pottery, slip decor., 3½" (A-E) 185
Plate, pottery, slip decor., black & white lines, 4½" (A-E) 300
Plate, pottery, slip decor., wavy lines & dots, 4½" (A-E) 150
Platter, redware, octagonal, green, white & black slip decor., 5½" (A-E) 2000
Platter, redware, octagonal, slip decor., rare (A-E) 375
Platter, redware, oval, white, green & black slip decor., drape & dot border, floral design, 5½"
    (A-E) 300
Platter, redware, slip decor., oblong, rare, 3"×4" (A-E) 850
Porringer, redware, olive-orange base w/brown decor., 2¼" (A-NE) 350
Porringer, taster, pewter, unmarked (A-E) 160
Pot, bean, olive to orange glaze (A-NE) 40
Pot, bean, orange, brown & black decor. (A-NE) 50
Pot, pottery, 1⅞" (A-E) 17
Powder horn (A-E) 37
Scales, hanging, well-crafted hooks (A-E) 65
Sconce, candle, tin, wall, pr. (A-E) 275
Scrubboard & washtub, wooden, pr., 2½"×3½" (D-E)............................. 25
Settee, cherry, ca. 1830 (D-E)... 350

Basket, miniature, 2-handled, w/lid, elaborate decor. on sided (A-E) $210

Desk, miniature, ogival skirt, fine grained decor., ca. 1790 $850
185

Blockfront secretary, mahogany, miniature. 16" h. (D-NW) $550

Sewing machine (A-E)	$ 30
Shovel, wood, painted w/scene on scoop, 18" l. (D-E)	20
Stand, goffering iron (D-E)	20
Stand, goffering iron, brass slub holder, iron base, 2¾"×4¼" (D-NE)	60
Steamer & double boiler, tin, rare, complete, 4"×9" (D-E)	50
Stove, cast, w/4 implements, 18th C. (A-SW)	70
Table, drop leaf, orig. paint, doll's (A-E)	60
Teakettle, copper, 5½" (A-E)	52
Teakettle, tin (A-E)	30
Teapot, child's, tin, 2½" (D-E)	18
Teapot, child's, w/side spout, 4½" (D-E)	24
Tea set, spatter w/overall blue & red, incls. teapot & 4 cups & saucers (D-E)	185
Trivet, for child's iron (A-E)	10
Wagon, Conestoga, w/6 carved horses & driver, cloth wagon top advertising George Smith, Schuykill Mills, 1818 (A-E)	1600
Washbowl & pitcher, blue sponge decoration, pitcher 4½" h., chip on underside, bowl mint (D-MW)	38
Weathervane, dog (A-E)	280
Wood carving, duck in boat, decorated (A-E)	125
Wood carving, white goose (A-E)	25

Paintings

Portraiture is perhaps the most recognized, and undoubtedly ranks as the foremost of our folk arts. Although professional artists did flourish in the more populated areas, most of our early American paintings fall under the heading of amateur work, painted by itinerant limners during the eighteenth and nineteenth centuries. Their inability to create a cohesive composition—and their lack of skill in depicting a true likeness or correct perspective—resulted in naive paintings with a juvenile quality that is extremely appealing to collectors.

Before the invention of photography, the nineteenth century was the most fertile period for paintings. Since the itinerant painter's stock-in-trade was individual and family portraits, they were the most popular type wall hanging, followed by still lifes, landscapes, intricate needlework, and fancy paintings done in velvet, "theorem" painting. This term simply means routine or theoretical exercises in painting, done on velvet or paper (rare), with the aid of stencils. This was an artistic skill taught in fashionable young ladies' seminaries from about 1810-1845. Topics included still lifes, showing colorful baskets of fruit or flowers with an occasional bird or butterfly, in addition to mourning pieces, portraits, and biblical or mythical landscapes.

Today, there are available to collectors many charming and beautiful paintings, drawings, prints, embroidery, etc., from all schools and periods of art. As with all fields of antiques, prices vary greatly with many factors—quality, size, artist's name, condition, etc., but in general, a beautiful original painting can be found to fit almost every budget. Collectors should never overlook paintings by unknown artists, or an unsigned work if it is good. It will not only bring the owner the esthetic pleasure of owning something beautiful and unique, but it also offers the practical quality of being a good investment.

* * *

Etching, "man & two children having a bite to eat," large, colorful (A-E)	$ 150
Oil, "a winter scene" by V. Shearer, 1913, 13"×25" (A-E)	110
Oil, "blacksmith" (A-E)	52
Oil, "boy dressed in blue w/white collar, holding toy gun in hand" (A-E)	450
Oil, "courting scene", signed Edward B. Bensell (D-E)	375
Oil, "gentleman", gold leaf frame (A-E)	110
Oil, "gentleman holding book," gold leaf frame, 25"×35" (A-E)	220
Oil, "Indian" (A-E)	42
Oil, "lady dressed in gown, long curls," attributed to John Wolloston, 1757, large (A-E)	375
Oil, "lady," gold leaf frame (A-E)	100
Oil, "lady sitting, dressed in gown," 41"×51" (A-E)	90
Oil, "lady with lace collar holding book," framed (A-E)	82
Oil, "moonlight harbor scene," attributed to Turner or Whistler (A-E)	775
Oil, "mountain landscape," by C. H. Shearer, 1884, 24"×34" (A-E)	260
Oil, "mountain top landscape," by F. Spang (A-E)	80
Oil, "old man holding book," unframed (A-E)	95
Oil, "square-rigged sailing boats" by T. Maes, 18" h., 22" w. (A-NE)	95
Oil on academy board, "winterscape of red squirrel on tree roots w/nest of partridge chicks," by Hardy Gregory, Patterson, N. J., ca. 1870-80, 8½"×6½" (A-NE)	150
Oil on bed ticking, "American allegorical," relined, ca. 1825, 28"×28" (A-NE)	250
Oil on bed ticking, "May day celebration," w/over 50 people & animals dancing, feasting & listening to band, illegibly signed, dated 1819, 22"×28" (A-NE)	3000

Oil on board, British soldiers on dress parade, Penna. countryside, rail-snake fence, rolling hills, stone farm house, 18th C. (A-E)..$ 3500

Oil on board, child in green jacket w/brass buttons, holding hammer & board w/tacks, by Henry Ward, Mass. (A-E) 4700

Oil on board, "cottage scene," by Groves (A-E)... 30

Oil on board, "girl," colorful, birds-eye frame (A-E) 75

Oil on board, katydid on dried maple leaf w/landscape background, painted in half round, labeled "painted by Byron Sutton of New York", dated (pencil) 1872, orig. frame, 9"×6½" (A-NE).. 225

Oil on board, portrait of Linus Greene, by William M. Prior, 1835, relined, 20"×23" (A-NE) ... 1100

Lithograph, Currier & Ives, American Homestead winter scene, small folio, 1868 (A-E) $170

Important American theorem, on paper, "The Summer Treat", signed by F. Coburn (A-NE) $2750

Watercolor of Col. Isaac S. Hottenstein, 1st Regiment, 2nd Brigade, 6th Division, Pennsylvania Militia, in full dress regalia (A-E) $4900

Oil on board, portrait of young man in black waistcoat & tie, signed "Lock, by W. M. Prior, 1835, in Portland, Ma.," 20"×24½" (A-NE) 1300

Oil on board, prior-Hamblen school portrait of Henry Ward, Lynn, Mass.; child in green jacket w/brass buttons & white collar, holding hammer & board w/tacks; inscr. "$2.00-Mrs. Ward", 12"×16" (A-NE) 4700

Oil on canvas, American fruit still life, ca. 1840, 36" w. × 29" h. (A-NE) 3200

Oil on canvas, "Annie R. Lewis, a 3-masted ship sailing off a lighthouse," by W. P. Stubbs, 20"×30" (A-NE) 1700

Oil on canvas, "basket of flowers & tulips," old, 29"×38" (A-E) 15

Oil on canvas, boy (James Edward Thacher) holding hoop & stick, dressed in collar & jacket w/brass buttons, sunset background, by Edward A. Conant, orig. frame (A-NE) 1000

Oil on canvas, "chicken in pen," framed, early, 22½"×31½" (A-E)...................................... 110

Oil on canvas, "chicks & duck," by Ben Austrian, good frame (A-E) 1000

Early portraits, by unidentified American artist (A-NE) $4300

Oil on canvas, child sitting on step w/doll in hand, colorful (A-E) ....$ 65
Oil on canvas, foothills of White Mountains, 3 figures on bank & footbridge, by H. B. Brown, orig.
frame, 13"×25" (A-NE)..   850
Oil on canvas, full length portrait of seated boy (Alfred Churchill Thacher), in pantaloons,
opening family jewel box & listening for ticking of watch, by Edward A. Conant, 1841, early
relining, no repaint, 30"×38" (A-NE)   3500
Oil on canvas, "horse and rider," by Walter Gilman (A-E)   375
Oil on canvas, "kittens in the hay," maple frame, 20¾"×24¾" (A-E)....................................   170
Oil on canvas, "Litchfield, Maine homestead," by Wesley Webber, 8 figures, 5 farms, horse in
barn, split-rail fence, rolling Maine hills, orig. ornate frame, 16"×26" (A-NE).....................   2600
Oil on canvas, mounted on board, "peaches," kitchen primitive, 9"×13" (A-NE)....................   150
Oil on canvas, mounted on board, "two women on rocks w/gray sea beyond," 9"×10" (A-NE)   40
Oil on canvas, portrait of Frederick Howard Thacher, seated & holding white rabbit, w/pleated
bib, velvet waistcoat w/brass buttons, ¾-length, by Edward A. Conant (A-NE)   5750
Oil on canvas, portrait of lady w/ruffled white bonnet, 21"×27" (A-E)   140
Oil on canvas, primitive, "young man and his dog," orig. stretcher, 25"×30" (A-E)   450
Oil on canvas, "Rip Van Winkle arriving home after his 20 year sleep," mounted on board, 19th
C., 10"×13" (A-NE)   250
Oil on canvas, "seascape", frame, ca. 1900 (D-E)   60
Oil on canvas, "seated girl in red dress," gilded frame (A-E)..   1800
Oil on canvas, "South Hampton, squared rigged 3-master, sailing off headlands," signed Knight,
1868, 22"×28" (A-NE)   700
Oil on canvas, Sylvia Sheppard of Norwalk, Conn., seated in landscape w/dress, holding straw
bonnet w/flowers, ca. 1830, 22"×28" (A-NE)...   350
Oil on canvas, "view of the waterfront at Liverpool," England, ca. 1825, 36" w., 26" h. (A-NE) ..   1000
Oil on canvas, "wooded scene & stream" by V. Shearer, goldleaf frame, 37"×23" (A-E)..........   320
Oil on ivory, "gentlemen," shell gold frame (A-E)   105
Oil on panel, pine, by J. C. Johnsen, "large 3-masted sq. rigger, Anna, under sail w/3 other sq.
riggers & 3 sm. ships sailing in foreground, flying flags," 22"×39" (A-NE)   800
On tin, "view of Berks County Almshouse," 1894 (A-E)..   9800
Oil, on wood, men sitting at table, drinking (A-E)..   430
Oil on wood panel, four figures standing over slain deer w/birch canoe in background, by Walter
Manley Hardy, Maine, unsigned, 8"×10" (A-NE)...   300
Oil on wood panel, "sheep & ducks," by N. H. Trotter, 1893 (A-E)......................................   65
Oil on wood, "young hunter with rifle," ca. 1840, 13½"×14½" (A-NE)   175
Oil, portrait of man, 18th C. (A-E)...   300
Oil, religious subject attributed to John Valentine Haidt, 1757 (A-E)....................................   75
Oil, "Saco River" (A-E)   110

Oil, "ship at sea, men on row boat going toward ship," (A-E) ....$ 65
Oil, small child sitting on chair dressed in yellow dress, holding apple, primitive (A-E) 1250
Oil, still life, basket of flowers & ferns on pine panel, 13½"×20" (A-NE)............................. 200
Oil, "winter farm scene," by Hicks (A-E) 750
Oil, wooded scene w/stream, goldleaf frame, by V. Shearer, 15"×24" (A-E)........................... 75
Oil, "young lady seated on sofa," 24"×29" (A-E).. 110
Oil, "young man," unframed (A-E)... 30
On cloth, circus broadside, black man w/three snakes standing in thick green foliage, 39"×70"
   (A-NE).. 185
On cloth, circus broadside, fat lady in bathing suit on shore of lake, 39"×70" (A-NE) 185
On cloth, circus broadside, gorilla in thick green foliage, 39"×70" (A-NE) 185
On panel board, fireplace, "domed cathedral, red lion at bottom" (A-E) 800
On porcelain, girl dressed in colorful cloth, beads & cross & two vases, gold leaf frame, signed "K.
   P. M." 6¾"×9½" (A-E).. 425
On porcelain, "lady," brass frame (A-E) 70
Painting, 1st American converted sail to steamship, 1896, signed J. S. Wright (A-E) 35
Painting, "lady with bonnet," primitive, minor repair (A-E) 75
Painting, "Maryland farm scene," primitive, signed C. P. Russell, 29" w. × 17" h. (A-NE) 1400
Painting, ship, "morning star" of Boston, Mass., ca. 1850, 40" w. × 28" h. (A-NE) 1400
Painting, well-dressed man w/beaver hat & carved cane on footbridge, signed Chadwick, 1845,
   relined, 12" h., 9" w. (A-NE) 900
Pastel on paper, "Annie R. Lewis" sailing off a lighthouse, rowboat w/2 figures," 22"×28" (A-NE) . 900
Pastel, portrait, "Anna Thomas," Chester Co., oval gilt frame (A-E)................................... 65
Portrait, child in shepherd's costume w/dog & basket of fruit, primitive, 18th C., 25" w. × 30" h.
   watch, orig. frame, 22"×27" (A-NE)... 2500
Portrait, lady, dressed with lace collar, holding purse, 31" w., 37" l. (A-E) 200
Portrait, child in shepherds costume w/dog & basket of fruit, primitive, 18th C., 25" w. × 30" h.
   (A-NE).. 1500
Portrait, young woman, by William M. Prior, inscr. on back & dated 1830, 19" w. × 23" h. (A-NE) .. 1300
Reverse on glass, "Burke," 7¾"×10" (A-E)... 225
Reverse on glass, "death of Nelson" (A-E)... 225
Reverse on glass, "Franklin," 7¾"×10" (A-E) 500
Reverse on glass, girl, "Lucinda" (A-E) 120
Reverse on glass, "Jackson," 9½"×11¾" (A-E)... 475
Reverse on glass, "John Adams," 6¾"×9" (A-E)... 375
Reverse on glass, "Lafayette" (A-E) 800
Reverse on glass, "Lafayette," 8"×10¼" (A-E) 400
Reverse on glass, "little Jesus, John & Virginia" (A-E)... 70
Reverse on glass, "Martin Van Buren," 9½"×11¾" (A-E).. 250
Reverse on glass, "Governor Wolf, first Governor of Pennsylvania" (A-E) 200

Hand colored print,
14" × 22" (D-MW)
$150

Reverse on glass, "T. Napoleon" (A-E)..$ 200

Reverse on glass, "old school house," mahogany frame (A-E)............................... 85

Reverse on glass, two hunters in front of log cabin w/hunting dogs, rifles & game, Maine
landscape, 19th C. (A-NE) 325

Reverse on glass, "view of New York from Brooklyn Heights," dated 1824 (D-MW) 375

Reverse on glass, "Washington" (A-E) 280

Reverse on glass, "Washington," 7⅜"×10" (A-E) 475

Reverse on glass, "Washington," 14"×14" (A-MW).. 130

Reverse on glass, "Washington," 14"×14" (D-W).. 130

Reverse on glass, w/tinsel, "vase of flowers" (A-NE) 275

Still life, pears, gold frame, 6" h. × 8" w. (A-NE) 200

Theorem, "fruit basket," by W. Rank, framed (D-E).. 70

Theorem, "horses," oil on velvet (A-E).. 35

Theorem, "landscape," people, bridge & trees, blues on darkened velvet, 22"×27" incl. frame
(D-MW) 110

Theorem, on velvet, stenciled eagle w/banner reading "Liberty & Union, one & inseparable"
above 2 stenciled vases of roses & pansies, 12"×18½" (A-NE)................................... 400

Theorem, watercolor, on paper, flowers, grapes & scroll w/verse, by Barbara Roudebush, 1845, 18"
h. × 16" w. (A-NE).. 250

Theorem, watercolor, on paper, "the summer treat", incl. watermelons, grapes, pears, etc., orig.
frame, signed F. Coburn, 23½" × 20" (A-NE) 2750

Theorem, watercolor, on paper, vase of flowers, 12" × 15" (A-NE)............................. 175

Tinsel painting, flowered, orig. frame (A-NE) 150

Watercolor, "autumn scene," by Hattie Brunner, 10½"×14½", framed (A-E).................... 600

Watercolor, "bird on branch," primitive, 5½"×6" (A-E)... 75

Watercolor, "bird on rose bud spring," red, yellow & green w/black beak (A-E) 225

Watercolor, "birds & flowers" (A-E).. 90

Watercolor, "birds, tulips & animals" (A-E) 100

Watercolor, "by the lake," by Caroline Lash (A-E) 20

Watercolor, Col. Isaac S. Hottenstein, 1st regiment, 2nd brigade, 6th div., Pa. militia, in full dress
regalia; cannon wheels, trees & fence background (A-E) 4900

Watercolor, "farm scene," Roy J. & Hattie K. Brunner, small (A-E).............................. 250

Watercolor, fruit (pear, apple, grapes, leaves), blue, red, yellow & green, framed size, 8"×9½"
(D-NE).. 32

Watercolor, "gentleman," 5½"×8½" (A-E) 105

Watercolor, "gentleman," by J. Maentil (A-E) 45

Watercolor, "girl," colorful (A-E) 75

Watercolor, girl holding book, sitting on chair with cat, primitive, 5"×7" (A-E).................... 120

Watercolor, girl holding flowers, sitting on chair (A-E) 110

Watercolor, girl reading book, sitting on Windsor chair, 8"×10" (A-E) 450

Watercolor, "country sale of antiques at old farmstead," by Hattie K. Brunner, Pa., folk artist
(contemporary) (A-E) 180

Watercolor, heart, tulip, two parrots, by Magdalene Wieber, 1845 (A-E).............................. 60

Watercolor, horses, birds, deer, ducks, small (A-E) 80

Watercolor, "Jacob B. Kauffmann," man holding cigar seated on Windsor chair (A-E) 875

Watercolor, lady holding book, 8"×10" (A-E) 150

Watercolor, "lady in black holding blue parasol" (A-E)... 750

Watercolor, "lady in black holding flowers" (A-E)... 475

Watercolor, lady in red w/white flowing hankerchief (A-E)...................................... 200

Watercolor, lady sitting on Windsor chair holding book, 7½"×9" (A-E) 210

Watercolor, "lady quilting," 8"×10" (A-E) 410

Watercolor, "love birds & sunflower" (A-NE) 60

Watercolor, man, colorful dress suit, silk hat, 9½"×11" (A-E).................................... 1000

Watercolor, man w/full dress suit, high silk hat, blue vest, tie, signed, 7½"×9" (A-E) 170

Watercolor, man w/silk hat, blue coat, brown pants, yellow & black boots, 8"×11" (A-E) 170

Watercolor, pr. of parrots on rose bush, framed, 11"×13" (A-E)................................. 250

Watercolor, "parrot & pot of tulips" (A-E) 375

Watercolor, portrait of Mr. Gaylom holding ring & high hat, by Emery Mudge, early 19th C., 4"×7"
(A-NE).. 300

Small watercolor, "Jacob B. Kauffman" (A-E) $875

Early theorm painting, of fruits w/butterfly & parrot, unframed, 15½" × 18" (D-MW) $250

Watercolor, portrait of gentleman in double-breasted waistcoat & boots, holding sealed letter, orig. pine frame in blue & red, full-length, 6½"×9" (A-NE) ....$ 750

Watercolor, "pot of flowers," Mary Gingrich (A-E).. 55

Watercolor, race horse called "British Pistol", color, 1829 writing on reverse side, Washington Henry Jackson (A-E) 120

Watercolor, "rampant spotted lion & yellow unicorn on green earth," good frame (A-E) 550

Watercolor, religious verse & death certificate, red, orange & yellow; birds, hearts, flowers (A-E) 300

Watercolor, "Eli Rothermel 1844," child in red dress on high chair (A-E) 800

Watercolor, Rutland Col. Merrill Railroad, dated 1804 (A-E) 500

Watercolor, "seashells," by Elizabeth Fisher, 1846, 5"×6" (A-E)... 80

Watercolor, scene of country store showing much early advertising, dated 1909, 12½"×16", framed (D-MW).. 95

Watercolor, ship, "Marie Butler", traveling on sea (A-E)... 525

Watercolor, silhouette of attractive woman, 4¾"×5½" (A-NE) 150

Watercolor, silhouette of gentleman holding red book, 3"×4½" (A-NE)............................... 225

Watercolor, Mrs. W. W. Stanley of Minot, Me., orig. frame, ca. 1820, 3½"×4½" (A-NE)......... 475

Watercolor, three maidens at graveside in mourning, by Prudence March, 1805, inscr. "a mourning piece no. 2 Aug. 18, 1863," oval, 12¼"×9" (A-NE) 625

Watercolor, "tulip & birds," frame, colorful (A-E).. 90

Watercolor, 20 colorful girls, different poses, walnut frame (A-E) 70

Watercolor, two men, woman & horse in landscape w/early houses on hillside, by Prudence March, 1805, inscr. "a landscape no. 1 Aug. 18, 1863, Oliver March property," 10"×8½"(A-NE) . 850

Watercolor, "Washington on horseback," 8"×10" (A-NE).. 280

Watercolor, "winter scene," by Hattie Brunner, 12½"×15½", framed (A-E) 775

Watercolor, "winter scene," by Hattie K. Brunner, 27½"×19" (A-E).................................... 1500

Watercolor, woman standing over hooded rush cradle, bearing sleeping child, by Prudence March, 1805, inscr. "infancy no. 5 August 18, 1863, Oliver March property", 7¼"×7" (A-NE). 850

Pewter

The pleasure of pewter lies not only in its softly rounded forms, but in its glowing surface, as though one of the metals that went into its making gave off light. Because its interesting forms reveal the brilliant workmanship of an earlier day, pewter has long been one of America's most costly and treasured collectibles.

Be it the bicentennial influence, nostalgia, or both, pewter products are the "in" metal today.

Pewter has been produced from the mid-1600s for countless everyday articles—with the exception of cooking utensils—and continued to be made and used well into the last century, when its popularity declined with the increased usage of porcelain and glass. By 1850 pewter was nearly forgotten.

Pewter is softer than other metals. It can be scratched, dented or bent very easily, and can be ruined by close contact with heat. It is an amalgam of base metals, chiefly tin and copper, plus varying amounts of other metals. Its color is determined by the variance of the chemical composition; some pieces will have an almost silver-like appearance, while others will be bluish-gray. Only the pewterer knew the exact components that made up his mixture.

Colonial pewterers never organized themselves into strict guilds, as the English craftsmen, where standards regulated the mix for each grade of pewter. Therefore, American pewter varies enormously from maker to maker.

The majority of American pewter available today is marked; however, there are many fine, early unmarked examples of pewter still available to collectors, at realistic prices, that can be attributed to American pewterers because of their shapes and designs.

The value of a piece of pewter is determined by the quality of its shape and form, the condition of the metal, and its touchmark. Objects produced by well-known pewterers generally command the highest prices. Pewterers adopted individual touchmarks which were impressed on the underside of the finished piece; however, some appear elsewhere, such as on the handles of porringers. The mark might include a name, two or more initials, a series of symbols, an eagle, ship, dove or rose.

Collectors who have purchased American-made pewter objects over the years, that were made by well-known pewterers, have been generously rewarded, since the value of their acquisitions has apreciated much faster than English or Continental objects.

Today, there is a new generation of pewter that combines the tradition of classic colonial shapes with advances in modern casting techniques. The new products no longer contain lead, since other minerals such as antimony have been used to strengthen the metal, so that it is as safe to use as it is practical. Most pieces are well-marked, in addition to the word PEWTER, which indicates that the objects are contemporary.

Beginning collectors should be most cautious of numerous imports that have found their way into antiques shops across the country in recent years, especially sets of measures. One grouping of six bears a "James Yates" touchmark sandwiched between the word "England," and a mark incorporating a crown.

Another set of seven tankard-shaped measures bear a square touchmark with a grouping of four symbols, including a crown and wreath.

New pewter lacks the minute scratches, dents, bruises and the inimitable patina that early pewter acquired only through years of usage. Moreover, edges will be nicely rounded from wear; and, although its surface will look smooth, it will feel slightly rough to the touch because of many scars, due to the softness of the metal.

* * *

Basin, 9" (D-N)..$	60
Basin, Richard Austin, 8" d. (D-NE)	850
Basin, Bordman, 6½" (A-E)..	280
Basin, Samuel Danforth, 6⅝" diam. (D-NE)	475
Basin, 8" diam. (A-E)	47
Basin, good imprint of Samuel Hamlin, 8" (A-E).....................................	400
Basin, Thomas Swanson, ca. 1760, 12½" (A-E).......................................	45
Basin, Thomas Swanson, ca. 1760 (D-NE)	165
Basin, Thomas & Townson, 8" (A-E)	75
Basin, Townsend & Compton, 9" (D-E)..	60
Basin, unmarked, 7⅞", 1¾" deep (D-E)	85
Basin, unmarked, 8" overall, tapering to 6" at base, 2" deep (D-E)........	135
Basin, unsigned, ca. 1800, 1¾" h. × 6½" across top (D-S)	125
Basin, baptismal, TD&SB, 4⅞" h., 7 ¹³/₁₆" diam. (D-NE).........................	875
Beaker, 3½" t. (D-E)	45
Beaker, Timothy Boardman, 3½" h. (D-NE)	425
Beaker, Ashbil Griswold, 3" h. (D-NE)	375

Plate, pewter, by Jacob Whitmore, 18th C., 11" diam. (D-MW) $475

Teapot, pewter, small, marked R.B. (D-E) $290

Water pitcher, pewter, marked "Boardman & Co.," 6" h. (D-E) $235

Beaker, pint size (A-E) ....$	30
Beakers, footed, pr., 3½" h. (D-E)..	68
Bottle, hot water (D-E)	170
Bowl, Gersham Jones eagle mark, 7½" (A-E)	325
Bowl, baptismal, unsigned, ca. 1825, 4" t. × 6½" across top (D-S)	175
Bowl, deep, 9¼" (D-E)	125
Bowl, marked "I. H.", 9½" d. (A-E)..	60
Bowl, sugar, covered, handled urn shape, lid w/acorn finial, pedestal base, 19th C., 8"h. (A-MW) .	70
Bowl, sugar, hinged, marked "P. C. G.", 1804 (A-E)	37
Bowl, sugar, marked "H. Homan" (A-E)	85
Bowl, sugar, unmarked, small (A-E)...	65
Bowl, sugar, w/lid, urn shape on pedestal base w/inverted & everted upper rim & double scroll handles, 6" h. (D-MW)	55
Bowl, sugar, w/wooden double handle (A-E)...	95
Bowl, sugar & creamer, Sellew & Co., Cinn., Ohio (D-E).......................	950
Can, bullbous, mark of Englefields, London, 19th C., 4¾" h. (A-MW)	50
Can, circular concave, touch mark of Nester, 19th C., 5⅜" h. (A-MW)	50
Can, tobacco (A-E)...	115
Caster frame, 5-bottle, heart shaped handle, pedestal base, 19th C., 11½" h. (A-MW)...........	25
Caster set, 5-bottle, Roswell Gleason (D-E)	165
Caster set, complete (D-NE)	40
Caster set, w/3 bottles (A-E)	27
Chalice, attributed to Boardman & Co., 7½" h. (D-S)	225
Chalices, communion, pr., 6½" h. (A-E)..	30
Chalices, handled, attributed to Israel Trask, pr., 7" h. (D-E)	750
Chalices, Reed & Barton, pr. (D-MW)...	325
Charger, 11¼" (D-E)	170
Charger, 12" (A-E)	95
Charger, 13" (A-E)	80
Charger, 13½" (D-MW)	250
Charger, 14½" (D-E)	190
Charger, 16½" (A-E)	100
Charger, 16½" (D-E)	300
Charger, deep bowl & plain rim, marks worn, late 18th C., 16½" diam. (D-MW)	85
Charger, shallow bowl, heavy, flaring rim, 16½" diam. (D-MW)...............	125
Charger, touch mark of James Dixon & Son, Sheffield, 19th C., 12" diam. (A-MW)	55
Charger, Townsen, 12" (A-E)	75
Coffee mill, hamper, all orig. (A-E)	80
Coffeepot, Boardman & Hall, Phila., 11" (D-E)	300
Coffeepot, Boardman & Hart, ex. cond., 11½" (A-E)...............................	475
Coffeepot, Boardman & Hart, N. Y., 12" h. (D-NE)	425
Coffeepot, Boardman lion mark, 11½" t. (D-NE)....................................	400
Coffeepot, Rufus Dunham, ca. 1845, approx. 8½" tall (D-E)	285
Coffeepot, Reed & Barton, Mass., wooden handle, early (D-MW)..............	135
Coffeepot, R. Gleason, pigeon breasted (D-E)..	200
Coffeepot, A. Griswold, 11" (D-E)..	390
Coffeepot, H. Homan (A-E)	65
Coffeepot, William McQuilkin, Phila., 1845-53 (D-E)	175
Coffeepot, Morey & Smith (A-E)	45
Coffeepot, F. Porter, 11½" t. (D-NE)	425
Coffeepot, lighthouse, bright-cut cartouche & line work, 9¼" t. (D-NE)......	660
Coffeepot, lighthouse style, 10¾" t. (D-NE)	350
Coffeepot, lighthouse, unmarked, 11" (D-E)	200
Coffeepot, H. B. Ward & Co., Wallingford, Conn., ca. 1840, 8½" (D-W)	135
Coffeepot, rectangular, gadroon border, ball feet, 19th C., 12¼" l.	45
Coffeepot, simple rounded baluster body on short pedestal base, hinged lid, scroll handle, 11"h. (D-MW)	150
Coffeepot, Smith & Co., low style, marked no. 11 on base (A-E)...............	220
Coffeepot, unsigned, 9" t. (D-E)	125

Funnel, pewter,
unmarked, 6½" h.
(D-E) $325

Communion service, 5-pc., Brittania ware, pair 10" plates, pair 7" chalices, 12¼" wine tankard, plates w/mark of Meridan Brittania Co., 19th C. (A-MW) ....$ 275

Communion set, 6-pc., Leonard, Reed & Barton, flagon, 10½" t; 2 chalices 7" t; 3 plates 10" diam.; marked, ca. 1835 (D-NE).. 1500

Container, covered, bulbous w/screw lid, 19th C., 6½" h. (A-MW) 50

Cup, baby (D-MW)... 45

Cup, church, 2-handled, 6⅛" h., top diam. 6½" (D-E) 490

Cup, church, 2-handled, strap base on handle, unmarked, 6⅛" t., 6½" top diam. (D-NE)....... 490

Cup, communion, by Leonard, Reed & Barton, ca. 1850, 7" h. (D-MW) 35

Dish, deep, 13" (A-E) 115

Dish, deep, N. Austin (A-E) 195

Dish, deep, Boardman & Co., N. Y., w/double eagle marks, ca. 1825, 9½" (D-E) 345

Dish, deep, T. Danforth, Phila., 13½" (A-E) 130

Dish, deep, Ashbil Griswold, 13" (D-E) 375

Dish, deep, by Samuel Kilbourn, 11" (D-NE).. 450

Dish, deep, "Love", 8⅞" diam. (D-NE) 375

Dish, deep, Jacob Whitmore, 18th C., 13½" diam. (A-E) 200

Dish, warming, hot water base, w/double handles decor. w/star design in oval relief, 10½" diam. (D-MW) 75

Flagon, Boardman & Hart (D-NW) 645

Flagon, communion, flaring base, single rib design top & bottom of body, double scroll handle ending in heart decor., domed lid, ca. 1850, 15½" h. (D-MW)... 225

Flagon, communion, Roswell Gleason, 10" h. (A-E) 425

Flagon, communion, Leonard, Reed & Barton, flaring tiered base, cylindrical body encircled by double raised ribs w/large curving handle & semi-domed lid & thumb lift, ca. 1850, 10½" h. (D-MW) 200

Flagon, E. Smith, 10¾" h. (D-E) 725

Flagon, E. Smith on inside of bottom, 10¾" h. (D-NE) 725

Flagon, Smith & Feltman, 11" h. (D-NE) 490

Flagon, unmarked, 12" t. (D-E) 250

Flagon, wine, hinged lid, shell-shaped thumb lift, brass finial (D-MW) 60

Flask, chestnut type, unmarked (A-E) 30

Fork, triwave, rat-tail (D-E).. 45

Funnel (A-E)... 22

Funnel, Frederick Basset, 7½" h. (D-MW) 150

Funnel, Frederick Bassett, 7½" h. (D-W) 90

Funnel, large (D-E) 125

Funnel, unmarked, 6¾" (D-E) 290

Goblet, 6" (D-E) 45

Inkwell (A-E).. 90

Inkwell, covered (A-E) 22

Inkwell, orig. blue pottery insert, ca. 1820-30, ex. cond., 9" base, 3" t. (D-NE) 135

Inkwell, round, 1½" (D-E) 135

Inkwell, round, dome roll top, 5" base (D-E) 65

Inkwell, round, insert (A-E) 35

Inkwell, round, unmarked, 3⅛" (D-E)... 150

Inkwell, 7¾" (A-E) 50

Inkwell, wide flat base, 6½" d. (A-E) 75

Insect duster (A-E).. 30

Ladle, Lewis Kruiger, orig. wood handle, ca. 1830, 14" l. (D-E) 190

Ladle, orig. wood handle, 14" l. (D-NE) 190

Ladle, J. Weeks, N. Y. C., small (A-E) 35

Measure, half-gill (D-E) ....$ 20
Measure, pint, tulip-bodied w/double-c handle (A-E) 70
Measure, quart, side spouted, inscription, 6″ h. (A-E) 65
Measure, quarter pint gill, 3″ (D-E) 35
Measure set, 7 pcs., American marked, matching, cylinder form, graduated, 19th C. (A-MW). 450
Measure set, 7 pcs., matching, cylinder form, graduated, 19th C. (D-E) 550
Mirror, Babbitt & Crossman, ring for hanging, ca. 1824-27, 4⅛″ diam. (D-E) 675
Mirror, circular w/ring for hanging, 4⅛″ diam. (D-NE) 675
Mold, chocolate, w/small pewter quarter gill, marked Kell & Chambers, Birmingham, 19th C.
   (A-MW) 25
Mold, ice cream, airplane (D-NE) 16
Mold, ice cream, apple (D-E) 9
Mold, ice cream, banana (D-E) 9
Mold, ice cream, bearded fisherman (D-E) 16
Mold, ice cream, bell (D-NE) 14
Mold, ice cream, billiken (D-E) 15
Mold, ice cream, bunch of grapes (D-E)... 14
Mold, ice cream, bust of clown (D-E) 12
Mold, ice cream, chicken (D-E) 12
Mold, ice cream, chicken coming out of egg (D-E) 16
Mold, ice cream, Christmas wreath (D-E) 21
Mold, ice cream, corn ear (D-E)... 18
Mold, ice cream, cupid (standing) (D-E) 15
Mold, ice cream, daisy bouquet (D-E) 12
Mold, ice cream, duck (D-E) 25
Mold, ice cream, Easter lily, 2-pc. (D-E) 10
Mold, ice cream, egg (D-E) 18
Mold, ice cream, football (D-E).. 8
Mold, ice cream, golfer, lady (D-E) 20
Mold, ice cream, golfer, man (D-E) 20
Mold, ice cream, harp (D-E) 22
Mold, ice cream, high hat (D-E) 14
Mold, ice cream, Irishman (D-E).. 18
Mold, ice cream, old shoe (D-E) 12
Mold, ice cream, orange (D-E).. 9
Mold, ice cream, orchid, marked ''1892'' (D-E) 20
Mold, ice cream, oval basket (D-E) 12
Mold, ice cream, peach (D-E) 9
Mold, ice cream, Ping-Pong racket (D-E) 12
Mold, ice cream, playing card (king of diamonds) (D-E) 20
Mold, ice cream, playing card (queen of spades) (D-E) 21
Mold, ice cream, pumpkin (D-E) 22
Mold, ice cream, question mark on box (D-E) 10
Mold, ice cream, railroad locomotive (D-E) 45
Mold, ice cream, Santa Claus (D-NE) 16
Mold, ice cream, sea shell (D-E) 11
Mold, ice cream, stars & stripes (D-E) 18
Mold, ice cream, Statue of Liberty (D-E).. 225
Mold, ice cream, stork w/baby (D-E) 14
Mold, ice cream, tulip (D-E) 38
Mold, ice cream, turkey (D-E) 30
Mold, ice cream, turkey (D-MW) 28
Mold, ice cream, 2 cooing doves (D-NE) 14
Mold, spoon, large (D-NE) 200
Molds, 3-compartment, ½ pint & 1 quart of cylinder form w/fruit molds, 19th C. (A-MW) 50
Mug, T. S. Derby, 3 5/16″ h. base diam. 2⅞″ (D-NE) 675
Mug, 1 quart (D-NE).. 150
Mustard pot, circular, hinged cover w/finial, 19th C., 4¼″ h. (A-MW) 45
Nozzle, 18″ l. (A-E).. 25

Pepper pots, American, pr., 7" h. (D-E) ....$ 300
Pitcher, covered, 10½" h. (D-NE).. 575
Pitcher, R. Dunham, Portland, Me., ca. 1840, 6½" t. × 6" at widest point (D-S).................. 325
Pitcher, handled, traditional shape, inscribed, 19th C., 5⅞" h. (A-MW) 55
Pitcher, lid, Boardman lion mark, Hartford, Conn., ca. 1860, 10" t. (D-S)............................ 595
Pitcher, Wm. McQuilken, covered, 10½" h. (D-E) 575
Pitcher, F. Porter, 3" h. (D-NE) 375
Pitcher, F. Porter (circle mark), 6⅜" h. (D-E) 375
Pitcher, syrup, covered, 5½" (D-E).. 150
Pitcher, water, Boardman & Co., N. Y., 6" (D-E) 290
Pitcher, water, 7½" (D-E)... 80
Pitcher, water, slightly flaring base, ca. 1820, 8" h. (D-MW).......................... 90
Plate, 7½" (A-E) 20
Plate, 8½" (A-E) .... 22 ·
Plate, American, 8½" (D-E) 90
Plate, Nathaniel Austin, Charlestown, Mass., ca. 1770, 8⅜" diam. (D-S) 395
Plate, Richard Austin, 7⅞" diam. (D-NE).. 425
Plate, Thomas Badger, Boston, ca. 1790, 8½" diam. (D-S)............................... 325
Plate, Nathaniel Barker, ca. 1780, 13¼" (D-E) 190
Plate, B. Barnes (A-E).. 175
Plate, B. Barnes, Phila., 7½" (A-E) 135
Plate, B. Barnes, Phila., ca. 1815, 7⅞" diam. (D-S) 250
Plate, Boardman, 6½" d. (A-E) 350
Plate, Boardman & Co., Hartford, Conn., deep, ca. 1825, 9⅜" diam. (D-S) 325
Plate, John Carpenter, 9¾" (A-E) 45
Plate, church, Reed & Barton, marked, ca. 1860, 10½" diam. (D-S) 125
Plate, Compton, 8½" (A-E) 47
Plate, Joseph Danforth (A-E).. 170
Plate, Samuel Danforth, 11⅜" (A-E) 300
Plate, Samuel Danforth, 7⅞" diam. (D-NE) 325
Plate, Samuel Danforth, 7⅞" diam. (D-NE) 385
Plate, T. Danforth (A-E) 220
Plate, T. Danforth, Phila., 7½" (A-E).. 190
Plate, T. Danforth, Phila., 7½" (A-E).. 130
Plate, T. Danforth, Phila., 7½" (A-E).. 65
Plate, double, "Ashbil Griswold" touch, 8" d. (A-E) 250
Plate, footed, ca. 1720, 11⅜" diam. (D-NE).. 325
Plate, G. L., 9½" (A-E) 45
Plate, large, 15" (A-E) 110
Plate, Leonard, Reed & Barton, 10" (D-E) 250
Plate, "Love," 8½" (A-E) 275
Plate, "Love," 8½" diam. (D-E) 160
Plate, "Love," Phila., ca. 1800, 8" diam. (D-S) 295
Plate, "Love," surface slightly marred, 7¾" diam. (D-E) 180
Plate, marriage, monogrammed, 18th C., ca. 1740, 13½" diam. (A-MW)............. 100
Plate, David Melville, Newport, R. I., 8" (A-E).. 115
Plate, David Melville, Newport, R. I., ca. 1780, 8¼" diam. (D-S) 385
Plate, Havel Parrer, 8" (A-E).. 40
Plate, Samuel Pierce, 8" (D-NE) 250
Plate, scalloped edge, w/deep bowl, ca. 1741, 9½" diam. (D-MW) 145
Plate, Thomas & Townson, deep, 10½" (A-E) 75
Plate, Thomas & Townson, w/dove, 8½" (A-E) 52
Plate, unmarked, 8" (D-E) 85
Plate, unmarked, 9" (D-E) 70
Plate, Jacob Whitmore, 11" diam. (D-MW) 475
Plate, Jacob Whitmore, 7⅞" diam. (D-NE) 395
Platter, Thom. Danforth II, 12" diam. (D-NE)... 485
Platter, S. Ellis, decor. w/single incised line around rim, 13½" diam. (D-MW) 120
Platter, large plate w/dipping rim, 18th C., 12½" diam. (D-MW) 200

Platter, oval, marked w/"ray star", 11" (A-E)..................................$	45
Porringer, basin shape, unmarked, ca. 1825, 3¾" w. (D-S)	225
Porringer, Boardman, 3¼" (A-E)	135
Porringer, Boardman, Lee, or Lewis, heart design handle (A-E)	130
Porringer, Boardman, Lee, or Lewis, heart design handle (A-E)	120
Porringer, crown handle, 5" diam. (D-E)	240
Porringer, crown handle, IC or G cast, 4½" diam. (D-E).............................	275
Porringer, S. E. Hamlin, Jr., Providence, R. I., eagle mark, flower handle, 5½" diam. (D-NE) .	875
Porringer, heart & crescent handle, 3⅜" diam. (D-E)	220
Porringer, R. Lee, good cond., 2⅞" diam. (A-NE)	875
Porringer, marked I. G. (A-E)	95
Porringer, marked TD & SB, 5⅜" (A-E)	400
Porringer, marked TD & SB (D-N)	280
Porringer, marked TD & SB in rectangle, 4½" diam. (D-NE)	695
Porringer, small (A-E)	160
Porringer, 2 reticulated handles, 19th C., 5⅜" diam. (A-MW)	40
Porringer, unmarked (A-E)	100
Porringer, unmarked, 3⅞" w. (D-S).............................	195
Porringer, unmarked, crown handle, 5" diam. (D-NE).............................	240
Porringer, unmarked, heart & crescent handle, 3⅜" diam. (D-NE).............................	220
Porringer, unmarked, small (A-E)	60
Pot, short, marked Ashbil Griswold, Meriden, Conn., ca. 1830, 6½" t. (D-S)	295
Pot, tall, marked F. Porter, Westbrook, Me., ca. 1840, 11¾" h. (D-S).............................	465
Sugar scuttle, circular, fluted, pedestal base, floral engraving, 19th C., 4½" l. (A-MW)..........	27
Sugar shaker, 4½" h. (A-E)	30
Spoon, invalid (A-E)	105
Spoon warmer, 19th C., nautilus shape, rockwork base w/hinged cover, floral engraving, 6" l. (A-MW)	50
Spoons, serving, set of 9, ca. 1790 (D-E)	350
Table articles, 4 dinner forks, 12 spoons, various sizes & shapes, 19th C. (A-MW)	144
Tankard, Manning-Bowman & Co., ca. 1865, 8½" h., 4¾" w. (D-S)	350
Tankard, syrup, cylinder shape w/hinged cover & spout, 19th C., 6¼" h. (A-MW)	90
Teaspoon, marked L. B. (D-E)	25
Teaspoon, marked C. Parker (D-E).............................	18
Teapot, Babbitt, Crossman & Co., Mass., 1825-1827 (D-N)	120
Teapot, Boardman (A-E)	190
Teapot, Calder, Providence, 9" h. (A-E)	225
Teapot, J. Danforth, 7¼" (D-E)	200
Teapot, J. Danforth, repair in bottom, hinge needs repair (A-E)	150
Teapot, T. S. Derby, 19th C., 8½" h. (A-MW).............................	200
Teapot, R. Dunham, 7½" h., 6" w. ex. of spout & wooden handle (D-S)	325
Teapot, fluted, wooden handle, 1829, 8" t. (D-NE).............................	285
Teapot, Roswell Gleason, 9" t. (D-NE)	285
Teapot, globular, unmarked, 7½" t. (D-NE)	175
Teapot, Grover & Whitlock, Troy, N. Y. (D-N)	255
Teapot, individual size, indistinct touch, wooden handle, 4¼" h. (A-E).............................	75
Teapot, marked TD & SB (D-E).............................	125
Teapot, marked T. G., wooden handle (D-E)	135
Teapot, pear shape, serrated edge on lid, small (A-E)	175
Teapot, Shaw & Fischer, melon-shaped (D-SE)	100
Teapot, Shaw & Fischer, ornate (D-E)	55
Teapot, small (D-E).............................	145
Teapot, small, good cond. (A-E)	100
Teapot, Smith & Co., Boston, ca. 1850, 8½" t. (D-S)	235
Teapot, unmarked, 8½" (D-E)	185
Teapot, H. B. Ward (A-E)	110
Teapot, wooden handle, 6" h. (A-E)	50
Teapot, H. Yale & Co. (A-E)	90
Tumbler, inscription, 4" h. (A-E)	40

Pottery

Pottery belongs to the broad category of earthenware which includes all objects made of common clay. Its body is opaque, and usually porous until glazed. Pottery may be shaped completely by hand, or on a potter's wheel. Little is known about the earliest American potters, but records indicate that pottery was made as early as 1625 at Jamestown, Virginia.

The past few years have seen a marked increase in interest focused upon American country pottery. Presently the most popular types are stoneware, redware, sponge-decorated objects, yellowware, blue-white pottery, and the flint enamel and Rockingham glazes, all of which are covered in separate categories within this volume. But, there is also a wide variety of other collectible country pottery which was produced by skilled craftsmen in an assortment of types, glazes and decoration. Almost every flourishing community once had a pottery, and the number of eighteenth and nineteenth century potters is enormous. Since most of the craftsmen did not identify their work, it is often difficult to determine the origin of a particular piece. However, regional characteristics are sometimes helpful in identifying pieces, especially examples from New England and Pennsylvania.

Pottery examples discussed in this particular category include the commonplace wares, unmarked and undecorated, the elusive marked pieces produced by the Bell family for over a century, and the collectible "Old Sleepy Eye" and Peoria pottery vessels. And, as in other fields of collecting, prices vary widely, depending upon location and awareness of current trends.

* * *

Batter jug, brown glaze, new wooden top, bail handle (D-S) ....$ 38
Batter jug, dk. brown glaze, complete w/top & spout cover (D-MW)................................... 45
Batter jug, gray w/molded floral designs in blue, complete w/matching lid, wire bail handle w/wood grip (D-MW)... 65
Bedpan, brownware glaze (A-MW) 8

Pitcher, pottery, John Bell, well-crafted, attractive, decor. w/bright colors, large (A-E) $500

Pitcher, pottery, with black splash decor., 8" h. (A-E) $275

Bean pot, brownware (D-MW) $15

Jug, pottery, green & tan w/black decor., 8" h. (A-E) $440

Bean pot, cover & side handle, 1 gal., brownware, 9" h. (D-MW) ....$ 10

Bowl, "Sleepy Eye," 6½" d., 4" h. (D-MW)   90

Butter tub, "Sleepy Eye," 4" h., signed (D-MW)   95

Chamber pot, strap handle, 8½" diam., brownware glazed (A-MW)   20

Creamer, "Bell", red, green & white slip, 6¼" h. (A-E)   110

Crock, butter, brownware, peacock in relief, cov. orig., 6" diam. (D-MW)   45

Crock, dk. brown glaze, Peoria, 2 gal. (D-MW)   16

Crock, double handled, w/wooden lid, 12" d. (D-E)   75

Coffeepot, brownware, 1 gal., ovoid (D-MW)   65

Coffeepot, brownware glazed, 1 gal. size, comp. w/orig. cover (D-MW)   48

Dish, brownware glaze, deep w/ribbed bottom, 11½" d. (A-E)   30

Flower pot, signed W. B. Smith, Womelsdorf, Pa. (A-E)   100

Flowerpot, John W. Bell, green & brown glazes (D-MW)   45

Ice tub, open handles, brownware glazed, 8¾" d. (D-MW)   55

Jar, S. Bell & Son, cobalt blue floral decor. (D-NE)   175

Jar, black glaze, 8" (A-E)   35

Jar, brown glaze, 2 gal., signed Peoria pottery (D-MW)   15

Jar, canning, brown glaze, 1 qt., signed Peoria Pottery (D-MW)   12

Jar, canning, brown glaze, 1 qt., signed Peoria Pottery (D-N)   8

Jar, canning, brown glaze, 2 qt., signed Peoria Pottery (D-W)   18

Jar, canning, buff glazed, pt., complete w/bail cover (D-W)   22

Jar, Galena, orange, wide mouth, 19th C., 8¾" h. (A-MW)   25

Jar, Ohio, brown, wide mouth, 19th C., 8¾" h. (A-MW)   25

Jar, sewer pipe, brown, wide mouth, 19th C., 14½" h. (A-MW)   25

Jug, black glaze, double handle, 19" h. (A-NE)   85

Jug, brown glaze, double handle, 16" h. (D-E)   12

Jug, small, mottled orange & olive glaze (A-E)   55

Jug, water, lt. brown glazed (A-E)   40

Mold, cake, Turk's head, dk. brown glazed (D-SE)   18

Mold, cake, Turk's head, tan/brown glazed (D-MW)...   30

Mold, fish (A-E)   22

Mug, black splash decor., 5½" (A-E)   130

Mug, handled, circular line decor. & black splash, 3½" (A-E)   170

Mug, "Sleepy Eye," 4½" h. (D-MW)   75

Mug, "Sleepy Eye," 4½" h. (D-W)   55

Mugs, brownware, panel ribbed design, 2, each 3⅛" h. (A-MW)   25

Pitcher & basin, octagonal, paneled sides, 11¾" h., brownware glaze (A-MW)   60

Pitcher, John Bell, large, small hair line at lip orig. when fired (A-E)   500

Pitcher, Peter Bell, green speckled glaze, 10½" h. (D-NE)   200

Pitcher, Peter Bell, multicolored glaze, 8¾" h. (D-E)   185

Pitcher, black glaze, w/side spout & inside strainer, 5" (A-E)   55

Pitcher, black stripe design, 3" (A-E)   175

Pitcher, blue bands on white ground, tankard, 8" h. (A-E)   35

Pitcher, brownware, tankard shape, 8½" h. (A-E)   95

Pitcher, large ovoid form, black decor., 8½" (A-E)   100

Pitcher, mocha, blue & black slip on white background, 8" diam. (A-E)   350

Pitcher, mocha, floral design, ex. cond. (A-E)   175

Pitcher, red glazed, covered (A-E)   52

Pitcher, 6 matching mugs, strap handles, brownware glazed, tankard shape (D-MW)   65

Pitcher, "Sleepy Eye," 5¼" h. (D-MW)   75

Pitcher, "Sleepy Eye," 4" h. (D-MW)   50

Pitcher, "Sleepy Eye," 9½" h. (D-MW)   90

Pitcher, "Sleepy Eye," 9½" h. (D-W)   125

Pitcher, "Sleepy Eye," Indian head handle & side decor., signed, 7¾" h. (D-E)   58

Pitchers, (3), "Sleepy Eye," Western Stoneware Co., 9" h., 5" h., 4" h. (A-E)   110

Rooster, brown glazed, 4½" h. (A-E)   30

Teapot, brownware glazed, embossed (D-E)   12

Teapot, brownware glazed, ovoid shape, 1 qt. (D-MW)   22

Vase, "Sleepy Eye," signed, head of Indian, frog, dragonfly & rushes on rev. side, 8" h. (D-N) .   90

Quilts

Collecting quilts has become a very fascinating hobby during recent years. With an increase in demand has come an increase in prices which have risen sharply and shows no signs of stabilizing, despite our sluggish economy nowadays. Most of the finer examples available today were made during the present century. Therefore, it should be noted that the nearer a quilt approaches the contemporary status, the more it becomes merely a very good collectible, not an antique. Quilts dating from the last century are extremely scarce, commanding top prices when found.

Today there seems to be some misuse of the term "quilt" and "comforter " which should be clarified. In America, the word "quilt" has come to mean that type of covering which has at least two layers of material fastened together by running stitches. The term "comforter" applies to a tied bed cover which also consists of at least two layers of fabric, but lacks the running stitching of quilting.

The majority of quilts available today are the appliqued examples and the pieced or patchwork type. Embroidered quilts, in which fancy stitchery is the only decoration, were also made, but these are scarce. Appliqued quilts were made by sewing pieces of fabric to a backing, while the pieced quilts were made of separate pieces of fabric which were sewed together. Of the two types, there seems to be more of the latter available, perhaps because this was actually a salvage art—something made economically from what was readily available to the creator—usually leftovers from women's and children's clothing, and men's suits and shirts.

Experience in handling quilts helps greatly to determine their age. Very few old quilts are entirely free from wear or strain, and too, many are bleached here and there from exposure or sun, or may be dye-eaten in spots The sense of smell can also be helpful, since most quilts will have a musty odor from storage. And of course, much interest lies in the quilting itself, which does not have to be a close or complicated design, but finely done, with as many as twelve or fifteen stitches per inch.

Quilt, Star of Le Moyne, ca. 1880 (D-E) $175

Quilt, Triple Irish Chain, ca. 1880 (D-E) $175

In this day of do-it-yourself, many of the old patterns have been copied or reproduced. Of course, the signs of newness are quite obvious due to the type of fabrics available today, and the majority of quilts being made now are machine-stitched. Many of the finer examples—especially those that have been hand-stitched—are quickly becoming collectors' items, and should be treasured.

The current interest—and the prices being paid now—are sufficient to lure heirlooms away from their present owners. The most desirable of the genuinely old quilts are those which bear an early date, or a name or initials.

* * *

Aaz, feather filled, shades of blue & pink, full size (D-E) ....$ 260
American flag, made from approx. 10 flags, full size (D-NE)................................ 350
Amish, patchwork, deep red/blue/lavender (A-NE) 325
Amish, geometric pattern, mauve, lt. pink & purple, baskets of flowers around border, full size (D-W) 150
Applique, baskets of flowers on light pink ground, bound in white w/white muslin backing, used, ex. cond. (D-Mont.).. 85
Applique, "basket" w/red, yellow flowers, green leaves on white ground, 68"×78" (D-MW).... 65
Applique, blazing sun, shades of yellow on white ground, full size (D-MW) 130
Applique, bride's, Baltimore, John & Rebecca Chamberlin, 1848, 3-dimensional effect, 25 panels w/border of roses & violets, 105"×108" (A-E)...................................... 3800
Applique, butterfly, on yellow/green/white squares, fine hand quilting, 80"×92" (D-MW)....... 200
Applique, child's crib, red & blue, leaf quilting between panels & on border, 16 panels (A-E) 130
Applique, child's crib, white flannel animals on pink ground, fancy stitchery, unused (D-E).. 75
Applique, designs w/hunting scene, boat scene, eagle, flag & shield center, flowers & fruits, displayed at Harrisburg State Museum (A-E) 1000
Applique, floral bouquet, pink & yellow flowers on white ground, 89"×89" (D-NW).............. 150
Applique, floral, red, yellow & green, full size (D-E) 100
Applique, flower & feather pattern, blue & red (A-E) 160
Applique, 4 lg. panels of red, green, yellow & pink, 4 branch flower sprigs, 4 triple flower bunches & 4 corner circled designs, grapevine border, 80"×82" (A-E)................................. 400
Applique, 4 lg. panels of red, green, yellow stars w/feather swirls, 5 stars in center, border of tulips & pink roses, 81"×81" (A-E) 425
Applique, friendship pattern, bright colors w/25 panels w/names, initials & dates, 102"×104" (A-E) 1200
Applique, heart & clover pattern (D-E) 350
Applique, large flowers in red & yellow w/gray leaves, white background, full size (A-E) 200
Applique, North Carolina rose, alternating red roses & leaves w/green stripes on white blocks, full size (D-MW)... 115
Applique, oak leaf, green leaves, red circles & squares on white blocks, full size (D-MW)...... 185
Applique, oak leaf pattern w/sawtooth patchwork borders, yellow ochre ground w/lt. blue & mulberry applique, cotton, 86"×84" (A-NE) 250
Applique, padded floral decor. in brown, green & yellow, full size (A-E)............................ 210
Applique, pansy, purple/orchid/yellow pansies on white ground, 87"×90", fine cond. (D-MW) 165
Applique, poinsettias w/green leaves, set in yellow baskets on white ground, diamond quilted, bound in red, matching sham, full size (D-MW) 250
Applique, poinsettias on soft green ground framed w/white, green binding, unused, early (D-N)... 165
Applique, pomegranate, shades of red w/green on white ground, ca. 1890, full size (D-E) 195
Applique, potted rose design in green, red, yellow & pink, vining border (A-E).................. 400
Applique, presentation, eagle in each corner, blocks w/wreaths, in red/green/yellow unbleached cotton, 19th C. (D-MW) 525
Applique, red & white, ca. 1860, full size (D-E) 100
Applique, red on white, dated, full size (A-E)... 175
Applique, rose cross, pink roses, ecru ground, green leaves & stems, ex. cond. unused, 87"×72" (D-MW) 175
Applique, rose & oak leaf, red roses, green leaves on white ground, cond. fine, full size (D-E).. 175

Applique, rose petal, floral blocks w/plain white blocks, full size (D-MW)............................$ 150

Applique, "spirit of St. Louis," yellow w/American eagle (D-MW) 150

Applique, star of Bethlehem, tulips border each star, different colored & designed star in each corner, ca. 1875 (D-NE) 625

Applique, star & feather pattern, pink speckled (A-E) 140

Applique, sunburst, diamond patches in shades of brown/orange, bordered w/stars & streamers, w/oak leaf in each corner, full size (D-MW) 375

Applique, tulips, red/yellow w/green leaves, full size w/matching sham (D-MW) 300

Applique, tulips, red/yellow/orange/pink, on white, full size, ca. 1890 (D-E) 195

Applique, 20 panels of blue eagles & stars w/green borders on white ground, 89"×108" (A-E) . 375

Applique, white background w/flowers in shades of dk. red, violet & purple, machine quilted, 128"×90" (D-MW) 60

Applique, white tulip pattern, unused, full size (D-MW) 260

Applique, wreath of grapes, bluish purple grapes w/green leaves, lattice bordered w/grape leaves, full size, ex. cond. (D-MW).. 230

Applique, wreath of roses, 2 tones of yellow bordered w/running leaf design, bound in yellow, full size (D-MW).. 185

Quilt, Princess Feather, ca. 1875 (D-E) $325

Quilt, Pinwheels & Tulips, ca. 1875 (D-E) $275

Applique, wreath & star, floral wreath w/8-point star in center, framed w/sprays of roses & green leaves, full size, ca. 1930 (D-MW) 225

Applique, lobster, red & white blocks with alternating red/white lobsters, full size (D-MW) ... 145

Applique, melon patch, pink & green melon-like forms, scalloped edge, full size (D-E) 135

Birds in air, pieced patches in form of triangles, multicolored, early, full size (D-MW)........... 280

Blazing star, full size (D-NE).. 425

Bow-tie, multicolor, full size (D-MW)... 150

Bow-tie & star, full size (A-E) 85

Broken pierced star, pink/white, diamonds & Quaker path quilting set w/pink stripes, bound w/white muslin, 88"×96" (D-E) 100

Butterflies on white squares w/pink borders, pink muslin back, block stitching, full size (D-W) 125

Centennial heirloom, made from 9 Centennial handkerchiefs, Phila., full size (D-NE)............ 650

Child's, orange, red, yellow & green floral, on white ground, fine quilting, 31"×31" (A-NE) ... 325

Child's, sunbonnet babies, pastel colors, fine quilting, 42"×54" (A-E) 87

Chintz, brown & blue one side; other side w/30 round star panels in red, blue & green, full size (A-E) 375

Chintz, floral design on light tan background, full size (D-MW)... 325

Comforter, applique, butterflies on pink ground, tied w/yellow string, full size (D-S) 37

Comforter, multicolored squares, Jersey string tied, 80"×92" (D-MW) 95

Comforter, patchwork, fancy stitchery, tied w/yellow string, ex. cond., full size (D-MW)........$ 55
Cornucopia, shades of yellow & brown on white background, full size (D-MW)....................   190
Crib, handmade, red, brown & white (D-NE)..   50
Criss-cross stitchery in brown on white ground, trimmed w/brown & white checkered gingham,
   back same, bound w/brown, matching sham (D-W)...   175
Double Irish chain pattern, green & red calico on white, floral border, full size (D-NE)   225
Dresden plate, ecru w/sawtooth edge, white background, coral sawtooth & solid, 92"×73"
   (D-MW)   150
Dresden plate, 1920s, good cond., full size (A-MW)   28
Dresden plate, striped w/solid yellow around white blocks, unusual pattern, swirl, 64"×79"
   (D-MW)   200
Dresden plate, white background, (1920-30), twin size (D-MW)   75
Drunkard's path pattern, red, white, yellow, blue & green, diamond stitching, 68"×70" (D-W) .   95
Drunkard's path, white & green, 82"×80" (D-MW)   150
Embroidered, pink w/saw tooth edge, 74"×95" (D-MW)   125
E Pluribus Unum, eagles in blue, dated 1844, excellent quilting, full size (D-NE)   625
Flower garden, Vermont, full size (D-NE)   650
Flowers in basket, hexagon, white background, browns, yellows, orchids, reds, blues, 68"×150"
   (D-MW)   200
Foliage wreath, shades of green on white background, twin size (D-MW)   95
Friendship, red print w/solid red & white, full size (D-N)   140
Gingham puff, pink, blue & yellow, 51"×82" (D-MW)   80
Goose tracks, blocks of dark blue w/white patches, full size (D-MW)   160
Grandmother's fan circle, old calicos, finely quilted, full size (D-MW)   250
Hen & chickens, triangles of green & pink on white background, twin size (D-MW)   95
Hexagon, bright pink, green calico, yellow patchwork prints, twin size (D-MW)..................   135
Hourglass, white w/blue patches, double bed size (A-E)   100
Linsey-woolsey, diamond & flower pattern, ca. 1780-1800 (D-E)....................................   150
Little giant, shades of blue & green on white background, full size (D-MW)........................   80
Log cabin, red, white & blue, crib size (D-NE)   55
Log cabin, straight furrow, reds, browns, blues, yellows, 96"×78" (D-MW)..........................   225
Lone star, blue, brown & gold, full size (D-MW)   175
Lone star (Texas), red, white & blue, full size (D-S)..   100
Lone star, white background, star orange, gold, yellow & 3 shades of brown, 86"×86" (D-MW) .   225
Nine patch, lavender plaid 1" sqs. w/white diamond stitching, lavender border & binding, pale
   unbleached muslin back (D-E)   100
Nine patch, multicolors w/light green background, 72"×83" (D-MW)................................   100
Nine patch square, small print back; red, brown, & blue solids, 72"×84" (D-MW)   100
Oak leaf wreath, light green & yellow w/solid brown acorns, beige background, full size
   (D-MW)   145
Ocean waves, pieced, dusty pink, multicolored triangles, 78"×87" (D-MW)..........................   150
Orange peel, orange, yellow & soft beige, full size (D-MW)   100
Patch triangle, blue & tan, full size (D-E)..   70
Patchwork, dark olive wide edge, red stripes alternate w/patchwork stripes (D-NE)...............   85
Patchwork, bound w/red, white muslin back, ex. cond., late 19th C., full size (D-SW)   135
Patchwork, multi-colors (A-E)   20
Patchwork, pink-red candystripe material, dark print diagonal stripes (D-NE)   85
Patchwork, poor stitching, ca. 1920, full size (D-S)   20
Patchwork, red & white (A-E)   60
Patchwork, red, white & blue, twin size (A-E)   50
Patchwork, red, white & blue, used but cond. good, full size (D-W)   45
Patchwork, "ribbon," early prints, 70"×75" (D-E)..   75
Patchwork, yellow, red, green w/fine quilting, late 19th. C. (A-NE)..................................   225
Patriotic, "cross trail" pattern, red/white/blue, 74"×82" (D-MW)   60
Peacock, hand stitched, twin size (A-E)   55
Pennsylvania Dutch, hex signs, mustard color on white ground, bound w/mustard (D-E).......   105
Pennsylvania Dutch, peasant motif in central wreath, hearts in each corner, cream background
   (D-MW)   180
Peony, shades of green & yellow, appliqued border, full size (D-MW)   170

Philadelphia Centennial, full size (D-NE) ....$ 650

Pieced, shades of brown & other colors in geometric pattern, cut-out corners for bed posts, 112"×100" (A-E)... 200

Pineapple, shades of yellow & orange diamonds on white background, full size (D-MW)....... 140

Pine tree & snowflake, blue & white, full size (D-E) 145

Pinwheel, old top, new quilting, blue, 70"×94" (D-MW) 125

Prairie flower, squares of white w/half wreath designs in rose & pink, full size (D-MW)........ 255

Print, w/handwoven backing, full size (D-E).. 55

Coverlet, jacquard, woven by John Smith, Lancaster County, Penna., ca. 1835 (D-E) $375

Coverlet, jacquard, double-woven, ca. 1835 (D-E) $350

Quilt, Star of Bethlehem, ca. 1880 (D-E) $375

Quilt top, wedding ring, pink/white & multicolor prints, ca. 1930, full size (D-W)................$ 35
Quilt top, postage stamp, ginghams, framed w/blue (D-W)   25
Reel, shades of blue on white background, twin size (D-MW)...   75
Reversible, turquoise/white, all quilted, 102"×89" (D-MW) 300
Rings, blue ground, white binding, used but good, full size (A-E)......................................   50
Robbing Peter to Pay Paul, pumpkin yellow, quilted, full size (A-E) 120
Rose of Sharon, brilliant colors, ca. 1870, full size (D-MW) 250
Rose of Sharon, pink & green, twin size (A-E)   50
Sawtooth, multicolored triangles on white background, border w/2 rows of saw teeth, full size
   (D-MW) 165
Sawtooth, pink/white, feather quilting, bound in pink & backed w/white muslin, 81"×83" (D-E). 150
Schoolhouse, calico house w/red checked roofs, used but v. g. cond., twin size (D-NE)   65
Schoolhouse, patchwork, houses on white sq. ground w/navy trim, background color rose, ca.
   1890, 82"×90" (D-E)... 600
Six-pointed star, blue ginghams w/red & white patches, good cond., full size (A-E)   45
Six-pointed star, star in pinks & navy on white, green print contrast, old calico, 5" blocks,
   55"×88" (D-MW).. 100
Snowflake, red/green flakes on white ground finely quilted w/pin wheels, green binding, fine
   cond. ca. 1920s, 78"×86" (D-MW)   80
Square & cross, child's, pieced patches of pink & blue (D-MW)...................................... 110
Square within a square, dark green calico, cotton, unused, 1875, full size (D-MW) 250
Star, fractured star corners, full size (A-E)... 195
Star, mustard & white, twin size (D-MW)... 145
Star, sawtooth edges, red w/red prints on white ground, won 1st prize in 1912 at Sears Century
   of Progress Quilt Centennial, full size (D-W)... 175
Star, shades of yellow, full size (D-NE).. 110
Star within a star, light & dark blue prints w/dark blue binding, 82"×91" (D-E) 100
Stars & roses, green, red & pumpkin yellow, full size (A-E) 125
Stepping stones, diamonds & triangles in red & brown, lt. tan background, full size (D-MW)   95
Storm at sea, patchwork blocks of blue w/white, solid blue border, full size (D-MW)............. 125
Sunbonnet babies & overall boys, figures on white muslin ground w/med. blue borders, twin
   size (D-W)... 135
Sunburst, burnt orange, ochre & yellow coloring (A-NE) 325
Thistle, scalloped edges, dated 1859, red, green on white, full size (D-E) 200
Tree of life, figured calico in green shades for tree foliage, white background, full size (D-MW) 170
Triangle, red, white & blue, full size (D-NE)... 115
Triangle, red & white, twin size (A-E)   65
Triple sunflower, full size (D-MW).. 115
Tulip, orange/yellow/green on white ground, orange bound, fine quilting, full size (D-MW)... 275
Tulip, red/yellow/green on white ground, early, much use, full size (D-N)   65
Tulip, rose & pink tulips w/green leaves, full size (D-MW)... 190
Twinkling star, light gray blocks alternating w/patched blocks of dark blue, border of small blue
   triangles, full size (D-MW).. 165
Virginia's star, pieced patches, multicolored, early, full size (D-MW)................................ 115
Wedding ring, peach background, blue & multicolor rings, 96"×78" (D-MW) 105
Wedding ring, w/yellow trim, 72"×96" (D-MW).. 150
Wedding ring, double, bound in purple w/white background, 74"×74" (D-MW).................... 150
Wedding ring, double, fine cond., full size (A-MW)..   35
Wedding ring, double, good colors, ex. cond., 101"×74" (D-NE) 150
Wedding ring, double, pink trim, 82"×74" (D-MW).. 150
Wedding ring, double, prints set w/yellow/mustard on brown ground, bound w/yellow, muslin
   back, unused, full size (D-N)   95
Wedding ring, double, white background, bright pink, multicolor rings, 64"×90" (D-MW) 200
Wheel, twin size (D-MW)...   35
Whig rose, pieced blocks in shades of yellow, blue, rose & green, scalloped edge, full size
   (D-MW) 165
Yo-yo, old calicos, green border, cotton, ex. cond., 1900, 77"×105" (D-MW) 350
Yo-yo pattern, pastel prints w/deep pink, unlined, full size (D-MW)..................................   95
Yo-yo pattern, pastel prints w/solid blue, unlined, full size (D-S)   65

Redware

Redware is one of our most popular forms of country pottery which was made in many areas of the United States. It has a soft, porous body and its color varies from warm reddish-brown earth tones to light orange or deep wine shades. It was produced in mostly utilitarian forms by potters working on their farms or in small factories to fill their everyday needs. The earliest examples were shaped by hand, and when dry, they were treated with a glaze, either brushed on the object or dipped. The glazes were used to intensify the color, and more importantly, to make the objects nonporous. After glazing, the pottery was fired in ovens heated by wood. Because wood fires are difficult to control, temperatures were often uneven, causing warping and other imperfections.

Hollow redware pieces such as jugs, churns, crocks, and large milk coolers, as well as pie plates, platters and deep dishes, were usually left unglazed on the outside. The pie plates almost always have fire blackened undersides as they were used frequently for baking the delicious pies that became a high culinary art in rural areas.

Although all forms of redware are very collectible, the most desirable objects are the slip-decorated pieces, or the exceedingly rare and expensive "sgraffito" examples which have scratched or incised line decoration. This type of decoration was for ornamentation, since examples were rarely used for ordinary utilitarian purposes, but were usually given as gifts. Hence, these highly prized pieces rarely show wear, indicating that they were treasured as ornaments only. Decoration ranged from Pennsylvania Dutch inscriptions to elaborate motifs. Flowers and birds were the most typical decoration, in addition to animals and human figures showing wedding couples or a spirited horseman. The peacock, distelfink or other birds signified good fortune and happiness; the tulip or lily represented the Holy Trinity, while the heart symbolized love or friendship.

Slip decoration was made by tracing the design on the redware shape with a clay having a creamy consistency in contrasting colors. When dried, the design was slightly raised above the surface. Because these pieces were made for practical usage, the potter then pressed or beat the slip decoration into the surface of the object. The simplest forms consist of lines and dots, but the most interesting pieces bear the name of the owner, a national hero, or the inscription "Apple Pie," "Lemon Pie," "Mary's Dish," etc.

Another interesting type of decoration is the manganese glazed pieces, artistically decorated by sprinkling or smearing manganese on the object to be fired, creating interesting "shapes," and raising the common pot to a more artistic level.

A few American potters continue to produce the traditional ware, and their work is collected today for its fine quality. The new objects made by Lester Breininger, Jr., and decorated by his wife, Barbara (Robesonia, Pennsylvania), are decorated in the traditional Pennsylvania Dutch designs, and are well-marked and almost always dated. An original example of the Breininger work—a "combed dot" decorated plate—was recently purchased by the Philadelphia Museum of Art.

The contemporary redware pieces causing the greatest concern today, generally from west of the Mississippi, are the imports. Much of this ware is of Mexican origin, and with some usage a spurious piece can fool the unknowledgeable collector. A few signs of age (unfortunately, some are imitated) include the overall hardness of earlier examples, making it difficult to penetrate the surface on the backside of a redware plate, bowl, etc. And, when penetrated, the clay will be darkened. When the backside of a new piece of redware is penetrated with a knife or a pin, the texture of the clay is soft and will have a clean, bright appearance which lacks the charred or black appearance of the older wares. Finally, there are the minute surface scratches made by knives over the years; and almost always, an early example will show crazing over its glazed surface.

* * *

Apple butter crock, dark brown glaze inside, handled, hairline near bottom, 6½″ t. (D-NE) ...$ 27
Barrel, green & white slip decor., rare, 4¾″ (A-E) 500
Bedpan, w/manganese splotches (D-E) 75
Bird, on double tree stump, feather design on bird & bark design on stump, border of circular indentation (A-E) 425
Birdhouse, unglazed (A-E) 95
Bird whistle, 1 lg. dove, 4 smaller birds, brown & white slip (A-E) 350
Bird whistle, slip decor. (A-E) 850
Bottle, 4-sided, reddish glaze w/shades of color, 6½″ t. (D-NE) 95
Bottle, harvest, ring-shaped, red-brown glaze, ca. 1870, 7¾″ diam. (D-MW) 75
Bowl, beaded decor. on rim, w/handle, 5″ (A-E) 120
Bowl, black glaze, 2¾″×5″ w. (A-NE) 125
Bowl, black, green & white slip decor., 2 handles, 7″ (A-E) 160
Bowl, cream & green decor., 13″ d. (A-E) 120
Bowl, cream & green decor., 13½″ d. (A-E) 140
Bowl, deep, tulip bud & "v" w/dots, 10″ (A-E) 350
Bowl, double-handled, mocha decor. (D-MW) 325
Bowl, floral decor., canary yellow, scalloped top rim (A-E) 250
Bowl, grape hyacinth design, black, green & white, 5″ (A-E) 525
Bowl, gray ground w/black speckles & brown &,black dripped decor., 11½″ (A-NE) .. 425
Bowl, green & tan w/black drip decor. on outside rim; orange, red & green inside, 5½″ (A-E) 180
Bowl, horizontal & vertical slip line decor., 11″ d. (A-E) 325
Bowl, large, w/sponge decor. (A-MW) 135
Bowl, Penna., small, 6½″ diam.(D-NE) 28
Bowl, pouring, w/black sponge decor., 9″ diam. (A-E) 350
Bowl, shallow rimmed w/brownish glaze, 6½″ (D-NE) 26
Bowl, shallow, reddish-brown mottled glaze, early, 5″ (D-NE) 26
Bowl, sugar, covered, w/brown ground, w/green & yellow slip decor., 8″×5″ (A-NE) .. 225
Bowl, sugar, handles (A-E) 52
Bowl, sugar, lid, glazed, sunflower decor., light color (A-E) 400
Bowl, sugar, lid, red brown decor. (A-E) 105
Bowl, sugar, open, bulbous, brown glaze, 3½″×4″ (D-E) 60
Bowl, sugar, signed on base, "S. B., Sept., 9, 1840" (A-E) 115
Bowl, sugar, white, green & black slip decor., w/2 handles, 4″ (A-E) 450
Bowl, yellow border, 11″ (A-E) 70
Bowl, yellow slip decor., rectangular, Penna., 11½″×15″ (A-MW) 190
Butterstamp, unglazed, strawberry, 4″ (A-NE) 375
Canteen, field, w/olive ground & red speckled decor., 11½″ (A-NE) 250
Caster, covered, handled, green & orange ground w/brown decor., 4¾″ (A-NE) 500
Colander, signed "MB" (Moulton Bodge), 13½″ (A-NE) 175
Coffeepot, w/orig. lid, white & dark slip sponge decor., 7″ (A-E) 625
Cows, 2 white & brown & 1 small brown w/white spots on base (A-E) 47
Creamer, black splash decor., 5″ (A-E) 140
Creamer, black sponge decor., ovid, 5½″ (A-E) 350

Creamer, green & tan, 4" (A-E) ....$ 75
Creamer, small chip, 7" (A-E)   45
Creamer, white & black sponge slip decor., matching lid, 5" (A-E)   400
Cream pan, green glaze inside, 17" diam., 4" deep (D-E)   120
Crock, black smear decor. near top, 2 handles, 8"×8½" (D-E)   48
Cup, cottage cheese, handled, reddish-brown glaze inside, ex. cond., 5½"×4" (D-NE)   35
Cup, custard, Maine glaze (D-W)   12
Cup, custard, red glaze at bottom w/dark glaze around top, drizzles down sides, 4"×2" (D-NE) .   80
Cup, handled, w/slip decor. (A-E)   100
Cup, pouring, handle & spout, white & green slip decor. (A-E)   80
Cup, slip decor. design, dk. brown base w/olive, green, cream & brown glazing, 3½" (A-NE)   100
Cups, custard, pr., 4" (A-E)   70
Dish, brown glaze, speckled in black, 7" diam. (A-E)   42
Dish, brown speckled glaze, old chips, 6¼" d. (A-E)   20
Dish, deep, slip decor., 8" (A-E)   45
Dish, deep, slip decor., 7" (A-E)   25
Dish, deep, white, green & black slip decor., running deer in center, 14" (A-E)   600
Dish, deep, white slip decor. lines around border, 8" (A-E)   85
Dish, loaf, w/yellow loop decor., 8"×13" (A-E)   160
Dish, oyster, 14" diam. (A-E)   50
Dish, soap, rectangular, 2"×3½"×7½" (D-E)   58
Dish, sponge cake, turks head (A-E)   17
Dish, sponge cake, white slip decor., w/brown splash, 9¼" (A-E)   42
Dog, brown glazed (A-E)   50
Dog, on base w/flowers (A-E)   290
Dog, sewer tile (D-S)   25
Dog, sitting & holding basket (A-E)   225
Dogs, cocker spaniels, green & brown, pr. (A-E)   500
Doorstop, dog, lt. green, brown & yellow glaze (A-E)   110
Doorstop, thrown in a flat round shape w/acorn finial, blue & gray glaze, 6" d. (A-E)   40
Flask, dark brown glaze, 6½" h. (D-NE)   65
Flask, dark red glaze, ovoid, 7½" t. (D-E)   45
Flask, pinched, 6¼" (A-NE)   250
Flowerpot, drip tray, 1-pc., incised rings at top, yellow glaze/brown splotches, 4½" diam.
    (D-NE)   75
Flowerpot, orange to olive ground & white & brn. decor., 4½" (A-NE)   90
Flowerpot, scratch work decor., 6" (A-E)   85
Flowerpot, spotted slip decor., 4½" (A-E)   55
Flowerpot, tan & brown decor., 5½" (A-E)   75
Flowerpot, yellow & brown decor. (A-E)   25
Flowerpots, marked "I. K. T.," pr. (A-E)   90
Flowerpots, pr. (A-E)   17
Fly or insect trap (D-E)   45

Platter, redware, oblong, deep, wavy slip decor.,
18" l. (A-E) $375

Plate, redware, fine detailed yellow slip decor. 11¾" diam. (A-E)
$700

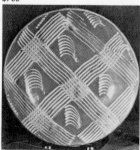

Footwarmer, w/orange glaze, 9½" h. (A-NE)..$ 70
Holder, ink & pen, 2-hole, brown glaze (D-E) 70
Holder, spill, olive ground w/brown decor., 4" (A-NE) 250
Holder, string, rare (A-E) 47
Jar, black & cream feather pinwheel decoration, 8" (A-E)... 275
Jar, black splash decor., w/lid, 8½" (A-E)... 52
Jar, black sponge decor., ovoid, 5" (A-E) 160
Jar, brown ground & dk. brown striping, 5¼" (A-NE) 275
Jar, brown spotting, yellow drip decor. & green spots, salmon colored, incised lines, 8", Maine
(A-E) 350
Jar, canning, blackish glaze inside & out, 6" t. × 4¾" (D-NE) 25
Jar, canning, dark glaze, 6¼" (D-NE) 18
Jar, cookie, w/lid & rope handles, good cond., 7" (A-E).. 300
Jar, covered, double entwined, by David Manderville, N. Y., incised "William Hurtin", 9½"
(A-NE) 450
Jar, covered, handled, w/green base & orange spots, 7¾" (A-NE)................................... 325
Jar, covered, olive cream ground & brown decor., 5½" (A-NE) 550
Jar, covered, olive-green-orange-lt. & drk. brown decor., 6½" (A-NE) 550
Jar, covered, olive ground, orange & bold brown drip decor., 6" (A-NE) 400
Jar, covered, olive ground, red-brown spotting, w/handle, 8½" (A-NE)........................... 300
Jar, covered, orange-red ground w/brown spots, 18th C., 8½" (A-NE)............................. 950
Jar, covered, salmon ground w/black speckled & drip decor., 9" (A-NE) 300
Jar, covered, sgraffito of tulips, hearts, hex signs, dated 1822 (A-MW) 2500
Jar, covered, yellow slip & brown dipped decor., w/incised line w/ochre ground; 8" (A-NE) ... 350
Jar, decor., cylindrical, incised wiggley band, 8" h. (D-MW)... 45
Jar, double-handled, olive ground w/brown tree decor., rare, 11" (A-NE) 475
Jar, eagle & date 1842, black decor., 8" (A-E) 575
Jar, 4-line slip decor., alternating in green & white rows, slip vertical lines around lip, w/2
crimped handles, 7" (A-E)... 1500
Jar, green w/brown decor., 18th C., ca. 1777, 8" (A-NE) 200
Jar, incised slip decor., w/double entwined handles, orange ground w/cream slip, green &
brown decor., early 18th C., 6" (A-NE) 175
Jar, handled, brown ground, green & yellow slip & brown decor., early 18th C., 9" (A-NE).... 150
Jar, handled, covered, green, 9½" (A-NE) 575
Jar, handled, green-gray glaze & pink mottling, 8¼" (A-NE) 375
Jar, handled, green, orange & red-brown decor., 8¼" (A-NE) 375
Jar, handled, green to orange glaze w/brown decor., 9" (A-NE) 425
Jar, handled, greenish-red ground w/brown decor., 6" (A-NE) 325
Jar, handled, olive-gray ground, orange spots, 7" (A-NE) 350
Jar, handled, olive ground w/orange & brown spots, 8½" (A-NE).................................... 250
Jar, handled, orange glaze w/brown decor., w/incised lines, 11" (A-NE) 225
Jar, handled, red ground w/lg. black spots, 8¾" (A-NE) 225
Jar, handled, tan ground w/brown decor., 9½" (A-NE) 150
Jar, incised "tea", olive gray ground w/red brown decor., 7" (A-NE)................................ 300
Jar, jelly, red glaze, 5" (A-E) 20
Jar, large, small opening, black splash designs, incised lines, 8" diam. (A-E) 210
Jar, mustard, covered, gray-brown ground slip spotted decor., 18th C., 3½" (A-NE)............. 200
Jar, mustard, handled, signed "Jaryan", red-brown base w/black speckles, 3 bold black lines,
3¾" (A-NE) 325
Jar, olive background w/orange & brown decor., Maine, 6" (A-NE).................................. 250
Jar, olive ground w/green & brown spots, 9" (A-NE).. 400
Jar, open mouthed, green & tan w/black sponge decor., circular lines incised, 10½" (A-E)...... 295
Jar, orange base w/brown decor., 8½" (A-NE) 375
Jar, orange-olive ground w/green & brown decor., 8" (A-NE) 450
Jar, orange, triple twisted handles, incised "MC", 5½" (A-NE)....................................... 175
Jar, preserve, covered, orange ground w/brown decor., 7" (A-NE) 210
Jar, preserve, covered, orange ground w/brown spots, 8¾" (A-NE).................................. 250
Jar, preserve, orange ground, brown decor., 8" (A-NE) 150
Jar, preserve, orange ground, brown decor., Conn., 11" (A-NE) 150

Jar, preserve, red ground w/brown spots, 12½″ (A-NE)..$ 200
Jar, red & cream scratch crow's foot decor., 5″ (A-E) 60
Jar, red & tan glaze, w/incised lines, 6½″ (A-NE) 400
Jar, red ground & black decor., 5″ (A-NE) 250
Jar, tulip & daisy slip decoration, 8″ (A-E) 650
Jar, white slip decor., circles & dots, w/2 handles & lid, 6″ (A-E)...................................... 1500
Jars, tan glaze w/brown splash decor., pr., 4½″ (A-E) 140
Jug, bulbous, N. E. origin, black glaze, 18th C., 6½″ (D-NE).. 45
Jug, black glaze, 8″ (D-NE).. 28
Jug, brown, 11¼″ (A-NE) 110
Jug, brown decor., 11″ (A-NE).. 80
Jug, by Matthias Norcross, Farmington, Maine, 7″ (A-NE) 300
Jug, decor. w/green, tan & black, 8″ h. (A-E) 440
Jug, gray, w/brown speckles, 6½″ (A-NE) 225
Jug, green, black & tan decor., 5″ (A-E) 200
Jug, green, early, 10¼″ (A-NE)... 50
Jug, green ground w/orange & brown spots, brown base, 7¾″ (A-NE) 375
Jug, handled, glazed inside, Penna., 5½″ h. (A-MW) 25
Jug, handled, olive ground w/red speckled decor., incised lines near top & on spout, Maine, 9″
   (A-NE)... 350
Jug, handled, orange ground & black specks, 2½″ (A-NE).. 200
Jug, handled, pear-shaped, lt. green to orange w/dk. brown spotting, 7″ (A-NE) 525
Jug, handled, red & orange ground w/brown decor., 11½″ (A-NE) 275
Jug, New Hampshire, ca. 1790-1800 (D-W) 100
Jug, ochre ground w/speckled red earth colored decor., w/3 incised lines around mouth, 9″
   (A-NE)... 100
Jug, (or vinegar cruet) unusual shape & size, black glaze, 7½″ (D-E) 28
Jug, red ground & olive & black dripped decor., 6″ (A-NE) 300
Jug, salmon, brown speckles, 7½″ (A-NE) 300
Jug, tan ground w/brown ground, 6½″ (A-NE) 300
Keg, salmon-orange ground w/green & brown decor., 7″ (A-NE) 250
Lion, dark glaze, 11″ l. (A-E)... 100
Master ink, cream ground, green speckles & wine colored drip decor., 5½″ (A-NE).............. 300
Master ink, tan ground & brown vertical drip decor., 5½″ (A-NE) 600
Match safe, old ochre, dk. red & brown paint, 3″ t., 3½″ diam. (D-E) 14
Milk bowl, reddish-brown glaze, 19″ diam. (D-NE) 145
Milk pan, dk. brown glaze, 14″ (D-NE) 35
Milk pan, dk. glaze, 14″ diam. (D-MW) 35
Milk pan, dk. glaze, 14″ (D-W)... 35
Mold, cake, brown glaze w/brown spots, 11″ (A-NE) 150

Turkshead cake mold,
redware (D-MW) $45

Pitcher, redware,
covered, hairline
crack in base
(A-E) $60

Bowl, redware, slip
glazed, large (D-MW) $35

Mold, cake, Penna. Dutch, 5½" h. (A-MW) ....$ 50
Mold, fish, good cond. (A-E)   70
Mold, turks head, black sponge decor. (D-E)..   35
Mold, turks head, black sponge decor. (D-N)..   42
Mold, turks head, ex. cond., 9" diam. (A-E)   65
Mold, turks head, orange, green & brown glaze, 7" diam. (D-MW)   40
Mug, green, w/black decor., 4¾" (A-NE)..   350
Mug, green, w/green & brown decor., 5" (A-NE)..   400
Mug, greenish ochre ground & brown decor., 3¾" (A-NE)..   325
Mug, handled, green, white & red glaze, signed Soloman Bell (A-E)   320
Mug, red ground w/black decor., 5" (A-NE)..   400
Mug, shaving, w/interior soap receptacle (D-E)   85
Nursing bottle, orange to olive glaze w/br. decor., 6¾" (A-NE)..   700
Pan, loaf, slip decor., w/9 wavy yellow bands, Penna., 15¾" (D-W)   285
Pan, loaf, yellow slip decor. (D-NE)   155
Pie plate, 11" diam. (D-E)   75
Pie plate, crow's foot decor., 8" (A-E)   115
Pie plate, sgraffito decor., peacock center,wreath of flowers, dated 1792; brown/green/cream
   colors, 8½" diam. (A-E)   1300
Pie plate, sgraffito decor., tree, tulips, fish & bird, crimped edge (A-NE)..............................   415
Pie plate, sgraffito decor., tulips/flowers w/star center, 8" diam. (D-NE)   495
Pie plate, slip decor., green/black wavy lines, crimped edge (D-MW)..................................   169
Pie plate, slip decor., green/brown stripes, 8½" diam. (A-E)..   157
Pie plate, slip decor., green/brown stripes, 8" diam. (D-W)..   55
Pie plate, slip decor., white/green/black lines, 8" diam. (D-S)   90
Pie plate, slip decor., yellow lines, 7" diam. (A-E)   90
Pie plate, slip decor., yellow wavy lines, crimped edge, 8" diam. (D-W)   75
Pitcher, black splash decor., 8" (A-E)..   275
Pitcher, black splash decor., 10" (A-E)..   475
Pitcher, brown patterned dripped decor., olive, w/incising, 9" (A-NE)   700
Pitcher, bulbous form, some mottling (D-E)   125
Pitcher, covered, w/tan ground w/lt. brown decor., 5¼" (A-NE)..   400
Pitcher, dark glaze, 6¼" (D-NE)   35
Pitcher, glazed inside, dk. spots outside, 4½" h. (A-MW)   80
Pitcher, handled, w/spout, gray-green ground w/orange spotting, 6" (A-NE)   300
Pitcher, incised lines & circle & indentations, black splash decor., 8" (A-E)   360
Pitcher, olive background w/brown dripping, 6½" (A-NE)   525
Pitcher, olive & brown decor., 8" (A-NE)..   350
Pitcher, olive-gray w/brown decor., 9⅛" (A-NE)   425
Pitcher, pink-gray ground w/bold brown decor., 8" (A-NE)   725
Pitcher, red ground w/brown decor., 5¼" (A-NE)..   275
Pitcher, tan glaze w/decor., 6" (A-NE)..   325
Pitcher, tan ground, w/warm brown, drk. brown & green decor., 8" (A-NE)   525
Planter, double entwined handles w/triple crimped banding yellow to orange decor., inscribed:
   "Hannah Allcut the 10th month, 1823, 7¼" (A-NE)..   350
Plate, deep, slip decor. fine combed lines on yellow ground, 11" diam. (A-E)   145
Plate, marked "W. Smith, Womelsdorf" (A-E)   150
Plate, sgraffito by Spinner, 8½" diam. (D-E)   700
Plate, sgraffito, fish & flower decor., 12½" (A-E)..   400
Plate, sgraffito, made in Stahl pottery 1937, copy of plate made for Mrs. Eleanor Roosevelt,
   repaired, 10" (A-E)   60
Plate, sgraffito, Meddinger, much green w/tulip plant in pot (A-E)   975
Plate, slip, cross lines of white w/black dots & 4 green leafy designs in angles, 7½" (A-E)   675
Plate, slip decor., deep reddish-brown glaze w/simple yellow line decor. in center, 9" diam.
   (A-E)   62
Plate, slip decor., diamonds and S's, 11½" (A-E)   500
Plate, slip decor. form of Spencerian pen work, 14" (A-E)..   600
Plate, slip decor., green spotted, 13½" diam. (D-NE)..   350
Plate, slip decor., large, green & cream Adeline Sweet & other decor., 14½" (A-E)   950

Plate, slip decor., lines & dots, 10" (A-E) ....$ 130
Plate, slip decor., orange/red ground w/3 yellow lines around border, 10" diam. (D-E) 200
Plate, slip decor., pot of tulips in yellow-green & brown sgraffito, 11½" (A-E) 140
Plate, slip decor., triple lines, 8" (A-E)... 95
Plate, slip decor., triple lines, 10¾" (A-E) 145
Plate, slip decor., unusual, sponge border decor., white slip dots in middle, 10" (A-E) 300
Plate, slip decor., wavy lines, bush tree decor., 9" (A-E) 175
Plate, slip decor., wavy lines, key decor., 9¼" (A-E) 125
Plate, slip decor., yellow wavy lines on deep reddish-brown glaze, 8½" diam. (A-E) 75
Plate, slip, elaborate red/yellow/black line decor., 13" diam. (A-NE)..................................... 950
Plate, slip, grape hyacinth plant design, green, black & white, 7¾" (A-E) 750
Plate, slip, serrated edge, orange/red, 9½" diam. (D-E) 300
Plate, slip, yellow pretzel type decor. & crows' feet, 14" diam. (D-E)................................... 80
Plate, tulips & flowers in scratch design, white background, flowered border, 8" (A-E) 60
Platter, 4 3-line slip decor., 8×11½" (A-E).. 525
Platter, oblong, deep, 4-line slip decor., 18" (A-E) 875
Platter, oblong, deep, 4-line slip decor., orange-red background, 14" (A-E)............................ 750
Platter, oblong, 4-line slip decor., 16" (A-E)... 675
Platter, oblong, sq. corners, triple slip designs, 14¾" l., 10½" w. (A-E)............................... 340
Platter, oval, triple slip lines, 18" (A-E) 460
Porringer, handled, black, 1⅝" (A-NE) 125
Porringer, handled, red ground w/olive gray & black spotted decor., 3½"×5" (A-NE)............... 275
Porringer, w/orange ground w/blk. decor., 3"×5" (A-NE) 150
Porringer, lt. brown ground w/dk. brown decor., 3¼" (A-NE) 175
Porringer, olive-orange base w/brown decor., 2¼" (A-NE) 350
Porringer, orange ground & brown decor., 3½" (A-NE) 275
Pot, bean (A-MW) 15
Pot, bean, brown glaze (A-MW) 20
Pot, handled, decor. w/green & white slip, white, black & green slip on body of jar, tulips & star
  flower design, serrated lip & lid, 7" (A-E) 1700
Pot, handled, glazed inside, signed John W. Bell, patina, 12" (A-E) 500
Pot, handled, outside unglazed, patina, 4¾" (A-E) 40
Pot, honey, handled, w/incised lines w/orange brown base w/yellow slip & gr. decor., 18th C., 4"
  (A-NE) 225
Pot, jelly, 5" (A-E) 22
Pot, jelly, orange-yellow glaze, 4½" (A-E) 55
Pot, jelly, red glaze, 5" (A-E) 35
Pot, oven, brown glazed interior w/brown & natural unglazed red exterior, 7¼" h. (A-E) 30
Pot, oven, speckled glaze on interior only, incised line below opening, 5" h., 3¾" diam. (A-E).. 70
Pot, small, like dyepot, dark glaze, 3¾" (D-NE) 18
Pot, small, sgraffito decor. (D-E) 75
Pot, stew, orange & green ground w/brown spots, 6 incised lines on shoulder, 6" (A-NE)....... 225
Pot, 2 handles, decor. w/white wavy lines & dots, 6½" (A-E) 375
Pot, unglazed, w/slip birds, eagle & flowers, 7½" (A-E) 55
Rooster, painted, ex. cond., 5¼" (A-E) 40
Sander, Maine, 2" (A-NE) 100
Salt, glazed, footed (A-MW)... 55
Salt, greenish-gray ground w/green spots, 2¼" (A-NE) 425
Snuff jar, labeled "Maccaboy Snuff", Salem, Mass. 5" (A-NE) 125
Snuff jar, mottled gray & red-brown decor., 4" (A-NE) 200
Strainer, Penna., conical shape, 19th C., 13" diam. (A-MW) 65
Teapot, ca. 1850 (D-E) 75
Teapot, raised bead decor., small (A-MW) 10
Trivet, round, brown decor. (D-S) 5
Tureen, double handled, w/red ground w/cream marbleized slipped black decor., 13" (A-NE) . 600
Vase, large (A-E).. 50
Witches ball, gray-green ground w/orange spots & brown decor., 5" (A-NE)........................ 425
Wren house, barrel, dk. glaze, J. L. Blaney, Cookstown, Pa. (A-E) 65
Wren house, barrel, signed John N. Bull, 1848, York County (A-E).. 100

Rugs

The refreshing freedom from artistic conventions, so typical of country art, is nowhere more apparent than in the early handmade rugs. These were obviously designed by the makers to please themselves, showing an originality in the usage of pattern and color that few folk arts of any culture have surpassed.

Typical country floor coverings were: patched rugs made of woolen fabric; braided rugs made from leftover clothing, bedding, etc.; rugs of animal hide; wool-crocheted or embroidered-type rugs; or the hand-hooked rug, which has proven to be the most popular with collectors. Their beauty is such that many collectors are willing to overlook their lack of durability. Therefore, it is almost impossible to find one that doesn't show signs of wear. They can be found in all shapes and sizes, from small rectangles to large carpets and stair runners. The earlier examples had a foundation of linen, homespun wool, or unbleached cotton, with burlap being used for the later rugs.

Hooked rugs were made principally on the Eastern seaboard, in some rural areas in the Midwest, and in the Pennsylvania Dutch country where regional influences were characteristic decoration. Rugs made here were small, but because of their quaint folk designs, they are a favorite with many collectors. They reached their height of popularity during the 1850s, but it wasn't until around the turn of the century that their primitive folk quality disappeared—when commercial designs replaced the quaint, early patterns.

For information concerning rugs, see *Indian* category.

* * *

Braided, round, 10 ft. diam., ca. 1920, fine condition (D-MW) ....$ 200
Braided, wool, oval, 11'6"×14'6" (A-MW)... 375
Hooked, abstract composition in blue, black, yellow, green & brown, 2'6"×4'10" (A-NE) 75
Hooked, alternating sq. panels of floral & scenic views, 3'×5' (A-MW)................................ 100

Hooked rug, fruit & flowers, 25½" × 40" (D-E) $485

Hooked rug, floral motif, 28½″ × 46″ (D-E) $395

Hooked rug, bright floral on natural background, 31″ × 520 (D-E) $450

Hooked rug, lions, 26″ × 38″ (D-E) $450

Hooked rug, Boston sidewalk, 31″ × 48″ (D-E) $295   **Hooked rug,** cat & kittens, 27″ × 42″ (D-E) $450

Hooked, alternating sq. panels of floral & scenic views, 4′×6′ (A-MW)...............................$ 100
Hooked, beige floral, sq. paneled on beige background, 6′×9′ (A-MW)   135
Hooked, black background, large red leaves, center floral, red, green & beige, 38″×73½″ (D-NE)   55
Hooked, black edge, center tan, floral roses, forget-me-nots, daisies, green leaves, 28″×49″
    (D-NE)...   40
Hooked, braided border, multi-colored feather & floral interior design, 5′6″×3′7″ (A-NE).......   150
Hooked, brown edge, center tan/basket of flowers in rose, maroon, green leaves, 24″×42″
    (D-NE)...   32
Hooked, circular geometric design, shades of grays & reds, 3′4″×6′7″ (A-NE)   70
Hooked, depicting dog (A-E)   35
Hooked, depicting train, engine & 2 cars of early stagecoach type on 4-wheel frames, mid-19th
    C., 19″×49″ (D-E)...   200
Hooked, floral center against beige, leaves pale brown, rust against tan background, 28×49″
    (D-NE)...   40
Hooked, floral center in red, green, beige on black background, surrounded by lg. red leaves,
    73½″×38″ (D-NE)   55
Hooked, floral decor. on beige background, 4′×6′ (A-MW)   90
Hooked, floral, early, 5′×8′ (D-E)   575
Hooked, floral, large flower heads in maroon, old rose, green leaves on tan background, 20″×38″
    (D-NE)...   35
Hooked, geometric design, reds, blues, grays, & browns, cubes illusions, primitive, ex. cond.,
    66″×35″ (D-NE)   100
Hooked, geometric, multicolored, 23″×40″ (A-NE)..   40
Hooked, geometric, sm. squares in reds, blues & earth colors, 2′8″×5′1″ (A-NE)   150
Hooked, geometric, squares bisected w/serrated lines, various colors, 2′9″×6′3″ (A-NE)   250
Hooked, girl chasing goose (D-E)   85
Hooked, house pattern (D-E)   90
Hooked, lion & cub, shades of brown, 26″ w., 32″ l. (D-E)   190
Hooked, Liberty Bell design, circular, 4′ (A-MW)..   80
Hooked, log cabin design, shades of brown & green, 7×10′ (A-E)....................................   170
Hooked, multicolored floral on beige background, oval, 8′×10′ (A-MW)   225
Hooked, multicolored floral on beige background, 10′6″×14′6″ (A-MW)   225
Hooked, multicolored floral square panels, 6′×9′ (A-MW)...   160
Hooked, multicolored w/orange floral w/sq. panel design, 4′×6′ (A-MW)   100
Hooked, multicolored floral w/oval center medallion, 3′×4′6″ (A-MW)   90
Hooked, oval, beige & tan floral, 2′6″×4′ (A-MW)...   30
Hooked, oval, floral design, 3′×5′ (A-MW)   80
Hooked, pale gray center, tan basket w/maroon & red flowers, brown, dk. gray & black edges,
    24″×41″ (D-E)   32
Hooked, petit-point type, pastel floral on beige background, approx. 8′×10′ (A-MW)...........   260
Hooked, petit point type, pastel floral on light blue background, 18″ × 26½″ (D-E)   165
Hooked, reclining male lion, rust, tan & black on beige oval background, rust-red chain around
    oval, green leaf sprigs, 31″×61″ (D-E)   225
Hooked, red & olive green, off-white center w/red roses, black background, 64″×32″ (D-E).....   95
Hooked, rooster weather vane decor., 3′×3′6″ (A-MW)..   50
Hooked, square panel design, multicolored & orange floral, 4′×6′ (A-MW)   90
Hooked, tan center w/roses, forget-me-nots, daisies, green leaves, black edge, 28″×49″ (D-NE).   40
Hooked, tan background, leaves pale brown, rust, center floral on beige, 28″×49″ (D-NE)   40

Salopian

The history of Salopian or Caughley ware—the term is interchangeable
—began during the mid 1770s when Thomas Turner moved to Caughley,
England to establish a porcelain factory. He had previously worked at
Worcester as a designer, hence his wares closely resembled those of the Worcester factory in shape, style of decoration, and in the general type of body. The
output at Caughley seems to have been mostly practical tableware, oftentimes
described as being truly elegant and beautiful. The blue printed Caughley
porcelains are generally marked with a "C" or "S," a crescent, or with various
Chinese-style numerals, all printed in underglaze blue. The impressed mark
"Salopian" appears on a variety of late tableware produced here, which appealed
to the Pennsylvania Dutch.

Salopian ware is delicate and fragile, which accounts for its scarcity; however,
many choice pieces can still be found in the "Dutch" country. This ware has an
all-over transfer design in colors predominantly blue, brown, orange, or gold.

In 1799, Thomas Turner sold the Caughley Works to John Rose, Edward
Blakeway and Richard Rose of Coalport Porcelain Manufacturers.

* * *

Bowl, acorn & flower pattern, 5" (A-E)	$ 190
Bowl, cottage & sheep tender pattern, 5" (A-E)	30
Bowl, sheep tender pattern (A-E)	60
Bowl, sugar, bird of paradise pattern, rare (A-E)	200
Bowl, sugar, Chinese pattern (A-E)	120
Bowl, sugar, pheasant & bird pattern, covered (A-E)	200
Bowl, sugar, yellow bird pattern, covered, 5½" h. (A-E)	210
Bowl, sugar, yellow bird pattern, rare (A-E)	80
Bowl, yellow bird pattern, 6" (A-E)	190
Bowl, yellow pheasant pattern, rare (A-E)	190
Chalice, basket weave pattern, ram's head impressed handle, footed (A-E)	80
Creamer, castle, cottage & sheep pattern (A-E)	100
Creamer, yellow bird pattern, 5½" h. (A-E)	310
Creamer, yellow pheasant pattern, stamped "Brameled-4" on bottom (A-E)	140
Cup & saucer, acorn & flower pattern, 5" (A-E)	130
Cup & saucer, basket weave pattern, small (A-E)	170
Cup & saucer, bird of paradise pattern (A-E)	345

*Salopian ware (A-E), back
row, left to right:* **sugar
bowl,** covered, Bird of
Paradise pattern, $130; **cup
& saucer,** Sheepherder &
Cottage pattern, $150;
teapot, Bird of Paradise
pattern, $130; *front row, left
to right:* **cup & saucer,** Deer
pattern, $180; **cup & saucer,**
Flower & Acorn pattern,
$130

Salopian ware (A-E), *top row, left to right:* **cup & saucer,** Shepherd design, $150; **cup & saucer,** Bird of Paradise & Rose design, $200; *center row, left to right:* **cup & saucer,** Boy Grooming Cow, slight discoloration in cup, $190; **cup & saucer,** Oriental design, slight chip on cup, $90; *bottom row:* **cups & saucers,** Mill & Bridge scene in center, w/butterflies & floral border, hairline in 1 cup, matched pr., $300

Cup & saucer, bordered thatch roof cottage pattern (A-E) ....$	50
Cup & saucer, boy & cow pattern (A-E)..	210
Cup & saucer, double deep (A-E)..	60
Cup & saucer, fleur-de-lis pattern (A-E)	95
Cup & saucer, girl & boy tending sheep pattern (A-E)..	110
Cup & saucer, sheep tender & lady friend pattern (A-E)	110
Cup & saucer, yellow bird pattern (A-E)..	200
Cup & saucer, yellow bird pattern, large (A-E)	160
Cup & saucers, deer pattern, pr. (A-E)	180
Cup & saucers, sheep herder & cottage pattern, pr. (A-E)	150
Gravy creamer, fleur-de-lis pattern (A-E)	155
Mug, bow & cow pattern, impressed handles (A-E)	85
Mug, deer pattern, w/handle, rare, 2¼″ (A-E)	300
Pitcher, cream, bird of paradise pattern (A-E)...	140
Pitcher, gravy, yellow bird & lace pattern (A-E)	200
Pitcher, water, castle & cow pattern, 6½″ (A-E)	85
Plate, bird of paradise pattern, 7¼″ (A-E)	125
Plate, boy & girl sowing seed pattern w/flower border, rare, 8½″ (A-E).............................	220
Plate, Chinese pattern, open edge, 8″ (A-E)	150
Plate, Chinese pattern, 10″ (A-E)...	170
Plate, Chinese pattern, octagonal, 9″ (A-E)	200
Plate, Chinese pattern, open edge, rare, 8″ (A-E)	150
Plate, floral & lace pattern, 8½″ (A-E)...	85
Plate, robin red breast perched on tree guarding nest of eggs pattern, flowered border, rare (A-E)	250
Plate, sheep tender pattern, 5¼″ (A-E)	190
Plate, sheep tender pattern, 5¼″ (A-E)	200
Plate, sheep tender pattern, 7¼″ (A-E)	210
Plate, soup, Chinese pattern, 10″ (A-E)	170
Plate, wheat reaper pattern, signed Lavinia (A-E)	70
Plate, yellow bird & lace pattern, 7¾″ (A-E)	210
Teapot, bird of paradise pattern, w/lid (A-E)	130
Teapot, boy & cow pattern (A-E)	180
Teapot, girl milking cow pattern, rare (A-E)	255
Teapot, yellow bird pattern (A-E)	210
Teapot, yellow bird pattern, 5½″ (A-E)...	130
Toddy plate, acorn pattern, 4½″ (A-E)	200
Toddy plate, bird of paradise pattern, 4½″ (A-E)	185
Toddy plate, deer pattern, 5¼″ (A-E)	200

Samplers

The term "sampler" is used to describe those lovingly created, or dutifully executed embroideries, used primarily as a means of recording an assortment of stitches, in addition to learning to read and write; hence, the use of alphabets and verses.

The majority of samplers still available to collectors are those that were produced by children and young women during their teens, dating from the first half of the last century. Colonial examples are rarely found.

Most of the early samplers were tall and narrow strips of hand-woven linen approximately 6 to 8 inches wide. Some were as long as 28 inches. During the eighteenth century the proportions generally became squarer.

The vast majority of samplers were simple exercises in cross-stitch, with sets of alphabets, numerals, occasionally a pious verse, and a twining border. Many lack the letter "J", as this was not included in the Roman alphabet. Those having the date, the name of the embroideress—and perhaps the name of her town—are much valued today.

Samplers were done on linen in loosely twisted hand-dyed silk or wool thread, worked in blues, browns, greens and white. Stitches most frequently used during the early period were the angular, petit-point, and cross-stitch. Other colored backgrounds used were dark green, blue, and mustard.

Although the most desirable samplers are from the eighteenth century, there is much to be said for the more attractive ones that date from the early years of the nineteenth century, when a variety of fancy stitchery was being used. Moreover, samplers were now characterized by more naturalistic designs, including barnyard scenes, human figures, a child's home, a schoolhouse, public building, or occasionally an American eagle. Such scenes first appeared near the base of the sampler, then gradually worked upward to the center.

These delightfully quaint examples of fine stitchery became a lost art around the turn of the last century.

* * *

Sampler, Abigail Cloey Barber, Ladies Academy, Georgetown, Mass., strawberry border, 1 alphabet, lg. basket flowers, butterflies, flame stitch, scroll line, 20¼"×15½" (D-NE) ....$ 125

Sampler, Delphina Bell, age 12, 1826, green, white, old gold floral border, 3 alphabets, 2 baskets of flowers w/birds in black, green & white, 13½"×17¼" (D-NE)...................................... 100

Sampler, bookmark, tan background, black, 2 ABC's, 7½×2½, numbers initialed, backed in blue chintz, dated 1861 (D-NE) 18

Sampler, Martha Cheever, aged 15 yrs., 3 alphabets, floral pattern edge goes into cornucopias, verse, grass, trees, basket of flowers, subtle colors, 21½"×26¼" (D-NE) 145

Sampler, Julian Clark, age 9, "two birds, strawberries, colonial house & roses", ca. 1830, 12"×18" (A-NE) 225

Sampler, Hannah Clay, ABC's w/lots of reds, done in 1770, homespun linen, framed, outlined birds at bottom, 18th C., 12¼"×8¼" (D-NE) 135

Sampler, Mary Eliza Darbys, 1839, age 8 years, lg., colorful (A-E) 170

Sampler, early, decor. w/trees, houses, small (A-E) 75

Sampler, early, tiger maple frame, green, yellow, pink, brown, ABC & numbers w/crewel trees, birds, & flowers, 1800s, 21"×16" (D-E) 125

Sampler, embroidery of woman seated in Windsor chair w/2 birds on string which she is holding; she is sitting next to apple tree bearing 2 large apples, 18th C., 8"×10" (A-NE)...... 550

Sampler, family record, large, 1871 (A-E) ....$ 50

Sampler, genealogy of family, husband & wife born in mid 1700s, list children of 1st marriage w/dates, second wife, children, by Harriet, aged 21, 1828; border solid crewel, 2" w., lettering in black on homespun linen, framed, 17½"×22½" (D-NE) 155

Sampler, genealogy, marriage of Sarah Davis & Samuel Fifield, 1797, birth dates & deaths, gold, lt. green & white, floral upper corners, 4 lg. flowerpots across bottom, geometric double border, 27"×22" (D-E) 155

Sampler, Elizabeth Heims, age 11, linen, 1839 (A-E) 55

Sampler, Nancy B. Jenks, 1826, 19th C., 12"×18" (A-MW) 130

Sampler, Sarah Ellen Johnson, 1851, colorful (A-E) 160

Sampler, Lempster, NH, 1811, several multicolor alphabets, nice edge, 20"×14", framed, fine branches at top, motto at bottom (D-NE) 115

Sampler, Betsy Needhan, born 1781, framed (D-NE) 115

Sampler, by Miss Pingst, age ten years old, Peoria, Ill., May 7, 1866, 19th C., 16"×25" overall (A-MW) 225

Sampler, Rachel Rinsey, 1829, colorful (A-E) 200

Sampler, several black alphabets, nice border, baskets of flowers w/blackbirds, framed, 1826, 17½"×13½" (D-NE) 85

Sampler, Mary Shipman, 1789, colorful (A-E) 145

Sampler, signed & dated 1842, linen (D-MW) 155

Pictorial sampler,
dated 1838
(D-E) $300

Sampler, linen & wool, 15¼ × 21" (D-MW) $135

Sampler, Margaret L. Smith, dated 1854 (D-NE) 155

Sampler, square, just alphabet done in black on tan linen, framed, no date or signature, early (D-NE) 25

Sampler, strawberry edge, baskets, several multicolor alphabets, good color, no date, but ca. 1810, framed, 19"×19½" (D-NE) 125

Sampler, Emily T. Ward, dated 1825 (A-E) 75

Sampler, Sarah Ward, dated 1826 (A-E) 75

Sampler, Mally Wolfenden, 1840, "birds, lamb, house, butterflys & girl," 28"×32" (A-E) 200

Sampler, Sarah Wood, age 13, 1784, American needlework, "Garden of Eden," orig. frame, 13½"×12¼" (A-NE) 2100

Sampler, Isabella Young, dated 1843, ex. color (D-NE) 120

Sampler, Madge Young, age 12 years old, 19th C., 20"×18" (A-MW) 175

Shaker Collectibles

The Shaker movement in America began in 1774 when Mother Ann Lee, an untutored English textile worker, arrived in this country with a small group of ardent followers. By the time of the Civil War, membership in "The United Society Of Believers In Christ's Second Appearing" had increased to 8,000 brothers and sisters living in 18 communities from Maine to Ohio. Deliberately withdrawing from the world around them, the members of this inspired religious communal sect have left us a heritage of simplicity and beauty in their furniture, architecture and life-style which is wholly without parallel in American history.

Shaker furniture is a major creative force in our decorative arts heritage because it is the only truly original American style of furniture. Harmony and quiet simplicity came naturally to the Shaker craftsman. His single-minded ambition was to produce works of the highest quality with the best materials to be found. He looked on the building of a chest, table or chair as a divinely inspired enterprise, tempered by functional need which would contribute to the good of his entire community. An artist in the truest sense, his goal was total perfection, nothing less.

In furniture, as in every other Shaker craft, the result was a unique contribution to our American heritage which is now being appreciated at its true value. The word "Shaker" has become a magic term to collectors, nowadays. Auctions attract this group, as well as the museum representatives, and their frenzied bidding has driven prices upward until many new heights have been realized for Shaker items during recent years.

Since the "discovery" of Shaker design during the late 1920s, a number of American museums have amassed distinguished collections of the sect's furniture and other artifacts. Two such collections are housed in former Shaker communities which are now being restored and operated as "outdoor" museums where the Shakers' arts and crafts may be seen in their native surroundings. These are Hancock Shaker Village, 5 miles west of Pittsfield, Massachusetts (open daily June 1 though October 15), and Shakertown at Pleasant Hill, 25 miles southwest of Lexington, Kentucky, open daily year-round.

Until recent years, no reproductions of Shaker furniture existed; but, in order to meet the growing demand for Shaker items, workshops have been established. The Guild Of Shaker Crafts, Spring Lake, Michigan, as well as Shaker Workshops, Inc., Concord, Massachusetts and #5 Ross Common, Ross, California, produce many fine items.

* * *

Armchair, ladder back, 4-slat w/rush seat, early New England style (D-E)	$ 300
Bag, flour, Shaker Mills (D-E)	200
Basket, garden, handled, round (D-E)	80
Basket, laundry, 28"×15"×14" (D-E)	125
Basket, laundry, w/handle, 13"×18"×9" (D-E)	55
Basket, notched handle, splint, 8½" (D-NE)	22
Basket, rectangular, splint, handle over top, green paint, 11"×16" (D-E)	22
Basket, sewing, marked "Sabbathday Lake" (A-E)	50
Basket, sewing, small, oval (D-E)	95

Basket, signed "S. Fisk," top handle, tight weave, 11" diam. × 8" (D-NE) ....$ 45
Basket, stationary handle, darkened splint, 11" diam. (D-E)..   35
Basket, sugar, good cond. (D-E)   60
Basket, swing handle, darkened splint, 13"×8½" (D-E)   45
Basket, top handle, open work, reinforced bottom, 11" diam. × 8" (D-NE)   34
Basket, top handle, tight weave, 9½" diam. × 7" (D-NE)   32
Basket, 2-handled, 26"×13" (D-S)...   110
Basket, 2-handled, 24" diam., 14" h. (D-SE)   200
Basket, 2-handled, ex. cond., 24" diam. (D-MW)...   90
Basket, 2-handled, splint, approx. 30" diam. (D-NE)...   225
Bed, rope, maple, cast iron & maple pegged feet, painted green (A-E)................................   200

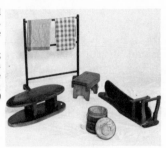

Shaker objects (A-E): **towel rack,** black finish, $105; **fabric,** hand-loomed, brown and white checked, 68" × 47" and 40" × 16½", $110; *left:* **wooden ironing sleeve,** $125; *center, top:* **wagon stool,** $45; *center,* **apple sauce firkin,** $120; *right,* **pressing board,** 22¾" l., $90

Shaker Objects (A-E): **Table** w/2 drawers, $425; **basket,** round, w/handle, $70; **funnel holder,** wooden, to fill bottles, $105; **swift,** maple, Hancock, w/table clamp, $170; **basket,** covered, signed Denison, $85

Candle dryer, Shaker, holds 30 candles (A-E) $400

Bed, rope, maple, painted green w/cast-iron & maple-pegged feet (D-MW)   180
Bed, pine w/detachable headboard & 4 detachable legs w/wooden wheels, 26" h., 66" l., 30" w. (A-E)   625
Bonnet mold, doll's w/bonnet (D-E)   60
Bonnet, splint, hand woven (D-E)..   60
Bonnet, straw, black & white (D-NE) ....$ 34
Box, cheese, interlapped, dk. blue, round, 14½" (D-NE)   40
Box, cheese, interwoven v-lap, unpainted, 14½"×7" (D-NE)   65
Box, document, dov. const., painted red (A-E)   115
Box, fingered, cherry, oval, w/cover (D-E)   115
Box, fingered, covered, oval, red paint, 6½"×9" (A-E)   90
Box, fingered, large, oval (D-E)   180
Box, fingered, oval, orig. red paint (D-E)   100
Box, herb, w/copper tacks, oval & open, straight lap, handplaned bottom, 12½"×7¼"×2¾" (D-NE)   35
Box, knife polishing, pine, primitive (D-E)..   100
Box, polishing, for knives, primitive (D-E)   100
Box, seed, 5 dividers (D-NE)..   60

Box, sewing (D-NE)	$ 35
Box, sewing, primitive, Sabbath Day Lake (D-E)	165
Box, wooden, covered, 2 fingers, copper rivets, 2¼"×3¼" (D-NE)...	32
Box, writing, side drawer & ink drawer (D-MW)	100
Box, sewing, blanket chest style (A-E)	275
Boxes, wood, 19th c., (4), circular & oval, one w/swing handle (A-MW)	150
Bread lifter, 2-pronged (D-E)	15
Brush, clothes, 5" l. (D-E)	25
Bucket, sap, tin, 9"×11" (D-NE)	30
Bucket, wood, bail handle (D-NE)	40
Bucket, wood, swing handles, 19th C., 9½" diam. (A-MW)............	45
Buckets, w/hoop handles, each 9½" diam., 19th C., pr. (A-MW)	110
Calendar, in wooden frame (D-E)	150
Can, spice, tin, round w/cover, small (D-E)	40
Carrier, oval, handled, 8"×10" (D-E)	120
Chair, rocker, mushroom arms, 4 slats, shawl rod at top of back (A-E)..............	175
Chair, rocker, mushroom arms & spindle back (A-E)	135
Chair, rocker, no. 3, pine, orig. cond. fine (D-MW).........................	175
Chair, rocker, no. 7 (A-E)...	450
Chair, rocker, no. 7, refinished (D-E)	400
Chair, rocker, shawl rod, orig. cond., label, no. 5 (D-MW)	225
Chair, rocker, tape seat & back, mushroom arms (D-E)	265
Chair, rocker, side, early, size 3 (D-MW)	175
Chair, sewing, rocker, shawl bar w/low seat in old rush (D-MW)	225
Chair, shawl bar (D-E)	225
Chairs, prayer, set of 4, ladder back (A-MW)	120
Chest, apothecary, w/plain wooden knobs, 24 drawers, refinished, 5' h., 36" w. (D-SE)..........	600
Chest, blanket, walnut (D-E)...	400
Chest, storage, 21-drawer, top w/4 reverse paneled cupboard doors all above 3 rows of 7 drawers, red stained, 82" h., 104" l., 18" d. (A-E)............	3750
Child's armchair, size 0, orig. finish (D-MW)...............................	295
Child's chair, rocker, no. 1, signed (D-MW)................................	185
Child's highchair, refinished (D-E)	500
Child's chair, rocker, no. 1, signed (D-MW)................................	185
Child's chair, rocker, no. 1, signed, refinished (D-E)	185
Churn, butter, w/handle, dasher, 21½" t. (D-NE)	525
Cider press, large, 53" h. (D-MW)	60
Clamp, leather maker's w/turnscrew device, maple (A-E)	65

Canterbury chest, Shaker, early, 28" h., 26" w., 15½" d. (A-E) $475

Churn, Shaker, early wooden, orig. red paint, 27" h. (A-E) $250

Coffeepot, large, tin, bail handle, copper bottom, 16″ t., base 17″ (D-NE) ....$ 135
Counter, 6-drawer, red-stain, cond. fair (D-MW) 275
Cradle, mortised slats & paneled sides, turned legs w/detachable rockers, old red paint, 42″ l.,
   18½″ w. (exclusive of rockers), 28½″ h. (A-E) 195
Cupboard, dough, oak, storage bins, roll top w/slide out board, dated 1888 (A-NE)............... 350
Cupboard, paneled, 2-door, orig. mustard paint (D-MW) 1800
Cupboard, pine, 2-door, 94″ h. (A-E) 800
Cupboard, pine, 2-door, 94″ h. (D-E) 800
Cupboard, setback, top w/2 doors, 2 drawers; bottom w/2 doors (D-E) 1650
Cupboard, setback, 2 doors & 2 drawers on top, 2 drawers & 2 doors on bottom (D-NE)........ 1650
Cupboard, weaver's cabinet, pine, 4-drawer base w/cupboard top w/1 narrow door (D-MW) .. 775
Dipper, tin (D-MW).. 22
Dipper, tin w/long handle (A-E) 75
Dustpan, tin, handmade, some pinholes, 14½″ w. (D-NE) .... 10.
Foot warmer, pine frame, pierced, red paint (D-MW) 60
Funnel, tin, w/strainer inside, 5″ (D-E) 8
Hanger, coat, handled, 40″ l. (D-NE) 35
Hanger, clothes, hangs w/ribbon (D-NE) 18
Hanger, clothes, on flat piece wood, curved wire hanging hook (D-NE)............................ 24
Hanger, dress, initialed (D-MW) 45
Herb masher, 4″ diam. head (D-E) 35
Lamp filler, side spout, 6½″ (D-NE) 38
Lamp filler, tin, 5½″ (D-NE) 35
Lamp filler, tin, side pour, 5¾″ (D-SE) 38
Lamp filler, tin, side spout (D-MW)... 30
Lamp, privy, tin, double-drop whale oil burner & screw top, 9¼″ l. (D-E) 90
Lap board, pine w/breadboard ends (D-NE) 130
Loom, dated 1775 (D-E) 250
Loom, maple & cherry, signed, 3′ h., 17″ w. 3″ l. (D-E)... 200
Masher, wooden, mushroom shape, yellow stain, 7″ l. (D-NE)...................................... 22
Measure, round, tin, 5¾″×3½″ (D-E) 25
Measure, round, wood, 5¾″×3½″ (A-E) 35
Mortar & pestle, small (D-MW) 65
Needlecase, bronze leather (D-W) 19
Pail, berry (growler), 6″ diam., 8″ tall (D-NE) 12
Pail, tin, covered & handled, 6″×8″ (D-E)... 10
Peg rail, 3 pegs (D-E) 25
Peg rail, pine, 11 cherry pegs, turned up ends, 45″ l. (D-MW) 75
Pincushion & thread holder, pedestal, w/attached needle holder, 5¾″ tall × 5″ base (D-E) 65
Press, cider, 53″ h. (D-MW).. 60
Press, napkin, maple, 11¼″ h. (D-N).. 85
Rack, drying (A-E) 55
Rack, drying, wooden w/openwork, 1″ splint-like woven top of pressed paper, rare, 17″×19″
   (D-NE) 45
Ruler, 6″ (D-E) 20
Scarn, hanging, 12 spools in 2 rows (D-MW)... 80
Scarn, hanging, 12 spools in 2 rows (D-MW)... 90
Scoop, apple butter, pine, large (D-W) 65
Sieve, hair, 4″ diam. (A-E) 25
Sieve, horsehair, 4½″ (D-NE) 45
Sieve, tallow, ex. cond., wooden rim put together w/iron staples, teardrop shape, 16″ l. (D-NE) 65
Sled, for carrying wood (D-E) 40
Sleeveboard, 22″ l. (A-E)... 52
Spice box, wood, 9-drawer, wooden pulls, orig. finish good (D-E) 390
Spice box, 9-drawer, wooden pulls, refinished (D-E) 390
Spinning wheel, large (D-NE) 375
Spool holder, maple (D-E) 40
Stove, with penny feet (D-E) 400
String holder, open work, fine weave, 2-pc., 4″ diam. (D-NE) 15

Chair, Shaker, ladder back, w/wheels on legs (A-E) $525

Rocker, Shaker, Union Village, 43″ h. (A-E) $425

Side chairs, Shaker, 2 from set of 5, all (A-E) $350

Rocker, Shaker, Hancock, early 1800s, 43½″ h. (A-E) $450

Swift, Hancock, old yellow paint (D-E)	$ 180
Table, syrup, large, label 65 (D-NE)	65
Table, tailoress's, maple, sewing cabinet w/drawer & legs, orig. finish (D-E)	450
Table, work, old red stain (D-E)	385
Table, work, orig. red stain (D-NW)	385
Table, work, pine & cherry, spider legs, 1 drawer, round (D-E)	600
Table, work, tailoress's, large, 1 drop leaf, wood knobs, 8 drawers (D-E)	490
Tailor's square, wood, 14½″×9½″ (D-E)	75
Teapot, tin, handled, 6″ h. (A-E)	80
Teapot, tin, handled, 6¾″ h. (A-E)	90
Tub, washing, wood w/handles (D-E)	110
Washstand, pine w/high splashboard & 3 graduating drawers, orig. finish good (D-MW)	450
Woodbox, w/drawer, pine, legs part of sides, 40″ h., orig. finish (D-MW)	275
Yarn swift, ochre (D-NE)	45

Soapstone

Soapstone is a soft rock having a bluish-gray smooth appearance that not only feels slick to the touch, but actually resembles soap. It is from these characteristics that it derives its name. Soapstone is a very durable mineral that is heat-resistant, nonabsorbent, and takes a high polish.

Large amounts of soapstone existed in the coastal regions of our country during the early years. The colonists quickly learned that pieces could easily be turned on the lathe, or cut with saws and knives. As a result, a variety of useful objects were produced, including pans, kettles, lamps, inkwells, foot warmers, as well as egg-shaped hand warmers, boot warmers, stoves, round and oblong griddles. Also, there were a few novelty items which are of much interest to collectors of this ware.

* * *

Bootwarmer, soapstone (D-E) $29

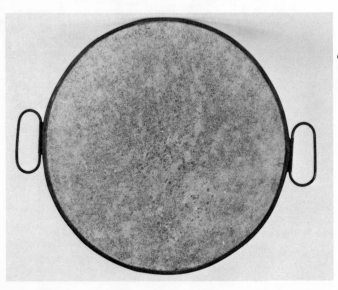

Griddle, soapstone, set in metal frame, 12″ diam. (D-MW) $22

Boot warmer, early, mint (D-W) ....$ 18
Foot warmer, w/wooden case & bail handle (D-E)   80
Griddle, oblong, 10″×15″ (D-W)   20
Mortar & pestle, w/wooden handle (D-E)..   80
Trivet, round (D-MW)..   12
Flatiron, Hood's patent, New Hampshire, soapstone worn, ca. 1867 (A-E)............................   55

Spatterware

Spatterware is a very colorful tableware, laboriously decorated with hand-drawn birds, buildings, flowers, etc., with "spatter" decoration chiefly as a background. It was produced by practically every export potter in Staffordshire, Scotland and Wales, especially for the American market. Very few pieces were marked. A variety of patterns were produced in considerable quantity from the early years of the last century up until around 1850. Although much of this ware was sent to New England and various points farther south, to this day spatterware, like Gaudy Dutch and Gaudy Welsh, is regarded everywhere as being characteristically "Pennsylvania Dutch," because of its popularity among the German settlers in that state.

The term "spatter" describes the effect achieved, rather than the actual technique used, in decorating this type tableware. The "spattering" was done with either a sponge or a brush containing a moderate supply of the liquid color, which was tapped repeatedly against the piece to be decorated. The spattered paint was either applied to the border, to the center, or completely covered the surface.

A great variety of designs and colors, or color combinations, were produced. The most popular pieces are those having a spatter border combined with a freehand center design, such as the widely collected Peafowl, Schoolhouse or Rose patterns. Yellow spatter examples are considered to be the rarest of all, followed by green, pink, red and blue. Purple, brown and black decorated pieces exist.

Stick-spatter is another type decoration that combines hand painting and transfer-painted bands in addition to "stick-spatter." This tableware was produced from the 1850s to the end of the last century. It was developed from the traditional Staffordshire spatterware previously described. Because this ware was very time-consuming and expensive to produce, manufacturers turned to an

Spatterware (A-E), *top row, left to right:* **creamer,** hexagonal, blue spatter, Rose pattern, 4½" h., $250; **plate,** red spatter, tulip center, 10½" diam., $275; **sugar bowl,** blue spatter, peafowl design, $150; *bottom row:* **plate,** deep, small, red spatter, w/peafowl, $200; **2 cups & matching saucers,** yellow spatter, Thistle pattern, $450; **toddy plate,** rainbow spatter, 5" diam. $190

easier process which greatly simplified production, in order to combat the efforts of competitors.

This type decoration is achieved by the use of small bits of sponge cut into different shapes such as leaves, hearts, rosettes, roses, vines or geometrical patterns. The sponge was mounted on the end of a short stick for convenience in dipping into the pigment. As the years passed, in order to meet the demands of a rapidly increasing population, it is not surprising that patterns themselves became simpler with transfer-painted bands or centers becoming part of the type decoration.

The colors used to produce this ware follow those of the traditional spatter, with blue and red predominating; but yellow is almost a rarity.

Although the majority of stick-spatter was produced in England, it was also imported from the Continent and made by some American manufacturers. Therefore, it is rather difficult to attribute an example to a particular manufacturer unless it is marked. Oftentimes American manufacturers included a pattern name in their mark on certain pieces. Marks found on English products include those of J. & G. Meakin Ltd.; W. Baker & Co. Ltd.; Elsmore & Forster; George Jones; and Malkin & Co. Ltd. Names were given to only a few of the English patterns at the time they were made. An example is the name "Virginia" which was used on a late English pattern decorated with bands or centers showing rabbits at play.

During recent years, Weaver's Ceramic Mold Company of New Holland, Pennsylvania has produced a variety of early Staffordshire forms, many of which have been decorated for display purposes by Mary E. Weaver. These colorful examples of new spatterware can occasionally be purchased from the firm. All pieces are marked with the impressed initials "M.E.W."

* * *

Creamer, rainbow, decor. w/wide bands of deep purple & blue vertically around body, 4½" globose helmet-shape (D-E) ....$ 95

Creamer, rainbow, pink & blue, octagonal, 6" (D-E) 120

Creamer, rose pattern, blue, hexagonal (A-E) 250

Creamer, schoolhouse pattern, primitive (A-E) 75

Cup, peafowl pattern, blue (A-E).. 32

Cup, peafowl pattern, overall purple (A-E)... 140

Cup plate, peafowl center, red, 4" d. (A-E)... 225

Cup & saucer, acorn, deep red spatter (A-E) 220

Cup & saucer, acorn, lavender (D-E) 130

Cup & saucer, Adams rose center, brown & black (D-W) 55

Cup & saucer, Adams rose center, purple (D-E) 125

Cup & saucer, Adams rose center, red & blue rainbow decor. (D-S) 100

Cup & saucer, the apple tree pattern, stamped by Meyer (A-E)... 2200

Cup & saucer, black cannon pattern, rare (D-NE).. 350

Cup & saucer, button center, red edge spatter (D-E).. 135

Cup & saucer, peafowl center & green leaves, plain white (D-E) 145

Cup & saucer, peafowl center, blue edge (D-E)... 190

Cup & saucer, peafowl center, green (A-E) 160

Cup & saucer, peafowl center, green (D-E)... 150

Cup & saucer, peafowl center, green (D-MW)... 110

Cup & saucer, peafowl center, green border (D-NE) 135

Cup & saucer, peafowl center, pink (A-E)... 90

Cup & saucer, peafowl center, red (A-E).. 160

Cup & saucer, peafowl center, red & green rainbow (D-E) 140

Staffordshire chop plate, spatterware, stick spatter border, decal center, 13" diam. (D-MW) $75

Bowl & pitcher, spatterware, blue spatter & Adams Rose decor. (A-E) $525

Cup & saucer, blue spatter, black cannon decor., rare (A-E) $5600

Washbowl & pitcher, spatterware, decor. w/red spatter & 3 peafowl (A-E) $1500

Cup & saucer, pinwheel pattern, large (A-E) ....$	37
Cup & saucer, rainbow, cup plain, saucer decorated (A-E)	125
Cup & saucer, rainbow pattern, blue & green (D-E)	110
Cup & saucer, rainbow pattern, red & blue (A-E)	75
Cup & saucer, rainbow pattern, red & yellow, blue flower w/green leaves (A-E)	325
Cup & saucer, rainbow, 3 wide bands of spatter horizontally around cup & saucer in dk. blue, green & red (D-E)	125
Cup & saucer, rainbow pattern, yellow & black (D-E)..	195
Cup & saucer, rooster pattern, blue, rare (A-E)..	320
Cup & saucer, rose center, pink & green (A-E)	50
Cup & saucer, rose center, rainbow border (A-E)	100
Cup & saucer, rose center, red & blue (A-E)..	275
Cup & saucer, spotted deer pattern, rare mottled pink (A-E)	300
Cup & saucer, sunflower pattern, rare blue & red (D-E)	165
Cup & saucer, thistle center, deep purple (D-E)	150
Cup & saucer, thistle center, yellow (D-E)..	290
Cup & saucer, tulip center, blue (D-E)..	140
Cup & saucer, tulip center, blue & red rainbow border (A-E)	340
Cup & saucer, tulip center, lt. blue (A-E)..	110
Cup & saucer, tulip center, rare purple (A-E)	210
Milk pitcher, rainbow pattern, large (A-E)	460
Muffineer, w/lid, pink/white decor. (D-NE)..	24
Mug, red & blue (A-E)	50
Pitcher, cream, black & brown (D-E)	130
Pitcher, milk, stick/transfer decor., red/blue/green floral w/rabbit border, rare, 8" h. (D-E)	155
Pitcher, rainbow pattern, green, brown, yellow & orange, 7½" t. (D-E)............................	200
Pitcher, water, rainbow, 9½" h. (D-SE)..	275
Pitcher, water, rainbow pattern, age mark in base (D-E)	300
Pitcher, water, shield & eagle center, blue spatter (D-E)..	175
Plate, acorn center, purple edge spatter, octagonal, 9" (D-E)	185
Plate, bread & butter, acorn center, purple, 6" (D-E)..	55
Plate, bread & butter, peafowl center, green, 5¼" (D-E)..	40
Plate, chop, stick/transfer decor., frog & rabbits center, floral border, 13" diam. (D-E)............	145
Plate, eagle center, blue spatter border, 9½" (D-E)	390
Plate, holly berry pattern, blue spatter, 9½" (D-E)..	95
Plate, peafowl center, blue, 6¼" (A-E)	55
Plate, peafowl center, blue, 8¼" (D-E)	70
Plate, peafowl center, blue, 9½" (A-E)	45
Plate, peafowl center, blue spatter edge & center, 7½" (D-E)	90
Plate, peafowl center, green, 8" (D-E)	140
Plate, peafowl center, green, ex. cond., 8¼" (A-E)..	210

Plate, peafowl center, pink, 7½" (A-E)	$ 130
Plate, peafowl center, rare blue, primitive, 9" (D-E)	250
Plate, peafowl center, red, 5" (A-E)	285
Plate, peafowl center, red, 6¾" (A-E)	60
Plate, peafowl center, red, 8½" (D-E)	125
Plate, peafowl center, red, 8½" (D-E)	175
Plate, peafowl center, red, 9¼" (A-E)	105
Plate, peafowl center, red spatter overall, 9¼" (D-E)	195
Plate, rainbow, purple & blue circle center, 9½" (D-E)	90
Plate, rainbow, thistle green leaf center, yellow & red spatter, 9¾" (D-E)	400
Plate, red flower, deep purple spatter, 8¾" (D-E)	150
Plate, red rose, red, blue & green spatter, 9½", ex. cond. (A-E)	145
Plate, schoolhouse center, pink spatter, 6" (D-E)	65
Plate, ship center, red, 8½" (D-E)	130
Plate, star center, lt. blue, 9½" (A-E)	180
Plate, star center, red, 9½" (A-E)	230
Plate, stick spatter, blue & green (D-E)	85
Plate, stick spatter, red & green, 8½" (D-E)	90
Plate, stick/transfer decor., red/blue/green floral border, rabbits & frog center, 9¼" (D-MW)	95
Plate, stick transfer decor., red/blue/green floral border, rabbits in center, 9½" (D-E)	125
Plate, stick/transfer decor., red/blue/green floral center, running rabbit border, clockwise, 9¼" (D-MW)	85
Plate, stick/transfer decor., red/blue/green floral center, running rabbit border, counter clockwise, 9¼" (D-E)	75
Plate, soup, peafowl center, blue overall, 10¼" (D-E)	190
Plate, soup, peafowl center, red, 9" (A-E)	195
Plate, thistle center, blue, 8" (D-E)	75
Plate, thistle center, 6¼" (D-E)	60
Plate, thistle center, yellow & red, 8" (A-E)	500
Plate, tulip center, blue, 9¼" (A-E)	175
Plate, tulip center, red, 10½" (A-E)	275
Saucer, peafowl pattern, deep red spatter, 5¾" (D-E)	65
Saucer, rainbow pattern w/wide vertical bands of deep purple & blue, 6" (D-E)	45
Saucer, red sponge & stick spatter decoration (A-E)	20
Sugar bowl, black & brown (D-E)	150
Sugar bowl, cockscomb pattern, dk. blue, covered, w/footed globular body, 5" h. (D-E)	200
Sugar bowl, drape pattern, w/blue flower, red & yellow spatter (A-E)	55
Sugar bowl, flower & green leaf (A-E)	40
Sugar bowl, green & blue, covered (A-E)	40
Sugar bowl, maroon & blue spatter (D-E)	120
Sugar bowl, peafowl pattern, blue (D-MW)	150
Sugar bowl, peafowl pattern, blue (A-E)	90
Sugar bowl, rainbow, pink & green (D-E)	140
Sugar bowl, sailboat pattern, w/lid, pink, 3½" h. (A-E)	320
Sugar bowl, schoolhouse pattern, blue, open (A-E)	60
Tea set, blue & red overall, incl. teapot & 4 cups & saucers (D-E)	185
Teapot, leaf pattern, green spatter (A-E)	40
Toddy plate, acorn center, blue edge spatter, 5" (D-E)	140
Toddy plate, peafowl center, green, 4" (D-E)	95
Toddy plate, peafowl center, red, yellow tail, ex. cond. (A-E)	160
Toddy plate, rainbow pattern, 5" (A-E)	190
Toddy plate, tulip center, blue edge spatter, 5" (D-E)	145
Tureen, Adams rose, deep blue spatter, covered, 12" (D-E)	175
Vegetable dish, eagle & shield in black transfer, octagonal, blue, 11½" l. (A-E)	225
Vegetable dish, rainbow pattern, blue & maroon, 8½" (D-E)	90
Washbowl, bird & fountain center, deep blue spatter, 13" (D-E)	320
Washbowl & pitcher, opera Adams rose pattern, rare blue spatter (A-E)	525
Washbowl & pitcher, rainbow spatter, red & blue, pitcher handle repaired (D-E)	450
Washbowl & pitcher, 3 peafowl decor., red spatter, rare (A-E)	1500

Spongeware

Spongeware, as it is known, is a decorated white earthenware made by applying the color—usually blue, blue/green, blue/brown, brown/tan/blue—to a white clay base. The object is then bathed in clear alkaline glaze. Because the desired hue was often applied with a color-soaked sponge, the term "spongeware" became common for this ware. Bowls, pitchers, bean pots and cookie jars are the most commonly found pieces, and marked examples are rare. Blue is the most popular color.

* * *

Bowl, blue/gray/buff, 10″ (D-MW) ....\$	35
Bowl, mixing, blue/brown, large (D-E)	28
Bowl, mixing, blue/orange, large (D-N)	45
Bowl, mixing, blue/white, 8″ (D-E)...	32
Bowl, mixing, blue/white, 10″ (D-W)...	48
Bowl, mixing, blue/white, 12″ (D-E)	38
Bowl, mixing, blue/white, 12″ (D-MW)	55
Bowl, mixing, blue/white, banded, 2 qt. (D-MW)	38
Bowl, yellow/green, 10″ d., 3½″ h. (D-MW)...	38
Bowl & pitcher set, blue/white (D-E)...	175
Bowl & pitcher set, blue/white, gold trim (D-W)...	90
Butter crock w/cover, brown/green/yellow, 5″ d. (D-MW)...................................	85
Butter tub, blue/white, 9½″×6¼″ (D-NE)...	48
Butter tub, blue/white, large open w/"butter" embossed on side (D-E)................	80
Cookie jar, blue/brown/buff, w/orig. cover, 12½″ h. (D-MW)	32
Cookie jar, blue/brown/gray, w/cover (D-S)	45

Pitcher, spongeware, multicolored (D-NE) $65

Dinner plate, blue & white spongeware (D-NE) $90

Blue & white, spongeware (D-MW), *left to right:* **pitcher,** marked UHL, $90; **crock w/bail,** $38; **bean pot,** $65; **pitcher,** $75

Blue & white spongeware (D-MW), *left to right:* **milk pitcher,** 7½″ h., $85; **water pitcher,** banded, 8¾″ h., $70; **water pitcher,** tankard, 9¼″ h., $80; **pitcher,** jug-shaped, 9″ h., $65

Bowl, covered, blue & white spongeware (D-NE) $150

Mush bowl & saucer, blue & white spongeware (D-NE) $185

Cup & saucer, blue & white spongeware (D-NE) $175

Cover, blue/white, for tin dough riser, 18″ diam. (D-W)	$ 22
Cup & saucer, blue/white (D-N)	28
Cuspidor, blue/white (D-N)	58
Cuspidor, blue/white (D-W)	75
Cuspidor, black/white, 5½″ h., 7¼″ d. (D-MW)	75
Grease tub, blue/white, w/pouring spout, wire handle, wood grip, 4″ h. (D-MW)	55
Jugs, blue/brown/white, matched pair (A-MW)	135
Pitcher, blue/white, bulbous, mkd. "UHL Pottery Co.," 8″ h. (D-MW)	95
Pitcher, blue/white, sponged hearts, tankard shape, 8″ h. (D-MW)	85
Pitcher, blue/white, squatty (D-W)	50
Pitcher, blue/white, tankard, 8″ h. (D-SW)	48
Pitcher, blue/white, tankard, 8½″ h. (D-MW)	65
Pitcher, blue/white, tankard shape, sponged arrows, 8″ h. (D-MW)	90
Pitcher, blue/white, tankard, sponged circles, 9″ h. (D-N)	69
Pitcher, milk, brown/buff (D-MW)	18
Pitcher, water, blue/white, 2 1″ white bands (D-NW)	22
Pitcher, blue/white, white banded center 4″ w., w/embossed blue flower on each side, 8½″ h. (D-S)	65
Pitcher, brown/green on buff ground, shaped & molded like keg (D-MW)	32
Plate, blue/white, 9″ (D-MW)	38
Plate, blue/white, 7″ (D-MW)	32
Platter, blue/white, oval, 13″ l. (D-S)	75
Salt crock, w/cover, blue/white, 9″ h. (D-MW)	90
Teapot, brown/green on buff ground (D-S)	12
Vegetable dish, blue/white, oval (D-MW)	75
Vegetable dish, blue/white, round (D-W)	65

Stoneware

Stoneware is another type of country pottery that swung into prominence during the last decade. Its production in America got underway around the mid 1700s and, because of its popularity, it was mass produced until the waning years of the last century.

Stoneware is a weighty, durable, dense pottery made from clay mixed with flint or sand, or made from very siliceous clay that vitrifies when heated to form a nonporous base. The common household vessels were glazed inside and/or outside to prevent porosity and resist chemical action. Most of the ware produced is salt-glazed. To produce this type of glaze, common table salt was heated and then thrown into the ware-filled kiln when firing was at the maximum temperature. The intense heat caused the salt to vaporize instantly, covering the objects with a clear, thin glaze; hence the term "salt-glaze" Quite frequently, the salt particles hit the vessels before being transformed into vapor, creating a pitted or pebbly surface on the stoneware.

When not salt-glazed, stoneware was coated with a slip glaze—often referred to as brown "Albany or Texas-slip"—which consisted of a mixture of rare clay mixed with water and, when applied as a finish, the mixture would fuse into a natural smooth glaze at certain firing temperatures.

Prior to 1850, stoneware crocks and jugs were thrown in an ovoid or egg-shaped form. Classic and graceful, these vessels are far more appealing than the later straight-sided objects which were either molded or formed in a semi-mechanical manner.

Fancy stoneware (A-NE), *top row, left to right:* **jug,** pear-shaped, marked Lyman & Clark, Gardiner, Maine, w/umber flower decor., 4-gal., 16" h., $375; **crock,** w/basket of flowers, by J & E Norton, Bennington, Vermont, 6-gal., $300; **crock,** double spotted deer decor. in blue, by J & E Norton, Bennington, Vermont, cracked w/flaking, $400; **jug,** marked Lyman & Clark, Gardiner, Maine, 2-gal., 13" h., $425; *bottom row, left to right:* **jug,** blue peacock decor., by J & E Norton, Bennington, Vermont, 3-gal., $250; **jug,** decor. in cobalt blue, very large primitive snowflakes, cracked, 16" h., $250; **crock,** bluebird on limb decor., by J & E Norton, Bennington, Vermont, 4-gal., $150

A century ago, country housewives stored, salted, and pickled much of their food in the heavy stoneware vessels. To brighten their tasks, they often chose fanciful, decorated containers that showed a craftsman's individuality. Subjects—usually in cobalt-blue, but occasionally in brown—included birds, fish, animals, insects, a human profile or figure, a patriotic symbol, quaint landscape scenes, or flowers and leaves.

The very earliest stoneware was plain and unadorned but, by the turn of the nineteenth century, potters were using splashes of cobalt blue at the handles to decorate the gray and tan jugs and crocks. Gradually, their first squiggles evolved into the highly sophisticated freehand figures of the mid-1850s and '60s, then to the usage of stenciled patterns as interest declined. And, by the last quarter of the century, few potters were using any decoration at all.

The most interesting decorative work was done in the Midwest and the northeastern areas, but any decorated object that can be attributed to a southern or western pottery is considered a rarity.

Interest in stoneware today is not in its beautiful forms or colors, but in its decoration, the maker's name, location, and in rare instances a date, painted or incised into the clay. As a general rule, the more cobalt blue decoration, the higher the price.

There is a vast quantity of mediocre unmarked, undecorated or sparsely decorated stoneware still available to the collector. For the most part, prices for these pieces have stabilized during the past year, but values for the fanciful, decorated vessels continue to increase, forcing the serious collector to be more discriminating.

Although stoneware is still being produced and used in several regions in our country, it is easily distinguished from the earlier examples because of its color, form, and decoration. However, many new, decorative stoneware imports have come on the market in recent years. To the novice, who isn't aware of their existence, these spurious pieces look very convincing when placed alongside authentic examples. The new objects examined by the writer have a very bluish-gray surface color, sparsely decorated with cobalt designs. Moreover, they are lightweight, unmarked, and rarely show any signs of wear because of their hard texture.

* * *

Bed warmer, w/iron bail (D-E)..$	35
Bottle, ale, brown glaze (D-NE)..	12
Bottle, ale, marked in blue (D-NE)..	10
Bottle, ale, ochre blended tan glaze (D-NE)..	10
Bottle, beer, deep blue neck & top, marked, 10″ (D-E)	18
Bottle, beer, donut top, blue (D-E)...	14
Bottle, beer, marked in lg. blue letters, "J Devine" (D-E)	16
Bottle, beer, neck and top blue (D-NE)...	16
Bottle, blue on top, 10¼″ (D-NE)..	10
Bottle, blue-gray, dated 1874 (D-E)	50
Bottle, brownish/tan glaze, marked "Day", 10″ (D-NE)	10
Bottle, ink, shaded ochre glaze, marked "H. R. Clark," 7″ (D-E)	18
Bottle, old gold glaze, marked, 10″ (D-NE)	10
Bottle, signed "O. Tinkham," dated 1847 (D-E)	45
Bottle, stamped in blue, marked "A. L. Walker," 10″ (D-NE)................................	10

Bowl, Albany slip glazed, A. L. Hyssong, Pa., 11½" diam., 6" d. (D-NE) ....$ 55
Bowl, punched through to make strainer, glazed inside gray, outside red/brown, incised decor.,
8"×4½" (D-E)   48
Box, salt, gray-blue underglaze, round hole for hanging (D-E)...   18
Box, salt, hanging, gray, w/blue decor. (D-MW)   18
Butter tub, blue sponge decor., no cover, 9"×6½" (D-NE)   48
Churn, blue slip decor., handled, 19th C., 7¼" h. (A-MW)...   50
Churn, C. Boynton, Troy, cobalt blue flower decor., ca. 1829, 3 gal., 15" h., ovoid shape (D-E) ..   100
Churn, cobalt blue flowers w/leaves, unmarked, ca. 1850, ovoid, 3 gal. (D-MW)....................   75
Churn, Sam'l. Irvine, Newville, Pa., decor. (A-E)   175
Churn, quill lines on bands, mark whites, Utica, N. Y., 3 gal. (D-E)................................   125
Churn, syllabub, brown, complete, rare (D-E)   160
Churn, syllabub, N. Y. S., brown glaze, 8" t. (D-E)   225
Churn, whites Utica, N. Y., 3 cobalt blue bands & quill lines, ca. 1865, 3 gal., 15" h. ovoid
(D-MW)   120
Crock, barrel shape, dk. glaze w/rings (D-E)..   18
Crock, blue, bird decor. (A-E)   80
Crock, bird, Fulper Bros., N. J. (A-E)   85
Crock, bird on a trunk, eared, 2-gal. (D-NE)   90
Crock, blue bird decor. (A-N)   57
Crock, blue, bird decor., marked "Reidinger & Caire, Poukeepsie, N. Y." (A-E)   115
Crock, blue bird, handle, unsigned, 1½-gal. (D-NE)   45
Crock, blue color portrait & trees, rare (A-E)   900
Crock, blue decor., 20-gal. (A-E)..   25
Crock, blue decor., double handled (D-S)   65
Crock, blue decor., handled, 9" (A-E)   45
Crock, blue eagle stencil decor., Penna., 11½" (D-E)   100
Crock, blue, floral decor. (A-E)..   42
Crock, blue, floral decor. (A-E)..   22
Crock, blue, floral decor. (A-MW)..   35
Crock, blue, leaf decor. (A-E)...   27

Stoneware (A-E), top row, *left to right:* **jar,**
tulip decor., signed Hamilton Beaver,
6-gal., $55; **crock,** 3 incised eagles
w/banners in blue, 6-gal., $25; **jar,** ovoid,
primitive tulip decor., signed T. Reed,
4-gal., $95; *second row, left to right:* **crock,**
decor. w/squiggles & grapes, 3-gal., $55;
jar, floral sprig decor., signed Campbell,
Penn Yan, hairline crack, 1-gal. $40; **crock,**
floral decor., $45; *third row, left to right:*
crock, poorly stenciled eagle, 2-gal., $20;
jug, stoneware, hole for spigot, decor.
w/cobalt blue bird, marked S. Hart, Fulton
& L. A. Griffin. Oswego Center, N. Y.,
$40; **jar,** ovoid, w/lid, signed I. M. Meade
& Co., $55; *fourth row, left to right:* **jug,**
stenciled Alderman & Scott, Belpre, Ohio,
2-gal., $65; **crock,** single bird decor.,
4-gal., $40; *fifth row, left to right:* **crock,**
double tulip decor., hairline crack, 5-gal.,
$55; **churn,** marked "6", single flower &
leaves, 6-gal., $75; **jar,** tulip & garland,
chip on lip, 4-gal., $50

Crock, blue slip, decor., blue branches, dated 1880, small (A-E).................................$ 50
Crock, blue slip decor., handled, 19th C., 3-gal., 10¼" h. (A-MW)   55
Crock, J. Boynton, eared, ovoid, cobalt blue decor. w/tree, 4-gal., 14¾" t. (D-NE)   350
Crock, bronze salt glaze, American eagle w/banner "E Pluribus Unum", arrows & olive branch in
    claws, 3-gal., 11" h. (D-E)   750
Crock, brown glaze, signed E. E. Wallace, "choicest butter." (D-MW)   10
Crock, bulbous, decor. w/cobalt garlands of tulips, 4-gal. (D-E)   195
Crock, bulbous eared, deep cobalt scrolls sym. design, signed "H. Weston, Honesdale, Pa.,"
    4-gal. (D-E)   60
Crock, bulbous, floral decor., blue (A-E)..   42
Crock, bulbous, open, signed "From Hamilton & Jones, Greensboro, Pa.," cobalt slip heavy
    swags, 2-gal. (D-E)   68
Crock, butter, blue decor., large (A-E)   35
Crock, butter, covered, embossed sides, heavily glazed blue, 7"×5" (D-E)   22
Crock, butter, lidded, large, decor., 14" (A-E)   100
Crock, J. B. Caire & Co., N. Y.-potters, cobalt blue decor. w/2 stemmed flowers, eared, ovoid,
    2-gal., 9½" t. (D-NE)   65
Crock, cobalt blue decor. of bird standing on tree stump w/bushes, 2-gal. (D-MW)   75
Crock, cobalt blue double bird, mkd. S. Hart Fulton, ca. 1840 (D-MW)   135
Crock, cobalt blue decor., flower, eared, ovoid, 2-gal. 11½" t. (D-NE)   600
Crock, cobalt blue 5-pointed star decor., eared, semi-ovoid, 4-gal., 11" t. (D-NE)   200
Crock, cobalt floral decor. (D-E)...   175
Crock, cobalt blue peafowl decor., no ears, ca. 1820, 3-gal., 14" h. ovoid (D-E)..................   350
Crock, cobalt blue pecking chicken, 4-gal., 11¾" h. (D-MW)   90
Crock, cobalt decor., signed "Goodwin & Webster," ovoid, 2-gal. (D-E)   250
Crock, cobalt design, floral (D-E)..   45
Crock, Cowden & Wilcox, Harrisburg, Pa., cobalt blue feather-like decor., 1½-gal., 9" h. (D-E)   45
Crock, decor., bulbous, marked "I. G. Nash, Utica" (A-E)   50
Crock, daisy cobalt blue decor., ovoid w/ears, ca. 1800, 3-gal., 13¼" h. (D-E)   125
Crock, decor. w/3 2" t. impressed swans stroked w/cobalt blue, 4-gal., 11½" t. (D-NE)   65
Crock, eared, semi-ovoid, cobalt blue brushed flowers w/leaves, brown-orange salt glaze,
    2-gal., 11" t. (D-NE)   90
Crock, encircling cobalt design, ovoid, 4-gal. (D-E)   60
Crock, floral decor., 2-gal. (D-E)   40
Crock, Goodwin & Webster, ovoid, eared, cobalt trim, ca. 1810 (D-E)   90
Crock, gray w/leafy design in blue, 2-gal. (D-E)   70
Crock, Harrington & Burger, floral decor., 2-gal. (D-E)   22
Crock, C. Hart, Potters, cobalt blue oak leaf decor., ovoid, 1-gal., 8" t. (D-NE)..................   60
Crock, S. Hart & Fulton, sylized birds, 6-gal. (A-E)...   100
Crock, lion, eagle, full spread, 2-gal. (D-E)..   350
Crock, med. brown glaze w/dk. brown speckles & smears, small, 6½"×6" (D-E)....................   18
Crock, H & G Nash, Utica, cobalt blue, eared, ovoid, 8¼" t., ca. 1832, 2-gal. (D-E)   70
Crock, J & E Norton, Bennington, Vt., basket of flowers decor., 6-gal. (A-NE)   300
Crock, J & E Norton, Bennington, Vt., bird on limb decor., 4-gal. (A-NE)............................   150
Crock, J & E Norton, Bennington, Vt., cobalt blue farm scene w/house/trees/fence, 2-gal. (D-E) .   1200
Crock, J & E Norton, Bennington, Vt., double spotted deer decor., 4-gal. (A-NE)..................   400
Crock, J. Norton Co., Potters, cobalt blue floral decor., ovoid, 4-gal., 13½" t. (D-NE)   175
Crock, Norton & Son, umber decor., 11" d. (D-E)..   200
Crock, ovoid, eared, cobalt blue incised leaves & branch, ca. 1800, 9½" h. (D-E)..................   500
Crock, ovoid, eared, double wreath, N.Y.S., ca. 1830, 2-gal. (D-E)   60
Crock, ovoid, scant blue decor. (A-E)...   40
Crock, W. Roberts, Binghamton N.Y., longtailed bird on branch in cobalt quill work, 6-gal.
    (A-E)   115
Crock, single flower in blue, marked "E. Jones" (A-E)..   25
Crock, A. E. Smith & Sons, Mfg., N. Y., eared, cobalt blue w/stemmed flowers & hundreds small
    dots, 2-gal., 9¼" t. (D-NE)   85
Crock, stenciling in blue (A-E)   30
Crock, J. Swank & Co., blue decor. (A-E)   90
Crock, tapered, w/blue scratch decor. (A-E)..   115

Crock, M. Tyler Mfg., cobalt blue, "cluster of leaves," eared, ovoid, 1-gal., 8½" t. (D-E) ....$ 58

Crock, J. A. & J. C. Underwood, N. Y., cobalt blue, "bird on branch w/leaves," eared, ca. 1865-67, 1½-gal., 7¾" t. (D-E) 65

Crock, unusually decor. w/handled tankard, 1-gal., 7½" t. (D-NE) 150

Crock, Whites Utica, w/whites bird decor., polka dot body, ca. 1865, 2-gal. (D-E) 135

Crock, L. Willard & Son, Ballardville, Mass., cobalt blue cow decor., quilled & brushed, 5-gal., 12" h. (D-E) 250

Crock, Woodruff, Cortland, 3-gal. (D-E) 70

Cuspidor, blue flower decor. (D-E) 35

Cuspidor, blue sponge decor. (A-E) 25

Cuspidor, 4 cobalt "face flowers," wrapping sides & slip leaves around spillway, bell shape, 7"×12" (D-E) 140

Cuspidor, R. C. R., Phila., blue decor. (D-NE) 65

Doorstop, w/molded date "1814" (A-E) 35

Flask, ca. early 1800s, 7" t. (D-NE) 45

Flask, decor. w/primitive bird & spray of leaves, ca. 1800, 8¼" t. (D-NE) 275

Fruit, apple, natural alabaster (D-NE) 12

Fruit, banana, natural alabaster (D-NE) 12

Fruit, bunch of grapes, off-white color w/brown stem (D-E) 20

Fruit, bunch of grapes, yellowish (D-NE) 28

Fruit, fig, red & green (D-NE) 12

Fruit, grapes, reddish color (D-NE) 28

Fruit, green fig, lg. (D-NE) 12

Fruit, green fig, natural alabaster (D-NE) 10

Fruit, natural pear (D-NE) 12

Fruit, orange (D-NE) 15

Fruit, orange, natural alabaster (D-NE) 12

Fruit, pear, natural alabaster (D-NE) 12

Fruit, pears, figs, peach, plum, 7-pc. (D-NE) 72

Inkwell, 3¾" d. (A-E) 20

Inkwell, ca. 1800, 3" diam., 1¼" t. (D-NE) 32

Inkwell, chip-carved edge, round (D-E) 30

Inkwell, one center hole, 3¼" diam. (D-E) 36

Butter churn, stoneware, marked "Harts-Fulton," 5-gal. (D-MW) $75

Jar, stoneware, white, 1 qt. (D-W) $23

Batter jug, stoneware, buff, w/blue embossed decor. (D-W) $55

Inkwell, oversized, red-brown glaze, "GWR" marked on side, dk. brown down side, 4 pen holes, rope pattern around top, 5" diam. × 2" (D-NE) ....$ 95

Jar, blue w/slip line decor., dated 1835, gray, 10½" h., 5½" d. (D-E) 100

Jar, Brady & Ryan, N. Y., cyl., gray, underglaze blue chicken eating corn, 10" h. (D-E) 175

Jar, bulbous, flower decor., marked "Whites Utica" (A-E) 90

Jar, Burger & Lang, N. Y., Potters, cobalt blue decor. of fern leaves tied in bow, eared, 2-gal., 11¼" t. (D-NE) 42

Jar, canning, gray glaze, wavy band, reddish-green decor. (A-E) 45

Jar, canning, orig. tin cover, 8¾" (D-NE) 10

Jar, cobalt U. S. shield & wreath stencil, 2-qt. (D-E) 100

Jar, covered, dk. brown glaze, "cookie jar" size, 9" t. (D-NE) 15

Jar, full eagle, shield & banner in cobalt stenciling, "Eagle Pottery" in banner, 3-gal. (A-E).... 160

Jar, ginger, gray w/blue band top and base, bulbous, high glaze, 5"×6" (D-NE) 18

Jar, glaze shades from brown, russet, mustard, ochre, incised lines around top, 9"×6" (D-E)... 24

Jar, Goodwin & Webster, Conn., ovoid, eared, cobalt blue decor., ca. 1810-40, 2-gal., 12½" t. (D-NE) 75

Jar, Hamilton & Jones, handled, cobalt decor. (D-E) 42

Jar, Hart & Fulton, blue decor., 2-gal. (A-E) 40

Jar, mottled tan glaze, beading around edge attributed to Willoughby-Smith, 10" h. (D-NE) ... 32

Jar, narrow flared neck, blue stripes & wavy lines (D-E) 65

Jar, Nichels & Co., Pa., decor. 2/man's face in moon (D-E) 950

Jar, ovoid, blue-gray flower decor. (D-E) 35

Jar, preserve, M. & N. C. Bell Pottery, N. Y., cobalt blue decor. w/impressed "1" w/leaves, 1-gal., 9¼" t. (D-NE) 50

Jar, preserve, for wax sealing, brown (D-MW) 5

Jar, preserve, for wax sealing, mottled brown (D-MW) 6

Jar, preserve, for wax sealing, steel-gray (D-MW) 3

Jar, preserve, for wax sealing, tan (D-MW) 4

Jar, N. White, Utica, ovoid, bulfous, cobalt blue, ca. 1838-49, 3-gal., 12¾" t. (D-NE) 50

Jar, wide mouth, blue slip decor., marked Graham & Stone, General Merchandise, Jackson, C. H. / W. V. A., 19th C., 10½" h. (A-MW) 45

Jar, wide mouth, gray w/blue flower & leaf decor., 4½"×8½" (D-NE) 60

Jars, matching pr., 9½" (D-NE) 20

Jug, Armstrong & Wentworth, Norwich, Conn., pear shape, blue glaze top & bottom of handle, ca. 1825, 16" h. (D-W) 45

Jug, batter, bulbous, brown, spout & handle, 10" h. (D-W) 27

Jug, batter, stemmed flower & leaves under spout, 9½" h. (D-NE) 50

Jug, blue bird design, 12" h. (A-E) 50

Jug, blue decor., 14" h. (A-E) 55

Jug, blue decor., stamped "A. J. Butler, New Brunswick, New Hampshire" (D-E) 225

Jug, blue decor., stamped "J. F. Weiler," made in N. Y. (D-E) 198

Jug, blue-gray, Utica, dated 1863 (D-E) 120

Jug, blue peacock, 3-gal. (D-NE) 90

Jug, bulbous, signed G. F. Brayton & Co., Utica, w/prim. cobalt flower, 1-gal. (D-E) 50

Jug, Charlestown, Mass., no decor., gray, ovoid (D-NE) 75

Jug, Charlestown, Mass. Potters, ovoid, ca. 1812-50, 3-gal., 16¼" t. (D-NE) 63

Jug, cobalt blue bird on branch, signed "Brady & Ryan, Ellenville," 3-gal. (D-E)............... 60

Jug, cobalt blue decor., marked Smith & Day Mfg. Conn., ovoid, 2-gal., 14" t. (D-NE)........... 65

Jug, cobalt blue decor., "Max Stiner & Co., N. Y." written by hand, 2-gal., 15" t. (D-NE) 20

Jug, cobalt blue decor., squiggley circle around impressed name w/flames, P. Mackey, N. Y. Potters, handle, 1-gal., 12¾" t. (D-NE) 50

Jug, cobalt blue strawberry decor., I. Seymour, Troy Fact, N. Y., gray-tone salt glaze, ovoid, 2-gal., 15" t. (D-NE) 95

Jug, cobalt blue, sunflower decor. (A-E) 75

Jug, cobalt fancy flower, signed "Lyons," ovoid, 2-gal. (D-E) 60

Jug, cobalt free form slip letter "S., etc.," signed "S. Hart & Son, Fulton," 2-gal. (D-E).......... 35

Jug, cobalt pine tree, signed "N. A. White & Sons, Utica," 1-gal. (D-E) 25

Jug, C. Crolius Mfg. N. Y., ovoid, cobalt blue decor., 1-gal., 12½" t. (D-NE) 135

Jug, dk. brown w/single flower decor., ca. 1883, 1-gal., 11½" h. (D-W) 75

Jug, decorated, 14" (A-E) ....$ 110
Jug, early, pear shaped, brown glaze, 9½" (D-NE) 16
Jug, early, pear shaped, flint glazed, 10" h. (D-NE) 160
Jug, early, reddish/brown glaze (D-NE) 34
Jug, D. Goodall, Hartford, blue around handle & name, ovoid, 19th C., 12" h. (D-NE)............ 38
Jug, Jacob Henry Hudson, Potters, cobalt blue decor., ovoid, 1-gal., 12½" t. (D-NE) 50
Jug, impressed mark Troy, N. Y., open leaf bold slip lines, 19th C., 14½" h. (A-MW)............ 50
Jug, impressed 2" swan stroked w/cobalt, 2-gal., 14¾" t. (D-NE) 60
Jug, Karrsville, N. J. written in blue (A-E) 37
Jug, lg. primitive snowflakes, decor. cobalt blue, 16" (A-NE) 250
Jug, line drawing of house, Binghamton, N. Y., 3-gal. (D-E) 1700
Jug, Lyman & Clark, Gardiner, Me., umbra decor., 2-gal. 13" h. (A-NE) 425
Jug, marked "Goodale, Hartford," blue around handle & top, 12" (D-NE) 38
Jug, marked Lyman & Clark, Me., pear shaped w/umber flower decor., 4-gal., 16" h. (A-NE).. 375
Jug, marked E. & L. P. Norton, Bennington, Vt., cobalt blue flower decor., 2-gal., 14¾" h. (D-E) . 90
Jug, E. Norton & Co., Bennington, Vt., cobalt blue flower, 1-gal., 11½" h. (D-W) 80
Jug, J & E Norton, Bennington, Vt., blue peacock decor., 3-gal. (A-NE) 250
Jug, J. & E. Norton, Bennington, Vt., cobalt blue "pheasant," 2-gal., 14" h. (D-E) 400
Jug, J. & E. Norton, Bennington, Vt., cobalt blue star decor., 3-gal., 15½" h. (D-E) 500
Jug, Orcutt & Crafts, Portland, Maine, green, ovoid, 1-gal. (D-E) 75
Jug, Orcutt & Montague, Troy Potters, cobalt blue decor., ovoid, 1-gal., 12" t. (D-NE) 75
Jug, ovoid shape, cobalt blue incised flower decor., ca. 1810, 1½-gal., 13¼" h. (D-MW) 300
Jug, signed C. Link Exeter, 9½" (A-E) 25
Jug, R. C. Remmey, Phila., ovoid, 3-gal. (D-E) 40
Jug, slip trailed flower decor. (A-E) 45
Jug, A. States & Co., Conn. Potters, cobalt blue decor., 2 incised bands around neck, ovoid, 2-gal., 14" t. (D-NE) 100
Jug, tannish gold bottom, dk. brown around top, 5" (D-NE)... 10
Jug, Troy, N. Y., cobalt blue decor., ca. 1861-81, 1-gal., 11½" t. (D-NE) 12
Jug, warbling bird in blue, 11½" h. (A-E) 95
Jug, West Troy, N. Y., ca. 1880, 2-gal., 15¼" t. (D-E)... 55
Jug, West Troy Pottery, blue decor., 1-gal. (D-NE) 35
Jug, N. A. White & Son, N. Y., lg. bird w/flowers-leaves decor., ca. 1882, 2-gal., 14½" h. (D-E). 200
Mallet, cone shape, blue band, wood handle (D-NE).. 27
Mug, barrel shape, cobalt blue w/incised band top & bottom, 4¾" t. (A-NE) 45
Pan, milk, w/pouring lip, 3 decor. of swags in buff brushstrokes, 10" diam. (D-S) 35
Pan, pouring, 11½" (A-E) 60
Penny bank, beehive, blue floral decor., rare design, 7" (A-E) 650
Pitcher, beer, Carl Wingender, N. J. Potters, cobalt blue decor. of tulips & vines, pewter lid, ovoid, 14½" t. (D-NE) 375
Pitcher, blue decor. lined collar at top, ex. cond., 13" (A-E) 230
Pitcher, blue floral decor., 7" (A-E) 525
Pitcher, cobalt blue, flowers & leaves over entire spout & bulbous portion, 8¾" t. (D-NE)...... 135
Pitcher, cobalt blue leaf decor., ca. 1850, 9¼" h. (D-E) 150
Pitcher, decor. (A-E) 45
Pitcher, floral decoration & incised lines on side (A-E) 105
Pitcher, flowered, all-over blue decor. (A-E) 210
Pot, bean, lid, 9½" (D-NE)... 14
Pot, chamber, blue decor., 11½" (A-E) 120
Pot, chamber, 2 applied handles, decor. w/bust of woman in brown & blue on side, rare, 11½" h. (A-E) 550
Pot, butter, Norton, Worcester, Mass. (D-E) 35
Pot, chamber, cobalt bird on branch, 2-gal. (D-E) 85
Pot, salt, blue floral slip decor., side mounted strap handles, 19th C., 10" h. (A-MW) 60
Pots, bean, with lids, pr., 7" (D-NE)... 18
Water cooler, blue bands, 5-gal. (D-MW) 45
Water cooler, cobalt blue raised bands span entire cir. & spout, 3-gal., 11¼" t. (D-SW)........ 50
Water cooler, 6 matching mugs, pinkish, fruit decor. w/green leaves & vines, ca. 1930, 3-gal., 14" h. (D-MW)... 80

Textiles

The early settlers brought to these shores the best handworked patterns and techniques of their native lands. The women were accomplished with the needle, and their creations were a matter of pride, as well as necessity. They adapted their native arts from England, Germany, France, the Netherlands, and later, the Slavic and eastern countries, literally threading themselves into the patchwork of a new American life-style as they settled in their new environment. Every handcrafted, surviving early example is a tasteful expression of folk art.

Practically all of the fabric for early American clothing, bedding, linens, etc., was made from flax, wool, and cotton which was spun and woven in the home by the women. They spent untold hours preparing flax for spinning and, after the thread was spun, it was woven into cloth which could later be dyed and made into clothing, bedding, etc. Homespun fabric made from flax fiber was lightweight; this was called linen. The heavier winter clothing was a combination of flax and woolen threads, and this was known as "linsey-woolsey."

The hatchel, like the spinning wheel, was an essential tool used for producing home textiles. On its long iron teeth, flax stems were untangled and separated into long silky strands which could later be spun into thread. The number of times flax was hatcheled determined the quality of the thread. Many of these tools were made with two sets of teeth, a long coarse set, and a short fine set. The shorter coarse fibers that remained in the teeth of the hatchel were called "tow." These were also used for spinning rope or making coarse thread for rough material. Many were still being used in isolated rural areas until around the turn of the present century.

Early homespun fabric found today is usually small pieces, varying in size. Perhaps the most desirable homespun article produced was the woven coverlet. The earliest were made on simple and limited size looms, usually in two parts, and later sewed together in the center.

Coverlets were made with several types of weaving techniques, including the overshot, summer and winter, and the Jacquard. The overshot was a loose weave, consisting of wool weft on a linen or cotton warp. These were made in simple geometric designs. The summer and winter reversible coverlet is a double weave employing two colors, usually blue and white. There were also coverlets made on looms using a Jacquard, or similar attachment, which were always the work of professional weavers. Joseph Jacquard, a Frenchman, literally revolutionized the weaving industry in America. Since the loom required a skilled operator, these

A variety of early linen homespun panels (A-E), *left to right:* **brown & white checked,** 18″ × 24″, $50; **blue, brown & white checked,** 18″ × 20″, $50; **small-checked,** blue, brown & white, 142 × 26″, $50; **blue, brown, & white checked,** 16″ × 17″, $50; **fine-checked design,** blue & brown, rare, 76″ × 41″, $210; **large-checked,** brown & white, 76″ × 58″, double, $400

coverlets were made by professional weavers whose products were usually marked in the corner, giving the name of the weaver, or the name of the owner, the date and place made. Few dated coverlets are found after the 1840s.

The fly shuttle was invented in England by John Kay during the early 1700s, but it was not in general use in America until the 1860s and '70s. It was the introduction of the fly shuttle and similar mechanisms that eventually enabled coverlets to be woven in full width.

* * *

Bedcover, candlewick, embroidered w/eagle & star (D-MW) ....$ 400
Bedspread, candlewick design, large (A-E).. 32
Bedspread, decor. in blue & white (A-E) 20
Bedspread, hand crocheted (A-E).. 25
Bedspread, homespun, brown, blue & white, large (A-E)... 85
Bedspread, linen & dimity, large (A-E).. 22
Bedspread, linsey-woolsey, red & blue check, repaired, 18th C. (A-E) 105
Bedspread, Marseilles design, large (A-E) 42
Bedspread, Marseilles, single (D-E)... 20
Bedspread, rose color, fox chase scene (A-E) 62
Bedspread, white crocheted, pink roses (D-MW)... 500
Blanket, homespun wool, seamed center, blue double cross-hatch, lg. pattern, on natural, 82"×96" (D-NE) 50
Blanket, homespoun wool, seamed centers, blue double cross-hatch, small pattern, on natural, 80"×62" (D-NE) 40
Blanket, homespun wool, seamed centers, blue & yellow on natural, windowpane stripes, 85"×80" (D-NE) 55
Blanket, homespun wool, seamed centers, dk. blue plaid on natural, 80"×84" (D-NE) 40
Blanket, homespun wool, seamed center, edge w/large cross stitch embroidery in dk. rose & navy (D-NE)... 30
Coverlet, bird & flower decor., blue, green, red & white (A-E) 125
Coverlet, blue & white, double weave, Jacquard, birds of paradise & Penelope's flower pot w/tulip border, white discolored, 2-pc., 86"×79" (A-E) 125
Coverlet, blue & white double weave Jacquard, "eagle & star 1838," also has Washington on rearing horses bearing swords, one edge bound, 2-pc., 76"×84" (A-E)................................ 285
Coverlet, blue & white, double weave, Jacquard, medallion center, eagle in corners, peacock border, white discolored, 2-pc., 90"×84" (A-E).. 175
Coverlet, blue & white, double weave, Jacquard, railroad border on sides, single on ends, ex. cond., 2-pc., 76"×86" (A-E) 1350
Coverlet, blue & white, double weave, Jacquard, small eagles & stars in center, border w/views of the Capitol Building, Washington, D. C., edges worn, 2-pc., 74"×84" (A-E)...................... 225
Coverlet, blue & white, marked "Mary Carpenter," 1842, decor. w/animals, birds & trees, full size (A-NE)... 285
Coverlet, blue & white, reversible, woven, full size (A-E) 75
Coverlet, Bostontown, pink, blue & white, bordered w/scenes of Boston, full size (D-MW)..... 180
Coverlet, chintz, red, white & blue, full size (D-E)... 450
Coverlet, crib, wool, white, brown & orange (D-E) 135
Coverlet, decor. w/eagle in each corner, red & blue on white background, full size (A-NE)..... 165
Coverlet, dk. blue/natural, wavy geometric pattern, some small mends, 78"×68" (D-NE)......... 50
Coverlet, double woven, blue & white (D-E) 85
Coverlet, double woven, blue & white, dated 1836, 79"×79" (D-MW)................................. 250
Coverlet, eagle center w/oak leaf border & flowers in corner; ochre, green, red on white, full size (A-E) 255
Coverlet, eagles on four corners, red & white, wool (D-E) 390
Coverlet, early blue & white double weave, attributed to James Alexander, 1826, N. Y., "agriculture & manufactures are the foundation of our independence, July 4, 1826, Gnrl Lafayette-S. Bottowland," minor wear, edges bound, 96½"×76" (A-E).. 325
Coverlet, homespun check, blue, red & navy (A-E) 130

Coverlet, Jacquard, dove border, interwoven, full size (A-NE) ....$ 375
Coverlet, Jacquard, dove border, dated 1843 (D-N).. 375
Coverlet, linen & wool, dated & signed "Hannah K. Bortz," made in Mounty Airy, Berks Co.,
1841, good cond. (A-E) 210
Coverlet, made by W. Stein & T. Montgomery, 2 shades green, blue & red on white, ca. 1846,
full size (A-E).. 225
Coverlet, overshot, blue, rust & cream (D-E) 100
Coverlet, overshot, gold, blue & white, full size (A-E) 135
Coverlet, red, white & blue, dated 1848, signed "made by Phillip Rossweller, Millersburg"
(D-E) 265
Coverlet, red, white & blue double bird border & F. Thornton on border, ca. 1845 (A-E) 350
Coverlet, red, white & blue, double weave, Jacquard, "Capitol in Washington 1846," Ohio
weaver, 1 edge bound, minor wear, 2-pc., 82"×80" (A-E) 330
Coverlet, red, white & blue; man on horse in corners, architectural bldgs. on border; acorn &
oak leaves in center, full size (A-E) 190
Coverlet, red/white, eagle pattern, dated 1848, cond. ex. (D-E)..................................... 750
Coverlet, red, white, blue & green single weave, Jacquard, vintage pattern, border is backward
looking birds & houses, "Ohio 1855, G. Engle weaver," 2-pc., 85"×74" (A-E).......................... 375
Coverlet, signed, Ohio, 1853, green, red & white w/birds & houses on border (A-E) 150
Coverlet, wheel of fortune, red, woven, w/woven fringe, made by Jane Grey, Buckfield, Mass.
(A-NE).. 275
Coverlet, wool, green, red & white, small (D-E)... 170
Coverlet, wool, red & white (A-E) 95
Coverlet, woven, dated & signed, "Susan C. Garrett, Aug. 1, 1851" (D-E)............................ 250
Coverlet, woven, red, eagle pattern, dated 1848 (D-NE) 750
Coverlet, woven, red & white w/eagles on border, marked "Fredericks Co., Maryland" (D-E). 155
Coverlet, woven, white roses on navy blue ground (D-E)... 220
Doorstop, needlepoint (A-E) 6
Embroidery, framed, worked on homespun in silk, geometric, center pale shrimp pink, 1-pc.,
12¼"×10¼" (D-NE)... 10
Handkerchief, copperplate, printed in blue, "four & twenty blackbirds," 10¼"×6¾" (D-NE).. 10
Handkerchief, linen, handmade, ca. 1850 (D-MW) 7
Linen, blue & brown checked, early (A-E) 170
Linen, blue & brown checked, 20×18" (A-E)... 65
Linen, blue & brown checked, early, 20×18" (A-E) 80
Linen, blue & brown checked, 1-pc., 76×41" (A-E) 210
Linen, blue, brown & white checked, 1-pc., 18×20" (A-E) 50
Linen, blue, brown & white checked, 1-pc., 26×14" (A-E) 50
Linen, blue, brown & white checked, large, rare (A-E) 100
Linen, blue checked, 1 lg. pc. (A-E) 65
Linen, blue & white checked, 1-pc. (A-E) 20
Linen, brown & white checked, 1-pc., 18×24" (A-E) 50
Linen, brown & white checked, 1-pc., 19"×51" (A-E) 50
Linen, brown & white checked, 20×52" (A-E).. 140
Linen, brown & white checked, blue pin stripes, 18"×36" (A-E) 105
Linen, brown & white checked, double, 1-pc., 76×58" (A-E) 400
Linen, brown & white checked, early (A-E)... 90
Linen, homespun, 1-pc. (A-E) 2
Linen, large blue, brown & white checked, rare, 15½"×36" (A-E) 105
Linen, large blue, brown & white checked, rare, 43×39" (A-E)...................................... 150
Linen, large blue checked, 1-pc. (A-E) 30
Linen, large blue checked, 1-pc. (A-E) 50
Linen, large double checked blue, white & brown, rare, 17"×32" (A-E) 100
Linen, multicolored, checked, early (A-E) 90
Linen, small blue, brown & white checked, 1-pc., 16×17" (A-E).................................... 50
Linen, small blue & walnut brown checked, rare, 40×76" (A-E) 200
Mat, chair, braided (A-E) 6
Mat, chair, hooked (A-E) 6
Mittens, child's, handmade from red dyed homespun (D-E)... 10

Towel, homespun, spread eagle motif, the words "the United States of America Declared July 4th, 1776, Washington Elected President of the Federal Union March 1789, E Pluribus Unum" (D-NW) $75

Fancy stitchery, on paper, 4″ × 6″ (D-S) $35

Panel, door, dated 1844 (A-E) ....$	45
Panel, door, dated 1846 (A-E)	40
Panels, door, (6) linen (A-E)	15
Pillow, made from early quilt, cotton w/silk tape, contemporary back (D-E)	45
Pillow, patchwork (D-NE)	30
Pillowcase, natural color, homespun (D-E)	2
Pillowcases, appliqued, pr. (A-E)	20
Quilt, see quilt section	
Robe, buggy, pink & green floral design, 48½″×54″ (D-MW)..	57
Rugs, see rug section	
Shawl, Amish, wool, fringed (D-MW)	15
Shawl, homespun, blue plaid, 36″ sq. (D-MW)	22
Sheet, homespun wool, 2 36″ panels, natural, full size (D-E)...	20
Sheet, linen, homespun, 7¼×6′ (D-MW)..	25
Sheet, linen, homespun, seamed center (D-NE)	20
Tablecloth, (bedcover) ecru, crocheted, 75″×60″ (D-MW)...	150
Tablecloth, homespun, gray flowered (A-E)	15
Tablecloth, red fringed (A-E)	30
Tablecloth, red & white w/fringe edge (A-E)	20
Towel, door panel, linen, crochet design (A-E)	110
Towel, door panel, linen, dated 1808 (A-E)	100
Towel, door panel, linen, decor., heart & peacocks, 1836 (A-E).....................................	650
Towel, door panel, linen, decor. in red, 1836 (A-E)	325
Towel, door panel, linen, decor. red & blue, flowers, 1839 (A-E)	180
Towel, door panel, linen, signed Mary Landis 1838, decor. w/birds & flowers (A-E)	350
Towel, door panel, wedding presentation, 1813, decor. profusely (A-E)	275
Towel, homespun, natural color (D-E)	1
Towel, linen, homespun (D-NE)..	2
Towel, show, colored, 1831 (A-E)	15
Towel, show, linen, plain, 1-pc. (A-E)...	4
Towels, linen, 2, thin red cross-hatch on natural, homespun, never laundered, hand-hemmed (D-NE)	5

Tinware

Tinware—actually sheet iron painted or coated with tin to resist rusting—has taken a wide variety of forms and purposes in America since the eighteenth century. Edward Pattison is credited with establishing the first tinware factory in Berlin, Connecticut in 1770, importing his tinplate from England. The tin industry in America didn't begin until about 1830. However, American tinmen continued to import plate from Britain's plentiful supply until 1890, when the McKinley Tariff Act made this impractical. By the turn of the century, its use was so widespread that the light, bright and inexpensive utensils became popular household items.

Early advertisements indicate that tinsmiths were active in many areas, transforming the metal into almost every scarce or non-existent item needed—plates, bowls, dishpans, cups, mugs, pots, pans, graters, candle molds, sieves, funnels, lighting devices—and literally hundreds of other objects. It was during this period that the tin peddler went on horseback from door to door peddling his wares in baskets. He has become a legend to everyone interested in this field of collecting because of his vital contribution to the economy of the rural areas.

Patent records show that, beginning in 1804, the tin craftsman utilized small machines to simplify and speed up production of his wares. However, the greatest amount of tin was produced after the Civil War, when cookstoves became more generally used, and the housewife replaced the heavy iron pots and pans for new types of kitchen utensils designed for use on the top of the stove. And, from about 1880 to 1930, a great variety of goods sold in retail shops, was packaged in or dispensed from bright tin boxes in all sizes and colors.

Most of the collectible tinware available today is of nineteenth century origin. Its simple beauty has a charm that appeals to all antiquarians. The most popular items are the small, decorative objects, in addition to pierced tin lanterns and coffeepots of various shapes and sizes. Of the latter group, it is the Pennsylvania Dutch examples, ornamented with punched designs, that fetch the greatest amounts.

A vast amount of new tinware in old forms has been produced in recent years because of the escalating interest in this field. Some of the finer examples are being made by reputable contemporary craftsmen in the old tradition. Their marked examples are actually works of art and should be collected. But, as in almost every field, there are those spurious examples that have been aged deliberately to deceive the collector that cause the greatest problems. The majority of these objects are European in origin, having a surface so overly distressed to resemble usage—rough, pitted, and occasionally painted—that even the beginning collector becomes suspicious.

* * *

Bake oven door, handmade for fireplace oven, swing cover on flue opening (D-NE)..............$ 35
Bathtub, child's (D-MW) 18
Bathtub, wood frame on legs, adult's (D-MW) 75
Beaker, horn, large, inset bottom (D-NE) 22
Beer warmer, fireplace, lidded & shoe shaped, 13″ l. (D-E) 24
Biscuit cutter, early, heart shape (D-E) 16

Biscuit oven, hinged cover, footed (D-E)..$ 75

Bottle corker, metal (D-W)...   4

Bottle, nursing, article inside by "Rudolf Hommel" on "brief history of old nursing bottles"
(A-E)   290

Bottle, nursing, w/shaped handle (A-E)   270

Bowl, barber's (D-NE)..   35

Bowl, sugar (D-NE)   45

Bowl, sugar, no color, darkened (D-NE)   38

Breadbox, painted wood grain, label (D-E)..   8

Bread mold, log shaped, 2-pc. (D-E)   12

Bread pan, corrugated (D-E)...   16

Broiler, fish & meat, iron swivel joint & long handle (D-E)   165

Bucket, bail handle, early (A-MW)..   6

Bun dish, solid bottom, cut out sides, 10"×2½" (D-NE)   8

Cabinet, w/bins for condiments & flour (A-MW)..   195

Cake closet, wooden knob, japanned, 15½"×11"×10" (S-MW)...   28

Cake/cracker box w/cover, labeled "cake", japanned (D-S)...   20

Canister, darkened, 7½" (D-W)   8

Canister, darkened, 8" (D-NE)   8

Canister, lg. orig. asphaltum, 12½" (D-NE)   11

Canister, tea, orig. asphaltum, red/gold swag w/"tea," 6" (A-E)   16

Canister, tea, octagonal, 4"×4" (D-E)   15

Case, violin, handmade on wooden back (D-E)   24

Cheese mold, handled & footed, round, pierced (D-E)...   30

Cheese mold, heart shaped (A-E)   55

Cheese mold, heart shaped (D-NE)   35

Cheese mold, heart shaped, hex sign pattern, pierced, tubular feet, 4½"×4½" (D-E)   65

Cheese mold, heart shaped, pierced, footed (D-E)..   55

Cheese mold, heart shaped, pierced, footed (D-MW)..   25

Cheese mold, heart shaped, punched (D-E)..   65

Cheese mold, heart shaped, punched design (D-W)   18

Cheese strainer, heart shaped (D-E)   35

Cheese strainer, heart shaped, cut type (A-E)   37

Cheese strainer, heart shaped, pierced tin, handled & footed, 3½" h., 5½" l. (A-NE)   50

Cheese tester, for large country cheeses (D-NE)   6

Chocolate mold, large elephant (D-W)   35

Chocolate mold, Little Red Riding Hood (D-W)...   35

Chocolate mold, Little Red Riding Hood, large (D-E)   35

Chocolate mold, owl, large (D-E)   35

Chocolate mold, rooster, 9" h. (D-E)...   35

Chocolate mold, rooster, 4½" (D-NE)   12

Chocolate mold, turkey, 4" (D-NE)...   9

Churn, cream, all orig. & complete, 9" h. (D-E)...   40

Churn, square, tin 2 gal. cont. set in iron frame, early 20th C., good working cond. (D-MW) .   35

Left to right: **7-hole muffin pan** (D-E) $18; **6-hole maple sugar mold** (D-E) $22

Cookie cutter, tin, Penna. Dutch, early, 6" l. (D-MW) $35

Coffeepot, gooseneck, blocked tin (D-MW) ....$ 250
Coffeepot, gooseneck, blocked tin, Pa. (A-E).. 250
Coffeepot, gooseneck, punched tin, tulip decor., dated 1867 (A-E) 1750
Coffeepot, punched, decor./tulip & star flowers (A-E)... 900
Coffeepot, punched, domed lid, gooseneck spout, urn decor./flower buds on slender stems, 3
  rows of diamond shaped chains/5 dot centers (A-E)... 1350
Coffeepot, punched, stars, pots of flowers & leaf design, ex. cond. (A-E) 1550
Coffeepot, rare, scratched decor. motif of eagle w/American flag, opposite side, tulip-floral
  decor. Pa. Dutch, ca 1800 (D-E) 1900
Coffeepot, straight side spout (A-E) 55
Coffeepot, straight spout, brass finial, 9" (D-NE) 32
Colander w/two handles (A-E).. 40
Comb case, embossed "combed case," 7¼" w., 2¾" d., 5½" h. (D-S) 10
Comb case, hanging, japanned, arch top, 5"×7" (D-E).. 22
Comb case, painted, w/mirror (D-E) 6
Comb case, wall, orig. stencil on back, worn on front, 7"×5½" (D-NE) 22
Cookie cutter, bird, 6" (D-NE) 60
Cookie cutter, bird w/lg. round handle, 6½" h. (D-MW) 5
Cookie cutter, chicken, Pa. Dutch, 4½"×4" (D-MW) 8
Cookie cutter, dog, Pa. Dutch (D-E) 7
Cookie cutter, eagle, early (D-E) 25
Cookie cutter, eagle, 4" (A-NE).. 45
Cookie cutter, eagle, early Pa. Dutch, 4½"×7¼" (D-E) 28
Cookie cutter, fish, Pa. Dutch, 5"×3" (D-MW) 8
Cookie cutter, gentleman w/high hat, early (A-E) 27
Cookie cutter, hatchet, early, 4½"×8" (D-NE) 18
Cookie cutter, heart, long, 2¼"×3½" (D-NE)... 25
Cookie cutter, heart, Pa. Dutch, 3½"×5½" (D-E)... 22
Cookie cutter, horse, Pa. Dutch, 4"×7" (D-E) 10
Cookie cutter, man on horse, mounted & framed, early (A-E)... 110
Cookie cutter, man w/derby hat, round handle, 6½", early (A-NE) 180
Cookie cutter, rabbit, Pa. Dutch, early, 5½"×7" (D-MW)... 6
Cookie cutter, rabbit, upright, 4½" t., early (D-E)... 20
Cookie cutter, rocking horse, Pa. Dutch, 9" h. (D-E) 38
Cookie cutter, rooster, early (A-E).. 30
Cookie cutter, rooster, Pa. Dutch, 5½"×4" (D-MW) 10
Cookie cutter, teapot, early 5¼"×8" (D-E) 22
Cookie cutter, tulip, early Pa. Dutch, 6" h. (D-E)... 18
Cookie cutters, set of 5, mounted on cardboard, chicken, hen, rabbit, tulip, pine tree, early
  (A-E) 55
Cookie cutters, set of 12, animals, teapot, roosters, eagle, fish, early (A-E) 47
Cookie cutters, (2) shape of men, early (A-E)... 30
Cover, food, handled, 9¼"×7½" (D-NE).. 15
Cranberry picker, wooden handle (D-MW) 45
Cream can, cover, handled, orig. paint, 5½" (D-E) 16
Creamer, covered, 5" h. (D-E).. 18
Cream whipper, 8½" h. (D-MW) 25
Cup, long handle, decoration (A-E).. 20
Cup, shaving (D-W).. 4
Cup, toddy, handled & covered, 3" diam. (D-MW) 16
Cup, toddy, handled & covered, 4" h. (D-E)... 18
Cup, toddy, handled, sits into footed base for hot coals, 8" h. (D-E) 35
Cupboard, hanging, punched design in reverse to keep out preying rodents, 36" l., 30" h., 26" d.
  (D-MW).. 125
Cupboard, hanging type suspended by rope from ceiling or trees to keep out rodents, pierced in
  reverse, 30" l., 24" h., 26" d. (D-S) 200
Cuspidor, shape of turtle (A-E)... 62
Cuspidor, turtle, step-on head (D-E) 35
Decoy, Canada goose, orig. paint ex., hinged (D-MW) 32

Coffeepot, punched tin, profuse decor. on both sides, large tulip & star flowers on slender stems, $900

Coffeepot, tin (D-W) $28

Coffeepot, tin, spread eagle on round disc on underside, marked H. F. & Co., 10¾" h. (D-MW) $95

Decoy, mallard drake, orig. paint good (D-MW) ....$ 22
Decoy, mallard hen, orig. paint good (D-N) 18
Decoy, nodding goose (D-MW) 35
Decoy, snipe (D-W) 28
Dipper, 15" (D-NE) 12
Dipper, 15½" (D-NE) 15
Dipper, 19" (D-NE) 18
Dipper, 12½" (D-NE) 12
Dipper, 20", handle has swirl pattern, deep 7" diam. bowl (D-NE) 24
Dipper, water (D-NE) 18
Dish, chafing (D-NW)... 95
Donut cutter w/open top, hole cutter supported by 3 bands from center to rim, wide tin handle, arched, 2¾" d., 2½" h. (D-S)... 12
Dough riser, w/orig. lid, large (A-E)... 17
Dough riser, w/orig. lid, large (D-W).. 25
Down spout head, large, dated 1841 (A-E) 250
Down spout head, pineapple & stars, dated 1854 (A-E).. 190
Dredger, flour, top opens, hasp closing, handled, 11¾"×4½" diam. (D-NE)...................... 25
Dustpan (D-E)... 10
Dustpan, early handmade (A-MW) 12
Dustpan, early, rolled edges & braced handle, 15½"×8½"×2½" (D-NE) 28
Dustpan, large, early (D-E) 50
Ear trumpet, old (D-E) 25
Fireman's helmet, w/brass eagle at top, from Kodak Park, N. Y. (D-E) 55
Flask, w/brass top (D-W) 18
Flour dredger, opens ends w/hinged closings, handless, 14" l. (D-E) 35
Fly trap, "pines fly trap, ketch the flies, save the babies," 5½" t. (D-E)............................ 18
Food warmer, open top, open sides, torch type, lamp inside, 4½" diam. (D-NE)............... 20
Food warmer, orig. camphene oil lamp (D-MW) 65
Foot warmer, oval (rare shape), Pa., pierced hearts/geometric design, wood frame, copper pan (D-E) 125
Foot warmer, round (rare form), nicely pierced decor., set in pine frame, 9" diam. (D-E)........ 88
Foot warmer, square, turned maple frame, pierced tin box, insert pan (D-E) 70
Foot warmer, square, wood frame, pierced geometric designs, no pan (D-W) 55
Foot warmer, square, wood frame, pierced heart designs, no insert pan (D-MW) 70
Foot warmer, square, wood frame, pierced heart & diamond design, tin insert pan (D-MW) .. 75
Foot warmer, square, wood frame, tin insert pan, 8"×9" (D-MW) 42
Foot warmer, wood frame, pierced heart design, w/tin coal carrier (D-E) 85
Fork, 2-tine, punch, dated 1813, signed "H. C. H." 18" l. (D-E) 165
Funnel, canning jar (D-MW) 2
Grater, coffin ends, rolled edges (D-E).. 38
Grater, nutmeg, flat, sliding wood holder, 4" (D-NE)... 10
Grater, nutmeg, hanging, 5" l. (D-E) 8
Grater, on pine board, half-round, shield, back hole for hanging, initial "W" in pierced tin (D-NE)... 38
Grater, paddle-shaped, pierced (D-W)... 32

Grater, snuff (D-W)	$ 30
Ice cream freezer, 1 gal. size, complete (D-MW)	22
Kettle, steamer w/punch tin decor., w/handles, 12" diam. (D-MW)	80
Kitchen cabinet, w/bins for condiments & flour (A-NE)	350
Ladle, w/punched decor., ex. cond. (A-E)	45
Ledger marker, black & gilt (D-E)	16
Maple sugar mold, fluted shape, 8 on tin frame (A-E)	30
Maple sugar mold, heart shaped, 6 on tin frame (D-MW)	50
Maple sugar mold, 30 sections, rectangular (D-E)	45
Maple sugar molds, set of 4, crimped/fluted, individual, 1"×3" (D-NE)	12
Match holder, hanging, embossed matches w/lid (A-E)	8
Match safe, faded orig. stencil, 3¾" (D-S)	18
Match safe, hanging, curved lid, blue, cylindrical (D-E)	36
Match safe, painted red, crimped, 7¾" h., 4" w. (D-MW)	30
Match safe, pedestal base, 3¾" (D-NE)	20
Measure, half-pint (D-MW)	8
Measure, 1 pint (D-W)	6
Measure, 1 quart (D-MW)	12
Milk can, handled, good cond. (A-E)	15
Milk can, handled, 2-qt. (D-E)	15
Milk pail, small (A-E)	20
Mold, copper top in form of American eagle (D-N)	150
Mold, egg (D-E)	15
Mold, melon, fluted, 2-pc., 7½" l. (D-W)	5
Mold, pudding, fluted & ribbed, bundt type (D-E)	5
Mold, pudding, melon shaped (D-NE)	5
Mold, round, fruits in bottom, cathedral type sides (D-NE)	12
Mold, turkey, full size (D-W)	45
Muffineer, 4½" (D-NE)	18
Molds, muffin (6), heart shaped (A-E)	55
Muffineer, 4½" (D-MW)	15
Muffineer, 4½" h. (D-S)	22
Mug, w/inlaid brass "Jessie" label, 18th C., 4" t. (D-E)	59
Mustache cup, miner's (D-SE)	18
Nurser, baby, w/spout (D-E)	125
Oil can, handled, 9" (D-E)	12
Pan, angel food cake, fluted, 9½" diam. (D-W)	5
Pan, cream, 15" diam., 4" deep (D-MW)	5
Pan, bread dough, large w/lid (A-E)	22
Pan, "flour" embossed on side, 10" diam., 5" deep (D-S)	12
Parrot cage, unusual (D-NE)	120
Pie lifter, 2-tine, brass ferrule, wooden handle (D-NE)	12
Pie plate, scalloped edge, 7¾" (D-MW)	5
Pie plates, 6" scalloped edge, pr. (D-NE)	12
Plate, ABC, embossed words "who killed cock robin" (D-MW)	38
Plate, ABC, letters & numerals in center (D-E)	12
Plate, ABC, "Liberty" (D-MW)	40
Plate, ABC, 6¼" (D-NE)	18
Plate, deep, scalloped edge, 7¾" (D-NE)	6
Plates, dinner, set of 6, scarce (D-E)	30
Post lamp, w/eagle finial, dietz, large (A-E)	190
Quilt pattern design, American spread eagle, early (A-E)	230
Quilt pattern design, bird, early (A-E)	50
Quilt pattern design, Indian w/bow & arrow, early (A-E)	240
Quilt pattern design, perched bird (A-E)	240
Quilt pattern designs, grape, star & leaves (6) (A-E)	200
Quilt pattern designs, stars (5) (A-E)	125
Quilt pattern, design, tulip, 3"×5" (D-E)	180
Ratchet stick, early, w/mid-drip (D-E)	295

Spice container, tin, rollback front, orig. red finish, gold trim (D-MW) $95

Egg & cream beater, tin (D-N) $32

Flour dredge, tin, hinged cover (D-MW) $38

Foot warmer, oval, fine pierced tin decor., copper pan for coals, set in cherry frame (D-MW) $90

Foot warmer, tin, pierced, set in walnut frame, pan missing (D-MW) $65

Roaster, bird, handled, shield, tray, 6 hooks, 18th C. (D-NE)	$ 125
Roaster, bird, w/handle & hooks (D-E)	125
Roaster, meat, rectangular w/spit (D-S)	80
Roasting oven, w/spit (D-W)	65
Roasting oven, w/spit & skewers, 20″ l., cylindrical in shape, early, footed, rare (D-E)	200
Scales, balance type, 13″ tin pan, 30 lb., chatillons (D-MW)	22
Scoop, for skimming maple syrup (D-E)	10
Scoop, tallow, 4″ handle (D-MW)	28
Scoop, tallow, 14″ handle (D-E)	50
Scoop, tin handle, 12″ l., 6″ wide blade (D-W)	8
Salt box, hanging, wooden lid (A-E)	17
Shaving mug, w/compartment, 4½″ h. (D-E)	20
Sieve, w/handle (A-E)	17
Skimmer, cream (D-MW)	6
Skimmer, round handle w/geometric pattern, 11″ (D-E)	18
Skimmer, shell-shaped (D-W)	12
Skimmer, without pierced holes (D-NE)	5
Spatula, pierced flipper & scrolled hook, 16″ l. (D-E)	28
Spatula, solid flipper, flat, 12″ l. (D-E)	28
Spill holder, corset-shaped (D-E)	28
Sprinkler, clothes, early, 8″ (D-N)	20
Sprinkler, clothes, handled, cylindrical (D-E)	28
Squeezer, lemon, hinged (D-NW)	15
Steamer, fish, on legs (D-E)	55
Strainer, 3-footed, 7½″ diam. (A-E)	35
Sugar shakers, black, large, pr. (A-E)	12
Tart cutter, 2 parts fit together, 1 cuts round bottom, 1 cuts donut or cookies (D-NW)	10
Tea caddy, undecorated (D-W)	12
Teakettle, drop type for early wood stove, heavy (D-MW)	52
Teakettle, handmade, "Rogers" on handle (D-MW)	62
Teakettle, straight spout (D-SW)	25
Teapot, approx. 1½ cup, early, 5″ (D-E)	20
Teapot, gooseneck spout, 10″ h. (D-MW)	35
Teapot, off center spout, 6½″ (D-NE)	18
Teapot, 6½″ (D-NE)	20
Teapot, straight spout, tin cover for the end, 4½″ h. (D-NE)	15
Tea strainer, ribbon handle (D-E)	12
Tray, bun, 12″ (D-NE)	15
Tray, ex. pattern in gold leaf & paint, 8″×10″ (D-NE)	35
Tray, handled, w/6 small spice cans (A-E)	35
Tray, Indian decor. (D-E)	25

Toleware, or Decorated Tinware

The correct term for this gaily decorated American tinware of the Dutch country and New England is simply AMERICAN PAINTED TINWARE. There is really no justification for labeling it "tole," a term that arises from a much more stylish nineteenth century type of painted iron decoration done by French workmen. But, nevertheless, as time passes more collectors are referring to decorated tinware by the French term, to the point that it seems to come under one general classification, "toleware."

American painted tinware became popular during the first quarter of the last century, and continued to be produced throughout the century. A great variety of shapes were decorated by talented artists. Many designs were quite simple, others were lavish, especially pieces decorated with Pennsylvania Dutch motifs.

And too, many pieces were japanned which describes the applying and kiln drying of a lustrous tar-based varnish used to imitate the lacquer finish of the Japanese. Another method of decoration is known as flowering, which identifies decorations done freehand, using oil paint.

Collectors became interested in painted tinware during the 'thirties. As a result, it has become quite scarce with values reaching lofty heights when pieces turn up in shops or at auctions.

Because of its popularity, much new decorated tinware has been reproduced, and some genuinely old undecorated forms have been decorated. Moreover, many of the once-decorated old pieces have been redecorated. Therefore, collectors should examine pieces carefully before making purchases.

It is rare to find an early piece of decorated tinware in perfect condition. Decoration will almost always have a faded appearance, paint at points of wear will be rubbed off, and the painted surface will be criss-crossed by tiny age cracks, not only in the background, but in the design as well. This is known as "crazing" or "alligatoring," caused by age and heat over the years.

For serious collectors of tin and decorated tinware, suggested references are Margaret Coffin's book, *The History & Folklore of American Country Tinware 1700-1900* (Thomas Nelson & Sons); and *Antique Tin & Tole Ware* by Mary Earle Gould (Charles E. Tuttle Company).

* * *

Bowl, sugar, decor. (D-E)	$ 400
Bowl, sugar, japanned ground w/red fruit w/white, yellow & green decor., 3¾" h. (A-E)	460
Can, watering, peaches & grape design, 18th C. (D-E)	105
Canister, spice, band of decor. in yellow, orange, red, green & black, initials & Phila. on bottom, 4½" h. (A-E)	85
Coffeepot, black decor. (A-E)	375
Coffeepot, decor., w/red, green & yellow, ex. cond. (A-E)	1100
Coffeepot, decor. w/red rose w/many florets, rare (A-E)	2000
Coffeepot, dark japanned ground, bright decor. in yellow, green & red, mint cond., 10½" h. (A-E)	1100
Coffeepot, dark japanned ground, decor., in yellow, red & dark green, mint cond., 10¼" h. (A-E)	1200
Coffeepot, good decor., part of spout missing (A-E)	190

Coffeepot, toleware, decor., red & yellow predominating, dk. green leaves, side spout (A-E) $1600

Coffeepot, toleware, decor., gooseneck spout (A-E) $2800

Decorated toleware (A-E), *top:* **syrup jug,** $450; *bottom, left to right:* **tea caddy,** $200; **octagonal tray,** $180; **tea caddy,** $160

Coffeepot, gooseneck spout, decor. w/bright colors (A-E)	$ 2800
Coffeepot, gooseneck, orig. decor. worn thin in spots, 11" h. (D-MW)	125
Coffeepot, gooseneck, red, blue & yellow decor. (A-E)	325
Coffeepot, rare scratched decor., motif of eagle w/American flag, opposite side decor. w/tulip (D-NE)	1800
Coffeepot, side spout, decor. red & yellow, green leaves, ex. cond. (A-E)	1600
Coffeepot, straight spout (A-E)	475
Creamer, covered, tole decor. (A-E)	65
Holder, knitting needle (A-E)	47
Jug, syrup, decor. w/red, green, white & yellow (A-E)	600
Jug, syrup, decor. w/traditional colors (A-E)	450
Match holder, wall, unapinted (A-E)	27
Match safe (D-E)	35
Match safe, asphaltum scratch surface, blue japanned, 4" t. (D-E)	35
Match safe, hanging, stenciled (D-E)	25
Mold, candle, 2-hole (D-E)	65
Muffineer (D-MW)	22
Mug (A-E)	12

Decorated toleware (A-E), *left to right:* **syrup jug,** $600; **handled mug,** mint, 5½" h., $425; **tea caddy,** $200

Mug, handled, bright decor., 5½" (A-E)	$ 425
Mug, handled, colorful (A-E)	180
Pitcher, molasses (A-E)	22
Plate, ABC, "Liberty" (D-NW)	40
Scoop, tallow (D-MW)	50
Tea caddy, black ground w/freehand decor. in red, white & yellow, 2¾" h. (A-E)	160
Tea caddy, dark background, red, green, yellow & white colors, ex. cond. (A-E)	200
Tea caddy, decor. bright green, red, yellow, med. size (A-E)	200
Tea caddy, decor., large (A-E)	55
Tea caddy, decor. rose red (A-E)	160
Tea caddy, good decor. (A-E)	85
Tea caddy, reddish-gold background, floral design (A-E)	27
Tea caddy, slant lid, green, block front, 4"×4"×6" (D-E)	44
Teapot, oval, decor. w/red, green & yellow flowers (D-E)	215
Teapot, spout on side, brown painted (A-E)	42
Tray, bread, bright decor. (A-E)	90
Tray, bread, fine decor. (A-E)	80
Tray, bread, floral design (A-E)	65
Tray, bread, red background, yellow, green, white, blue & black decor., rare w/blue (A-E)	400
Tray, bread, tulip decor. (A-E)	200
Tray, Chippendale, old (A-E)	20
Tray, Chippendale, old decor. (A-NE)	20
Tray, decor., eagle on world (A-E)	50
Tray, decor., farm scene (A-E)	45
Tray, decor., large (A-E)	30
Tray, decor., painted bird & flowers, orig. (A-E)	20
Tray, decor., peacock, ex. cond. (A-E)	25
Tray, oblong, red tulip decor., 9" (A-E)	390
Tray, octagonal, colorful decor., black background, 5¾"×8¾" (D-MW)	85
Tray, octagonal, decor., good colors (A-E)	180
Tray, octagonal, red, green & white, 8¾" (A-E)	55
Tray, octagonal, red, yellow & black, 8½" (A-E)	135
Tray, orig. bird of paradise decor., 16" (A-E)	17
Tray, orig. decor. fruit & peacock (A-E)	27
Tray, orig. flower & fruit decor., black ground w/yellow banding, 12½" (A-NE)	140
Tray, razor edge, gold background covers tray, edge pat. white w/black, 3 flowers each end, red, yellow, green, lt. green brush strokes, center decor., opp. sides w/black flowers w/white veining, sm. yellow flowers w/red centers, black & green brushstrokes, 8"×10" (D-NE)	45
Tray, snuffer, tin, w/orig. decor. in blue (D-NE)	32

Tools

Old tool collecting—automatically a masculine category—is relatively wide-spread and long established. And, amazingly countless men are serious tool collectors without realizing it, because few are ever willing to discard an old tool no matter how worn or obsolete it has become.

By necessity, the early settler was a jack-of-all-trades. He not only had to be a tiller of the soil, but oftentimes had to be his own carpenter, cobbler, cooper, blacksmith or butcher. Being resourceful, he developed a variety of tools that were necessary and useful. Practically all of the smaller surviving examples in this field found their way into coveted museum collections long ago. Most of those available to the collector nowadays date from the late years of the last century, and are mass-produced products.

Hand tools—particularly woodworking tools—are the most widespread type collected, while others prefer farming or household tools. When the collector has familiarized himself with particular tool designs, he will note that they reveal distinct changes over the years, just as does anything else. But the very basic design changes slowly because there is an enormous amount of resistance to radically different concepts among tool-users.

Precisely how tools are collected is largely a matter of personal choice. Many collect over a broad, general spectrum, while others prefer to specialize in one or several types of tools, or tools related to a particular period, geographic region, craft or trade. In any event, tools of all types have proven to be very desirable collectors' items.

* * *

Auger, hand, 5" (D-E)	$ 14
Auger, hub, wheelwright's, handwrought, 13" red wood handle, 13½" l. iron part (D-NE)	15
Auger, hub, wheelwright's, handwrought, wood "T" handle, tapered, 13" l. (D-E)	15
Auger, 12" bit (D-MW)	50
Ax, cooper's, 9½" blade (D-MW)	50
Ax, cooper's, orig. Portland, Maine (D-E)	110
Ax, goose wing, wrought iron w/wooden handle (D-NE)	245
Ax, hewing, goose wing decor., signed "J. C. Flicker" (A-E)	275
Ax, hewing, goose wing decor., signed "N. Gilbert," high quality (A-E)	375
Backscratcher, primitive, 23" l. (A-NE)	40
Bag spreader, bow-shape, 9"×14" (D-E)	30
Bag spreader, bow-shape, all wood, 9"×14" (D-W)	22
Bark peeler (D-E)	22
Bark spud, w/wood handle, early, 23" (D-E)	15
Barrel, corn shelling, w/round drilled holes in sides & bottom, lapped hoops, 33" h. × 23" w. (A-NE)	130
Bed jack, maple (D-E)	12
Bellow, blacksmith, leather & iron hdwe., ca. 1850 (D-E)	90
Bellows, fireplace, painted & decor. in yellow, red, w/green stenciled leaves & gold fruit (A-NE)	100
Bellows, leather w/brass nailheads (A-MW)	22
Bellows, orig. decor., big red apples & green leaves on yellow smoked background, orig. leather, 16" (D-NE)	48
Bellows, turtleback, orig. decor. (A-S)	45
Bellows, turtleback, orig. decor., orig. leather, good cond. (D-NE)	60
Bit brace, brass throat (D-MW)	49
Bit brace, walnut, all wood, slip-on chuck, 18th C., 14"×4½" (D-MW)	175

Bit brace, walnut, slip-on chuck, 18th C., 4½"×14" (D-E) ....$ 195
Blueberry picker, wooden teeth (D-NW).. 45
Box, carpenter's, pine, hand grip, dovetailed, unfinished, 20" l. (D-W) 30
Branding iron, hand-forged, "flying H" (D-SW) 18
Branding iron, hand-forged, "running R" (D-W) 22
Branding iron, handwrought, ends cinch up into handwhittled wooden handle, initial "A"
  carved in handle, 24" l. (D-MW)... 32
Broadax, curved handle, signed "Wm. Beatty & Son, Chester, Pa.," bull design (A-E) 135
Broadax, long handle (A-E)... 80
Broadax, long handle (A-E)... 90
Broadax, marked Shapleigh Day & Co., wide blade, 11" (D-W)............................. 65
Broadax, wing, by Wm. Beatty & Son, Chester, Pa. (A-E) 90
Bucket, Fire, w/ball, leather, red, black & white, "S. Tullinghast no. 2, 1812" (D-E)........... 160
Bull rake, 4½' across base (D-MW)... 33
Bung spigot, pine, hand-hewn, tubular, 20" l. (D-E).................................... 12
Bung spigot, pine, hand-hewn, tubular, 18" l. (D-MW).................................. 8
Caliper, outside, hand-forged, w/bent shaped thumbscrew, 11" l. (D-E) 35
Caliper, wooden, handmade (D-E).. 20
Calipers, hand forged outside, w/heart shaped thumbscrew (D-E) 45
Calipers, inside-outside (comical), shape of female legs (A-E) 22
Candle drying rack, revolving crossbars above pedestaled tripod base (D-MW) 80
Carpenter's dividers, w/brass thumbscrew, 12" (D-E) 12
Carpet beater, batwing (D-MW) 8
Charcoal iron, smokestack (D-NE)... 12
Child's bucksaw, complete, 15" (D-E).. 20
Chisel, corner (D-E).. 19
Chisel, handwrought, signed "Gilbert," high quality (A-E)............................... 375
Clamp, "C", handwrought (D-MW) 12
Clamp, pegged & mortised, early (D-E) 10
Clamp, pine, w/wooden screw, 22" l. (D-MW) 35
Clamp, w/wooden screw, 12" l., ¾" diam., jaws, 10" l., 1½" sq. (D-MW)............... 28
Comb, curry, horse & rider carved at top, name reverse side (D-NE).................. 25
Comb, flax, cover (D-MW).. 45
Comb, flax, pine, decor., metal teeth (D-E)... 45
Compass, handwrought, "heart," thumbscrew (D-E).................................... 49
Compass, heart-shaped thumbscrew, hand gorged, 18th C., 14½" l. (D-E)............... 40
Compass, pine (D-W)... 35
Compass plane (D-E).. 16
Corkscrew, 4¼" l. (D-MW) 5
Corn dryer, 10 prongs (D-MW)... 7
Corn dryer, 12 prongs (D-MW)... 10
Corn dryer, 12 prongs (D-W).. 10
Corn planter, wooden, early, 1868 patent date (D-W) 125
Corn sheller, tabletop, complete & workable (D-MW)................................... 45
Crane plate, footed w/hanging ring, 18th C., 13½×16" (D-NE)......................... 65
Croze, cooper's (D-E).. 40
Croze, cooper's (D-MW).. 22
Croze, cooper's, burl (D-E).. 75
Croze, cooper's, unusual (D-E).. 33
Dividers/compass, barn builder, handwrought, 17" (D-E) 25
Dowel cutter (D-E).. 8
Drawknife, cooper's, curved (D-E)... 15
Drawknife, cooper's, tang through handle & bent, signed (D-E)......................... 14
Drawshave, cooper's (D-E).. 15
Drill, pump (D-MW)... 90
Farrier's buttress, small crack in handle (D-E).. 12
Fence stretcher, early (D-MW) 8
Fid, hand-carved, sailor's tool used for working w/rope (D-E)......................... 85
Flail, handle 47" l., beater 31½" l., refinished (D-MW)................................ 12

Flail, and sickle, early, signed "Hamilton" (A-E) ....$ 30

Flail, wooden swivel (A-E) 20

Flat plane, w/push handle behind blade, sm. plate missing on throat (D-E)........................ 21

Froe, cooper's, handwrought, 9", w/10½" handle (D-W) 25

Froe, grafting, 9" l. (D-E) 22

Froe, splitting, curved (D-E) 24

Gauge, marking, for post & rail fence (D-E) 55

Gauge, slitting, mortise & pegged, wooden handle missing, early (D-E) 25

Grist mill, Enterprise, table, w/wheel, working, no. 750 (for shelling corn) (D-MW) 20

Grass seed stripper, refinished (D-MW).. 35

Gauge, handwrought, w/wood handle, early, 16" (D-E) 12

Hammer, claw, handwrought, wood handle, 4" head (D-E) 15

Hammer, hand-forged, claw w/wood handle, 4" head (D-E) 18

Hammer, tack, handwrought, w/wooden handle, 3¾" l. head (D-E)................................... 12

Hayfork, long wooden ash handle, 1 end split into 3 branches, refinished (D-E).................. 45

Hayfork, 3 tines (D-MW)... 52

Hay hook, short rod w/hook (D-MW) 1

Hone block, pine frame, pink shale, 3"×9" (D-E) 50

Hook, bale, T-shape w/wooden handle, hook 9" l. (D-MW).. 4

Hook, cant, pattern, pegged (D-NE) 12

Hook, hay, handwrought (D-MW) 5

Hook, hay, long rod w/hook (D-MW) 3

Hook tool, w/L-shaped wood handle, end of rod is split & curled in opposite directions, 14" (D-E) . 16

Hoop, covered wagon, original finish (D-MW) 15

Ice saw, early, 32" l. (D-E).. 38

Ice tongs (D-MW)... 10

Ice tongs (D-N) 6

Ice tongs (D-W) 7

Ice tongs, small (D-SE) 12

Jackknife, black & gilt trade sign, movable, blade 8" l. (D-NE) 115

Jam pike head, lumberman's, w/hook (D-E) 6

Key, dental, folding w/tooth puller (D-E) 25

Kiln, pipe, handwrought, 10¼" l. × 10½" h. (D-E)... 235

Kiln, pipe, handwrought (D-NE) 260

Corn planter, early, refinished (D-MW) $35

Berry basket form (D-NE) $55

Drag shoe (D-MW) $18

Bog shoes (D-S) $22

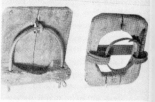

Clamp, pine, pegged, refinished (D-MW) $39

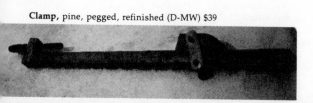

Knife, bleeder trip, handwrought, w/tin cup receptacle (A-E) ....$ 30
Knife, chamfer, curved, hand-forged iron w/wood handles, 15″ l. (D-MW)   20
Knife, chamfer, handwrought, w/wood handles, cooper's, curved, 15″ (D-E).....................   20
Knife, flax, 27″ (D-NE)   18
Lasts, infants' (D-E)   32
Lasts, men's boot (D-MW)   55
Level, cherry, 26¼″ (D-NE)   22
Level, wooden (D-MW)   5
Log, hand hewed, for oiling wagon wheels, 4′ l. (D-E)   35
Mallet, burl, 14½″ (A-E)   105
Mallet, burl w/oak handle (D-W)   10
Mallet, burl w/ash handle (D-E)   45
Mallet, maple, primitive, mid-19th C., refinished (D-NE)   28
Marking gauge, burl slide, early thumbscrew (D-E)   17
Marking gauge, rosewood, round slide, wooden screw, signed (D-E)   15
Mortar, grain, from hollow tree trunk, 3 ft. h. w/orig. pestle for grinding grain (D-E)   125
Nail puller, handwrought, 13″ l. (D-E)...   8
Nail puller, handwrought, 12″ l. (D-MW)..   7
Peel, used on crane plates, handwrought, rare size, 20″ (D-E)   35
Pipe tongs (D-E)   150
Pipe tongs, handwrought, notched decor. on spring loaded handles, acorn finial, 15″ l. (D-MW) .   125
Pitchfork, long handle (D-MW)   35
Pitchfork, wood w/iron tips (A-E)..   27
Plane, block, 8″ (D-SW)...   12
Plane, carpenter's (D-W)   8
Plane, grooving (D-W)   15
Plane, handmade, adjustable, maple, w/hand forged cutting blade (D-E)..............................   55
Plane, horned, primitive (D-E)   14
Plane, jointer, cooper's, solid tiger maple, 4′ (D-NE)   225
Plane, jointer, wooden, 26″ l. (D-S)...   8
Plane, plow, adjustable, fence adjusts by wooden screws, signed Edward Carter, Troy, N. Y.
    (D-E)   23
Plane, plow, adjustable, ivory runners (D-E)   114
Plane, plow, carved out saw grip, fence adjusts on wooden screws (D-E)......................   22
Plane, plow, long, hand grip on top, wedged fence (D-E)   27
Plane, rabbet (D-E)   12
Plane, smoothing, dated 1870 (D-E)   22
Plane, smoothing, horned (D-E)   22
Planes, matched set of tongue & groove (D-E)   12
Potato fork/digger w/wooden teeth, long handle w/carved grip (D-MW)   30
Pot rake w/iron ring & 30″ l. wooden handle (D-E)   32
Press, lard or fruit, 8″ diam., 10″ h. (D-NE)   20
Pulley, small, w/ring at top, mkd. 1880, 2″ w., 2″ d., 3½″ h. (D-MW)...........................   8
Pulley, w/wheel (D-MW)   5
Pump, barrel, w/wooden plunger & handle, refinished (D-E)..   45
Pump drill, primitive (D-N)   90
Pump handle, handwrought, 1 long drop bar, 1 spring bar (D-E)   27
Race wheel, handwrought, 8½″ diam., 15″ l. (D-E)...   30
Race wheel, handwrought, traveler wood handle (D-W)   17
Rake, wooden, long whittled handle, 18 long whittled teeth, refinished (D-E)   35
Rake head, all wood w/12 long whittled teeth, handleless, refinished (D-MW)   12
Ratchet, hanging light holder, all wood, 2 3-ft. lengths, 19 notches (D-E)   125
Router, coachmaker's, handwrought iron (D-E)   28
Router, coachmaker's, maple & cast steel bladed, 7½″ w., 7½″ l. (D-E)   30
Router, coachmaker's, maple & cast steel bladed, 7½″ w., 7½″ l. (D-W)   22
Rug stretcher, wooden (D-W)..   15
Rye straw press, handmade & pegged, ca. 1800 (D-E)..   190
Sawhorse, early (D-E)   20
Saw, keyhole, maple handled, 12½″ l. (D-E)   12

Saw, log, 1-man (D-MW) ....\$ 6
Saw, stair-maker's, ex. cond. (D-NE) 45
Scissors, expanding type for lifting hot coals from fire (D-NE) 45
Scorper, bowlmaker's (D-E) 32
Scorper, bowlmaker's, closed, 2″ diam. blade, 15″ overall (D-E) 35
Scorper, cast steel, square double handle, 4½″ × 5″ (D-E) 25
Scorper, cooper's, cast steel blade, double wood handles, 5″ w. (D-W) 15
Scorper, corset-shape (D-E) 25
Scorper, curved wooden handle, unusual, 1″ blade, 21″ l. (D-MW) 34
Scorper, square, double handle, cast, 4½″×5″ (D-E) 25
Screwdriver, hand carved wooden handle, 7″ l. (D-E) 12
Scythe, barley, handwrought (D-W) 27
Scythe, wooden handle, 18th C. (N-E) 20
Shaving horse, oak & pine, complete, unfinished (D-W) 35
Shaving horse or bench, handmade, complete (D-SE) 125
Sheep stamp, old red wood block, leather letter (D-E) 25
Shovel, ash, w/brass top, 18th C. (D-MW) 24
Shovel, grain, carved from 1 pc. wood, 3½″ h. (A-NE) 75
Shovel, grain, poplar, deep ovoid bowl & long handle, refinished (D-MW) 45
Shovel, long handle, curled top (D-E) 65
Shovel, snow, metal-tipped lip, turned handle (D-MW) 8
Sifter-scoop, charcoal, 30″ wooden handle (D-W) 30
Skewer holder, handwrought, brass inlay, signed "ER 1806," complete w/skewers (A-E)........ 1025
Slick, long handle, signed, 4″ w. blade (D-E) 35
Slick, lumberman's, wooden crossbar handle, handwrought, 21″ (D-NE) 25
Spade, iron, hand-forged, wooden handle (D-E) 85
Spoke pointer (D-E) 10
Spoke shave (D-MW) 12
Spoke shave, curved copper sole, knobby handles, large (D-E) 17
Spoke shave, rounded grips, brass sole, 13″ (D-E) 18
Spool holder, maple (A-E) 50
Spool holder, w/sand filled base, carrying ring, 2 tiers, orig. old red paint, 5½″ t., 5½″ diam.
   base (D-NE) 55
"T" square, adjustable, for drafting, rosewood, w/brass trim, 22″ (D-E) 22
Square, wooden, 24″ (D-W).. 12
Stamp, tool, handwrought, 1-pc., w/ring handle (D-W) 22
Stitching horse, oak, complete, refinished (D-MW) 55
Strainer, varnish, decorator's, inset of wire mesh acts as strainer, brass devoe plate/1850s patent
   (D-NE) 12
Striker, handled, handmade w/pumpkin shaped "head," 10″ (D-NE) 14
Trammel, handwrought, 20″ l. (D-W) 12
Trammel, iron & tin, extends to 58″ (D-MW) 82
Trammel, long crane (D-E) 55
Trammel, small crane (D-E) 40
Trammel, s-scrolls, 18th C. (D-E) 145
Racewheel/traveler, cooper's, all wood (D-E) 40
Racewheel/traveler, hand-forged iron, 8½″ diam., 15″ l. (D-E) 32
Traveler, wheelwright's (D-E) 15
Traveler, wheelwright's, pine, 25″ circum. (D-NW) 75
Traveler, wooden handle (D-E).. 35
Vise, wooden (D-N).. 125
Wagon ax holder, Conestoga, handwrought, fish design (A-E) 450
Wagon jack, oak, complete (D-W) 45
Wagon wrench & bit brace comb., w/iron bit, wood handles, 10″ l., 6″ w. (D-E) 55
Whetstone holder, handle, carved from hollow log, 12″ l. (D-MW)........................... 30
Whetstone holder, pine, carved (D-E)... 38
Wrench, pipe & monkey combination (D-MW) 10
Wrench, wagon wheel (D-MW) 7
Wrench, wooden, hand-hewn (D-E) 18

Toys

Early, interesting old toys—especially the hand-carved examples—are truly vivid expressions of the American craftsman's art of imagination. They are continuously in demand and prices increase sharply each year. Those worthy of consideration as folk art are toys from the Pennsylvania and New England provinces, as both areas were centers of craft tradition in America.

Among the most interesting of the early toys are the carved wooden dolls, squeak toys, jointed wood and metal jumping figures, wood and chalk animals, whistles, miniatures, and the ever-popular "Sunday" toys, when boisterous play was banned. The carved Gardens of Eden and Noah's Arks were especially designed for this purpose. The latter oftentimes contained as many as fifty minutely carved and decorated animals, in addition to human figures. Among the most sought-after are the carved and polychromed groupings that can be attributed to Wilhelm Schimmel.

The American toy industry was brought into being during the first decades of the nineteenth century. William S. Tower of South Hingham, Massachusetts, a carpenter by profession, has often been called the founder of the toy industry in America. In spite of the availability and wide usage of wood during the period, an increasing number of tin toys were made, along with cast iron examples. It wasn't until after 1865 that the latter was used at all extensively. It was during the 1870s that the cast iron mechanical banks were evolved.

Because of the scarcity of earlier examples, today there is a rapidly growing band of enthusiasts buying up toys, almost regardless of the era. Sometimes the items haven't been around as long as those doing the prospecting! But, whether it is indicative of a universal yearning for the good old days, or simply a case of monkey-see, monkey-do, the rush is on.

* * *

Acrobat, clockwork, American Toy Co., ca. 1880 (A-MW)	$ 610
Acrobat, mechanical, tin, ca. 1925 (A-MW)	50
Airplane, iron, nickel wings & propeller, Hubley, 3½" (D-W)	20
Airplane, replica of Lindy's "Spirit of St. Louis" (D-E)	40
Alligator, mechanical, tin, ca. 1920 (A-MW)	15
Ark, wooden (D-MW)	70
Ball player, mechanical, tin, ca. 1910 (A-MW)	210
Banjo player, clockwork, secor, ca. 1880 (A-MW)	2700
Banjo player, clockwork, secor, ca. 1880 (D-E)	2000
Bareback rider, mechanical, tin, ca. 1900 (D-MW)	200
Barn, wood (D-MW)	160
Beetle, mechanical, tin, early (D-W)	25
Bellringer, dancing boy & girl, Watrous Mfg. Co., Conn. (A-MW)	325
Bellringer, on velocipede, clockwork, animated (A-MW)	425
Bicycle rider, on string, American flyer (A-MW)	50
Billiard player, mechanical, tin, ca. 1915 (A-MW)	155
Bird, whistling, mechanical, tin (A-MW)	45
Blocks, puzzle, McLaughlin Bros., ca. 1890 (A-MW)	130
Blocks, set, w/box, wood (D-MW)	80
Board game, slate, played w/marbles, 9" sq. (D-NE)	19
Boat, clockwork, "three friends," tin (A-MW)	35
Boat, friction driven, early 1900s (A-MW)	50

Boat, live steam, ca. 1890 (A-MW) ....$ 375
Boat, windup, small, ca. 1920 (A-MW)   40
Boat, windup, tin, ca. 1920 (A-MW)..   130
B. O. Plenty, mechanical, tin, Marx (A-MW)   55
Boy, naughty, windup, Lehmann (A-MW)   375
Boy on sled, friction, tin (D-E)   75
Bucking broncho, windup, Lehmann (A-MW).................................   300
Cab, hansom, cast iron (A-MW)   700
Cab, hansom, w/horse, tin (A-MW)..   80
Cake walkers, clockwork, Ives, ca. 1880 (A-MW)   400
Cannon, w/soldier, W. W. I, tin (D-MW)   10
Car, electric, 1905, wood w/metal chassis & wheels (A-MW)   250
Carousel, mechanical, tin, ca. 1910 (D-MW)   175
Cart, baggage, w/3 metal wheels (D-W)   75
Cart, donkey, cast iron, Hubley (A-MW)   175
Cart, dump, cast iron (A-MW)..   80
Cart, horse, tin, ca. 1870 (A-MW)   90
Cart, one-horse, cast iron (D-E)   75
Cart, road, small, cast iron (A-MW)   100
Checkerboard, complete (D-MW)..   25
Clown, on pig, mechanical, tin, ca. 1915 (A-MW)   110
Clown, rocking, mechanical, tin, ca. 1915 (A-MW).........................   110
Clowns, on mechanical see-saw (A-MW)   80
Coffee grinder, w/middle drawer, iron (D-NE)   45
Colored dancers, mechanical, tin, ca. 1900 (A-MW)   400
Concert, Thomas, clockwork, animated (A-MW)   300
Coupe, iron, Kilgore, traces orig. paint, 5″ (D-W)...........................   40
Cowboy, mechanical, Decamp (A-MW)   60
Cribbage board, complete (D-MW)   18
Crone, with basket, mechanical, tin, walks, ca. 1910 (A-MW).........   200
Dancer, tap, Negro, ca. 1880 (D-MW)   175
Dancers, clockwork, Ives, ex. cond., ca. 1890 (A-MW)   600
Dancers, Jack Sprat & wife, mechanical, tin, ca. 1900 (A-MW)   300
Dancers, on mirrored stage, automatic, clockwork, ca. 1865 (A-MW)   275
Dirigible carousel, mechanical, tin, ca. 1910 (A-MW)   300

Horse, wooden, hand-carved, on iron stand, late 19th C., 36″ l. (D-W) $150

Horse, wooden, hand-carved & decor., 8″ h. (D-MW) $45

Cow, on stand, hand-carved, orig. old red paint, 8½″ h. (D-MW) $55

Boat, hand-carved (D-MW) $18

Trolley, pine, orig. red paint, 5½″ l. (D-W) $10

Sled, decor., painted green w/red trim, yellow & white flowers, early, 32″ l. (D-MW) $90

Doll cradle, Penna. Dutch, orig. untouched finish, 17½″ l. (D-W) $39

Doll bed, spool-turned, orig. old blue paint (D-W) $35

Dog, pine, carved (D-E)	$ 50
Doll bed, wooden frame, wire mattress (D-E)	27
Doll blanket chest, pine (D-E)	85
Doll blanket chest, pine, dov. const., w/4 ball feet (A-NE)	135
Doll chair, Chippendale, 5¼" h. (S-MW)	22
Doll coach, baby buggy, 1870 (A-NE)	200
Doll cradle, old blue paint (A-E)	35
Doll cradle, softwood, w/hooded top (A-E)	45
Doll cradle, ribbon weave (A-E)	15
Doll cradle, swinging, slipper feet, turned black knobs, 20" l. (A-E)	325
Doll cradle, Windsor, fanback, old decor. (D-E)	350
Doll cradle, wood, 16" l., 11½" w. incl. rockers, 5½" h. (D-MW)	25
Doll crib, wicker, 11½" h. (D-E)	22
Doll dishes, tin, 24-pc. (D-E)	20
Doll, figure of man, jointed legs & arms, wood carving (D-E)	85
Doll, milliner's model, papier-mâché head, well modeled hairdo, wooden arms & legs, leather body, orig. underclothes, ex. cond., 11" t. (D-NE)	115
Doll, Popeye, wooden, jointed (D-E)	30
Doll, rag, handmade, black stocking hat, buttons & skirt red yarn, 12½" (D-NE)	10
Doll table, drop leaf, orig. paint, miniature (A-E)	60
Dolls, early, handmade, knitted, black, pr., 15" (D-NE)	35
Dominoes, set, worked in ivory & ebony, joined by brass rivets, dated, red & blue (D-W)	25
Donkey cart, cast iron, Hubley (A-MW)	200
Duck, running, mechanical, tin, ca. 1910 (A-MW)	55
Duck, walking, cloth-covered, tin (A-MW)	30
Elephant, with rider, mechanical, tin, ex. cond. (A-MW)	175
Engine, steam (A-MW)	725
Engine, steam, Weeden, self-propelled (D-MW)	200
Evangelist, male, Ives, ca. 1880 (A-MW)	625
Express, windup, early friction type, Lehmann (A-W)	100
Fire patrol, cast iron, dent (A-MW)	350
Fire pumper, cast iron (A-MW)	375
Fire pumper, cast iron, Wilkens (A-MW)	285
Fire pumper, mechanical, Wilkens, ca. 1919 (A-MW)	300
Fire pumper, wind-up, tin, "Wilkens," comp. w/driver, rubber tires (D-W)	90
Firetruck (A-E)	50
Flatiron (D-E)	4
Fox & duck, mechanical, tin, ca. 1910 (D-MW)	125
Game, peg board, early, complete (D-E)	18
Game, peg, wooden, handmade, 8 pegs, 1-pc., 5½" sq. (D-W)	16
Giraffe, wooden, jointed, painted black splotches on natural pine, 6"×11" (D-NE)	30
Girl, hunchback, clockwork, animated (A-MW)	300
Girl, swinging, clockwork, Ives, ca. 1880 (A-MW)	850
Goat, mounted on iron base w/iron wheels & pull bar (D-NE)	90
Goat, on treadmill, hand-crafted, one of kind (A-MW)	100
Ham & Sam, mechanical, tin, F. Strauss (D-NE)	125
Hi Way Henry, mechanical, tin, ca. 1925 (A-MW)	700
Hobby-horse, glass eyes & wooly mane & tail, 3" h. (D-NE)	250
Hobby-horse, small, wood, ca. 1850 (D-E)	150
Hobby-horse, wood, painted red, ca. 1850 (D-E)	115
Hook & ladder, cast iron (D-E)	65
Hook & ladder, cast iron, Hubley (D-MW)	350
Hook & ladder, cast iron, w/horses, Hubley, ca. 1910 (A-MW)	300
Hook & ladder, cast iron, w/horses, Hubley, ca. 1915 (A-MW)	250
Horse, carved, pine (D-E)	50
Horse, colorful, wood (A-E)	25
Horse feeding, mechanical, clockwork (A-MW)	160
Horse, wood carved (D-E)	70
Horse, wood carving, apple green on dk. green base w/metal wheels, 9½"×8¾" (A-NE)	375

Horse, wooden, w/jockey rider, animated (D-E) ....$ 150
Horse & buggy, clockwork, American Toy Co., ex. cond., ca. 1875 (A-MW)   1500
Horse & buggy, iron (A-E)   40
Horse & buggy, metal & wood (A-MW)...   120
Horse & carriage, cast iron, dent (A-MW)   210
Horse & cart, mechanical, tin, erratic motion, G & K (A-MW)   80
Horse & cart, tin (A-MW)   180
Horse & wagon, cast iron, dent (A-MW)..   300
Horse & wagon, tin (A-MW)   100
Horse race attachment, for steam engine, can be hand operated (D-MW)   60
Horses, pulling circus wagon, iron (D-NE)   125
Horses (3), pulling fireman's ladder, iron (D-E)   190
Horses, tin, early, pr. (A-MW)   50
Jack-in-the-box, tin (A-MW)   60
Jazzbo Jim, mechanical, dancing banjo player, good cond. (D-E)   100
Jenny the balking mule, mechanical, tin, ca. 1920 (A-MW)   75
Jocko the golfer, mechanical, tin, ca. 1925 (A-MW)   110
Joe Penner, mechanical (D-E)   115
Kettle, iron (D-E)   7
Kiddie-car, 4-wheeled, orig. paint (A-E)   42
Komical cop, mechanical (D-E)   60
Lamb, in cage, wood (D-MW)..   75
Landau, cast iron, Wilkens (A-MW)   1500
LeClown orchestra, F. Martin, ca. 1900 (A-MW)...   450
Locomotive, w/coal car, friction, tin & wood, red & yellow decor. (D-MW)....................   60
Magic lantern, early (A-MW)   50
Magic lantern, early (A-MW)   70
Man & goat, mechanical, tin, ca. 1915 (A-MW)...   160
Man at grindstone, mechanical, tin (A-MW)   15
Man on motorcycle, mechanical, tin (A-MW)   150
Mickey Mouse band, Marx, mechanical, tin (A-MW)..   200
Menagerie, in cage, wooden, metal wheels (D-S)   150
Milk wagon, red, w/horse & milk cans (A-E)..   325
Monkey and the coconut bellringer, cast iron (A-MW)   175
Monkey, pushing drum, mechanical, tin, 1915 (A-MW)..   90
Motorcycle & cop, iron, "champion," 7" (D-W)   30
Motorcycle & cop, iron, (Harley Davidson) Hubley, 5" (D-W)   22
Motorcycle, w/side car, iron, nickel wheels (D-W)   15
Mule, balking, tin, Lehmann, ex. cond. (D-W)   58
Music box, animal act, clockwork, mechanical, tin (A-MW)..   300
Music box, circus performers, animated, rare (A-MW)..   400
Music box, bass fiddle player, clockwork, tin (A-MW)   150
Music box, clown on elephant, animated, rare (A-MW)   525
Music box, dog trainer, clockwork, mechanical, tin (A-MW).......................................   225
Music box, dog trainer, clockwork, mechanical, tin (A-MW).......................................   300
Music box, mechanical band, clockwork, tin, ca. 1900 (A-MW)...................................   275
Music box, musician, animated, ca. 1900 (D-S)..   200
Music box, pig, crank tail (A-MW)...   100
Music box, ringmaster & rider, clockwork, animated, one of kind (D-S)   300
Music box, Scots Piper, mechanical, tin (A-MW)   100
Noah's ark, w/animals & birds, carved, late 19th C. (D-NE)......................................   200
Negro woman shopper, mechanical, tin (A-MW)   150
Nodder, chestnut mare & colt on wheels, colorful wood & papier-mâché, 6"×8" (D-E)   75
Nodder, goose, tin, 2"×4½" (D-W)   16
Nodder, Happy Hooligan, Kenton, cast iron, ca. 1911 (A-MW)   1100
Nodder, wood carved (D-E)   100
Oarsman, single, clockwork, Ives, ca. 1880 (A-MW)...   500
Onkel, windup, Lehmann, man tips hat-parasol turns (A-MW)   310
Organ, gem (A-MW)..   180

Ox cart, tin, ca. 1870 (A-MW)	$ 90
Ox cart, wood, orig. paint (D-MW)	50
Oxen, cast iron (A-MW)	120
Paddy's dancing pig, windup, Lehmann (A-MW)	200
Pail & child's cup, tin, ca. 1870 (A-MW)	5
Paper toy, clockwork, animated, ca. 1885 (A-MW)	125
Peacock, mechanical, tin (A-MW)	75
Phaeton, cast iron, Hubley (A-MW)	600
Piano, upright, ca. 1900 (D-MW)	50
Pig, mechanical, Decamp, leather covered (A-MW)	160
Pistol, cap, cowboy, 4" (D-E)	37
Pistol, cap, iron, 4½" (D-E)	10
Pistol, cap, single shot, iron (D-E)	8
Pistol, pop, tin (D-E)	6
Police patrol, Happy Hooligan, cast iron, Kenton, unusual, ca. 1910 (A-MW)	4000
Pony, mechanical, fur-covered (A-MW)	50
Popgun, wooden, bow-shaped spring, 10" l. (D-E)	45
Potato masher, wood, 4¼" (D-E)	8
Pretzel vendor, windup, Lehmann (A-MW)	225
Printing press, cast iron (D-E)	95
Pull toy, bisque figures, musical instruments, animated (A-MW)	400
Pull toy, bisque head doll & swinging girl, animated (A-MW)	600
Pull toy, butterfly, tin, 10" wing span, wings flap, wooden base, decor. w/red, green & yellow, 26" l. (D-NE)	55
Pull toy, chef, animated (A-MW)	120
Pull toy, cow, leather, moos when head moves (A-MW)	190
Pull toy, horse & rider, wood, early (A-MW)	400
Pull toy, monkeys, swinging, cast iron (D-MW)	300
Pull toy, old witch, animated (A-MW)	35
Punch, walks, mechanical, tin, ca. 1910 (A-MW)	450
Quack quack, windup, Lehmann (A-MW)	90
Rabbit, mechanical, fur-covered, ca. 1920 (A-MW)	200
Racer, w/driver, iron, nickel wheels, Hubley, 5" (D-W)	25
Railroad coach, Continental type (A-MW)	180
Railroad transfer, clockwork, George Brown, ex. cond., ca. 1870 (A-MW)	5500
Range, gas, iron (D-E)	12
Rickshaw, "Masuyama," windup, Lehmann (A-MW)	400
Rocking horse, carved wood, double saddle horns, well-shaped head & neck, serrated edge on tail (A-E)	900
Rocking horse, double, pine, unpainted, 26" h. (A-NE)	60
Rocking horse, on orig. red rockers w/yellow decor., leather saddle (A-E)	50
Rocking horse, pine w/smoke decor., 45" l. (A-NE)	350
Rocking horse, shaped wooden saddle, horse's head small, good cond. (A-E)	500
Rooster, in cage, wood (D-MW)	125
Rooster, mechanical, tin (A-MW)	20
Rooster & chicken, mechanical, tin (A-MW)	25
Sand toy, Oriental, boy pops in & out (A-MW)	300
Schoolboy, four problems, mechanical, tin (A-MW)	400
See-saw, clockwork, Ives, ex. cond., ca. 1875 (A-MW)	4000
See-saw, clockwork, woman pops out of chimney, ex. cond. (A-MW)	2100
Sewing machine, Singer (D-NE)	7
Sewing machine, Singer, tin, painted red (D-E)	15
Shooting gallery, beaver eating tree, iron, 6×16" (D-E)	125
Skating girl, mechanical, tin (A-MW)	75
Skier, footboard, mechanical, tin, ca. 1915 (A-MW)	150
Skier, mechanical, tin, ca. 1910 (A-MW)	210
Sled, orig. decor. finish, ca. 1880 (D-E)	150
Sleigh, orig. red paint, w/green & yellow floral decor., pulls in form of goose head & neck attached to runners, metal (D-MW)	100

Sleigh, orig. yellow paint, w/green stencil & red sleighs, dated 1860 (A-E) ....$ 130
Sleigh, 2 horse w/woman, cast iron, Hubley (A-MW) 600
Sleigh, w/wrought iron hdwe. & decor. details, painted in plaid design (red, yellow, blue &
 orange on cream background) with red runners striped in white, all orig., plush seat, 33"
 exclusive of handle (A-E).. 300
Soldier, windup, Lehmann (A-MW).. 150
Squeak, bird cage (A-E) 22
Squeak, cardinal (D-E)... 100
Squeak, chicken coop (A-E) 40
Squeak, donkey (A-E).. 40
Steam roller, iron (D-W) 125
Stove, iron, nickel plated "Royal," complete w/cooking pots & stove pipe (D-SE) 65
Stove, & utensils, cast iron (A-MW).. 100
Stove, wooden, handmade, painted black (D-E).. 45
Street cleaner, horse-drawn, cast iron, Wilkens (A-MW) 1050
Stubborn donkey, windup, Lehmann (A-MW) 50
Sulky, cast iron (A-MW) 100
Sulky w/driver, iron, 5" (D-W) 25
Surrey, cast iron, Hubley (A-MW) 925
Swing, children's, mechanical, ca. 1900 (A-MW).. 200
Teeter-totter, w/2 seated figures, Gibbs, tin (D-W) 30
Tin lizzie, windup (A-MW) 60
Tin penney, child's highchair converts to table (A-MW) 45
Tin penney, oarsmen (A-MW).. 45
Tip top porter, mechanical, tin, ca. 1920 (A-MW).. 80
Tractor, iron, Arcade, 3½" (D-W).. 20
Tractor, iron, w/wooden wheels, 3½" (D-W)... 10
Train, clockwork, Penn R. R. (A-MW) 120
Train, Lionel, engine w/tender, no. 310 (D-E) 22
Train, Lionel, engine w/tender, no. 2025 (D-E) 27
Train, Lionel, engine w/tender, no. 2037 (D-E) 25
Train, pull, cast iron, carpenter (A-MW)... 100
Train, tin, clockwork, 5-pc. (A-MW) 1100
Train, wooden, 6 pieces, late 19th C. (D-MW) 42
Trolley, horse, lithographed, tin, ca. 1880 (A-MW)... 750
Trolley, open air, Morton converse, ca. 1890 (A-MW) 675
Trolley, w/riders, Hill Climb Co., friction (D-E).. 65
Truck, dump, iron, comp. w/driver, Arcade, 10" (D-W).. 115
Truck, dump, iron, Kilgore, 8½" (D-W)... 60
Truck, fire pumper, iron, w/rubber tires, Kenton, 7" (D-W) 40
Truck, hook & ladder, Ives (D-E) 195
Truck, Mack, cast iron (D-E)... 125
Velocipede, clockwork, ca. 1870 (A-MW) 400
Velocipede, clockwork, Stevens & Brown, ca. 1870 (A-MW) 600
Velocipede, 2 wheels w/fenders, Toledo (D-W) 250
Velocipede, w/rider, mechanical, tin (A-MW).. 210
Wagon, circus, overland, cast iron, Kenton (A-MW).. 160
Wagon, contractor's, cast iron (A-MW) 120
Wagon, contractor's, cast iron, Hubley (D-MW) 125
Wagon, delivery, cast iron, Kenton (A-MW)... 200
Wagon, delivery, w/horses, covered, tin (A-MW) 235
Wagon, metal wheels, red & black (D-E)... 65
Wagon, U. S. mail, early, tin, ca. 1870 (A-MW) 225
Water mill attachment, for steam engine, ca. 1905 (A-MW) 70
Water pump, tin, ca. 1890 (A-MW) 120
Woman & churn, clockwork, Ives, ca. 1880 (A-MW) 450
Woman's rights, clockwork, Ives, ex. cond., ca. 1880 (A-MW).. 1200
Woman with sweeper, mechanical, tin, ca. 1900 (A-MW) 175
Zilatone, Wolverine, mechanical, tin (A-MW) 135

Trade Signs

One of the most fascinating fields of collecting today is that of advertising signs. They appeal to both young and old, and are an excellent specialty for the collector who has a limited space available for display. Regardless of size or shape, these objects are actually works of art especially designed to capture the attention of the public.

During the horse-and-buggy days, stores displayed trade signs of every conceivable shape, either above their doors or on the sidewalks. This is the silent group of trade signs, as their very existence was sufficient to inform anyone that here was a particular kind of business. A big hat signified the hat manufacturer, while a giant pair of glasses indicated the optical supply manufacturer. The jeweler displayed a large dummy clock, the pharmacist a mortar and pestle, the barber a colorful striped barber pole, and the cigar store a wooden Indian.

By the Civil War, a considerable proportion of the trade signs were standardized and mass-produced. In most instances, a merchant simply ordered the desired trade sign from a catalog supplied by a wholesale manufacturer who carried them in stock.

* * *

 Tavern sign, handwrought, Indian chief on horseback, 19th C., 54" h. (A-E) $600

Fish-seller's sign, carved & painted Atlantic salmon, 34" l., 9½" h., 5" w. (A-NE) $1050

American flag, painted, w/applied sandpaper letters reading "American 5 cent cigar," 28" l. (A-NE) ....$ 1200
Ax blade, tin, 11½" l. (D-NE) 90
Ax, wooden, 58" (D-MW) 90
Barber, handwrought iron, razor w/wooden handle (A-NE) 25
Blacksmith shop, wood horse, ca. 1900, 30" l. (D-MW) 280
Blacksmith, w/words "blacksmith, horseshoes & axe," carved in relief, black paint, weathered condition, 8½' l., 20" h. (D-E) 400
Boat, large, wooden, old paint (D-W) 70
Bootmaker, poplar, actual boot, 3-dimensional, 36" h. (D-W) 350
Clock, wood, 2 black & white tin faces, 21"×30" (D-MW) 185
Clockmaker, cast iron clock (D-NE) 160
Fish seller, carved & painted, "Atlantic salmon" 34" l. × 9½" h. × 5" w. (A-NE)............. 1050
Fish, wood carved, yellow paint (D-E) 82
Gunsmith, 9' double barrel shotgun, orig. cond. (D-N) 1500
Gunsmith, 9' double barrel shotgun, wood, orig. cond. (D-E) 1500
Knife sharpener, form of jackknife, wood, painted (D-E) 215
Livery stable, "teams to let," painted, 17×116" (D-E)... 65
Pipe tobacco, large, ca. 1860 (A-E) 75
Pork, painted in orange & black, reads "pork" on one side & "soap" on other, 15" h. (A-NE). 90
Poultry, hand-carved, wood, form of rooster (D-E).. 215
Rubber boots, large, Boston Shoe Co. (D-E) 55
Screwdriver, hollow iron shaft w/red wood handle, 43" l. (D-NE) 150
Shoeing, G. C. Wells, large (D-NE)... 275
Watch repair, cast iron, ca. 1800 (D-E) 150

Tramp Art

Tramp Art dates from the remaining years of the last century. The name applies to numerous articles made by tramps, literally "foot walkers." These gentlemen gathered discarded wooden cigar boxes—the basic ingredient of their craft—and after having acquired a supply, the carver was ready to produce an item he could either peddle or trade for food and lodging as he roamed the countryside.

Examples of Tramp Art were often embellished with notches cut from the board ends. This type of chip carving resulted in maximum decoration with minimum tool requirements, usually only a good sharp pocketknife. The favorite item produced was the comb and brush holder. However, a number of very desirable objects were made ranging from trinket boxes to furniture. Today, most experts consider these objects to be the last remnants of American folk art still available at reasonable prices.

* * *

Trinket box, tramp art, hinged lid (D-MW) $23

Trinket box, tramp art, 12" l., 6½" h. (D-W) $18

Art pedestal, w/double fronted drawer, 21" l., 13" h. (A-NE)	$ 175
Box, trinket, footed w/hinged cover, 6" h., pyramidal decor. (D-W)	16
Cane, walking, painted gold (D-E)	38
Chest, jewelry, 2 drawers, lift-top compartment, footed, 7¾" h. (D-E)	65
Comb box, large, ca. 1900 (D-E)	60
Comb-brush holder, 11" h. (D-MW)	32
Comb case, hanging w/mirror & towel bar, pyramidal decor. (D-E)	65
Doll bed (D-E)	18
Doll dresser (D-E)	32
Frame, picture, orig. gold paint, 8"×10" (D-W)	10
Frame, picture, carved pyramidal decor., 12"×18" (D-MW)	22
Frame, picture, carved pyramidal decor. painted gold, 12"×18" (D-MW)	22
Frame, picture, notched edges, orig. gold paint, 11"×13" (D-MW)	12
Frame, picture, 10 layers of wood, painted brown, porcelain pin head decor., 18" × 22" (D-E)	35
Lantern, glass panes, 8" sq., 12" h. (D-W)	65
Match safe, 7½" h. (D-E)	18
Mirror w/frame, carved pyramidal decor., 18×24" (D-MW)	32
Pencil box, 8" l., 3" h. (D-E)	28
Washstand, w/hex signs (D-E)	125

Weapons and Accessories

Settling America's wilderness during the sixteenth and seventeenth centuries was largely accomplished by men carrying firearms. The gun was as essential a part of the home equipment as a piece of furniture. Colonists relied on it for much of their food, and some of their clothing, as well as protection. Today, the appeal of guns is perhaps as great as any of the tools or articles that are classified as collectible Americana.

The earliest weapons used in America were the matchlocks and wheel locks which were brought by the colonist from Europe. But available evidence suggests that the one weapon so often associated with the first American colonists—the blunderbuss—did not find its way to America until much later.

Existing conditions stimulated the inventive genius of American settlers to develop the so-called "Kentucky" rifle during the early 1700s. It was the result of the efforts of gunsmiths in Pennsylvania, Virginia, Maryland, and the Carolinas to produce a weapon which would not only meet the needs, but please the eye of the American frontiersman. The confusing term Kentucky rifle simply reflects the long rifle's use in settling Kentucky, not its origin. Although the rifle acquired regional characteristics, because each state developed several schools of rifle-making, its one obvious feature was its down-sloping, gracefully narrow butt.

Most stocks were curly maple; however, cherry, walnut and apple woods are known to exist. Some were handsomely carved, but the great majority were richly decorated with silver or brass inlays of many designs. Some of the earlier examples weighed less than ten pounds and measured fifty-five inches in length. Genuine Pennsylvania long rifles are extremely rare. Many were converted from flintlock to later systems of ignition. These, of course, are not as popular with the serious collector, but they are still considered to be very respectable and command quite good prices.

The American long rifle reached its artistic maturity in the two decades following the American Revolution and, by 1835, it was being replaced by the heavy-barrel, half-stock plains rifles of the Hawken type.

Other names associated with this field—and of course of much interest to collectors of firearms—are Winchester, Remington, and the famous Colt hand guns developed by Samuel Colt during the 1830s. In 1836 he formed the Patent Arms Company at Paterson, New Jersey, producing the first percussion revolver.

Also associated with the various types of early American weapons are a number of accessories which are very desirable collectibles, such as containers for gunpowder, powder flasks, jugs and horns. The most highly prized are the powder horns engraved with maps, or sketches of historic battle scenes, a fort or town.

* * *

Bear trap, large (D-E)	$ 90
Bear trap (D-E)	95
Bear trap, no. 6 (A-W)	165
Bullet mold, old musket size (D-NE)	18
Cannon, signal, Civil War, ca. 1860 (A-NE)	700

Flask, brass fit, leather shot, game birds (D-E) ....$ 27
Gun gauge, brass (A-E)..   7
Horn, fox, pine carved, ca. 1820 (D-E)   80
Horn, priming, small, flat (A-E)..   30
Horn, tally-ho, tin (A-E)..   50
Hunting bag, w/hunting knife, sheath & powder horn, animal skin (A-E)   425
Knife, crooked w/shape of hand & wrapped leather handle, carved, 10" l. (A-NE)   450
Pistol, blunderbuss, early, flint lock, brass wire inlay (A-E)   190
Pistol, flintlock, brass barrel & engraving, carved walnut stock, 13" (A-E)............................   350
Pistol, flintlock, walnut stock, marked "S. North," Middletown, Conn., w/eagle (D-NE)........   265
Pistol, hand, double barrel, percussion (A-E)   45
Pistol, Kentucky, homemade, full octagon barrel, rare left-hand lock (A-E)..........................   140
Pistol, Manhattan, 6-shot rotary, E. A. Mfg. Co. (A-E)   85
Pistol, martial, smooth bore, flintlock (A-E)   140
Pistol, martial, smooth bore, orig. flint converted to percussion (A-E)   95
Pistol, pepper box, 6-shot, by Washington Arms Co., engraved, good cond. (A-E)...............   120
Pistol, percussion, H. Aston (A-E)   190
Pistol, percussion, single shot, small, rifled (A-E)   35
Pistol, pocket, percussion (A-E)...   25
Pistol, pocket, Williamson (A-E)...   95
Pistol, single octagon barrel, experimental cap (A-E)   30
Pistol, single shot, homemade, breech-loading, percussion (A-E)   45
Pistols, dueling, John Derr, signed, rare rings crafted on barrel ends, pr. (A-E)   5200
Powder flask, brass, copper & zinc (A-E)..   30
Powder flask, brass w/embossed bust of George Washington & liberty cap at top (A-E).........   180
Powder flask, "Colt's patent" (A-S)   70
Powder flask, copper, 7" t. (A-MW)   30
Powder horn, carved w/initials "E. M.", 4 lg. sq. rigged 3-masted ships w/2 American flags ea., 1
    lg. 2-masted side-wheeled steamboat w/4 American flags, 3 1 & 2 masted sloops, 3 fish,
    lighthouse, canoe w/2 people, ca. 1830, 13¾" l. (A-NE)   750
Powder horn, dog head, rare (A-E)   42
Powder horn, engraved w/covered wagon, signed "John Hollingsworth" (A-E)   250
Powder horn, engraved w/full rigged ship & compass, signed "William Billings" (A-E)..........   170
Powder horn, engraved w/name & date, 1807, man engraved on horseback w/gun & sword (A-E)   70
Powder horn, engraved w/ship, anchor, signed "Joe Morgan" (A-E)   80
Powder horn, large, plain (A-E)..   40
Powder horn, leather pouch (A-E)..   47
Powder horn, Scrimshaw, rare, w/human figures (A-E)..   210
Powder horn, showing Susquehanna River & towns (A-E)   260

Rifle, flintlock, double-barrel, octagonal, full length curly maple stock profusely inlaid w/silver, minor repair to stock, flint hammers replaced (A-E) $2800

Kentucky rifle, flintlock, octagonal, full length curly maple stock (A-E) $1200

Kentucky rifle, w/silver plate w/engraved eagle & shield (A-E) $1000

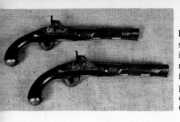

Dueling pistols, silver wire inlay, initial "R" on nameplate, orig. flint converted to percussion, Ketland & Co. locks, 18th C., pr. (A-E) $4900

Hunting bag, animal skin w/fur, including knife & sheath & powder horn (A-E) $425

Powder keg, wood, 10 hoops, labeled rifle, Laflin & Rand (D-E) ....$	55
Revolver, 6-shot (A-E)..	30
Revolver, Smith & Wesson (D-E)	500
Rifle, cane (A-E)	140
Rifle, compressed air, B. S. A. target range (A-E)	30
Rifle, flintlock, by D. Nippes, marked U. S. 1840, L. S. (A-E)	350
Rifle, Kentucky, ca. 1845 (A-NE)..	575
Rifle, Kentucky, curly maple stock, full octagon barrel, rifled, by D. Derr (A-E)..............	375
Rifle, Kentucky, curly maple stock, orig. rifling (A-E)	375
Rifle, Kentucky, curly maple stock, rifled barrel, pierced & engraved patch box (A-E)	350
Rifle, Kentucky, curly maple stock, flint hammer changed to percussion, signed "G. Kopp" (A-E)	650
Rifle, Kentucky, flintlock, full stock, curly maple, octagonal barrel, engraved patch box, inlaid star, carved stock (A-E)	1900
Rifle, Kentucky, flintlock, full stock, curly maple, octagonal barrel, patch box (A-E)	1200
Rifle, Kentucky, full stock, curly maple, rifled by D. Derr (A-E)	450
Rifle, Kentucky, full stock, 15 pcs. silver, I. H. Johnson (A-E)	900
Rifle, Kentucky, full stock percussion, curly maple w/silver & silver wire inlay, brass patch box, inlay of squirrel & acorns on butt, barrel signed "A. T. W", barrel 36" l., O. A., 51¼" l. (A-E)	725
Rifle, Kentucky, full stock, tiger maple (A-E)	350
Rifle, Kentucky, full stock, tiger maple, engraved patch box (A-E)	340
Rifle, Kentucky, half stock, octagon barrel, double trigger (A-E)...................................	200
Rifle, Kentucky, half stock percussion, curly maple w/silver inlay, barrel 33" l., O.A. 47½" l. (A-E)	475
Rifle, Kentucky, half stock, percussion, rifled, set triggers (A-E)...................................	200
Rifle, Kentucky, half stock, 30 pcs. brass, Jos. H. Golcher (A-E)	450
Rifle, Kentucky, large bore, rifled, walnut stock (A-E)...	300
Rifle, Kentucky, orig. flintlock, engraved & pierced patch box, silver inlays (A-E)	1500
Rifle, Kentucky, over & under, inlaid running deer, engraved lock plates, half stock (A-E)	320
Rifle, Kentucky, over & under, 1 barrel rifled, 1 barrel smooth bore, by J. Harder (A-E)........	300
Rifle, Kentucky, over & under, pierced & engraved patch box, barrels rifled, by C. Young (A-E).	300
Rifle, Kentucky, over & under, pierced patch box, barrels rifled (A-E)	365
Rifle, Kentucky, over & under, silver inlays (A-E)	395
Rifle, Kentucky, over & under, tiger maple stock, both barrels rifled, engraved & pierced patch box (A-E)	350
Rifle, Kentucky, over & under, tiger maple stock, engraved & pierced patch box (A-E)	340
Rifle, Kentucky, over & under, walnut stock, both barrels rifled, eagle inlay (A-E)	300
Rifle, Kentucky, pierced patch box (A-E)...	330
Rifle, Kentucky, side-by-side double barrel, walnut stock, engraved barrels, silver deer inlay (A-E)	400
Rifle, Kentucky, silver plate w/engraved eagle & shield, wood carving on stock (A-E)	1000
Rifle, Kentucky, tiger maple stock, smooth bore (A-E)	400
Rifle, Kentucky, tiger maple stock, rifled (A-E)	375
Rifle, Penna., made by Bird & Bros., orig. flintlock w/"cockback & pull trigger," ex. cond. (A-NE)..	950
Rifle, Springfield, VPI, 1861 (A-E)	85
Shot case, oak, "self-lighting" patent 1881, complete (D-W)	350
Shotgun, double-barrel, side hinged, breech, Ethan Allen, 1865 (A-E)	70
Shotgun shell holder w/tools for measuring (D-W)	45
Shot pouch, leather, embossed w/"dead game" scene (A-E)...	25
Sword, cavalry, Civil War (A-E)	65
Turkey call, made from wing bone of turkey, ca. 1800 (D-E)	10

Weathervanes

The weathervane is one of the oldest of weather instruments. This device turns freely on an upright rod and points in the direction from which wind comes; and, the part of the vane which turns into the wind has taken on a variety of shapes through the years. These decorative, yet utilitarian objects, have been made in a combination of woods, tin, iron and copper. Although never intended to be "arty," many of the earlier wooden vanes with their crude but vigorous designs actually resemble modern sculpture in their clean, dynamic lines.

The talented wood carvers contributed clever designs for vanes. Along seaports the fish was common in addition to sailors with swinging arms. The charging buffalo was frequently a western choice, while flying geese and eagles were popular in the south. There were even trade weathervanes, such as the druggist's mortar and pestle, or a revolving pig for the butcher, and an exaggerated boot for the shoemaker. Moreover, there were also handsomely carved silhouetted buggies and human figures, along with a variety of animals including the stag, horse, fish, cow, and the ever-popular cockerel.

Exposed as these objects were to the elements, many have suffered wear and tear. But, since the folk art explosion, collectors have become very understanding on this score, realizing that finding a perfect example just isn't possible; hence, allowances are made, especially when the carvings have been well-executed.

These treasured and early pieces of wooden sculpture should never be repainted or retouched in any way because, in this instance, any improvements will only distract from the original decoration and decreases values.

During the eighteenth century, weathervanes were to be found on the ridges of important public buildings; but, by the middle of the nineteenth century, their manufacture was a prosperous trade, and the American countryside became dotted with professional, new, metal vanes which were painted, gilded, and often striped.

Despite the ominous number of new weathervanes now on the market, the value of early examples continues to advance steadily because of the brisk demand.

* * *

Weathervane, tin, w/arrow & flag, early, large (A-E) $105

Weathervane, copper, horse & jockey, gold, 41"l. (A-NE) $1550

Airplane, copper, fashioned from 1900-1904 Bleriot monoplane, 4'8" l., 4'9" wingspan, 3' h.
(A-NE) ....$ 8500
Arrow & flag, tin, early, large (A-E)... 105
Arrow, old, orig. red paint, no directionals, 24" l. × 5" h. (D-NE) 125
Arrow, wood, old red paint, no directionals, 24" l. × 5" (D-NE) 125
Ball, pine, w/metal arrow (A-E) 85
Coach & four, tin, 48" h. (A-MW) 80
Cow, copper, w/orig. weathered green patina, 28½" l., 16" h. (A-NE) 1150
Cow, molded tin w/fine details (A-E) 290
Cow, sheet metal on copper stand (D-MW) 50
Cow, tin, brass fittings, milk glass ball, complete (D-MW) 125
Cupid, w/horn, wooden, cut-out (A-E) 32
Deer, copper, full directionals, ex. cond. (A-MW) 170
Deer, leaping, copper w/orig. patina & directionals, 20" l. (A-NE) 450
Deer, leaping, copper w/good natural patina (A-NE) 1000
Deer, running, tin, 20"×25" (A-E) 120
Deer, tin (A-E).. 140

Left to right: **cow weathervane,**
molded tin, fine detail (A-E)
$290; **cock weathervane,** tin,
cut-out & punched construction
(A-E) $300

Deer, walking, copper, gold finish, 26" h. × 29" w. (A-NE)... 1450
Dragon, wrought iron, large (A-E) 140
Eagle, spread wings, copper, perched on orb, 36" h., 44" l. (D-E).. 1250
Eagle, spread wings, copper, perched on orb, w/directionals & rod standard (D-E).............. 785
Fish, on cupola, wood (D-E) 650
Horse, copper, directionals (A-E) 180
Horse, copper, small, directionals (D-E) 275
Horse, copper, traces orig. mustard colored paint, 4' l. (D-MW)... 550
Horse, leaping through hoop, copper, orig. patina, 30" l. (A-NE) 1350
Horse, metal, large (A-E) 75
Horse, orig. parcel gilding on tin, blue, 1860 (A-E) 950
Horse, running, copper (D-E) 400
Horse, tin, 33½" l., 21½" h. (A-E) 120
Horse, tin, directionals (D-MW) 37
Horse, tin, full directionals (D-E) 300
Horse, tin, hollow, large (A-E) 95
Horse, trotting, copper, full bodied, orig. gold leaf, no directionals, 30" (D-MW)................ 300
Horse, trotting, copper, gilt good, orig. decor. (D-E) 425
Horse, trotting, tin (A-E) 90
Horse & jockey, copper, in gold, 41" l. (A-NE) 1550
Horse & sulky, copper, horse, gold & black, jockey, red & white, 34" l. (A-NE) 1700
Indian, tin (A-E) 30
Indian w/hatchet, standing on arrow weather vane, handwrought iron (A-E)........................ 535
Indian, w/tomahawk, tin, on wrought iron pole, decor., 49" h. without pole (A-E) 475
Locomotive & tender, wood-burning, pine, traces orig. black paint, orig. iron & wood directionals (A-NE).. 320

Weathervane, man in silk hat on horseback, hollow tin (A-E) $1100

Weathervane, tin, Indian w/tomahawk on wrought iron pole, 49″ h. without pole (A-E) $475

Locomotive, woodburning, pine, w/tender, orig. directionals (A-E) .... $ 3200
Man on horseback, small, tin (A-E) 220
Man with silk hat, on horseback, hollow, tin (A-E) 1100
Peacock, iron, Penna. Dutch, 19th C., 21″ l., 9″ h. (D-E) 200
Pheasant, flying tail, iron, ca. 1870 (D-MW) 250
Pheasant, flying tail, tin, full directionals (D-E) 250
Rooster, cast iron (D-MW) 125
Rooster, copper, on stand (A-E) 110
Rooster, copper, orig. blue paint (D-E) 850
Rooster, copper, orig. weathered green paint, 28½″ l., 16″ h. (A-NE) 1150
Rooster, copper, w/orig. yellow coloring, 22″ h. (A-NE) 775
Rooster crowing, tin, w/full directionals & cupola (D-MW) 225
Rooster, crowing, iron, full directionals, cupola (D-MW) 110
Rooster, tin (A-E) 25
Rooster, tin (A-E) 35
Rooster, tin, cut-out & punched const. (A-E) 300
Rooster, tin, full directionals, red painted decor. (D-N) 55
Statue of Liberty holding flag, punched copper, gilded (D-S) 280
Whale, copper, New Bedford area, ca. 1880 (D-NE) 1700

Wireware

During the latter half of the nineteenth century, country stores began stocking articles made of wire. The largest manufacturer was Woods, Sherwood & Company, Lowell, Massachusetts. Their 1878 catalogue listed literally hundreds of items. Most of the objects were utilitarian, including pie lifters, potato mashers, rug beaters, egg boilers, vegetable washers, corn poppers, flytraps, toasters, vegetable skimmers, tea and coffee strainers. Moreover, there was an array of decorative articles, such as fancy epergnes, compotes, cake stands, fruit baskets, knife rests, napkin rings, and pickle and celery holders with glass containers. To complete the long list, pieces of furniture were also produced, including chairs, flower stands, etc.

There are many interesting pieces of wireware available today at modest prices at antiques shops, shows or at flea markets across the country.

One exception, however, is the decorative round wire basket which has been extremely popular over the years. These were made in a variety of styles, and some could even be folded into different designs. When collapsed flat, many even serve as a trivet.

* * *

Bacon hanger, slab, 10 hooks (D-MW)	$ 10
Bacon hanger, slab, 12 hooks (D-MW)	7
Bacon hanger, slab, 16 hooks (D-S)	10
Boiling basket, 6½" h. (A-E)	42
Boiler, potato, nice patina, ca. 1830, 8"×11" (D-E)	58
Broom holder (D-S)	6
Chair, twisted wire, ca. 1870 (D-W)	25
Chimney cleaner, 16" l. (D-W)	15
Cornucopia, centerpiece (D-MW)	38
Cornucopia, fancy weaving (D-E)	45
Egg basket, collapsible (D-MW)	18
Egg basket, collapsible, footed, carrier handle, ex. cond. (D-MW)	32

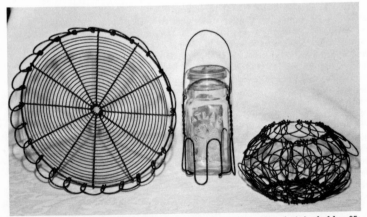

Grouping of wireware (D-MW), *left to right:* **trivet,** 12" diam., $18; **fruit jar holder,** $5; **egg basket,** $23

Potato basket, wireware, early (D-MW) $50

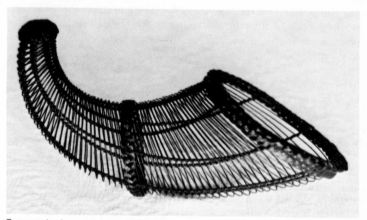

Cornucopia, fancy wireware (D-W) $20

Egg basket, collapsible, small (D-E)	$ 15
Eggbeater (D-E)	3
Fly cover, round (D-W)	6
Flytrap, pyramid type (D-E)	8
Flytrap, w/wire screen, funnel & cylinder shape, 9" h. (D-W)	27
Jar holder, canning w/bail handle (D-MW)	4
Milk carrier, 6 sect. (D-E)	7
Mousetrap, w/wheel (D-E)	12
Ox muzzles, 11" (D-MW)	18
Pie lifter (D-E)	8
Rattrap, 18" l. (D-W)	15
Rattrap, oval shape, 16" l., 8" h. (D-MW)	15
Rattrap & cage, oblong, oval shape, 8½"×15" (D-W)	13
Sack holder, store, graduating shelves, 24" h. (D-W)	25
Sifter, hair, 14" diam. (D-E)	35
Sifter, hair, 14" diam. (D-W)	28
String holder, circular, 14"×14" (D-W)	27
Toast holder, wire trefoils w/wooden handle, 19th C. (D-W)	35
Trivet or stand, 12" diam. (D-MW)	7

Wood Carvings

The artistic ingenuity and inventive craftsmanship of the American woodcarvers has contributed greatly to our cultural history. Much of their work was quite primitive while other specimens were intricately carved and well-executed. Appreciation for the fanciful objects produced by these naive, non-academic, native artists and craftsmen has developed slowly over the years, to the extent that they are sought by private collectors and museums alike.

Best known to collectors of fine rural folk art are the works of the almost legendary, wandering whittler, Wilhelm Schimmel who, according to tradition, tramped throughout southeastern Pennsylvania for a period of about thirty years after the Civil War, carving toy figures and fierce-looking eagles in various sizes. One of the most outstanding characteristics that identify examples of the latter is that of crosshatching, a process in which each feather on the wings and body of the eagle is made to stand out clearly. The wings of the eagle were made separately and pegged into the body. Schimmel figures, like other carvings, were occasionally decorated in naturalistic colors. Traces of brown and black are found on most birds with many having touches of red and black at the eyes, or traces of yellow on the beak and feet.

The amount of original paint found on carvings depends largely on the care they have had over the years.

Nowadays, whether the object be a decorative carved bird, animal, a figure group, weathervane—or something purely utilitarian, such as a handsomely carved butter print or springerle cookie board—it is classified as an example of "American Folk Art." Prices are reaching new heights as each day passes.

* * *

Bird, black striped wings (A-E)	$ 47
Bird, blue w/white wings (A-E)	52
Bird, green w/black striped wings (A-E)	60
Bird, on stump (A-E)	410
Bird, painted in gray & red w/painted base, 6" h. (A-NE)	375
Bird, perched on wooden base (A-E)	110
Bird, winged, brown & gray (A-E)	35
Birds, humming, pr. (A-E)	110
Blackbird, red & yellow winged, round base (A-E)	225
Bluebird, w/metal legs, wood base, 5" (A-NE)	230
Blue jay (A-E)	300
Brown wood thrush, w/yellow breast (A-E)	200
Cane, hand-carved, primitive face carved in handle (D-NE)	20
Chicken, picking corn (D-E)	150
Chicken, red comb & yellow bill, decor. wings & feathers (A-E)	1000
Dog, Aaron mounts type (A-E)	825
Dog, begging position, under arch w/double acorn decor., 1-pc. wood, 4-legged stand, 20" h. (A-NE)	350
Dog, painted & polychromed, w/tin teeth & marble eyes, 40" l. × 27" h. (A-NE)	1800
Dog, poodle, lg., Aaron mounts, 1865, carved under Schimmel (A-E)	950
Dog, Schimmel, colorful (A-E)	350
Donkey (D-E)	20
Eagle, coiled snake, ca. 1860, 15" h. (D-NE)	85
Eagle, from public bldg. in Painesville, Ohio (D-MW)	950
Eagle, orig. beige paint, carved base, 9½" (A-NE)	450

Eagle, painted shield, wall, 48″ (A-NE) ....$ 625
Eagle, pilot house, on ball, full-bodied, gilded (A-NE) 1700
Eagle, pilot house, standing on wood block carved w/large letter "D", leaf decor., 51″ wingspan, 34″ h. (A-NE) 700
Eagle, pine, beige on wooden blue, red painted base, 13″ h. (A-NE) 950
Eagle, Schimmel, 17″ spread wings, 10″ h. (A-E) 2400
Eagle, Schimmel, decor., polychrome, 5½″ h., 5½″ w. (A-E) 210
Eagle, stylized (A-MW) 450
Face, on old board, primitive, 3-dimension, 6″×10″ (D-E) 100
Fish, 10″×20″ (D-E) 135
Forest type, in color, man, deer, dog, trees (A-E) 75

Wood carvings (A-E), *left to right:* **parrot,** decor., primitive, Schimmel type, beak repaired, 6½″ h., $450; **parrot,** decor., Schimmel type, 5½″ h., $625

Dog, wood carving, pine, typical Mounts type (A-E) $825

Wood carving, man sitting on stump, coat painted blue, early 17½″ h. (A-E) $675

Indian in canoe, red & green whirligig, scarce (D-E) 165
Lion, pine, traces gray paint, 33″ h. incl. base (A-NE) 800
Man, blue & orange w/2 pegs projecting from flat torso, 12″ h. (A-NE)................ 110
Man, jointed legs & arms, doll (D-E) 85
Man, sailor top & knickers holding fishing pole, 5″ (A-NE) 160
Man, sitting on stump, coat painted blue, 17½″ t. (A-E) 675
Mourning figure, under tree by tomb, black paint, 19″ (A-NE) 250
Noah's ark, w/17 painted animals, blue & red decor., 11″ t. (D-E)........................ 75
Owl, attacking lamb, carved from tree stump (A-E) 240
Owl call, shape of bird, 6″ (D-E).. 50

Wooden plaque, hand-carved, signed Haines Butler, 18½″ × 16¾″ (D-W) $175

Pilothouse eagle, on ball, wood carved & gilded, Massachusetts origin, most important (A-NE) $1700

Owl, polychromed, 7″ h. (A-E)	$ 110
Parrots, pr. on base, 6¼″ h. (A-E)	600
Pheasant, full size, by Tyler Crisfield, Maryland, dated 1957 (D-NE)	150
Pigeon, painted, glass eyes, metal beak (D-E)	55
Puppet, Negro minstrel, orig. clothing (D-NE)	145
Ram (D-E)	25
Redbird, w/black wings, sq. base (A-E)	275
Redbird, w/metal legs, cork base, 5½″ (A-NE)	200
Robin, w/orig. paint & metal legs, mounted on wood base, 9″ l. (A-NE)	250
Rooster, large (A-E)	160
Rooster, primitive (A-E)	62
Rooster, Schimmel, small (A-E)	725
Seagull, ex. cond. (D-MW)	115
Snake, from old birch root w/painted head & rattle tail (A-NE)	175
Squaw, 40″ h., ca. 1860 (D-NE)	75
Squaw, w/headdress & papoose, cigar store counter top figure, carved in the round, ex. quality w/early paint, 20½″ h. (A-NE)	2000
Squirrel, eating nut, all orig. (A-E)	125
Stencil pattern, square, traces blue-gray paint, 7¼″ (D-E)	42
Sunfish, painted in shades of orange, green, blue & white (D-MW)	175
Whirligig, w/2 Indians paddling canoe, orig. paint in yellow, reds & greens, ex. cond. (A-NE)	1200

Woodenware

Woodenware has been produced in America from the earliest times. From the Indians, the colonists learned the art of making utilitarian objects such as trenchers, porringers, noggins, bowls, etc. The completely hand-shaped pieces are prized by collectors, as no two were ever alike. Oftentimes cutting lines left by the craftsman are clearly evident on the surface of the object. Moreover, vessels may even bear signs of crude decoration—having an incised geometric design, initials, a date or a name—which, of course, enhances the value. Surprisingly, in some of the more remote regions, many people were still eating from woodenware up until the time of the Revolution.

During the early years crude lathes were common in many areas. Having only half a revolution, an object had to be cut or turned in two stages. But when the mandrel lathe was developed in the seventeenth century, it eliminated the need to turn the work in order to complete both sides, since it had a continuous action. From that point in time the variety of wooden utensils produced is almost endless.

Although numerous kinds of wood were available to the colonists, it was the bulgy growth scar tissue found at the base of certain trees that was favored. This was known as "burl." Its grain, instead of running in the usual parallel lines, was twisted and coiled and produced an unusually attractive grain. Burl, of course, was harder to work, but objects made from it were quite durable and rarely cracked or warped. In this field, it is the burl examples that fetch the highest prices when sold.

Bowl, burl, w/carved burl paddle, 16" diam. (A-E) $525

Woodenware (A-E), *left to right:* **Butter mold,** tulip leaves & lined crescent moons, 4¾ diam. $150; **dough scraper,** brass collar & wooden handle, Peter Derr, signed P.D. 1840, $425; **candlestick** w/wrought iron push rod, $95; **miniature whiskey "Feslen" cask,** Peter Derr, $230; **liquor cup,** sampler, tooled brass, by Peter Derr, small, ca. 1840, $125

Commercial production started during the early years of the eighteenth century and, by the turn of that century, woodenware markers were numerous, especially in New England. Those that pursued this craft were known as "coopers," and there were several groups. The "white" cooper or dish turner made small household articles such as plates, spoons, bowls and pitchers, to name a few. Their articles are oftentimes referred to as "treen" ware. The word, of Old English derivation, means "made of trees." This is actually a catch-all term for these small objects.

The second group of coopers made strong vessels—and here there were two different classes—the "wet" or the "dry" cooper. The latter group produced kegs or barrels for dry bulk commodities, sugar and flour. Their counterparts manufactured large kegs or casks for holding liquids. And then there was the "noncooper" that made every variety of woodenware without regard to specialization.

The desirability of collecting woodenware, whether it be plain, handcarved or handpainted, has spiraled in recent years because of the all-American trend, natural and nostalgic. Moreover, the approaching bicentennial has revived even more interest in this field, and values continue their upward trend.

Because of the popularity of wooden objects, a variety of reproductions exists. The majority of these new pieces are machine-made and can easily be detected. Many can be purchased in department stores or at supermarkets across the country. But, there are always those new items that look awfully convincing, especially to the novice. The majority of the new cookie boards available are easily detected. These range in length from 39 inches to 10½ inches. There is always one carving on each board, a human figure or an animal.

The new butter prints and molds have caused the greatest confusion in this field. Examples of the latter consist of three pieces: the handle, case and screw-on press. When assembled, the molds stand 5½" high and are available in the following patterns: Daisy, Flower Pineapple, Swan, Wheat, and Bird In Tree.

The new butter prints measure 4¼ inches across, and they are available in six patterns: Wheat, Acorn, Cow, Heart, Eagle and Geometric.

When examining a piece of woodenware, it is always wise to remember that stains and odors are great telltale clues to age. Even though a piece has been refinished, it rarely loses its odor of grease or soured milk and butter. Finally, time brings lightness and a warm, worn, burnished patina to early woodenware that does not exist in the ware currently being produced.

* * *

Apple butter bucket, staved, iron bindings (D-E) ....$	22
Apple butter bucket, staved, iron bindings (D-MW)	22
Apple butter scoop, fine, smooth, carved handle (D-E)......................................	75
Apple butter stirrer, long handle w/16" l. paddle-shaped head, refinished (D-NW)	12
Apple butter stirrer, pine, handle 42" l., paddle 14" l., refinished (D-MW)............................	22
Apple butter stirrer, pine, w/handle 16" l., paddle 5", holes (D-W).......................................	6
Apple corer, maple, complete (D-W)	60
Apple corer, primitive (D-E)	65
Apple corer & slicer, pine, late 19th C., refinished (D-MW)	135
Apple grinder, pine, wood teeth, complete, refinished (D-W)............................	75
Apple parer (D-MW)..	55
Apple peeler, leather belt driven (D-E)	80
Apple peeler, old red paint w/branded mark "C. Woodbury," 12" l. (A-NE)	175

Apple peeler, primitive (D-E)..$ 65
Apple slicer, box w/inset blades, complete & refinished (D-MW)   135
Barber pole, orig. decor., hanging, 24" l. (D-MW)   165
Barber pole, orig. decor., hanging, 40" l. (D-S)   225
Barrel, carved from single log, 18th C., 22" h. (D-E)   115
Barrel, cider, staved & hooped (metal), 5 gal., refinished (D-MW)......................   22
Barrel, handmade w/orig. cover, bark hoops, 19th C., 20"×13¼" (D-NE)   60
Barrel, hickory, w/4 brass rims (A-E)   220
Bee box, partitions, 2 glass covers, 4-section (D-E)   45
Bellows, curly maple (A-NE)..   60
Biscuit cutter, knob handle, all wood, 1-pc., 2⅛" diam. (D-E)..........................   27
Biscuit cutter, maple (D-E)   28
Biscuit cutter, maple, 1-pc. (D-W)   6

Sugar bucket, pine, fine
condition, refinished (D-MW) $45

Keeler, pine, oval, refinished (D-MW) $245

Bobbin winder, maple, orig. paint (D-E)   170
Bootjack, all wood, folding (D-W)..   18
Bootjack, bird's-eye maple, scalloped, 12" l. (D-E)   25
Bootjack, carved, dated 1800 (D-NE)   100
Bootjack, cherry, carved & dated 1800 (D-NE)   100
Bootjack, pine, folding (D-W)   18
Bootjack, walnut, folding, 10" l. (D-MW)   10
Bootjack, walnut, folding (D-W)   19
Bootjack, wooden (D-E)   10
Bootmaker's tray, pine, w/16 round cup-like bowls, 7 on each side, 2 end holes serve as handles,
    carved steer's head (longhorn) on each side serve as feet, 7" w., 32" l. (D-SW)....................   47
Bowl, bird's-eye maple, nice patina, 10" d., 5½" d. (D-MW)...............................   12
Bowl, burl, ash, finely speckled, 8½" diam. (D-E)......................................   190
Bowl, burl, ash, footed, 1-pc., rare, 17¾" diam. (D-NE)...............................   1285
Bowl, burl, ash, ex. cond., 12½" d., 3" d. (D-W)   22
Bowl, burl, bottom initialed, 5½" d. (A-E)   225
Bowl, burl, carved burl paddle, good cond., 16" diam. (A-E)   525
Bowl, burl, ex cond., 22½" (A-E)   375
Bowl, burl, 15¼" diam., 4" h. (D-MW)   125
Bowl, burl, maple, ex. cond., 14½" (A-E)..   175
Bowl, burl, maple, 14" l., 5" d. (D-E)   400
Bowl, burl, maple, 17" (A-E)   125
Bowl, burl, 19th C., 13" diam. (A-MW)...   210
Bowl, burl, 6" (D-NE)..   115
Bowl, burl, speckled, round (D-E)   165
Bowl, burl, 12" diam., 6" d. (D-E)   185
Bowl, butter, curly maple, 14" (D-MW)..   45

Bowl, butter, locking lid, carved from 1 piece of wood, rare, some worm holes, 8" across, 4" h. (D-MW) ....$ 50

Bowl, butter, old yellow paint (D-MW) 45

Bowl, butter, rectangular shape w/old red stain (D-N) 85

Bowl, butter, tiger maple, refinished, 24"×13"×4" (D-MW) 65

Bowl, cheese, rare treen, footed, drain hole, 6"×7" diam. (D-MW) 65

Bowl, chopping, old green exterior & old red interior, 25" diam., 8" h. (A-NE) 160

Bowl, chopping, old mustard yellow, rectangular, handplaned, hanging hole, 22½"×11"×4½" (D-NE) 60

Bowl, chopping, old red exterior, carved finger grips, 22" l. × 18" w. × 7" h. (A-NE) 190

Bowl, chopping, very deep, handled, refinished, rectangular, 17¾"×9¼"×5½" (D-NE) 55

Bowl, deep, oblong, 23" (A-E) 32

Bowl, deep, oblong w/wooden handles on ends, 31" (A-E) 40

Bowl, deep, round, 25" (A-E) 45

Bowl, eating, shallow, 7¼"×7¾" (D-NE) 38

Bowl, fruit, tiger maple, turned, 10" side, 3" h. (A-NE) 230

Bowl, handturned, ridged, old dk. blue, 15" diam., early (D-NE) 35

Bowl, maple, deep w/dipper, hook handle (D-N) 60

Bowl, maple, oblong, 22" (A-E) 45

Bowl, maple, some chips in rim, 16¾" l., 9¼" w., approx. 2¼" h. (D-MW) 24

Bowl, nut, curly maple (D-S) 15

Bowl, oblong, 24" (A-E) 35

Bowl, old red paint, Maine, 6"×25" (A-NE) 150

Bowl, open, treen, double-tiered, pine, orig. finish, 5½" t. (A-NE) 60

Bowl, oval, 18" (A-MW) 80

Bowl, oval, 24" (A-MW) 95

Bowl, pine, oval, 19"×10½" (D-MW) 39

Bowl, pressed fiber, mark of United Indurated Fiber Co., Lockport, N. Y., U. S. A., patent dates in 1880s, 19th C., 16¼" diam. (A-MW) 35

Bowl, sugar, covered, turned maple, 5½" diam. (D-E) 150

Bowl, sugar, flared lip, bulbous, turned maple, 5½"×3½" (D-SE) 40

Bowl, sugar, turned, round, 7"×8" (D-E) 225

Bowl, 13"×20" (A-E) 30

Bowl, tiger maple, 10" diam., 3" d. (D-MW) 45

Bowl, tiger maple, 10½"×11" (D-E) 55

Bowl, turned, old olive green paint, early, 8" (D-NE) 34

Bowl, turned, old red paint, 9" (A-NE) 20

Bowl, turned, remnants of red inside, blue outside, 6" (D-NE) 22

Bowl, 20"×58" l. (A-E) 45

Breadboard, cherry, oval shaped, stub handle, Pa. Dutch, 17" l., 12" w. (D-MW) 65

Breadboard, knife, deep carved w/acorns & leaves (D-E) 75

Breadboard, maple, round, carved, 12" diam. (D-E) 45

Breadboard, maple, 10¾" diam. (D-MW) 35

Breadboard, pine, handled, 1-pc., 16" diam. (D-E) 85

Breadboard, rectangular, deep carved hex sign, 8"×11" (D-MW) 65

Breadboard, rim carved w/feather design & flowers, 11⅞" diam. (D-E) 68

Breadboard, round, handled, good color & wear, early, 15¼" diam. (D-NE) 28

Breadboard, some age cracks, approx. 12" diam. (D-MW) 12

Breaboard, w/word "bread" at top, small flower at bottom, 11½" diam. (D-MW).......... 68

Bread peel, cherry, refinished, 45" l., 8½" w. (D-S) 65

Bread peel, maple, refinished, 48" l. (D-MW) 35

Bread peel, pine, 1-pc., 14" w., 32" l. (D-E) 50

Bread peel, pine, charred tapered blade, well-used, 1-pc., 45½" l. (D-E) 38

Bread slicer, walnut, ca. 1880, 7½"×24" (D-NE) 35

Broom, hearthside, split hickory, ca. 1820, 4" (D-E) 65

Broom, oven, splint, ca. 1830, mint cond. (D-E) 30

Broom, peeled splint, early (D-NE) 65

Broom, peeled splint, large, ex. cond., rare, 38" (D-NE) 65

Broom, splint, handmade, split up from bottom 6", unused, 30" l. (D-NE) 35

Spoon rack, orig. green paint, 28" l. (A-E) $325

Tankard, burl, 5¾" h. (D-MW) $200

Spice mortar, covered, maple, hollowed to thinness w/deep cavity, orig. red stain, 4½" h. (D-MW) $65

Bucket, blue w/red stars, flags, horses, miniature, 3½" h. (D-E)	$ 45
Bucket, grease, complete (D-NE)	85
Bucket, grease, complete w/orig. set-in cover (D-E)	85
Bucket, grease, Conestoga wagon, 1-pc., 9" h. (D-E)	50
Bucket, lg. composition style (A-E)	15
Bucket, maple sugar, staved/hooped w/single handle, refinished (D-E)	55
Bucket, oak, w/iron handle (D-E)	18
Bucket, pickle (built in top with 4" hole in center), bail handle, refinished, 11¾" h. (D-W)	28
Bucket, pickle, staved w/3 iron bands, 13½" h., center opening in top 4½" d., refinished (D-S)	45
Bucket, pickle, staved w/metal bands, inset top w/4" hole in center for removing pickles, refinished (D-W)	35
Bucket, pine, staved, bail handle w/wooden grip, orig. mustard ex. paint good, 6½" h. (D-SE)	28
Bucket, red w/black bands, 11" h. (A-E)	50
Bucket, sap, hickory bands (D-E)	35
Bucket, sap, iron bands at top & bottom (D-W)	22
Bucket, sap, pine, staved, metal loops, refinished, 9¼" h. (D-N)	22
Bucket, sap, pine, wood hanger, refinished (D-NE)	35
Bucket, sugar, lid, 10" h. (D-MW)	25
Bucket, sugar, pine, w/lid, refinished, dated 1776-1876 (D-W)	65
Bucket, sugar, pine w/thin wood bindings, loop handle, orig. top (D-NW)	45
Bucket, sugar, pine w/thin wood bindings, loop handle, orig. top marked "Centennial best, 1776-1876," refinish fine (D-MW)	65
Bucket, water, handled, strapped, gray paint (A-NE)	70
Bucket, water, staved w/iron hoop & handle attached to stave ears, rare (D-E)	100
Buckets, sugar, old yellow over gray, V lapped, covered, handled, bottom of smaller one fits top of large one, stack perfectly, 12" × 11¾", 10½" × 10½", pr. (D-NE)	65
Buggy step, w/arm to attach to carriage, step is 4¼" diam., w/6"×2½" front plate (D-W)	45
Busk, love, early, initialed, carved w/heart crisscross pattern, large hex sign, design of circles, 12¾"×2½" (D-NE)	95
Butter box/carrier, Penna. Dutch, w/handle, & 6 boxes, pine, untouched cond. good (D-E)	135
Butter box/carrier, pine, complete w/6 boxes, refinished (D-MW)	85
Butter ladle, curved, deep stripe tiger maple, 9½" l., scoop, 4½"×5½" (D-NE)	55
Butter ladle, tiger maple, 12" l. (D-E)	45
Butter mold, beaver, round, ½ lb. (D-E)	95
Butter mold, bird, primitive, ½ lb. (D-E)	30
Butter mold, cherries, rose tips & raspberries, four 2×2 prints, 5½"×6"×3½", case w/wood knob handle (D-MW)	46
Butter mold, concentric circles, plunger type, 3⅝" diam. (D-E)	72
Butter mold, cow design (A-E)	60
Butter mold, cow, glass case & plunger, wooden handle (D-E)	45
Butter mold, cow, round, screw hole in body of cow, 3¼" diam. (D-MW)	95
Butter mold, double acorn pattern, oblong (A-E)	85
Butter mold, double acorn, plunger type, round, 3¼" diam. (D-E)	36
Butter mold, double heart, tulip & 6-pointed stars, line carved & notched on rim (A-E)	500

Butter mold, eagle (D-W)..$ 80
Butter mold, eagle, 4¼" diam. (A-E) 200
Butter mold, Ephrata lily growing out of heart, carved, rare, long handle & oblong block form, dated 1786 (A-E).. 725
Butter mold, floral design, ½ lb. (A-E) 15
Butter mold, flower design, 4-petal (D-MW)... 28
Butter mold, flower in pot, 4 star flowers, 5" diam. (A-E).. 275
Butter mold, flowers (forget-me-not), w/fern type leaf, round, refinished, 4½" diam. (D-MW) 32
Butter mold, maple, 2 lb., composed of 8 ¼-lb. prints, 1-pc., 5¼" w., 11" l. (D-MW)............ 55
Butter mold, maple, 2 lb. (New England), composed of 4 interchangeable ½-lb. prints, 3½" w., 12" 1. (D-MW).. 90
Butter mold, nut & leaf, plunger type, dated Apr. 17, 1866, 1 qt. lb. (D-NE)........................ 100
Butter mold, ½-lb. size w/floral design (D-MW) 27
Butter mold, patented 1886 (D-E).. 85
Butter mold, pine, acorn, plunger type, 1⁷/₁₆" diam. (D-MW).. 23
Butter mold, pineapple, ½ lb. (D-E).. 30
Butter mold, pineapple, round, 3⅝" diam. (D-E) 33
Butter mold, pine, box type, Prints Inc., carrot, beet, radish & pineapple, refinished, 5¼" × 4⅜" (D-MW) 75
Butter mold, pine sprig, 3½" diam. (D-E) 36
Butter mold, pine tree, 1 lb. (D-MW) 37
Butter mold, pine twigs & stars, plunger type, round, deep cut, 1⁵/₁₆" diam. (D-MW)........... 25
Butter mold, poplar, pine leaf, round, 3½" diam. (D-MW) 43
Butter mold, rare design, 6 running dogs & multi-stars, 5½" diam. (A-E) 425
Butter mold, rose, 1 lb. (D-MW) 42
Butter mold, Santa Claus w/Christmas tree, carved (A-E) 110
Butter mold, schoolhouse w/chimney, windows & door, sides & roof separate, rare (A-E) 360

Primitive butter molds (A-E), *left:* tulip, $250; *right:* oblong, initialed H.M., dated 1823 on back, $450

Butter mold, maple, 8 separate prints, 2 lb., New England, refinished (D-MW) $59

Butter mold, shamrock, 1 lb. (D-E) 36
Butter mold, sheaf of wheat, miniature, 2" diam. (A-E)... 42
Butter mold, single berry & leaves, plunger type, handcarved, rare, 3¼" diam. (D-E) 90
Butter mold, 6-pointed star, round, 3⅝" d. (D-E).. 35
Butter mold, 6-star design w/notched border, hand carved (A-E)................................ 175
Butter mold, strawberry, round, 3¾" diam. (D-E) 65
Butter mold, swan, 1 lb. (D-MW) 85
Butter mold, swan, print & handle one piece, knob larger on handle than plunger, hole in case (D-MW) 66
Butter mold, tulip design, carved, 4" (A-E).. 250
Butter mold, tulip design w/cross lines, carved (A-E).. 275
Butter mold, tulip & 2-pointed star, long handle, carved (A-E) 950
Butter mold, tulip design, 3 series double lines, 4½" diam., 2" thick (A-E) 300
Butter mold, tulips & leaves, lined crescent moons, 4¾" diam. (A-E) 150
Butter mold, tulip in pot, carved, initialed "M H," 2½"×4" (A-E) 450
Butter mold, tulip w/sunflower & leaves, 3½" diam. (A-E) 200
Butter mold, 2 butterflies, 1 8-pointed daisy, 1 aster, 4 print box w/brass hooks, 5⁵/₁₆"×4⅝" (D-E) 30
Butter mold, 2 8-pointed daisies & 2 leaves, 4-print box w/brass hooks, 5¼"×4½" (D-E)........ 30

Examples of Lehn ware (A-E), *left to right:* **sugar bucket,** $550; **cup,** decor., $200; **saffron box,** w/lid, decor., $275; **cup,** decor., dated 1878, $120

Butter mold, 2-star design, rectangular, 5½" l., 3¼" w. (D-MW) ....$	18
Butter mold, 2-star pattern, rectangular, brass hdwe., complete (D-W)................................	35
Butter mold, wheat pattern, square (A-E)	35
Butter paddle, bird's-eye maple, w/handle hook, 9" l., paddle 5" l., 5" w. (D-E)	20
Butter paddle, burl (D-MW)...	35
Butter paddle, carved, green paint, 9¼" l. (A-NE)..	80
Butter paddle, corrugated, ridged (D-MW)...	18
Butter paddle, corrugated roller (D-MW)...	75
Butter paddle, curly maple, hand-whittled, hook handle, 10½" l. overall (D-N).....................	12
Butter paddle, early, 13" l. (D-NE)	5
Butter paddle, flat bottom, almost vertical handle, handmade (D-NE)	35
Butter paddle, geometric, bird's head design (D-NE)...	225
Butter paddle, handcarved, hook handle, 13" (D-NE)...	18
Butter paddle, handle hook, 8¼" w., paddle, 4" l., 4½" w. (D-E)	18
Butter paddle, handle hook, paddle 5½" l., 4½" w. (D-MW)...	16
Butter paddle, handle hook, paddle 4" w., 4¼" l. (D-MW)	8
Butter paddle, handle hook, 9" l., paddle 4½" l., 4¾" w. (D-E)	12
Butter paddle, hickory, 9½" l., paddle 4" l., 4" w. (D-E)	8
Butter paddle, machine-made, 4½" w., 4¾" l. (D-E)...	6
Butter paddle, machine-made, paddle 4¾" l., 4" w. (D-MW)	6
Butter paddle, maple, w/handle hook, 9½" l., paddle, 4" l., 5" w. (D-MW).........................	16
Butter paddle, Penna. Dutch, carved intaglio symbols, rare, 1-pc., 10" l., 5" handle (D-E)	200
Butter paddle, Penna. Dutch, early, w/print, refinished (D-W)..	45
Butter paddle, pine, complete (D-S)...	65
Butter paddle, pine, paddle portion w/hand carved grooves, refinished, 17" l. (D-E)	37
Butter paddle, pine, thin shell bowl, hook handle, refinished (D-MW)	24
Butter paddle, shallow bowl, w/hook handle, 5" w., 8¼" l. (D-N)...................................	22
Butter paddle, unusual shape, 7" (D-NE)	18
Butter paddles, palette type, pr. (D-MW)	18
Butter paddles, "Scotch hands," corrugated, pr. (D-MW)	6
Butter print, acorn w/leaves, 4¼" (D-NE)	40
Butter print, American eagle & shield, 4" diam. (D-E)...	95
Butter print, bluebell design, round, small chip on rim, 3¼" diam. (D-E)............................	63
Butter print, compass type pattern, handmade w/scalloped edge like multi-petaled flower, back sloped to flat center, early, 4½" (D-NE)	38
Butter print, cow design (D-MW)	90
Butter print, cow design, octagonal, 3" (D-E)	80
Butter print, cow, hand-carved, round (D-W)	65
Butter print, designs on both front & back, diagonal bars & diamonds on one side, other w/four hearts w/tips all pointing to center, 4½"×3" (D-E)	75

Butter print, eagle design (D-MW) ....$ 125
Butter print, eagle design, 4½" (A-E) 105
Butter print, eagle design, round, handcarved, 3½" diam. (D-E) 125
Butter print, eagle & shield design (D-E) 85
Butter print, heart design, half-round (D-MW) 75
Butter print, hex design, side handle, 8½" l. (D-E).. 85
Butter print, maple, strawberry design, rolling type (D-E)..................................... 75
Butter print, mold, 4 pieces (A-E) 45
Butter print, pineapple, 3½" (D-NE) 38
Butter print, pineapple design, side-handled, 6¾" l. (D-E)..................................... 165
Butter print, pine, pine twig & fern design, 4⅝" diam. (D-MW) 30
Butter print, pine, 2 flowers, bud & leaves design, 3¹⁵/₁₆" diam. (D-MW) 105
Butter print, sheaf of wheat & floral pattern, carved, half-round, 3¼"×7" (D-E)........ 125
Butter print, sheaf of wheat design, oblong, 5" (A-E)... 52
Butter print, sheaf of wheat design, rare, ½" diam. (D-E) 125

Pickle bucket, traces of orig. green paint, refinished (D-MW) $35

Conestoga wagon jack, ratchet, wooden (A-E) $50

Butter print, sunflower design, 3½" (D-W).. 25
Butter print, swastika design, handle, rare, 4" (D-E) 175
Butter print, 3 feathers design, 3¾" (D-NE).. 36
Butter print, tulip design, 2¾" (A-E) 85
Butter scoop, burl, large (D-E).. 90
Butter scoop, curly maple, hook end (D-E) 32
Butter scoop, hand-hewn, 15½" l. (D-MW) 18
Butter scoop, handmade (D-NE) 18
Butter scoop, splintered at edge of scoop, 8½" l. (D-E) 30
Butter scoop, tiger maple, hook handle (D-MW) 35
Butter spade, heart carved handle (D-E)... 32
Butter spade, maple (D-SW)... 12
Butter tamp, cherry, flat, 3½" head (D-MW)... 28
Butter tester, handled, narrow, 16" l. (D-S).. 8
Butter tub, orig. paint, white inside, dk. green outside, 10"×4¾" (D-NE) 18
Cabbage cutter, arched top w/heart cut-out (D-E).. 36
Cabbage cutter, pine, large, complete & early, refinished, 5½" w., 22" l. (D-W) 45
Cabbage cutter, walnut w/knife blades, 17" l. (D-E)... 22
Cakestand, maple, hand-hewn, tazza, 1-pc. (D-E)... 135
Calendar, peg, 1-week, w/orig. blue paint (A-E) 35
Candy mold, cherry, star & leaf pat., 2-part, 5"×2½" (D-NE) 75
Candy mold, marzipan, Penna. Dutch, 1¾" thick board, orig. patina, 8" × 10" (D-E)............. 200
Cane, head in shape of dog (D-MW) 38
Cane, head in shape of man's head (D-N)... 22
Canister, treen, w/grained, sponged & rolled decor., burnt sienna on yellow ground, inscr. "made for Mary Cook by her father John Cook, 1828, Arcoda, Wayne Co., N. Y.", 4½" h. (A-NE)... 550
Canister, treen, w/sponged & rolled decor., burnt sienna on yellow ground, 3½" h. (A-NE) ... 375
Canteen, lapped veneer & nailed, early (D-E) 35

Canteen, round wooden w/old blue paint, 18th C. (D-E) ....$ 90
Canteen, small, painted yellow, made from hollow log, 4½" h. (A-NE) 90
Cask, water, w/wooden carrying handle & stopper, 10" round, 6" thick (A-E)...................... 67
Chalices, painted black, New England origin, pr., 7¾" h. (A-NE) 275
Checkerboard, early, red w/black squares (D-NE)... 25
Cheese basket, round, signed, 18th C. (D-E) 125
Cheese drainer, all wooden frame, tapered, square, perforated bottom, w/orig. cheese ladder,
   refinished (D-E) 95
Cheese drainer, attached ladder, mint & refinished (D-E)... 150
Cheese drainer, pine, flared sides & slat bottom (D-N) 45
Cheese drainer, pine, round sticks, 16" diam. (D-E) 75
Cheese drainer, pine, square w/slats, 12" (D-E) 65
Cheese ladder, cherry, 9½"×27" (D-E) 30
Cheese ladder, hickory, pegged & mortised, 18th C., 8"×13" (D-W)................................. 27
Cheese ladder, maple (D-N).. 22
Cheese ladder, refinished (D-E).. 22
Cheese press, complete, pegged (D-N) 300
Cheese press (D-W) 75
Chintz polisher, maple, shoe shape, 8" l. (D-E).. 55
Chopping knife, wooden handle, early (D-MW) 12
Churn, ash, staved, steel bands, orig. plunger, signed "Babcock Co." (D-W)...................... 50
Churn, barrel, 9½" diam., 20½" high (A-E).. 12
Churn, barrel, 13" diam., 22" high (A-E) 62
Churn, barrel, orig. red paint (D-NW)... 50
Churn, barrel, pump type, walnut w/orig. plunger & cross bars, wood hoops, carved from log
   (D-E) 300
Churn, bentwood, on legs, marked, complete, refinished (D-NW)...................................... 165
Churn, bucket type, w/cover & steel bands, complete, 22" h. (D-W).................................. 45
Churn, pine, staved w/wooden hoops, rare (D-E) 165
Churn, plunger type, complete, cedar w/metal hoops (D-W) 55
Churn, plunger type, staved, wooden hoops, complete, refinished (D-MW) 125
Churn, plunger type, staved w/3 metal bands, wooden handle, complete, refinished, 16" h. (D-N) . 70
Churn, primitive, dasher type, w/rosette nails, orig. handle & top, 8" d., 12" h. (A-E)............ 200
Churn, pump type, orig. plunger & cross bars, staved w/wooden bands (D-W)..................... 125

Pelt board, pine, refinished,
6½" w., 27½" l. (D-W) $8

Legt to right: (A-E): comb box, wall, decor. w/birds in relief, $220; footstool,
3-leg, decor. red & white, $150; Betty lamp trammel, wooden, sawtooth,
rare, $300

Churn, pump type, staved, metal & wire bands, orig. plunger & cross bars, complete (D-SW) 190

Churn, rocking, early, orig. red paint (D-NW)..$ 200

Churn, stave constructed, lid, old blue paint, 23″ h. (A-E).................................... 110

Churn, table syllabub, maple, complete, small, covered, 7″ diam., 12″ t. (D-E)...................... 90

Cigar mold, 10-tube (D-S).. 12

Cigar mold, 20-tube (D-NE).. 32

Cigar molds, 24-tube, pr. (D-MW) 35

Clothespin, chestnut, handmade, well-turned (D-NE).. 5

Clothespin, hand-carved, 5¾″ l. (D-E).. 5

Clothespin, handmade (D-W) 22

Clothespin, handmade, 5½″ (D-NE) 14

Clothespin, handmade, once painted white, 7¼″ (D-NE) 7

Clothespin, lathe turned, early (D-W).. 18

Coat hanger, hand-hewn straight rod w/arched wire top (D-NE) 10

Coat hanger, handmade, 16″ (D-E) 14

Coffee grinders & coffee mills, see Iron category

Coffee grinder, bolted on wood top & grinder w/lower drawer (D-MW)............................... 28

Coffee grinder, dovetailed, iron fittings, complete & working (D-E) 75

Coffee grinder, hand, decorated handle & knob, dovetail pewter under bowl, wood all dov.
cond. (A-E).. 125

Coffee grinder, metal top, 1 drawer (A-E) 35

Coffee grinder, pine w/iron hopper, 1 drawer, dovetailed, refinished (D-MW)...................... 28

Coffee grinder, pine w/iron hopper, 2 drawers, orig. finish fair (D-MW)........................ 18

Coffee grinder, pine w/iron top, working, 2 drawers, unfinished (D-S)............................ 22

Coffee grinder, tall, "challenge fast grinder" w/orig. label, screw on cap over holding compartment (D-MW) 70

Coffee grinder, walnut, brass hopper, one drawer, refinished (D-MW) 32

Comb, hand carved, lg. & sm. teeth, 6″ (D-NE) 8

Comb, horse's mane & tail, wooden teeth (D-E) 35

Comb, ladies, w/l. wooden teeth (D-MW) 12

Comb, long toothed, w/carved handle, 10″×3½″ (D-NE) 14

Compact, pine, w/early mirror, 2-pc. (D-N).. 12

Container, handled, round, green paint (A-NE) 40

Container, soap, pine, cylindrical (D-E).. 60

Cookie board, carved diamond pattern, 5″×7″ (D-E).. 35

Cookie board, rectangular, carved rooster/flower, walnut, 3½″×5¾″ (D-E) 165

**Variety of woodenware objects, attached to a pine Shaker pegboard w/cherry pigtail
hooks, 48″ l. (D-MW) $55.** *Left to right:* **butter paddle,** bird'seye maple, $18; **rolling pin,**
curly maple, 1-pc., $22; **rolling pin,** maple, thin grooved, stub handle, 1-pc., $23;
spatula, pine, $8; **butter scoop,** curly maple, $28; **meat pounder,** maple, corrugated
grooves, $8; **scoop,** $39; **doughnut cutter,** $16; **dipper,** maple, deep bowl & hook handle,
$48; **biscuit cutter,** $23; **funnel,** maple, 1-pc., $39; **butter scoop,** deep, maple, hook
handle, $32; **cookie rolling pin,** $15; **spoon,** bird's-eye maple, $12; **stirring spoon,** maple,
hook handle, $20; **herb masher,** Shaker, $38; **rolling pin,** maple, thin, 1-pc., 18½″ l., $18;
potato masher, maple, $8 (all items, D-MW)

Cookie board, springerle, rooster, early, 10″×14″ (D-E) ....$ 50
Cookie mold, leaf motif, early (A-NE) 170
Cookie mold, 6 designs, flying bird, castle, beehive, cat, sitting bird & grapes, 6″ l., 3½″ w. (D-E) 6
Cookie roller, darkened wood, 12¼″ l. (D-NE) 8
Cookie roller, maple, worn, 27″ l. (D-MW)........................... 12
Cookie roller, springerle, 7″ (D-NE) 35
Cookie roller, springerle, 7″ (D-W)................................. 30
Cookie roller, waffle pattern, roller 6″ l., 2″ diam., 9½″ overall length (D-NE) 65
Corkscrew, carved, figure of man (A-E) 12
Corn board, Penna. Dutch, cut-out hearts in legs of stand, 11″ l., 4½″ h. (D-E) 28
Corn cutter, for stripping fresh corn from cob (D-MW) 8
Cottage cheese mold, iron bands, 12″ l., 7″ w., 5½″ h. (D-MW)........... 23
Cottage cheese mold, signed (D-MW)................................. 30
Cranberry picker, horseshoe shape, wood toothed (D-E)............... 140
Cranberry picker, long handle (D-MW) 50
Cranberry picker, maple (D-E) 90
Cranberry picker, refinished (D-S) 55
Cranberry scoop, w/wood prongs, stenciled "F. L. Buckingham Mfg. Plymouth, Mass.," approx. 19½″ w., 20½″ h., 8½″ d., incl. handles (D-MW) 105
Cup, burl w/handle for hanging, maple, early (D-NE)................ 100
Cup, drinking, burl, maple, handled (D-W) 55
Curd breaker, all wooden box, pegged (D-W)........................ 75

Set of seed dippers, pine, refinished (D-MW) $32.

Bowl, chopping, maple, refinished, 18½″ l. (D-MW) $45

Measures, cherry, orig. finish, matched set (D-MW) $290

Curd breaker, crank, wood tooth (D-E)........................... 75
Curd breaker, pine (D-NE) 225
Curd knife, maple, curved handle, handcarved, 27″ l. (D-N)......... 22
Curd knife, maple, curved handle, refinished (D-MW) 28
Curd knife, maple, decorated, dated 1847 (D-E)................... 65
Curd knife, early, unfinished, 27″ l. (D-NE) 18
Curd knife, maple, 18″ l. (D-MW) 28
Darning knob, maple, short handle (D-MW)......................... 6
Darning knob, pine, for long stockings, 12″ handle (D-MW) 8
Darner/masher, mushroom shaped, 6¼″ l., base 4¾″ diam. (D-MW) 10
Date board, 1809 (A-E) 50
Dipper, burl (D-E)... 125

Dipper, drinking, maple, 1-pc. (D-E) ....$ 80
Dipper, drinking, pine, hand-carved from 1 pc., early, orig. patina good (D-E) 24
Dippers, seed, pine, mkd. Cornell Seed. Co., St. Louis, ½ cup, ¼ cup, ⅛ cup (D-MW) 32
Dish drainer, old (D-MW) 24
Dish rack, drying (D-MW)... 25
Dish, soap, hand-carved (D-MW) 18
Doughnut cutter, all wood w/handle (D-NW) 17
Doughnut cutter (D-W) 28
Doughnut cutter, maple (D-E) 35
Drum, pre-Civil War, w/preserved eagle painting, 16½" diam., 12½" deep, orig. drum head
    w/much wear, orig. label "H. C. Schmidt, Mfr. of military drums of all kinds" (D-E).......... 500
Drying rack, old red paint, 37" h. (A-NE) 225
Dustpan, large, refinished (D-E) 50
Egg carrier, 1 dozen, cardboard dividers, refinished (D-E) 12
Egg carrier, 1 dozen, cardboard dividers, refinished (D-MW) 20
Egg carrier, 1 dozen, orig. dividers, refinished (D-S) 22
Egg carrier, 6 dozen, w/cover, no dividers, refinished (D-W) 35
Egg carrier, 12 dozen, no dividers, cover, refinished (D-MW)...................................... 18
Egg carrier, 12 dozen, no dividers, orig. top, unfinished (D-E) 10
Egg carrier, 24 doz. w/cardboard dividers, orig. cover, refinished (D-MW) 24
Egg cup, turned, small, 2¾" h. (D-E)... 28
Egg cup, turned wooden pedestal, 1-pc. (D-W).. 25
Egg, hen, pine painted white (D-MW).. 3
Embroidery frame, maple, round, tabletop attachment, complete & fine (D-NE).................... 145
Embroidery frame, pine, rectangular, adj. w/large wooden screws, orig. untouched cond. ex.
    (D-E) 165
Embroidery frame, pine, square, adjustable wooden screws, approx. 12"×12" sq., rare (D-NE) 120
Feather bed fluffer, rare, 23¼" l., some worn holes (D-E) 38
Firkin, early w/orig. top (A-E) 155
Firkin, V-lapped, greenish-blue, 14" × 13½" (D-NE) 45
Firkin, V-lapped, handled, copper tacks, old yellow paint over old blue, good cond., 9½" tall ×
    9½" (D-NE) 40
Flax breaker, handmade, 20½" (D-NE) 10
Flax breaker, handmade, initialed (D-MW) 25
Flax hatchel, cherry, rectangular, multi-spike, 18th C. (D-E) 75
Flax hatchel, joined entirely w/wooden pipe, Penna., 1782, 19¼" l. × 3½" w. (D-MW) 75
Flax hatchel on board, chip carving (D-E) 65
Flax hatchel, spike tooth, on cherry board, 4"×22" (D-W) 15
Flax wheel, all orig., signed "J. Platt" (D-E) 150
Flour chest, pine, lift top, three bins for flours & meal, 2 comp. below for pans, orig. finish fine
    (D-MW) 250
Flour chest, pine, slant top, dovetailed, bun feet, orig. dark finish good (D-N) 285
Flour sifter (A-MW) 35
Foot warmer, wooden, square type without pan, w/geometric design (D-MW) 35
Fork, 3 sharpened tines, 17th C. (D-E).. 32
Fork, tipped handle, 4 tines, w/finial, 18th C. (D-E) 25
Funnel, cider, pine (D-MW)... 18
Funnel, hand-hewn, small (D-W)... 30
Funnel, large, handmade inset whittled funnel end, used to fill cider barrels, 13" diam., 12½" t.
    (D-NE) 95
Funnel, large, 1-pc., 17½" l. (D-E) 65
Funnel, maple syrup, 1-pc. (D-E) 35
Funnel, sap, maple, 1-pc., 4" diam., 6" t. (D-E) 40
Funnel, sap, maple, turned, refinished, 4½" diam., 6" l. (D-W)................................... 30
Funnel, vinegar (D-MW) 45
Glove duster, talc, turned, maple (D-E) 60
Glove powderer, turned (D-W).. 17
Glove stretcher, maple (D-MW) 5
Grain measures, hickory, iron bound, nest of 4, unfinished (D-E)................................. 32

Grinder, all wood, pegged (D-W) ....$ 100
Hat rack, walnut, folding, 7 pegs, refinished (D-S).. 28
Hen's nest, in the rough, 14½"×14½", 7½" h. (D-MW).. 10
Hens' nests, 4 units, refinished (D-MW) 35
Hens' nests, 6 units, refinished (D-MW) 55
Herb dryer, w/5 natural growth branches, orange-brown paint, 23" h. (A-NE)...................... 275
Honing stone, fitted into box, initials "H H K" on box, approx. 8¾" l., 3" w., 2½" h. (D-MW) .. 19
Horn, 9½" t. (D-NE) 40
Horses' legs, gray & black paint, from early horse shoeing shop, 19th C., pr. (A-NE) 90
Hourglass, early, free blown sand chambers enclosed in pine holder, orig. red paint, 7½" h.
  (A-NE)..
  525
Hourglass, oak, mounted, 2 hours (A-E).. 300

Pie crimper, wooden,
5" l., w/1" carved wheel
(D-E) $45

Pie crimper,
hand-carved, 5½" l.,
wheel 1½" diam.
(D-MW) $35

Ink sander, pounce, turned, orig. yellow paint, 3½" t. (D-E) 35
Ink stand, signed "J. R. Chappell," 3¾" diam. (D-MW).. 45
Inkwell, Silliman label intact, 4 quill holders, glass insert, decor., 4" diam., 2½" h. (D-NE).... 45
Jar, covered, tall, Lane type, decor. (A-E).. 110
Jug, handcarved from 1 block of wood (D-MW) 30
Keeler, pine, pegged, 26" l., 19" w., 9" h., rare (D-E) 225
Keeler, pine, shallow, wood hoops, open handles, 14" diam. (D-E) 90
Keeler, pine, staved & pegged, held by hoops, oval, 28" l., refinished (D-MW)................... 200
Keg, bail handles, metal hoops, 1 gal. (D-NE) 35
Keg, cedar, w/metal hoops, small, unfinished (D-N) 12
Keg, oak, staved & hooped w/wooden bands, 18" h. (D-E) 65
Keg, oyster, refinished (D-MW).. 12
Knife board w/sharpening stone, box type, refinished (D-MW)................................... 38
Knife, scouring tray, wooden center for working knife on pumice, raised, 9½" × 15½" (D-NE). 40
Knife tray, bird's-eye maple (D-E) 50
Knife tray, maple, dovetailed, covered w/orig. porcelain pulls, center carved handle refinished
  (D-MW) ....
  75
Knife tray, old red paint, strawberry decor., approx. 12"×9" (D-MW) 42
Knife tray, walnut, arched carrying handle, dov. const. (D-MW).................................. 36
Knife tray, walnut, covered, porcelain pulls, dovetailed (D-MW) 65
Knife tray, walnut, dovetailed, 14"×10"×3½" h., handle, orig. varnish finish (D-S) 38
Kraut cutter, triple blades (D-MW).. 17

Ladle, burl, long handle, 11½" deep (D-N) ....$ 85
Ladle, maple w/perforated bowl, hook handle 7" l. (D-W)   35
Ladle, turned bowl, 14" handle w/hook (A-MW)   14
Lap board, striped black walnut & pine, 30" l., 25" w. (D-E)   32
Lemon squeezer, hinged (D-NW)   14
Lemon squeezer, hinged arms, round projected head (D-SW)   28
Lemon squeezer, hinged, refinished (D-MW)   32
Lemon squeezer, maple, hinged, 2 arms, refinished (D-E)...   30
Lemon squeezer, 1-pc., 9½" l. (D-E)   45
Lemon squeezer, hinged, wood frame w/white ironstone juicer (D-NW)   18
Lemon squeezer, maple, refinished, 10½" l. (D-E)   35
Lid, crock, 8" diam., 1" thick (D-E)...   3
Maple sugar mold, dog, 2-part (D-E)..   75
Maple sugar mold, dog, pine, 2-pc., 3½" × 3½" (D-E)   60
Maple sugar mold, dogs, maple, 6, 2"×9¼" (D-W)   22
Maple sugar mold, flower, scoop type w/handle, overall length 9", scoop measures 4¾" l., 3¼"
   w., 1¾" d. (D-MW)...   40
Maple sugar mold, heart, initials "E P Y" carved into heart, 9"×8"×3¼" (D-MW)   62
Maple sugar mold, hen-on-the-nest, 9½" l., 4½" h. (D-MW)   70
Maple sugar mold, maple, 5-unit, 2½"×22½" (D-E)   75
Maple sugar mold, maple, reindeer, hinged, 2-section, rare (D-MW)..............................   62
Maple sugar mold, 1-pc. for pound cake of maple sugar, rectangular (D-E)   55
Maple sugar mold, penny cake, makes 96 indiv. pieces (D-E).....................................   125
Maple sugar mold, pine, heart, spade & diamond, 1-pc., 17" (D-E)   39
Maple sugar mold, rabbit, crouching, 7¾"×4¾" (D-MW)   35
Maple sugar mold, squirrel, solid block of pine, unfinished, 5¾" sq. (D-NE)   55
Maple sugar mold, turkey & rabbit, refinished, 12"×4¾", 2" thick (D-E)   65
Maple sugar molds, soldier on horseback, birch, held by 4 wooden pins & 2 iron pins, 7½" h.,
   10¾" w., 1¾" thick (D-E)..   300
Maple sugar molds, 2 fish, maple, pieces held by 4 wooden pins, 11¾" l., 3¾" w., 1¾" thick
   (D-MW)   90
Marzipan board, hardwood, Hudson River Valley, basket of flowers in fancy circle, 11" sq. (D-E)   500
Marzipan board, hearts & flower motif, Penna. Dutch, 8" sq. (D-E)   225
Masher, 1½" l., head 2½" l., 2¼" diam. (D-E)   8
Masher, bell-shaped, 9¾" l. (D-E)...   11
Masher, bell-shaped, 10" l., head 3½" l., diam. 3" (D-E)......................................   16
Masher, good cond., 5½" l., head diam. 1¼" (D-MW)   6
Masher, minor age cracks, small, 5¾" total length, head measures 2¼" w., 2" h. (D-MW).......   6
Match holder, maple, hanging, 6" h., 2" w. (D-E)..   35
Match holder, maple, hanging, cylinder-like picket, unfinished w/traces of bark on back, 14" h.,
   2⅜" w. (D-W)   45

Apple corer & slicer,
   pine & maple
   (D-MW) $135

Curd breaker, pine, wooden teeth, all orig. (D-W) $75

Match holder, pine, hanging, carved, Penna. Dutch, 3″ w., 6″ h. (D-E) ....$	28
Match holder, round base, 1-pc., 4″ h. (D-NE)...	15
Match holder, whittled, Penna. Dutch, 3½″×6″ (D-E)..	28
Match safe, owl design w/green eyes, label on base (D-W)...	75
Measure, large size, round, heavy construction, old orangy red, 15″×7″ (D-NE)	28
Measures, or noggins, cherry, matched set inc. qt., pint & ½-pint, orig. finish ex. (D-MW)...	290
Meat block, large, turned oak legs, refinished (D-MW)...	150
Meat board, hanging, 8 hooks, w/scratched Penna. Dutch designs (D-W)	32
Meat grinder, traces orig. paint, 29″ l. (D-MW)...	27
Meat pounder, w/corrugated tapered head, refinished (D-W)	12
Meat tenderizer (noodle cutter), handled (D-NE)...	5
Meat tenderizer, rolling pin type, some metal, 11¾″ l. (D-E)	12
Mortar & pestle, 22½″ h., 12″ w. (A-NE)	275
Mortar & pestle, burl, 7″ h. (A-E)	450
Mortar & pestle, herb, 1-pc., shallow (D-E)	30
Mortar & pestle, maple, 7½″ h. (D-W)	40
Mortar & pestle, maple, burl (D-W)	45
Mortar & pestle, maple, for snuff, mkd. Jabez Burns & Sons, New York, 3″ h. (D-W)	25
Mortar & pestle, marked "Jabez Burns & Sons," 3″ mortar, 3½″ grooved pestle (D-MW)	40
Mortar & pestle, orig. red paint (A-E)	27
Mortar & pestle, poppy seed, handle on pestle doweled & nailed, mortar 10″ h., base diam. 2″ (D-MW)	63
Mortar & pestle, red, black, green & gold paint (A-NE)	110
Mortar & pestle, small, age splits in sides of mortar, 5½″ h. (A-E)	38
Mortar & pestle, spice, deep turnings, early, remnants of old red paint, 6″ (D-NE).................	38
Mortar & pestle, turned wood, 19th C. (D-MW)	35
Mortar & pestle, turned wood, wide pedestal base, 19th C. (D-MW)	35
Mortar, pill, weighted (D-E)	55
Mousetrap, crude, wide block of wood w/spring device (D-E)..	35
Mousetrap, label, 1877, mascotte, blue (D-NE)..	36
Niddy-noddy, carved & painted, orange/brown, incl. notch carving (A-NE)	60
Niddy-noddy, maple, pegged ends, 18″ l. (D-MW)	30
Niddy-noddy, maple, pegged, refinished (D-MW)	23
Niddy-noddy, pine, carved heart, willow tree, fir tree, house & moon & signed L. C. (A-NE)	250
Niddy-noddy, turned center section, braced ends, 18½″ (D-NE)	28
Noggin, cherry wood, 13-sided, 6¾″ h., base diam. 4¼″ (D-MW)	100
Noggin, maple, from 1 pc. of wood, refinished, 9″ h. (D-NE)	135
Noggin, maple, from 1 pc. of wood, round, 5½″ diam., 11″ h., refinished (D-MW).................	165
Noggin, maple, perfect, 3″ diam., 5½″ h. (D-E)...	135
Noggin, pine, pint size, orig. untouched cond. fair (D-E)	45

Noggins, cherry, matched set, qt., pint & ½-pint, orig. finish, ex. cond. (D-MW) ....$ 290
Nutcracker, handcarved, figure of owl (D-MW) 25
Nutmeg grater, wood & tin w/hinged flap top (D-MW) 5
Nutmeg grinder, barrel top (A-E) 38
Paddle, stirring, 17" l. (D-MW) 4
Paddle, stirring, w/2 round holes in end, 18" l., 1½" w. (D-MW) 7
Peel, pine, oven, well-preserved w/fine patina, 48" l. (A-E) 90
Pickle dipper, maple, deep bowl w/3 holes, 16" handle (D-W) 15
Pickle dipper, 3 holes in bowl (D-W) 15
Pie board, round, pine, 20" diam. (D-E) 45
Pie crimper, maple, crude, handcarved w/points on end of handle to prick air holes in crust
    (D-NE) 55
Pie crimper, maple, double wheel, 2 sizes, ex. cond. (D-E) 75
Pie crimper, maple, turned, hand carved wheel, 5" l. handle (D-MW) 35
Pie crimper, much wear, 5½" l. (A-MW) 17
Pie crimper, pine, turned 4½" handle, notched wheel, 1½" diam. (D-MW).................... 28
Pie crimper, scrimshaw, curved handle, double wheel, ex. cond. (D-NE) 90
Pie crimper, turned handle (D-NW) 30
Pie crimper, wooden handle, bone jagger (D-NW) 38
Pie crimper, wooden handle, iron wheel (D-SE).. 29
Pie crimper, wooden handle, pewter wheel (D-W) 32
Pie lifter, 2-prong, w/handle (D-E) 14
Pie lifter, 2-tine, handle, 20" l. (D-W) 15
Pie lifter, wire w/wood handle, 19" l. (D-W) 15
Pie peel, handle, scarred as should be, 1747, 9" diam. (D-MW) 95
Pie peel, 3" stub handle w/hole for hanging, 15¼" l., 9¼" w. (D-W) 12
Pie peel, 5" stub handle w/hole for hanging, 18" l., 11" w. (D-MW) 65
Piggin, milk, one stave elongated as handle (D-E) 80
Piggin, pine, staved and hooped, 6" h. (D-MW).. 55
Piggin, staved w/lapped hoops, mustard yellow, 9" diam. (D-E) 95
Piggin, staved w/metal hoops, refinished, 14" h. (D-W) 65
Pill roller, apothecary (D-MW) 42
Pipe rack, fitted for 3 pipes w/small drawer, 19th C., 4 clay pipes, 16½" h. (A-MW) 90
Pipe rack, glass door in back, small (D-E) 150
Pitcher, iron bands, lip & handle, 9¾" tall (D-E) 47
Pitcher, milk, made in Lockport, N. Y., 1883, 1-pc., 5" t. (D-E) 20
Plate, 7½" diam. (D-E) 80
Plate, bread, bird's-eye maple, round (D-E) 65
Plate, eating, 18th C., 9" diam. (D-E)... 90
Plate, treen, early 19th C., 7"×6⅝" (D-NE) 90
Plate, treen, round, 13" (D-NW)... 250
Plate dryer, old brown paint, w/4 heart cut-outs (A-NE) 260
Porringer, burl, w/ring handle (D-NE) 350
Porringer, walnut, handled, 3"×4" (D-E) 85
Potato masher, 10¾" l. (D-E) 7
Potato masher, curly maple, 11" l. (D-NE) 15
Potato masher, double heads on both ends, different sizes, 14½" l. (D-E)..................... 10
Potato masher, pine (D-W) 6
Pump, barrel, small w/wooden plunger & handle, mkd. "barrel pump, Sabina, Ohio," re-
    finished (D-W) 60
Rattle, baby, carved, painted in red, blue & white, made of over 80 pc. of wood, 4½" h. × 10"
    (A-NE) 125
Rattle, baby, carved, robin's egg blue, made of 9 pieces of wood, filled w/seeds (A-NE) 120
Rattle, baby, handmade, splint (D-E) 30
Rattle, baby, pine, handcarved, approx. 12" l. (D-MW) 33
Rattrap, primitive, large hollowed wood block w/spring attachment & metal shaft (D-S)......... 32
Rattrap, primitive, large wooden block w/spring attachment & metal shaft (D-MW)............... 30
Rolling pin, applewood, small knobs for handles, 1-pc., 14" l. (D-E)............................ 28
Rolling pin, bird's-eye maple, 1-pc., 18½" l. (D-E)... 16

Rolling pin, cherry, 1-pc. (D-MW) ....$ 22
Rolling pin, corrugated, shaped handles (D-NW).. 18
Rolling pin, curly maple, 1-pc. (D-MW) 28
Rolling pin, curly maple, shaped handles, all 1 pc. (D-NW) 20
Rolling pin, curly tiger maple, 17" l. (D-W) 18
Rolling pin, cookie, 12¼" l. (D-MW).. 20
Rolling pin, cookie, maple, 11¾" l. (D-MW) 16
Rolling pin, egg shaped handles, 1-pc., 19" l. (D-E) 6
Rolling pin, maple & cherry striped roller, cherry handles, 16" l. (D-E) 65
Rolling pin, maple, handleless, 1" diam. (D-NW)... 18
Rolling pin, maple, narrow roller, 1-pc., 16" l. (D-SW)...................................... 15
Rolling pin, maple, 1-pc., w/tapering ends, thick center (D-E)............................ 24
Rolling pin, maple, tapering ends (D-NW) 15
Rolling pin, maple, 2-handled, 14" l. (D-E) 58
Rolling pin, maple, w/handles, 1-pc., 1½" diam., 10" l. (D-MW) 18
Rolling pin, noodle, maple, 18" l. (D-MW)... 23
Rolling pin, noodle or spaghetti, 1820 (A-E)... 10
Rolling pin, pine, shaped handles, all 1 pc. (D-NW) 10
Rolling pin, pine & cherry, turned handles, 15" l. (D-MW)................................. 22
Rolling pin, pine w/tapering ends, thick center (D-S) 18
Rolling pin, springerle, animals & birds, 1-pc., 16" l. (D-W) 32
Rolling pin, springerle, fruit & animals, pine, hand carved, rev. cherry handles (D-E)........... 35
Rolling pin, wafer type, leaf decor. (A-E) 32
Ruler, metric, curly maple, 20" (D-E) 55

Cookie board,
maple, reversible,
28" l., 5" w. (D-E)
$190

Rumlet (keg), marked, dated 1781, 3¼″ × 4″ (D-NE) ....$ 65
Salt, burnt wood, "poker work" (D-S)   8
Salt, open, 2 compartments, Penna. Dutch hex sign & initialed (D-MW)   150
Salt, walnut, 1 drawer, hinged cover, refinished (D-NW)   80
Sander, pounce, lignum vitae (D-MW)   38
Sander, pounce, octagonal (D-E)   24
Sander, pounce, desk (D-E)   25
Sauerkraut stomper (D-W)   35
Sausage trough, oblong, 37½″ (A-E)   40
Scoop, 16″ (D-NE)   38
Scoop, blueberry, handle (D-E)   28
Scoop, candy, maple, 5″ l. (D-S)   18
Scoop, candy, pine, 3½″ l. (D-S)   12
Scoop, early, 12½″ (D-NE)   24
Scoop, flour/sugar, maple, short handle, 1-pc. (D-SE)   65
Scoop, grease, long handle, hook (D-E)   45
Scoop, long handled (D-E)   28
Scoop, maple sugar, burl, notched handle, 19th C., 6″ diam. (A-MW)..............   275
Scoop, melon ball, w/handle, brass ferrule, steel scoop, 6½″ (D-E)   5
Scoop, plum pudding, speckled ash burl, 9″ l. (D-E)   100
Scoop, small, long handled, 11″, scoop measures 1¾″ l., 1⅜″ w. (D-E)   24
Scoop, soft soap (D-S)   20
Scoop, soft soap, hole in handle for hanging, 1-pc., 10½″ l. (D-E)...................   36
Scoop, 3½″ vertical handle, deeply scooped 5″ bowl (D-NE)   14
Scotch hands, machine-made, paddle 5″ l., pr., 3″ w. (D-MW)   14
Scrub board, cherry & maple, 13½″×26½″ (D-E)..   38
Scrub board, early (D-S)   40
Scrubstick, hand-hewn, maple, handle, 1-pc., 3″ × 25″ (D-E).........................   58
Scrubstick, long, 1-pc. (D-E)   70
Scrustick, Maine, oak scrub surface worn, 28″ (D-NE)   75
Scrubstick, maple, 6″ w., 24″ l. (D-MW)   40
Seat, spring wagon (D-NE)   40
Sewing bird, pine, complete, traces of red paint, dated 1845 (D-N)   125
Shoehorn, primitive, 14″ l. (A-E)   15
Sieve, round, brass screening, 3″ d., 6½″ diam. (D-NE)   10
Sifter, hair, 10″ diam. (D-E)   60
Singletree, curled ends, complete, refinished, 31″ l. (D-MW)   15
Skimmer, cream, great patina & wear (D-E)   50
Skimmer, cream, pine, shell shape, oval, tin, 5″×7″ (D-E)   75
Skimmer, cream, pine, stub handle (D-W)   15
Skimmer, shell-shaped (D-MW)   38
Skimmer, short handle (D-MW)   35
Smoother, cheese or butter, handled, 13″, grayish-brown (D-NE)   4
Smoothing board, maple, w/stick, 2-pc. (D-W)   38
Sour cream tub, w/cover, iron hoops & handle, pine (D-SE)   35
Spatula, 8″ l., paddle 4″ l., 3″ w. (D-E)   8
Spatula, 9½″ l., paddle 4″ l., 3¾″ w. (D-E)   6
Spatula, 9¹⁄₁₀″ l., paddle 4″ l., 3¼″ w. (D-E)   7
Spatula, pine, carved heart, 10″ l. (D-E)   18
Spatula, 10½″ l., paddle 4″ w., 3″ l. refinished (D-MW)   6
Spice grinder, wheel in trough (D-E)..   200
Spoon, bride's, maple, hand-carved, 18½″ l. (D-N)   28
Spoon, bride's, hand-carved, heart, geometric designs & initials "FGMM" carved into handle,
  21¾″ l. (D-E)   30
Spoon, eating, early, 7½″ (D-NE)   16
Spoon, hand-carved, tablespoon size, back has shell carving, maple or birch, 10″ (D-NE).......   22
Spoon, hasty pudding, w/snubbed end & straight handle for stirring, 18″ l. (A-NE)..............   40
Spoon, long handled, handmade, 27½″ (D-NE)   18
Spoon, 13¼″ l., bowl of spoon 4¾″ l., 3″ w. (D-E)......................................   20

Spoon holder, lignum vitae, turned pedestal, 4½" w., 14¼" h. (D-E).....................................$ 65
Spoon holder, Penna. Dutch, hanging, carved w/orig. finish (D-MW)...................................190
Spoon, initial ''M'' or ''W'' carved into handle, 12¼" l. (D-E) 21
Spoon rack, pine, chip carved, Penna. Dutch, w/8 unmarked pewter spoons, early (D-MW) ... 250
Spoon rack, pine, 8 carved slots for spoons, hanging, orig. dark finish, 18th C. (D-NE)......... 185
Spoon rack, scalloping on all sides, green paint, 28½" w. (A-E)... 325
Spoon rack, triangular, traces of old blue paint, 18" h. (D-MW) 20
Spoon rack, hanging type, Penna. Dutch, dov. const., orig. red paint, 12"×18" (D-E)............. 95
Spoon rack, walnut, chip carving, Penna. Dutch hex signs (D-MW) 125
Spoon, stirrer, pine, for maple syrup, 20" handle, deep bowl (D-W) 36
Spoon, stirring, bird's-eye maple, ex. cond., refinished (D-MW).. 6
Spoon, stirring, maple, shallow bowl, 10" handle, slotted for hanging (D-W)....................... 18
Spoon, stirring, maple, w/flat back, 16" l. (D-MW) 9
Spoon, tablespoon size (D-NE).. 4
Spoon, tasting, solid tiger maple, long handle (D-E)... 35
Squeezer, lemon, all wood, 10" l. (D-MW) 27
Stirrer, early, crude, 15" (D-NE).. 20
Stirrer, 15¾" l., round paddle-like stirring end, 2¼" l., w/2¾" diam. (D-E)........................... 11
Stirrer, narrow, overall length 14¼", paddle 3" l., 1¼" w. (D-E) 7
Stirrer, paraffin, 13½" l. (D-E)... 6
Stirrer, 17" l., paddle 3¾" l., 3½" w. (D-E) 13
Stirrer, some chips & worm holes, length 18¼", paddle 5" l., 3¼" w. (D-E) 7
Stirrer, toddy, 7" turned handle w/head shaped like small spoon (D-W) 8
Stirring stick, long scooped end, 44½" (D-E)... 28
Stirrups, early (D-NW)... 35
Stirrups, hand-hewn, early, refinished (D-E)... 24
Stirrups, 19th C. (D-MW) 30
Stirrups, wood covered w/leather, ca. 1900 (D-MW) 8
Swift, free standing (D-MW)... 25

Maple sugar or cookie mold,
reversible, animals on 1
side, human figures on
other side, deep carving,
5½" w., 25" l. (D-MW) $175

Swift, held by carved female hand, carved designs (A-NE) ....$ 1100
Swift, inlaid, w/masonic emblems, American shield w/6-pointed stars & other geometric designs, signed "S. E. E." (A-NE) 170
Swift, pinwheel design carved in base, green & red paint, 24" diam., 27" h. (A-NE) 175
Swift, table, Shaker, ca. 1800 (D-MW) 85
Swift, tabletop (D-E) 350
Swift, yarn, tabletop, pine, complete (D-E) 135
Swizzle stick, 7½" l. (A-E) 9
Tablespoon, handmade, 10" (D-N) 24
Tablespoon, handmade, carved shell on back side, 10" (D-MW) 24
Tankard, burl, turned barrel body w/shaped handle, 19th C., 5" h. (A-MW) 140
Tankard, w/cover, staved & hooped (D-NE) 100
Tankard, w/cover, staved & hooped, 6" h. (D-MW) 85
Tape loom board (D-E) 72
Tape loom board, birch, early, knee cut-outs on sides, 7½"×18" (D-E).................................. 95
Tape loom board, pine, crude, 27" l., 8" w. (D-NE) 70
Tape loom board, small, pine (D-E) 80
Tape loom, early, 18"×17" (D-NE) 70
Tape loom, early, small size, 18" (D-NE) 65
Tape loom, traveling, dove-tailed walnut box w/slide cover (D-E) 250
Tea bin, pine, w/tin door in orig. green paint w/gold lettering "Oolong," w/hand painted crane, weeds & cattails, 16" t. (A-NE) 150
Toddy stick, 11¼" (D-NE) 12
Toddy stick, 9¾" l. (D-MW)... 12
Toddy stick, 14¼" l. (D-MW) 12
Toddy stick, cherry, turned w/captive rings, 12" l. (D-E) 35
Toddy stick, maple, flat head 2" diam., 8" l. (D-MW).. 18
Toddy stick, maple, good turnings, 7" l. (D-E).. 4
Tongs, asparagus, 11½" l. (D-E) 21
Towel rack, maple, 2 turned wooden rings hold bar 1½" diam. w/tapered ends, 18" l. (D-MW) . 18
Towel rack, wall hanging, very primitive, 18" l. (D-E) 18

Bride's washing fork, cherry (D-W) $30

Washer, wooden, 19th C., refinished (D-MW) $85

Towel roller, maple, 18¼" l. (D-W) ....$ 22
Towel roller, walnut, 14" l., w/14" l. shelf (D-MW) 38
Tray, cheese, pine, refinished (D-S) 30
Tray, pine, w/half moon shape cut-out for handles, orig. old blue paint, 14½"×19½"×3" deep
   (A-E) 42
Tray, walnut, 10" l., 9¾" w. (D-MW) 46
Trencher, carved masonic emblem, 8½" diam. (D-E) 95
Trencher, deep rim, 8½" diam. (D-E) 115
Trencher, old, pine, 11¾" diam. (D-E) 102
Trencher, primitive w/tool marks, darkened, worn wood, handmade, round (D-NE) 35
Trencher, round (D-E) 90
Trencher, serving bowl, pine, flat, 16½"×17½" (D-NE) 85
Trencher, small, hard maple (D-NE) 120
Trencher, w/wire repair (D-NE) 105
Vase, striped wood, maple & cherry, 6" h. (D-E) 45
Vegetable slicer, w/shaped top, 10" (A-NE) 40
Wagon seat, maple, orig. rush seats, slat backs, signed "John Penovar," ca. 1820 (D-E) 450
Wagon, wheel, 20"×24" d. (D-E) 7
Wagon wheel, small, Conestoga wagon (D-E) 75
Walking cane, curly maple w/stag horn handle, dated 1754 (A-E) 65
Washboard, all wood frame w/vertical wooden rollers resembling spool turnings, refinished
   (D-N) 48
Washboard, carved from 1 flat piece of walnut, 18th C., refinished, 15¼"×6¼" (D-E) 85
Washboard, early, handmade, 17"×4½" (D-E) 75
Washboard, hand-carved, pine, 12" w., 18" l. (D-N) 55
Washboard, pegged & mortised, 12½"×23" (D-W) 22
Washboard, pine frame, metal corrugations, 19th C., refinished (D-MW) 12
Washboard, pine, narrow tin corrugations, refinished frame (D-W) 28
Washboard, zinc scrub surface, wood frame w/soap well, 12½"×24" (D-W) 12
Washer, "handy washer" patent Nov. 22, 1892, complete, refinished (D-MW) 90
Washing fork, maple, 22½" l. (D-MW) 9
Washing fork, maple, 2 tines at one end, refinished, 27¼" l. (D-W) 18
Wash stick, bride's, fancy cherry, never used, heart carved handle, 30" l. (D-E) 65
Wash stick, cherry, professionally hand carved (A-NE) 90
Wash stick, handmade, 2-tine, 1-pc., 31" l. (D-W) 10
Weaving shuttle, initialed, dated 1795, 18th C., 11" (D-NE) 25
Whetstone holder, octagonal, maple, 1-pc., 9½" t. (D-E) 29
Woodbox, pine, rectangular, slant front, refinished (D-MW) 75
Woodbox, pine, rectangular, top front open, in the rough (A-MW) 22
Wringer, wash, w/1 roller corrugated; other smooth & smaller, 14½" l. w/iron crank, wooden grip,
   base, 19½" l. (D-S) 22
Yardstick, seamstress, relief carved name & date, "Karolina Beutler, 1868" (A-E) 135
Yarn winder, framed, painted, 8 spokes on wheel axle, hand crank (A-E) 175
Yarn winder, heart shaped base, 3 small, pegged legs, 13¼" l., 11¼" h. (D-MW) 75
Yarn winder, maple, refinished, signed & dated 1905 (D-MW) 35
Yarn winder, maple, w/table attachment (D-E) 65
Yarn winder, pine, 4 vertical, adjustable spokes, refinished (D-E) 80
Yarn winder, 6 side arms w/cross bars for holding yarn, good turnings, 3 turned feet at base (A-E) . 65
Yarn winder, upright, green & red, bold cross bar base, gouged dec., 4 arms w/slanting verticals
   (A-E) 200
Yoke, animal, hickory (A-E) 40
Yoke, goat, pine, single (D-E) 75
Yoke, goat, walnut (A-MW) 25
Yoke, goose (D-E) 60
Yoke, ox, oak, complete w/hoops & iron ring, 4½" l. (D-W) 150
Yoke, sap carrier, shoulder, maple, refinished (D-NE) 75
Yoke, sap carrier, shoulder, maple, refinished (D-W) 42
Yoke, sap carrier, shoulder, pine, unfinished (D-NE) 22
Yoke, shoulder, orig. old red paint good (A-E) 45

Yellowware

Yellowware was the most economical and unadorned form of earthenware produced, spanning at least a hundred years, from the 1840s. Its body texture is finer, less dense and vitreous, than stoneware. Forms were almost always simple and utilitarian, with colors varying from deep yellow to pale buff, having a clear glaze that intensifies its color. Occasionally pieces such as bowls, pitchers, storage crocks, teapots or coffeepots were banded with slip rings of brown, white, yellow, blue or black.

Only a small amount of yellowware was marked, therefore very few pieces can be attributed to a particular factory. Most of its production was made in Ohio, at Zanesville, Cincinnati, and East Liverpool. However, a few pieces were produced at Bennington, including pie plates, deep custard cups, pipkins, a few figures, cow creamers, and Toby snuff jars. These objects are considered to be rarities by most enthusiasts.

For today's budget-bound collectors of earthenware this is a fertile field, as many pleasing forms are waiting to be discovered in shops across the country at moderate prices.

* * *

Bowl, covered, blue/white bands, 1 qt. (D-MW)	$ 30
Bowl, flare-out sides, 5½" h., 12½" diam. (D-E)	45
Bowl, mixing, 11½"×5" deep (D-E)	7
Bowl, mixing, white bands, 2 qt. (D-MW)	18
Bowl & pitcher set, crazed surface, otherwise perfect (D-MW)	85
Bowls, mixing, flare-out sides, set of 6 (D-MW)	125
Bowls, mixing, rounded sides, set of 6 (D-W)	50
Canister, or preserve jar, 8" tall × 5¾" base × 3" opening (D-MW)	28
Coffeepot, white bands, 12" h. (D-MW)	75
Colander, 11¾" top × 6½" base × 4" tall (D-MW)	75
Crock, butter, w/cream colored band around middle, "butter" in brown letters, 5½" h., 7½" diam. (D-MW)	24
Crock, 2 qt., patent 1856, Phila. (D-E)	60
Cup, baking, 2⅛" h., 3½" diam. (D-MW)	12
Cuspidor, blue bands (D-W)	12
Dish, serving, octagonal, 11⅝"×9"×2" deep, tapers to 7"×5" (D-E)	65
Dish, serving, oval, 9½"×7"×1½" deep (D-MW)	28
Dish, soap, 5½"×4½" at top × 2" h. (D-MW)	48
Jar, preserve, 1 qt., ovoid w/ears (D-E)	75
Mold, jelly, flared-sides, corn center, 7½" l., 3½" d. (D-MW)	45
Mold, pudding or jelly, 5¼" at top, 3" base, 2¾" h. (D-E)	28
Pitcher, 6" tall × 3" dia. base approx. 4" at widest part (D-MW)	20
Pitcher, milk, 2 brown & 1 white band around center, 6½" h. (D-E)	18
Pitcher, water, blue bands (D-MW)	18
Pitcher, water, white bands, tankard shape (D-E)	30
Plate, pie, 9½"×1" (D-MW)	25
Plate, pie, 10"×1" (D-MW)	28
Plate, pie, 10⅝"×1½" (D-MW)	32
Plate, pie, 10¾"×1¼" (D-MW)	30
Pot, seaweed decor., 8" diam. (A-E)	27
Rolling pin, w/wooden handles, pottery portion 8¼" long × 3¼" dia. (D-MW)	23
Teapot, blue bands (D-MW)	28

Glossary of Terms

Frequently, names sprang into existence with the making of different pieces, and only those who lived in certain localities could explain their meaning; hence the writer felt a glossary of terms would be helpful.

Adze: a cooper's tool used to hollow out bowls, ladles, etc.

Apple butter stirrer: long handle with paddle-shaped head which was set at right angles to the handle. Holes were drilled in the head to reduce friction when stirring the thick apple butter.

Bed wrench: tool for tightening bed ropes.

Bird-spit: a wrought iron or steel device with projecting prongs used for holding a bird for roasting near hearth.

Bracket foot: a term used to describe the base of a case piece of furniture, meaning the foot is shaped like a bracket.

Butter worker: a fan-shaped tray with corrugated roller with handle at one end. Used for removing excess water from butter.

Butterfly Table: A small drop-leaf table with leaf supports shaped similar to a butterfly's wing.

Cabinet: term given to any set of drawers, regardless of size.

Cannon-ball bed: popular name for a post bed having large round finials. Type popular from about 1825–1850.

Carpet cutter rocker: a chair having wide, thin boards cut in the shape of a food chopper knife blade. Found on early rocking chairs.

Case furniture: term applied to furniture having drawers or portions which are enclosed in a case, such as cabinets, cupboards, chests of drawers or book cases.

Chair table: sometimes called "hutch-chair" meaning any chair with a separate back designed to swing over the chair arms, and usually secured by wooden pins.

Chalice: a container for sacramental wine.

Charger: an early name given to any kind of dish or plate.

Chill: an open four cornered fat lamp with wick channels at each corner.

Clock reel: a device used for reeling yarn for hanking, having a counter operating by several wooden gears.

Coffee bean roaster: a cylindrical-shaped tin or wire head with metal frame, having a small side opening for coffee beans. A metal spike extended from the base of the cylinder, and on the opposite end, a long metal arm set into a wooden handle. The roaster rested on the long metal spike in front of the fireplace. Later examples had a metal spring around the arm, attached to the wooden handle. When pushed down, this action would rotate the cylinder. Round, iron coffee roasters were made but rarely found.

Cooper: a specialist in woodcraftsmanship. The "wet" or "tight" cooper made watertight containers—large barrels, and casks, whereas the "dry" or "slack" cooper made containers for dry products—sugar, flour, and meal. The "white" coopers produced small household articles—bowls, tubs, plates, etc.—all of which are extremely collectible today.

Cupboard: a case with shelves for display and storage of cups, earthenware, etc. Doors, solid and glass were a later addition.

Dough trough: a deep, slope-sided wooden box with cover, used by housewife for mixing and kneading bread. When on legs, referred to as a "Dough Box-Table" or "Dough Table."

Fire dogs: andirons, are metal devices used on the hearth.

Firkin: a vessel or keg used for measuring liquids or solids like butter.

Flagon: an early name given to a vessel with handle and pouring spout.

Flax wheel: flax fibers were spun into thread on the flax wheel, then stored on bobbins. Made with four splayed legs, they are smaller than the larger wool spinning wheels, usually having nice turnings.

Jenny Lind furniture: became a popular name for furniture—especially those with spool turnings—after the Swedish singer toured the U.S. during the mid-1800s. The early examples had head and foot boards the same height, with straight lines. Later, cabinet-makers produced bed having curved or rounded foot and headboards.

Kas: a large wardrobe or cupboard with heavy moldings and cornices. Popular case piece made by Dutch settlers.

Keeler: a shallow, round or oval hooped tub having two protruding stave handles. Used for cooling milk.

Lehn ware: Joseph Lehn, born in 1798, spent the long winter months on his Pennsylvania farm producing small, turned wooden containers — egg cups, vases, pin cups, spice holders, saffron cups, etc. — all of which are very collectible today. He died in 1892.

Marzipan candy mold: a board used in making candy, particularly at Christmas time. Carved intaglio, which causes the decoration to stand out in relief.

Niddy-Noddy: a slender wooden tool having a central bar with crosspieces or ends set at right angles. Resembles a double-ended anchor. Used for winding yarn to form a skein.

Noggin: made from one block of wood, having a carved handle on side opposite from pouring spout. Used as a pitcher or a measuring container.

Peel: a device for removing hot baked goods from oven. Bread peels are long-handled, flat-headed, whereas pie peels have a wider head and shorter handle.

Pumice box: flat tray with end compartment for pumice, used for scouring knives. The long knife blade was placed on flat section for cleaning with pumice and water.

Rabbit ear: term applied to the upright end of chair posts which are flattened near the end on front side. Frequently found on ladder back chairs.

Rundlet: a wooden keg originally intended to measure 18 gallons of liquid — rum or water.

Sawbuck table: a long table having a two-board top with either cleated or breadboard ends, and an X-shaped leg at each end. A horizontal stretcher joined the ends.

Scrubbing stick: the first washboards were called scrubbing sticks. These were a thick, narrow slab of wood, about two feet long and six inches wide, with a protruding handle at one end, having *sharp* grooves or corrugations.

Settle bench: high-backed bench with protruding sides and oftentimes partially hooded. Seat was often used as a storage unit, having a lift top or a drawer. Settles were generally used near the fireplace for protection from drafts. Date from early 17th C. to 19th C.

Six-board chest: a common term for blanket chest made of six wide boards.

Smoothing board: before the appearance of flatirons, the smoothing stick was an ironing aid. These long, round rods — 2-3 feet in length — had slight indentations. The fabric, such as a sheet, was sprinkled, then rolled tightly around the stick.

Spill: thin slivers of wood, selected twigs, natural straw, or coiled paper, used as a match to convey flame from the hearth to a pipe, candle or lamp. These small combustible pieces were kept in a wall box or a holder near the fireplace.

"Sticking Tommie": term used for an iron miner's candlestick, made to permit attachment anywhere. Includes hanger for hanging a miner's cap.

Swift: an adjustable, revolving reel, used for winding yarn. Made of a framework of thin, narrow slats, usually of wood, but ivory examples are known. Both table models with clamps as well as free-standing types were made.

Swigler: a small cylindrical wooden, pottery or stoneware keg used for rum or whiskey.

Tap table: low, rectangular table usually having breadboard ends. Common in taverns, hence the name "tap."

Traveler: a tool used for measuring the distance around wooden wagon wheel for iron rim size.

Trencher: common early term for any wooden plate.

Wrought iron: any iron object which has been forged and wrought by hand.